Malaysian Politics

Gordon P. Means, M.A., PH.D.
Associate Professor, McMaster University, Canada

New York · New York University Press
London · University of London Press Ltd

Library of Congress Catalog Card Number: 78-91692
SBN: 8147–0469–7

Printed in Great Britain

Contents

Preface		9
Introduction		11
1	The Malays	15
2	The Chinese	26
3	The Indians and Others	36
4	The Colonial Legacy	42
5	Malaya's Colonial Government in Transition	51
6	The Malayan Communist Party	68
7	The Radical Nationalists, 1945–48	81
8	The Conservative Nationalists, 1945–48	98
9	Communalism and the Emergency	118
10	The Introduction of Elections	132
11	The First Federal Elections	153
12	The *Merdeka* Constitution	170
13	The Alliance Government	193
14	The Challenge of the Opposition	225
15	The Communist Challenge	265
16	The Federation of Malaysia	292
17	Malaysia under Attack	313
18	The Internal Challenge to Malaysia	333
19	Political Realignment: Partition and Peace	353
20	Eastern Malaysia: The Politics of Federalism	371
21	An Interpretation of Malaysian Politics	391
Bibliography		421
Index		437

List of tables

1 Racial-Ethnic Composition of Malaya (excluding Singapore), 1921–64   12

2 Economically Active Population by Race and Industry with Selected Subdivisions   16

3 Student Enrolment in Malaya according to Medium of Instruction   19

4 Student Enrolment in Malaya in English-medium Schools by Race 1962   19

5 Student Enrolment in Each Faculty at the University of Malaya by Race, 1962/1963 session   20

6 Chinese Enumerated in Past Population Counts in Malaya and Singapore   26

7 Proposals for the Composition of the Legislative Council, 1954   63

8 Selective Comparisons of Public Investments, First and Second Five-Year Plan   216

9 Seats Won in Selected Local Authority Elections   251

10 Seats Won in Parliamentary and State Elections   252

11 Comparison of State and Federal Elections, 1955 and 1959   253

12 Estimated Population by Racial-Ethnic Groups, December 31, 1945   294

13 Political Party Representation in North Borneo, 1963   303

14 Elections to Council Negri Sarawak, by Divisions, 1963   304

15 Party Distribution in Singapore Legislative Assembly Before and After September, 1963, Elections   334

16 Comparison of Parliamentary and State Elections in Malaya, 1959 and 1964   338

17 Party Distribution in House of Representatives   339

18 Distribution of Party Seats within the Sabah Alliance   375

19 Inter-Party Contests in Sabah Legislative Assembly Elections, 1967   378

20 Results of Sabah Legislative Assembly Elections, 1967   379

21 Ethnic Distribution on a Percentage Basis for Malaya and Malaysia   405

22 Ethnic and Tribal Distribution in Malaya and Malaysia 1964, by Percentages   405

Preface

This study concentrates upon the political developments in one of the emerging states where the problems of nation-building are particularly acute. The cultural and ethnic variety found in modern Malaya makes it a country of equisite charm. Yet, such a diverse mixture of cultures, languages and races has also created the political and social tensions which hinder the development of national loyalties and a sense of national identity. Even so, after its independence in 1957, Malaya experienced a remarkably high degree of political stability and began making substantial progress toward integrating its mosaic of peoples into a fairly harmonious whole. In 1963, however, the problem became even more complex as Malaya undertook to join in a larger political union with Singapore and the British-protected states of Borneo. That this wider Federation of Malaysia was even proposed, let alone formed, is a testimony to Malaya's progress toward a solution of its most vexing problems. Thus, before Malaya had integrated its own population, it assumed a major responsibility for establishing political stability in a far wider union, and for creating a nation out of states with even greater contrasts of cultures, languages, religions and stages of economic development.

There was implicit in the Federation of Malaysia proposals the assumption that some of the experience of Malaya could be successfully applied to meet the greater challenge of nation-building facing the wider Federation of Malaysia. Malaya not only provided the political leadership for the new union, but it also defined the issues and thus determined the basic political cleavages for the new union. Consequently, the primary focus of this study is upon the political developments within Malaya. However, the politics of Singapore and the Borneo states are given some attention, primarily when political developments in these states have influenced or become a part of the wider Malayan scene. Of course, after the formation of Malaysia, political developments in Malaya, Singapore and Borneo have become increasingly interrelated, so the politics of these other states are not ignored.

The initial research for this book was begun in 1954 and 1955 while I was in Malaya on a Ford Foundation Research and Travel Grant. After returning to the United States I completed a Ph.D dissertation entitled *Malayan Government and Politics in Transition* which was submitted to the University of Washington in 1960. During 1962 and 1963 I returned to Malaya on a Smith-Mundt Visiting Professorship to the University of Malaya at Kuala Lumpur. At that time I began to revise and up-date my earlier study of Malayan politics. Ultimately, only a small proportion of the dissertation was retained in its original form and so much new material was added that the present volume bears little resemblance to the dissertation, but it is, nonetheless, an "offspring" of it.

In the course of preparing this study I have received the cooperation and assistance of many people. I cannot acknowledge my dept to all of them individually, but I must mention a few who have been particularly helpful. My dissertation advisor, Dr. Charles E. Martin, gave me guidance and encouragement. In 1955 he came to Malaya and helped me to plan my field research activities. At various stages during its preparation, the manuscript was read by Professor C. Northcote Parkinson, W. L. Blythe (formerly Colonial Secretary of Singapore), and Professor Wang Gung-wu of the University of Malaya. Much of the basic research involved the use of materials in the following collections: Raffles Museum Library, the National Archives Malaya, University of Malaya Library and University of Singapore Library. My research was facilitated by the cooperation I received from the staff of these libraries. During the time while I was away from Malaya, I relied upon a number of friends to secure documentary material for me. In this category Mr. Leong Mun-tong and Mr. Benjamin Hang deserve special thanks for the time and effort they donated to the task of assembling and sending to me a large collection of materials on contemporary developments in Malaya.

Part of the research on this book involved interviewing party politicians, staff at political party headquarters, newspaper reporters and government officials. To encourage a frank exchange of views and observations on the political scene, I always promised to keep the interviews "off-the-record". Consequently, I have not quoted anyone on the basis of these interviews, and have made no citations to indicate the source of information gained through interviews. Rather than attempt to give a full list of all the people I have interviewed and express my thanks to them individually, I would prefer instead to acknowledge a debt to all the people of Malaysia, since it is they who are the actors and the subjects of this volume. My hope is that I have been able to write an account of their political life that is reasonably accurate and objective.

Is it really necessary to add the usual caveat found at the end of most "acknowledgments"? It should be obvious that sole responsibility for the views and statements of fact found in this book rest with the author.

Introduction

The Second World War marked the beginning of a period of political upheaval and revolutionary change in vast areas of Asia and Africa where major European powers had previously established their colonial domains. Today nearly all of these former colonies have secured their independence and are now engaged in the tasks of developing the political and social institutions necessary to sustain that independence. Many of these new states owe their existence to the legacy of colonial rule, and have few ties of unity and identity apart from those provided by their common experience under a single, fairly unified colonial administration. Consequently, as the colonial powers departed and political attention shifted from the "anti-colonial struggle" to internal problems, domestic tensions and centrifugal forces became so intensified that the very existence of many of the new states was and still is being threatened.

Political leaders in these new states have been hard pressed to find and develop new bonds that can bring together the frequently very diverse social, cultural and racial elements within their country so that political independence will not degenerate into anarchy and civil conflict. The contemporary term used for this undertaking is "nation-building". It is a slow and often painful process which involves more than frantic repetition of slogans condemning the former colonial regime. Rather, it eventually must be based upon the development of basic loyalties and a common concensus concerning the fundamental institutions which hold the political and social system together. The politics of a country reflect this process, for it is in the political and governmental sphere that the major adjustments are made between the competing demands and aspirations of the diverse elements in society. In the long run, the nation becomes the product of the conflicts and accommodations which charactarize the political process.

All political description and analysis must focus on certain main themes, issues and events, and in doing so lesser ones must of necessity be de-emphasized. In part, such focus and concentration on dominant themes is accomplished by the political system itself, since major issues of politics will tend to submerge and apparently obliterate the lesser ones, much as the stars appear to vanish when the sun illuminates the sky. E. E. Schatt-schneider, in his perceptive little volume, *The Semisovereign People*, explains how every viable political system narrows the issues of conflict through displacement and substitution.

There are billions of potential conflicts in any modern society, but *only a few become significant*. The reduction of the number of conflicts is an essential part of politics. Politics deals with the domination and subordination of conflicts. A democratic society is able to survive because it manages conflict by establishing priorities among a multitude of potential conflicts.

Any political system which attempted to exploit all of the tensions in the community would be blown to bits. On the other hand, every combination involves the dominance of some conflicts and the subordination of others.[1]

Since the end of the war, the central issues of Malayan politics have been those of a communal character. These questions have so dominated the political scene, that other potential conflicts and lines of political cleavage

TABLE 1
Racial-Ethnic composition of Malaya (excluding Singapore) 1921–64

Population in thousands and percentages

Year	Race Malays	Chinese	Indians	Others	Total
1921	1,569 54·0%	856 29·4%	439 15·1%	43 1·5%	2,907 100%
1931	1,864 49·2%	1,285 33·9%	571 15·1%	68 1·3%	3,788 100%
1947	2,428 49·8%	1,885 38·4%	531 10·8%	65 1·8%	4,908 100%
1957	3,125 49·8%	2,334 37·2%	707 11·3%	112 1·8%	6,279 100%
1960*	3,510 50·0%	2,595 37·0%	785 11·2%	126 1·8%	7,017 100%
1964*	3,963 50·1%	2,918 36·8%	884 11·2%	153 1·9%	7,919 100%

All figures are rounded

* Official estimates

Source: Federation of Malaya Official Year Book 1962 Vol. XI (Kuala Lumpur: Government Press 1962) p. 40. The estimate for 1960 is taken from *Monthly Statistical Bulletin of the Federation of Malaya, May 1962* (Kuala Lumpur: Department of Statistics 1962) p. 3. The 1964 estimate is based on "Malaysia Population Statistics, Estimated Population by Race and Sex as at 31st December 1964" (mimeographed), Department of Statistics, Malaysia 1965. The category "Malays" in these figures also includes all persons of Indonesian or aboriginal ethnic origin. Pakistanis and Ceylonese are counted with "Indians" in the above table.

have been fairly effectively subordinated. This is not to suggest that other issues do not play a part in the politics of the country. However, even non-communal questions are evaluated on the basis of their effect on the communal contest, and thus practically all issues assume a communal coloration. No doubt the dominant communal cleavage in Malayan politics conceals many questions and issues that have never come to the surface, but may well do so once communal issues become less important. Despite the wishful predictions of a number of observers who would like to see the political system articulated with non-communal political alignments, this has not yet happened, and there is little evidence to suggest that it will occur in the near future.

It is for this reason that we begin this study of Malayan politics with an account of the general character and structure of each of Malaya's three major ethnic-cultural communities. However, before turning to that account, it may be helpful to note the size of each ethnic community, since the calculus of politics depends in part on population distribution.

Perhaps the most important figure in Table 1 is the one which reveals that the Malays constitute 50 per cent of the population in the country which they claim as their traditional homeland.[2] More than any other factor, this has promoted a fundamental political cleavage between the Malays and the non-Malays. Yet, politics is far more complicated than counting heads and calculating percentages. This will become more apparent as we examine the economic and socio-cultural texture of Malayan society.

[1] E. E. Schattschneider, *The Semisovereign People* (New York: Holt, Rinehart and Winston, 1960) pp.66–67.

[2] The terms Malaya, Malay, Malayan, Malaysian and Malaysia are often loosely used and therefore the cause of confusion. Here they will be employed in their accepted meanings, which are as follows: "Malaya" refers to the geographical areas of the Malay peninsula (the nine Malay states plus Penang and Malacca). Malays are defined by law as the traditional subjects of the Sultans, and the people whose native tongue is the Malay language and whose religion is Islam. "Malayan" used as a noun refers to someone who is a permanent resident of Malaya, regardless of race. The term "Malaysian" formerly was applied to any of the Malay-Indonesian ethnic stock peoples indigenous to the Malay peninsula or insular Southeast Asia. More recently it has assumed a more restricted meaning, embracing only the inhabitants of the Federation of Malaysia, namely, Malaya, Sarawak, Sabah and (for a time) Singapore.

1 The Malays

The Malays are usually considered to be the indigenous people of Malaya even though historical evidence suggests that they were not the earliest inhabitants of the area. The ancestors of the Malays came to Southeast Asia in prehistoric times, probably migrating from Indo-China or Yunnan over 3,500 years ago.[1] They gradually settled in the coastal areas and the better agricultural lands, while the various aboriginal peoples of Negrito and Austroloid-Veddoid ethnic strains retreated into the interior mountainous and dense jungle areas where some have survived and still perpetuate their more primitive cultures. Today the peoples of Malay-Indonesian ethnic stock constitute the basic population of most of insular Southeast Asia. The great island empires which flourished from the second century until after the arrival of the Europeans were their creation. Internecine warfare accompanying the rise and fall of these empires and numberless lesser kingdoms, resulted in frequent migrations, which have continued into the present era. Consequently, many of the Malays now living in Malaya are the product of fairly recent migrations from insular Southeast Asia.[2] However, regardless of their diverse geographical origins or their length of domicile, today the Malays have a strong sense of communal-cultural identity, and, what is perhaps even more significant, their status as the indigenous people is not a subject for political or even academic debate.

Traditionally, Malay village life has been rather simple. After the essentials of food and shelter were acquired, the villager allocated his time to leisure, entertainment or religious duties. The thought of one's heirs was no spur to the acquisition of material possessions, since land was free to those who would make the effort to clear and cultivate it. Many western observers have commented on the easy-going style of life of the Malays, characterizing them as inherently lazy, leisure-loving and stolid.[3] This is somewhat unfair to the Malay peasant who at times engages in strenuous labor for long hours; but it does illustrate the fact that the padi peasant or fisherman enjoys periods of inactivity at certain times of the year. This may partially account for the Malay's tendency to avoid economic pursuits which do not permit such periodic leisure for sport, religion and social activities. The traditional Malay villager has a style of life which has a graciousness and charm of its own, but it places low priority on the values of individual initiative and the competitive ethic. These traditional habits and attitudes are being challenged primarily by urban and educated Malays who are increasingly disturbed by the Malays' economic backwardness, particularly in comparison with the other communities in Malaya.

The Economic Position of the Malays

In spite of the effort of the government to improve the economic position of the Malays, they remain the poorest of Malaya's communities. The productivity of the Malay peasant is low. He cannot easily escape the limitations of a rather static traditional way of life, and is not easily induced to change his method of livelihood. Social customs force the Malay to spend a disproportionate part of his income on feasts and ceremonial celebrations. Traditional credit and market practices[4] add to the econonic burden and contribute to the high incidence of indebtedness among the rural Malays.

TABLE 2
Economically active population by race and industry with selected subdivisions

Industry	Malaysians	Chinese	Indians	Others
Agriculture, forestry, fishing	749 (thou)	310	174	10
rice	381	9	0·5	6
market gardening	23	54	1	0·1
rubber	260	200	150	2
coconut	26	4	9	0·1
Mining, manufacturing	36	136	16	2
Commerce	32	127	32	3
Other Industries and Services	180	174	80	38
government services	17	5	8	2
police, home guard	43	4	2	1
armed forces (Malayan and other governments)	15	2	3	23
Total economically active population	1,023	771	312	56

Source: 1957 Population Census of the Federation of Malaya, Report No. 14 (Kuala *History* Vol. 1, no. 1 (March 1960) pp. 9–15.

A number of government programs have been initiated to give the Malays a greater share in the wealth of the country. Rural credit and consumers cooperatives have been sponsored by the government to provide improved credit and marketing facilities for the peasant.[5] In 1950 the Rural and Industrial Development Authority (later renamed Majlis Amanah Ra'ayat) was founded having as its primary objectives economic development and improved social services for rural areas where peasant Malays constitute the bulk of the population. In 1956 the Federal Land Development Authority was formed to undertake land reclamation and jungle clearing projects to open up new land for cultivation of high yield rubber and cash crops, primarily but not exclusively, for Malay peasants on overcrowded and fragmented land holdings. In commercial licensing, particularly in the road transport industry, the Malays enjoy preferential treatment through a quota system designed to give them an increasing share of commercial licenses. Preferential Malay quotas have also been established for educational scholarships and for recruitment into the public services. Similarly, the government has been trying to persuade private industry and commercial firms to recruit more Malays so that they will have an increasing share of the better paid jobs in the more advanced sectors of the economy. Unfortunately, it is frequently difficult to find Malays with the educational background to fill the better paid positions. So often the Malay is not educationally or culturally prepared to exploit fully the available opportunities designed for his self-advancement.

Whether these policies will substantially increase the Malays' share of the Gross National Product remains to be seen. The number of Malays who move into the more advanced sectors of the economy do not begin to match the natural increase in the rural Malay population.[6] Even if the Malays are receiving an increasing share of the country's wealth (which appears doubtful), they have a very long way to go before they can match the per capita income of the Chinese and the Indians. On the basis of estimates of the division of income by racial communities, the Malays will have to double their share of the national income before they achieve the per capita income of the non-Malay communities.[7] To accomplish this goal, the standard of living of the Malays will have to be improved at a considerably faster rate than that enjoyed by the non-Malays. The political implications of such a re-distribution of national income is obvious. Whether the goals are met or not, the issue promises to be potentially explosive for the forseeable future.

The Place of Islam in Malay Society

By constitutional and legal definition a Malay is and must be a Muslim.[8] To abandon Islam would mean the renunciation of his Malay way of life (for the two are intertwined) and the loss of all legal and political privileges afforded to the Malays on the basis of their claim of being the indigenous people.[9] All Malays go through the outward observances demanded by the Islamic faith, and special Muslim courts established in every state enforce Muslim law and the religious obligations of Islam.[9]

Islam gives the Malays bonds of communal identity as strong as those developed by social or political institutions. For the Malay the sense of community is inextricably bound up with the concept of the community of true believers. *Masok Melayu* is the common term to denote conversion to Islam. In rough translation it means "to enter the Malay community". While some have argued that the concept of being a Malay is more religious than racial, in practice it appears that most Malays have a strong sense of racial identity re-inforced by Islamic attitudes toward the infidel. As a result, communally-oriented politicians often play upon the Malays' religious devotion when attempting to mobilize Malays for political action.

Although non-Muslims are prevented in most states from propagating their faith among Muslims,[10] it is doubtful whether the repeal of these restrictions would soon result in an appreciable number of Malay converts. The social and religious structure of Malay society make the Malays virtually unassimilable into any of the other religious or ethnic communities. This does not mean that they do not marry non-Malays, but when such a marriage takes place, the non-Malay must accept the Muslim faith. Since there can be no compromise for the Malay on matters of religion, it follows that Malaysia cannot become the cultural or religious "melting pot of the Orient" unless the other communities are willing to adopt the Muslim-Malay religious and cultural patterns. Malay and Chinese resistance to such a proposal makes it essential that Malaysia develops the political and social institutions which permit multiple cultural streams to exist and flourish side by side.

In the social structure of Islam, women have a clearly defined restricted role, and their status is subsidiary to that of men. In part this is due to Muslim marriage laws which permit a man to have four wives and gives to the husband dominant rights over the wife or wives. The present-day move toward the emancipation of women and feminine equality is beginning to be reflected in a growing discontent among the upper class and urban Malay women with their inferior status. Although poorly organized and generally scorned, particularly by religious leaders, the feminists are becoming an increasingly important factor in political and social affairs. With universal suffrage, women can make their weight felt in politics. Today, the leadership of women's organizations sponsored by political parties seeking the Malay vote tends to be drawn from the upper class urban Malay women who are more willing to challenge their traditional role in Muslim society.[11]

Malay Education

Free government schools have been provided for the Malays dating from the last century. These Malay schools were designed to meet the minimal educational needs of the rural Malays. Practically no Malay secondary schools were built until after the war. However, in 1903 the colonial government did establish a Malay College at Kuala Kangsar to educate the children of Malay royalty and the hereditary aristocracy, and in 1922 the Sultan Idris Teachers Training College was founded at Tanjong Malim to provide teachers for Malay schools.

Malay education has been supplemented by a variety of Muslim religious schools, both private and government operated.[12] Although a Muslim College was established at Klang in 1955 to provide Muslim religious teachers and officials for the administration of Muslim affairs, for years the teachers in these schools were recruited from students who received their education in Islamic schools in Egypt, Arabia or Indonesia. Consequently, a significant distinction can be made between Malay elites who are primarily a product of the government Malay schools, those who are a product of the English-media schools and those who have an Islamic school background. The latter are generally more radical in their political views, having been exposed to the radical nationalist and reformist Islamic doctrines emanating from Al'Azhar University in Cairo, the Wahhabi movement of Arabia, or Sarekat Islam in Indonesia. By contrast, the Malay government schools have tended to produce more parochial and conservative Malays with strong attachments to the Sultans and the traditional authority structure of Malay society, while the traditional Malay elites have generally received an English education and thereby retained their leadership role in government and over Malay society.

Until recently, the demand for education among the Malays has been small, and the performance of the average Malay student has been very poor—not because of inferior abilities, but rather because of poor motivation and because Malay schools were of low quality. Too often Malay youth looked upon education as the necessary price for entry into government service, with all its prestige and security. Consequently, education was viewed as a burdensome hurdle, rather than as an opportunity for increased knowledge and technical competance. For many, these attitudes continue to persist, contributing to the high drop-out rate among Malay students.[13]

TABLE 3
Student enrolment in Malaya according to medium of instruction

| | Type of school | | | |
	Malay-medium	English-medium	Chinese-medium	Indian-medium
Primary				
1957	428 (thou)	164	358	48
1962	486	238	358	62
Secondary				
1957	2	76	33	0·3
1962	2	168	31	none

Sources: Federation of Malaya, Annual Report on Education 1957 (Kuala Lumpur: Eastern Press, n.d.) pp. 65–68; 1962 figures obtained directly from the Ministry of Education in a private letter.

The Malay school system has not prepared the Malays for higher or technical education. Malay schools suffer from poorly qualified teachers and a curriculum that emphasizes Malay language, culture and religion. Until recently, there were comparatively few Malay secondary schools, partly because of the high Malay drop-out rate, and partly because, neither the Malays nor the government gave a high priority to Malay secondary education. Most Malays who wanted a secondary education transferred to English-medium schools. But such a transfer put the Malay at a disadvantage in comparison with the students coming from the English-medium primary

TABLE 4
Student enrolment in Malaya in English-medium schools by race 1962

	Malay	Chinese	Indian	Others	Total
English Primary Schools	63	113	56	4	238
English Secondary Schools	56	89	21	1	168
Total	119	202	78	6	406

Source: Compiled from figures obtained directly from the Ministry of Education in a private letter.

schools. The few in Malay secondary schools faced the same difficulty later on if they wished to continue their education beyond the secondary level. Malays who began their primary education in English-media schools were far more likely to continue to the university level, since Malay school education was a liability to those wishing to pursue higher studies.

TABLE 5
Student enrolment in each faculty at the University of Malaya by race 1962/1963 session

	Malay	Chinese	Indians	Ceylonese	Eurasians	Others
Faculty of Agriculture	6	56	6	6	0	0
Faculty of Arts	247	319	90	42	9	16
Faculty of Engineering	5	185	24	9	4	1
Faculty of Science	16	228	41	25	3	5

Source: University of Malaya, Document No. AR 344/62 p. 2.

It has been difficult to find qualified Malays for admission to technical schools and universities either in Malaysia or abroad, despite government scholarships and admission standards that discriminate in their favor. Likewise, few Malays pursued technical or professional careers in Malayan industry, preferring instead to hold a government position if they could qualify for it. At the University of Malaya in 1963, even with favored admission quotas, the Malays constituted only 20 per cent of the student body and comprised only 4·6 per cent of the students in the Science and Engineering Faculties. Well over half of the Malay students were pursuing Malay Studies or Islamic Studies,[14] both fields in which they could more easily excel, but hardly subjects likely to be of much practical value. However, for access to the administrative public service, a degree in one field counts as much as a degree in any other field, provided it is from a recognized university. It is therefore apparent that the Malays are yet to develop an advanced and scientifically trained intelligentsia, let alone keeping pace with the rapidly expanding professional and technical ranks of the other communities.

Political Culture of the Malays

Despite the strong bonds of race and religion, Malays tend to be rather provincial in their habits, attitudes and loyalties. This is especially characteristic of the rural Malay. Apart from the village, his only contact with government is that of the state government, run, for the most part, by his fellow Malays and administered in the name of the state's Malay Ruler to whom he pledges his loyalty. Since the Second World War, mass political parties have helped to break down some of the provincial perspective of the Malays by focusing their attention on the continuing drama of national politics and by political campaigning on the basis of their common interests as Malays. Nevertheless, local and provincial pressures remain a characteristic of Malay politics, even within the strongest of Malay political parties.

In the traditional political systems of the Malay States, an hereditary aristocratic *raja* (or *periai*) class monopolized positions of power. This class was closely associated with the institution of the Sultanate.[15] Persons from the *raja* class, many of whom traced their lineage from royal descent, had great prestige and status and the major offices in the state were distributed among them according to their rank and aristocratic title. Under British rule the members of the Malay aristocracy were more likely to get an English education in Malaya or England and they were frequently recruited into government service and given positions of some responsibility. Consequently, even under colonial rule they remained the political elite of Malay society. When Malay nationalism began to burgeon forth after the war, these same aristocratic Malay elites were able, in many instances, to become the leaders of the political parties which appeared on the scene. Such a transformation of roles was made easier because of the common Malays' loyalty to their Sultans and the aristocracy associated with the court circle. Furthermore, in the case of the largest Malay political party, the United Malays National Organization (UMNO), the power stucture of Malay society, from the Malay Rulers down to the *kampong* headman, was relied upon for the political mobilization of the Malay masses. In most instances, UMNO merely incorporated the existing Malay political and administrative office-holders into the party, thus capitalizing on a political communication and authority system already in existence. These same elites continue to hold a substantial share of the top offices in UMNO, which is today the dominant party in the Federation of Malaysia.

The influence of the Malays in politics is greater than that of the other communities. They enjoy a superiority of numbers, and an even greater superiority at the polls because, unlike the other communities, all Malays automatically qualify for citizenship. In addition, they are fairly easy to organize for political action through their traditional political institutions. There are few other organizations or associations which can divert the Malay's energies or compete for his loyalties. Since the Malays predominate in the civil service and the police force,[16] it is only natural that they are more directly concerned with government and politics than people engaged in other pursuits. Likewise, because the Malay tends to view government as his particular preserve, and looks to government to raise his economic status, he is even more inclined to be politically active. Consequently, the Malays have been able to mobilize their political power more effectively than have the Chinese or the Indians. It may be that the Malays expect too much to be accomplished by government action, but one can hardly accuse them of being unrealistic in hoping to meet their social and economic problems through new or expanded government programs, particularly since they can command the political power to translate into public policy most of their demands.

Early Malay Political Associations

British colonial policy in Malaya was designed to protect the Malays and enable them to preserve their customary way of life and their traditional political system. In the long run, this policy only delayed the impact of modernization and western cosmopolitan influences upon Malay society. Consequently, Malay traditional patterns continued longer than the immigrant communities, and modern political and nationalist movements were comparatively late in developing. It is not surprising, therefore, that the first Malay political associations were begun among Malays of Singapore, for there the Malays were in a minority and enjoyed no special privileges or protective laws. They were also more urbanized and generally better educated than their kin across the causeway. Feeling beleaguered and politically isolated, they were more receptive to nationalist currents from abroad.

In the early 1920s an influential segment of Malay society became agitated over issues of Islamic reform and modernism. The Malay press engaged in an extended debate between two schools of religio-political thought: *Kaum Tua*, representing the conservative doctrines of the traditional court-centered Muslim hierarchy in Malaya; and *Kaum Muda*, representing the modernist, Muslim reformist element who were disciples of the pan-Islamic revivalist ideology emanating from Egypt.[17] Although this controversy stirred Malay opinion and introduced ideas of pan-Islamic nationalism to a small number of literate Malays, neither *Kaum Tua* or *Kaum Muda* had the organization to be counted as an early political party. Likewise, various Malay sports or literary clubs became involved with some public issues, but in a rather oblique fashion, so that one has to stretch a definition to claim that they were the first Malay political associations.

Rather this honor seems to belong to the Kesatuan Melayu Singapura or Singapore Malay Union (SMU), which was founded in 1926 shortly after the first Malay, Inche Mohammad Eunos bin Abdullah, was appointed to the Straits Settlement Legislative Council. He believed that his views would carry more weight in the Council if he had the organized support of the Malays of Singapore. The founding of the SMU by Inche Eunos marked the beginning of organized political activity by the Malays of Singapore, who, at the time, were fearful of being engulfed by alien majorities and were demanding Malay reservations and other special privileges and guarantees in the Straits Settlements. By 1937 branches of the SMU were formed in the other Settlements of Malacca and Penang.[18]

Not until the 1930s did Malay political associations begin to form in Malaya. In 1935 Tunku Ismail (a Malay lawyer from Kula Lumpur) and Raja Uda bin Raja Muhammad (later Governor of Penang) founded the Persatuan Melayu Selangor or Selangor Malay Union (sometimes called the Selangor Malay Association).[19] This was the first of a number of similar Malay associations formed in other Malay states. It appears that this Malay political activity was greatly stimulated by anxiety over the 1931 proposals of the High Commissioner, Sir Cecil Clementi, to form a Pan-Malayan federation, and by Malay concern over the effect of the depression on opportunities for Malay employment in the government service.

Seeking to build the foundation for Malay political unity, Tunku Ismail took the initiative of convening in Kuala Lumpur the first Pan-Malay Congress in

1937, to which various state Malay associations sent representatives. Before the outbreak of the war, four Malay Congresses were held: the second met in Singapore in 1938, the third in Kuala Lumpur in 1939, the fourth in Singapore in 1940, while the fifth Malay Congress was scheduled for Ipoh in 1941 but had to be cancelled because of the Japanese invasion.[20] In general, the leadership of the Malay associations that were represented at these annual Malay Congresses remained in the hands of the traditional Malay aristocratic elites and those Malays who held government positions. While expressing a form of Malay nationalism against colonial rule, they did not become exponents of radical doctrines that challenged the power and authority of the traditional elites of Malay society and government.

Some Malays held far more radical and revolutionary views, but they were few in number and more likely to be found in Singapore than in Malaya. Indonesian refugees from the abortive 1926 Communist-led revolt against the Dutch helped to swell their numbers and provide a more coherent revolutionary ideology. Even so, a radical Malay nationalist party was not formed until 1937 when the *Kesatuan Melayu Muda* (KMM) or Union of Malay Youth came into being through the efforts of Ibrahim Yaacob and Ishak bin Haji Mohammad, both of whom came from the Temerloh district of Pahang. Shortly after, the KMM became a political rival to the Malay organizations associated with the Malay Congress, and began attacking the Sultans for having "sold the country to the British". It preached a militant Malay nationalism, which held out the promise of political salvation for the Malays by means of expulsion of the British and the union of Malaya with a yet to be formed independent Indonesia. Immigrants from Indonesia were attracted to the KMM and they contributed to its radical and revolutionary flavor. When war in Asia became more imminent, the British were fearful that the KMM might collaborate with Britain's enemies, so all the activists in the KMM were imprisoned in 1940 and remained in detention until released by the Japanese after the fall of Singapore.

Although the Kesatuan Melayu Muda probably never had more than a few hundred members, it helped to stimulate Malay political consciousness and helped to focus the attention of the Malays on the nationalist movement of Indonesia. The existence of rival nationalist organizations, even in embryonic form, tended to divide Malay political opinion between the moderate nationalism of the traditional leaders, and the radical revolutionary Indonesian-inspired nationalism of the KMM. A somewhat similar ideological cleavage can be discerned in Malay politics even today.

---

[1] Historical evidence of the origins of the Malays is scanty and inconclusive. See Tom Harrisson, "The Peoples of North and West Borneo," in Wang Gungwu (ed.), *Malaysia—A Survey* (New York: Frederick A. Praeger, 1964) pp. 163–178; M. W. F. Tweedie "The Stone Age in Malaya," *Journal of the Malayan Branch of the Royal Asiatic Society* Vol. 26 Part 2 (October 1953) pp. 1–100; Sir Richard Winstedt *The Malays, A Cultural History* 3rd ed. (London: Routledge & Kegan Paul Ltd., 1953) p. 11.

[2] The Achinese, Menangkabau, Bugis, Javanese and Siamese are among the more recent infusions into the Malay population of the peninsula.

3 For example see Sir Frank Swettenham *British Malaya* (London: George Allen and Unwin Ltd rev. ed. 1948) pp. 136–137; L. Richmond Wheeler *The Modern Malay* (London: George Allen and Unwin Ltd 1928) p. 212.

4 Traditionally the Malay peasant secured credit from the local store keeper and money lender who frequently was Chinese. The *padi kuncha* system was the most common form of credit which was secured by a promise of a future delivery of a specified quantity of padi, calculated far below the market price. By 1961 the government claimed to have eradicated the *padi kuncha* system by providing alternative sources of credit through cooperative societies. See *Report of the Rice Production Committee*, Council Paper No. 52 of 1953 Federation of Malaya p. 21; *Second Five-Year Plan* 1961–1965 Cmd. 3 of 1961, Federation of Malaya p. 6.

5 See Lim Tay Boh *The Co-operative Movement in Malaya* (Cambridge: Cambridge University Press 1950).

6 T. H. Silcock and E. K. Fisk (eds.), *The Political Economy of Independent Malaya* (Canberra: The Australian National University, 1963) p. 175.

7 T. H. Silcock makes the following estimates for the racial distribution of national income for Malaya and Singapore combined as of 1957: Malays M$1,225–1,345m. or 23–25 per cent; Chinese M$3,215–3,395m. or 60–63 per cent; Indians M$555–615m. or 10–11 per cent. *Ibid.* pp. 276–281.

8 *Malaysia, The Federal Constitution* Art. 160 (2).

9 Islam is the official religion of the Federation of Malaysia. In the Malay States the Ruler is the legal head of the Muslim religion while in the other states this function is performed by the Paramount Ruler. In the Malay States the administration of Muslim affairs rests with a Council of Religion, a State Department of Religious Affairs and a system of Kathis Courts. In most cases the highest Muslim official is the *Mufti* who is responsible for preserving orthodoxy and has the power to issue *fetuas*, which are legally binding interpretations of Muslim law or doctrine. By law no one may teach or espouse "unorthodox" doctrines or religious beliefs among Muslims. Islam is supported by regular state funds and by *zakat* and *fitrah* alms taxes which are levied on all Muslims. See Gordon P. Means, "State and Religion in Malaya and Malaysia" in M. M. Thomas and M. Abel (eds.) *Religion, State and Ideologies in East Asia* (Bangalore: East Asia Christian Conference, 1956) pp. 101–126; Gordon P. Means "The Role of Islam in the Political Development of Malaysia" *Comparative Politics* Vol. I, no. 2 (January 1969) pp. 264–284.

10 Article 11 of the Constitution of Malaysia states, "Every person has the right to profess and practise his religion and, subject to Clause (4), to propagate it." Clause (4) provides that "State law may control or restrict the propagation of any religious doctrine or belief among persons professing the Muslim religion." All the Malay States plus Penang and Malacca have passed laws prohibiting the propagation of unorthodox or non-Muslim religious doctrines among Muslims. Sarawak, Sabah and Singapore have no such statutes at present. In the Borneo States a statute under Clause (4) would require the approval of a two-thirds majority in the state Legislative Assembly.

11 A women's political organization succeeded in getting the Council of Rulers to agree in principle that Muslims should not have more than one wife, but the Rulers did not agree to change Muslim law on that point. This was quite a concession to feminist demands considering Muslim tradition and the fact that a majority of the Rulers practise polygamy themselves. See *Malayan Times* November 10 1962, p. 1.

12 Muslim schools are of three general types. The *surau* schools are privately supported evening mosque schools for rudimentary religious training of both students and adults. The *pondok* schools (literally "hut schools") are private Islamic schools usually established by a religious teacher and offering a regular course of Islamic studies of from two to five years. The *madrasah* schools are more advanced Islamic schools teaching in Arabic and frequently government-assisted or operated by the state Religious Affairs Department. See Rozhan bin Kuntom "A General Survey of Muslim Religious Schools in Malaya" (Singapore: University of Malaya, B.A. Honors thesis, 1957).

13 Most Malays who did not plan to try for government positions left school before they were twelve. The drop-out rate for girls was much higher due to the widespread belief that education of women was a waste of time and money. The literacy rate for Malay females between 20 and 55 years varied in 1957 from 3 per cent to 33 per cent depending upon age, while that of the Malay males in the same age groupings varied from 41 per cent to 73 per cent. See *1957 Population Census, Report No. 14, op. cit.*, p. 93.

14 Compiled from figures obtained directly from the Departments of Malay Studies and Islamic Studies, University of Malaya.

15 See J. M. Gullick *Indigenous Political Systems of Western Malaya* (London: The Athlone Press 1958) pp. 65–94.

16 Because the British ruled Malaya through treaties with the Malay Rulers, there was never any doubt that the basic character of the Malay States should be preserved by using the Malay symbols of legitimacy and by giving Malays privileged access to the public services, particularly in administrative and clerical positions. Since 1953 these practices have become formalized into rules requiring a recruitment ratio for the Malayan Civil Service of 4:1 in favor of the Malays with a similar ratio of 3:1 for the External Affairs Service. See Robert O. Tilman *Bureaucratic Transition in Malaya* (Durham, N.C.: Duke University Press 1964) pp. 96–97 and 110.

17 The revitalization of Islam became the primary objective of the Wahhabi movement of Arabia, and later of the "Al-Manar Circle" in Cairo, named for the journal of Islamic opinion *Al'Manar*, which became the major organ for propagating those views. For an excellent account of Malay politics before the Second World War see William R. Roff *The Origins of Malay Nationalism* (New Haven, Yale University Press 1967) especially chapters 3, 4, 6 and 7.

18 Radin Soenarno "Malay Nationalism, 1900–1945," *Journal of Southeast Asian History* Vol. 1, no. 1 (March 1960) pp. 9–15.

19 Mohammad Yunus Hamidi *Sejarah Pergerakan Politik Melayu Semenanjong* (Kuala Lumpur: Pustaka Antara, n.d. [1961?]) pp. 1–5.

20 *Ibid.*, pp. 5–6.

2 The Chinese

Chinese contacts with the Malay Peninsula are recorded as early as the fifth century.[1] However, significant Chinese immigration to Malaya did not begin until after the Portuguese captured Malacca in the sixteenth century, and only after the commencement of British rule did the Chinese begin to immigrate in substantial numbers. In the nineteenth century Chinese flocked to the rich tin fields of Larut and Selangor. Before 1850 there were only three Chinese in the Larut Valley. In little more than a decade 20,000 to 25,000 Chinese had arrived, and by 1872 their number had swelled to 40,000. By 1901 the Chinese constituted 65 per cent of the population of Selangor and 46 per cent in Perak.[2] After 1905 the fast-growing rubber industry began to create new demands for labor. Fortunately, the rubber industry absorbed many of the Chinese laborers who were displaced by the increased mechanization of tin mining after the turn of the century.[3]

TABLE 6

Chinese enumerated in past population counts in Malaya and Singapore

Year	States included in count	Total
1750	Malacca	2,161
1812	Penang	7,558
1842	Penang and Malacca	16,597
1871	Penang, Malacca and Singapore	104,615
1881	Penang, Malacca and Singapore	173,861
1891	Penang, Malacca, Singapore, Perak, Selangor, Negri Sembilan, Pahang	391,810
1901	Penang, Malacca, Singapore, Perak, Selangor, Negri Sembilan, Pahang	584,036
1911	All states and settlements	874,200
1921	All states and settlements	1,221,138
1931	All states and settlements	1,708,966
1947	Malaya and Singapore	2,614,667
1957	Malaya and Singapore	3,424,351

Source: M. V. del Tufo, *Malaya, A Report on the 1947 Census of Population* (Singapore: Government Printing Office, 1948) Appendix C, pp. 584–588; *1957 Population Census of the Federation of Malaya*, Report No. 14 (Kuala Lumpur: Department of Statistics, 1960) Table 1, p. 51; Singapore Annual Report 1958 (Singapore: Government Printing Office 1959) pp. 27–28.

The ups and downs of Malaya's economy are reflected in the figures of Chinese immigration and emigration. Yet, even in the midst of economic slumps, the new arrivals surpassed the number returning to China. Even in boom years Malaya could absorb only a limited number of immigrants, and when the depression hit the rubber and tin industries, the surplus labor force was more than apparent from the swelling ranks of the unemployed. To meet this problem the government introduced the first immigration restriction scheme in January 1933. Since that date there have always been some limitations on immigration from China.

In the years before the First World War Chinese immigration to Malaya was promoted by what came to be called the *sin-kueh* system. With exaggerated stories of quick wealth Chinese labor brokers recruited peasant coolies in China for the labor market of Malaya. The broker arranged the passage; in return the coolie had to sign a contract to work for any employer chosen by the broker. After arrival in Singapore or Penang, the broker would contact employers desiring additional labor, who would in turn pay a cash sum for the coolie to the broker. Under the terms of the contract the coolie was then required to work for the employer until the amount paid for him by the latter had been paid off, with interest. The employer had a vested interest in keeping his laborers in debt since their contracts would be prolonged. The system was finally abolished in 1914.[4] Of course, many Chinese came to Malaya through private means, and continued to do so in ever increasing numbers, as those already in Malaya frequently assisted their relatives to follow them.

Colonial Government and the Chinese

In reviewing Chinese immigration, it is significant to note that almost none of the Chinese came to Malaya with the idea of becoming permanent residents, but for the purpose of making a fortune and eventually returning to China. Moreover, government policies toward the Chinese until the Second World War were based on the same assumption: namely, that the Chinese were resident aliens and did not have the same rights or claims to government services as indigenous nationals of Malaya. Nevertheless, after living in Malaya for years, many Chinese lost contact with their homeland and others were forced to remain because of debts, vested economic interests, or due to war and famine in China. For many, Malaya became their permanent home.

The Chinese always posed a problem for the effective administration of law and order. As they established communities in Malaya they quite naturally brought with them their existing social and political organizations. During the early days of Chinese immigration government authorities left the Chinese community largely to itself. The Chinese established their own schools, at first without government assistance, and some welfare and social services were secured largely through their own initiative.

The early government of the Chinese was achieved through a system of headmen, with the title "Kapitan China", who were appointed by the authorities and held responsible for the maintenance of law and order among the Chinese community. While the headman was nominally chosen by the government, in practice the choice was made from among the already established leaders of the particular clan which settled in each village or section of a town. This system of indirect rule was continued into the turn of the century, although in later years, the title became increasingly honorary as more and more direct authority over the Chinese was assumed by the government. The establishment of the Chinese Protectorate (in 1877 in Singapore and in 1884 in Malaya) marked the beginning of more direct rule over the Chinese and the increasing determination of the government to combat some of the social problems of the Chinese community, such as prostitution, opium smoking, gambling, extortion, gang robberies and secret societies.[5]

Secret Societies and Chinese Politics

Even after the "Kapitan" system terminated, the importance and power of the Chinese clan leaders continued, as they exercised power through the ever-present Chinese secret societies.[6] Because secret societies often provided the only effective power over the Chinese communities in the early days, their power was given *de facto* recognition through the appointment of the secret society or clan leader as the "Kapitan China". This system worked well enough when each community was isolated and had little to do with people from a different community. But almost from the beginnings of Chinese settlement in the Malay States, conflicts arose between secret societies and with Malay political authorities over innumerable questions of political and economic control.[7]

When the relationship between the authorities and the secret societies remained harmonious, the government was lenient toward them on the assumption that they performed valuable services for the Chinese community by settling differences, maintaining order and providing welfare services. However, since they were an effective *imperium in imperio*, they presented a continuing threat to internal order. Finally, all Chinese secret societies were outlawed by the Societies Ordinance, 1889, but provision was made for the registration of other societies formed for "Recreation, Charity, Religion and Literature".[8] Many of the less troublesome and odious secret societies were re-organized as legal, benevolent associations, and were duly registered with the Registrar of Societies. Those societies having a criminal aspect were unable to qualify under the enactment and went underground or sponsored a "front" organization in an attempt to carry out their activities despite continual police harassment.

In contemporary Malaya and Singapore a large proportion of organized crime can be traced to the continued operation of illegal secret societies. They have their protection rackets among shopkeepers, hawkers, prostitutes and coolies. Their operations also extend to the Chinese in rural areas. The natural inclination of the Chinese not to report illegal activities in his community to the police gives these societies a great advantage. They will operate popular gambling games or lotteries that are generally "fixed" but not sufficiently so to arouse the wrath of their customers. In some cases, action against a secret society will accomplish little more than creating resentment against the government by the Chinese in that community.

We cannot leave the topic of secret societies without giving some attention to their political activities. It is a well-known fact that Dr. Sun Yat-sen's power as a revolutionary leader came from his association with anti-Manchu secret societies. The history of the Kuomintang from its inception is a story of intrigue and secret society politics. The Kuomintang was formed in February 1912 as a coalition of factions in five revolutionary anti-Manchu secret societies, the most important of which was the T'ung Meng Hui. Sun Yat-sen had been president of the latter for a number of years prior to 1912.

Dr. Sun first visited Malaya in 1900 seeking support from the overseas Chinese for his revolutionary movement. Between 1905 and 1911 he revisited Malaya seven times, during which period he founded the Singapore branch of the T'ung Meng Hui, which became the nucleus of the subsequent Kuomintang organization among the Chinese of Southeast Asia.[9] Eleven months after the formation of the Kuomintang the first branch was formed in Singapore and duly registered under the provisions of the Societies Ordinance. The Kuomintang continued to exist as a legal registered society in Malaya until 1925 when its registration was cancelled because of failure to provide the information required under the Societies Ordinance.[10]

A number of secret societies became actively associated with the Kuomintang in Malaya. Later, when the break developed within the Kuomintang between the right and left wing following Chiang Kai-shek's purge of the Communists in 1927, some secret societies followed the lead of the right-wing group which remained in control of the Kuomintang, while other societies identified themselves with the left wing which split off to form the Chinese Communist Party. The Ang Bin Hoey and the Wah Kei Society together with their legal "front" organizations and clubs formed the backbone of support in Malaya for the Kuomintang.[11] The Chinese Communist Party was backed by the Chi Kung Society. Although a branch of this organization was formed in Malaya in 1925, it was not very active. After the war the Chi Kung Society split into two groups, both claiming to be authentic, one of which followed the lead of the Malayan Communist Party.[12] When the MCP began its guerrilla war in 1948, the Communist oriented half of the Chi Kung Society supported the MCP by collecting money and by combating the influence and activities of the secret societies backing the Kuomintang.

With the introduction of elections to Malaya, secret societies turned their attention to the organization and control of voters. In the Singapore by-elections of July 1957, both the winning candidates secured the aid of secret societies to act as ward organizers, distribute literature, put up election posters and drive voters to the polls. Voters who supported opposition candidates or who refused to ride to the polls in a car marked with the symbol of the society's chosen candidate were intimidated.[13] While the police were alert to the threat to democratic processes posed by secret societies, it was difficult to stop candidates making informal agreements with secret societies, particularly since secret societies have shown that they are able to deliver the votes in certain Chinese constituencies. Although the most flagrant abuses have been revealed in Singapore, it is common knowledge that they have also been active in Malaya during elections.

Chinese Religion

Unlike the Malays, the Chinese practice many faiths. In 1931 97·7 per cent professed to what the census enumerated as the "Chinese national religion".[14] The very fact that the census employed this category illustrates one of the most important features of Chinese religious beliefs. While most Chinese confess to one or more of the three great religions of China, it is extremely difficult to categorize them as Buddhist, Taoist or Confucian. In their religious practices and beliefs they are eclectic, choosing to worship both Buddhist and Taoist deities, heroes or Bodhisattvas, and performing the ancestral rites associated with Confucianism. One often finds Buddhist and Taoist deities worshipped in the same temple, and in some cases the priests do not even know which deities are associated with which religion.

The wide latitude of Chinese beliefs makes them extremely tolerant in matters of religion. They show almost no religious fanaticism, and they make little attempt to spread their faith through missionary activities. However, these attitudes have made the Chinese suitable subjects for conversion to other religions. Thus in 1931 more than thirty thousand Chinese gave their religious affiliation as Christian, while three and a half thousand were counted as Muslims.[15] By now these figures have probably more than doubled.

With the increasing number of western-educated Chinese, many traditional Chinese beliefs are gradually dying or being undermined. Likewise, an ever growing number of people are secular to the point of professing no religious beliefs, while some Chinese are seeking to re-evaluate the essentials of their religious traditions, separating them from the great mass of superstitions, lore and legend that typifies so much of Chinese religious beliefs. The variety of religious beliefs and philosophies found among the Chinese make them more willing to accept a person of another religious faith without exhibiting attitudes of contempt or scorn. Their lack of religious dogmatism or crusading zeal is in marked contrast to the attitudes of many Malays toward Islam.

Nearly all Chinese, whatever their religion, participate in the major festivals and holidays observed in China. The lore and legend of Chinese history and religious literature give a sense of unity which helps to overcome the divisions of dialect and clan groupings. Observances of traditional holidays are considered to be a part of Chinese culture and they provide the occasion for the reassertion of the ties binding together the Chinese community.

Economic Position of the Chinese

Among the three major communities of Malaya the Chinese control the greatest proportion of the country's economy. In the early days of Chinese immigration, the Chinese contribution to the Malayan economy was largely a matter of labor. Industrious and diligent, the Chinese quickly adapted themselves to the new conditions of living and to the hardships of early Malaya. They also exhibited exceptional imagination and private initiative. Small trading, shopkeeping, open-cast tin mining and transportation rapidly became their economic preserve.[16] From these vantage points the Chinese expanded into rubber growing and processing, banking concerns, tin dredging companies, and the newly developing manufacturing industries. Increasing Chinese investments in European companies operating in Southeast Asia make it difficult to distinguish between Chinese and European capital invested in the country. What is perhaps even more significant, however, is the fact that the Chinese are most often found in the expanding and dynamic sectors of the economy.

Because there has been no systematic collection of statistics on the racial distribution of national income, it is difficult to determine the total wealth of the Chinese community. However, selective surveys and estimates have been made which give some indication of their economic position.[17] From these, Professor T. H. Silcock has calculated the 1947 per capita income of the Chinese at M$656, while the Malays earned M$258 per capita and the Indians M$560. He also estimated the total profits, rents and interests for 1947 were distributed as follows: Malays, M$20m; Chinese M$450m and Indians M$30m. As reported above, Professor Silcock concludes that the Chinese community receive from 60 to 63 per cent of the national income of Singapore and Malaya combined.[18] Since only 44 per cent of the combined population of Singapore and Malaya are Chinese, it can be seen that their stake in the economy is very large indeed.

The dominant economic position of the Chinese has influenced their attitudes toward recent political developments in Malaysia. They are aware of the thinly disguised antagonisms against them from the other communities who are jealous of the Chinese wealth or fear economic domination at their hands. Most Chinese recognize that their fortunes are dependent upon Malaysia's future, and for both economic and political reasons they demand to be counted as fully-fledged citizens. Otherwise, they fear that their economic stake in the country will be undermined through restrictive legislation passed by a government with an "anti-Chinese" bias. Any legislation designed to redistribute the national income would benefit many poorer Chinese, but it also raises the specter of forceable expropriation of Chinese wealth for distribution to the poor Malay masses. In politics, economic and communal issues become interwoven due to the disproportionate distribution of the national income among the racial communities.

Political Aspects of Chinese Society

The Chinese in Malaya are not a homogeneous community. While most of them came from South China, they speak a wide variety of dialects which have helped to preserve their provincial differences.[19] Thus, unified Chinese political activity is difficult and organizations seeking the support of all Chinese are frequently plagued by rival factions forming along linguistic, provincial or clan lines. The Japanese occupation of Malaya made the Chinese think more in terms of communal unity because they were singled out for exceptionally brutal and repressive measures.

Despite the upsurge of Chinese nationalism and political awareness during the war, Chinese participation in political affairs has been limited and episodic. Since no comprehensive studies of public attitudes have been made in Malaya only tentative partial explanations can be suggested. For one thing, many Chinese are fatalists, and fatalism is antithetical to the ideas of democratic participation in politics. Until recently the ordinary Chinese did not believe that government could be improved, much less did he believe that good government demanded political activity and a positive commitment on the part of the masses. The traditional Chinese view of an ideal government is one that maintains necessary public works but leaves the ordinary man in peace to pursue his ecomonic and social activities without undue interference. Government was viewed as a necessary evil to be avoided if at all possible. Traditional Chinese political theory held that government, like any profession requiring special skills, should be run by those trained for that purpose. In the eyes of the tradition-bound Chinese, when the government seeks to secure widespread democratic participation in the policy-making process, it exhibits its weakness and its prestige drops.

Under colonial rule the government was alien and frequently unsympathetic to Chinese demands. After Malayan independence, the government still appeared to most Chinese as an alien government and still largely unsympathetic to their demands. Consequently, Chinese participation in politics has frequently been rather negative, involving such activities as demonstrations, mass meetings, hartals, or passive resistance against government policies which seem to be unjust or discriminatory against the Chinese. The more militant among the younger generation can be moved to violence in street riots or acts of political terror in these moments of crisis when Chinese passions become inflamed. Occasional outbursts of anomic political activity are too often followed by periods of withdrawal and for some a form of sullen resignation The Chinese as a whole seem hesitant to give their full support to political parties that do gain access to government and share in the power and responsibility of policy-making. In lar gemeasure, this may be due to the essentially negative traditional view of government, reinforced in part by their experience in Malaya.

Before the Second World War, few Chinese in Malaya would have willingly renounced their ties with China. However, the circumstances of the postwar years have forced most of the Chinese to recognize that for all practical purposes Malaya was their permanent home. Return to China was difficult, and re-entry into Malaya was made even more difficult, so that the Chinese had little to gain by voicing loyalty to China. Rather they found it advantageous to apply for Malayan citizenship, even though they were determined to preserve their Chinese culture and their separate identity as Chinese. Today, their profession of loyalty to their adopted country is undoubtedly contingent upon government policies which permit them to preserve their culture and enable them to participate fully in the political and economic life of the nation.

While the Chinese demand to be included as partners in the nation-building processes, they are not readily assimilated with either the Malays or the Indians. There is an almost universal feeling among the Chinese that they are superior in both individual attributes and culture to the Malays and the Indians. This attitude may be partly the result of their awareness of their great cultural heritage, and partly the result of an increasing sense of Chinese nationalism. But whatever the reason, the attitude is significant when political issues arise involving the question of building a "Malayan" citizenry with a "Malayan" outlook and a distinctive "Malayan" way of life. When a Chinese becomes a "Malayan Chinese" what is changed—his domicile, his political loyalties, his language, his education, or his whole culture? The determination of the content and meaning of the word "Malayan" has become the heart of many of the political issues revolving round the problems of citizenship, schools, immigration, national service and voting rights. Now that the wider union of Malaysia is a reality, even more complex is the definition and meaning of "Malaysian Chinese".

The political unrest and instability among the Chinese stems from the fact that they tend to face in two directions at once. On the one hand, they want to remain Chinese, with Chinese culture, language, traditions and loyalty to China (though not necessarily to a particular political regime in China). On the other hand, as a community, they want to be counted as loyal Malaysians with the rights of permanently domiciled citizens. Where these two sets of values conflict, they find themselves either in a quandary of indecision and internal divisions, or pursuing somewhat contradictory objectives.[20]

1 D. G. E. Hall *A History of South-East Asia* (London: Macmillan & Co., 1955) p. 33.

2 W. L. Blythe *Historical Sketch of Chinese Labour in Malaya* (Singapore: Government Printing Office, 1953) pp. 2–3. (This is a reprint from *Journal of the Malayan Branch, Royal Asiatic Society* Vol. XX, part 1, June 1947.)

3 By employing floating dredges, the amount of labor required for a tin mine could be reduced to one-third or less of that previously used.

4 Blythe, *op. cit.*, pp. 15 and 20–25. See also J. Norman Parmer, *Colonial Labor Policy and Administration, A History of Labor in the Rubber Plantation Industry, c. 1910–1941* (New York: Association for Asian Studies 1960) pp. 27–37 and 79–108.

5 Victor Purcell *The Chinese in Southeast Asia* (London: Oxford University Press 1951) pp. 321–339.

6 Nearly all Chinese secret societies in Malaya trace their origins to secret societies formed in China. It is difficult to say what aspects of Chinese society stimulated their growth, but it is likely that they represented a reaction on the part of local districts to the coercive power of the Chinese Imperial Government, particularly during the foreign Manchu dynasty. The semi-anarchical rule in Malaya during the nineteenth century provided an ideal opportunity for secret societies to flourish. See Wilfrid Blythe *The Impact of Chinese Secret Societies in Malaya* (London:

Oxford University Press 1969), pp. 1–275; L. F. Comber, *Chinese Secret Societies in Malaya* (Locust Valley, New York: Association of Asian Studies, J. J. Augustin, Inc., 1959), pp. 1–31; W. L. Wynne, Triad and Tabut, (Singapore: Government Printing Office 1941), pp. xv–lvii, 1–151, 202–430.

[7] In the mid-nineteenth century, Chinese secret societies engaged in a bloody struggle over the control of the tin-rich lands of Perak and over the succession to the Perak throne. The full-scale fighting which erupted in Perak during the 1860s and 1870s became known as the Larut Wars. Upon the initiative of the Governor, Sir Andrew Clarke of Singapore, the leaders of the warring Chinese societies and the Malay chiefs in Perak met to negotiate the famous Pangkor Engagement of 1874. The Chinese agreed to destroy their fortifications, and the Sultan agreed to accept a British officer "whose advice must be asked and acted upon in all questions other than those touching Malay religion and custom". This treaty was the first in a series of treaties that provided the basis for British indirect rule in the Malay States. The anarchy resulting in part from the large influx of Chinese enabled the British to assume the role of keeper-of-the-peace and arbiter in the disputes arising from Malaya's growing multi-racial population. For a thorough account of this period see C. Northcote Parkinson *British Intervention in Malaya, 1867–1877* (Singapore: University of Malaya Press 1960).

[8] Comber, *op. cit.*, pp. 266. Earlier attempts at registration and control of secret societies had been made in 1869, 1882 and 1885 but they were evaded and totally ineffective. See *ibid.*, pp. 129–153 and 247–266.

Wang Gungwu, "Sun Yat-Sen and Singapore", *Journal of the South Seas Society* Vol. XV, part 2 (December 1959) pp. 55–68. See also Png Poh Seng, "The Kuomintang in Malaya, 1912–1941", *Journal of Southeast Asian History* Vol. 2, no. 1 (March 1961) pp. 1–32.

[10] *Federated Malay States Government Gazette, 1925* p. 1971 (L.N. 7741). Although the KMT was not registered after 1925, it continued to exist with little attempt at concealment and few prosecutions. In 1930, the new Governor and High Commissioner Sir Cecil Clementi was alarmed by public announcements of KMT meetings appearing in the Chinese press. He forthwith summoned seventeen top members of the KMT and warned them "that the Government was not prepared to allow the Kuomintang to function in the Malay States or the Straits Settlements". See *Malay Mail*, February 20, 1930 p. 11. This statement has led to erroneous reports that the KMT was not banned until 1930.

[11] Leon Comber reports that 100,000 Chinese in Penang and Province Wellesley were members of the Ang Bin Hoey Society in 1946. The Ang Bin Hoey and the Wah Kei were reported to have held a secret meeting in May 1948 at which they decided to cooperate to fight their common enemy, the Communists. See Norton S. Ginsburg *et al.*, *Area Handbook on Malaya* (Preliminary Edition; University of Chicago: Human Relations Area Files 1955) pp. 591–596. (Appendix A in this volume entitled "Chinese Secret Societies" is written by Leon Comber.) The former Secretary for Chinese Affairs, W. L. Blythe, in a private communication to the author, disputes Mr. Comber's interpretation of the May meeting, saying rather that it produced an agreement for joint protection against police action.

[12] From a private communication with W. L. Blythe.

[13] *Straits Times* April 16 1958, pp. 1 and 9. (This is a newspaper summary of the *Report of the By-Election Corruption Commission*.)

[14] del Tufo, *Malaya, A Report on the 1947 Census of Population, op. cit.*, pp. 123 f. No attempt has been made to collect data on religious affiliation since the 1931 census.

[15] *Loc. cit.*

[16] See R. N. Jackson *Immigrant Labour and the Development of Malaya, 1786–1920* (Federation of Malaya: Government Press, 1961).

[17] See F. C. Benham *The National Income of Malaya, 1947–49* (Singapore: Government Printing Office 1951); *Household Budget Survey of the Federation of Malaya, 1957–1958* (Kuala Lumpur: Department of Statistics).

[18] T. H. Silcock and E. K. Fisk (eds.) *The Political Economy of Independent Malaya* (Canberra: The Australian National University, 1963) pp. 276–281. Also see *supra* pp. 17 and 23n.

[19] Today the Malayan Chinese exhibit a widespread desire to become proficient in *Kuo Yu*, the Chinese national language. By making that dialect the common medium of instruction in all Chinese schools, the Chinese hope to create a sense of identity with modern Chinese nationalism and stimulate greater cultural and political unity among themselves. The 1957 census gives the following distribution for the Chinese by "Specific Community":

	thousands	%		thousands	%
Hokkien	740·6	31·7	Kwongsai	69·1	3·0
Hakka	508·8	21·8	Hockchiu	46·1	2·0
Cantonese	505·2	21·7	Hengkwa	11·9	0·5
Tiechieu	283·1	12·1	Hokchia	9·8	0·4
Hainanese	123·0	5·3	Other	34·3	1·5

From *1957 Population Census, Report No. 14, op. cit.*, p. 14.

[20] Robert S. Elegant examines the political aspects of the overseas Chinese in his book *The Dragon's Seed*, (New York: St. Martin's Press, 1959).

B

3 The Indians and Others

Indian literature contains evidence that the first Indian contacts with Southeast Asia date back to the sixth century B.C. However, the Indian cultural impact probably remained slight until the first or second century A.D.[1] Despite the cultural debt Southeast Asia owes India, there is no evidence that Indians migrated to the area in substantial numbers until after the arrival of the Europeans. When the British founded their settlement at Penang in 1786, they brought with them Indian Sepoy troops, and Indian laborers were employed in the construction of public works and harbor facilities. Indian traders soon followed to cater to the Indian community and to share in the expanding trade with the Malay States. Yet, at no time prior to the mid-nineteenth century did the Indian population in Malaya exceed 20,000.[2]

A steady flow of immigrants from India began after the turn of the century when Europeans began to recruit Indians for plantation labor. The exceptional growth of the rubber industry after 1905 stimulated the demand for Indian laborers who were desired because they were hard-working and dependable. Likewise, Indians were sought for the construction of railways and roads.

To promote Indian immigration, the governments of the Federated Malay States and the Straits Settlements established in 1907 an Indian Immigration Fund, from which Indian laborers were given free passage and accommodation from the Indian ports of Negapatam and Madras to their place of employment in Malaya.[3] Indian agents, known as *kanganies*, were sent to India by employers to persuade laborers to apply to the Emigration Comissioner in India for free passage to Malaya. Indians who came to Malaya with government assistance under the *kangany* system were considered to be the special responsibility of the government. However, this meant little more than government officials overseeing the conditions of labor on the estates, and the provision of financial assistance for return to India when their period of labor was completed.[4]

Estate and railway workers remained in Malaya for short periods before return to India. They lived as isolated communities in specially constructed "labor lines" under the supervision of an Indian labor foreman, and thus had very few contacts with other racial communities. Indian merchants and office workers in the cities were better integrated into the life of the country, but even so often had only superficial contacts with Malays or Chinese. After the war the Indian population has become much more stable, and now Indians can with greater justification claim to be permanent residents of the country.[5]

The pattern of Indian immigration has favored South Indians—Tamil,

Malayali and Telegu. Recruitment under the *kangany* system attracted primarily peasant and lower caste Tamils. Apart from the South Indians, the Punjabis and Sikhs comprise the next largest Indian sub-communities.[6] An even smaller number of those enumerated as "Indians" are from Bengal in present-day East Pakistan. However, some confusion results from a common practice in Malaya of calling any Indian a "Bengali" if he is not from southern India.

Indian Economic Activities

Indian immigrants found a fairly small number of economic pursuits open to them. Laborers were employed on estates, public works or the railways. The 1957 census reveals that over 48 per cent of the Indian working population were employed in the cultivation of rubber.[7] While some Indians work their own rubber smallholdings (in 1953 7·6 per cent of the total rubber acreage was owned by Indians), very few of the larger rubber estates are Indian-owned.[8] Rather, the vast majority of Indians employed in rubber cultivation work as wage earners on the larger estates operated by European companies.

In the cities Indians are usually engaged in commerce or are employed in the public services. Government sponsorship of Indian immigration contributed to the high incidence of Indians in government employ. Indians brought to Malaya to construct railways and public works have remained in these occupations through the years. Indians who secured an English-media education have been attracted to the lesser posts in the civil service or to teaching in the government-aided schools. The prestige of a "white collar" job is great for nearly all Asians, but this is particularly true of Indians who are partly influenced by a "caste attitude" toward employment.[9]

When compared with Chinese commercial enterprise, the Indians are outnumbered about four to one. Yet they are an important part of the business community, and in proportion to their numbers are a close second to the Chinese.[10] Indian traders cater to the special demands of the Indian population in addition to extensive retail trading to all Malayan communities. They often specialize in cotton goods, clothing, jewelry and sundries. Most of the goods imported from India and a large proportion of the imports from Japan are marketed by Indians. Except for the Chettiars,[11] Indian business has not expanded to a significant extent into the lucrative tin and rubber export markets.

Indian Education

The government helped to establish Indian primary schools wherever Indians were concentrated. The Labor Code made estates employing Indians provide for schools if more than ten school-age children were on the estate. Government grants-in-aid paid the teachers' salaries in these estate schools. Government-operated schools were also built to accommodate children of Indian laborers employed by the government. The quality of these vernacular schools was poor because of poorly trained teachers, some as young as sixteen years of age. Few students attending Indian schools completed the six years of education.[12] Where it was available, Indians generally preferred an English education. Thus, in the cities, large numbers of Indians enrolled in the excellent English-media schools.[13] Consequently, an important educational-socio-economic division developed within the Indian community between the primarily rural laboring and lower caste Indians who received a poor vernacular education, and the urban business, professional and white-collar workers who received a good English-media education.

The relative importance of the Indians in Mayasia is derived from the large number who have acquired an English education and have become part of Malaysia's intelligentsia. In the English-media schools 19·3 per cent of the students are Indian, many of whom go on for higher degrees and enter professions, particularly those of law and medicine.

Indian Religion

Most Indians profess one of the two major religions of India—Hinduism or Islam. Since Hinduism is the dominant religion of South India, the over-whelming number of émigrés to Malaya were Hindu. Because Hinduism in Malaya is an exclusively Indian religion (if the Ceylon Tamils may be counted as Indian), it tends to reinforce with religious sanctions the communal exclusiveness of the Indian community. Yet the great diversity of beliefs within Hinduism seems to make the Hindu tolerant of other religions and it is easier for a Hindu to accept another faith than for a Muslim. Thus, Christian missionary endeavor has borne fruit among Hindu Indians, especially those of the lower castes who seek to escape from their low status in the caste system and from among those Indians who have attended the English-media mission schools.[14]

Because of his religion the Muslim Indian has closer ties with the Malays. There are few mosques which cater exclusively for Indian Muslims, so they participate in religious services with the Malays. While Indians are not accepted into Malay society as equals, intermarriage between Indian Muslims and Malays is becoming quite common. Indian (or Pakistani) Muslims have also assumed an active role in the leadership of the Muslim community, being represented on such bodies as the Muslim League and the All-Malaya Muslim Missionary Society.

Prewar Indian Political Associations

Before the Second World War most of the Indians in Malaya still considered India to be their home and were largely unconcerned about politics in Malaya, except as related to India. Rather their attention was fixed upon the Indian nationalist movement in its political struggle with the British over the issues of national independence. Since opposition to the British became one test of Indian nationalism, Indian politics began to carry over into Malaya.

The two decades before the Second World War witnessed the growth of a number of Indian organizations in Malaya, some of which developed semi-political objectives. The Indian Chamber of Commerce, the Indian Merchants' Association and the All-Malaya Nattukottai Chettiars Chamber of Commerce were all active in representing Indian commercial interests. But of greater importance politically were the organizations which were formed to better the working conditions of Indian laborers, for these became the forerunners of later Indian political organizations. In 1922 M. K. Ramachandran formed the Young Men's Indian Association (YMIA) which later merged with the Indian Independence League during the Japanese occupation. The Malayan Indian Association (MIA) was founded in 1932 by G. V. Thaver to represent the permanently domiciled Indians. It survived the war, although politically it has been of no account. The Central Indian Association of Malaya (CIAM) was organized in 1936 by S. N. Veerasamy to bargain with employers after the failure of the attempt by the Indian Government to negotiate better conditions for Indian laborers in Malaya following the depression. During the thirties the CIAM became an important vehicle for Indian nationalism in Malaya, and later it assisted in the formation of the Indian Independence League. However, after the war, the CIAM ceased to exist apparently because of the opposition of the returning British who objected to its previous associations with the Japanese and its alleged Communist ties.[15]

In summary, we may note that relatively small numbers of Indians were involved in these embryonic political organizations, and that the few western-educated political militants tended to have their eyes focused on India. Demands for full and equal participation in Malayan politics were being made, but could be safely ignored because they represented a minority of a fragmented Indian community having only inchoate attachments to Malaya.

Other Minorities

We cannot end this survey of the human geography of Malaya without some mention of very small but significant minority groups. The Ceylonese, divided into Sinhalese and Ceylon Tamils, are a minority community, even though they are often classified with the Indians because, in Malaya, most of the Ceylonese are Ceylon Tamils and are very similar in culture, religion and ethnic characteristics to the Indian Tamils.[16] The Ceylonese are quite conscious of their communal identity which is strengthened by such organizations as the Ceylon Federation and the Malayan Sinhalese Association. Since the Ceylonese have been denied membership in many Indian organizations, including the Malayan Indian Congress, they have been forced to play an independent role in politics. For such a small community, this has proven to be both difficult and frustrating.

The Eurasians constitute another important sub-group of about 11,000 in Malaya and a similar number in Singapore. A small tightly-knit Eurasian Catholic community has existed for over three hundred years tracing its origins to the Portuguese who ruled Malacca before 1641. The Portuguese

Eurasians are fiercly proud of their heritage and are jealous about preserving their identity as a community. Many other Eurasians are the product of Anglo-Indian, -Malay or -Chinese unions. These offspring are frequently torn between two cultures, and often are fully accepted by neither society. Although these Eurasians may develop a sense of community among themselves, they frequently suffer from anxiety and uncertainty over their identity.[17] As a community they lack the capacity to act in concert, but, because of their frustrations and sense of grievance against the discriminations of English colonial society, individual Eurasians have frequently been at the forefront of militant anti-colonial nationalist movements. At the same time, other Eurasians have been among the staunchest defenders of colonial rule, and with the approach of national independence, some of them exercised their rights as British nationals to emigrate to England.

1 See G. Coedes *The Making of South East Asia* (Berkeley: University of California Press 1966) pp. 50–75; Brian Harrison *South-East Asia— A Short History* (London: Macmillan 1954) pp. 9–20.

2 T. E. Smith *Population Growth in Malaya* (London: Royal Institute of International Affairs 1952) pp. 83–84.

3 The Indian Immigration Fund was administered by the Indian Immigration Committee, composed of several government officials, the manager of the Malayan Railways, and a number of prominent European planters. This fund was maintained by a per capita tax levied against employers of Indian laborers. See R. N. Jackson *Immigrant Labour and the Development of Malaya, 1786–1920* (Federation of Malaya: Government Press 1961) pp. 57–69, 96–126; J. Norman Parmer *Colonial Labor Policy and Administration: A History of Labor in the Rubber Plantation Industry in Malaya, c. 1910–1941* (Locust Valley, New York: J. J. Augustin for Association for Asian Studies, 1960) pp. 38–78; G. E. Turner, "Indian Immigration", *The Malayan Historical Journal*, Vol. 1 (December 1954), 80–84.

4 In the 1930s the number of unassisted Indian immigrants gradually increased. In 1938 the *kangany* system was outlawed by the Government of India and all immigration since then has been without government subsidy.

5 By 1957 only 34·3 per cent of the Indians had been born in India, while the male-female sex ratio in the 35–39 year age group had shifted from 439 : 100 in 1921 to 134 : 100 in 1957. See Smith, *op. cit.*, p. 86; *1957 Population Census of the Federation of Malaya, Report No. 14*, (Kuala Lumpur: Department of Statistics 1960) pp. 16 and 68.

6 The 1957 census gives the following distribution among those enumerated as "Indians":

	1947		1957	
	thousands	%	thousands	%
Indian Tamil	418·7	78·9	556·5	78·7
Malayali	34·6	6·5	51·2	7·2
Telegu	23·7	4·5	27·1	3·8
Others	53·5	10·1	72·4	10·2
Total	530·6	100·0	707·1	99·9

The 1947 census gives the following figures (in thousands) for other Indian sub-groups: Sikh, 10·2; Punjabi, 20·5; Pathan, 3·1; Bengali, 3·8; Gujerati, 1·3; and Marwari, 1·4. Similar figures for 1957 are not available.

7 See Table 2 above, p. 16.

8 *Federation of Malaya Annual Report 1953* (Kuala Lumpur: Government Printer 1954) p. 114.

9 Although the Indians comprise less than 12 per cent of the total population of Malaya, they constituted over 31 per cent of those employed in "public administration and defense" in the 1947 census and 26 per cent of those employed in "government services" as tabulated in the 1957 census.

10 Of the working Indians, 10·5 per cent are employed in "commerce" as compared to the Chinese figure of 16·4 per cent. Calculated from *1957 Population Census, Report No. 14, op. cit.,* p. 107.

11 Numbering only about 2,000, the Chettiars are the most wealthy of the Indian sub-groups. There are about 800 Chettiar firms, mostly in banking and investments. In 1941 Chettiar investments in Malaya were estimated to be M$270m and since then they have grown considerably. See Usha Mahajani *The Role of Indian Minorities in Burma and Malaya* (Bombay: Vora & Co., 1960) pp. 99–100.

12 In 1957, 55 per cent of the pupils in government-aided Indian schools were in the first or second year of school, while only 5·2 per cent were in the sixth year. See *Federation of Malaya Annual Report on Education, 1957* (Kuala Lumpur: Eastern Press, n.d.) p. 73.

13 In 1962, 78,281 Indians were attending English-media schools, while 62,318 were in Tamil-media schools. These figures were compiled from information obtained directly from the Ministry of Education, Federation of Malaya.

14 The last census to collect data on religion was in 1931, at which time 81·6 per cent of the Indians were counted as Hindus, 9·0 per cent as Muslims and 5·8 per cent as Christians. See M. V. del Tufo *Malaya—A Report on the 1947 Census of Population* (Singapore: Government Printing Office 1948) p. 123.

15 Mahajani *op. cit.* pp. 121–128.

16 Of the total Ceylonese population of 28,030 in Malaya, 24,616 were Ceylonese Tamils. See *1957 Population Census, Report No. 14, op. cit.,* pp. 56–57.

17 For an introspective essay on the problems of the Eurasians as seen through the eyes of an Eurasian see C. H. Crabb *Malaya's Eurasians—An Opinion* (Singapore: Eastern Universities Press, 1960).

4 The Colonial Legacy

Some appreciation of prewar British policy is essential to an understanding of the major constitutional and political changes in postwar Malaya. British rule in the nine Malay States had been extended gradually and indirectly by means of what came to be known as the residential system. This device had been secured through separate treaties with the Ruler of each state, by which he agreed to "receive and provide a suitable residence for a British Officer to be called Resident, who shall be accredited to his Court, and whose advice must be asked and acted upon on all questions other than those touching Malay Religion and Custom".[1] Treaties were made with Perak and Selangor in 1874; Negri Sembilan came under the system by stages between 1874 and 1895, while the treaty with Pahang dated from 1888. Each state was administered separately until 1895 when these four British-protected states joined to form the Federated Malay States with a fairly centralized administrative structure.

Five Malay States remained out of the Federation and were identified by the curious title: Unfederated Malay States. Of these states, Johore was the largest and most important. It came under British protection in 1885, but the treaty providing for the assistance of a British administrative officer (called General Adviser) dates from 1914. The four northern Malay States of Perlis, Kedah, Kelantan and Trengganu were under nominal Siamese suzerainty until the Anglo-Siamese treaty of 1909, which transferred to Britain rights of suzerainty and protection. Later, treaties were made for "British Advisers" to assist in the administration of these states, the dates being: 1910 for Kelantan and Trengganu, 1923 for Kedah and 1930 for Perlis.

Colonial rule in Malaya thus operated through a confusing patchwork of legal and administrative structures. In the Federated Malay States British rule was of longer duration, more complete and more uniform, with the British Resident in each State subject to the central direction of a Resident-General and the High Commissioner (who was also the Governor of the Straits Settlements). The Unfederated Malay States, coming rather late under British rule, retained greater autonomy, and remained more traditional in their political system and backward in their economic development. For these states, the principal administrative officer, the British Adviser, exercised less control over the Malay Ruler and fewer British officers were employed in administration, so a more predominantly Malay administration centered about the royal court prevailed.

Rather than examine the constitutional and administrative system of indirect rule,[2] we need only consider the broad outlines of British policy in prewar Malaya. The resident system was initially designed primarily as a means of bringing law and order to the Malay States. The Malay governments remained, and in legal theory sovereignty rested with the Sultans—not with the British Crown. In a number of cases British courts recognized the ultimate sovereignty of each Sultan, restricted only by the terms of the treaties made with the British.[3] Even so, the "advice" given to the Sultans by the British Residents or British Advisers had to be "acted upon" so that the British very quickly assumed nearly complete control of the decision-making powers of government. While the forms of government retained their Malay trappings, the functions of government were carried on with a fairly efficient bureaucratic administration staffed in the higher positions by British officials. The government attracted little public attention and cautiously avoided political controversy.

Under such arrangements British policy followed these principles: (1) the legal position of the Sultans was safeguarded, as laid down in the treaties; (2) the government was preserved as the distinctly Malay government which antedated any of the treaty arrangements made with the British; (3) the Malays were considered the indigenous people, and the government accepted special responsibility for their welfare and the preservation of their rights as the "subjects of the Sultan" in each state.

The "pro-Malay" policies of the prewar regime helped to preserve the traditional patterns of Malay society and its peasant-based economy. At the time, these policies seemed both benevolent and appropriate, but they did not help the Malays to come to terms with the modern world or adapt themselves to a competitive economic system. Furthermore, the privileged status of the Malays created an undercurrent of resentment among the other racial communities. The British legal frame of mind probably accounted for the extension of the original objectives of the treaties beyond the time when they were politically appropriate.

Although the colonial government established State Legislative and Executive Councils, their membership was appointed rather than popularly elected, and these Councils were never given power to be more than advisory bodies to the government. Pledged to the preservation of the existing autocratic Malay sultanates, British policy left no room for substantial reforms leading to the eventual popular participation in democratic institutions. So long as the economy remained buoyant, and the government remained benevolently humanitarian toward the immigrant communities and gave preferential privileges to the Malays, few complaints were voiced. Demands for self-government were seldom made, and then only in the forms of hints and friendly requests. So as not to surrender its authority, the colonial regime tried to respond to grievances before they became too intense. In this sense, the colonial government was responsive, without being responsible, to the people it ruled.

Although British colonial policy was remarkably effective in discouraging widespread political activity, prewar Malaya did, as we have seen, develop some organizations having political objectives, and nationalist movements in China and India produced counterparts in Malaya. While early Malay political activists were more concerned with developments in Malaya, even they became politically motivated, partially as a result of reactions to events in Egypt, Turkey and the Dutch East Indies. Thus, with few exceptions, prewar politics was dispersed and fragmented in the sense that these early political associations tended to be oriented toward issues arising beyond Malaya's borders, and their activities in Malaya were somewhat incidental to their primary concern. Consequently, racial communities were not as inclined to view each other as political protagonists, since their political enemies were being defined outside the arena of domestic politics. This may provide a partial explanation of the relatively low intensity of communal conflict in the prewar era, despite serious communal antagonisms which were submerged but nonetheless evident.

The Impact of Japanese Rule

With the Japanese invasion, the British colonial system came crashing to the ground. What had seemed to be the "superior protecting power" had suffered a disastrous and humiliating defeat after little more than two months of ineffective fighting. The aura of invincibility and permanence could never again clothe British rule in Malaya.

Because Japanese policy was not uniform in its treatment of Malaya's racial communities, the occupation produced different responses and attitudes within each community.

The Japanese hoped to win over the Malays to their cause and sought to utilize them in the administration of the country. Before the invasion, Japanese agents established contacts with *Kesatuan Melayu Muda*, and during the military campaign some of its members were given special duties under the command of a Major Fujiwara.[4] When Singapore fell Ibrahim Yaacob, Ishak bin Haji Mohammad and Ahmad Boestamam were released from British imprisonment to be given employment in the Japanese administration. Ibrahim Yaacob became the Commanding Lieutenant-Colonel of the Japanese-sponsored volunteer military force called *Pembela Tanah Ayer* (PETA) meaning "Avengers of the Country". While the KMM was revived, its value to the Japanese was short-lived, and by June 1942 the Japanese outlawed it. However, Ibrahim Yaacob recruited his KMM supporters into PETA thus keeping the KMM organization intact as a political force in fact, if not in name.[5]

Initially the Japanese Military Administration had planned to abolish the status of the Malay Sultans, and it announced a policy of racial equality of all Asians under the "Great Spirit of Cosmocracy" which supposedly was a guiding principle of the Greater East Asia Co-Prosperity Sphere.[6] What appeared to be the renunciation of the pro-Malay policies of the British was soon forgotten because the Japanese needed the cooperation of the Malays in the civil administration of the country. Under Japanese military control,

Malays continued to perform routine administrative and policing duties. By January 1943 the Occupation authorities enunciated a new policy of recognizing the honorific position of the Sultans, of confirming their status as head of Islam in each State, and of supporting them with allowances comparable to prewar days.[7] Although not entirely successful, this policy made it easier for the Malays to cooperate with the Japanese. Thus, despite the rigors of the Japanese occupation, most Malays in the civil administration gave at least nominal cooperation to the Japanese.

The occupation had less impact upon the ordinary Malay peasant. While inconvenienced by the shortage of certain consumer goods, he did not suffer the deprivations of the urban population because of his self-sufficiency in food. For the most part, the Japanese interlude had little immediate effect upon the ordinary Malay who remained politically inert. By contrast, Malays in government service assumed fairly high positions of responsibility upon the sudden departure of their British superiors, so gaining valuable administrative experience and confidence in their abilities to run the country without assistance. These Malays became more politically motivated, and were to provide the leadership for the postwar Malay nationalist movement.

In the early stages of the war, the Japanese cautiously encouraged selected Malay political leaders to organize support among the Malays. A few were even taken to Japan to receive training and indoctrination in the principles underlying the "Greater East Asia Co-Prosperity Sphere" and the Japanese claim to the leadership of Asia. However, a damper was placed on Malay nationalist movements since the Japanese hoped to keep Malaya under their control for many years.

As the tides of war turned, Japan became more favorably disposed toward nationalist movements in Southeast Asia, hoping to turn these forces against her enemies. In August 1943 Burmese "independence" was proclaimed, followed in October by a similar declaration for the Philippines. By September the following year the Japanese Government announced that Indonesia would be granted independence in the future. This news was greeted with enthusiasm by radical Malays especially in Singapore. Ibrahim Yaacob and his *Kesatuan Melayu Muda* followers in the PETA armed force requested that Malaya be granted independence as a part of Indonesia. The concept of *Indonesia Raya* or Greater Indonesia had long captured the imagination of militant Malay and Indonesian nationalists who saw it as a means of uniting into a single nation all peoples of Malay-Indonesian ethnic stock. The proponents of this idea saw it as a means to resolve problems posed by alien minorities in Southeast Asia and by the threatened return of colonial powers.

In July 1945 Japanese military administrators from Java, Sumatra, Celebes and Malaya met in Singapore to discuss these demands and decided to promote a Malay nationalist movement based on the *Indonesia Raya* concept. Accordingly, the Japanese sanctioned the formation of a Malay political organization known as KRIS, which name was an abbreviation of a longer title. Apparently at first it was decided to call it *Kesatuan Ra'ayat Indonesia*

Semenanjong (Union of Peninsular Indonesians), but later the title *Kekuatan Ra'ayat Istimewa* (Supreme Effort of the People) was adopted. Ibrahim Yaacob assumed the leadership of KRIS while preparations were made for its first meeting in Kuala Lumpur, which finally came just two days after the Emperor issued his imperial rescript announcing Japan's surrender and just as Indonesian independence was being proclaimed by Sukarno.[8] About twenty representatives of Malay organizations attended the meetings.[9] Although the plan for Malaya's union with Indonesia collapsed because of Japan's sudden surrender, it was agreed that the nationalist struggle would be continued in Malaya. The leadership of KRIS passed to Dr. Burhanuddin since Ibrahim Yaacob remained in Singapore until his flight to Jakarta a few days following the KRIS convention. While KRIS disintegrated as a political organization as soon as the British returned to Malaya, its impact on Malay politics was considerable, since it provided the nucleus for the later formation of the Malay Nationalist Party, and it gave to early postwar Malay politics a radical pro-Indonesian hue.

In summary, we have seen that the Japanese occupation exposed the Malays to new currents of nationalism, but the Japanese, nonetheless, failed to create a dynamic mass nationalist movement among the Malays, either in support of or in opposition to their rule. However, the growing nationalism in Indonesia during the war did attract considerable attention on the part of some Malays who became enamored with the vision of *Indonesia Raya*.

After years of reading reports of Japanese brutality in China, the Chinese were quite naturally terrified when the Japanese war machine began its conquest of Malaya. Some Chinese joined a volunteer military unit called Dalforce and fought in the last few days of Singapore's defense. While the Japanese talked about the equality of all Asians, they assumed that the Chinese were completely hostile, and when Singapore surrendered, the Japanese military issued orders for the execution of 50,000 Chinese who were suspected of being Communists, Nationalists or of having participated in Dalforce. The Japanese found it impractical to execute this number and brought the massacres to a halt after the elimination of perhaps about half that number, but oppressive measures such as arbitrary terror, confiscatory taxation and compulsory loans were employed against the Chinese.[10]

Because "foreign" political parties had been outlawed in Malaya since 1929 (the KMT had been banned four years earlier), it might appear that a number of Chinese organizations or secret societies would have become skilled in the techniques of underground activity. Yet, only the Malayan Communist Party was prepared for an active anti-Japanese insurgency. While the Japanese were still fighting on the peninsula, the leader of the MCP, Loi Tak, approached the British authorities and obtained their assistance in training and arming about 200 Communists to provide the nucleus for their guerrilla force.[11] Calling itself the Malayan Peoples Anti-Japanese Army, the Communist-led resistance movement attracted widespread support among the Chinese, who suffered most from the calculated brutality of the Japanese. Although not all Chinese were willing to take the risks or were in a position to participate in anti-Japanese activities, a large proportion of them found some way to assist the guerrilla movement.

Substantial changes in the leadership of the Chinese community occurred during the occupation. The traditional leaders of Chinese society either fled the country with many of the Europeans, or they remained and were eliminated or forced to come to terms with the Japanese who easily identified them and kept them in line through coercion and intimidation. Consequently, the prewar elites of Chinese society were discredited and frequently despised. Their place in the Chinese community tended to be filled by the Communists, who were not so easy to identify, who were mostly from a younger generation, and who had the courage and ingenuity to establish an effective politico-military organization in the midst of the Chinese community and under the noses of the Japanese.

Besides these changes in the structure of Chinese society, the war experience strengthened Chinese nationalism and their sense of communal identity. In addition, the Chinese became more accustomed to violence, intimidation and extortion, and the leaders and "heroes" of the Chinese during the war were those who had perfected the use of these techniques to pursue their political objectives. Considering these factors, it is little wonder that the Chinese community became a source of much political turmoil in the postwar years.

As the war clouds darkened over Asia, the Indians in Malaya were torn between conflicting desires. The politically conscious ones hoped that British rule in Asia would be broken through the misfortunes of war. But they found it difficult to become enthusiastic supporters of Japan, especially since the Japanese conquest of China was far worse than any of the excesses of British rule in India. For their part, the Japanese attempted to capitalize upon the nascent nationalism in many parts of Asia with their talk of a "Greater East-Asia Co-Prosperity Sphere". Their propaganda fell on the receptive ears of many Indian nationalists who hoped that Japanese adventuring in Asia would facilitate Indian independence.

During the 1930s the Japanese had encouraged, aided and given asylum to a number of Indian nationalists in the hope that the Indians would collaborate with the Japanese if trouble developed with England. Rash Behari Bose, an Indian revolutionary given asylum by the Japanese, laid plans for India's liberation through the joint efforts of Japan and the overseas Indians under the banner of his Indian Independence League (IIL) and its parallel military force, the Indian National Army (INA).[12]

When the Japanese invaded Malaya, the Indians were faced with a difficult problem of political affiliation. The brutality of Japanese rule was evident to all. They hardly acted like the "liberators of Asia". Yet, the Japanese made positive overtures to the Indians. Rash Behari Bose and a Japanese political officer, Major Fujiwara, worked closely together to win Indian support for the Indian Independence League. When Singapore capitulated, approximately 60,000 British Indian troops were captured. Of these, about

5,000 agreed to join the Indian National Army after appeals by Bose and a promise of release from the prisoner-of-war camps. By vigorous recruiting, the IIL is reported to have expanded its membership to 95,000 by May, 1942.[13]

The leadership of Rash Behari Bose was soon eclipsed by the more dynamic Indian nationalist, Subhas Chandra Bose. He had been in Germany trying to get a promise of material support from Hitler for his revolutionary cause when the war in the Pacific broke out. He arrived in Singapore in July after a journey in a German submarine. He quickly turned his energies to building up the Indian National Army (renamed *Azad Hind Fauj*), which ultimately expanded to about 50,000 recruited from all of Southeast Asia. Having to rely upon the Japanese for most of its arms and rations, the INA made a rather poor showing in its only campaign in Burma. S. C. Bose also helped to form a Provisional Indian Government, in the name of which the Japanese broadcast their propaganda to India.[14]

Despite Japanese support for the Indian Independence League, their policies toward the Indians was not entirely consistent. While some received favored treatment, most Indians suffered greatly under Japanese rule. The ravages of war had upset the rubber industry, and the Indian estate population had difficulty in finding sufficient means of support. Inflation hit the urban population, especially those on fixed income in "white collar" positions. But the most dreadful feature of the occupation for the Indians involved the Japanese use of forced labor for the construction of the vital railway link from Bangkok to Rangoon. Since there were insufficient prisoners-of-war for this project, laborers were conscripted ruthlessly and arbitrarily from the local people. The Indians employed as construction laborers by the Malayan Railways were drafted in great numbers, and the unemployed Indian estate population was another ready source of labor. Many thousands of Indian laborers were forcibly transported to Siam to work on the infamous Bangkok to Rangoon "death railway". Contrary to the popular impression created by the film, *Bridge on the River Kwai*, more Indians than British prisoners lost their lives constructing the railway.[15]

Under these circumstances, it is easy to see that the Indians' reaction to the Japanese occupation was not uniform. A few became open and active collaborators in order to secure the benefits the Japanese gave to their supporters. Many more were associated with the Japanese through the IIL and the INA. Although most Indians disliked the Japanese because of their arrogance and inhumanity, very few of them became active in the anti-Japanese resistance movement.

Through all the hardships and deprivations of the war, the Indians became more conscious of the impact of world events upon their own future, and their growing political consciousness was gradually diverted from India to their immediate interests in Malaya.

Political Uncertainties After Japan's Defeat

Almost a month elapsed between Japan's initial suing for peace and the arrival of British troops in Malaya. The sudden collapse of Japan had precluded adequate planning, and little consideration had been given to many of the problems standing in the way of Malaya's rehabilitation. Malayans themselves were in a state of shock and felt as though they were being swept along by events beyond their control. After the brutality and hardships of the Japanese occupation, most Malayans were more than happy to welcome back the British to accept the surrender of Japanese forces and to re-establish orderly government. But, beyond that, few political organizations had clearly articulated objectives and demands. Neither had they decided upon the most suitable methods for the political activity.

The determination of political objectives and methods depends in large measure upon an assessment of what the future has in store and how it may be shaped by organized political action. Except for the Communists, few political activists had a rigid ideology purporting to foretell the "wave of the future". Yet, all had some assumptions and expectations which undoubtedly influenced their choice of goals and operational methods. Nearly universal among them was their high expectations for democracy and self-government, and their belief in the inevitable demise of colonialism. The events of the war, coupled with the growing nationalist movements throughout Asia helped to convince political leaders of all shades of opinion that colonialism would soon give way to a new order of independent democratic nations. Yet, there seemed to be great differences of opinion as to how the colonial regime would be replaced and what political system should take its place. At one extreme were those who believed that colonialism would be displaced only after a violent revolution against diehard foreign imperialists. At the other extreme were those who hoped that colonialism would gradually develop into a permanent cooperative partnership between the colonial power and its former colonies. Most political elites appeared to be uncertain how the British would respond to their rising nationalist demands. Generally, the more radical the doctrine of a group, the more it anticipated an intransigent response on the part of the British, and the more it assumed that violent means would be required to achieve their goals. When the British Military Administration first assumed command in Malaya, no political groups appeared ready to eschew all forms of violence in their political activities. However, the militants were far more ready and willing to resort to such tactics than the moderates. The policies of the British administration to each of the various political groups in Malaya became a primary factor in determining the group's choice of means for political expression.

The immediate postwar years were a period of fundamental re-alignments in politics as new issues of power and policy had to be decided upon for the new Malaya. Since the British re-established the basis of their authority and worked out the constitutional forms for postwar Malaya, indigenous politics developed within an environment largely established by the institutions and policies of the returning colonial government. Therefore, we will examine the major outlines of British policy and postwar constitutional developments leading up to Malayan independence before we turn to the main account of Malaya's emerging political alignments.

[1] The first treaty of this kind, the Pangkor Engagement of 1874, is reproduced in C. Northcote Parkinson *British Intervention in Malaya 1867–1877* (Singapore: University of Malaya Press 1960) pp. 323–324.

[2] An account of British rule in Malaya before 1941 can be found in the following: Roland St. John Braddell *The Law of the Straits Settlements—A Commentary* 2nd ed. 2 vols., (Singapore: Kelly and Walsh, 1931); Rupert Emerson *Malaysia—A Study in Direct and Indirect Rule* (New York: The Macmillan Co., 1937); S. M. Middlebrook and A. W. Pinnick, *How Malaya is Governed*, 2nd ed., (London: Longmans Green, 1949); Sir Frank Swettenham *British Malaya* 3rd ed. rev., (London: George Allen & Unwin, 1948).

[3] For example see *Duff Development Co. v. Government of Kelantan* (1924) A.C. 797.

[4] T. H. Silcock and Ungku Abdul Aziz, "Nationalism in Malaya", in William L. Holland (ed.) *Asian Nationalism and the West* (New York: The Macmillan Co. 1953) p. 292.

[5] Radin Soenarno, "Malay Nationalism, 1896–1941", *Journal of Southeast Asian History* Vol. 1, no. 1 (March 1960) pp. 19–20.

[6] Lee Ting Hui, "Singapore Under the Japanese", *Journal of the South Seas Society*, Vol. XI, part 1 (1961) pp. 55–56. "Cosmocracy" was defined as "Universal Brotherhood".

[7] Yoichi Itagaki, "Some Aspects of the Japanese Policy for Malaya Under the Occupation, With Special Reference to Nationalism," published in K. G. Tregonning (ed.) *Papers on Malayan History* (Singapore: Journal of South-East Asian History 1962) p. 257.

[8] Radin Soenarno and Yoichi Itagaki present conflicting evidence on the dates of the first meeting of KRIS. The former cites the dates August 16 and 17, while the latter states that KRIS met on August 17 and 18, 1945. See Soenarno, *op. cit.*, p. 21 and Itagaki *op. cit.*, p. 264.

[9] The list of those affiliated with KRIS includes: Dr. Burhanuddin, Dato Onn bin Jaafar, Hasan Manan and Ahmad Boestamam.

[10] Lee Ting Hui, *op. cit.* 31–69. Also see Victor Purcell *The Chinese in Southeast Asia* 2nd ed., (London: Oxford University Press 1965) p. 306.

[11] Harry Miller *Menace in Malaya* (London: George G. Harrap & Co., 1954) pp. 37–38. Also see F. Spencer Chapman *The Jungle is Neutral* (New York: W. W. Norton & Co., 1949).

[12] Usha Mahajani *The Role of Indian Minorities in Burma and Malaya* (Bombay: Vora & Co., 1960) pp. 141–143.

[13] *Ibid.*, pp. 145–147.

[14] Subhas Chandra Bose was a former President of the Congress Party (1938–39) and leader of its militant "left wing". He was killed toward the end of the war on his way to Japan. For a number of years after the war rumors circulated in Malaya to the effect that he was still alive and would shortly make a dramatic appearance in Malaya or India.
An interesting account of Bose's selection as leader of the IIL and the mass rally staged by him in Singapore is contained in *Malai Sinpo*, July 5, 1943, p. 1. Also see Sivaram, M. *The Road to Delhi* (Rutland, Vermont: Charles Tuttle & Co., 1967), pp. 111–135.

[15] T. E. Smith estimates the Indian mortality was about 20,000 per annum during the war years. See T. E. Smith *Population Growth in Malaya* (London: Roya Institute of International Affairs 1952) p. 82.

5 Malaya's Colonial Government in Transition

During the war, the British Colonial Office concluded that the prewar political system would be unsuited to the conditions likely to prevail when the British returned to Malaya. It was argued that Malaya needed a more rational and uniform system of government. The confused patchwork of four Federated and five Unfederated Malay States plus three Settlements had hindered the development of a uniform system of law and administration. The legal fiction of the sovereignty of the Malay Sultans in each state was considered to be an anachronism. The constitutional position of the Rulers hindered democratic reforms and made it virtually impossible for non-Malays to secure rights and privileges of citizenship. Thus, prewar policies and legal doctrines would have denied political rights to about half of the population. Whitehall realized that changes would be required to meet the anticipated demands for democratic reforms and eventual self-government.

To this end, the Colonial Office began examining proposals for constitutional and legal reforms.[1] The opinions of prominent Malayans who had fled to exile during the war were solicited,[2] although no attempt was made to draft formal proposals for a new constitution. The period immediately following the liberation of Malaya was considered to be the most appropriate time to initiate the needed reforms.

On September 5, 1945, British troops under Admiral Mountbatten landed at Singapore to accept the surrender of the Japanese forces in Malaya.[3] Under his authority, the British Military Administration ruled the country until a new civil government was inaugurated almost seven months later. During this period the Colonial Office took the necessary steps to insure that a new constitution would contain those reforms considered to be essential for Malaya's future.

The MacMichael Treaties and the Malayan Union

To prepare the legal groundwork for the new civilian administration, the British Government sent Sir Harold MacMichael to Malaya in October 1945 to negotiate new treaties with the Malay Rulers. At the same time he investigated the conduct of each Ruler during the Japanese occupation, and, in the case of a disputed title to the throne, determined which claimant was rightful sovereign. Because of these circumstances, the Malays later claimed that the treaties were made under duress from a tacit threat of deposition.

It is difficult to evaluate this charge, but MacMichael was in each state only a few days and was able to make his investigation and complete the treaties with the Rulers in all nine Malay States. It is apparent, however, that the Rulers did not fully realize the implications of the treaties they signed.[4]

The treaties provided that the Sultans were to accept "such future constitutional arrangements for Malaya as may be approved by His Majesty" and "full power and jurisdiction" was transferred to Britain.[5] The purpose of these treaties was to nullify the legal sovereignty of the Sultans so that the British Government would have a free hand in establishing constitutional reforms. Fear of stirring up local controversy caused these treaties to be made in haste and with considerable secrecy. As a result, public opinion was not given a chance to crystallize on the fundamental issues involved.

By January of 1946 MacMichael returned to London with the treaties. The British Government almost immediately issued a White Paper on the proposed arrangements for a Malayan Union and for Singapore.[6] This document stated the case for more equal treatment of the immigrant populations and proposed a more unified and centralized government in a union to include all the Malay States plus the former Settlements of Penang and Malacca. The decision to retain Singapore as a Crown Colony is explained as follows:

> At least for the time being Singapore requires separate treatment. It is the centre of entrepôt trade on a very large scale and has economic and social interests distinct from those of the mainland. It is recognized, however, that there were and will be close ties between Singapore and the mainland, and it is no part of the policy of His Majesty's Government to preclude or prejudice in any way the fusion of Singapore and the Malayan Union in a wider union at a later date should it be considered that such a course was desirable.[7]

With Singapore separated from the Malayan Union, the Malays outnumbered the Chinese, but still did not comprise a majority of the population. If Singapore had been included, however, the Chinese would have become the largest community. For this reason the proposal that Singapore remain a Crown Colony was not too controversial in view of the concessions already proposed for the Chinese. Likewise, British trading interests supported the decision to retain Singapore as a separate Crown Colony.

On the crucial and controversial question of political rights for non-Malays, the White Paper stated ". . . all those who have made the country their homeland should have the opportunity of a due share in the country's political and cultural institutions".[8] It then proceeded to outline citizenship proposals which called for the inclusion of all persons born in Malaya or Singapore or residing therin for ten out of the preceding fifteen years, with the occupation period disregarded, while naturalized citizenship could be acquired after a residence of five years in Malaya or Singapore. These proposals were viewed favorably by the Chinese and Indians, since a majority could qualify for citizenship.

Under these proposals British control was to remain approximately the same as before, but the legal reforms were to give essentially equal recognition to all who lived in Malaya. This revision of British policy was explained as follows:

> . . . the pre-war system will not lend itself to that political adjustment which will offer, through broad-based institutions in which the whole community can participate, the means and prospect of developing Malaya's capacity in the direction of responsible self-government.[9]

Reaction to the Malayan Union

Shortly after the announcement of British policy toward the proposed Malayan Union, Malay agitation against the proposals became surprisingly severe. In fact, the Malayan Union proposals provided the spark which roused the Malays from their political lethargy. Mass demonstrations and rallies were held throughout the country by Malays in all walks of life, who suddenly became fearful of being overrun by the non-Malay communities. For the Malays it seemed that they were in danger of losing "their country".

In London a number of retired British civil servants who had served in Malaya began to carry the "case for the Malays" to Whitehall,[10] and encourage key Malay leaders to agitate for their rights in Malaya. However, the Labour Government was determined to push ahead with its plans. On December 19, 1945, the Straits Settlements Repeal Bill was introduced in the House of Lords and was finally passed by the House of Commons on March 18 after several lively debates.[11] At the close of debate the Government promised that the question of common citizenship would not be included in the Order in Council establishing the Malayan Union. The Colonial Secretary explained:

> The Government cannot abandon this basic principle of common citizenship . . . I assure the House, in the light of the criticisms made in regard to the Orders in Council, that these will be considered, and that, so far as this Order relating to citizenship is concerned, it will not be issued for a while until these consultations have been made possible. The House should be under no illusion that the British Government must push on with this policy. We believe it to be right, and in the best interest of Malaya. We want Malayan cooperation, and we believe, in their interest, that this policy alone can further general prosperity and social happiness.[12]

Subsequent Orders in Council[13] established the constitutional framework for the Malayan Union and for Singapore, which supplanted the British Military Administration. Both constitutions became operative April 1, 1946.

Although the preliminary statement of policy toward Malaya was made on October 10, 1945,[14] and a clarification of policy was contained in the White Paper of January, specific constitutional provisions were not made public until less than a month before the Malayan Union came into effect. During this period there had been no opportunity for Malayans to participate in drafting a constitution. Such representations as were made by Malayans had to be through the normal channels of communication to Whitehall. The Malay Rulers of Johore, Kedah, Perak, Selangor and Negri Sembilan all made strong objections to the provisions of the Malayan Union. While their objections were noted, little was done to allay the misgivings of the Malays about their political future under the new constitution. As a result, the Malays rallied to the support of their Sultans in their decision to boycott the new constitution. None of the Malay Rulers attended the installation ceremonies of Sir Edward Gent, the new Governor of the Malayan Union. Rather, the Malays wore white mourning bands for seven days, and Malay members refused to participate in the deliberations of the Advisory Council.[15]

At the same time, in London, the Under-Secretary for the Colonies announced that the government would continue to press for the Malayan Constitution Bill which supplemented the Order in Council setting up the Malayan Union. The government was still determined to force through the scheme for creating a common citizenship, and to provide for the constitutional form of government which would deprive the Malays of their privileged position in the government of Malaya.

The Sultans, with the considered advice of a number of former British officials, continued to make strong protests against the implementation of the Malayan Union. Before the new government was a month old all nine Malay Rulers prepared a petition to be sent directly to the King against the "annexation of Malaya".[16] The communalism that had flared up just after the liberation was again returning in the form of overt Malay hostility toward the non-Malay communities. Finally it became apparent to the British Colonial Office that some adjustment would have to be made to accommodate the strong resistance of the Malay communities to the constitutional forms and the avowed policies of the Malayan Union. Accordingly, the governor, Sir Edward Gent, announced that:

> His Majesty's Government can rightly expect us in Malaya to settle our own temporary differences and this can only be done by full and free consultation here. I hope that no further time will be lost in doing so, because I regard unnecessary prolongation of the present transitional arrangements under the Order in Council as highly unsatisfactory.[17]

In the latter part of May a two-man Parliamentary mission composed of Lt. Col. D. R. Rees-Williams (Labour) and Capt. L. D. Gammons (Conservative) arrived in Malaya to hear the representations on various aspects of the British Government's policy toward Malaya. On May 29, the Parliamentary mission attended the conference of all the Malay Rulers held in the Palace of the Sultan of Perak at Kuala Kangsar.[18] Here the Rulers presented their objections along with a set of proposals that had been drafted earlier through consultation among themselves and the newly formed United Malays

National Organization,[19] representing most of the politically vocal segments of the Malay community. The talks continued behind closed doors for several days. Probably few substantive decisions were made, since the object of the mission was to report to the Colonial Secretary on the constitutional and political situation.[20] However, later events reveal that the substance of the Rulers' proposals received sympathetic consideration, and they became the basis for the re-negotiation of constitutional arrangements for Malaya.

Drafting the Federation of Malaya Agreement

For over a month extensive discussions were held between the Colonial Office, the Governor-General Mr. Malcolm MacDonald, Governor Sir Edward Gent, the Malay Rulers and representatives of the United Malays National Organization. Finally, on July 3, 1946, the Colonial Office agreed to the substitution of a federal form of government for the Malayan Union, and the substitution of a High Commissioner for the Governor as symbolic evidence that governmental authority was derived from the Malay Rulers rather than the British Crown.[21] The Colonial Office also indicated a willingness to abrogate the MacMichael Treaties if some agreements were reached along the lines of the proposals discussed during the Rulers Conference.

To facilitate a review of the constitution, Governor Gent announced the formation of a committee of twelve to seek an agreement on "tentative proposals with a view to recommendations being submitted to His Majesty's Government which will be acceptable to all concerned in Malaya".[22] Known as the Working Committee, it consisted of six Government members, four Malay Rulers and two representatives of the United Malays National Organization.

Once it became clear that the Malay Rulers and UMNO were to have initial responsibility for drafting a new constitution, the non-Malay communities became alarmed over a possible reversion to the pre-war system of colonial rule with its openly "pro-Malay" policies. Thus, the Malay reaction against the MacMichael Treaties was followed by a similar non-Malay reaction against procedures which gave primary responsibility for the new constitution to the traditional elites of Malay society and to the Colonial Government. A mounting chorus of protests against the unrepresentative character of the Working Committee came from the non-Malay communities, the very active English-educated nationalists, the Malayan Communist Party and some radical Malay nationalist organizations.[23] A number of organizations opposing the formation of a Federation of Malaya, as proposed by the Working Committee, joined together in an association called the Pan-Malayan Council of Joint Action (later changed to the All-Malaya Council of Joint Action).[24] Although the AMCJA became the spokesman of the non-Malays seeking an equality of status in Malaya, it claimed to be "the only body which embraces all Asiatic communities of Malaya and with which the Government may conduct negotiations on Constitutional issues".[25] In view of the massive antipathy of the Malays toward the Malayan Union, the Colonial Office chose first to negotiate a constitutional formula which the

Malay Rulers and UMNO would be willing to support, and then to give the domiciled non-Malay populations an opportunity to criticize and suggest changes, provided they did not too seriously alienate Malay opinion. Such a procedure clearly denied representation to the non-Malay communities at the most important stage of the constitution making process.

After two and a half months of consultations the Working Committee presented its recommendations and proposed draft treaties to supplant the MacMichael Treaties and provide the basis for the new constitution.[26] Following the publication of this report a "Consultative Committee on the Constitutional Proposals" was formed to hear representations of all persons or organizations wishing to present their views on the proposed constitutions.[27] The All-Malaya Council of Joint Action decided to boycott the Consultative Committee because the AMCJA did not wish to take the "pro-Malay" Working Committee Report as the basis for discussions on constitutional revision.[28] Instead, it tried to discredit the procedures of constitution making and attempted to mobilize public opinion against the proposed federation. Nevertheless, the Consultative Committee completed its report on March 21, 1947, and recommended a number of substantial changes in the draft proposed by the Working Committee.[29] Recommendations of the Consultative Committee were then transmitted to the Colonial Secretary, and the original Working Committee was re-convened to consider modifications to their earlier draft constitution. Finally, a Plenary Conference of the Government, the Malay Rulers and UMNO was held on April 24, 1947,[30] at which time some of the recommendations of the Consultative Committee were accepted. The final constitutional draft which emerged was ratified by His Majesty's Government on July 24, 1947, signed by the Malay Rulers in January 1948, and the Federation of Malaya came into being on February 1, 1948.

The Federation of Malaya Agreement

While the Federation of Malaya Agreement represented substantial concession to Malay demands, the views of the non-Malay communities were not ignored, and on many constitutional issues the Agreement represented a compromise which generated criticism from the more communally-oriented political leaders, both Malay and non-Malay. Even so, the new constitution was a document the Malays could live with and one the non-Malays found difficult to reject completely.

The position of the Malay Rulers was strengthened under the new constitution by ensuring their position as constitutional monarchs within each of the Malay States. For the federation as a whole, they acted through a body called "The Conference of Rulers". Any proposed changes in immigration laws required the approval of this body, and any major changes in salary schemes for public officers or government re-organization proposals were to be submitted to the Rulers Conference for discussion prior to enactment.[31] These subjects are of particular interest to the Malays, who fear non-Malay encroachment into their more privileged position in the public services and strongly oppose any relaxation of immigration restrictions against non-

Malays (excepting Indonesians). In this constitutional scheme, the Rulers were conceived as having a special responsibility for protecting the interests of the Malays, rather than being impartial heads of state outside the arena of politics.

The federal form of government represented another concession to Malay criticism of the unitary Malayan Union, as Malays looked upon the States as the primary bulwark against the political demands being made by non-Malays. Malay politicians and civil servants dominated the state governments. These were the very people who had successfully organized Malay opinion against the Malayan Union, which threatened their "power base" at the state level.

The federal system created by the Agreement did little to guarantee the autonomous authority of the States since the Federal Government had complete legislative powers, except for matters related to Islam and Malay custom. A substantial number of powers were shared by both the Federal and State Governments, but in all matters of conflict, federal authority was supreme. The States were assured revenues from certain sources, the most important being fees and taxes on land, licenses (other than vehicle), revenues of local authorities, court fees and fines, and revenues from sale and rent of state property and land. State expenditure for many subjects (under 65 headings) were to be financed from federal revenues, and the States were given executive responsibility for the administration of a number of subjects, including: schools, local authorities, land laws, Malay Reservations, agriculture, forestries and aborigines.[32] However, in all these areas the Federal Government could exercise both legislative and executive responsibility if it cared to do so. In short, the federal system was nearly unitary in legislative powers, yet permitted, and to a degree assured, a decentralized state administration in a number of important subjects. Perhaps most important, however, was the psychological impact of the word "federalism" which gave the Malays an assurance that the Malay States were not to be swallowed up in a "union" which had no apparent historical ties with traditional Malay forms of government.

The citizenship provisions incorporated into the Agreement made the Malays and a few others citizens, and established legal means for non-Malays to acquire federal citizenship after fulfilling certain requirements of domicile, language, birth and oath of allegiance.[33] While the Malays considered the new citizenship requirements very generous to the immigrant communities, the non-Malays considered the citizenship requirements too restrictive and designed to deny the non-Malays full legal and political rights in Malaya. Likewise, the restrictive immigration policies were viewed as discriminatory and a device to check the political power of the non-Malay communities.

The government under the Federation Agreement was centered on the High Commissioner who, as representative of His Majesty, was responsible for the functioning of the government. He was given full executive authority for the Federation Government, and had the power to constitute public offices, and appoint or dismiss persons from public office. In the performance of his executive responsibilities, he was aided by a Federal Executive Council composed as follows:

Official Members	*Unofficial Members*
Chief Secretary	5 to 7 Members not holding an office of
Attorney General	emolument under any government in the
Financial Secretary	Federation
	Any number of other Unofficial Members holding an office of emolument as the High Commissioner considers suitable.

All the Members of the Executive Council were appointed by the High Commissioner, the regular term of office being three years. The High Commissioner was required to consult the Council on all matters involving the exercise of his powers, except where "the public interest would sustain material prejudice", or for matters that were too unimportant or too urgent to be considered. However, the High Commissioner alone made the ultimate decision as to the exercise of his powers and did not have to give any reasons for his decisions. He presided over the Executive Council, and he alone had the power to submit questions to the Council for discussion. However, individual Members of the Council could submit requests to the High Commissioner and have their requests recorded in the minutes of the Council. The official languages of the Executive Council were Malay and English, although it is doubtful that the proceedings were ever conducted in Malay since no High Commissioner became very fluent in the language.

The 1948 Federation Agreement provided for a Legislative Council which was composed as follows:

The High Commissioner (Presiding Officer)	*ex officio*	
The Chief Secretary	*ex officio*	Must be Federal
The Attorney General	*ex officio*	Citizen or British
The Financial Secretary	*ex officio*	Subject under the
11 Officials (holding an office of emolument under the Federal Government or the Crown)	appointed by the High Commissioner	discipline of the Government
9 Presidents of Councils of State (in the Malay States)	*ex officio*	
2 Representatives of Settlement Councils	*ex officio*	Must be Federal Citizen
50 Unofficials (not holding an office of emolument under the Federal Government or the Crown)	appointed by the High Commissioner to represent various communities and economic interests	May speak and vote as they wish

The responsibility for the administration of the Government rested entirely with the fifteen appointed and *ex officio* Official Members. This number comprised the Government in the Legislative Council, and each Official Member was individually responsible, not to the Legislative Council, but to the High Commissioner, who, in turn, answered to the Secretary of State for the Colonies in London. The Legislative Council acted upon all legislation, but the High Commissioner possessed reserved powers permitting him to override any action by the Legislative Council or to make enactments without the consent of the Legislative Council if he "shall consider it is expedient in the interests of public order, public faith, or good government . . ."[34] Appointed State and Settlement Councils and Town Councils were established at the lower levels of government, having similar functions and subject to the limitations of higher authority.

The preamble of the Agreement explicitly provided for the transitional nature of its constitutional provisions by proclaiming as a policy,

> . . . that progress should be made toward eventual self-government, and, as a first step to that end, His Majesty and their Highnesses have agreed that, as soon as circumstances and local conditions will permit, legislation should be introduced for the election of members to the several legislatures to be established pursuant to this Agreement . . .[35]

During the first few years of the Federation, little was done to implement this statement of policy. In 1950 the first steps in the evolutionary approach toward self-government were taken at the local level when members of a number of town councils were popularly elected. In 1951 and 1952 further progress was made in the extension of elections to local authorities, and a number of important ordinances were enacted to facilitate the creation of popularly elected local government.[36]

The introduction of popularly elected local and town councils, while significant, did not require any substantial changes in the constitutional structure of the Federation. These changes were accomplished through federal and state enactments. Intense political activity did not accompany the introduction of local elections since local issues were of lesser importance and did not raise the fundamental political questions involving the relationships between the diverse elements in the body politic and the questions of constitutional structure for democratic government.

Introduction of the Member System

Rather than start with the introduction of elections for the Federal Legislative Council, the British first sought to develop Malayan political leaders and gradually confer upon them a larger share of responsibility for administration and leadership in the Legislative Council. As a first step on the gradual road to self-government, Whitehall decided to introduce a modified cabinet system which would enable both Officials and Unofficials to be appointed as ministerial department heads and to participate in the responsibility of formulating government policy. This constitutional modification came to be known as the Member System.[37]

When the Member System was first proposed, the reaction of the local political leaders was neither enthusiastic nor severely critical. The most influential Malay paper, *Utusan Melayu*, is reported as regarding the plan as meaningless without the introduction of elections to the Legislative Council.[38] Generally, indigenous politicians remained unresponsive to the Member System proposals until the proposals were submitted to the Legislative Assembly for approval. An amendment introduced by a European Unofficial Member seeking to postpone the Member System, brought forth a flurry of indignant emotion from prominent Malayan Members who then hastened to support the government's proposal to share responsibility with Unofficials.[39] Unfortunately, the debate centered on the single issue of postponing the plan, and the Member System was adopted without a close examination of some important constitutional questions. The responsibility of the individual Ministers was never precisely defined. An Unofficial appointed to a ministerial post by the High Commissioner was required to resign if the Legislative Council should pass by a two-thirds majority a vote of no confidence in him. But Official Members appointed to a ministry were not subject to removal by the Legislative Council.[40] Perhaps any attempt to define precisely the lines of responsibility of the ministers would have prevented the gradual transition which the Member System implied. In effect, all the ministers were individually accountable to the Legislative Council, but the ultimate authority to assure the stability of the Government rested with the High Commissioner, armed with the reserved powers permitting him to override the actions of the Legislative Council. Significantly, the success of the Member System rested, not upon precise legal formulae, but upon the spirit of cooperation that developed between Officials and Unofficials comprising the ministry.

When the new ministry assumed office under the Member System, it was composed of five Unofficials and five Officials in addition to the Chief Secretary. The portfolios of Home Affairs, Health, Education, Lands Mines and Communications, and Works and Housing were awarded to Unofficials, while Officials retained the portfolios of Economic Affairs, Defense, Chinese Affairs, Industrial and Social Relations, and Railways and Ports.[41]

Under the Member System the administration was no longer centralized under the authority of the Chief Secretary. His duties changed from that of being the "chief administrator" to that of a coordinator of the ministry, in a manner analogous to that of a prime minister. Similarly, the Member System involved a revision of the role of the High Commissioner. As more and more responsibility for government policy was assumed by the Members holding portfolio, the position of the High Commissioner, as presiding officer in the Legislative Council, became anomalous and inconsistent with the professed move toward parliamentary government. Consequently, in September 1953, eighteen months after the inauguration of the Member System, the High Commissioner retired as President of the Legislative

Council and was replaced by a Speaker, who assumed a role similar to that of the Speaker in the House of Commons.[42] Thus, by stages the Member System introduced many features of parliamentary government before the introduction of elections and before the establishment of "parliamentary supremacy". The British authorities undoubtedly assumed that the early introduction of national elections would have released such strong demands for immediate self-government that the transition to self-government would have been unduly abrupt. The Member System seemed to provide a more gradual means of transferring responsibility.

If the object of the Member System was to give administrative experience in top policy-making positions to Malaya's future political leaders, the experiment must be judged to be largely a failure because only two members of the Alliance Party (which has dominated Malayan politics since the first elections) were given portfolios.[43] However, the Member System probably had a number of intangible effects on Malayan politics which no doubt made it a worthwhile experiment. For one thing, it seems likely that parties represented in the government came to appreciate the sincerity of the British authorities in trying to make Malaya's transition to independence as peaceful and smooth as possible. Perhaps also, political leaders became more aware of the complexity of government and developed an appreciation of the difficulties facing the government. But this is a conjecture which cannot be tested.

Introduction of Elections for the Federal Legislative Council

In the development of self-government and independence, the introduction of national elections is one of the most difficult steps to undertake. Elections determine the political power of all groups in society and allocate the positions of leadership. Consequently, the first national elections put a severe strain upon the political and social unity of the nation since many of the most fundamental political issues have to be faced by the electorate in their first trip to the polls. There is no reservoir of fundamental agreement established over a period of time in previous political battles.

Malayan politicians were well aware of the importance of elections and the constitutional changes which were required to determine their form. They did not wait for election proposals to come from Whitehall or the High Commissioner.[44] Indeed, by 1953 the major political groupings were already jockeying for position by trying to sponsor competing proposals for elections to the Federal Legislative Council and for constitutional revision in anticipation of self-government.

In view of the preliminary political skirmishes that were under way over the issues of Federal elections, Whitehall decided to prepare the groundwork for elections to the Legislative Council. The Malay Rulers were approached by the High Commissioner, and together they agreed to support a proposal for the formation of a committee to examine the question of elections and future constitutional changes. This proposal was announced in the Legislative

Council by the Deputy High Commissioner in May 1953.[45] A committee of 46 members was selected by the High Commissioner to prepare comprehensive election proposals. The Elections Committee first met in August and after five months its report was completed. During that time the Committee became the focus of political attention for all parties.

The Elections Committee reached a large measure of agreement but on a number of key issues it was badly split. Two rival parties[46] represented on the Committee clashed with such vigor that the election proposals became a major test of strength between the two parties, and ultimately the clash developed into a rather severe constitutional crisis. The contest revolved around the following questions: the number of members to be elected in the new Legislative Council; the date for the first elections; the eligibility of government servants to stand for election; and the use of the limited vote in multiple member constituencies.[47]

Because elections entailed basic constitutional changes in the Federation Agreement, the Report of the Committee, with both majority and minority views, was submitted to the process of negotiation between the Rulers and Her Majesty's Government. The High Commissioner and the Rulers considered the Report at two meetings of the Rulers Conference before reaching final decisions on the substance of the Report. The amendments to the Report agreed upon in the Rulers Conference were approved by the Colonial Secretary, Mr. Oliver Lyttelton, in April 1954.[48]

The proposals that were finally accepted by the Rulers and Her Majesty's Government represented a compromise between the majority report and the several minority reports of the Elections Committee. Where the Committee had split 26 to 18 in favor of barring a government servant from standing for election, the ultimate decision was made to allow government servants in the junior grades to stand for election by taking one month's leave without pay prior to election day. The successful candidate would be required to resign from the public service, with opportunity for reinstatement within ten years upon the completion of membership in the Legislative Council. Where the Committee had split 28 to 14 in favor of a limited vote in multiple member constituencies,[49] the High Commissioner's dispatch avoided the issue by hinting that multiple member constituencies of over two members would be unlikely, and the issue need not arise. One of the most bitterly contested issues was the demand by a minority of 13 that elections should be held not later than November 1954. This minority report, backed by the Alliance Party, was rejected with the statement that the date "would not permit the proper completion of the work necessary before the electors can go to the polls". However, elections were promised on the "earliest practicable date in 1955".[50]

The most important minority report concerned the composition of the new Legislative Council. A majority of 29 on the Committee called for an elected minority of 44 out of a total Legislative Council membership of 92. The minority, however, demanded the election of 60 members in a Council of 100. Likewise, they proposed eight fewer appointed positions to be filled by the

High Commissioner. The proposals finally accepted at the Rulers Conference compromised between the minority and the majority reports, and provided for an elected majority of 52 in a Council of 99, and the "nominated reserve members"[51] were fixed at 5. The majority proposals, the minority proposals and the final decision on the composition of the Legislative Council are summarized in the table below.

TABLE 7
Proposals for the composition of the Legislative Council 1954

Majority report	Minority report	Final proposals accepted by Rulers Conference
1 Speaker	1 Speaker	1 Speaker
3 Ex officio	3 Ex officio	3 Ex officio
11 State and Settlement Members	11 State and Settlement Members	11 State and Settlement Members
20 Scheduled Interests	20 Scheduled Interests	22 Scheduled Interests
6 Commerce	6 Commerce	6 Commerce
6 Planting	6 Planting	6 Planting
4 Mining	4 Mining	4 Mining
2 Agriculture and Husbandry	2 Agriculture and Husbandry	2 Agriculture and Husbandry
2 Trade Unions	2 Trade Unions	4 Trade Unions
3 Racial Minorities	3 Racial Minorities	3 Racial Minorities
2 Official Members	2 Official Members	2 Official Members
8 Nominated Reserve		5 Nominated Reserve
44 Elected Members	60 Elected Members	52 Elected Members
Total 92	100	99

The decisions of the Rulers Conference were severely criticized by the Alliance Party which was in a minority on the Elections Committee. Indeed, the Alliance, claiming to have a popular mandate, sought to enforce their demands by calling upon all their members to resign from all government positions on executive and legislative councils—local, state and federal. An Alliance delegation travelled to London to present its demands to the Colonial Secretary, but he refused to re-open negotiations with the Rulers to alter the proposals accepted by the Rulers Conference. By this time, the major point at issue was the proportion of elected members in the Legislative Council. As the political crisis became more severe, the High Commissioner made a concession to the Alliance which helped to resolve the dispute. He agreed to consult the party winning a majority of the elected seats before appointing the five "nominated reserve" members.[52] By this means, whichever party might win a majority of elected seats was assured of the control of five additional seats through appointment, and under these terms the boycott of government by the Alliance Party was ended.

Shortly before the Rulers Conference had acted upon the election proposals, a three-man Constituency Delineation Commission was appointed by the High Commissioner to divide Malaya into election districts of approximately equal population with some "weightage" for area. This report[53] was made public during the height of the controversy over the election proposals, but it attracted almost no criticism and was accepted in its entirety.

The constitutional changes made during the years between 1945 and 1955 prepared the way for Malayan independence. Each change in the constitutional framework also stimulated new developments in the country's politics. Many of the constitutional reforms altered the balance of political forces, and the discussion of new constitutional forms generated political activity, especially as elements in the population began to become aware of the fact that their welfare hinged upon the provisions of the constitution. Our attention must now turn to these emerging political forces in postwar Malaya.

[1] In 1932 Sir Samuel Wilson drafted proposals for the administrative unification and reorganization of the Malay States. These proposals had to be abandoned because of the opposition of the Malay Rulers, but, with the war, they could be reconsidered and may have become the basis for many of the constitutional changes being prepared by the Colonial Office. See Robert O. Tilman *Bureaucratic Transition in Malaya* (Durham, North Carolina: Duke University Press, 1964) n. 66, pp. 32–34. Also see *Parliamentary Debates—Commons*, (Fifth Series) 1945–46, Vol. 420, 709–710.

[2] Tan Cheng-lock was one of the exiled Malayans who, during the war, submitted memoranda to Whitehall concerning constitutional reforms.

[3] N. I. Low and H. M. Cheng *This Singapore* (Singapore: Ngai Seong Press 1948) pp. 161–173.

[4] Criticism of the tactics and policies of Sir Harold MacMichael were aired in the House of Commons. See *Parliamentary Debates—Commons*, (Fifth Series) 1945–46, Vol. 420, 648–665.

[5] Sir Harold MacMichael *Report on a Mission to Malaya* Colonial No. 194 (London: His Majesty's Stationery Office 1946).

[6] *Malayan Union and Singapore* Cmd. 6724, (London: His Majesty's Stationery Office, 1946).

[7] *Ibid.*, p. 3.

[8] *Ibid.*, p. 1.

[9] *Ibid.*, p. 2.

[10] Note Articles by Sir George Maxwell, Sir Roland Braddell, Sir Arnold Robinson and Sir Frank Swettenham in *Straits Times*: November 14, 1945, p. 2; November 15, 1945, p. 2; November 16, 1945, p. 2; November 29, 1945, p. 2; February 8, 1946, p. 2; February 11, 1946, p. 2; and March 7, 1946, p. 2. An article by Sir Cecil Clementi appeared in the *Malay Mail*, April 27, 1946, p. 2.

[11] *Parliamentary Debates—Commons*, (Fifth Series) 1945–46, Vol. 420, 637–727, 1540–1565. *Parliamentary Debates—Lords*, 1945–46, Vol. 139, 17–45, 312, 435.

[12] *Parliamentary Debates—Commons*, (Fifth Series) 1945–46, Vol. 420, 727.

[13] *Statutory Rules and Orders*, 1946, Vol. 1, (London: His Majesty's Stationery Office, 1947), 543–571 (O. in C. No. 463), 1539–1557 (O. in C. No. 464).

[14] *Parliamentary Debates—Commons*, (Fifth Series) 1945–46, Vol. 414, 255–256.

[15] *Straits Times*, April 2, 1946, p. 1.

16 *Straits Times*, April 18, 1946, p. 3; April 25, 1946, p. 3; April 30, 1946, p. 1.

17 *Malay Mail*, April 29, 1946, p. 1.

18 *Straits Times*, May 26, 1946, p. 1; May 30, 1946, pp. 1 and 3.

19 An account of this political party is given in later chapters.

20 For the report of Mr. Gammons and Mr. Rees-Williams to the House of Commons see *Parliamentary Debates—Commons*, (Fifth Series) 1945-36, Vol. 425, 301-312, 316-318.
   The Malay Rulers and UMNO secured the assistance of Sir Roland Braddell in the preparation of draft proposals which were considered by the Rulers Conference and submitted to the Colonial Office.

21 *Straits Times*, July 5, 1946, p. 1.

22 *Straits Times*, July 26, 1946, p. 5.

23 Note *Straits Times*, July 16, 1946, p. 3; August 2, 1946, p. 4; August 8, 1946, p. 4; August 9, 1946, p. 4; August 12, 1946, p. 5; August 16, 1946, p. 5.

24 An account of this political organization may be found in Chapter VII.

25 Telegram of Tan Cheng-lock to the Secretary of State for the Colonies, December 22, 1946, published in *Constitutional Proposals for Malaya, Report of the Consultative Committee*, (Kuala Lumpur: Government Printer, 1947), p. 183.

26 *Ibid.*

27 The Consultative Committee was formed in January 1947 and consisted of four members chosen by the Governor from the Malayan Union Advisory Council (a transitional quasi-legislative body), two from the Government (the Chairman and the Secretary to the Committee), and four prominent Malayans nominated by each of the four chosen from the Advisory Council. No Malays were among the Members of the Consultative Committee. This must have been a deliberate attempt to balance the predominantly Malay Working Committee with a non-Malay Consultative Committee.

28 *Straits Times*, January 30, 1947, p. 6.

29 *Constitutional Proposals for Malaya, Report of the Consultative Committee, op. cit.*, pp. 7-14.

30 *Straits Times*, April 25, 1947, p. 1.

31 *The Federation of Malaya Agreement, 1948*, reprinted 1952 with amendments, (Kuala Lumpur: Government Press, 1952), pp. 27-30.

32 *Ibid.*, Second, Third and Fourth Schedules, pp. 58-70.

33 In brief summary, the following persons were defined as federal citizens by operation of law:
   a a subject of the Ruler of any State (i.e. the Malays in the Malay States);
   b a British subject born in Penang or Malacca and permanently resident in Malaya (i.e. most of the second generation Malayans from Penang and Malacca);
   c a British subject born in Malaya whose father was also born in Malaya, or who became a permanent resident of Malaya;
   d any person who habitually speaks the Malay language and conforms to Malay custon (i.e. all Malays and nearly all Indonesians who wish to claim citizenship);
   e any person born in Malaya, both of whose parents were also born in Malaya and who is permanently resident in Malaya (i.e. third generation Malayans);
   f any person whose father is a federal citizen at the date of that person's birth.
   In addition, citizenship could be secured by naturalization. The applicant had to meet the following requirements:

a he must be born in Malaya and resident for eight out of the preceding twelve years, or for fifteen out of the preceding twenty years;

b he must be "of good character";

c he must have an adequate speaking knowledge of Malay or English; (This requirement was waived for applicants 45 years of age or older who had also been resident in Malaya for 20 years. After 1950, both speaking and reading knowledge was required for those tested in Malay.)

d he must take a citizenship oath of allegiance to Malaya.

See: *The Federation of Malaya Agreement, 1948, op. cit.,* pp. 40–43 (Par. 124 and 125). For more detailed citizenship regulations see also: *The Federation of Malaya Agreement (Amendment) Ordinance, 1952,* Council No. 23 of 1952 (L.N. 534).

[34] *The Federation of Malaya Agreement, 1948, op. cit.,* p. 23.

[35] *Ibid.,* p. 2.

[36] *Report of the Select Committee on Policy to Provide for Elections to Local Government Authorities,* Council Paper No. 26 of 1950, Federation of Malaya.

Report on the Village Council Bills, 1952, with Bill, Council Paper No. 40 of 1952, Federation of Malaya.

L. C. Hill *Report on the Reform of Local Government* (Singapore: Government Printing Office, 1952).

Harold Bedale *Establishment, Organization and Supervision of Local Authorities in the Federation of Malaya* Council Paper No. 14 of 1953, Federation of Malaya.

[37] The Member System was proposed in April 1950, approved by the Legislative Council in January 1951 with minor revisions, and put into effect in March of the same year. See: *Memorandum Relating to the Proposal for the Introduction of a System Under Which Departments of Government Will Be Grouped and Placed Under Members Who Will Be Responsible Therefor to the High Commissioner and Certain of Such Members Will Be Appointed From Among Unofficial Members of the Legislative Council,* Council Paper No. 49 of 1950, Federation of Malaya.

[38] *Straits Times,* October 10, 1950, p. 6.

[39] *Legislative Council Debates, 24th January 1951,* Federation of Malaya, 14–29.

[40] In the debates the Chief Secretary explained that forcing an Official Member to resign would automatically throw him out of employment and this would "be an intolerable burden, both upon Your Excellency and upon the Official . . ." *Ibid.,* 15–16.

[41] *Legislative Council Debates, 25th April 1951,* Federation of Malaya, 2.

[42] The first Speaker was Dato Mahmud bin Mat, who had been the Member for Lands, Mines and Communications since the inception of the Member System.

[43] In fact, the members of the Alliance Party were reluctant to accept any portfolios under the System, apparently fearing the political consequence of cooperation and close association with the British colonial regime. The High Commissioner, Gerald Templer, did persuade Tunku Abdul Rahman to get two Alliance members to accept portfolios, and accordingly, Dr. Ismail and Colonel H. S. Lee were appointed. The hesitant caution on the part of the Alliance Party was well-founded since the rival Party Negara (which was more closely associated with the British regime) discovered that the cooperation and encouragement of the British became a political "kiss of death".

For an account of some of the behind-the-scenes negotiations over these appointments see Harry Miller, *Prince and Premier* (London: George G. Harrap & Co. Ltd., 1959), pp. 123–128.

[44] In the debate on the High Commissioner's speech to the Legislative Council in March 1953, Tunku Abdul Rahman, who subsequently became Malaya's first Prime Minister, criticized the government for failure to propose the introduction of elections to the Federal Legislative Council. Note *Legislative Council Debates, 18th, 19th & 20th March 1953,* Federation of Malaya, 223–226.

45 Speech of Sir Donald MacGillivray *Legislative Council Debates, 6th & 7th May 1953*, Federation of Malaya, 285.

46 Party Negara was strongly represented on the Committee and its views were largely incorporated into the majority report of the Committee. The Alliance Party objected to its minority representation on the Committee because of its recent victories in state and local elections. It demanded that the Committee adopt the Alliance proposals because of the "popular mandate" which it claimed to enjoy.

47 M. J. Hogan (Chairman) *Report of the Committee Appointed to Examine the Question of Elections to the Federal Legislative Council*, Council Paper No. 21 of 1954, Federation of Malaya.

48 *Introduction of Elections to the Federal Legislative Council*, Council Paper No. 21 of 1954, Federation of Malaya.

49 A limited vote means that in multiple member constituencies the voter is given fewer ballots to cast than seats to be filled from the constituency. Thus, in a three member constituency, the voters might be awarded only two ballots to cast. This system is designed to aid minority groups by making a bare majority unlikely to obtain all the seats in a multiple member constituency.

50 *Introduction of Elections, op. cit.*, p. 6.

51 These members were to be appointed by the High Commissioner to represent "any important element which had not found adequate representation through the electoral process". See Hogan, *op. cit.*, p. 7.

52 *Malay Mail*, July 8, 1954, p. 5.

53 *Report of the Constituency Delineation Commission*, Council Paper No. 36 of 1954, Federation of Malaya.

c

6 The Malayan Communist Party

Marxist-inspired political movements began to develop in Southeast Asia during the first and second decade of this century. By 1920 an embryonic Communist Party had been established in Indonesia,[1] but this party did not become the main vehicle for the spread of Communism to Southeast Asia. Rather, the prime organizer for Communist parties in this area became the Chinese Communist Party. Although it was founded in 1921, the appearance of other independent Communist parties in Southeast Asia was delayed for some years, partly because of the 1923 agreement reached between the Comintern agent Adolph A. Joffe and the founder of the Kuomintang, Sun Yat-sen. The Soviet Government agreed to help reorganize and strengthen the Kuomintang, and in return, the Chinese Communists were permitted to join and work within the Kuomintang.[2] This agreement meant that the Chinese Communists operated as a faction within the KMT until 1927 when Chiang Kai-shek purged the KMT of its Communist wing.

In Malaya a Communist oriented left-wing faction of the Kuomintang developed in the mid-1920s.[3] The Comintern's Far Eastern Bureau in Shanghai helped to direct the activities of Chinese Communists in the KMT, who in Malaya formed the Malayan Revolutionary Committee of the KMT.[4] The open breach between the Kuomintang and the Chinese Communist Party in 1927 was duplicated in Malaya by a purge of KMT "extremists". Shortly afterwards, five representatives of the Comintern came to Singapore to organize the new Nanyang (South Seas) Communist Party.[5] It was disbanded in 1930 when the Malayan Communist Party was founded to take its place. During the following year Communism suffered a severe setback when the Singapore Police detected the presence of the French Communist, Joseph Ducroux, who had been sent to assist the MCP with advice and money. When Ducroux was arrested, the Police obtained evidence which led to a number of arrests of important Communists in Singapore, Hong Kong and Shanghai.[6] Despite these reverses, the Malayan Communist Party is reported to have increased its membership from 1,500 in 1931 to 37,000 on the eve of the Second World War.[7]

During its first decade of activity, the Malayan Communist Party concentrated on fomenting strikes and political disturbances against the British. This policy continued after the outbreak of war in Europe, but was abruptly reversed after the German attack on Russia in June 1941, at which time the MCP decided not to undermine the British war effort. When the Japanese attacked Malaya, both the Malayan Communist Party and the Kuomintang offered to give full support to the British to resist the Japanese invasion. A Mobilization Committee headed by the prominent Chinese millionaire, Tan Kah-kee, hastily recruited a Chinese military unit which fought in the defense of Singapore.[8] Mention has already been made of the arms and training given by the British to MCP cadres for the purpose of establishing guerrilla resistence forces.[9] Later in the war, an Allied unit called Force 136 was formed to supply and direct guerrilla activities in several Southeast Asian countries.[10]

The Communist Guerrillas

The Communist-led guerrillas called themselves the Malayan Peoples Anti-Japanese Army (MPAJA). The name helped to create an impression of strength far beyond their military capability. They never engaged in any sizeable military actions, although the organization consisted of an extensive network of supporters who sustained the main force of 5,000 to 7,000 guerrillas living in the heart of the jungle. Because the guerrillas had to depend on "subscriptions" from the civilian population, they were forced to devote an inordinate proportion of their energies to collecting "subscriptions" and protecting their supporters from informers and "traitors". By the end of the war, the guerrillas had inflicted a few hundred casualties on the Japanese, while, in the same period, 2,542 "traitors" were eliminated.[11]

With the sudden collapse of Japan in August 1945, Japanese forces retired to their military installations, waiting to surrender to the British forces, which did not arrive from India for almost a month. During this interval the Communist guerrillas emerged from the jungle as victorious heroes. Their victory celebrations were followed by reprisals staged as "trials" against those believed to have collaborated with the Japanese. No acquittals were given and particularly brutal methods of executions were employed.

British officers in Force 136 attempted to persuade the Communist guerrillas to abide by directives issued from the Allied Southeast Asia Command headquarters in Ceylon. Earlier the Communists had agreed to recognize the superior authority of the Allied military command in return for Allied arms, but some guerrilla units now became openly hostile to the few British officers on the scene. While they might have utilized the interim period to seize control of some areas where they were strong, they were hesitant to make such a defiant show of force. Once the main British forces landed in Malaya such a course was out of the question. The Communist leadership then had to adjust their tactics to contend with the new conditions created by British rule.

The British Military Administration, as the new interim authority, was anxious to deactivate all the guerrilla forces as soon as possible so as to minimize threats of dacoity or insurgency. The Communists, on the other hand, wished to retain their military organization to strengthen their political position. An agreement was finally reached whereby the guerrilla units were to be disbanded. Each guerrilla soldier was to receive M$350 and a ration of rice as a discharge allowance, while members of the original guerrilla units trained by the British were to receive an additional M$30 per month for a period of three years. At the time of discharge, each guerrilla was to turn in his arms.[12] During December 1945, 6,800 guerrillas were demobilized and given their discharge payments. Of these, fewer than 500 failed to turn in weapons.[13]

When the Malayan Communist Party finally consented to disband the MPAJA, they issued a statement encouraging members of the guerrilla forces and supporting organizations to continue their "friendship" and "association" in order to "rebuild a new and democratic Malaya".[14] Shortly afterward an Ex-Service Comrades' Association was founded to transform the guerrillas into a highly disciplined para-military arm of the Malayan Communist Party.[15]

Postwar Communist Objectives

Of all the political groups in Malaya, the Communist Party was the best organized and most powerful political force immediately following the war. After commending the Communists for their leadership of the resistance movement, the British were in no position to prevent the Malayan Communist Party from operating as a legal organization. Communist leaders seized this opportunity to revive their General Labour Union, which, before the war, had been banned. Using both persuasion and intimidation, subsidiary unions were established for nearly every trade and industry. The Party exercised an effective system of control through the General Labour Union.[16] Union dues extracted from the workers were channelled through the GLU into the coffers of the Communist Party, providing it with the funds to employ the bulk of the MCP membership as full-time organizers and agitators.[17] Extremely low wages and food shortages stimulated labor unrest and helped to create favorable conditions for Communist exploitation of the mushrooming labor union movement.[18]

To provide the physical "persuasion" for union disputes, a Workers' Protection Corps was formed by the MCP. This corps carried out strong-arm tactics and "militant" activities. Needless to say, it operated beyond the law and became the object of considerable attention from police authorities.[19]

As the Communist Party consolidated its power in the labor union movement and in numerous Chinese schools and front organizations, it began a well-directed campaign to pursue its political objectives. Before the war ended the MCP had issued a manifesto proclaiming the following objectives:

(1) to drive the "Japanese Fascists" out of Malaya and to establish a republic; (2) to establish a government with representation from all the nationalities, improve living conditions, and develop industry, agriculture, and commerce; (3) to give freedom of speech, association, etc., and abolish the old oppressive laws; (4) increase wages, abolish high taxation and money-lending at high interest; (5) reorganize the guerrillas into a National Defence Army; (6) establish free education in the several languages; (7) confiscate Fascist property and restore

property confiscated by the Japanese; (8) practise tariff autonomy; and (9) combine with Russia and China to free the oppressed peoples of the East.[20]

After the war, on August 25, 1945, this "nine point program" was revised to the "Eight Great Proposals" of the MCP by substituting "British" for "Japanese Fascists" and omitting point (9) to give the impression that the MCP was not allied with international Communism.[21]

In January 1946 the MCP called a plenary meeting of its Central Committee to consider both its tactical line and the revision of its program. The leadership of the Party was split on the question of immediate tactics. Although the MPAJA guerrillas had been demobilized and ostensibly disbanded, one group favored an immediate civil struggle against the government to create "liberated areas" from which the Communists could operate as a competing revolutionary government. This policy has been called the "Chinese Line" because it followed the example of the Chinese Communist Party in its struggle against the Kuomintang. The second group, led by Loi Tak (Lai Teck), the MCP Secretary-General, proposed a more moderate policy which may have been patterned on Soviet revolutionary tactics and followed the Comintern line at the time.[22] In his report of the meeting, Loi Tak summarized the alternatives which were considered.

Today, the colonial problem can be resolved in two ways: (i) Liberation through a bloody revolutionary struggle (as in the case of Vietnam and Indonesia); or (2) through the strength of a National United Front (which embodies total popular solidarity with harmony established between all political parties and factions).[23]

The Central Committee decided that the conditions were not favorable for the first policy, deciding instead to pursue with all the means at its command the victory of the revolution "through the strength of a National United Front". Two weeks later the Party issued a long document explaining its policies and calling for both a "United Racial Emancipation War Front" and a "Great United Democratic War Front" to conduct an "All Peoples' Anti-Imperialist Strife".[84] In short, the MCP hoped to achieve its initial objectives by claiming the banner of Malayan nationalism and anti-imperialism in order to forge a mass movement under its direction which would dominate the political scene and make the position of the British increasingly untenable. In this proposed United Front, the associated "parties and cliques" were promised that their independence would be "respected".

The Communist Campaign Against Colonial Authority

As the Communists re-organized the structure of their party they began to test their strength and the reaction of the British authorities through a series of "incidents". These "incidents" were designed to accomplish some of the following objectives: to embarrass the government; to mobilize support for the MCP; to promote the formation of a mass United Front under their leadership; to tighten party control and discipline, and to generate a militant mood in politics. A brief recital of a few of the party's activities will illustrate its tactics and provide examples of the issues it chose to dramatize its cause.

Shortly after the British returned, a number of criminal cases were tried involving extortion, larceny and murder by ex-guerrillas, some of whom had become "union organizers" for the Party. These cases were handled just as any other criminal case in spite of their obvious political implications. One such person tried for extortion was Soong Kwong, General Secretary of the Selangor Peoples' Anti-Japanese Union. His case came to trial three times since, at the first two trials, the three assessors and the President of the Court disagreed on the question of his guilt.[25] When he was finally convicted, the MCP decided to make his trial the basis of a challenge to the government with the objective of obtaining the release of some thirty other Communists also in detention awaiting trial on similar charges. A general strike was called for January 29, 1946. It was most effective in Singapore where, according to the figures of the General Labour Union, 173,000 participated in the strike.[26] The strike was less effective on the peninsula, but Malaya's only coal mine at Batu Arang was organized by a Communist union which did force a work stoppage and threatened to disrupt the supply of coal to Malaya's railways.[27] After one day the general strike was suddenly called off, apparently because the MCP anticipated more public support, and the failure of the labor movement to maintain its "solidarity", even though 3,500 intimidators helped to enforce the strike. Four days later the government released Soong Kwong on a M$2,000 one year good behaviour bond.[28]

The next Communist inspired "incident" was staged on the anniversary of Singapore's capitulation to the Japanese. In accordance with legal requirements, the Communists had applied for permission to hold public meetings on February 15 as a day of "humiliation" and to "commemorate the members of the MPAJA who died fighting the Japanese". The authorities refused to grant permits for these meetings because it was obvious that the Communists sought to celebrate the defeat of the British. When the MCP called for public defiance of the ban on February 15 celebrations, the police raided the Singapore headquarters of the Malayan Communist Party, the New Democratic Youth League, the General Labour Union, and the Ex-Service Comrades Association. When the day came, police clashed with Communist demonstrators in Singapore and Penang, while in Johore fifteen persons were killed in the most serious incident. A number of Communists were taken into custody and were later tried and convicted of joining an "unlawful assembly and assaulting a police officer".[29]

Another contest developed over the Communist attempt to secure control over the Singapore waterfront unions. The Singapore dock workers were employed by an agency of the Singapore Government, the Singapore Harbour Board. Before the war two non-Communist unions had represented Harbour Board employees. These unions re-established themselves immediately after the cessation of hostilities, and in May 1946 negotiated a new contract calling for a 20 per cent wage increase and other benefits. In the meantime, the Communist-sponsored General Labour Union began its campaign to gain control of Singapore's strategic waterfront by means of a competing union, the Singapore Harbour Labourers' Union (SHLU). Labor violence against rival unionists staged by the Workers Protection Corps occurred at frequent intervals during strikes in the latter part of 1946. By February 1947 the Communist unions and the Singapore Government appeared close to a show-down as the number of unions on strike approached the proportions of a general strike, which was threatened, but never materialized.[30] Tensions eased slightly during the latter half of 1947, but a new crisis developed when the Harbour Board announced that the labor contract system was to be dis-continued and that wages were to be paid directly to the workers. Formerly, wages went to a labor contractor who, in turn, paid his crew. Since the unions had supplanted the traditional Chinese labor contractors, this system gave the unions excessive powers over the workers. By 1947 the SHLU had become the dominant waterfront union, so this change threatened to undermine one means of its control over the workers. Finally a temporary settlement was reached whereby the Harbour Board agreed to delay the introduction of the new pay system in return for a promise of two months of labor peace.[31] Shortly after that agreement expired the Communists began their revolution-ary war.

Government Restrictions on Communist Activity

The Labour Government in Britain was anxious to encourage the development of a healthy trade union movement in Malaya, but it recognized the menace posed by the widespread Communist infiltration and control of trade unions. As the Communists began to assume a posture of increasing defiance of the government, the British responded with a number of measures which were designed to break the Communist Party's control of unions and to encourage the formation of independent trade unions. During the British Military Administration, Communist activity was restricted by taking action against the individual labor agitators who frequently employed illegal strong-arm tactics to organize workers. Banishment to China was one penalty more feared than regular prison sentences, partly because the Chinese Government at that time was more severe in its treatment of Communists than were the British authorities.

To provide additional control over union activities, a law was passed in July 1946, providing for the registration of all unions with the government's Registrar of Trade Unions. To qualify for registration each union was required to submit a list of its officers, its rules, its membership, and periodic financial reports to the Registrar of Trade Unions. The law regulated elections within the union and prohibited the use of union funds for political purposes. Violations could result in prosecution of union leaders and cancellation of the union's registration, thus making it an illegal organization.[32]

The Communist-organized General Labour Union sought to avoid registration by changing its name to the Pan-Malayan Federation of Trade Unions, thereby claiming not to be a trade union within the definition of the law. But the authorities made it clear that the PMFTU would be declared illegal if it failed to register.[33] Eventually most of the Communist unions registered and were subjected to increasing government scrutiny. Even so, Communist domination of the labor union movement remained a serious problem. Of the 289 unions in Malaya (excluding Singapore), the Labour Department report for 1948 stated:

> Nearly half of these were under the direct control of the Communist PMFTU and about a hundred more were believed to be practically under that control. Only 63 unions were considered to be independent, most of these being unions of Government employees.[34]

However, the government's Trade Union Adviser, Mr. John Brazier, in 1948 claimed some success in encouraging unions to resist infiltration or domination by the Communists. From the beginning of 1948 the PMFTU began to decline in strength and membership.[35]

On several occasions the authorities initiated action against Communist publications for their inflammatory articles. Between November 1945 and February 1946 charges of sedition and incitement to violence were brought against the editors of the following Communist newspapers and journals: *Ming Shin Pao, Shi Tai Jih Pao, Da Chung* and *New Democracy*.[36] After these convictions, the more militant articles appeared in pamphlets which were secretly published by the Communist Party to avoid prosecution.

Political Activity of the MCP

When the Malayan Union constitutional proposals were published in January 1946, the Malayan Communist Party gave them little public notice. Rather than become an active participant in the early political controversy which developed over these proposals, its political energies were expended in other directions. But when the political opposition to the Malayan Union became sufficiently organized and vocal to force the authorities to abandon the Malayan Union, the Communist Party entered the political arena in opposition to the proposed Federation which gave substantial concessions to the Malays. The Communist Party was particularly interested in a constitution that would put the immigrant communities on an equal political and legal status with the Malays, since any constitutional or legal provisions that discriminated against or under-represented recent immigrants would detract from their political strength. The party severely criticized the Colonial Office for opening secret discussions on the new constitution with the Sultans and the United Malays National Organization, who were jointly described by the Communists as being "reactionary and feudalistic elements of Malayan society".[37]

Despite the strong Communist objections to the anticipated changes in the Malayan Union, the Communists were not able to assume leadership of the opposition to the constitutional changes incorporated in the Federation Agreement. The All-Malaya Council of Joint Action (AMCJA)[38] became the principal organ of this opposition, and while the Communist Party, as a part of its "United Front" policy, was affiliated with the AMCJA, it was unable to gain control of the AMCJA. Thus, the Communist Party found itself in the embarrassing position of claiming to be the center of a mass protest movement, when it was obviously only one of many political organizations seeking to prevent the concessions to Malay opinion embodied in the Federation proposals.

The first elections were held in March 1948 for six seats to the Singapore Legislative Council. The Communist Party boycotted this election on the grounds that the Legislative Council was undemocratic in that only six of the twenty-two members of the Council were to be chosen by popular vote.[39] Consequently, the Malayan Communist Party chose not to make an open test of its strength at the polls when the opportunity presented itself. Rather it preferred to organize for other forms of political action.

The Road to Revolution

Although the Communist Party had been able to play a significant role in the political and economic life of Malaya from 1945 to 1948, the leadership of the Party was not satisfied with its progress. In 1945 the MCP had emerged as the only effective political force on the political horizon. By the end of 1947 the picture had changed until the Communist Party was being challenged not only by the government, but by rival political organizations which competed for the loyalty of large segments of the populace. Even among the Chinese, the Communist Party's political leadership was being challenged by such groups as the Chinese Chambers of Commerce, the Kuomintang and numerous secret societies, while in the very stronghold of Communist strength—the trade unions—a growing opposition to Communist leadership was developing.

Communist policy after the war had sought to capitalize on the Party's new legal status, while continuing its covert program to undermine the government. But by 1948 the MCP discovered that the increasing effectiveness of law enforcement meant that a choice had to be made between illegal revolutionary activity and legal, openly organized political activity. Although previous Communist policies had brough forth both strong measures by the government and the political activation of non-Communist organizations, it would have been possible for the Communist Party to redirect its energies into open and legal activities. It is interesting to speculate on the probable position of the Communist Party in Malaya today had that decision been taken. However, the Communist Party decided to embark on a policy of active revolution to throw the British colonial administration out of Malaya, and replace it by force of arms with a Communist Peoples Republic.

Although Malaya had become increasingly inhospitable to the Communist

Party, it appears that the decision to revolt was based more on the dictates of international Communism than upon immediate developments in Malaya.[40] In 1945 the Communist world was suspicious of the West, yet outwardly the wartime alliance had not been renounced. By 1948, after the threats of Soviet expansion had been answered by the Truman Doctrine and the Marshall Plan, Moscow was ready to call upon Communist parties the world over to pursue a more militant policy toward "capitalist" governments of the West. This new line was enunciated by A. A. Zhdanov in a speech to the inaugural meeting of the Cominform in September 1947.[41] For the colonial areas, Communists were urged to intensify the anti-imperialist struggle and not make the mistake of "overrating the strength of the enemy". These views were later communicated to Communists in Southeast Asia at the Southeast Asian Youth Conference[42] and the Congress of the Indian Communist Party which met consecutively at Calcutta in February, 1948. In attendance were delegates from New Democratic Youth Leagues and Asian Students' Associations, and a host of other Communist front organizations. representing nearly every country in Southeast Asia. Experienced Communist leaders explained the world situation according to Moscow's current analysis of Marxism, and encouraged "the struggle for national liberation" in Southeast Asia. Key Asian Communists were taken aside for special consultation and advice by the bigger names in international Communism. Mr. Sharkey of the Australian Communist Party had long discussions with the representatives of the Malayan Communist Party, both during the conference and some weeks later in Singapore. Whether a coordinated policy for Communist parties in Southeast Asia emerged from the meetings in Calcutta is still uncertain.[43] However, within a few months Communist revolts had begun in Malaya, Burma, the Philippines, and Hyderabad, not to mention Indonesia and Vietnam where Communists had earlier taken to arms.

The decision to start the revolution undoubtedly came as a shock to some of the elements in the Malayan Communist Party who had been supporters of the previous "moderate" policy, including the Secretary-General, Loi Tak. While he had held the top position in the Party since 1939, Loi Tak could see that he was about to be held responsible for postwar Communist setbacks. Rather than subject himself to the discipline of the Party, he disappeared in March with a large sum of money from the coffers of the Party. His whereabouts or his fate have remained a mystery ever since. The Communist Party immediately set up an "Examination Committee" to investigate the circumstances surrounding the disappearance of Loi Tak, and rumors began to circulate in the Party concerning his previous misconduct.[44] The chairman of that committee, Chin Peng (Chen Ping), was subsequently selected to succeed Loi Tak as Secretary-General of the MCP and has held this post to the present day.

Whatever the circumstances that surrounded the mysterious disappearance of Loi Tak and the election of the new Secretary-General, it is clear that the change in leadership was accompanied by a drastic revision of party policy. The "moderate" policy was renounced at a meeting of the Central Committee in March 1948, and the Party prepared to pursue the "Chinese line" in an attempt to emulate the tactics of the Chinese Communist Party, which was then in the process of securing its victory in China through military action.

About three months elapsed between this meeting of the MCP Central Committee and the full-scale initiation of guerrilla war by the Communist military units. Extensive preparations for guerrilla operations were made in this period, and the Party appeared to have gone underground by stages, the top leaders being the first to vanish into the heart of the Malayan jungles.

The developments in April gave the first overt indications of the Party's willingness to resort to violence. The two month's no-strike "truce" between the Singapore Harbour Board and the SHLU expired on April 10. Shortly before this date, pamphlets and literature began to appear calling for violence and bloodshed as a means of securing workers' demands. When the pamphlets were traced to the SHLU, the police made a surprise raid on the offices of the SHLU and the Singapore Federation of Trade Unions,[45] and nine members were charged in court with being active in the illegal Workers' Protection Corps.[46]

With the increasing defiance of the law by Communist organizations, the authorities decided to cancel the permission earlier granted to the PMFTU to hold a May Day rally in Farrer Park. May Day passed without incident probably because the Communists did not want to reveal their hand before they were ready.[47]

By the middle of May the number of strikes and incidents of violence reached alarming proportions. The Singapore Rubber Workers' Union was implicated in a number of arson attempts including the fire which burned the Bin Seng Rubber Factory at a loss of M$1,750,000. After a police raid 129 members of the union were detained and 48 were later charged in court, including its leader.[48]

As it became more apparent that the Communists were using their leadership of the trade unions for revolutionary political purposes, the Government countered with a number of amendments to the Trade Unions Ordinance which were designed to aid in combating the Communist Party's domination of the trade union movement. The first amendment, which became law on June 11, outlawed federations or combinations of unions comprising dissimilar trades. This measure had the effect of outlawing the Pan-Malayan Federation of Trade Unions and the General Labour Union in the Federation of Malaya (but not in Singapore).[49] The second amendment forbade holding an office in a trade union by anyone who had not served for a period of at least three years in the trade represented by the union, or by anyone who had been convicted of a criminal act. It had the effect of disqualifying from office many of the Communist trade union leaders who had been placed in leadership by virtue of their position in the Communist Party. Few Communist labor leaders had had any experience in the trade of the union they controlled. The latter amendment did not become effective until July 6.[50] By this date the Communists had already issued their call to arms and insurrection was in full swing. The open political activity of the Malayan Communist Party had come to an end and all that remained was for the Government to give legal recognition to this fact. Although the Communist insurrection, referred to in Malaya as the "Emergency", is dated from June 1948, the Emergency Regulation Ordinance did not go into effect until July 15, and the Communist Party and its subsidiary organs were not officially outlawed until July 23.[51]

1 J. H. Brimmell *Communism in South East Asia* (London: Oxford University Press, 1959) pp. 77–88.

2 David J. Dallin *The Rise of Russia in Asia* (New Haven: Yale University Press, 1949) pp. 210–211.

3 For other accounts of Communism in Malaya see Brimmell, *op. cit.*; F. Spencer Chapman *The Jungle is Neutral* (New York: W. W. Norton & Co., 1949); Gene Z. Hanrahan *The Communist Struggle in Malaya* (New York: Institute of Pacific Relations, 1954); Captain Malcolm Kennedy *A History of Communism in East Asia* (New York: Frederick A. Praeger, 1957); Harry Miller *Menace in Malaya* (London: George G. Harrap & Co., Ltd., 1954); Rene Onraet *Singapore—A Police Background* (London: Dorothy Crisp and Co., n.d.); and Lucian W. Pye *Guerrilla Communism in Malaya* (Princeton, New Jersey: Princeton University Press, 1956).

4 Kennedy, *op. cit.*, p. 65.

5 Miller, *op. cit.*, p. 21.

6 Ho Chi-minh was one of the Communists arrested in Hong Kong.

7 Miller, *op. cit.*, pp. 22–32.

8 This unit went by the name "Dalforce". See Victor Purcell *The Chinese in Southeast Asia* 2d ed. (London: Oxford University Press, 1965) p. 305.

9 See above, p. 46.

10 The leader of the Special Training School was Spencer Chapman who was also with the Communist guerrillas during the war. See his book *The Jungle is Neutral op. cit.*

11 The latter figure is from Communist sources. See Hanrahan, *op. cit.*, p. 44.

12 *Malaya Tribune*, November 23, 1945, p. 1.

13 Most of the weapons supplied to the guerrillas by the Allies were returned. But the guerrilla arsenal also included weapons collected from the battlefields of Malaya as well as those obtained through guerrilla action and by Communist disarmament of some Japanese units before the arrival of the British. Few of these weapons were turned in. Rather, they were placed in secret caches so that they might be used again if the Communists so decided, as they finally did in 1948.

Some guerrillas remained in the jungle and lived by intimidating local people into giving them support, just as they had done under the Japanese. Since the MCP disclaimed responsibility for their actions, these groups were called "bandits" and the police tried to eliminate these bands, most of whom were concentrated along the Perak River and near the Siamese border. A few of the "bandits" were former members of a small Kuomintang guerrilla force called the Malayan Overseas Chinese Self-Defence Army (MOCSDA), while others may have been dedicated Communists who disagreed with the MCP decision not to engage in an immediate revolution against British rule.

14 *Malaya Tribune*, November 23, 1945, p. 1.

15 This organization has also been called the MPAJA Old Comrades Association, and the MPAJA Ex-Comrades Association.

16 When civil authority was restored the General Labour Union was divided into two sections to comply with the separate labor union laws in the Malayan Union and Singapore. The central Communist labor organ in Singapore was the Singapore Federation of Trade Unions, while the Malayan Union equivalent was the Pan-Malayan Federation of Trade Unions. See S. S. Awbery and F. W. Dalley *Labour and Trade Union Organisation in the Federation of Malaya and Singapore* (London: His Majesty's Stationery Office, 1948) pp. 26–28.

17 Pye, *op. cit.*, pp. 77–79.

18 Charles Gamba, *The Origins of Trade Unionism in Malaya* (Singapore: Eastern Universities Press, 1962) pp. 180–213.

19 Awbery, *op. cit.*, p. 7.

20 Victor Purcell, *op. cit.*, p. 310.

21 From a private communication with W. L. Blythe, former Secretary for Chinese Affairs, Malayan Union.

22 Hanrahan, *op. cit.*, pp. 49–50.

23 Lai T'e (Loi Tak), "Report Given at the Eighth Enlarged Plenum of the Central Committee of the Malayan Communist Party", January 22–27, 1946 (in Chinese), p. 15, as quoted in Hanrahan, *op. cit.*, pp. 51–52.

24 "Letter to the Brethren of All Races in Malaya from the Central Executive Committee of the Malayan Communist Party on the Realization of the Compendium of Democracy, February 5, 1946", published as an appendix in Gamba, *op. cit.*, pp. 479–487. In this document the MCP also announced its revised platform entitled "Compendium of Democracy". Its nine planks included the following (in summary): (1) to establish a Malayan Autonomous Government, (2) to form a Pan-Malayan State Council and formulate a democratic constitution, (3) to realize democratic politics by giving freedom of speech, publication, organization, assembly, strike and liberty of person, (4) to establish customs and excise autonomy, (5) to increase wages and rations, (6) to abolish the enslaving educational system and establish in its place democratic free education, (7) to practise the 8-hour day and improve living conditions, (8) to recognize the equality of men and women in political and social status, (9) to unite all oppressed races of the Far East and support their independence.

25 *Malaya Tribune*, December 5, 1945, p. 1.

26 *Straits Times*, January 30, 1946, p. 3.

27 An earlier strike had been called in November 1945, but that strike had concentrated on issues of pay, retroactive wages for the returning work force, and conditions of work. This earlier strike strengthened the position of the Communist union at Batu Arang, thus posing a potential threat to Malaya's transportation system. Note *Malaya Tribune*, November 16, 1945, p. 1; *Straits Times*, January 28, 1947, p. 1; February 7, 1947, p. 1; February 28, 1947, p. 5.

28 *Straits Times*, February 5, 1946, p. 3.

29 *Straits Times*, May 10, 1946, p. 3.

30 See *Straits Times*, February 7, 1947, p. 1; February 9, 1947, p. 5.

31 Gamba, *op. cit.*, p. 323. Also see *Colonial Annual Reports—Malaya, 1948* (London: His Majesty's Stationery Office, 1949), p. 6.

32 *The Trade Union Ordinance, 1946*, (No. 12 of 1946) reinstated the prewar *Trade Union Enactment, 1940*, of the Federated Malay States (No. 11 of 1940). See *Government Gazette of the Federated Malay States, 1940*, pp. 1942c–1942n (L.N. 4961e); *Supplement to Malayan Union Gazette, 1946*, pp. 373–374 (L.N. 940).

[33] *Straits Times*, October 31, 1946, p. 5.

[34] *Federation of Malaya Annual Report of the Labour Department, 1948*, (Kuala Lumpur: Government Printer, 1949), p. 4.

[35] Alex Josey, *Trade Unionism in Malaya* (Singapore: Donald Moore, 1954), pp. 15–16.

[36] *Straits Times*, February 5, 1946, p. 3. See also Virginia Thompson and Richard Adloff, *The Left Wing in Southeast Asia* (New York: William Sloane Associates, 1950), pp. 134–135.

[37] See the account of the MCP rally at Farrer Park, Singapore, which drew a crowd of about 20,000, in *Straits Times*, September 15, 1946, p. 5.

[38] A more complete account of this organization may be found in Chapter 7.

[39] *Straits Budget*, March 11, 1948, p. 17.

[40] The Communists blamed the guerrilla war on the provocations and aggressions of the British against the Malayan peoples. See Victor Purcell, *Malaya: Communist or Free?* (Stanford, California: Stanford University Press, 1954), pp. 131–134.

[41] Brimmell, *op. cit.*, pp. 249–255.

[42] The full title is the Conference of the Youth and Students of Southeast Asia Fighting for Freedom and Independence. It was sponsored by the World Federation of Democratic Youth and the International Union of Students.

[43] Although evidence is lacking, Mr. Brimmell seems to argue that Cominform directives to begin wars of national liberation were transmitted at the Calcutta meetings and coordinated plans were probably formulated. See Brimmell, *op. cit.*, pp. 255–263.

[44] Loi Tak left the Party amid charges that he had betrayed many top Communists to the Japanese during the war in order to save his own life, and, incidentally, also to do away with opposition to him within the ranks of the Party. Apparently he enjoyed the confidence of the Japanese who never realized that he was Malaya's top Communist who was playing the double role of being an informer for the Japanese. This allegation is reported in Harry Miller's book, *Menace in Malaya*, *op. cit.*, pp. 65–73. However, since Miller's source is a Communist document explaining the reasons for the purge of Party leadership, it may be questioned whether the charges against Loi Tak are entirely correct.

[45] *Straits Times*, April 18, 1948, p. 1; April 20, 1948, p. 7; *Singapore Free Press*, April 28, 1948, p. 1.

[46] *Straits Times*, April 29, 1948, pp. 7 and 10; April 30, 1948, p. 6.

[47] In the Federation, incidents of "banditry" increased sharply. After "anti-bandit" operations, the police found a training camp capable of accommodating 500 persons and learned that former leaders of the MPAJA were already in the jungle training for guerrilla warfare. Other camps were discovered in Johore during April. Note *Straits Times*, April 12, 1948, p. 1.

[48] *Singapore Free Press*, May 24, 1948, p. 1.

[49] *Straits Times*, June 14, 1948, p. 1; June 15, 1948, p. 1.

[50] *Straits Budget*, July 8, 1948, p. 17.

[51] The following organizations were outlawed: the Malayan Communist Party, the New Democratic Youth League, the Malayan Peoples Anti-Japanese Army Ex-Comrades Association, and *Ikatan Pembela Tanah Ayer Malaya* (PETA). See *Federation of Malaya Government Gazette*, July 23, 1948 (L.N. 2037).

7 The Radical Nationalists 1945–48

The political activities of the non-Communist left in Malaya are much more difficult to trace than those of the Communist Party. This is partially due to the fact that non-Communist political associations in this period were weak and poorly organized. But a greater difficulty lies in the fact that political issues of the postwar period were so blurred that leftist and conservative groups frequently paraded under a common banner to promote political objectives not easily definable in terms of leftist v. rightist politics. Nevertheless, leftist and radical nationalist opinion tended to be first to organize independently of the Communist Party.

Because the non-Communist left had no effective means of expression at the time of the liberation, a number of self-appointed leaders came forward claiming to represent large segments of political opinion in Malaya. Indeed, almost anyone could form an association, no matter how small the following, and thereby claim to be the leader of an indigenous nationalist political movement. Nearly all the founders and leaders of the early leftist political groups came from professional and semi-professional elites. Frequently, they represented those who had not been fully accepted by their profession or had found it difficult to obtain positions of authority and status in government service. Lawyers, doctors, teachers, and those with some higher education whose expectations of employment and social status had not been fulfilled were among the more active members of the non-Communist left.

Marxism developed a following among non-Communists in Malaya during and after the Japanese occupation. Yet the strong nationalist sentiment that emerged in this period was much more dominant. It appears, with a few possible exceptions, that the non-Communist left used Marxism more to re-inforce nationalism than to determine a political ideology. Leninist theories of imperialism are especially useful when nationalists seek to interpret their colonial past and to develop popular slogans to justify their immediate nationalist objectives.[1]

Although nationalism was a common ingredient of the leftist groups that were founded after the occupation, their brand of nationalism was not identical. On the one hand there were a number of radical nationalist groups which sought support primarily among the Malays by trying to develop a sense of nationalism, ostensibly on a non-communal basis, but usually by emphasizing the national aspirations of all the people of Malaysian stock in Southeast Asia. On the other hand, there were the nationalist groups that were formed by the non-Malay elements of the population, who, nonetheless, looked upon Malaya as their permanent home, and therefore expected to enjoy full legal and political rights in the Malaya of the future. For the latter, "non-communalism" meant no discrimination against the more recent immigrants to Malaya. It is significant that very few Malays became active in the leftist political associations which genuinely attempted to follow a non-communal form of Malayan nationalism. Consequently there was little over-lapping of membership and appeal between the Malay-oriented radical nationalist associations and the other professedly non-communal leftist-nationalist groups. Although both brands of leftist-nationalism formed a loose alliance to further common objectives, they deserve separate attention because they represent wholly separate elements in Malayan society, each developing a new and distinctive sense of political and national consciousness.

The Westernized Left

For several years after the war, a group known as the Malayan Democratic Union (MDU) was the major representative of the emerging non-Malay leftist nationalism. This organization attracted to its fold a substantial portion of the politically active English-educated and westernized elements among the Chinese, Indian and Eurasian communities, particularly in Singapore. The chairman of the MDU was Philip Hoalim, but a Eurasian lawyer by the name of John Eber became its most vigorous spokesman and its public image. He had been interned by the Japanese during the occupation, and after the war he became intensely involved in public affairs, writing and speaking on political issues and criticizing the policies of the British Military Administration. The Malayan Democratic Union was viewed with considerable suspicion by the authorities, although the British Military Administration was careful to state that government employees might join the MDU if they so desired.[2]

The majority of active members of the MDU lived in Singapore and were in government service or in the professions. It had a large following among the teachers in the English media schools in Singapore, especially among the members of the Singapore Teachers' Union. The influence of these teachers is evident in an MDU statement on educational policy which proposed a unified system of education for all Malayan racial communities. At the primary level, education was to be conducted in the student's mother tongue, but at the secondary level, it was proposed that all education be in English, with Malay as a compulsory language.[3] The proposals clearly added up to a compulsory non-communal western system of education.

The major political manifesto of the Malayan Democratic Union was drafted in December 1945 before the British plans for Malaya were made public. This document enunciated the following MDU platform:

1. Self-government for Malaya within the British Commonwealth of Nations.
2. Legislative Assembly for Malaya composed of freely elected represen-tatives of the people.
3. Votes for all Malayan citizens above the age of 21 years irrespective of race, sex, religion, or property.

4. Complete freedom of person, speech, Press and meeting.
5. Educational reform including free elementary, secondary, and technical education for all.
6. A social security scheme including free medical services throughout Malaya.
7. Improved standard of life for all.
8. Complete equality in the employment of Malayans and removal of colour restrictions.

In the accompanying explanatory section of the manifesto, the MDU also called for the incorporation of Singapore within the new Malayan Union.[4]

The Malayan Democratic Union assumed its most active role in the political disputes arising from the Malayan Union and its replacement with the Federation Agreement. In early 1946, the MDU was critical of the Malayan Union constitution for not giving full power to a completely elected legislature. But their criticisms of the Malayan Union largely ceased when it became apparent that the Malayan Union was about to be replaced by a new constitution to meet the objections of Malay opinion regarding citizenship and special rights for Malays. John Eber wrote a number of articles putting forward the thesis that the only way to win the loyalty of the immigrant communities is to treat them all as Malayan nationals, and not to define the rights of citizenship in terms that give preference to the Malays. Because the Sultans had offered the strongest opposition to the Malayan Union constitution and were the symbol of Malay special rights, he attacked the Sultans and the Malay supporters of the Sultans as being remnants of a feudal order that was incompatible with democracy and national self-determination.[5]

The political inspiration for the MDU was the British Labour Party, particularly its left-wing faction. Because the Labour Party was then in power, the MDU became a source of considerable embarrassment to the Malayan authorities, particularly since the MDU kept making demands which were patterned on the Labour Party's domestic policies. Not only did it make demands for universal suffrage and equal political rights for all, but it also demanded labor legislation patterned on the British model which permitted unions to engage actively in politics.[6] The MDU appeared to view itself as the future "Labour Party" of Malaya and attempted to espouse the cause of trade unions whenever it could. Although the MDU was clearly not a Communist organization, its left-wing orientation made it a ready target for Communist "united front" infiltration attempts which were partially successful.

The All-Malaya Council of Joint Action

Because of the MDU campaign for equal rights and privileges for all Malayans regardless of race, the MDU attracted support from all the political elements who suddenly became aroused over the capitulation of the government to conservative Malay opinion. The MDU leaders feared that the opposition to the new Federation proposals would become dissipated by division and contradictory demands from the various communities in Malaya. Consequently, the MDU issued an invitation for all political groups to meet and "join hands in submitting proposals on the future Malayan constitution".[7] Eleven political organizations and communal bodies met at the MDU headquarters in Singapore on December 7 to form what was initially known as the Council of Joint Action,[8] but which later became the Pan-Malayan Council of Joint Action (PMCJA) and finally assumed the title of All-Malaya Council of Joint Action (AMCJA). From then on nearly all the determined opposition to the proposals for the Federation for the non-Malay communities was represented through the Council of Joint Action. Three Malay radical nationalist groups joined the AMCJA for a short while,[9] partly because they had been rebuffed when they attended the founder meetings of the United Malays National Organization, which they had hoped to dominate. Consequently, they too opposed the UMNO-inspired Federation proposals. However, their objections were based on different premises from those of the organizations who opposed the Federation proposals for its "pro-Malay" bias. Rather, they joined the AMCJA because they viewed the Federation proposals as permitting the continuation of colonial rule, which they opposed under any circumstances. These Malay organizations later withdrew from the AMCJA to create a separate "front" opposing the new constitutional proposals. This move made it all the more apparent that the AMCJA was the spokesman for non-Malay political opinion in the fight over the Federation Agreement.[10]

Initially the AMCJA sought to force the British Colonial Office to break off its negotiations with the Sultans and the United Malays National Organization on the question of the revision of the Malayan Union. The AMCJA claimed that it was the only body representing all Malayans—Malays, Chinese, Indians and others—and that the negotiations should therefore be conducted between the British Government and the AMCJA. The Colonial Office was apparently not much impressed by the demands of the AMCJA and continued its talks with the Sultans and the United Malays National Organization. After the British consultations with the Sultans and UMNO had reached a certain state, a Working Committee was formed from representatives of UMNO, the Sultans and the British. Only after this Working Committee had produced a draft constitution was opportunity given for representations from the non-Malay communities. A Consultative Committee was specially created to hear non-Malay views and objections, and prepare revisions to the Working Committee draft. At every juncture the All-Malaya Council of Joint Action fought this procedure. It was unwilling to accept the draft constitution produced by the Malay-dominated Working Committee as a framework for the new constitution. Consequently, when the Colonial Office finally gave the non-Malay communities the opportunity to present evidence before the Consultative Committee, the AMCJA preferred to boycott the proceedings and did not make any representations to that body.[11]

Rather than participate in the process of constitution-making as provided by the Colonial Office, the All-Malaya Council of Joint Action turned its energies to drafting a separate constitutional document of its own and tried to use it to stimulate an expression of Malayan nationalism that would force the British to accede to the political demands made by the AMCJA. Initially, the AMCJA had enunciated the following principles:

1. A united Malaya, inclusive of Singapore.
2. Responsible self-government through a fully elected central legislature for the whole of Malaya.
3. Equal citizenship rights for all who make Malaya their permanent home and the object of their undivided loyalty.[12]

In 1947 these principles were incorporated into the AMCJA draft constitution, which, with some defiance, was entitled "People's Constitutional Proposals". This "constitution" provided for immediate and complete independence for Malaya, including Singapore. Citizenship was to be automatically given to anyone who had been born in Malaya, or whose father was a Malayan citizen or who was a woman married to a Malayan citizen. Citizenship by naturalization would be available to those who had resided in Malaya for eight out of ten years, and who at the time of naturalization were over 18 years of age. The Federal Legislative Assembly was to be directly elected by citizens over 18 years of age. For the first nine years the Malays were to be assured a majority of 55 per cent in the Assembly by the addition of defeated Malay candidates to extra seats in the Assembly if less than 55 per cent of the seats were won by Malays in the regular elections. Any bill which was discriminatory on racial or religious grounds was deemed to be unconstitutional—a principle to which the Constitution itself did not adhere. The upper chamber was given a three-year suspensive veto if it decided by a majority that a bill was discriminatory. A minority might also delay a bill for a lesser period on the same grounds. This higher chamber, to be called Council of Races, was to have two members representing each racial-ethnic group in Malaya (nine such groups were mentioned). Malay was to be the official language in government, but the use of any other languages in government was not to be proscribed. An extensive list of individual rights was incorporated into the AMCJA constitution, including, complete equal rights for women, the rights to leisure, to education, to two weeks vacation with full pay per year, to two months maternity leave with full pay, and to maintenance for old age and sickness. The Malay Sultans were to remain as constitutional monarchs, shorn of all their prerogative powers. Matters pertaining to Islam and Malay Custom were to be regulated through separate institutions set up solely by the Malays.[13]

Armed with these proposals the AMCJA and its allied political groups attempted to stir up a wave of nationalistic sentiment which it hoped would defeat the Federation proposals and thereby dislodge UMNO from its dominating position in Malayan politics. In pursuance of this objective, the AMCJA promoted a "passive" national demonstration patterned along the lines of Indian political resistance tactics. It appears that Tan Cheng-lock conceived of the idea of a national "hartal" during which an attempt was to be made to halt all business and economic activity. He first sold this idea to the Associated Chinese Chambers of Commerce, and later the AMCJA and the Communist unions agreed to support the demonstration. During the first "hartal" on October 20, 1947, Chinese business interests affiliated with the Chinese Chambers of Commerce combined with the Communist-affiliated unions to halt certain economic activities for a period of one day.[14] Generally speaking, however, the hartal affected only Chinese businesses and a few factories. It certainly was not the kind of economic weapon that could secure from the British any major political concessions.

A second hartal was scheduled for February 1, 1948, the date the Federation Agreement became the constitution for Malaya. However, it was called off at the last minute and the AMCJA coalition announced instead its intention of boycotting the new Constitution by refusing to permit members to accept appointments to government legislative and advisory bodies.[15] Likewise, when the first elections were held for the Singapore Legislative Assembly in March 1948, the AMCJA decided to boycott the elections. The latter decision was explained by the statement that it "did not want to give sanction to an undemocratic legislative council".[16] However, there seem to have been other practical considerations influencing this decision. The AMCJA would have been hard pressed to maintain its unity if it had to select candidates to contest elections. There was little likelihood that the AMCJA coalition would hold together in an election, since neither the Communist-dominated wing nor the conservative Chinese wing could have agreed upon candidates that both factions would have supported.

The All-Malaya Council of Joint Action had retained an apparent front of unity in opposition to the Federation Agreement proposals. But when it undertook to outline a specific program of its own, it ran into divisions within its ranks. In January 1947 all the Malay radical nationalist groups withdrew to form a separate "front" of Malay opposition to the Federation proposals, under the name PUTERA. Although these Malay associations later cooperated with the AMCJA in an attempt to block the introduction and implementation of the Federation Agreement, and also participated in drafting the "People's Constitutional Proposals", their cooperation was always very tenuous because of differences on racial-communal issues.[17]

Another significant division in the AMCJA occurred over the issue of income taxation. The government had proposed the introduction of a progressive income tax. The Advisory Councils for both the Malayan Union and Singapore had opposed this measure. Although the reserved powers of the Governor were almost never used, they were employed on this occasion to secure passage of the income tax measures over the objections of the Advisory Councils.[18] The Communist Party, the trade unions, and the Malayan Democratic Union supported the income tax measures, while the Chinese Chambers of Commerce strongly opposed income taxation. This created a sharp division within the ranks of the AMCJA. It also produced the anomalous situation where the Communist Party and the MDU were aligned in favor of the exercise of the Governor's reserved powers. The AMCJA retained its coalition by ignoring the income tax issue, permitting each of its member associations to act independently on the issue.

Throughout the active political life of the All-Malaya Council of Joint Action, the Malayan Democratic Union played a decisive part in the leadership of the coalition. Yet the MDU never commanded a mass following in Singapore, and it had very few members on the peninsula. The fact that the MDU retained a strong position of leadership in the AMCJA has been attributed to the energy and foresight of its leaders. But perhaps a more important reason was that the MDU political viewpoint represented a middle position between the major groups opposing the constitutional concessions made to conservative Malay opinion. The withdrawal of the Malay radical nationalists from the AMCJA made the latter even more predominantly Chinese than before.[19] Yet none of the more powerful political groups in the AMCJA wanted the opposition to the Federation proposals to be identified with communal partisanship. The conservative Chinese who were very active politically were perfectly willing to let the MDU speak for them in championing the equality of all communities in Malaya. The Communist Party also found the MDU to be an energetic and vociferous spokesman for a "colonial liberation movement". Indeed, the Communist Party used the AMCJA as a vehicle for implementing its "national front" policy during the period when the Party was committed to its "moderate" line.

The Malayan Democratic Union, and, for that matter, all the elements comprising the "westernized left", were placed in a very difficult predicament in 1948 by the sudden change in policy adopted by the Malayan Communist Party. Many of the "westernized left" were very idealistic, believing themselves to be national saviors in a colonial liberation movement. Armed violence and the excesses of revolutionary terror ran counter to the idealism of most of them. However, they were proud of their militant anti-colonialism and did not want to associate themselves with the Government's attempt to put down the wave of violence that preceded the final "declaration of war" between the Malayan Government and the Communist Party. Indeed, the leaders of the MDU sought to explain the violence as the product of a colonial administration. They even went so far as to say that the primary cause of the violence was the unworkability of the Federation Agreement. When the Communist delegates returned from the now famous Calcutta Conference, the MDU, rather than the MCP, sponsored a welcoming celebration for the very persons who were returning with the decision to revolt and who, within two months, were to lead the Communist guerrillas in the fight against the government.[20] With a considerable amount of naïveté, the MDU leaders could not bring themselves to believe that the Communist Party did not represent an essentially progressive democratic nationalist movement.

By the time the Communist front groups went underground at the start of the "Emergency", the All-Malaya Council of Joint Action was no longer an effective political coalition. With half of the AMCJA coalition gone, the Malayan Democratic Union lost its position at the center of the coalition, and could not continue to operate as the spokesman and the apparent leader of all the groups within the AMCJA. In addition, the MDU was further weakened by division in its own ranks between those who wished to support the Communist revolution and those who could not stomach the violence, the bloodshed and intercommunal friction created by the Communist insurgents. In a few short months, the leaders of the MDU had moved from an apparently commanding position in Malayan politics to a position where they could muster practically no political following. On June 25, 1948, the MDU announced that "in view of the serious curtailment of civil liberties and the chaotic political situation" the MDU could no longer serve any useful purpose.[21] The MDU blamed its demise on the government and its use of emergency measures rather than on the Communist decision to revolt which forced the MDU into a political "dead end". In the final pronouncement, the leadership of the MDU still sought to attach all blame for Malaya's social and political ills upon the British colonial administration.[22]

Radical Malay Nationalists

Before the war, Malay political activity was confined to a small number of Malays affiliated with societies designed to preserve and stimulate Malay culture. Some of the Malay intelligentsia saw that the traditional Malay way of life was being threatened by the influx of immigrants from China and India. They also saw that the apparently benevolent policies of the British did not help the Malays to keep pace with the other communities in Malaya. Concern for the problems of the Malays attracted the attention of these literary and cultural societies, although ideas of Malay nationalism did not become a strong political force until after the war.[23]

While the Japanese occupation had some impact upon Malay attitudes, Malays were not unified nor greatly motivated to political action by the experience. Rather, it appears that the events following the collapse of Japan startled the Malays, perhaps even more than the occupation itself. For a few short weeks the Communist guerrillas tried to rule the country. Then, when the British returned, the Malays found that the prewar understanding and accord between the British and the Malays had been strained by the events in the intervening years. The British praised the Chinese for their resistance to Japanese rule at the same time that they began to investigate the actions of individual Malays (and Indians) for pro-Japanese activity during the occupation. It is little wonder that the Malays felt a sense of frustration and a lack of direction in the midst of these fast-moving events over which they had so little control.

As the war ended, the most politically active Malays were those who held radical views, were contemptuous of traditional Malay elites, and wished to pattern Malay nationalism after the Indonesian nationalist movement. The organizational base for these radical Malay sentiments had shifted from the *Kesatuan Melayu Muda* to PETA and finally to KRIS.[24] But since KRIS had the stigma of Japanese sponsorship, it did not survive beyond its founding date, which coincided with the time when Japan surrendered. Nonetheless, radical

Malay nationalists, while small in number, were politically aroused, and only needed a new organization to mobilize their number and espouse their cause.

The Malay Nationalist Party

When the British returned they jailed some of the former leaders of KMM, PETA and KRIS for their collaboration with the Japanese. However, they soon found it to be impolitic to impose such punishment for war-time collaboration and released the accused leaders. Despite these obstacles, *Kesatuan Melayu Muda* was revived by Dr. Burhanuddin[25] who established party headquarters in Ipoh and began publishing a newspaper to publicize KMM doctrines.[26] Meanwhile, the Malay Nationalist Party (MNP) (*Party Kebangsaan Melayu Sa-Malaya*) was founded in October 1946 by Mokhtar U'd-din, who became its first president.[27] Within a few months the KMM merged into the MNP and Dr. Burhanuddin assumed the presidency of the enlarged MNP, which thus became the political heir to the KMM-PETA-KRIS legacy.

Despite its professedly radical-revolutionary complexion, the British gave the MNP semi-official recognition as a spokesman for the Malays by inviting it to name a member for the committee which was formed in early 1946 to consider the issue of citizenship for the Malayan Union. [28] Later that year the MNP presented a memorandum to the Government calling for a united Malaya under a central government with a legislative council comprised of three-quarters elected members, half of whom were to be Malay. It also proposed that Malay be made the only official language of the country. In explaining its objectives a spokesman for the MNP stated:

> We must rise as one man with increased national consciousness to become a new nation. We must not be deceived by such sweet and flowery words as that Malaya belongs to the Malays when actually the Malay masses do not have a voice in the way they are ruled.
>
> . . . We appeal to the Sultans, rajas and religious leaders to come out and work with the real leaders of the ra'ayat [the common Malays] to construct a new Malaya and emulate the spirit of the Indonesian leaders. Do not let our Malay race decline and rot in submission to the old colonial rule of 1941.
>
> . . . As in Indonesia, we shall not neglect the minorities and other communities in order to lay the basis for harmonious co-operation between all men of goodwill in this country.[29]

In its first platform of 1945, the MNP stated that "Malaya should be a part of Greater Indonesia".[30] The object was to create a vast national state embracing all the indigenous peoples of Malaysian stock. Whether the boundaries were to be drawn along ethnic or religious divisions was never quite made clear. For many of the radical Malay nationalists, this idealized pan-Malaysian empire (variously called *Indonesia Raya* or *Melayu Raya*) was like an apocalyptic vision, in that it became a major ultimate goal, but it was postponed into the indefinite future and seldom openly discussed or debated.

In its campaigning the MNP tried to sustain the claim that it represented the interests of the common Malays. The party leaders hoped to build the MNP into the foremost Malay party through the mobilization of the Malay masses. However, when the Malayan Union and the MacMichael Treaties suddenly aroused Malay opinion, the conservative Malay elites commanded far greater popular support.[31] The MNP sent a delegation to the Pan-Malayan Malay Congress in March 1946 and to the subsequent meetings in May which resulted in the formation of the United Malays National Organization. But after several sharp political clashes, the MNP withdrew amid charges of "dictatorial methods", and with ill-will on all sides.[32] Understandably, the MNP later became incensed when the British opened secret negotiations with the Sultans and representatives of UMNO—its primary competitor for the political loyalty of the Malays. While the MNP demanded that the Government convene a "people's representative conference" to draft a revised constitution, it hinted that its real objective was to be included as an equal partner with the Sultans, UMNO and the British in the secret negotiations then under way.[33] But since the MNP was ignored as a representative of Malay opinion in these negotiations, it turned to more radical opposition to "colonialism", and began to look around for political allies.

By aligning itself in opposition to the product of the British-Sultans-UMNO negotiations, the MNP travelled a political course parallel to that of other political forces which were forming under the banner of the All-Malaya Council of Joint Action to fight the Federation proposals. The MNP, in company with other minor Malay radical associations, found itself in a difficult political position. Should it join forces with all groups resisting the Federation proposals? Or should it fight the proposals from a strictly Malay point of view? The first alternative would align the MNP with those who objected to special concessions and privileges for the Malays, while the second would divide and weaken the opponents of the Federation.

When the All-Malaya Council of Joint Action was in its formative stages, the MNP and an affiliated Malay group were invited to participate. Although the MNP sent an observer to the first sessions of the AMCJA, it decided against participation in that coalition the following month. Later it also sent observers to the UMNO Congress in January, perhaps in a move to explore the possibilities of a rapprochement. If such a course was seriously contemplated, it came to nothing, for the MNP once again announced its determination to fight the federation proposals because they "did not prepare Malaya for democratic government" and because "real power was given to a few officers dancing to the tune of the Colonial Office".[34]

PUTERA

Taking its example from the AMCJA, the Malay Nationalist Party decided to organize a distinctly Malay council of joint action to agitate for its demands for constitutional revision. This radical Malay anti-UMNO coalition was called *Pusat Tenaga Ra'ayat* (Central Force of the Malay People) but was universally known by the abbreviation PUTERA.[35] The MNP was careful to leave the way open for cooperation with the AMCJA by stating that the creation of PUTERA would not rule out the possibility of Malay participation in the AMCJA.

Radical Malay opinion was denied effective representation in the constitution-making procedures employed to draft the Federation Agreement of 1948. It may be recalled that the first stage of drafting proposals had been undertaken by the British-Sultans-UMNO Working Committtee. The second stage Consultative Committee was formed to permit non-Malays to present evidence and suggest revisions. Non-British representation on the first committee was entirely Malay, while on the second it was entirely non-Malay. Although the non-Malay Consultative Committee was prepared to receive evidence from Malay parties, PUTERA understandably felt that its views would not receive a fair hearing. When its demand that Malays be included on the Consultative Committee was not met,[36] PUTERA and its affiliated organizations boycotted the Consultative Committee.

The fact that PUTERA and the AMCJA objected to the procedure for drafting the Federation Agreement for antithetical reasons[37] did not prevent the formation of a joint AMCJA-PUTERA coalition to oppose the Federation proposals. From mid-1946 until the demise of the AMCJA the public actions of PUTERA were coordinated with those of the AMCJA. Although the leaders of both coalitions were aware of the conflict between the demands for equal rights on the part of non-Malays in AMCJA and the demands for Malay privileges and restrictive definition of citizenship by PUTERA, there is no evidence that their fundamental differences were resolved. It is true that PUTERA formally supported the "People's Constitutional Proposals" which it had helped the AMCJA to draft. Concessions to Malay opinion had been made when the two agreed that the "national flag of Malaya" should be the Indonesian-inspired red and white MNP flag, that the constitution should guarantee 55 per cent Malay representation in Parliament, and that Malay should be the official language of government. But other fundamental communal differences were either glossed over or ignored when the AMCJA and PUTERA joined forces to fight the Federation Agreement. Rather, they both preferred to stress the "undemocratic" features of the Federation and to affirm their "anti-colonial" stand against British control which was being perpetuated under the new constitution.

Angkatan Pemuda Insaf

An important offshoot of the Malay Nationalist Party developed from a faction within its ranks that flirted with ideas of revolution against the British colonial regime. The leader of this faction was Ahmad Boestamam who had worked with the Japanese during the occupation and had graduated from one of the Japanese propaganda schools. He became the secretary of the MNP shortly after it was formed, but at the December 1946 meeting of the party he was not re-elected. Instead, he was elected chairman of the youth branch of the MNP,[38] called in English, the Malay Nationalist Youth Corps. Its Malay name, *Angkatan Pemuda Insaf*, means roughly: Organization of Youth for Justice. The abbreviation API is the Malay word for "fire", truly an appropriate sobriquet for a revolutionary group! API under the leadership of Boestamam attracted the most radical and revolutionary of the Malay nationalists into its ranks. Although it retained nominal affiliation with the MNP, it pursued an independent political existence and issued separate political manifestoes.[39]

The Communist Party leaders were particularly interested in API because they hoped to develop it (and for that matter the MNP) into a Malay front under their own direction. Likewise, Ahmad Boestamam tried to use the Communist Party for his objectives. Although the MCP may have had some influence over API, if only by way of inspiration in the techniques of revolution, API was not a Communist front as some have suggested.

The authorities were alert to the potential revolutionary character of API, and in April 1947, Boestamam was arrested on a charge of sedition for urging Malays to use violence to secure Malayan independence. He was convicted of the charge but, after paying a fine, he resumed the leadership of API.[40] However, the matter did not rest there, for three months later the government declared API illegal and ordered it to dissolve.[41] The Malay Nationalist Party protested the banning, but the Government stood firm and refused to re-instate API to legal status.

In January 1948, an attempt was made to re-organize the former following of API. The assistant Secretary-General of the MNP, M. Mustaza, resigned from his post to become president and founder of a new left-wing Malay youth organization called PERAM, an abbreviation of *Pemuda Radikal Melayu* (Radical Malay Youth). Apparently PERAM was an outgrowth of another minor Malay youth group in Singapore called GERAM, a shortened form of *Gerakan Angkatan Muda* (Organized Youth Movement).[42] Just as the abbreviation API spelled a Malay word, so did PERAM and GERAM; the former means "fermenting" or "ripening", and the latter means "eager" or "impassioned". Following in the footsteps of API, these parties became a part of the PUTERA coalition. Delegates from PERAM were sent to the Southeast Asia Youth Conference in Calcutta at which the Communist parties in Southeast Asia received the instructions on the policy of revolution. Whether PERAM had any ties with the Malayan Communist Party is uncertain. In any event, both PERAM and GERAM were cut short by the outbreak of the Communist insurrection.

The Dilemma of Malay Radicalism

Malay radical politics in the period from 1945 to 1948 never captured the imagination of large numbers of Malays, and the identification of Malay radical organizations with the Indonesian nationalist movement tended to alienate the more provincial Malays. Nearly all Malays were in favor of Indonesian nationalism, but Malay loyalties were to their Rulers and their Malay state. It was difficult enough to think of pan-Malay nationalism, let alone the much more embracing pan-Malaysian nationalism based upon the Indonesian model. Because the radical Malay parties had not secured a mass following, they were not in an effective position to oppose the "anti-Malay" MacMichael Treaties and the subsequent Malayan Union constitution Instead, the "case for the Malays" was carried to Whitehall by the Sultans and the conservative United Malays National Organization. Consequently, most Malays considered the Sultans and UMNO to be the authoritative spokesmen for Malay opinion, while the Malay radical parties were identified with the vociferous and unstable elements, which sometimes appeared as interested in Indonesia as in Malaya. Not strong enough to be effective through independent action, radical Malay parties exhibited indecision and political opportunism that caused some of their original supporters to lose confidence in their leaders. The Malay Nationalist Party had claimed to oppose the Federation Agreement because it continued colonial rule. But, to many Malays, it appeared to be a case of "sour grapes" resulting from the inability of radical Malay leaders to share in the drafting of the new constitution.

Where the Sultans and UMNO appeared to champion the cause of the Malays, the MNP and its affiliates appeared to be closely allied with non-Malay political forces in the AMCJA. Unwilling to commit itself to a consistent policy either in favor of Malay "special rights" or in favor of the equal rights of all domiciled communities, the MNP emphasized instead radical anti-colonial aspects of Malayan nationalism. At times it avoided a distinctly *Malay* expression of nationalism, yet it remained Malay in character and continued to appeal to Malay nationalists by holding out the prospect of union with Indonesia—a union which would assure the dominant position of Malay-Indonesian ethnic communities. Although this had great appeal for a section of Malay youth, the bulk of Malay opinion wanted more immediate political guarantees as demanded by the Sultans and conservative Malay leaders. Despite bold beginnings, the radical Malay left never attracted a mass following even though it enjoyed the zealous support of students from Malay schools, particularly in Singapore.

The outbreak of the Emergency caught the Malay radical nationalists in much the same political dead end as the Malayan Democratic Union. In their opposition to the Federation Agreement, these parties had become associated with the Communist Party in a militant approach to politics. Yet, the Communist insurrection was not the kind of revolution radical Malay nationalists had in mind. A few Malays who had been active in API and PERAM joined the Communist insurgency, while the majority of the members of the MNP became frustrated political malcontents who did not want to be committed to support either the British or the Communists. In July 1948, the MNP issued a statement cautioning its members against violence or illegal acts and stating that its political creed was based solely on nationalism. Although the MNP was not banned, the authorities were extremely suspicious of its activities, and a number of its members were detained, including its president, Inche Ishak bin Haji Mohamed.[43]

[1] There is no evidence that a Trotskyite group was ever organized in Malaya.

[2] *Malaya Tribune*, January 18, 1946, p. 1.

[3] *Straits Times*, December 13, 1946, p. 4.

[4] The full MDU manifesto is reproduced in an appendix to Charles Gamba, *The Origins of Trade Unionism in Malaya* (Singapore: Eastern Universities Press, 1962), pp. 433–437.

[5] John Eber, "Sultans as Sovereign Rulers", *Straits Times*, August 8, 1946, p. 4; John Eber, "Loyalty to Malaya", *Straits Times*, August 9, 1946, p. 4.

[6] Gamba, *op. cit.*, p. 151.

[7] *Straits Times*, December 13, 1946, p. 1.

[8] Not all the organizations attending the initial meetings joined the AMCJA. The first membership of December 1946 comprised: the Malay Nationalist Party, the Malayan Democratic Union, the Singapore Federation of Trade Unions, the Clerical Union, the Straits Chinese British Association, the Malayan Indian Congress, the Indian Chamber of Commerce, the Ceylon Tamils Association. See *Straits Times*, December 16, 1946. By September 1947 the AMCJA listed the following affiliated organizations, the last three of which were clearly Communist front organizations: the Malayan Democratic Union, the Malayan Indian Congress, 12 Women's Federations in Malaya, the Malayan New Democratic Youth League, the Malayan People's Anti-Japanese Army Ex-Service Comrades' Association, and the Pan-Malayan Federation of Trade Unions. See AMJCA, *Constitutional and Political Developments from September 1945 to September 1947* (mimeographed by AMCJA, 1947), p. 4.

[9] The three Malay political organizations which temporarily joined the AMCJA were the Malay Nationalist Party, *Angkatan Pemuda Insaf* (API), and *Lembaga Kesatuan Melayu*. These three were part of a Malay radical movement which is examined as a distinct political force later in this chapter.

[10] Throughout the active life of the AMCJA, a determined effort was made to persuade the radical Malay parties to associate with the AMCJA in political action against the colonial regime. The AMCJA held out the promise of speedy independence and economic advances for the Malays, along with other minor concessions to Malay opinion. John Eber wrote an indignant letter to the *Straits Times* after its editors had suggested that the AMCJA was essentially a non-Malay political movement. The analysis of the *Straits Times* editorial writer was fundamentally correct, even though the AMCJA may have wished to conceal that fact for obvious political reasons. See *Straits Times*, December 18, 1946, p. 6. Although the original four elected officers included a Malay as Vice-Chairman, the real moving forces were the non-Malay leaders, particularly Tan Cheng-lock and John Eber. The first elected officers were: Tan Cheng-lock, Chairman; Mohamed Tahar, Vice-Chairman (MNP); John Eber, General Secretary (MDU); and A. M. Mitra, Treasurer (MIC). Shortly after its founding the AMCJA announced that the Treasurer would be a person selected by the Pan-Malayan Federation of Trade Unions.

[11] Despite this boycott some of the individual groups in the AMCJA did submit memoranda to the Consultative Committee. *Straits Times*, January 6, 1947, p. 1.

[12] *Straits Times*, December 23, 1946, p. 1. These basic principles were later expanded to six, the latter three calling for the retention of the Malay Sultans, the regulation of the Muslim religion and Malay Custom by Malays, and "Special attention to be paid to the advancement of the Malays". See AMCJA, *Constitutional and Political Developments, op. cit.*, p. 3.

[13] *Ibid.*, pp. 8–52.

[14] *Straits Times*, October 21, 1947, p. 1.

15 *Straits Budget*, January 1, 1948, p. 12; January 29, 1948, p. 17; *Straits Times*, January 20, 1948, p. 1.

16 *Straits Budget*, March 4, 1948, p. 9.

17 In 1948 there were reports of discussions between the Malay radical groups and the UMNO leaders on the possibility of merger into one single Malay party. See *Straits Times*, April 15, 1948, p. 6.

18 *Malay Mail*, November 26, 1947, p. 1; December 4, 1947, p. 1; *Straits Budget*, December 11, 1947, pp. 8, 10 and 14.

19 The AMCJA in September 1947 claimed a membership of 400,000, of which 300,000 were said to be members of the Pan-Malayan Federation of Trade Unions. It would be safe to assume that about 300,000 to 350,000 of the claimed membership was Chinese. Somewhat under 10,000 Malays could probably be claimed as members, but nearly all of them were members by virtue of trade union affiliation. See AMCJA, *Constitutional and Political Developments, op. cit.*, p. 4.

20 For an account of the welcoming celebrations, see *Straits Budget*, April 22, 1948, p. 16.

21 *Straits Budget*, July 1, 1948, p. 12.

22 John Eber, the person most closely linked to the MDU, continued to maintain some of his association with Communist elements through the illegal Singapore Peoples Anti-British League. On January 8, 1951, he was detained without trial under the Emergency Regulations for his activities in the SPABL and for his "Communist sympathies". Two years later he was released under restricted conditions. He left Malaya shortly afterwards for England where he tried to organize a left-wing movement among Malayan students.

23 See also below, pp. 89–93.

24 See above, pp. 21–23, 44.
For an account of the parallel PETA organization in Indonesia see George McTurnan Kahin *Nationalism and Revolution in Indonesia* (Ithaca, New York: Cornell University Press), pp. 109, 113–114, 122, 128, 135, 137. After the war the Malayan Communist Party tried to capitalize on the nationalist mystic of PETA by adopting that name for its ancillary organization designed to recruit militant Malay nationalists into the communist fold. Thus, the war time PETA was Japanese sponsored, while the post war version was a front for the Malayan Communist Party.

25 Dr. Burhanuddin bin Mohamed Noor also goes by the name Burhanuddin Al-Helmy. Born in Kota Bharu, Perak, in 1911, he attended school in Indonesia and then obtained a degree in homeopathic medicine in India. He says of himself that he was a journalist for *Kehidupan Dunia Akhiral* in 1936, was the editor of the magazine *Taman Bahagia* in 1937 and taught Arabic in Madrasah Aljunied, Singapore (a Muslim secondary school), from 1937 to 1940. He became one of the early members of the KMM. During the war he was a "high official" in the Japanese military administration.

26 Mohammad Yunus Hamidi, *Sejarah Pergerakan Politik Melayu Semenanjong* (Kuala Lumpur: Pustaka Antara, n.d. [1961?]), pp. 11–12. The KMM paper was called *Suara Ra'ayat* (Voice of the People). This source reports that the KMM attempted to sponsor a congress of Malay organizations, which collapsed for lack of support.

[27] Mokhtar U'd-din was born in the Dutch East Indies, and before the war went to Moscow, perhaps through his association with the Indonesian Communist Party. Later he came to Singapore as a correspondent for some Indonesian newspapers. He became a member of the MCP and during the war headed the Malay section of its "Anti-Japanese Union". No doubt the MNP high command considered his MCP ties to be a valuable asset for a political organization dedicated to resist British colonialism.

[28] *Malay Mail*, April 15, 1946, p. 1.

[29] *Straits Times*, October 21, 1946, p. 5.

[30] *Straits Times*, December 30, 1946, p. 4.

[31] Dr. Burhanuddin is reported to have given tentative approval of the idea of a Malayan Union while he was still president of the KMM. No doubt he was attracted to the promise of a unified democratic Malaya with the Sultans reduced to titular constitutional monarchs. Although he later reversed his stand, early support for some features of the Malayan Union later became a liability exploited by his opponents. See Mohammad Yunus Hamidi, *op. cit.*, p. 12.

[32] Some of the differences between UMNO and the MNP were over the questions of adoption of the red and white Indonesian flag as the Malay national flag, the union of Singapore with Malaya in the new constitution, the definition of "Melayu citizenship", and the membership of Malaya in *Indonesia Raya*. See Abdul Rahim Ibrahim, "The Malay Left Wing", *Straits Times*, March 10, 1948, p. 4; A. Samad Ismail, "The MNP Platform: A Reply," *Straits Times*, March 23, 1948, p. 6; Mohammad Yunus Hamidi, *op. cit.*, pp. 65–68; Usha Mahajani, *The Role of Indian Minorities in Burma and Malaya* (Bombay: Vora & Co., 1960), pp. 230–231.

[33] Note the article by an MNP leader in *Straits Times*, November 25, 1946, p. 4. For a time the MNP attempted to compete with UMNO for mass Malay support by sponsoring several political conventions representing radical anti-UMNO Malay organizations. The Pan-Malayan Malay Labour Congress and the All-Malaya Malay League were both designed to mobilize mass Malay support for the MNP political line. See *Malaya Tribune*, December 13, 1946, p. 1; December 25, 1946, p. 1.

[34] *Straits Times*, January 14, 1947, p. 5.

[35] The first name adopted for the coalition was Malay Council of Action. Later its English name was changed to United Malay Front and in Malay it became *Pusat Tenaga Ra'ayat*. It was patterned on the union of nationalist parties formed in Indonesia during 1943 under the leadership of Sukarno, and also called PUTERA. See George McTurnan Kahin, *op. cit.*, p. 106.

[36] *Straits Times*, January 24, 1947, p. 5.

[37] The AMCJA objected to the procedure for drafting the new constitution because the first stage Working Committee had only Malay-British representation, while PUTERA objected to the procedure because the second stage Consultative Committee had no Malay representation.

[38] *Malaya Tribune*, December 25, 1946, p. 1.

[39] The first API manifesto had seven planks, 1) demanding democratic government and "an open declaration of the sovereignty of the Malay people", 2) demanding the replacement of British and Indian soldiers by the Malay Regiment, 3) demanding the abolition of "the open door policy in Malaya", 4) demanding the removal of Dutch forces from Malaya, 5) demanding the repatriation of Japanese prisoners, 6) affirming support for the Indonesian independence struggle, and 7) promising to "contact the Federation of Democratic Youth". See *loc. cit.*

40 Virginia Thompson and Richard Adloff, *The Left Wing in Southeast Asia* (New York: William Sloane Associates, 1950), pp. 262–263.

41 *Government Gazette, Malayan Union, 1947* (17, July, 1947), p. 2285.

42 GERAM had been in PUTERA and was noted for its xenophobic attitude towards the "alien Chinese". Note A. Samad Ismail, "PUTERA and its Allies", *Straits Times*, November 10, 1947, p. 4; *Times of Malaya & Straits Echo*, January 22, 1948, p. 5. The president of GERAM and one of its founders was Abdul Aziz bin Ishak, the former Minister of Agriculture in the Alliance Government.

43 *Straits Times*, July 6, 1948, p. 9; July 19, 1948, p. 5. Ishak bin Haji Mohamed became president of the MNP in December 1947. Before that he was, along with Ibrahim Yaacob, a co-founder of *Kesatuan Melayu Muda* in 1937. He was jailed by the British after the Japanese invasion, but was released by the Japanese and edited a Japanese-sponsored paper, *Berita Malai*, during the war. He was sent by the Japanese to Tokyo, possibly for political indoctrination. Just as the British were returning to Malaya, Ishak fled to Karimoen, but later returned to join the MNP and became its third president. He is reported to have written a book during the war with the title *Persatulak Sekarang* in which he expounds the *Indonesia Raya* theme.

8 The Conservative Nationalists 1945–48

The political force of nationalism was increasingly evident among the educated middle-class Malays, both during and after the war. Yet, the bulk of the Malays in the *kampongs* remained politically inarticulate until the controversy over the Malayan Union jarred them out of their political lethargy. To prepare the way for democratic government, the Malayan Union constitution embodied three drastic revisions of traditional British policy toward Malaya. First, the Sultans were to be divested of their powers to permit the introduction of democratic reforms later on. Secondly, the confused patchwork of small states was to be replaced by a unitary government for all Malaya. Thirdly, all persons domiciled in Malaya were to be given an equal status for participation in Malay's future political life.

The Sultans and the Malay aristocracy were not the only ones who found themselves threatened by these new principles of "equalitarian democracy". The common Malays had always looked upon the government as a Malay institution which was obligated to protect their interests against the tide of immigrants coming to Malay. The Sultans, as the heads of the States, were evidence that the country and the government, while administered with the aid and advice of the British, was still Malay. The majority of educated Malays depended upon government employment, and government policies afforded the peasant Malay some protection from the excesses of economic domination by the immigrant communities. The Malayan Union, therefore, came as a heavy blow to Malays in all walks of life.

The first indication of the broad outlines of British policy for postwar Malaya was made by the Secretary of State for the Colonies, Mr. George Hall to Parliament on October 10, 1945. He stated:

> Our policy will call for a constitutional union of Malaya and for the institution of Malayan citizenship which will give equal citizenship rights to those who claim Malaya to be their homeland.[1]

A few Malays were quick to realize the implications of this statement. Within a week the Malay press, led by the influential *Utusan Melayu* urged Malays to revive their prewar Malay organizations in order to represent their views to the government. Within the next few months a host of "Malay unions" and political associations were being founded or revived. Before Sir Harold MacMichael returned to England with the new treaties with the Sultans, Malay protests were assuming mass proportions. Ten thousand

Malays are reported to have demonstrated in Kelantan when the MacMichael mission visited there in December.[2]

In Johore the opposition to the Malayan Union proposals was led by the Sultan and his adopted son and political advisor, Dato Onn bin Ja'afar.[3] The latter helped to found the Movement of Peninsular Malays (*Pergerakan Melayu Semenanjong*). By 1946, 100,000 members were recruited into this party through the efforts of Dato Onn who quickly became the leading figure in Malay agitation against British policy.[4] On February 10, shortly after the publication of the Malayan Union White Paper, he organized a mass protest rally at Batu Pahat. Before approximately 18,000 Malays Dato Onn attacked the White Paper and called for the formation of a "United Malays National Organization" to fight for Malay interests. Moves had already been made to form such an organization, but with the publication of the White Paper these proposals were pursued with greater urgency.[5]

As a first step, a Pan-Malayan Malay Congress (*Konggres Melayu Sa-Tanah Melayu*) was held in Kuala Lumpur from March 1 to 4. Forty Malay organizations sent delegations in addition to the hundreds of Malays from all walks of life who attended as individuals. After an opening speech by the Sultan of Selangor, Dato Onn was installed as Chairman of the Congress.[6] He invited all Malay political groups, from the right to the left, to join the Congress in its fight against the Malayan Union proposals. He also called upon the Sultans to repudiate the MacMichael Treaties, which were depicted as instruments of surrender to the British Crown. Because the Malayan Union draft constitution had been prepared by the Colonial Office without formal consultation with representative leaders from Malaya, Dato Onn hoped to secure a revision by demanding consultation with the Rulers, the State Councils and Malay political organizations which now were expressing their views through the medium of the Pan-Malayan Malay Congress.[7]

The Colonial Office realized that approval of its proposed "fundamental democratic reforms" would not be forthcoming from such a procedure for constitutional review. Consequently, it turned a deaf ear to these demands and proceeded to inaugurate the Malayan Union as scheduled. The inflexibility of the British Government inflamed Malay opinion even more than had the MacMichael Treaties. Under the leadership of Dato Onn, an "Emergency Meeting" of the Pan-Malayan Malay Congress met to organize a massive Malay boycott of the Malayan Union. None of the Sultans appeared for the inauguration ceremonies for the Malayan Union, and Malays refused to serve on Advisory Councils. Rallies were held throughout Malaya, and for a week politically active Malays wore white mourning bands on their black songkok caps to symbolize the loss of "their birthright and liberty".[8] The boycott continued in effect when the new Governor, Sir Edward Gent was installed on May 22.

The United Malays National Organization

At the first Pan-Malayan Malay Congress, a committee of five was appointed to draft a constitution for a United Malays National Organization (UMNO).[9]

The report of this committee was submitted to the second Pan-Malayan Malay Congress which met in Johore Bahru on May 11 and 12. The plans were approved and the United Malays National Organization was formally launched after the election of Dato Onn bin Ja'afar as the first president.[10] Approval was also given to draft proposals for an alternative federal constitution to replace the detested Malayan Union.

The tactics employed by UMNO to fight the Malayan Union were very effective. All the Malay Rulers and the leaders of UMNO worked hand-in-hand to prevent the Malayan Union from becoming operative. Evidence of serious Malay discontent so disturbed the British Government that a two-man Parliamentary delegation was sent to Malaya in May to investigate the situation and to explore possible means for resolving the crisis.[11] They witnessed Malay mass demonstrations, addressed Malay meetings, heard representations by the Rulers and leaders of UMNO, and were surprised by the intensity of Malay feelings. The orderly manner in which massive demonstrations were staged reflected on the highly developed and disciplined following of UMNO.[12]

The growth of the United Malays National Organization was perhaps the most phenominal occurrence in Malayan politics. Dato Onn's plea for a Malay political organization was made at a rally on February 10. Three months later at its birth, UMNO was a well-organized mass party. By July it had achieved its first objective—the agreement on the part of the British to abandon the Malayan Union and begin negotiations for a new constitution. By the end of July, UMNO became the only political party represented on the Working Committee which prepared the basic draft of the Federation Agreement. Furthermore, the constitutional proposals for a federal system which had earlier been drafted by UMNO became the basis for the negotiations with the British for the new constitution.

Although the political success of UMNO may be attributed to the fact that UMNO and the Malay Rulers presented a unified common front, that is not the whole story. UMNO was able to mobilize Malay opinion to a degree thought impossible by all except the most visionary Malay politicians.[13] How was this done? Of course, the drama of political crisis made mobilization of Malay political opinion much easier than ever before. But the leaders of UMNO were also able to add the ingredient of organization. Within a short period, UMNO was transformed from a loose association of Malay societies into a unified political party having its own separate membership, leadership and an effective system of political communication.[14] Malays in government service assumed leadership of the party, and through their position they were often able to use the administrative structure of the Malay States to accomplish the political mobilization of the Malays. Thus senior Malay government servants organized Malays working in the district offices, and they in turn secured the help of *penghulus* (village headmen) who recruited and propagandized for UMNO at the grass roots level. In this way the traditional power structure of Malay society was transformed into a mass political party.

Dato Onn's leadership of UMNO made him the dominant personality in Malay politics for a number of years. In its formative period, the party accepted his policies and his political views. In general, it may be said that Dato Onn sought to counter two political forces which he believed were threatening the stability of Malayan life—the Chinese communists, and extremist Indonesian-inspired nationalists operating in Malaya. Although he was an avowed spokesman of Malay nationalism, he expounded a mild nationalism which stressed gradualism and cooperation with the British provided they remained sensitive to Malay opinion. During the fight against the Malayan Union Dato Onn talked and acted like a rather narrow-minded Malay chauvinist. Yet, a year or two later, he stressed the importance of intercommunal harmony and appeared genuinely interested in accepting non-Malays into full status in Malaya's political and cultural life provided that their loyalty to Malaya was undivided. He was neither precise nor consistent on the question of which non-Malays should be given these rights, and his definition of what was required as evidence of "loyalty to Malaya" seemed to vary, partly depending on his own political fortunes. Even so, he voiced a recurring theme: immigrant Malayans should be encouraged to become loyal to the Sultans and a "Malay" Malaya. By implication, he rejected a "potpurri" Malaya in which multiple cultural streams would be given equal status. He did not expect Chinese and Indians to adopt Malay culture, religion and language as their own before they were accepted as citizens, but they had to be willing to break their overseas ties and give undivided loyalty to a Malaya that retained its basic Malay character and institutions.

Although Dato Onn fought bitterly against the Malayan Union, he was far from being "anti-British". He realized that the Malays were backward and needed the assistance of a sympathetic British administration to protect their interests. Indeed, it was not the continuation of colonial rule which caused his disillusionment with the British, but rather the postwar policy which promised to end colonialism in such a manner that the Malays would not inherit the mantle of governing authority. Too sudden acquisition of independence, he feared, would mean the political and economic domination of the Malays by the immigrant communities.

The views outlined above did not directly repudiate the central objectives of British postwar policy. They only called for a more gradualist approach to self-government and the introduction of democratic reforms so that the existing political system could accommodate non-Malay political activity by small stages and retain the continuity of an institutional structure based on the existing Malay state governments. These objectives are reflected in the terms of reference approved by UMNO, the Rulers and the British to guide the Working Committee which drafted the proposals for the Federation of Malaya:

(a) that there should be a strong Central Government so as to ensure economical and effective administration . . .

(*b*) that the individuality of each of the Malay States and of the Settlements should be clearly expressed and maintained;

(*c*) that the new arrangements should, on a long view, offer the means and prospects of development in the direction of ultimate self-government;

(*d*) that . . . a common form of citizenship should be introduced which would enable political rights to be extended to all those who regard Malaya as their real home and as the object of their loyalty;

(*e*) that, as these States are Malay States ruled by Your Highnesses, the subjects of Your Highnesses have no alternative allegiance or other country which they can regard as their homeland, and they occupy a special position and possess rights which must be safeguarded.[15]

For all practical purposes, the Federation Agreement resulted in the United Malays National Organization becoming the dominant party in government affairs. Government policy had been brought into essential harmony with the political objectives of UMNO, and, particularly at the state level, the key men in government were either UMNO members or conformed to the party's political ideals. In the controversy over the Federation Agreement, UMNO was the only party openly committed to its defense. It found that task more difficult to organize than its previous attacks on the Malayan Union. The strength of the AMCJA-PUTERA coalition which attacked the Agreement, alarmed many UMNO leaders. Later, when AMCJA-PUTERA staged their hartals against the Federation, UMNO made some moves to organize some Malays to provide the scarce goods and services, but it is doubtful whether UMNO-organized Malays contributed significantly to the relative impotence of the hartal as a political weapon.

When the Communist Party began its insurrection, UMNO gave its unqualified support to the government in the fight against terrorism and insurrection. Despite UMNO's cooperation with the British, the Communists never openly equated UMNO with "British colonialism". They appeared to be unwilling to antagonize the bulk of the politically active Malays who supported UMNO. Thus, while UMNO was almost completely identified with government policies, it enjoyed a certain status of non-belligerency in the battle being waged between government forces and Communist guerrillas.

Emerging Chinese Political Associations

Postwar Chinese political activity is difficult to trace because so many Chinese organizations become involved in public affairs at one time or another. In some respects, all Chinese business associations, benevolent societies and secret societies are political insofar as they act like pressure groups by seeking to protect and promote their economic and political interests. As long as government policies were not too detrimental to their interests they were generally content to approach the government through Chinese Advisory Boards, the Secretary for Chinese Affairs, or through

Chinese members appointed to legislative councils and government boards. After the war the older Chinese associations awakened to the importance of expanding their scope and became more like political action groups, at times actively engaging in political demonstrations or campaigning for votes.

Many Chinese interest groups tended to follow the lead of the Kuomintang, the Chinese Chambers of Commerce or the Straits Chinese British Association, each of which was fairly representative of the divisions of opinion found among the non-Communist Chinese.

The Kuomintang

Even though it was an illegal organization after 1925, the Kuomintang remained quite active during the twenties and thirties,[16] but found it difficult to compete with the Communists during the occupation years. Nonetheless, the KMT succeeded in supporting a guerrilla force called the Malayan Overseas Self-Defence Army (MOCSDA). Most of the wartime activities were directed against Chinese collaborating with the Japanese or the supporters of the rival Communist guerrilla forces. After the British returned to Malaya the KMT guerrillas were not demobilized and did not receive any discharge gratuity such as had been agreed upon between the Communist guerrilla leaders and the British Military Administration.[17] Consequently, the KMT guerrillas degenerated into extortion and bandit gangs that intimidated the population principally in the Slim River area and along the Siamese border.

As conditions became gradually stabilized, the KMT organized branches and its *San Min Chu I* Youth Corps in most centers of Chinese population. While the attention of the KMT was directed to the immediate political issues of China, it also became involved with Malayan political issues, often enlisting the aid of the Nationalist Chinese Government's diplomatic corps. Pro-KMT Chinese groups even met under the auspices of the Chinese Consulate in May 1946 to draft an eight-point manifesto on the Malayan Union. In it they expressed appreciation for the rights of citizenship anticipated under the Malayan Union, but also demanded the retention of all "prewar rights" enjoyed by the Chinese.[18] They hoped to preserve their status as Chinese citizens while claiming the proposed new rights of Malayan citizenship under the Malayan Union.

When the Communist Party began its insurrection, leading members of the KMT were among those singled out for extermination by the guerrillas. The toll was quite high among KMT members in the smaller towns near the areas where guerrilla forces operated. These assassinations were motivated by past KMT-Communist rivalry, and by the fear that the KMT members would provide information for government security operations.

Although the KMT was dragged into the conflict between the Government and the Communists, it avoided involvement in Malayan politics, and thus failed to play a significant role in Malaya. Several important political personalities were linked to the KMT, but it appears that their political activities were unrelated to their ties with the KMT. As Chinese in public life were challenged to demonstrate their "undivided loyalty to Malaya", membership in the KMT proved to be an increasing liability.[19] In May 1949, the government decided to curb the activities of "foreign political parties" by making them illegal. This action brought the KMT to an end as a legal political organization for the second time,[20] although the KMT, in shadow form, probably lingered on for a number of years.

Chinese Chambers of Commerce

Chinese businessmen frequently considered themselves to be the leaders of the Chinese community. Before the war the traditional leaders of Chinese society were usually engaged in business activities, but their leadership role was undermined during the Japanese occupation since many Chinese businessmen had to reach some accommodation with the Japanese and thus compromised their leadership position in the Chinese community. Their reassertion of leadership in the Chinese community became more pronounced once the Communists decided to launch their insurrection.

The major organization representing Chinese business interests was the Chinese Chambers of Commerce. It became very sensitive to political developments which might jeopardize the economic stake of the Chinese in Malaya. However, the Chinese Chambers of Commerce also tried to assume the role of being defenders of Chinese culture. Frequently, their notion of Chinese culture was a strange mixture of romantic attitudes toward the heritage of old China, combined with western ideas of scientific progress and nationalism. For the Chinese businessman, the preservation of "Chinese culture" all too frequently meant little more than the use of the *Kuo-Yu* dialect and the teaching of Chinese historical and religious literature in Chinese schools. This preoccupation with Chinese culture put many CCC leaders into the forefront of the continuing fight over education policy as it affected the Chinese-medium schools. Because of their substantial contributions to Chinese schools, Chinese businessmen were heavily represented on the schools' management committees, and for this reason the Chinese Chambers of Commerce became involved in communal issues rather far removed from their uniquely business interests.

While the members of the Chinese Chambers of Commerce were motivated by a strong sense of Chinese nationalism, they avoided involvement in the struggles over Chinese domestic politics. Rather, the CCC were among the first Chinese interest groups to give major attention to the Malayan political scene, perhaps because they were well aware that the protection of the political and economic interests depended upon developments in Malaya. In political affairs, the Malacca Chinese Chamber of Commerce assumed a dominant role, in large measure because of forceful leadership of its president, Tan Cheng-lock.[21] Because the CCC operated as a pressure group, its political role is difficult to trace apart from the activities of the political parties and political coalitions it chose to support.

The Straits Chinese British Association

Some Chinese business and professional people became thoroughly western-ized and developed pronounced "pro-British" sympathies. Most of these Chinese were second or third generation residents of Malaya, and a product of the English-media educational system. Although they did not abandon or disclaim their Chinese identity, they tended to adopt a more western style of life than the more culture-bound Chinese-educated Chinese. The proportion of westernized Chinese is highest in the former Straits Settlements of Penang, Malacca and Singapore. In these large urban centers there was a greater opportunity for access to the higher quality English-media schools, which helped to create a larger English-educated Chinese community. A high proportion of these individuals entered business or the professions.

All persons born in the Straits Settlements were "subjects of the Crown" and enjoyed the equal protection and privileges of the law. Therefore, second generation Chinese in Penang, Malacca and Singapore were jealous of the legal rights which were denied to Chinese in the Malay States. Chinese business interests were also fearful that incorporation into Malaya would mean the end of the free trade policy for Penang and Singapore. Thus, for a variety of reasons, westernized Chinese business and professional interests were favorably disposed toward British colonial rule, particularly when com-pared with the likely consequence of union in a Malay-dominated Malaya.

The Straits Chinese British Association, which had been founded before the war, became the primary spokesman of these interests. Its president, Heah Joo-seang, a Penang millionaire rubber dealer, waged a successful campaign for Penang's exemption from Malaya's tariffs. While the SCBA objected to a number of features of the Federation Agreement, it was more mild in its opposition than the groups affiliated with the AMCJA. By January 1948, the SCBA leadership was willing to avoid the issues raised by the Federation Agreement, saying that the new constitution was a *fait accompli* and that the issue would thus be dropped from its agenda.[22]

As the agitation for national independence grew in intensity, the political influence of the SCBA appeared to decrease. The title "the King's Chinese" used so proudly to refer to the members of the SCBA gradually became tarnished until it degenerated into a political epithet tinged with derision. Although the SCBA counted among its membership some of the most illustrious political figures in Penang and Singapore, it was too closely identified with the passing colonial era to be representative of the views even of the most westernized Chinese.[23]

Political Activities of Conservative Chinese

The political position of the established Chinese economic elites was greatly weakened by the events of the war. Japan's conquest of Malaya and her repressive measures against the Chinese tended to discredit the traditional

Chinese leaders, who were forced to cooperate with the Japanese, or who, having the money to do so, had fled Malaya during the occupation. This caused the leadership vacuum in the Chinese community which the Chinese leaders of the Communist Party were all too eager to fill. Furthermore, the conservative Chinese have always had a propensity to form many societies and associations resulting in overlapping membership and competing group loyalties so typical of plural societies. Weakened and divided, the conservative Chinese needed some time to become an effective political force. As these traditional Chinese elites attempted to regain their former positions of power in the Chinese community, they were forced to come to terms with the changed political realities, which often meant they had to make some accommodations to the leadership position which the Communists enjoyed at the close of the war. This fact helps to explain some of the strange alliances and maneuverings which characterized the conservative Chinese in the period between the war's end and the start of the Communist revolt.

When the Malayan Union was under consideration a number of Chinese associations submitted their views on the issues of citizenship, immigration, and the political rights of the Chinese. But each group tended to act separately, and no apparent attempt was made to strengthen their political position through the creation of a united front of Chinese conservatism. However, after the Sultans and UMNO had succeeded in forcing the British to abandon the Malayan Union, the established Chinese economic elites gradually woke up to the challenge of Malay nationalism. They began to look about for means to solidify their ranks in order to exert political pressure for the retention of the policies embodied in the Malayan Union.

In August 1946, the Chinese Chamber of Commerce in Malacca, under the leadership of Tan Cheng-lock, organized the Malacca Chinese Union. The objectives of this organization were "to promote the co-operation of the various Chinese Associations", and to protect the political, economic and cultural interests of the Chinese.[24] This was the first of many postwar political ventures by Tan Cheng-lock and others in the Chinese Chambers of Commerce following his lead. The Malacca Chinese Union did not prove to be of sufficient political strength, for within a few months, Tan Cheng-lock began to look about for possible political allies to mount an attack against the "anti-Chinese" Federation proposals. Shortly afterwards, he became one of the founders of the All-Malaya Council of Joint Action which was formed in December 1946 between the Communist front organizations, the Malayan Democratic Union, and the conservative Chinese under his leadership.[25]

During 1946 and 1947 the major political activity of the conservative Chinese elements were channelled into the All-Malaya Council of Joint Action. Both the Chinese Chambers of Commerce and the Communist Party were willing to provide money, organization, know-how and mass support for the AMCJA, while the Malayan Democratic Union acted as the spokesman for that strange coalition formed to fight the Federation proposals. However, during these two years the conservative Chinese also engaged in some independent political action, especially over the issue of the income tax proposed by the Government late in 1947. Both the MDU and the MCP came out in favor of income taxation, but the Chinese Chambers of Commerce staunchly opposed such a measure. Rather than let AMCJA be jeopardized by political in-fighting between its three wings, this issue was avoided within the AMCJA and each member organization proceeded to agitate for its own position on the matter.

The demonstrated need for independent political action by the conservative Chinese prompted attepts to build a unified political organization. In February 1947, the various Chinese Chambers of Commerce united to form a central organization—the Associated Chinese Chambers of Commerce. The new combination was headed by a Malayan Chinese who during the war had been an officer with the Chinese Nationalist Army, Colonel H. S. Lee.[26]

As the Malayan Communist Party began to intensify its militant activities through strikes, violence, and arson, the conservative Chinese businessmen became wary of their association with the pro-Communist elements in the AMCJA. More and more the Chinese Chambers of Commerce began to dissociate themselves from the AMCJA coalition. By March 1948, Tan Cheng-lock was proposing the formation of a new unified Chinese political association around the nucleus of the Chinese Chambers of Commerce. He also expressed the hope that an inter-communal "National Unity League" could be created to establish cooperation between communal associations for political purposes.[27] This appeared to be a "trial balloon" to test the possibility of the formation of a new inter-communal coalition that would exclude the Communists. His efforts in this respect were cut short by the start of the Communist insurrection.

When the Communist challenge to law and order became apparent, nearly all conservative Chinese leaders were quick to express their support for the Government. Even those who had sympathies for the Communist regime in China, such as Tan Kah-kee, called on the Chinese to cooperate with the authorities in the fight against insurrection. During the first stages of the Emergency the issues created by the Federation Agreement were temporarily shelved while the non-Communist Chinese leaders attempted to take stock of the new political climate.

Indian Political Associations

Indian political activity immediately after the war was greatly influenced by the legacy of the Indian Independence League. When the British returned to Malaya and Burma, they interned the armed units of the Indian National Army as hostile enemy forces, and within a short time the leaders of the Indian Independence League and the Indian National Army were charged in court for "collaborating with the enemy". Although the Indian Independence League passed out of existence with the termination of the war, many of the same Indians banded together in November 1945 to form the Indian National Army Defence Committee to help defend the Indians being tried on treason charges in Malaya. This committee helped to secure defense attorneys from India to defend the accused. It also made representations to the British Government calling for the release of all Indians held on treason and collaboration charges.[28]

Whether the Indian National Army Defence Committee was really instrumental in changing British policy is difficult to determine. Apparently, it did help to secure acquittal for both the former Chairman and the Secretary of the Indian Independence League, who were tried for delivering political speeches detrimental to the British Administration at a rally of Indians in November 1945.[29] After their acquittal the British pursued a more lenient policy and prosecuted only those who had committed gross brutalities during the occupation, or had acted as Japanese informers, knowing that the Japanese would take brutal action against the informed. Almost no Indians were convicted under this revised policy.

An outgrowth of the Indian National Army Defence Committee was the formation of the Indian Association which sought to act as the spokesman of the Indians in Malaya. It organized relief for destitute Indians in Malaya and helped to arrange for the repatriation of those who desired to return to India. In 1946 Jawaharlal Nehru visited Malaya and urged the Indians to strengthen and unify their political organization in order to pursue an active role in Malayan public affairs. On his suggestion, a conference was held in August 1946 and attended by 600 delegates from a number of separate Indian organizations. With the blessing of the Congress Party of India, the Malayan Indian Congress (MIC) was founded, superseding the Indian Association. The constitution which was adopted was patterned on that of the Congress Party. The following resolutions were among those passed at its first meeting in late 1946: a recognition of the services rendered by Subhas Chandra Bose to his country; an expression of sympathy for Indian patriots in Natal; a condemnation of the actions of the South African Government against Indians; an expression of support for closer economic ties between India and Malaya; the initiation of efforts to secure Hindi as the national language for Indians in Malaya; an expression of sympathy with the people of Indonesia, Burma and Indo-China in the struggle against colonialism.[30] The attachment of the MIC to the politics of India is demonstrated by the selection of MIC delegates to attend the annual meeting of the Indian Congress Party at Meerut, Uttar Pradesh, in November 1946. The delegation was led by the first president of the MIC, Mr. J. A. Thivy.[31] After Indian independence, Mr. Thivy became India's representative to Malaya.

The close ties between the Malayan Indian Congress and the Congress Party of India caused Muslim Indians to be unenthusiastic about the MIC. Right after the war the Muslim League in India sponsored the formation of branches in Malaya, but no attempt was made to unite Indian Muslims into a unified Malayan organization until after India and Pakistan had been formed as separate states. On December 30, 1947, the Muslim League of Malaya was formed under the presidency of M. J. Namazie.[32] Both Indian and Pakistani Muslims were encouraged to give their support to this new organization, but its small membership doomed it to a totally insignificant role in Malayan politics.

The Indians in Malaya, like the Chinese, favored the Malayan Union over the Federation Agreement, but did little to give the former active public support. Only after Malay political action had forced the abandonment of the Malayan Union did the Indians begin to agitate for its retention and fight against the Federation proposals. The Malayan Indian Congress was one of the founder members of the All-Malaya Council of Joint Action in opposition to the Federation, and remained with that coalition through 1946 and 1947 despite the increasing criticism of one faction within the MIC.[33]

In 1947 G. V. Thaver revived the Malayan Indian Association which he had founded in 1932 but which had been defunct during the war. This organization objected to the MIC's preoccupation with Indian affairs and its rules which permitted non-Malayans to be members. However, personal ambitions and jealousies may have been as important as policy differences in the formation of the MIA. Similarly, when the AMCJA decided to boycott the Singapore elections, MIC schisms over the issue led to the parallel formation of the Singapore Indian Association led by R. Jumabhoy, a former president of the Singapore MIC.[34] It may be added that the revived Indian Association never developed a significant following in either Singapore or Malaya.

As soon as it became apparent that the Communists were embarking upon a revolutionary course, the president of the MIC sought to disentangle his party from its alliance with Communist elements. While expressing fear that the Emergency Regulations might be employed to suppress "the legitimate expression of political opinions", the MIC strongly disavowed violence and condemned the Communists for their insurrection. At the same time, it reiterated its opposition to the Government's constitutional policies.[35] At this juncture, continued attacks on the Federation Agreement seemed to be a futile exercise.

Ceylonese Politics

The Ceylonese are frequently classified with the Indian community in Malaya. In many respects the Ceylon Tamils have a greater affinity for their Indian counterparts than their fellow Ceylonese who are not Tamil. Yet, the Ceylonese have remained a separate community and as such they have developed a slightly different outlook toward political developments. During the occupation, the Japanese tried to encourage the Ceylonese to join the Indian Independence League. The following is a report by the Government of Ceylon Representative made in 1946 on the activities of the Ceylonese in the IIL during the occupation:

. . . it was only later, after much agitation, that separate Ceylonese sections of the Indian Independence League were formed.

Leading Ceylonese in various areas in Malaya took office in the Ceylon section. The Indian National Army itself received little support from the Ceylonese.

The Independence League, however, performed one valuable function —it protected the Indians and Ceylonese from indiscriminate persecutions and the Ceylonese section through its office bearers was able to protect or warn Ceylonese of imminent trouble. The interest of the Ceylonese, however, in the movement was lukewarm and a general estimate could safely say that they derived more good in the way of personal protection and did little or no harm to the British cause to which they were consistently loyal.[36]

The Ceylonese were less nationalistic than the Indians and more moderate in their criticism of the British. As a very small minority they looked to the stability and justice of British rule for protection of their interests, and they were less inclined to stress the principles of unbridled majority rule. They feared that they might be overwhelmed by the larger communities in Malaya, particularly if the latter were motivated by extreme nationalism. Furthermore, few Ceylonese genuinely looked upon Malaya as their permanent home. When Malayan citizenship became available to them relatively few applied for it, preferring to plan for their return to Ceylon.[37]

Among the first to form a communal association after the war were the Ceylonese. E. E. C. Thuraisingham, a prominent western-educated attorney from Kuala Lumpur, helped to found the Ceylon Federation in 1945 and became its first president. This organization received fairly widespread support from the Ceylonese, who at the time were estimated to number about 25,000. A Malay Sinhalese Association was also formed to speak for that small sub-group in the Ceylonese community, but the two cooperated when the occasion arose. Very few Ceylonese became active in the Malayan Indian Congress, in part because they were eligible only for "associate membership". As political activity became more intense, an increasing number of Ceylonese joined the ranks of the "non-communal" political parties that were being formed.

When the Malayan Union was abandoned and the Federation proposals were under discussion, the Ceylonese did not associate themselves with either the extreme opponents or the avid supporters of the Federation. The many Ceylonese who were employed in government service had much in common with the Malays, who were seeking to preserve many of the prewar administrative arrangements. The major objection of the Ceylon Federation. to the Working Committee draft constitution was its absence of any provision for Ceylonese reserved seats.[38] The final Federation Agreement, however, remedied this obejction by giving the Ceylonese one reserved seat, to which E. E. C. Thuraisingham was appointed. He became one of the most influential members of the Legislative Council and a staunch defender of the Federation Agreement.

After the establishment of the Federation the Ceylonese moved into closer political association with the conservative Malays, who had resumed a dominant position in government. The outbreak of the Communist rebellion created little problem of political readjustment for the Ceylonese as the politically active Ceylonese had few, if any, associations with Communist organizations.

Eurasian Politics

The Eurasian community has always had difficulty finding a satisfactory role in Malayan society. During the colonial era they were not accepted in European social circles, nor did they wish to fit into the social patterns of the Asian communities, even if they would have been accepted, which appears doubtful. In Malaya they have much in common with the very westernized Chinese and Indians, but they have remained a distinctly separate community. Because they felt unattached to either the East or the West, many of them were in a quandary over their relations with the other communities in Malaya,[39] and tended to be uncertain and hesitant in their political objectives.

When the Japanese invaded Malaya the Eurasians were placed in a very difficult position. At first the Japanese were inclined to classify them with the Europeans, and many of them were interned and treated very poorly. However other Eurasians could see no advantage in identifying themselves with the British when the Japanese had become the new rulers of Malaya. A number of prominent Eurasians went out of their way to court favor with the Japanese, not only to secure individual favors, but also to secure greater leniency for the Eurasian community as a whole. After the British returned to Malaya the most celebrated treason trials were those of a number of Eurasians who had collaborated with the Japanese. Eventually these persons were either acquitted or given light sentences, but the Eurasians were embarrassed by the trials.

In the first year after the war a few Eurasians became active in some of the newly-formed political parties such as the Malayan Democratic Union, but for several years the majority of Eurasians appeared to be cautious about politics. Although Eurasian Associations were organized in most of the States and Settlements, they did not engage in political action until the issue of the Federation proposals forced the Eurasians to evaluate their position as one of Malaya's smallest minority groups. In January 1947 several Eurasian Associations joined to form the Eurasian Union which drafted a memorandum of the Federation proposals. Because some Eurasian families trace their origin to the Portuguese and Dutch who occupied Malaya in the sixteenth and seventeenth centuries, they sought to secure for themselves special rights as indigenous "subjects of the Sultans", just as the Malays were also claiming special rights. The Eurasians requested that their "status and rights in the Federation be the same as those of the Malays and [that they] be classed 'Non-Muslim Subjects of Their Highnesses' ".[40] They were particularly anxious to secure by this means a privileged access to the public service. However, the Malays in the United Malays National Organization and the Malay Chambers of Commerce objected to the Eurasian request, and no such provision was incorporated into the Federation Agreement.[41]

Throughout the period from 1946 to 1948 the Eurasians appeared to be disturbed by Malaya's rapidly changing political and social scene. One evidence of their frustration was the attempt to establish a completely Eurasian community in an isolated section of Dutch New Guinea.[42] These plans were so unrealistic that they never materialized into any Eurasian migration. Yet, the very fact that such plans were considered shows their disquiet over the course of Malayan affairs.

European Interests in Politics

During the colonial era European participation in political activity was partially concealed within the structure of administration. Yet, as indigenous groups became more active politically, European interests had to rely less and less on behind-the-scenes representations to promote their political objectives. Each of the major economic interests in Malaya has its spokesman in the form of trade and professional associations. For example, the rubber companies were represented by the United Planting Association of Malaya, the mining interests by the Chamber of Mines, and commercial trading interests by the Chambers of Commerce. Although European trade and professional associations often campaigned publicly for a particular government policy, they more frequently promoted their interests through informal channels where personal contacts were often decisive. Not only did the Europeans have easy access to the important Europeans in the administration, both in Malaya and Great Britain, but many of them had the "ear" of one or more Members of Parliament who could bring an issue to the attention of the British Government or of Parliament. The influence of European interests upon government policy was considerable throughout the period under consideration. But because European political activity is not within the scope of this study of evolving indigenous politics, this important aspect of Malayan politics will have to await a study of the records of the European associations as well as the private papers of the principal figures of the colonial administration.

An Evaluation of Political Developments, 1945–1948

When the war in the Pacific came to an end, all segments of Malayan society had to find ways of readjusting to the new and unexpected conditions of the postwar period. New relationships had to be worked out, not only with the returning British administration, but also between the separate elements of Malayan society. The political expression of each of these various parts developed unevenly in response to threats, real or imagined, to their interests.

We have seen that the first group to dominate the political scene was the

Communists, who, by virtue of their guerrilla forces and their control of labor unions had a large, well-organized following. The Communists looked upon themselves as the leaders of the anti-colonial movement and they viewed the British authorities as their primary political target. For the Communists, the real issue was "colonialism", and any evidence of lack of popular support for their "anti-colonial front" was explained as the result of deceitful colonial policies which "seduced" some of the colonial peoples by small favors and deceptive talk. The Communist theory of colonial politics explains internal political division by ascribing it to the evil design of the "imperialist" pursuing a policy of "divide and rule". A cursory examination of the events in Malaya may lend plausibility to this theory, for the major political divisions in Malaya were not openly in contention until the British constitutional plans for Malaya were made public. But what Marxist theoreticians fail to explain is the fact that the first constitution—that of the Malayan Union—was met by the massive resistance of the Malays because it was too equalitarian, too liberal and suggested a too rapid development toward self-government, all of which threatened the position of the Malays. The dialectic has to be stretched pretty thin to ascribe the amazing political awakening of the Malays to the manipulative abilities of the British authorities seeking to perpetuate their rule. As a consequence the Communist Party leadership was never prepared to participate in the development of Malayan politics as the representative of only one rather small segment of Malayan society. The Marxist-Leninist cosmology prevented the Malayan Communist Party from accepting such a role in Malayan politics because, for them, there are only the imperialists on the one side and the anti-imperialists on the other. The politics of class war leaves only two alternative policies toward "the opposition": a temporary and unfriendly truce—and open revolution. The first alternative must, in time, give way to the second. This is precisely what happened to Communist policy in 1948.

The second political combination to dominate the Malayan scene was the product of the opposition to the first postwar civil constitution. The United Malays National Organization was catapulted into its dominant political position on the wave of Malay nationalism, aroused by the Malays' fear of the economic power and numerical superiority of the immigrant communities. Malay nationalism sought to revert to the traditional patterns of prewar policy and administration as a means of preserving the Malay bias of government. Thus, Malay nationalism, represented by UMNO, was a reaction against too progressive policies planned and executed by the colonial authorities from their desks in Whitehall. With an inadequate assessment of the temper of local political opinion, the British were inflexible at first, and then were forced into a major retreat in the face of the ensuing massive resistance of the Malays. The Federation Agreement emerged as the political settlement between the British and the forces of Malay nationalism led by UMNO.

The third major force to come onto the political stage was the All-Malaya Council of Joint Action, representing the major non-Malay communities.

This political coalition was formed as a reaction against the conservative Malay orientation of the Federation proposals which had been the product of Malay nationalism. The AMCJA coalition did not have the internal cohesion of UMNO and it was unable to play a dominant role in Malayan politics.

It should be noted that each of the three major political forces mentioned above grew out of opposition to policies which threatened their respective segments of Malayan society. The political power of the Communists grew out of the Chinese opposition to the repressive policies of the Japanese. After the war the political appeal of the Communists was based on opposition to the returning British rule. The political power of UMNO was likewise the result of a policy which threatened a previously politically-dormant segment of Malayan society. For a short while the emergence of the Malays as a political force unbalanced the political scales and caused the government to give a disproportionate attention to the political demands of the Malays. The non-Malay AMCJA coalition was therefore also born out of the opposition to policies which threatened another previously politically-dormant segment of Malayan society.

Political consciousness did not come to all segments of Malayan society simultaneously. Rather, it developed in reaction to government policies which posed threats to the economic, cultural or political status of first one and then another segment of Malayan society. The overall political development may be likened to a chain reaction. As each segment of society became politically active it influenced public policy and, in turn, awakened another segment of society, until nearly all parts of society were politically mobilized and seeking ways to be politically effective.

Earlier the statement was made that the first question which the newly active political groups had to consider was that of the means by which they were to pursue their political objectives. In short, they had to determine whether they would engage in illegal, violent, revolutionary tactics or extra-legal passive resistance and obstructionist tactics; or whether they should operate entirely within the law and through the framework of representation provided by the forms of colonial government. No major political group chose the last alternative, that of entirely confining its activity within the framework of representation provided by the colonial administration. In part this was due to the inadequate representative institutions established during the period up to 1948. But a more important reason was that each of the major political groups was born in opposition to the government and, therefore, each was attracted to obstructionist tactics. Those political forces which remained in opposition, such as the Communists and the AMCJA, increased the intensity of their tactics. The United Malays National Organization began as an "opposition" employing obstructionist tactics, but after it had won its political victory in the form of the Federation Agreement, it confined most of its political activity to the representative institutions established under the constitution, for UMNO was in fundamental agreement with government policy after that victory.

As political groups began to get a stake in the political settlements of past battles, they became more willing to restrict their extra-legal or illegal activities. Only the Communists were determined to follow a course of violent revolution.

1 *Parliamentary Debates—Commons* (Fifth Series), 1945–46, Vol. 414, 255.

2 Ishak bin Tadin, "Dato Onn and Malay Nationalism, 1946–1951", *Journal of Southeast Asian History*, Vol. 1, no. 1 (March 1960), p. 60.

3 Dato Onn came from an aristocratic family, his father and several other members of his family having been *Mentri Besar* (Prime Minister) of Johore. He received some of his education in England and joined the Johore civil service to become District Officer in Batu Pahat. Before the war he helped to found and edit the Malay paper *Warta Melayu*. He attended the KRIS convention, but did not play a major role in its activities.

4 Daniel Eldredge Moore, "The United Malays National Organization and the 1959 Malayan Elections" (unpublished Ph.D. dissertation, University of California, 1960), p. 30.

5 The proposal to convene a Congress of Malay organizations has been traced to the Malay paper *Warta Negara*. Dato Onn publicly endorsed the idea on January 24, and plans were rather quickly worked out for such a meeting. See Ishak bin Tadin, *op. cit.*, p. 61.

6 Mohammad Yunus Hamidi, *Sejarah Pergerakan Politik Melayu Semenanjong* (Kuala Lumpur: Pustaka Antara, n.d. [1961?]), pp. 10–34.

7 *Straits Times*, March 2, 1946, p. 3; March 10, 1946, p. 4.

8 From Dato Onn's speeches as quoted in Ishak bin Tadin, *op. cit.*, p. 65.

9 The Malay name, *Pertubohan Kebangsaan Melayu Bersatu*, is hardly ever used. The organization is universally known as UMNO, pronounced as a single word, and not as four letters.

10 *Straits Times*, May 13, 1946, p. 1.

11 The Labour member was Col. D. R. Rees-Williams, who subsequently became Colonial Secretary, while the Conservative member was a former Malayan Civil Servant, Capt. L. D. Gammons.

12 Evidence of massive Malay backing for UMNO led Captain Gammons to conclude, "It's no good just to tinker about with the MacMichael treaties. We must make a fresh start and make a new treaty with the Malays under which their status is assured." See *Straits Times*, June 18, 1946, p. 3.

13 Dato Onn claimed the adherence of 70 to 80 per cent of the Malays after UMNO was only two weeks old! This was probably an exaggeration, but it appears that UMNO had secured the support of about that percentage of *penghulus* and of Malays who were either in government service or interested in political affairs. See *Sunday Times* (Singapore), May 26, 1946, p. 4.

14 A description of the organizational structure of UMNO is given in Moore, *op. cit.*, pp. 35–39.

15 *Constitutional Proposals for Malaya, Report of the Working Committee*, (Kuala Lumpur: Government Printer, 1946), p. 7.

16 For an account of the prewar activities of the Kuomintang see Png Poh Seng, "Kuomintang in Malaya, 1912–1941", *Journal of Southeast Asian History*, Vol. 2, no. 1 (March 1961), pp. 1–41.

[17] Arrangements were made for the demobilization of MOCSDA forces and payment of the same gratuities as were given the Communist MPAJA forces. However, at the last moment something went wrong and the MOCSDA forces did not parade for discharge and payment. This information was provided in a private communication from a former government official.

[18] *Straits Times*, May 11, 1946, p. 3.

[19] The most important political figure said to have ties with the KMT was Colonel H. S. Lee, who became the Minister of Finance in the first government formed after Malayan independence.

[20] *Straits Times*, May 10, 1949, p. 1.

[21] Born in Malacca in 1883, Tan Cheng-lock entered public life when he became a Malacca Municipal Commissioner in 1912. From 1933 to 1935 he was an Unofficial Member of the Straits Settlements Legislative Council and became recognized as a leading representative of the Chinese in Malaya. His postwar political activities centered around the formation of the Malayan Chinese Association, the account of which may be found in later chapters. For his vita see J. Victor Morais (ed.), *The Leaders of Malaya and Who's Who, 1956*, (Kuala Lumpur: The Economy Printers, 1956), p. 376.

[22] *Straits Budget*, January 22, 1948, p. 17.

[23] There are a number of interesting deviations from the three general patterns of Chinese conservatism described above. For example, some very wealthy Chinese who lived in Malaya for years became motivated by exceedingly strong ideas of Chinese nationalism predicated on the emergence of a "new China". They look with pride (or at least did so for a number of years) upon the radical program of the Communists in China, yet they have remained essentially conservative in their outlook on Malayan politics. This point of view is exemplified by Tan Kah-kee, who was a rubber magnate and one of the wealthiest Chinese in Malaya. He became active in the Penang Chinese Association's anti-civil war committee, seeking to aid the Chinese Communist Government. In later years he went to Communist China to represent the overseas Chinese in the Peoples Republic of China. For a number of years he was a leading member of the Overseas Chinese Affairs Commission in the Communist Government in Peking.

[24] *Straits Times*, August 17, 1946, p. 3.

[25] *Straits Times*, December 16, 1946, p. 5.

[26] *Straits Times*, February 24, 1947, p. 5. Later the Singapore Chinese Chamber of Commerce was included in a wider organization called the Pan-Malayan Chinese Chambers of Commerce.

[27] Tan Cheng-lock's original proposal was to form a Malayan Chinese League "to unite all the Chinese in Malaya". The subsequent formation of the Malayan Chinese Association the following year is often traced back to this earlier proposal. See *Malaya Tribune*, March 10, 1948, p. 1; *Straits Budget*, March 25, 1948, p. 15; May 6, 1948, p. 16.

[28] *Malaya Tribune*, November 24, 1945, p. 2; November 26, 1945, p. 1.

[29] *Straits Times*, January 16, 1946, p. 3.

[30] *Straits Times*, August 7, 1946, p. 3.

[31] *Straits Times*, November 19, 1946, p. 3.

[32] *Sunday Gazette*, January 4, 1948, p. 6; *Malaya Tribune* (Penang), December 30, 1947, p. 2.

33 An anti-AMCJA resolution was passed by MIC Malacca and similar sentiments were voiced in many other MIC meetings. See *Straits Times*, March 21, 1948, p. 3.

34 Usha Mahajani, *The Role of Indian Minorities in Burma and Malaya*, (Bombay: Vora & Co., 1960), pp. 121 and 237; *Straits Budget*, July 8, 1948, p. 9.

35 *Sunday Times*, July 4, 1948, p. 3; *Straits Times*, July 5, 1948, p. 5.

36 *Straits Times*, June 17, 1946, p. 5.

37 The Malayan Ceylonese were greatly disturbed by the 1958 racial riots in Ceylon, and the anti-Tamil policies of the Ceylon Government. A sudden increase in applications for Malayan citizenship by Ceylonese ensued, indicating a profound change in attitude toward Malaya.

38 *Constitutional Proposals for Malaya, Report of the Consultative Committee*, (Kuala Lumpur: Government Printer, 1947), p. 124.

39 For example, see C. H. Crabb, *Malaya's Eurasians—an Opinion*, (Singapore: Eastern Universities Press, 1960).

40 *Report of the Consultative Committee, op. cit.*, p. 140.

41 The Eurasian Union made a second attempt to accomplish the same result through definition of "Subject of the Sultans", but the Rulers Conference was not persuaded by the arguments. See *Straits Budget*, December 4, 1947, p. 13; December 11, 1947, p. 5.

42 If a Eurasian colony had been founded, it would have been caught up in the turmoil over Indonesia's militant campaign to acquire West Irian. See *Straits Times*, February 27, 1948, p. 6; *Sunday Times*, February 29, 1948, p. 1.

9 Communalism and the Emergency

Once the Communists began their insurrections, the political scene was drastically altered. Political coalitions formed to oppose the Federation Agreement disintegrated owing to the demise of the Malayan Democratic Union and the disappearance of Communist front organizations. As these coalitions broke up, policies became more fragmented. Moreover, the Emergency[1] forced a more cautious approach to politics. Those who sympathized with the insurrection faced the possibility of detention, or even deportation if they were not citizens, while those who sought to uphold the authority of government did not want to stir up controversy when the Communists were making their bid to seize power. All political activities were therefore dampened during the first year or two of the Emergency.

Counter-insurgency measures undertaken by the Government also tended to intensify communal antagonisms. Rural Chinese who cultivated vegetable plots or rubber smallholdings were uprooted for their often illegal land holdings and sent to detention camps for "screening" or, after 1950, to "new villages" where they could be brought within effective government control so as to prevent their giving willing (or unwilling) support to the guerrillas. The use of collective punishment, preventive detention and summary deportation were all measures employed almost exclusively to punish Chinese for proven or suspected support of the Communist cause. Food denial measures, which under severe circumstances involved communal cooking of food, added to the grievances of these resettled Chinese "squatters". Although the government provided physical amenities and social services to the new villagers, the total impact of government policy frequently caused hardship and grievances among the very people whose cooperation was essential for defeating the Communist guerrillas.[2]

While Chinese home guard units were formed in the "new villages" to provide protection against guerrilla attacks, the bulk of the security forces were composed of Commonwealth troops and Malays who were recruited by the thousands for the Police and the Special Constabulary Force.[3] Thus, the jungle fighting involved Commonwealth and Malay forces against Chinese guerrilla units. Although the war was never defined in racial terms by either side, it did complicate the problems of developing communal harmony and understanding.

Malay Politics and the Emergency

Because many leaders of UMNO were prominent officials in government service, they assumed new responsibilities for enlisting popular support for the fight against the Communists. Since the cooperation of the Chinese was essential for this effort, they tended to soften their earlier expressions of Malay "communal chauvinism". Inter-communal tensions increased when Malay communities responded to guerrilla terrorism by retaliatory attacks against neighboring Chinese. UMNO leaders warned the Malays against taking the law into their own hands and tried to function as peace-makers when disputes arose.

Radical Malay nationalists were under no such restraints, but nonetheless found it difficult to exploit the situation created by the Emergency. Their ambivalence toward the Communist revolution made the authorities suspicious of their activities. Some flirted with the idea of active revolution, but very few Malays joined the Communist guerrillas. In the first year of the Emergency no radical Malay party was banned, except for *Ikatan Pembala Tanah Ayer Melayu* (PETA)[4] which was the Communist Party's Malay front formed from a few remnants of the previously banned API. Nevertheless, individuals in radical Malay organizations which continued to function legally were closely watched to prevent possible affiliation with the Communist Party.[5] After the Governor of Sarawak, Mr. Duncan George Stewart, was killed in Sibu by two Malays who were later found to have been active members of a revolutionary organization, *Persatuan Permuda Melayu* (United Malay Youth),[6] the Malayan Government increased its vigilance against the possible formation of similar revolutionary groups in Malaya. Shortly after this, the Federation Government outlawed the Malay Nationalist Party, probably as a precautionary move, since no accusations against the party were made public.[7]

In December 1950, a number of radical Malay leaders seized upon the celebrated Maria Hertog case[8] to stir up Malay mobs in Singapore to frenzied hatred of Europeans and Eurasians. After severe rioting, the Singapore Government, acting under the provisions of the Emergency Regulations, detained the former leaders of the MNP, including Dr. Burhanuddin, Taha bin Kalu (former Vice-President of the MNP), and Abdul Mohamed Abdul Karim Ghani, an Indian Muslim and President of the Singapore Muslim League.[9] These events demonstrated the potentially explosive power of religion in politics. The experience of radical Malay politicians with this issue in 1950 may have been extremely significant in the long run, for when these individuals returned to active political life, Malay radicalism abandoned its earlier leftist secular stance to combine Malay nationalist radicalism with militant Islamic revivalism. However, in the short run, Malay radicalism received a setback, and some radical Malays left for Indonesia while others were recruited into UMNO or other new parties then in the process of formation.

The Founding of the Malayan Chinese Association

Non-Communist Chinese opinion appeared to be badly fragmented, un organized and disoriented following the outbreak of the guerrilla war The Kuomintang was not a suitable alternative for the Chinese and, in any event, was soon banned as a "foreign political party". Into this leadership vacuum stepped Tan Cheng-lock, who for years had been making proposals for some form of united Chinese organization, but had been unable to move much beyond the stage of proposal and exhortation.[10] However, after the Emergency began and the AMCJA disintegrated, the need for a new coalition of Chinese interests was obvious even to those Chinese who had avoided political involvement heretofore. The Chinese Chambers of Commerce and other conservative Chinese provided an initial impetus to the new organization, although avoiding the appearance of being its sponsor, while the British gave behind-the-scenes encouragement to those seeking to form a united non-Communist Chinese organization. After much planning the Malayan Chinese Association (MCA) was launched at Kuala Lumpur on February 27, 1949, under the leadership of Tan Cheng-lock, Leong Yew-koh and T. H. Tan.[11]

Realizing that the new conditions called for a re-evaluation of policy, these leaders of the MCA abandoned their pre-Emergency boycott of the Federation constitution and instead pledged full cooperation with the government. They claimed that the MCA would become an effective answer to the challenge of the Malayan Communist Party, thus speeding the end of the Emergency.[12] In return, they expected the government to give greater consideration to Chinese demands. In a move to command greater influence in government circles, all sixteen appointed Chinese members of the Federal Legislative and Executive Councils were included on the formative committee of the MCA. At its inception, the Malayan Chinese Association issued an appeal to all Chinese to join its ranks in order to fight Communism and strengthen the association in its representations to the government on behalf of the Chinese.[13] The government responded to the MCA pledge of cooperation by giving the MCA unofficial recognition as the principal representative of the Chinese in Malaya.

During 1949 the government began a program of resettling the scattered rural Chinese peasants into compact villages which could be more easily defended against guerrilla attack. It thereby hoped to deny the Communist guerrillas access to both their willing and unwilling supporters. In close cooperation with the government authorities, the Malayan Chinese Association assisted in the resettlement of these rural Chinese by helping them to rebuild their homes and adjust to life in the new villages. By concentrating on social welfare projects, the MCA hoped to win the confidence and cooperation of the rural Chinese peasants who were the object of so much Communist propaganda and intimidation. At the same time, the MCA aired Chinese grievances and prodded the government for policies favorable to the Chinese. These objectives were explicitly stated by Tan Cheng-lock.

It is morally and legally obligatory on all of us as good citizens to . . . co-operate with the Government to restore peace and order in the present disturbed state of the country, and it is equally the bounden duty of the Government to . . . co-operate with us to make such co-operation practicable.[14]

The Malayan Chinese Association increased greatly in strength after October 1949 when the Federal Government legalized lotteries for charitable purposes.[15] It began sponsoring periodic multi-million dollar lotteries, the proceeds of which were used to help the rural Chinese who were being resettled into new villages. Through this program the MCA provided financial assistance and social services to needy Chinese, but it also helped to increase its membership by means of "welfare patronage". As the size and profits from these lotteries increased, the Malayan Government began to be concerned about the political implications of welfare lotteries conducted by an organization that was both political and charitable. However, for several years the MCA exploited the Chinese love of gambling to pay for welfare programs which incidentally helped to consolidate its power among the Chinese of Malaya.

The Communists, of course, found the activities of the Malayan Chinese Association most detrimental to their revolution, and accused the MCA of being "running dogs and lackeys of imperialism". Less than two months after the founding of the MCA, the Communists attempted to assassinate Tan Cheng-lock with a hand grenade while he was delivering a speech at the Chinese Chamber of Commerce in Ipoh.[16] The attack contributed to his stature among the Chinese and after his recovery he continued his outspoken opposition to Communist terrorism.

Other Minority Groups and the Emergency

Since maximum Indian political influence depended upon some form of coalition with other parties, Indians had to wait for the regrouping of political forces after the Emergency before they could make their bid for access to power through coalition politics. Furthermore, several organizations competed for the loyalty of Indians so that bargaining on behalf of the entire Indian community was impossible. The Malayan Indian Congress had been split over questions of membership for non-Indians and its participation in the All-Malaya Council of Joint Action. The collapse of the AMCJA coalition left the MIC isolated from political allies, while having to contend with competition from the Indian Association and the Indian Chambers of Commerce. Thus for several years after 1948 Indian political influence was at a comparatively low ebb, and Indian politics were characterized by division, disorganization and indecision.

On the other hand, the Ceylonese, represented by the Ceylon Federation, had become identified quite closely with the Government, and by implication with UMNO.[17] Through the strategic location in government of respected and capable Ceylonese, that minority exercised influence over government policy far out of proportion to its size.

Following the declaration of the Emergency, the Malayan Democratic Union voluntarily closed down. However, individuals who had been active in the MDU tried to keep in contact with one another, hoping eventually to recoup their losses. Discussion groups were formed among these intellectual leftists, and various issues of current interest were studied, usually from a Marxist point of view.[18] The authorities suspected that these groups were affiliated with the Communist Party and in January 1951 the police detained a University of Malaya lecturer and six students. A few days later nine others were detained, most of whom had been active in the MDU, including its founder, John Eber; P. V. Sarma, president of the Malayan Teachers' Union; and Abdul Samad, an editor of the Malay newspaper, *Utusan Melayu*. With the aid of mine detectors, documents were found which the government alleged were "secret orders and other evidence of membership in a disciplined revolutionary body", later identified as the Singapore Peoples' Anti-British League.[19] Some of the detained persons were freed within a day or two, but John Eber, C. Devan Nair and Abdul Samad were held without trial under emergency detention orders which were renewed from time to time and approved by an Advisory Committee of jurists who examined the evidence *in camera*. Finally in 1951 the three men were released, but severe restrictions were placed upon their freedom of movement and political activity. John Eber left for England so that he could be free to voice his bitter criticisms of Malayan developments and he attempted to develop a political following among Malayan students in Britain.[20]

The John Eber case made westernized leftists more fearful of possible detention, while the accusations against him tended to implicate them with tacit support of violent revolution. Finding political activity difficult and hazardous, many westernized intellectuals with Marxist sympathies became disturbed and frustrated by the turn of events which had destroyed their imagined position of leadership of Malayan nationalism.

Experiment in Inter-Communal Cooperation—The Communities Liaison Committee

The constitutional issues that arose in connection with the Malayan Union and the Federation Agreement had the effect of bringing into bold relief the fundamental communal divisions of Malayan politics. Communalism, even in a mild form, threatened social cohesion, without which democratic government becomes difficult if not dangerous. The Communist revolt threatened to turn these communal tensions into massive communal violence, particularly since the Communists exploited the grievances of the Chinese to generate a following for their cause. Many people in and out of public life became concerned lest Malaya be torn asunder by communal warfare similar to that which had spread through India and Pakistan.

On the initiative of the Commissioner-General, Malcolm MacDonald, prominent Malay and Chinese leaders were called together at Penang to consider means to alleviate Sino-Malay tensions throughout Malaya. At this meeting in January 1949 a committee was formed consisting of five Malays and four Chinese with Mr. MacDonald acting as "liaison officer". It was initially known as the Malay-Chinese Goodwill Committee, but after its membership expanded to include representatives from other communities, its official name became the Communities Liaison Committee.[21] By August 1949 this committee consisted of six Malays, six Chinese, and one representative from each of the Indian, Eurasian, Ceylonese, and European communities.[22]

While the initial objective of the committee was to alleviate the immediate causes of inter-communal friction, its horizon soon broadened to encompass all political issues. The authorities very soon began to view the committee as an appropriate arena for the negotiation of compromise solutions to communal issues and perhaps eventually pave the way for a non-communal approach to politics. On this assumption, the committee took on the responsibility for making preliminary recommendations on such controversial issues as citizenship, education policy, the introduction of elections to local and federal councils, and economic policies to aid the Malays.[23]

In its first report of September 1949 the Communities Liaison Committee issued a general statement of the ultimate aims of Malayan political and constitutional development. It proposed the introduction of elections, first at the local level and finally for the federal legislature, as soon as conditions permitted. The committee suggested that the franchise should be based on federal citizenship, but it did not attempt to define the conditions for citizenship. It rejected reserved communal seats and communal electoral rolls which had been proposed by some persons who wanted to guarantee a proportionate communal representation in the Legislative Council. On the matter of educational policy the committee proposed "that the teaching of the Malay and English languages should be compulsory in all Government and Government-aided primary schools".[24] Later, in April 1950, the committee released another report which contained proposed amendments to the Federation Agreement in regard to federal citizenship and naturalization, as well as proposals for the economic improvement of the Malays.[25]

Although couched in general terms, the reports of the CLC represented significant political compromises reached through hard bargaining by communal leaders. The committee's proposals did not bind anyone, not even its members. However, many of its recommendations, particularly on the issues of education and citizenship, were incorporated into legislative proposals which were approved by the Legislative Council.[26]

The recommendations drafted by the Communities Liaison Committee were not always well received by the communal organizations whose leaders were on the committee. Indeed, committee members found themselves torn between their responsibility as leaders of communal organizations to promote communal interests, and their implied responsibility as members of the committee to seek "non-communal" answers to vexing political issues.

While the committee never developed a genuine non-communal approach to the problems confronting Malaya, it did demonstrate that significant communal compromise was more likely to emerge from semi-secret and "off-the-record" negotiations conducted by communal leaders. The experience of the CLC in inter-communal bargaining conducted beyond the view of the mass media may have been extremely significant in later years when political coalitions emerged to bridge communal cleavages.[27]

Non-Communalism versus Communalism within UMNO

One of the most important by-products of the Communities Liaison Committee was the remarkable change which it appeared to have made in the political stance of Dato Onn. In 1948 he had led the attack on the Malayan Union and had been the prime mover in the political awakening of the Malays. Yet, as a member of the Communities Liaison he professed conversion to the ideal of "avoiding communalism" in politics. Dato Onn tried to get both the Malay Rulers and UMNO to accept policies which, he hoped, would eventually create a unified and independent country. Although he did not abandon his solicitude for the Malays, he saw the necessity of admitting non-Malays to full rights of citizenship, provided that they were willing to give full loyalty to a Malaya having a predominantly Malay character to its institutions and cultural life. Under these conditions, he believed that Malaya could move toward democracy and national independence.

Dato Onn soon found it difficult to persuade the Malay public to accept the political course being charted by the Communities Liaison Committee. The Sultans, acting against the advice of their ministers, vetoed the CLC proposal to establish the post of Deputy High Commissioner, which was to have been filled by a Malay and was to have been a preparatory step toward independence. In protest Dato threatened to resign his position as Mentri Besar of Johore, but it was not until May 1950 that he finally relinquished that post. At the time he announced that he would devote all his energies to the United Malays National Organization,[28] perhaps because even more serious opposition was emerging from his own party.

When the Communities Liaison Committee made public its proposals on citizenship in April 1950, Dato Onn attempted to secure their approval by UMNO. An emergency general assembly of UMNO was convened in May to consider these proposals. Although no decision was reached, the delegates did authorize the UMNO Executive Committee to draft "counter proposals" to overcome some of the more serious objections from ultra-communal Malays who paraded under the slogan "Malaya for the Malays", and who had viewed the CLC with suspicion from the very beginning.[29] Another special UMNO general assembly was convened in June to approach the "counter proposals" on citizenship, prepared by the Executive Committee, but still patterned on the CLC proposals. Dato Onn made impassioned pleas to the delegates for approval of the principle that loyal non-Malays should be given the opportunity to acquire full rights of citizenship in Malaya. However, opposition was strong and well-organized. Some delegates accused Dato Onn of being a "traitor to the Malays"[30] since he had led the fight for Malay privileges, but was now proposing to surrender these hard-won victories without a fight. Although the proposal to liberalize the citizenship requirements of the Federation Agreement was never put to a vote, Dato Onn could sense impending defeat, so he dramatically announced his resignation from the leadership of UMNO, and the Executive Committee followed his example.

Dato Onn's resignation from the presidency of UMNO came as a shock to the Malays, most of whom had come to look to him for guidance and leadership as the "father of Malay politics". Within a short time a number of local UMNO branches pledged anew their support to him and begged him to resume the presidency. Yet, the opposition became increasingly vocal and critical of Dato Onn.[31] At the following annual meeting of UMNO the controversial citizenship proposals were finally approved and Dato Onn was re-elected president of UMNO by a vote of 66 to 3.[32] Although this appeared to be a decisive personal victory for Dato Onn, it did not mean that UMNO had been converted to his views on the necessity of pursuing a less communal approach to politics.

Tensions within UMNO became even more severe when Dato Onn made a new proposal that the name of the organization be changed to United Malayan National Organization and that its ranks should be open to members of any race on the basis of complete equality. He believed that UMNO should be a non-communal political party so as to be in a strong position to contest the elections which were first scheduled to be introduced at the local level during 1952. Although Dato Onn secured the approval of the UMNO Executive Committee for these changes, the rank and file opposed the idea of accepting non-Malays in UMNO, because it tended to imply the abandonment of Malay special rights and would also make it difficult for UMNO to champion the "cause of the Malays".[33]

Malay Opposition to Dato Onn

When the first report of the Communities Liaison Committee was being considered by UMNO, some dissident elements founded a rival party with the announced aim of opposing the policies of UMNO and Dato Onn.[34] Led by Inche Hashim Ghani, this party, *Persatuan Melayu Semenanjong* (Peninsular Malays Union—PMU), attracted the support of militantly communal Malays. Although the Peninsular Malays Union started as a very weak party, it continued to grow in strength after each new "non-communal" proposal of Dato Onn. By 1951 the PMU and its twin, the Malay Union of Singapore, were mounting an intensive campaign against Dato Onn's "unconditional surrender" to the non-Malays, and his attempt to recast UMNO into a multi-communal political party.

Dato Onn lost additional support to his critics when he insisted that the "Nadra" (Maria Hertog) case should be avoided as a political issue and that

125

its outcome should be left entirely for the courts to decide. After the Maria Hertog riots, Dato Onn condemned the violent outbreaks and the hot-headed radicals who had incited the mobs, and when the Malay rioters were sentenced for riot and murder, UMNO did not take the initiative in seeking to have their sentences commuted. By contrast, the PMU was implicated in the riots, agitated against the court decision, and took a lead in demanding the release of convicted Malay rioters.

By mid-1951 Dato Onn realized that he no longer commanded the un-qualified support of UMNO, despite the fact that a majority of its Executive Committee remained loyal to him and reluctantly approved his new policies. As he saw it, he had only two alternatives if he was to remain faithful to the ideal of "non-communal politics". He could continue his efforts to win the support of UMNO for his policies. Or he could break with UMNO and form a new party dedicated to Malayan nationalism and communal co-operation. He chose the second course of action, because, in his words, "Even if the principles . . . are accepted by the majority of UMNO, there would still be a powerful minority which would continue to sabotage or retard progress."[35] Without waiting for UMNO to vote on his proposals to make it multi-communal, he decided to form a new political party which would attempt to achieve Malayan independence "within seven years" by uniting the racial communities in Malaya behind a single nationalist banner. At first he hinted that UMNO might become the nucleus for such a party. However, a week later, he announced that he was breaking his ties with UMNO to form the Independence of Malaya Party (IMP).[36]

Experiment in Non-Communal Politics—The Independence of Malaya Party

In the planning stages for the Independence of Malaya Party, Dato Onn stressed only a few basic political objectives, while avoiding many more immediate controversial issues. Before the party had been formally launched, he made public its aims in an eight-point manifesto, the principal provisions of which called for: self-government within ten years, local elections by 1953, federal elections by 1955, free, compulsory education to the age of 12, and Malayanization of the public services.[37]

In order to form the base for a mass "non-communal" nationalist party, Dato Onn solicited support from as many prominent community leaders as possible. He also expected to bring a substantial portion of his political following from UMNO into the new party. At the annual general assembly of UMNO, he gave a major address as its retiring president, and invited all progressive Malays in and out of UMNO to join with him to work for an independent Malaya through the cooperative effort of all the races of Malaya.[38] He was given lavish praise for his leadership of UMNO, yet only a very small fraction of the UMNO membership followed his lead to join the IMP. Shortly after taking office the new president of UMNO, Tunku Abdul Rahman, [39] called upon all Malays to avoid any affiliation with the IMP. Later, he announced that the IMP policies were contrary to those of

UMNO and that members joining or showing sympathy for the IMP would be expelled from UMNO.[40] Most Malays were convinced of the sincerity and dedication of Dato Onn, but they were not persuaded that they would benefit from political union with the other communities, fearing that their political and economic privileges guaranteed by the Federation Agreement would thereby become jeopardized. One Malay writing to the *Straits Times* asked, "Is the IMP the banding together of lambs, lions and tigers to drive out the caretakers"[41] Communal considerations were still paramount.

While the Malay chauvinists provided the primary opposition to the formation of the IMP, most Europeans and many pro-British elements were apprehensive about the public pronouncements of Dato Onn. In one speech he said that "the British intentions on self-government are not above suspicion",[42] and he refused to commit the IMP to the goal of independence within the Commonwealth. He also castigated the Sultans for their gradualist approach to self government. Thus, some pro-British moderates feared that he was following a course of extreme nationalism which would lead to premature independence and the rejection of all ties with Britain. On the other hand, because the IMP was following the course chartered by the government-encouraged Communities Liaison Committee, many local people suspected that the IMP was being formed with the secret backing of the British.

On September 16, 1951, the Independence of Malaya Party was launched at a gala meeting held on the roof garden of the Majestic Hotel in Kuala Lumpur. In attendance were nearly all the members of the former Communities Liaison Committee, representing all the major communal organizations, as well as leaders from the Malayan Trade Union Congress and from two newly formed political parties—the Radical Party of Penang and the Selangor Labour Party. The founding ceremonies for the IMP were the most impressive of any party formed in Malaya. The array of distinguished political leaders who expressed their support for the IMP gave the impression that this new party would soon dominate the Malayan political scene.[43]

Although the IMP profoundly altered the course of Malayan politics, its founding marked the zenith of "non-communal" politics, rather than its commencement. In early 1952 the introduction of elections brought Malayan politics into a distinctly new stage of development which exposed fundamental political divisions that could not be bridged by restricting political issues to nationalism, independence, or inter-communal harmony. No issues are immune to the politics of elections, and the prize of office encourages all contestants, particularly in the first "race".

---

[1] The fight against Communist guerrillas is referred to as "The Emergency" in both the press and in official government publications.

[2] The guerrilla war and the counter-insurgency measures employed by the government fall beyond the scope of this work. Aspects of this subject may be found in the following: W. C. S. Corry, *A General Survey of New Villages*, (Kuala Lumpur: Government Printer, 1954); E. H. G. Dobby, "Resettlement Transforms Malaya", *Economic Development and Cultural Change*, Vol. 1, no. 3, (October 1952), pp.

165 ff.; Maynard Weston Dow, *Nation Building in Southeast Asia*, (Boulder, Colorado: Pruett Press, 1966), pp. 17–87; Federation of Malaya, *Detention and Deportation During the Emergency in the Federation of Malaya*, Council Paper No. 24 of 1953; Federation of Malaya, *Report of the Baling Talks*, Council Paper No. 25 of 1956; Federation of Malaya, *The Squatter Problem in the Federation of Malaya*, Council Paper No. 14 of 1950; Federation of Malaya, *Resettlement and the Development of New Villages in the Federation of Malaya, 1952*, Council Paper No. 33 of 1952; Federation of Malaya, *Regulations Made Under the Emergency Regulations Ordinance, 1948*, (Kuala Lumpur: Government Press, 1953); Gene Z. Hanrahan, *The Communist Struggle in Malaya*, (New York: Institute of Pacific Relations, 1954); J. K. King, "Malaya's Resettlement Problem", *Far Eastern Survey*, Vol 23, no. 3, (March 1954), pp. 33–40; Paul Markandan, *The Problem of the New Villages of Malaya*, (Singapore: Donald Moore, 1954); Harry Miller, *Menace in Malaya*, (London: George G. Harrap & Co., 1954); Ray Nyce, "The 'New Villages' of Malaya: A Community Study", unpublished Ph.D. dissertation, Hartford Seminary Foundation, 1962; Lucian W. Pye, *Guerrilla Communism in Malaya*, (Princeton, New Jersey: Princeton University Press, 1956); J. B. Perry Robinson, *Transformation in Malaya*, (London: Secker & Warburg, 1956); Anthony Short, "Communism and the Emergency", in Wang Gungwu (ed.), *Malaysia—A Survey*, (New York: Frederick A. Praeger, 1964), pp. 149–160; Sir Robert Thompson, *Defeating Communist Insurgency*, (New York: Frederick A. Praeger, 1966).

3 Within six months the Special Constabulary Force had grown to 30,000. By 1951 about 400,000 rural Chinese had been resettled, and by 1954 the figure had risen to about 600,000 persons living in 410 "new villages". Ultimately about 700,000 persons were resettled in the "new villages".

4 *Federation of Malaya Government Gazette*, July 23, 1948 (L.N. 2037). Although a different organization, this Communist front used the same initials as the Japanese sponsored Malay volunteer force *Pembela Tanah Ayer*, perhaps as a front to recruit radical Malays.

5 A few radical Malays were arrested for security reasons. Among them was the president of the MNP, Ishak bin Haji Muhammad. Criticism of his arrest in the Malay press elicited the following explanation: "Government holds evidence that, in his private capacity, he has been working with Communist elements for the overthrow of Government and the establishment of an alternative government by force." See *Straits Times*, July 28, 1948, p. 1.

6 An embryonic Malay underground organization composed of former API members was discovered in Perak the following month. See *Singapore Free Press*, January 12, 1950, p. 1.

7 *Federation of Malaya Government Gazette*, April 27, 1950, p. 809 (L.N. 988). The MNP remained a legal organization for a short while longer in Singapore.

8 Maria Hertog was the daughter of Dutch parents who had left her in the care of an Indonesian servant when they were about to be interned by the Japanese in the early stages of the war. After the war they could not find the servant or their daughter, but in 1950 they finally traced her to the east coast of Malaya where she was living as a Malay with their former family servant. Maria had been given the Malay name Nadra, had become a Muslim and did not want to return to her parents whom she did not remember. The parents secured a court order to obtain custody over Maria, who at the time was 13 years old. To forestall the court action, her Indonesian foster mother immediately arranged her marriage to a Malay. Under Muslim law this action made her legally the responsibility of her husband. The legal proceedings went through prolonged stages of appeals and hearings, and religious fanatics among the Malays attempted to make this an issue of Christianity versus Islam. In mid-December, rioting Malay mobs indiscriminately began attacking Europeans and Eurasians. Before order was restored by units of the Army, 18 persons had been killed and more than 180 had been injured. Eventually Maria was given into the custody of her parents and she was taken to Holland where she has been living ever since. For an account of the events leading up to and including the riots see Lionel Leach (Chairman), *Report of the Singapore Riots Inquiry Commission, 1951*, (Singapore: Government Printing Office, 1951).

9 *Straits Times*, December 19, 1950, p. 1.

10 Tan Cheng-lock was an active member of the Malacca branch of the Straits Chinese British Association during the First World War, and later was president of the SCBA's Malacca branch from 1928 to 1935. During the Second World War, while in exile in Bangalore, India, he considered the formation of a Malayan Chinese association, and later founded what he called the Overseas Chinese Association. It remained a paper organization of practically no significance. See Soh Eng Lim, "Tan Cheng-lock, His Leadership of the Malayan Chinese", *Journal of Southeast Asian History*, Vol. 1, no. 1 (March 1960), pp. 31–35. In May 1948 Tan Cheng-lock began reviving his earlier idea with talk about the formation of a "Malayan Chinese League".

11 Mr. Soh states that Leong Yew-koh was the originator of the idea of the MCA, and that it came into being largely through his organizational and administrative skills. See *ibid.*, p. 45. Also see *Straits Times*, February 28, 1949, pp. 1 and 5.

12 *Straits Times*, February 6, 1949, p. 1.

13 Membership of the MCA was open to any Chinese over 18 years of age who had resided in Malaya for five years and regarded Malaya as his permanent home and the object of his loyalty. Non-Chinese could become associate members, but without voting rights. *Rules of the Malayan Chinese Association* (mimeographed), Rules 4–7 and 42.

14 Tan Cheng-Lock, *Speeches of Tan Cheng Lock*, (Singapore: Ih Shih Press, n.d.), p. 18.

15 The MCA claimed a membership of 100,000 at the end of 1949, 188,000 in December 1951, 220,000 in June 1953, and 250,000 by January 1955. See *Malayan Chinese Association, Fifth Annual General Committee Meeting*, (January 1953), p. 4; *Malayan Chinese Association Annual Report Seventh Annual General Committee Meeting*, (January 1955), p. 2. The MCA earned 4 per cent on all lottery tickets, and by 1953 was earning an estimated M$1,000,000 annually from this source alone. See *Malayan Chinese Association, Paper No. 1 of 1953*, p. 10.

16 *Straits Times*, April 11, 1949, p. 1.

17 In 1949 the Ceylon Federation president, E. E. C. Thuraisingham became an associate member of UMNO at the invitation of Dato Onn. The close cooperation between the two gave the Ceylonese their primary access to government. See *Straits Budget*, September 1, 1949, p. 7.

18 A number of these political activists were affiliated with the Malayan Teachers' Union or the Singapore Cooperative Stores Society.

19 The Singapore Peoples' Anti-British League was a proscribed organization which the authorities claimed was supported by the Communist Party to propagate Communist doctrine and collect money for the guerrillas. See *Straits Times*, January 9, 1951, p. 1.

20 The case of John Eber became a *cause célèbre*, both for critics of colonial rule and for those who argue that the civil rights of the individual are to be valued above the alleged requirements of public order and safety. The Singapore Government's refusal to present its case in open court generated much criticism in both England and Malaya. After John Eber was released and arrived in England he tried to organize a far-left movement among Malayan students, and helped to edit the *Malayan Monitor*—a paper published in London claiming to be an organ of "PUTERA-AMCJA (Malayan People's United Front)". Later John Eber became General-Secretary for the "Movement for Colonial Freedom"—an association organized in 1954 by the Labour M.P., Fenner Brockway. Although closely associated with the Labour Party, the "Movement for Colonial Freedom" became an embarrassment for the Labour Party because of its opposition to the Malaysian Federation and its close proximity to the Communist line. The *Malayan Monitor* regularly published MCP documents and policy declarations, thus providing a valuable source for documentary materials on the Communists in Malaysia.

21 Earlier Malay-Chinese committees had been formed on the local level in areas where Sino-Malay clashes had occurred or had appeared imminent. See *Straits Times*, December 14, 1948, p. 5. Commissioner-General, Malcolm MacDonald, and Sir Roland Braddell are reported to have been the moving force behind the formation of a high level committee of communal leaders.

22 The Communities Liaison Committee selected E. E. C. Thuraisingham (president of the Ceylon Federation) to be chairman. Among the members of the committee were Dato Onn (president of UMNO), Tan Cheng-lock (president of the MCA), Dr. J. S. Goonting (president of the Eurasian Association) and C. C. Tan (Chairman of the Singapore Progressive Party). See *Straits Times*, August 10, 1949, p. 5. Earlier on December 31, 1948, Dato Onn invited 21 communal leaders to his home for informal discussions. He claimed to have done so on his own initiative, and thus claims some credit for the formation of the CLC. See Ishak bin Tadin, "Dato Onn and Malay Nationalism, 1946–1951", *Journal of Southeast Asian History*, Vol. 1, no. 1 (March 1960), p. 71.

23 *Straits Times*, March 16, 1949, p. 1; April 19, 1949, p. 1.

24 The first CLC report is reproduced in *Straits Times*, September 18, 1949, pp. 1 and 3. The second report may be found in *Straits Times*, April 19, 1950, p. 8.

25 The Communities Liaison Committee had come to the conclusion that the Malays would sacrifice their privileged political position only if they could be aided in securing a greater share of their country's wealth. As a direct result of the CLC recommendations, the Government created the Rural Industrial Development Authority (RIDA) in July 1950 to improve the economic condition of the Malays. Dato Onn became its first chairman, and won the praise of Malays of all shades of opinion for his untiring efforts to make RIDA effective. However, in the first years of its operations, RIDA raised the expectations of the Malays but was able to do little to alleviate their economic plight, despite substantial investments in a variety of rural development programs.

26 *The Federation of Malaya Agreement (Amendment) Ordinance, 1951* incorporated the substance of the CLC recommendations on citizenship. However, the opposition to the bill became so severe that it was referred to a Select Committee. Eventually revised proposals were incorporated into the *Federation of Malaya Agreement (Amendment) Ordinance, 1952*. For an excellent account of the issues of citizenship see K. J. Ratnam, *Communalism and the Political Process in Malaya*, (Kuala Lumpur: University of Malaya Press, 1965), pp. 66–101.

27 There is remarkable similarity between the communal bargaining which took place within the Communities Liaison Committee and the bargaining which has taken place within the Alliance National Council. In both, negotiations were secret, but the agreements were presented as "non-communal" and support for them was then solicited from communal political organizations represented at the bargaining sessions.

28 Dato Onn would probably have been appointed to the vetoed post. His resignation threat was repeated on several occasions. See *Straits Times*, June 22, 1949, p. 1; May 19, 1950, p. 1; *Straits Budget*, October 6, 1949, p. 15.

29 *Straits Times*, May 22, 1950, p. 1.

30 *Straits Times*, June 12, 1950, p. 1.

31 In an editorial of June 23, 1950, the Malay paper *Majlis* suggested that the Malays had lost confidence in Dato Onn's leadership. A translation of the article may be found in *Malayan Press Digest*, Federation of Malaya, No. 11/50, June 16 to June 30, 1950, p. 9.

32 *Malay Mail*, August 28, 1950, p. 5.

[33] Dato Onn asked that the UMNO slogan be changed from "Hidup Melayu" (Long Live the Malays) to "Merdeka" (Independence). One motive for opening UMNO membership to non-Malays may have been the desire to split and weaken the MCA which was then becoming a formidable political organization. Note Ishak bin Tadin, *op. cit.*, pp. 78–84.

[34] *Malay Mail*, December 17, 1949, p. 1.

[35] *Straits Times*, June 13, 1951, p. 1.

[36] *Straits Times*, June 6, 1951, p. 1; June 13, 1951, p. 1; *Malay Mail*, June 13, 1951, p. 5.

[37] *Straits Times*, June 23, 1951, p. 1.

[38] *Malay Mail*, August 27, 1951, pp. 3 and 6.

[39] An account of Tunku Abdul Rahman's selection as the new president of UMNO is contained in his biography by Harry Miller, *Prince and Premier*, (London: George G. Harrap & Co., 1959), pp. 105–108.

[40] *Malay Mail*, September 18, 1951, p. 7. Some UMNO members planned to join the IMP and remain active in UMNO, because Dato Onn explained that the two parties were not opposed. This announcement by Tunku Abdul Rahman forced the Malays to choose between the two parties, which in retrospect probably was the primary reason for the failure of the IMP.

[41] *Straits Times*, June 30, 1951, p. 9.

[42] *Straits Times*, June 13, 1951, p. 1.

[43] *Sunday Times*, September 16, 1951, p. 1; *Straits Times*, September 17, pp. 1 and 7. For a few months after its inception, Tan Cheng-lock and Dato Onn were reportedly working hard to build grass-roots support for the IMP. The seemingly harmonious cooperation between these two former protagonists was interpreted as additional evidence of the success of "non-communal" politics. However, as later events revealed, appearances were deceptive.

10 The Introduction of Elections

Prior to the introduction of elections, most political activity in Malaya was limited to that of making representations to the government or organizing public demonstrations in protest over various issues. Practically any person who espoused a political cause could claim to be a political leader, since leadership in some cases required little more than the ability to attract the attention of the public or, perhaps more correctly, to attract the attention of the press. As soon as elections became the primary vehicle to political success and power, political leadership was put to the new task of organizing popular support from diverse and often competing narrow interest groups. The introduction of elections can have a very chastening effect upon political activity, in that political leadership is put to a test and the emphasis of politics gradually shifts fom that of making public pronouncements or organizing protests and "civil disobedience" campaigns against public policies, to that of organizing the public to give positive support for particular public policies. In short, the creation of dependable majorities becomes the overriding consideration of all politics once it becomes established that elections are to be the sole avenue to political power.

The First Elections

The first elections in the Federation were for the Municipal Council of George Town on Penang Island, and were held December 1, 1951. The Radical Party of Penang, the Penang Labour Party, and UMNO were the three parties contesting the elections. The short, vigorous campaign turned on local issues and the personal popularity of individual candidates. The Penang Radical Party, campaigning on a "non-communal"middle-of-the-road platform, captured six of the nine seats.[1] Although the George Town (Penang) elections were watched with much interest by Malayan politicians they were not a test of strength between major political parties organized on a national basis, and thus provided very little evidence of future trends in Malayan politics.

Because of its position as the capital of Malaya, the Kuala Lumpur Municipal Council elections of February, 1952, attracted much more national political interest. In political circles it was common knowledge that Dato Onn and the Independence of Malaya Party would try to make a strong showing in the Kuala Lumpur elections as evidence to the British that Malaya was on the road to independence, and as evidence to Malaya that a "non-

West Malaysia

THAILAND

PERLIS

Kangar

LANGKAWI
ISLANDS

6°N

KEDAH

Alor Star

Baling

GEORGE TOWN

Butterworth   Grik

Prai

PENANG

PERAK

Taiping

Port Weld   Kuala Kangsar

IPOH

PANGKOR

Lumut

Perak R.

Telok Anson

Tanjong Malim

SELANGOR

Petaling Jaya

Port Swettenham

Klang Strait   Morib

STRAIT   OF   MALACCA

Kelanton R.

Kota Bharu

Kuala Krai

Kuala Gris

KELANTAN

Gunong Tahan
2190m (7186ft)

Cameron
Highlands

Kuala
Lipis

Benta

Fraser's
Hill

Bentong   Temerloh

PAHANG

Maran

Pahang R.

SOUTH   CHINA

SEA

Kuala
Trengganu

TRENGGANU

Kuala
Dungun

Kuantan

KLANG   KUALA LUMPUR

NEGRI
SEMBILAN

Seremban

Port
Dickson

MALACCA

Malacca

Batu Pahat

SUMATRA

(INDONESIA)

Gemas

JOHORE

Muar

Kluang

Johore
Bahru

SINGAPORE

TIOMAN

Mersing

2°N

International boundary ••••••••
State boundary ‑‑‑‑‑‑‑

0   50   100 Miles

0   50   100   150 Kilometres

100°E   102°E   104°E

East Malaysia (Sabah and Sarawak)

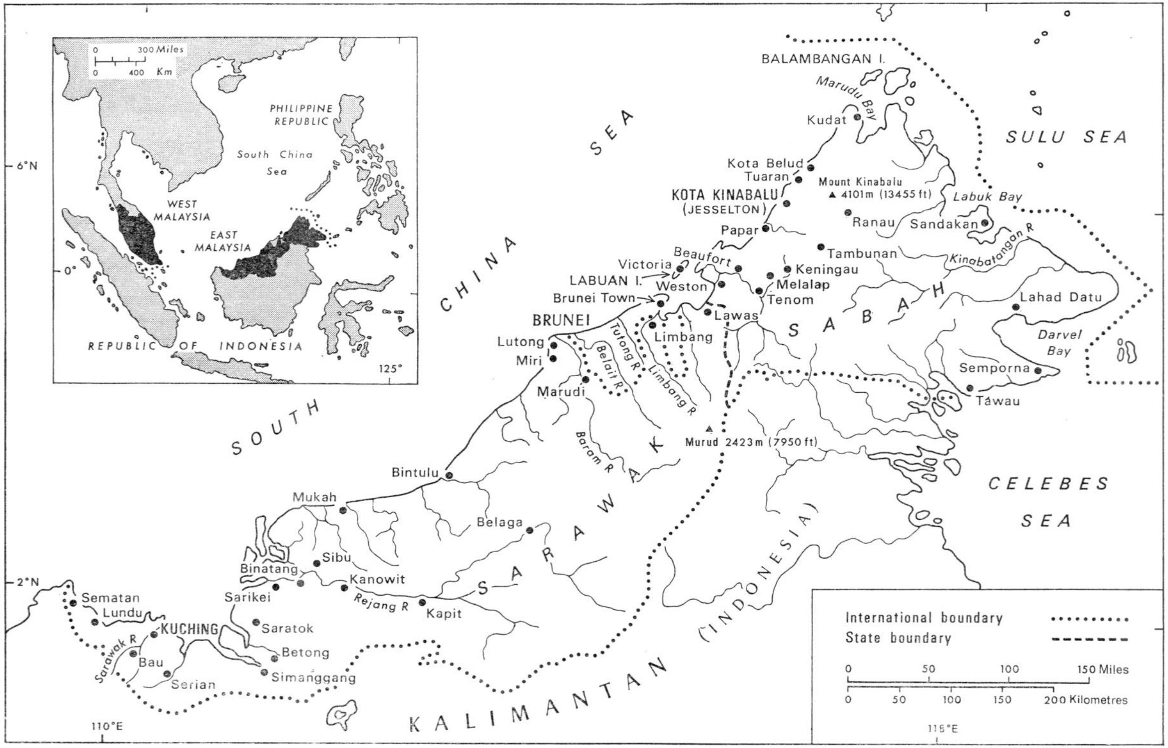

communal" approach to politics could unite the country for such independence. Kuala Lumpur was an ideal location for the IMP to test its power at the polls because the Malays, the Chinese and the Indians had established good relations with each other, and the people of the city were generally conceded to be more liberal in their communal attitudes than those in most other areas of Malaya. Furthermore, the IMP had been launched in Kuala Lumpur, and many of its strongest supporters were connected with the Federal Government. Any of the communal parties would have found it very difficult to win a majority with a strictly communal appeal to Kuala Lumpur's mixed communal constituencies. It was also obvious that the Selangor Labour Party offered no challenge to the IMP at the polls, because it was an embryonic party, having only a few hundred loyal supporters at the time. Five weeks before the Kuala Lumpur editions, it appeared that the IMP would have no serious opposition from any quarter.

On January 8, 1952, a most unexpected joint declaration was made by the Selangor branches of the United Malays National Organization and the Malayan Chinese Association announcing that these two parties would contest the Kuala Lumpur elections together in a common front.[2] Many political observers were unable to understand how UMNO and the MCA were able to reach a working agreement to band together to contest the Kuala Lumpur elections. Since this phenomenon is one of the most important turning-points in Malaya's political development it deserves some explanation.

The UMNO-MCA Alliance was created as a reaction to the Independence of Malaya Party. Both parties to this alliance had compelling reasons to oppose the IMP. Dato Onn and the IMP had charted a course that threatened to undermine the political support of UMNO among the Malays. The new president of UMNO, Tunku Abdul Rahman, wasted no time in trying to purge the party of those elements that still supported Dato Onn. He realized that if the IMP were to expand its power, UMNO would suffer proportionally. Consequently, UMNO was looking for the means to deal the IMP a decisive blow.

The Malayan Chinese Association also had reasons for joining a common front against the IMP. For one thing, Dato Onn's ideas of "non-communal" politics were based on the assumption that the immigrant communities would be accepted as full citizens of Malaya only after they had proved their loyalty and had measured up to certain standards. In other words, Dato Onn, being a Malay, tended to define a "Malayan" by reference to the Malays. Therefore, although the IMP was much more liberal with respect to non-Malay rights, citizenship and voting requirements than UMNO, it was still not above suspicion as far as the Malayan Chinese Association was concerned. Yet the IMP had received the implied blessing of the MCA when Tan cheng-lock had agreed to act as chairman for the founding meeting of the IMP, and when he later toured the coutry with Dato Onn to help organize IMP branches.

The most adequate explanation of the sudden turn-about of the MCA must take into account the personalities of Dato Onn and Tan Cheng-lock.

Both men were very dynamic, and both possessed too much of the quality of a *prima donna* on the political stage to be able to work together very well. Furthermore, personal animosities had developed between them during the extended political controversies over the Malayan Union and the Federation Agreement.   Although Tan Cheng-lock could have supported a "non-communal" political party, he could never have been an enthusiastic supporter of such a party if it also would have given Dato Onn an unassailable position of political supremacy in Malaya. Indeed, the political and personal rivalry between Dato Onn and Tan Cheng-lock was a major feature of Malayan politics for a decade after the war.

Both the MCA and UMNO realized that by themselves neither could hope to capture more than two or three of the twelve seats to be contested in the Kuala Lumpur municipal elections. By presenting a common front in the elections they hoped to be able to defeat the IMP and in the process secure additional seats for both the MCA and UMNO. By prior agreement MCA candidates ran in the predominantly Chinese constituencies, while UMNO candidates contested the predominantly Malay constituencies, and each party promised support for the other's candidates. No attempt was made to create a merger of the MCA and UMNO. Rather, this was a cleverly calculated maneuver designed to increase the strength of both parties at the polls. No attempt was made to draft a comprehensive common program between UMNO and the MCA. Indeed, political issues were avoided and the joint statement of the two parties even gave as one of the explanations for their alliance that "the purely local interests of the Municipality do not call for activities of a political character".[3]

The alliance between UMNO and the MCA made it difficult for the IMP to campaign against communalism in politics. All three parties contesting the election came out in favor of communal harmony, although admittedly the "communal harmony" of the UMNO-MCA was not quite the same as IMP's professed ideal of non-communal politics. However, the similarity between these positions was such that the election turned on personalities, and the organizational abilities of each party to reach the voters and bring them out on election day.

The results of the election for the Kuala Lumpur Municipal Council gave ample proof of the value of the UMNO-MCA strategy, for in combination they won nine of the twelve seats contested. The IMP captured only two seats while the remaining seat was won by an independent. All six Selangor Labour candidates were defeated. The total vote secured by UMNO-MCA was 10,240 while IMP polled 6,641. Although this was only a municipal election it was a severe defeat for Dato Onn and the Independence of Malaya Party.[4]

After-Effects of the First Elections

Because the Kuala Lumpur elections were the first to be contested by national parties they had a great influence upon subsequent political developments. The political agreement between UMNO and the MCA had been negotiated only between the Selangor branches of the two parties as a temporary political maneuver which did not involve the central organs or any of the other branches of either party. Their victory at the polls prompted both the MCA and UMNO to begin to explore the possibility of expanding their alliance to other municipalities where elections were to be held toward the end of the year. Two weeks after the Kuala Lumpur elections Tunku Abdul Rahman was quoted as saying that UMNO "will cooperate with other organizations, but we certainly want to preserve our identity".[5] The basic problem to be met was how to preserve the union at the polls while each party retained its separate identity and its separate political objectives.

Prior to the first elections the Malayan Chinese Association had attempted to maintain the fiction that it was a social, cultural and welfare organization. Although it had been active in submitting representations to the government on behalf of the Chinese, on several occasions it disclaimed being a political organization. After the Kuala Lumpur elections such a claim became even more absurd than before. Moreover, the British authorities had been encouraging the MCA to take a more openly political role to provide "an alternative standard (to Communism) to which loyal Chinese could rally".[6] Within a few weeks after the elections the Malayan Chinese Association began to prepare openly for active participation in elections throughout Malaya by reorganizing the party and centralizing some of its activities. The full-time staff was expanded and volunteer political workers were organized for contacting voters in their homes. To strengthen ties with the United Malays National Organization, the MCA also initiated a Malay Welfare Fund "to help in the economic uplift of the Malay community". The sum of M$500,000 was to be diverted from some of the profits of the sweepstake lotteries conducted every few months by the MCA, and officials of UMNO were expected to be appointed to the committee controlling the fund.[7]

The political relations between UMNO and the MCA were subject to severe strain in August and September, 1952, when Victor Purcell arrived from London to prepare a report on the Chinese at the invitation of the MCA. The Malays took strong exception to Dr. Purcell's visit because he was a well-known spokesman for the Chinese viewpoint on political and constitutional issues. Tunku Abdul Rahman forbade any UMNO officials to cooperate with Dr. Purcell, and, in apparent retaliation, the MCA withdrew its offer of M$500,000 to set up a Malay Welfare Fund to be administered in cooperation with UMNO.[8]

In the Federal Legislative Council, communal division became very sharp over such bills as the Immigration Control Bill, the Education Bill, and the Registration and Licensing of Business Bill.[9] The UMNO-MCA political alliance was subjected to severe strains over these issues. While little attempt was made to reconcile the differing political objectives of each party, efforts were made to preserve their common front at the polls which were to be held in six major towns and cities in the following months. Plans were laid for creating liaison committees between UMNO and MCA branches at all levels throughout Malaya so as to exploit fully their political advantage through cooperation and frank discussions.[10] Since both UMNO and the MCA remained communal political parties, they were torn between the objective of winning elections and the objective of vigorously championing their separate communal causes. The seeming irreconcilability of the two parties led to recurring predictions of the break-up of the "temporary" political agreement negotiated for the first Kuala Lumpur elections. Yet, the anticipation of further victories at the polls proved to be sufficiently strong to preserve this makeshift alliance.

The Independence of Malaya Party found it very difficult to recover from the setback received at the Kuala Lumpur municipal elections. It had entered politics with such confidence and such apparent power, only to suffer humiliating defeat. Moreover, the political union between UMNO and the MCA made it very difficult for the IMP to make communalism into the major issue of politics. Dato Onn made speeches suggesting that communal conflict might well seize Malaya, and he attempted to discount the inter-communal understanding that was claimed by both UMNO and the MCA as a product of their alliance. Indeed, Dato Onn and the IMP were in the anomolous position of attempting to make political capital out of the issues of communalism by overstating the threats to communal harmony and by referring to the "communal friendship" between UMNO and MCA as a "sham", which tactics tended to increase intercommunal frictions and mistrust. Moreover, the IMP could regain its position only with the breakup of the UMNO-MCA Alliance. And attempts to drive a wedge between these two parties meant that the IMP played up the very sensitive communal issues which divided the Malays and the Chinese. Thus, in some respects the "non-communal" IMP was more communal in its campaigning than either UMNO or the MCA. These tactics did not split the UMNO-MCA Alliance because their political "agreement" was based on the full understanding that dis-agreements on issues between them should not destroy the political advantage both secured through the common front presented during the elections. To some degree, the attempts of the IMP to divide the UMNO-MCA Alliance backfired, for the IMP lost the support of some members who looked with favor on the growing cooperation between UMNO and the MCA.

The defeat of the IMP at the first Kuala Lumpur polls prompted the IMP to attempt to widen its appeal and to form a coalition with other political forces. Since the IMP had campaigned against communal organizations in politics, it could not readily switch its professed "non-communalism" by entering into a political alliance with any communal associations. Yet very few other "non-communal" political parties existed and none of them was nationally organized. Before the second Municipal Council elections in Kuala Lumpur, the IMP and the Selangor Labour Party entered into an agreement to support each other's candidates.[11] However, being in its infancy the Labour Party added very little to the power of the IMP at the polls. In the other cities where municipal council elections were held there were no political associations which joined in coalition with the IMP.

Of the 37 municipal council seats contested in six cities of the Federation during the December elections of 1952, UMNO-MCA captured 26 seats, and the IMP was able to win only one seat when one of its members in Kuala Lumpur was re-elected. The UMNO-MCA Alliance did not contest the Penang elections, but UMNO put up candidates, in partnership with the Muslim League and captured one of the three Penang seats contested. The previous victor in the Penang election, the "non-communal" Radical Party, came in a poor third after UMNO and the Penang Labour Party. Out of the nine Johore Bahru seats the strongest IMP candidate polled less than half of the votes of the third-strongest UMNO-MCA candidate. Since Johore Bahru is the home of Dato Onn and a city where the IMP was expected to have some power, this was a particularly humiliating defeat for the IMP. These election results further confirmed the overwhelming strength of the UMNO-MCA Alliance.[12]

Partisan Politics in Government

Although the elections during 1952 had been fought over a comparatively few and insignificant seats on municipal councils, they greatly influenced political activity in both state and federal governments. Their alliance gave UMNO-MCA a commanding position for future elections, and they began to act together as a party convinced that it has a clear mandate to speak for the people. Yet. the UMNO-MCA Alliance remained a small minority in the state and federal legislative councils. By contrast, the IMP had been formed from the top with the support of a large number of appointed Federal Legislative Council members and in the state governments most of the *Mentris Besar* (Chief Ministers) and many of the top officials of the state governments had strong political ties with Dato Onn and were suspicious, if not critical, of the UMNO-MCA Alliance. Thus, in the state and federal legislative councils the IMP commanded decisive majorities, and in the higher administrative echelons the IMP wielded considerable behind-the-scenes political influence.

From its position of strength in the state and federal governments, the IMP attempted to foster a number of government policies that were politically detrimental to the Alliance. The opportunities for such political maneuvers are multiplied when a number of basic decisions regarding elections, citizenship and franchise requirements have yet to be made. When such decisions have to be made with the weaker party strongly represented in the councils of government, the stage is set for very bitter and acrimonious partisan conflict, both within and outside the formal structure of government.

The Lotteries Question

One of the first partisan political battles was waged over the question of banning or controlling lotteries run by political parties. It may be recalled that the Malayan Chinese Association had been permitted to operate "welfare" lotteries to aid Chinese in the rural areas who were being resettled in the new villages as part of the government's policy of denying to the Communists easy access to the civilian population. By the end of 1952 the lotteries were being held every couple of months and the prizes for each lottery were about M$1,500,000. Although few criticized the welfare work of the MCA in the new villages, many questioned the way in which the MCA had been able to use the lottery to build up its membership and to finance its other activities. When the MCA entered active politics in the Kuala Lumpur elections, members of the IMP sought to get from the MCA a public accounting of funds obtained from its lotteries. Although Tan Cheng-lock answered by a public letter to the *Straits Times* saying that all lottery profits went for "welfare projects" and not for "political purposes",[13] no accounting of the lottery profits was ever made public.

At the annual conference of the IMP in October a resolution was passed condemning lotteries run by political associations. The question was brought to the attention of the Legislative Council at its next meeting when the government introduced a bill to control all lotteries. Although this bill did not prohibit the MCA from conducting lotteries, it did establish a government lottery to collect funds for welfare projects which rivalled those of the MCA, and all other public and private lotteries were subject to a tax of 20 per cent on the profits unless exempted by the High Commissioner in Council.[14] Just prior to the passage of this legislation, the MCA attempted to meet the objections of its critics by restricting the sale of lottery tickets to MCA members, and it announced that funds would be allocated for Malay welfare projects and for the tuberculosis hospital in Kuala Lumpur.[15] However, this did not end the political controversy over lotteries, particularly since those Chinese who still wanted to buy tickets were given an added incentive to join the MCA for a very small membership fee.

Within a few months the dispute over the MCA lotteries became more than just a matter of partisan politics between the IMP and the MCA. In March and April of 1953 the MCA was becoming very obstructionist toward a number of government policies. The Malayan Chinese Association objected very strongly to the implementation of the new Education Ordinance which it believed threatened the Chinese media schools with a policy of developing a unified government-supported Malayan national school system. Moreover, some of the funds for the implementation of the new education policy were to be derived from a licence tax on all business. Because the business community is largely Chinese in composition, the Chinese reacted very strongly against this Licensing and Registration of Businesses Ordinance, and the Malayan Chinese Association threatened the Government with a business hartal along the same lines as the hartal previously staged by the All-Malaya Council of Joint Action against the Federation Agreement. As these threats from the Malayan Chinese Association mounted, the government authorities began to consider counter measures which would reduce the extraordinary political leverage of the MCA, derived in part from its great financial resources. First, the Government refused to exempt the MCA from the 20 per cent tax on lotteries, and then, after an internal fight in the MCA revealed that M$37,514 of the party's funds had been misappropriated, the Government banned all lotteries by political parties.[16] Although the MCA sought to have the Government reconsider its decision, the High Commissioner, Sir Gerald Templer, remained adamant in the face of bitter denunciations and allegations that he was "anti-Chinese". The MCA also intimated that the Government sought to prevent any political organization from becoming "too strong".[17] In retaliation, the MCA announced that it was abandoning all "social welfare" work. Also, it would no longer seek to recruit Chinese for the police force, and would cease other activities designed to gain the cooperation of the Chinese in connection with the rural resettlement program.[18] Thus, while the dispute over lotteries initially was raised by the IMP, it developed into a bitter controversy between Tan Cheng-lock and the MCA on one hand and the Colonial Office and Sir Gerald Templer on the other.

The Attempt to Censure Dato Onn

Another important partisan battle developed in 1953 over the political activities of Dato Onn who, as the Member for Home Affairs, gave the impression of speaking for the Government while campaigning for the Independence of Malaya Party. In a political speech to a meeting of the IMP in March, Dato Onn predicted that "we shall yet see a major clash of conflicting interests between two communities, a clash which may have disastrous consequences for this country." He went on to cite the determined Chinese opposition to the nationality laws, the Education Ordinance and their threats of hartals and boycotts, as well as their demands for the creation of a separate Chinese university to rival the University of Malaya. After linking the Malayan Chinese Association to the Kuomintang, he concluded that "Chinese organizations in Malaya are trying to make this country into the twentieth province of China." He also suggested that UMNO was selling the country to the Chinese for political gain. The object of this political attack was obvious. Dato Onn sought to break up the political alliance between the MCA and UMNO by playing on the sensitive issues which divided them. The Malayan Chinese Association, and the Chinese guilds reacted very strongly against this "anti-Chinese" attack. Special meetings of Chinese organizations were called to consider counter measures.[20]

The United Malays National Organization was also deeply disturbed by the political line employed by Dato Onn, particularly since it cultivated internal dissentions within UMNO over its association with the MCA. For example, Dato Panglima Bukit Gantang, the chairman of UMNO in Perak, had been the leader of the opposition to the policies of the UMNO central executive committee. In March he began to establish a separate political organization beyond the control of UMNO and on political issues he threw his support to Dato Onn. In April he was expelled from the party, but the Perak branches of UMNO gave him a vote of confidence by a 37 to 15 majority. UMNO president Tunku Abdul Rahman informed the Perak branches of UMNO that, if they continued to recognize Dato Panglima Bukit Gantang as UMNO chairman in Perak, they would be expelled from the party.[21] Finally a large segment of UMNO in Perak broke away under his leadership to form another party, the Perak National Party, which became politically allied with Dato Onn and the IMP.

Because the UMNO-MCA Alliance was being damaged by the revised political line expounded by Dato Onn, several attempts were made to have the High Commissioner either silence Dato Onn or denounce his intemperate political expressions. Sir Gerald Templer only went so far as to say that the disputed speech was made by Dato Onn in his private capacity, not in his capacity as an official of the Government. When the Legislative Council met in May, Mr. Tan Siew-sin, MCA publicity chairman, moved to censure Dato Onn for this speech "calculated to stir up inter-racial discord". After two days of acrimonious and partisan debate the motion was defeated 40 to 9 with 20 abstentions.[22]

The Attempt to Ban Communal Organizations from Politics

Other maneuvers for partisan political advantage became evident in many of the issues arising in legislative councils during 1953. The most blatant attempt to use legislative powers for partisan political advantage was through a motion made in the Perak State Legislative Council to ban communal organizations from contesting elections. The support for such legislation developed as an after-growth of the political infighting which had been in progress in Perak since 1952.

The Mentri Besar of Perak, Dato Panglima Bukit Gantang, had led the revolt of the Perak branch of UMNO in 1953, and later helped to found the "non-communal" Perak National Party, which comprised a large proportion of the higher officials in the state administration. It was dominated by the western-educated Malays in the "court circle" around the Sultan of Perak, but also enjoyed the support of a number of prominent Chinese and Indians closely identified with the state administration.

After this defection UMNO was very weak in Perak and, at the time, the MCA had not yet been very effective in its campaign to organize the Chinese for contesting elections. Because the state leaders feared the potential political power of UMNO and the MCA, they sought to block the UMNO-MCA Alliance from contesting state and municipal elections. When this motion was introduced in the State Legislative Council, the State Legal Adviser, a British official, promptly recommended that the vote be deferred on the grounds that it embarrassed a select committee which had been set up to recommend legislation for elections in the state. By this maneuver a direct vote on the highly controversial bill was avoided and the bill itself finally forgotten.[23]

These examples of partisan politics demonstrate that the political factions in control of the legislative councils were not averse to utilizing their official position to create favorable conditions for their participation in the elections which were shortly to determine the distribution of power in the state and federal governments. The personal and partisan rivalries that were evident greatly hampered the British authorities in their attempt to secure cooperation from all party leaders for policies designed to prepare Malaya for democratic government.

Competitive Nationalism in Politics

Nationalism in one form or another has influenced Malayan politics since 1945 or before. As soon as Malayan parties began to gird themselves for elections, they entered into greater competition for the support of a common electorate, and in so doing they all attempted to broaden their appeal by becoming more nationalistic. To the casual observer, this competitive nationalism may create the impression that all parties were unified behind a single cause—that of national independence. This widely acclaimed objective concealed the more real political contests for power between various segments of the body politic. At one time or another every major political party in Malaya attempted to become the core of a united nationalist movement.

Just before the "second round" of municipal elections, in September 1952, both the IMP and UMNO drafted proposals for the attainment of Malayan independence. The Central National Council of IMP passed a ten-point program which called for Malayan independence within the Commonwealth within nine years. The UMNO general assembly, meeting at the same time, was informed by Tunku Abdul Rahman that UMNO would invite all political parties to a round-table conference to consider the question of the attainment of Malayan independence.[24] Shortly afterwards, the chairman of the newly formed Pan-Malayan Labour Party, Inche Mohamed Sopiee called for the formation of a "Malayan National Congress" to work for a "united free democratic country".[25] Since the major political parties all professed to favor a united national front, many believed that the time was ripe to bring all the parties together for concerted action in the attainment of Malayan independence.

Without any preliminary hint, the Mentris Besar of seven of the nine Malay states announced on March 19, 1953, that a "National Conference" would be held on April 27 for "planning the way to a united, free and independent Malayan nation". Some thirteen political parties and communal associations were invited to send delegates to this conference, and no party, or communal group of any significance was ignored in the list of invitations.[26] Nevertheless, the enthusiasm for such a conference was not universal. Nearly all the sponsors of the "National Conference" were active members of the Independence of Malaya Party, and the chairman of the group was Dato Panglima Bukit Gantang, the expelled leader of UMNO in Perak.

Rather than immediately answer the call for a "National Conference", the UMNO-MCA Alliance stepped up their own plans for national independence. Liaison committees between UMNO and the MCA had previously drafted proposals on the introduction of federal elections, and at the metting of the Federal Legislative Council on March 20, Tunku Abdul Rahman sharply criticized the Government for not pressing ahead with plans for federal elections. As Member for Home Affairs, Dato Onn had to answer these criticisms and defend the Government's policies.[27] Because of the sensational victories of the UMNO-MCA Alliance at the municipal polls, the Alliance was pressing for federal elections as soon as possible, while the IMP and some other weaker parties cautioned against "too fast a pace" toward independence.

As the date for the first meeting of the Mentris Besar-sponsored "National Conference" approached, all political and communal bodies were forced to decide whether they would participate. Without turning down the invitation outright, the UMNO-MCA Alliance announced that it would attend a conference only with organizations "whose voting power shall prevail at the conference". Since the UMNO-MCA Alliance had been winning the municipal council elections by large majorities, it expected to have a majority representation on the "National Conference" being sponsored by the Mentris Besar. When these conditions were not agreed to by the sponsors of the "National Conference", both UMNO and the MCA refused to participate and they enjoined their members from participating. At the same time it announced its own election demands which called for federal elections by 1954 with the threat that all UMNO and MCA members in the federal and state councils would resign if these demands were not met by the Government.[29]

At the height of the partisan controversy over Dato Onn's speech and over the UMNO-MCA boycott of the "National Conference", the Deputy High Commissioner, Sir Donald MacGillivray, announced that the Government was going to appoint a committee "to examine the question of elections to the Federal Legislative Council and future constitutional changes arising therefrom; and to make recommendations".[29] This move appeared to head off the partisan dispute over the formation of a "National Conference" by placing the responsibility for making recommendations on elections directly with the appointed committee. However this expectation was very quickly shattered, for the day after the Legislative Council adjourned the UMNO-MCA Alliance announced that they were going to sponsor a "National Convention" to consider and adopt specific proposals for constitutional changes and federal elections.[30] Furthermore, the Peninsular Malays Union had also announced the sponsorship of an "All-Malay Round Table Conference" to consider the question of independence for Malaya from a strictly Malay point of view.[31] Thus, by mid-May three separate "national front" conferences were being planned, not to mention the Government-appointed committee which was officially charged with preparing recommendations on elections!

Although the ideal of creating a single national front to plan for independence had disintegrated, each amalgamation of political groups went ahead with plans for a conference and attempted to maintain the fiction that its conference was the authoritative representation of nationalist sentiment in

Malaya. Consequently, these conferences competed with each other in their expression of nationalist demands. But they also reflected the political interests of the groups that sponsored them. For a period of almost a year the principal efforts of the major parties were channelled through these conferences.

The "National Conference"

The Mentris Besar-sponsored "National Conference" attracted considerable public interest when it was first proposed. However, it degenerated into a small cluster of minor political groups following the lead of the Independence of Malaya Party and the seven Mentris Besar. The first session of the "National Conference" met on April 27, 1953, with five organizations in attendance: the Independence of Malaya Party, the Malayan Indian Congress, the Malayan Indian Association, the Selangor Pakistan Association, and the Straits Chinese British Association. A working committee was formed to draft a "plan for independence" comprising the seven Mentris Besar, one representative from each organization, and three members co-opted by the committee.[32] Thus the Malay Mentris Besar who were the moving force behind the "National Conference" were also on the working committee and were in a position to see their political views incorporated into the recommendations prepared by the committee.

After the initial meeting of the "National Conference" several informal and behind-the-scenes approaches were made to the leaders of UMNO and the MCA to see whether a compromise could be reached whereby they would become parties to the "National Conference", but the inflexible demands on each side over the question of representation made a compromise agreement impossible. Once it became clear that the UMNO-MCA Alliance could not be enticed to join the "National Conference", the working committee continued with its task as though it spoke for all interests in Malaya.

In view of their defeats in the municipal council elections of 1952 and 1953, the IMP leaders wanted to give the party time to build up its strength, so they favored a more gradual transition to self-government than did the UMNO-MCA Alliance. The recommendations of the "National Conference" working committee reflected this view. It proposed that municipal and state elections should precede the federal elections, the latter to be held toward the end of 1956. A Legislative Council of 90 with less than half elected membership was proposed as a first stage in the transition to self-government. When this report was submitted to the "National Conference" in September 1953, the Malayan Indian Congress objected to the timing of the federal elections, contending they should be held not later than 1954. The MIC's concurrent disagreement with the Government over education policy for Indian schools made it wary of identification with the IMP-led "National Conference", partly because the conference organizers were mostly government officials, including the Member for Education, E. E. C. Thuraisingham. The day after the conference adjourned, the Malayan Indian Congress announced its withdrawal from the "National Conference", causing rising speculation that the MIC might join forces with UMNO and the MCA.[33] However, for the time being, the MIC remained unaligned.

The "National Conference" failed to create a "national front" for the attainment of independence. To recoup its political losses, its leaders then attempted to utilize the conference for developing a broad-based political party to challenge the demonstrated power of UMNO-MCA at the polls.[34] No official action was taken by the "National Conference" until the end of February 1954, when a new party was formally launched.[35] Party Negara was the name which was finally selected. *Negara*, the Malay word for "nationalist", was designed to appeal to the Malays, who constituted the majority of the electorate. Although Party Negara was launched with great fanfare as a new party, it was really only a continuation of the Independence of Malaya Party, which merged into Party Negara and dissolved as a separate entity. All the other participants in the "National Conference" retained their identity even though all, except the MIC, were openly allied with this "new" Party Negara.

The "National Convention"

In early 1953 UMNO and the MCA had formed a top level liaison committee to prepare an agreement on federal elections. The agreement drafted by this committee was not immediately made public so that the draft proposals could be discussed in detail by both UMNO and MCA branches. In April the joint election agreement was approved by the annual UMNO general assembly meeting in Malacca. As revealed at that time the plan called for a Federal Legislative Council of 75 with 44 elected, 16 appointed by the High Commissioner, and 15 to be nominated by commercial and planting interests. The assembly also approved a statement that called upon all UMNO members to resign from their positions on local, municipal, state and federal councils if elections were not held by the end of 1954.[36] The recent victories of the UMNO-MCA Alliance at the municipal and local council polls had made them impatient to contest federal elections.

After the government announced that a committee would be formed to study the question of federal elections, the UMNO-MCA Alliance decided to call a "National Convention" to counter the "National Conference" which had been organized earlier under the leadership of the Mentris Besar. Although the UMNO-MCA Alliance did not announce their sponsorship of a "National Convention" until several weeks after the initial meeting of the rival "National Conference", no time was lost since the UMNO-MCA liaison committee had already prepared its election agreement, and substantially the same committee continued as the working committee for their "National Convention".

Just as the Mentris Besar-sponsored "National Conference" invited all parties to join, so too did the Alliance-sponsored "National Convention". Likewise, the representation in both was weighted in favor of the sponsors. For the "National Convention" the Malayan Chinese Association had ourteen votes, the United Malays National Organization had fourteen votes, and all other parties who were willing to participate were given two votes each.[37] Although the Pan-Malayan Labour Party had tentatively joined in sponsoring the "National Convention", it withdrew in June as a result of a dispute over the allocation of reserved seats for labor interests in the Legislative Council. When the first plenary session of the "National Convention" was held in August 1953, the only political parties represented were the Peninsular Malays Union, the Pan-Malayan Islamic Association, the *Persatuan Persetiaan Melayu* (Union of Malay Patriots), and the two sponsors—UMNO and the MCA.[38]

The "National Convention" did not approve a "blueprint" for federal elections until its second plenary session in October.[39] This "blueprint" differed only slightly from the election agreement prepared by the UMNO-MCA liaison committee early in 1953, but this time it was proclaimed with more vigor and determination.

Political controversy became more intense in February 1954, as a result of the release of the report by the Government-appointed committee on elections.[40] Because the major UMNO-MCA election demands had not been incorporated into the majority report of this committee, UMNO-MCA decided to call a third session of the "National Convention" to reiterate and revise their demands. The detailed election proposals passed in October were condensed down to six demands submitted to the High Commissioner in the form of a petition. This petition demanded the following: (1) a minimum of three-fifths elected majority in the Legislative Council, (2) permission for government servants to contest elections, (3) a simple majority to be deciding in both multiple and single member constituencies, (4) extension of the franchise to all adults who are either citizens, subjects of the Rulers, British subjects or born in Malaya and who have lived in Malaya for five years, (5) a two-thirds elected Executive Council to be chosen solely from members of the Legislative Council, and (6) the holding of federal elections not later than 1954.[41]

Since UMNO had a substantial following among the Malays in the lower ranks of government administration, the UMNO leaders were particularly anxious to secure permission for government servants to contest elections without having to give up their positions. Similarly, the Malayan Chinese Association had secured an agreement from UMNO to support the demand for the liberalization of the franchise which would greatly increase the number of eligible Chinese voters. Because the leaders of the UMNO-MCA Alliance were supremely confident of victory at the polls, they were in no mood to be cautious over the introduction of elections, nor were they willing to accept any constitutional changes which might prevent their assuming full control of both the Legislative and Executive Councils. At the time, they were claiming to have the support of 90 per cent of the potential electorate, and this confidence was reflected in the defiant tone of their resolutions and the uncompromising manner in which they advanced demands, particularly the demand for elections by the end of 1954.

The "All-Malaya National Congress"

The ultra-communal Malay nationalists were perplexed by the turn of politica[l] events during 1953. Many of them had broken away from UMNO durin[g] Dato Onn's leadership when he attempted to get UMNO to adopt les[s] narrowly communal policies. After Dato Onn's resignation from UMNO, th[e] ultra-communal Malays expected that UMNO would revert to a militant for[m] of Malay communal nationalism such as that expounded by UMNO durin[g] the height of the Malay opposition to the Malayan Union. However, th[e] expectations of these Malay communal nationalists did not materialize, sinc[e] UMNO entered into an alliance with the Malayan Chinese Associatio[n] shortly after Dato Onn's resignation. The ultra-communal Malays were in [a] quandary and vacillated between support for UMNO as the strongest Mala[y] political organization, and opposition to UMNO for its close association wit[h] the MCA. Some of these Malays were active within UMNO, particularly it[s] ancillary Youth Movement. But the Peninsular Malays Union became th[e] center of Malay communal chauvinism, attracting both public attention an[d] the active support of ultra-communal Malays, including many members o[f] UMNO.

When the Mentris Besar first announced their intention to sponsor [a] "National Conference", the Peninsular Malays Union accepted an invitatio[n] to participate, but withdrew on the eve of the conference. Instead, the PM[U] responded by proposing the formation of a strictly Malay "national front" t[o] which the Malay Rulers, the Malay Mentris Besar and all Malay politica[l] organizations were to be invited.[42] The PMU argued that national indepen- dence was strictly a question to be decided between the Malays and th[e] British since Britain's powers in Malaya depended upon treaties with th[e] Malay Rulers as the heads of the Malay States. However, the PMU was unable to get the cooperation of the Rulers and the Mentris Besar who were already in the process of promoting their "National Conference". UMNO, the biggest Malay political organization, could not be enticed to join an all-Malay "national front" since such a move would break up its winning combination with the MCA. Instead, UMNO sponsored a meeting of Malay organizations, including the PMU, in an attempt to win the support of dissident Malayans for the Alliance-sponsored "National Convention".[43] Three of the nine Malay organizations represented at the meeting did send representatives to the "National Convention", including the PMU.

At the plenary session of the "National Convention" held in August, the president of the PMU, Inche Hashim Ghani, rose to give an unexpected speech attacking the Malayan Chinese Association. He also proposed that a conference be called "with the protecting power on one side and the political bodies on the other".[44] The motion was pigeonholed by being referred to the convention constitutional committee which was controlled by UMNO and the MCA. Yet it did embarrass the Alliance leaders since the object of the conven- tion was to demonstrate the unity of the participants for the proposals prepared by the UMNO-MCA working committee.

Because of its opposition to the political course being charted by the Alliance-sponsored "National Convention", the Peninsular Malays Union finally broke away to form the "All-Malaya National Congress" composed entirely of minor Malay political organizations having a very communal and nationalist orientation. At the PMU-sponsored Congress a petition was drafted demanding a very restrictive form of "Malay" citizenship as opposed to the proposals which would give citizenship to the great majority of non-Malays who were permanently resident in Malaya. The Congress also proposed that Malay be the official language, Islam the official religion and that a Malay be selected to be the monarch for all of Malaya.[45] By comparison with the "National Conference" and the "National Convention", the "All-Malaya National Conference" was politically impotent. Yet it did provide an outlet for the political expression of the dissident Malay communal nationalists who were extremely perturbed by the recent developments in Malayan politics which tended to give more and more concessions to non-Malays.

Federal Election Plans Under Fire

The government was not a passive bystander during all the political manoeuvering over the formation of the various competing "national fronts". In July the High Commissioner appointed a 46-member Elections Committee, and the first sessions of this committee were held the following month. The final report of the Elections Committee was released in the latter part of January 1954.[46]

As might be expected, the contentious issues examined by the Elections Committee were the very ones which had been given prior consideration at the several "national front" conferences. Indeed, one of the most unfortunate consequences of these "national" front conferences was that the political groups had committed themselves to rigid demands from which they would not retreat when the time came for compromise.

The Elections Committee could not avoid reflecting the basic antagonisms and competition between the IMP (re-organized as Party Negara) and the UMNO-MCA Alliance. On the major contentious questions faced by the Committee, the proposals and counter proposals mirrored the election proposals prepared on one side by the "National Conference" and on the other by the "National Convention". In making his appointments to the Elections Committee, the High Commissioner took into account many of the same considerations of appropriate representation as were applied to appointments to the Legislative Council. Consequently, the Elections Committee tended to reproduce the same relative political strength which Party Negara commanded in the Legislative Council. Therefore, the majority proposals were very similar to those prepared by the Mentris Besar-sponsored "National Conference", while the minority reports expressed the demands made by the Alliance through the "National Convention" which it had sponsored.

If a minority recognizes itself as a minority, it is easier to concede the power of decision-making to the majority. The Alliance, however, did not accept its minority position on the Election Committee as a fair representation of its political importance, in view of its overwhelming successes in recent local elections. Instead it demanded that the minority reports submitted by its members on the Committee be accepted as the basis for the ultimate revision of the Federation of Malaya Agreement. Two weeks after the Report of the Elections Committee was published, the Alliance reconvened its "National Convention" to demand the complete acceptance of the minority reports by the government. Petitions supporting the Alliance demands for elections were sent to the Rulers and the High Commissioner even before the Rulers Conference had had an opportunity to act on the Elections Committee Report.[47] In addition, the Alliance tried to enter into direct negotiations with the Colonial Secretary by sending a three-man delegation to London. This move was made in spite of the Colonial Secretary's prior assertion that he would not engage in any talks or negotiations with Alliance spokesmen. He remained adamant in refusing to by-pass the negotiations then in progress with the Malay Rulers by meeting with the Alliance delegation.[48]

Negotiations between the High Commisioner, representing the British Government, and the Rulers resulted in an agreement on compromise proposals between the majority and the minority reports of the Elections Committee.[49] When these decisions of the Rulers Conference were made public, the Alliance became even more militant in demanding the complete acceptance of the Elections Committee minority reports. Once again the Alliance leaders announced their intention of opening direct negotiations with London for revision of the Federation Agreement along the lines proposed by the "National Convention".[50] After receiving several threats that the Alliance would call upon all its members to resign from government posts, the Colonial Secretary, Mr. Oliver Lyttelton, finally agreed to meet informally with Tunku Abdul Rahman, T. H. Tan and Dato Abdul Razak who had flown to London to present the Alliance demands.

The discussions revealed that the cardinal point at issue was the number of members to be elected to the new Council.[51] The two Alliance leaders would not back down from their demand for a 60 per cent popularly elected Council, or 59 (later changed to 60) elected members in place of the 52 provided for in the agreement reached by the Conference of Rulers. At the completion of the inconclusive discussions, Mr. Lyttelton gave the delegation assurances that if the majority party was unable to form an effective government as a result of the new election provisions, and the interference of an obstructive minority, he would "at once ask the High Commissioner to consider with the Conference of Rulers how the situation might be remedied" and he would also "be prepared, if necessary, to agree to amendment of the Federation Agreement in order to apply a suitable remedy".[52]

Although the delegation expressed some satisfaction with these assurances, two days after it returned to Malaya the Alliance announced new demands that the election proposals approved at the Rulers Conference be abandoned and an impartial Royal Commission be formed "to review immediately the question of Federal elections".[53] The Alliance also toyed with the idea of reconvening the "National Convention" of "all parties" to reaffirm their fundamental demands, and "decide upon steps to achieve an effective elected majority in the Federal Legislative Council". The Colonial Secretary announced the rejection of these new demands in a letter to Tunku Abdul Rahman made public on June 11.[54]

Faced with this impasse, largely of its own making, the Alliance was left with no satisfactory avenue for graceful retreat. It had the choice of being resigned to the new compromise election provisions, or following up on its threats by taking political action to force a governmental crisis by means of a mass boycott. The latter course was chosen.

On June 14 the Alliance issued orders that all party members must resign from federal executive and legislative councils, state and settlement councils, municipal councils and town boards. The Alliance headquarters in Kuala Lumpur was reported to have sent over 1,000 letters ordering members to resign from all government councils and official bodies.[55] Although not every Alliance member on a government body submitted his resignation, in a few days the Alliance had achieved an effective boycott in both state and federal governments.

Meanwhile, the election ordinances and amendments[56] were submitted to the Legislative Council, debated and passed without the participation of any Alliance members of the Council. Most of the debate was directed against the impetuous action of the absent Alliance members—some heaping scorn upon them for their "irresponsibility" while others pleaded with them to return and work for the successful introduction of elections.[57]

The Alliance boycott subjected the party to a number of internal strains. A few members refused to submit their resignation as ordered and, consequently, controversy arose over the enforcement of party discipline. Moreover, the Pan-Malayan Labour Party, a part-time affiliate of the Alliance, was completely divided over the use of the boycott tactic. Its chairman, Inche Mohamed Sopiee, resigned from the PMLP when it ordered all members to boycott the Legislative Council over the issue of "elections in 1954".[58] The unyielding stand of the Alliance appeared to many as an artificial crisis, since the difference between the Alliance demands and the decisions of the Rulers Conference were relatively slight and a matter of degree rather than of principle. Sixty versus fifty-two elected seats and "elections in 1954" versus "elections as soon as possible" did not appear to warrant the creation of a severe constitutional crisis by the resignation of all Alliance members from government positions. And many Alliance supporters were frank in expressing their criticism of this tactic.

Approximately two weeks after the commencement of the Alliance boycott, secret talks were undertaken between the new High Commissioner, Sir Donald MacGillivray, and the Alliance leaders with a view to breaking the deadlock.[59] On July 7, the High Commissioner made public the terms of a compromise solution which was acceptable to all parties. Rather than attempt to re-examine the question of the number of elected seats in the Legislative Council, the High Commissioner announced his "intention to consult with the leader or leaders of the majority amongst the elected members before making appointments to these [reserved] seats".[61] In this way the elected majority would be assured of support from the five nominated members. The other five demands of the Alliance were conveniently forgotten. With this compromise, the Alliance was able to retire gracefully from its position of intransigence. UMNO and MCA members were reappointed to positions on the various government councils, and preparations for elections continued without the complications of a continuing constitutional crisis.

[1] *Penang Gazette & Straits Chronicle*, December 3, 1951, p. 2.

[2] *Malay Mail*, January 9, 1952, p. 3. Before the first UMNO-MCA Alliance was agreed upon, the MIC sent out feelers to UMNO, the MCA, and the PMU suggesting a common election front. However, nothing materialized, so the MIC joined the IMP instead, only to withdraw a few months later. See Usha Mahajani, *The Role of Indian Minorities in Burma and Malaya*, (Bombay: Vora & Co., 1960), p. 245.

[3] *Malay Mail*, January 9, 1952, p. 3.

[4] *Malay Mail*, February 15, 1952, pp. 4 and 10; February 17, pp. 1, 2 and 12. On the IMP ticket were three MIC members, including MIC president, K. L. Devaser. He and one other MIC member were the only IMP candidates elected.

[5] *Straits Times*, February 28, 1952, p. 5; *Malay Mail*, February 22, 1952, p. 1.

[6] This quotation is from a letter written by the High Commissioner, Sir Henry Gurney, on October 5, 1951, the day before he was killed in a Communist ambush. It is reproduced in the *Straits Times*, May 27, 1952, p. 6; May 28, 1952, p. 6.

[7] *Straits Times*, July 14, 1952, p. 1; July 15, 1952, p. 7.

The increase of Sino-Malay tensions created by various issues prompted some people to suggest the revitalization of the Communities Liaison Committee. Of course, such a move was politically impossible because the Communities Liaison Committee was dominated by the persons who had become supporters of the IMP, and they could not have helped to create better understanding in a dispute which centered around the MCA and UMNO, their opponents in the previous elections. See *Straits Times*, August 25, 1952, p. 1; August 26, 1952, p. 1.

Legislative Council Debates, 19th, 20th, 21st, and 22nd November, 1952, Federation of Malaya, 661–712 and 731–749.

[10] *Straits Times*, September 25, 1952, pp. 5–6.

[11] *Malay Mail*, November 6, 1952, pp. 1–2.

[12] *Straits Echo & Times of Malaya*, December 8, 1952, p. 6; *Straits Budget*, December 11, 1952, pp. 4 and 14.

[13] *Straits Budget*, September 25, 1952, p. 2.

[14] *Legislative Council Debates, 19th, 20th, 21st, and 22nd November 1952*, Federation of Malaya, 780–789.

[15] *Straits Times*, November 15, 1952, p. 7.

[16] *Straits Times*, May 23, 1953, p. 1; June 13, 1953, p. 4.

[17] *Straits Times*, June 25, 1953, p. 1.

18 According to one reliable informant, the MCA had M$3·5m remaining in the "welfare fund" which was carefully invested to act as a continual source of income for the party. A total of M$33·6m worth of tickets were sold for the 18 lotteries sponsored by the MCA. Note *Straits Times*, February 3, 1955, p. 8.

19 *Malay Mail*, March 26, 1953, p. 2.

20 *Straits Times*, April 25, 1953, p. 7.

21 *Straits Times*, March 27, 1953, p. 8; April 4, 1953, p. 1; April 27, 1953, p. 3; *Sunday Mail*, May 3, 1953, p. 1.

22 The European Officials and the representatives of the Penang and Malacca Settlement Councils abstained. See *Legislative Council Debates, 6th and 7th May 1953*, Federation of Malaya, 328–347, 358–396.

23 In favor of the proposal were the IMP, the Federation of Indian Organizations, the Malayan Indian Congress, the Malayan Indian Association, the Perak Progressive Party and, of course, the Perak National Party which sponsored the motion. Opposed were UMNO, the MCA and a third party which at the time was flirting with the idea of joining the UMNO-MCA Alliance, the Pan-Malayan Labour Party (PMLP). See *Straits Echo & Times of Malaya*, July 2, 1953, p. 1.

24 *Straits Times*, September 15, 1952, pp. 1 and 7.

25 *Straits Times*, November 12, 1952, p. 2.

26 *Malay Mail*, March 20, 1953, pp. 1–2.

27 *Legislative Council Debates March 18th, 19th and 20th 1953*, Federation of Malaya, 225 and 250.

28 *Straits Times*, April 8, 1953, p. 1.

29 *Legislative Council Debates 6th and 7th May 1953*, Federation of Malaya, 285–286.

30 *Straits Times*, May 9, 1953, p. 8.

31 *Straits Times*, April 16, 1953, p. 8. The PMU was the ultra-communal Malay Party that had broken away from UMNO when Dato Onn was still its leader. The PMU was opposed to the "non-communalism" of the IMP and was suspicious of the "unholy" alliance between UMNO and the MCA.

32 *Straits Times*, April 28, 1953, p. 17. The *Malay Mail* reported seven organizations attending this first session: The Straits Chinese British Association, the Independence of Malaya Party, the Ceylon Federation of Malaya, the Eurasian Association, the Federation of Indian Organizations, the Malayan Indian Association, and the All-Malayan Islamic Association. The Peninsular Malays Union withdrew the day before. See *Malay Mail*, April 27, 1953, p. 1; April 28, 1953, pp. 1, 3, 7 and 10.

33 *Straits Times*, September 28, 1953, p. 17; September 29, 1953, pp. 4 and 6. Earlier speculation that the MIC might join with UMNO and the MCA was vigorously denied by the MIC with the explanation that the Alliance was "too communal". See *Straits Times*, February 27, 1952, p. 4.

34 In September the press published reports that the leaders of the "National Conference" were considering the formation of a new political party to be called Malayan National Progressive Party. Apparently this name was designed to counter some of the UMNO-MCA propaganda which pictured the IMP as reactionary and bureaucratic. See *Straits Times*, September 8, 1953, p. 4.

35 *Malay Mail*, March 1, 1954, pp. 7 and 10.

36 *Straits Times*, April 8, 1953, pp. 1 and 6.

37 *Straits Times*, August 5, 1953, p. 4.

38 *Straits Times*, August 24, 1953, pp. 1 and 7.

39 *Straits Times*, October 9, 1953, pp. 1–2; October 12, 1953, pp. 1 and 5.

40 M. J. Hogan (Chairman), *Report of the Committee Appointed to Examine the Question of Elections to the Federal Legislative Council*, Council Paper No. 20 of 1954, Federation of Malaya.

41 *Straits Times*, February 15, 1954, p. 7.

42 *Straits Times*, April 16, 1953, p. 8.

43 *Straits Times*, August 12, 1953, p. 1.

44 *Straits Times*, August 24, 1953, p. 1.

45 *Straits Echo & Times of Malaya*, March 6, 1954, p. 3.

46 Hogan, *op. cit.*

47 *Straits Times*, February 15, 1954, p. 7; February 25, 1954, p. 7.

48 *Straits Times*, April 15, 1954, p. 1; April 22, 1954, p. 1.

49 See Table 7, p. 63 above.

50 *Straits Times*, April 28, 1954, p. 8.

51 At first the Alliance delegation is reported to have demanded a "fully elected" Legislative Council, which was far beyond what the Alliance "National Convention" had proposed, or what was contained in the Alliance "minority report" of the Elections Commission. For an account of these negotiations see Harry Miller, *Prince and Premier*, (London: George G. Harrap & Co., 1959), pp. 134–141.

52 The text of Mr. Lyttelton's reply to the Alliance delegation is contained in: *Parliamentary Debates—Commons*, (Fifth Series) 1953–54, Vol. 528, 24–25.

53 *Malay Mail*, May 24, 1954, p. 1; *Straits Times*, May 26, 1954, p. 1.

54 *Straits Times*, May 25, 1954, p. 1; June 12, 1954, p. 1; *Malay Mail*, June 12, 1954, p. 4.

55 *Straits Times*, June 15, 1954, p. 1.

56 The Federation of Malaya Agreement (Amendment) Bill, 1954; The Legislative Council Elections Bill, 1954; The Registration of Electors Bill, 1954; The Local Councils (Amendment) Bill, 1954.

57 *Legislative Council Debates, 23rd and 24th June 1954*, Federation of Malaya, 257–353.

58 *Ibid.*, 284–291.

59 The behind-the-scenes maneuvers and negotiations to break the deadlock are reported in some detail by Harry Miller, *op. cit.*, pp. 147–161.

60 The letter from Sir Donald MacGillivray to Tunku Abdul Rahman is quoted in full in *Straits Times*, July 8, 1954, p. 1.

11 The First Federal Elections

Once the major constitutional provisions for federal elections were determined, all parties began preparations for electioneering. Yet, by itself, campaigning and party organization was hardly sufficient to assure victory, since no party was in a position to command a majority of the electorate on a national scale. Torn between the desire to preserve their ideals and programs intact, and the desire to share in power after elections, many parties began to seek political allies. During the federal election campaign nearly every party either affiliated with other parties or made overtures to do so. These coalitions reveal some of the problems of compromise and conflict between the active participants in Malaya's political arena. This account of the federal elections will commence with the minor parties because of the influence they had upon the tactics of the two major protagonists—the Alliance and Party Negara.

Indian Parties

After 1951 the Malayan Indian Congress became less oriented toward the Indian political scene, and began to represent the views of the more indigenous Malayan Indians. The first two presidents of the MIC, John Thivy and Budh Singh had returned to India, and K. L. Devaser, a Malaya-born Indian, was elected president that year. When V. T. Sambanthan became president in 1954, the "Malayan" character of the MIC became even more pronounced, and the MIC began to encourage Indians to become Malayan citizens so they could participate fully in Malayan political affairs.[1] Whether Indians should participate in politics through Indian organizations or through non-communal political parties was a subject of debate among Indian leaders. For federal elections, many Indians had agitated for a proportionate number of reserved seats for Indians to be contested and voted for only by Indians.[2] However, when the final election provisions did not establish guaranteed Indian representation, the Indians began to consider other means for securing adequate political representation.

In October the MIC entered into secret negotiations with the Alliance to secure Indian candidates on the Alliance ticket in return for MIC support.[3] The initial, temporary agreement for the municipal council elections was later expanded and extended to make the Malayan Indian Congress a full-fledged partner in the UMNO-MCA Alliance for the federal Legislative Council elections.

This move by the MIC was met with considerable opposition among some sections of the Indian community. The leading Tamil paper in Singapore said that "the Alliance is disposed to throw one or two seats to small communities and win them over to its side. The Devaser clique [leading the MIC] has fallen prey to such a move . . ."[4] In the midst of this dispute Prime Minister Nehru of India made a stop-over visit in Penang where he addressed a rally of the Malayan Indian Association at which he urged cooperation of Indians with other races of Malaya. He also commented favorably on the Malayan Indian Congress decision to join forces with the UMNO-MCA Alliance.[5] A controversy ensued over the question of whether Mr. Nehru had actually endorsed the action of the MIC.[6]

Although the Malayan Indian Congress remained a partner in the Alliance, Party Negara also attempted to win the support of the Indians. The most influential Indian in the Federal Legislative Council, Mr. P. Ramani, was a member of the central executive of Party Negara, and he tried to persuade Indians to abandon the lead of the MIC by joining Party Negara.[7] Although the MIC was sympathetic to "non-communalism" in politics, the prospect of sharing power with a party which had been a consistent winner at the polls proved to be the more compelling consideration. The rival Malayan Indian Association avoided any official identification with either the Alliance or Party Negara, but was generally believed to be supporting Party Negara's attempt to build an anti-Alliance coalition.

Minor Malay Parties

In mid-1955 an attempt was made to bring all the minor Malay associations into one common political front under the leadership of Dr. Burhanuddin, the former president of the banned Malay Nationalist Party. The venue for this combination was the All-Malaya Malay Youth Congress, which met in April at Kuala Lumpur.[8] It was partly an outgrowth of the defunct All-Malaya National Congress which had been sponsored by the Peninsular Malays Union during the height of the controversy over election proposals. It was reported in the Malay press that the All-Malaya Malay Youth Congress was organized through the joint efforts of the Peninsular Malays Union and Party Negara with the objective of winning Malay support away from UMNO.[9] Malay communal nationalism was the main theme which was used to attract the support of the 44 Malay organizations which sent delegates. A platform was drafted which was much more moderate in tone than the presidential speeches delivered to the Congress by Dr. Burhanuddin. Not only did he preach an extremist form of Malay nationalism, but he also was very critical of government policies for suppressing the Communist insurrection. He later attended the Afro-Asian Bandung Conference as a spokesman of the Malay Youth Congress where he distributed a memorandum demanding that "all foreign troops now in action in Malaya should be withdrawn . . . since Malaya is being turned into a battlefield for Asians who are being used to kill Asians . . ."[10]

Dr. Burhanuddin and the Malay Youth Congress came under sharp criticism from the United Malays National Organization, in part because it was reported that Burhanuddin had attempted to get former members of the banned MNP and API to resign from UMNO in order to re-establish a radical Malay party under his leadership. The UMNO leaders did everything possible to undermine the Malay Youth Congress which appeared to challenge UMNO's position as the dominant Malay political party.

One outcome of the Malay Youth Congress was the formation of a Malay Nationalist Front (*Barisan Kebangsaan Melayu*), which was little more than a steering committee of the Malay Youth Congress. Because Dato Onn was a member of the Malay Nationalist Front there was some speculation that the Front would become the vehicle for winning Malay support for Party Negara. But the radical Malay nationalists in these minor parties were still suspicious of Dato Onn's political objectives and previous maneuvers.[11] Dr. Burhanuddin remained the central figure in the Malay Nationalist Front despite Dato Onn's presence in its top echelon. Both were Malay nationalists, but Dr. Burhanuddin stressed an exclusive Malay communal chauvinism, while Dato Onn claimed to be promoting a "multi-communal" Malayan nationalism, yet based in large measure upon the Malays. Dr. Burhanuddin looked upon the non-Malays as alien to Malaya and was known to favor some form of union between Malaya and Indonesia as a means of assuring a dominant position for the Malays over the other communities in Malaya. For some ultra-communal Malays, this was the easy answer to their fears that the Malays would be overwhelmed by the non-Malay immigrants.

During the federal elections campaign Dr. Burhanuddin toured Malaya giving political speeches under the auspices of the Malay Nationalist Front, but he refrained from supporting either UMNO or Party Negara, even though the Front did not field any candidates of its own. These dissident radical Malay nationalists were frustrated and could do little more than criticize both UMNO and Party Negara as well as raise doubts as to the validity of the elections, regardless of their outcome. Nevertheless, the campaign was the occasion for an effort to rebuild the forces of radical Malay nationalism which had been disorganized since the time the Malay Nationalist Party and API were banned.

The Pan-Malayan Islamic Party (*Persatuan Aislam Sa-Melayu*)[12] was another Malay party which grew in strength during 1954 and 1955 through an appeal to the religious sentiments of the Malays. At one time the PMIP had participated in the Alliance-sponsored "National Convention", but it could not agree to the concessions which were made to the Malayan Chinese Association concerning citizenship and voting rights for non-Malays. After breaking with the UMNO-MCA Alliance, the PMIP recruited supporters from various Malay nationalist societies and from among those Malays who were attracted to ideas of a Pan-Islamic nationalist movement. In the federal elections the Pan-Malayan Islamic Party contested eleven seats in the overwhelmingly Malay constituencies of north western Malaya.

A number of other smaller Malay parties were quite active in a few scattered constituencies. In Perak, some Malays broke away from UMNO at the same time that Dato Panglima Bukit Gantang formed the Perak National Party. However, they rejected his leadership and revived the Malay League which had been in existence prior to the formation of UMNO in 1946. By 1955 the Malay League was quite strong in several districts of Perak, and in the federal elections, the Malay League and Dr. Burhanuddin's Malay National Front worked together to support several independent candidates, although neither party openly fielded a candidate of its own.

While potentially a major force in Malayan politics, the Malay racial and religious chauvinists were a disorganized and inchoate force which was not yet prepared to enter the political arena as a unified national party. Rather, these elements were to be found engaged in political agitation and attempts to influence existing parties, particularly Party Negara.

Labor and Leftist Parties

In the years since the war a number of attempts were made to form labor parties along the lines of the British Labour Party. These parties sprang up in the principal cities of Malaya and were led by a small nucleus of trade union leaders and non-Communist leftists. For a number of years these parties were little more than paper organizations with a few dozen self-proclaimed labor leaders disputing each other's right to use the "Labour Party" label. Labor parties developed independently of one another in the cities of Penang, Kuala Lumpur and Ipoh.

The Penang Labour Party was formed sometime prior to the first municipal elections in December 1951, which it contested without much success. Later, the Penang Labour Party joined with the All-Malaya Peasants Organization led by Mohamed Sopiee and representing primarily the rice-producing Malay peasants of Kedah. From this union emerged the Pan-Malayan Labour Party which was "Pan-Malayan" in name only, since nearly all its supporters were in Penang and Kedah. During the controversies over election proposals, the Pan-Malayan Labour Party participated in some sessions of the Alliance-sponsored National Convention; however, it never joined forces with the Alliance to contest any elections.

In Ipoh, a small group of Fabian-type socialists formed the Perak Labour Party about 1951, but it was beset by dissention and internal divisions. The party split in 1952 over the question of the introduction of jury trials in Malaya. One faction formed the Perak Progressive Party, while the weaker faction retained the name of Perak Labour Party. In 1954 the Perak Progressive Party joined with the UMNO-MCA Alliance at the local level to contest the Town Council elections in Ipoh. However, after these elections the PPP withdrew from its association with the Alliance after a clash over party leadership, discipline and the selection of candidates.[13] Later, the PPP attempted to recombine with the remnants of the Perak Labour Party, but as that did not prove feasible, the Perak Progressive Party contested two seats in the federal elections without aid from any other parties.

The Selangor Labour Party was another of several weak labor parties formed around 1951. In the first municipal elections in Kuala Lumpur it contested, unsuccessfully, six seats. It then moved into closer association with the Independence of Malaya Party. An agreement was reached to contest jointly the second municipal elections in December 1952. Again the Selangor Labour Party suffered complete defeat in Kuala Lumpur by the UMNO-MCA Alliance, although one IMP candidate did win in a tight race. It was reported by a person close to the Selangor Labour Party that the ranks of the dues-paying members had shrunk to 33 by May 1955. However, this was a low, since by the following month the membership had jumped to 800.

Before the federal elections the various state labor parties took steps to amalgamate into a national labor party. The Pan-Malayan Labour Party had become badly split when its chairman, Mohamed Sopiee, refused to abide by a party decision to follow the lead of the Alliance when it called the mass boycott of the legislative councils over the demand for "elections in 1954". Shortly afterwards, the All-Malaya Peasants Organization withdrew from the Pan-Malayan Labour Party, which move made the latter even less "Pan-Malayan" than before. To remedy this situation the Penang and Perak Labour Parties took the initiative in forming the Labour Party of Malaya, which expanded to embrace the Selangor Labour Party as well as receiving unofficial support from a number of trade unions in the Malayan Trade Union Congress.

In 1955 a further move toward labor unity was made when the newly formed Labour Party of Malaya called a conference to create a "Malayan Peoples United Labour Front" to unite all labor and leftist parties to contest the federal elections. However, this "front" never materialized since the Labour Party invited mostly anti-Alliance parties, and also required all parties to accept the entire 56-point manifesto of the Labour Party as a condition of membership in the "front".[14] Furthermore, several top leaders of the Malayan Trade Union Congress were on the executive committee of Party Negara and they were not persuaded to abandon their association with that party. The political action of the MTUC was partly channelled through Party Negara because it appeared to be a more promising challenge to the Alliance than any combination of labor parties, no matter how unified they might become.

All the labor and leftist parties campaigned on platforms of more corporate taxation and public ownership of certain basic industries. They were also similar in their demands for the revision or repeal of the Emergency Regulations, which restricted civil liberties in the alleged interest of public safety during the Communist insurrection. Although none of the parties mentioned above were pro-Communist, some of them held the belief that the Communist guerrillas could be persuaded to surrender if given liberal amnesty terms and permission to resume normal lives as citizens without fear of prosecution for their previous activities as guerrillas. On many other issues, the programs drafted by these parties did not differ markedly from the programs of the Alliance or Party Negara.

The weakness of the labor parties was not so much in their programs as in the nucleus of their support. They tended to rely too heavily upon the trade union movement which was not yet strong enough to command large blocs of voters. Because these parties were generally unwilling to compromise their programs or share leadership with other important elements of society, they had almost no hope of winning a single seat in the federal elections. The recognized futility of their effort led the Labour Party of Malaya to dub the elections a "farce" on the ground that complete independence was not yet obtained, and because the elections were being held in the shadow of the Emergency Regulations. They officially stated that the party was putting up candidates "with a view to using the elections . . . as a forum to expose the defects of the present system."[15]

Party Negara

When the federal elections campaign began in earnest in the latter part of 1954, Party Negara was struggling under a number of liabilities. The controversies over election proposals had caused it to become even more identified with the position of the government, since it had been defending the final elections compromise against the very militant attacks being made by the Alliance. Furthermore, Party Negara emerged from that controversy as the party which was pursuing the more leisurely course toward independence. In the mind of many, Party Negara appeared to be the representative of the entrenched, conservative, western-educated Malayans who were following in the footsteps of the British colonial administrators. Indeed, a great number of the active members of Party Negara were government servants in the higher civil service positions. Although the party was relatively strong in the legislative councils, it had not been able to build a party machine which reached effectively down to the "grass roots" of the common electorate. Moreover, the continued success of the Alliance at state and municipal elections cast an air of defeatism over the party, which made its rejuvenation all the more difficult.[16]

The defeats suffered first by the IMP and later by Party Negara at the hands of the Alliance convinced most politicians in Malaya that communalism could not be ignored. It was apparent that communal appeals were more effective with the voters than any other issues that might be raised. An electoral survey in 1955 estimated that out of a total registered electorate of 1,280,000, over 1,000,000 were Malays. With this fact in mind, Party Negara began to utilize the communal appeal more and more to counter the devastating power of the Alliance. Although it did not abandon its claim to be a "non-communal" party, it gradually redefined "non-communalism" in terms that gave almost exclusive consideration to Malay interests. Thus the Negara campaign focused upon Malay demands and practically ignored the existence of the non-Malay electorate. The party embraced the doctrine once renounced by Dat oOnn, that Malaya is in essence a Malay country and that non-Malays should be given rights as Malayans only in so far as they are willing to become part of a *Malay* Malaya. By this line of attack Party Negara not only hoped to win the support of the predominantly Malay electorate, but it also hoped to bring about a rupture within the Alliance over communal issues.

The manifesto prepared by Party Negara in January 1955 concentrated on a number of popular issues for the Malays. It proposed immigration restrictions to avoid the growing "imbalance between the three major races". Explaining its position it stated, "We are against any attempt at domination by a section of the Chinese community in this country."[17] During campaigning the appeal of Party Negara became more communal than might be indicated from the contents of the manifesto. In his speeches Dato Onn continually played upon the Malays' fears of being submerged by non-Malays after the attainment of independence. Time and again he brought up the threats of Chinese immigration and the high birth rates of the non-Malays. As a remedy to the "Chinese threat" he proposed to restrict the immigration of the Chinese and Indians while encouraging the immigration of Indonesians as a means of assuring the numerical superiority of the Malays. The Negara campaign played upon the theme that UMNO was betraying the vital interests of the Malays by its participation in an alliance with the Malayan Chinese Association.

The language issue was injected into the deliberations of the Legislative Council when a Party Negara leader introduced a motion to make Malay the only national language. Because this resolution sought to implement a plank of the Negara platform, Tunku Abdul Rahman charged that it was part of a crude campaign maneuver.

> But this Party [Negara], in its effort to break up the Alliance, because of their failure to win a single seat in all the elections, and having had to forfeit so many deposits, is just desperate. . . . They feel that since their party failed miserably in their aim to found a non-communal party no one else should.[18]

Although the Alliance decried the political motivation of this motion, they let it pass unanimously.

As the date for federal elections approached, it became apparent that Party Negara was able neither to break the Alliance, nor to win a sufficient number of converts among the Malays. The injection of Malay communalism in the campaigning created misgivings among non-Malays who had supported the party for its professed ideals of "non-communalism".[19] Even E. E. C. Thuraisingham, a leader of Party Negara and the foremost Ceylonese in Malaya, was quoted as saying that the party system "left him cold",[20] obviously because he was distressed by the more strident tones of communal electioneering. The few Chinese, Indians and Eurasians who remained loyal to Party Negara privately stated that the communal appeal to the Malays was necessary to secure the election of Negara leaders, several of whom were at the time holding seats in the Legislative Council. These Negara supporters tended to dismiss the resort to Malay communalism by the party as "so much campaign oratory". They preferred to look at the record of the Negara members in the Legislative Council as support for their belief that Negara was "less communal" than the Alliance; they still had faith that Dato Onn retained a balanced view of communal harmony, and retained as his ultimate objective "non-communalism" in politics.

During the early stages of the federal election campaign Party Negara announced its intention to contest all 52 elected seats in the Legislative Council. Later in the campaign it became obvious that Party Negara had not become sufficiently strong to challenge the Alliance in all constituencies without dissipating the energies of the party. Consequently, Party Negara decided to contest only a limited number of seats and make up for its deficiency through affiilation with other political parties outside the Alliance fold. In March, Party Negara began to send out feelers to other parties hoping to create an anti-Alliance front. Three months later, Dato Onn and E. E. C. Thuraisingham represented the party in informal negotiations at Ipoh with the Perak Progressive Party, the National Association of Perak and the Malay League. These negotiations to form an anti-Alliance block broke down over the question of the allocation of constituencies among the participating parties.[21] However, Party Negara did agree to throw its support to the National Association of Perak rather than contest any seats in that state. At one time Party Negara considered an election agreement with the Labour Party of Malaya, but it came to naught because of Labour's demand that associate parties embrace the Labour manifesto in its entirety.[22]

Behind the scenes other attempts were made to find political allies. The backing of the All-Malaya Youth Congress and the Malay Nationalist Front were sought, but Dr. Burhanuddin did not want to become associated with a party whose leaders at one time had renounced Malay communal nationalism and the radical Malay nationalist movement of the former Malay Nationalist Party. Yet Party Negara included at least four Malays who were active in radical Malay politics. One had been Information Officer for the Malay Nationalist Party; one had been a member of the *Kesatuan Melayu Muda*; one was the ex-chairman of API who had for a time been detained by the government undert he Emergency Regulations; and one was the Secretary-General of the Malay Nationalist Front.[23] Thus, Party Negara was able to pick up some of the radical Malay nationalist vote despite the unwillingness of Dr. Burhanuddin to become its formal ally.

Party Negara did succeed in reaching an understanding with the Pan-Malayan Islamic Party. This party enjoyed phenomenal growth during 1955 by means of its appeal to the Malays to preserve and strengthen the Muslim faith through religiously-inspired political action. The PMIP was strong in the northern states where Negara was weak and poorly organized. Consequently, Negara and the PMIP were able to reach an informal agreement to back each other's candidates, and (it was alleged by the Alliance) Party Negara also contributed funds to the PMIP for some of its campaign expenses.[24]

Two months before the federal elections Party Negara and the Alliance became engaged in a Legislative Council battle over two motions. One of these restricted the use of cars by political parties for transport of voters to the polls, and the other made election day a holiday. Because the Alliance was very well organized and by far the richer party, relying in part on the MCA lottery profit investments, Party Negara sought to restrict the use of cars by political parties on election day. Likewise, Party Negara opposed the creation of an election holiday since that would favor the Alliance, particularly in the areas where estate workers and the lower-class wage-earners had been organized by the Alliance political machine. The government officials did not take sides on these motions, leaving the decision to the remainder of the Council. The Negara position on both these motions was carried by one vote, the margin on the election holiday motion being determined by the vote of the Speaker after a tie.[25]

Following this defeat in the Legislative Council, the three top Alliance Members, Tunku Abdul Rahman, Colonel H. S. Lee and Dr. Ismail bin Abdul Rahman resigned their positions on the Council, charging that the government made the Negara victories possible as a result of the abstentions of government officials.[26] To the critics of the Alliance, this action appeared as just another one of its political tantrums.

The UMNO-MCA-MIC Alliance

The Alliance was in a position of exceptional strength when the federal elections campaigning got into full swing. It had amassed an impressive string of victories in municipal and state elections, and its coalition had been strengthened through the addition of the Malayan Indian Congress as its third partner. Moreover, the Alliance had the advantage of being popularly identified as spearheading the opposition to the government. Consequently, the Alliance could capitalize on any dissatisfaction with Government policies, even though it might be unable to present a clearly defined alternative. This image of opposition to the government had been perpetuated through a continuous series of attacks upon government policies, as well as through staged incidents such as the Alliance boycott in June 1954 and the resignation of the three top Alliance leaders from the Legislative Council in May 1955. The occasional use of noncooperation and boycott created the impression that the Alliance was the more militant nationalist party, regardless what alternative policies were being promoted by either the Alliance or Party Negara.

The power of the Alliance was dependent upon cooperation and agreement among its three partners. As a major objective of the Negara campaign was to split the Alliance, internal discipline and cohesion became the major task of the leadership of the trio of parties comprising the Alliance. Each communal organization contained within its ranks elements which resisted the concessions made to their communal partners. Thus each constituent party had to retain the support of its communally conscious members without antagonizing the other two to the point where their common political front would be jeopardized. The intra-Alliance tension was greatest when its "National Council" set about the task of allocating seats on the ticket to each respective party. The internal politics of the Alliance can best be discussed by reference

F

to the problem of compromise and discipline encountered by each of its constituent members.

At the UMNO general assembly in October 1954, Tunku Abdul Rahman came under sharp criticism for being too vague on policy matters and for not insisting upon a more positive program to preserve and promote Malay interests. His critics within the party wanted him to demand that the Alliance draft a concrete program committed to Malay special rights and the adoption of Malay as the official language of the country.27 Although he weathered this opposition within his party, he was again criticized at the next UMNO general assembly over the number of seats allocated to UMNO on the Alliance ticket. For the 52 seats to be contested, the Alliance National Council was reported to have selected 40 Malay candidates, 12 Chinese candidates, and no Indian candidates. Despite the favorable ratio of Malays on the Alliance ticket, the dissident elements in UMNO demanded that Malays should be nominated for at least 42 of the 52 positions on the ballot. In response to this criticism, Tunku Abdul Rahman spoke out vigorously against those who were leaning toward a "Malays only" policy and were attempting to revive the "Malaya for the Malays" policies which had been characteristic of UMNO in its pre-Alliance days. Only after he threatened to resign did he receive a vote of confidence from the UMNO general assembly.28

Although Malay communalism accounted for most of the demands for increasing the number of Malays on the Alliance ticket, some agitation along this line originated from a number of Malays who thought they deserved to be nominated, but were not selected because the aspiring candidates outnumbered the seats allocated to UMNO. Several disappointed UMNO members filed nomination papers as independents after they had been by-passed by the Alliance nomination committee, and UMNO was forced to take disciplinary action by expelling them from the party. At least one of these expelled UMNO members had been a leading critic of UMNO's cooperation with the MCA and had been attempting to persuade Malay voters not to vote for any non-Malays even though they might be running on the Alliance ticket.29 The women's division of UMNO, *Kaum Ibu*, also threatened to boycott the elections if no UMNO women were selected to stand for the federal elections as Alliance candidates.30 In short, many elements in UMNO were unaccustomed to making compromises and concessions which were essential to hold the Alliance coalition together.

The Malayan Chinese Association was also faced with the problem of reconciling the demands made by the Chinese communal interests and the concessions which it made to UMNO and the MIC to maintain their cooperation in the partnership of the Alliance. As an example, there were many within the MCA who wanted Chinese to be given a legal status as an official language of Malaya; and these persons agitated unceasingly for "multilingualism" which would have made possible the use of Chinese (and Indian) dialects in the elected state and federal councils. When the UMNO leaders heard of these demands, they immediately requested the MCA not to champion the cause of multi-lingualism for fear of antagonizing the Malays.

Since the Malays were estimated to comprise about 90 per cent of the voters in the Federation, these proposals for multi-lingualism were rejected by the Alliance National Council.[31] However, the more communally conscious Chinese in the MCA continued to agitate for multi-lingualism through other Chinese bodies such as the Chinese Guilds, despite the MCA commitment to defend the Alliance policy. To prevent Malay mistrust of the Chinese in the MCA, Tan Cheng-lock, as its president, went to great pains to try to dissuade the Chinese Guilds from submitting a petition to the Queen for multi-lingualism. However, the petition was not withdrawn and several MCA members resigned when they were unwilling to compromise their communal demands for the sake of harmony with the Malays in UMNO.[32]

When the Alliance National Council alloted only 12 out of 52 seats to the MCA, members criticized its failure to secure larger representation for the Chinese on the Alliance ticket. At least one MCA member resigned to contest the elections as an independent when not selected as an Alliance candidate.[33] The dissatisfaction with the number of seats allocated to the MCA must have caused the Alliance National Council to reconsider its earlier decision, for when nomination day arrived the Alliance slate included 15 Chinese.

Because the Malayan Indian Congress had joined the Alliance less than a year before the federal elections, it was at the disadvantage of being both a newcomer and the weakest partner in the Alliance. Furthermore, the MIC retained the confidence of only a segment of the Indian community, and it was the object of considerable criticism in the Indian press for its participation in the Alliance. Preliminary reports that no Indians were to be included on the Alliance ticket added to this wave of criticism of the MIC. Eventually, however, the MIC did secure two positions on the Alliance ticket.

The most severe threat to MIC participation in the Alliance came as a result of a political blunder made by the secretary and the publicity chief of the Malayan Chinese Association. Together they wrote a letter to the Chinese-owned English language paper, the *Singapore Standard*, complaining about its political viewpoint, stating: "Quite often, some of the articles are not only pro-Tamil, they are distinctly anti-Chinese—and this in a Chinese newspaper!" The letter went on to suggest as a remedy that all articles written by the *Standard* staff could be submitted for approval to the publicity chief of the MCA, Mr. Tan Siew-sin, the son of Tan Cheng-lock. Rather than follow the "suggestion" of the MCA, the *Singapore Standard* devoted one-half of the first page of its Sunday edition to publicizing and replying to this letter under the heading "A Prelude to Dictatorship".[34] The political repercussions were immediate. Some Indians took this letter as proof that the MCA, and hence the Alliance, was basically "anti-Indian". The Indian paper, *Tamil Murasu*, called for a boycott of the Malayan Indian Congress by all Indians.

> The quislings in the MIC have formed a treacherous pact with the Alliance to eliminate the Tamils. Those Tamils who act as the camp followers to the MIC, which dig graves for the Tamils, will be halter ropes to their community.[35]

163

This episode not only threatened the Indian participation in the Alliance, but it also weakened the political support of the MIC. Although the MIC accepted the denial by Mr. Tan Siew-sin that he was "anti-Indian", some considered the episode "merely an election stunt".[36] Secret talks were held by the Alliance to repair the mistrust and discord resulting from the publicity given this letter.

Much of this Indian criticism of the MIC undoubtedly stemmed from its being a weak third partner in a coalition dominated by the other two powerful communal bodies. The MIC had very little say in the political course charted by the Alliance and it could only hope for a few minor concessions. It was a question of choice between pursuing the politically possible and remaining steadfast for the political objectives of Indian communal interests narrowly defined. The MIC chose the former.

The Alliance manifesto was much more difficult to draft than that of any other party for the very reason that it was necessary to secure the approval of all three communal groups within the Alliance. After extended negotiations of almost half a year, a manifesto was approved by the Alliance National Council. Later, a booklet entitled, *The Road to Independence*[37] was published, presenting the manifesto along with explanatory "policy papers". Like all other parties contesting the elections, the Alliance promised increased social services, measures to promote economic development, and "Malayanization" of the civil service. Although Alliance leaders had been talking about independence in ten years, the manifesto promised independence within four years, one year sooner than the target date for independence set by Party Negara. The Alliance also promised to establish educational policies that would "promote" Malay as the national language. This was also in response to the Party Negara plank which pledged to make Malay the sole national language.

During 1954 the Alliance had been a staunch proponent of the union of Malaya and Singapore. While this general objective remained popular because of the importance of Singapore as a commercial and trading center for Southeast Asia, many Malays were fearful of Singapore's Chinese population which, when added to the Chinese in Malaya, would make the Chinese as numerous as the Malays. Furthermore, the Communist subversion of Chinese schools and labor unions in Singapore created problems which the Federation politicians preferred to have solved before union. After the Communist-led labor disorders and riots of April, May and June 1955, Tunku Abdul Rahman became less enthusiastic about the union of Singapore with the Federation. The Alliance manifesto avoided making a statement about eventual union of Singapore and the Federation after the attainment of independence, and no promises were made to achieve this goal in the election campaign.[38]

UMNO and the MCA were unable to agree on the question of citizenship and nationality rights for non-Malays. The Malayan Chinese Association held out for the principle of *jus soli* whereby citizenship would be automatically acquired by all persons born in Malaya, while the Malays in UMNO wanted to retain many features of the more restrictive citizenship requirements and naturalization process embodied in the existing Federation Agreement.

Inability to reach an acceptable compromise forced the Alliance to avoid a commitment on this issue. Instead, it proposed the formation of a special independent commission to recommend a policy on the nationality question and the future position of the Malay Rulers in an independent Malaya.[39]

During the campaign the Alliance leadership exhibited some ambivalence toward communal issues. On the one hand Tunku Abdul Rahman made a communal appeal for the support of the Malays, stressing such issues as "the alien danger" and the threat to the Malays posed by the immigration of "foreigners". On the other hand, he defended the Alliance manifesto which attributed the "alien danger" to the restrictive citizenship requirements which made it difficult for non-Malays to acquire full status as Malayan citizens. Thus, the Alliance tended to utilize the "foreign threat" issue in appealing to the Malays, but hastened to explain to its MCA and MIC members that the loyal Chinese and Indians in these two organizations were not a part of that "foreign threat". This is just one of many examples of ambiguous terms being employed successfully to keep incongruous elements united for common political action.

One particularly knotty problem was that posed by the continued activity of Communist guerrillas fighting to bring about the downfall of the government. While some radicals and a few optimists believed that the Communist insurrection would cease as soon as Malaya obtained independence, a majority of Malayans feared that the Communists would probably continue their revolutionary tactics even after independence. The problem of meeting the challenge posed by the Communist guerrillas was closely linked to the question of attaining independence. Some doubted that independence could become final until the Communist guerrillas were eliminated. Tunku Abdul Rahman expressed this view at the UMNO general assembly in October 1954.[40] Thus, as the Alliance began to place more emphasis upon the goal of independence, the problem of Communist terrorism loomed larger and larger. Toward the end of 1954 political leaders from the major political parties were appointed by the government to the War Executive Committee which reviewed the strategy and operations of the Security Forces against the Communist bands. After thus obtaining an inside view of the Emergency operations, several Alliance leaders attempted to draft a program which would hasten the end of the Emergency.

In January 1955, Tunku Abdul Rahman made two proposals: Singapore should shoulder one-third of the yearly costs of the Emergency in the Federation; and an amnesty should be offered all "terrorists" who, after surrender, should be given the option of remaining in Malaya as law-abiding citizens or returning to their country of origin.[41] The first proposal, while popular in the Federation, raised a storm of protest in Singapore, and little came of it. The second proposal was coolly received by leaders of other political parties and by the government, which rejected the proposal, stating that the Communist guerrillas were perfectly free to surrender as individuals, and they were offered opportunities to start a new life if they had not committed atrocities for which they must stand trial.[42]

When the Alliance manifesto was published in May, amnesty for all "terrorists" was included as one of the major planks. More attention was given this one proposal than any other provision of the platform. By stressing the amnesty issue, the Alliance was able to keep the political initiative and divert political attention from communal issues that might cause internal division, and hence, weakness.

Although the Alliance amnesty proposal presented nothing drastically new, it was popular because it appeared to point out means for ending the guerrilla war which was in its eighth year. People in Malaya were tired of both the restrictions of the Emergency Regulations and the continued fear of and losses from Communist terrorism. The issue of amnesty stole the political spotlight, particularly in the last weeks of the campaign after the Government had made public on June 24 a letter sent by the Communist "Supreme Command Headquarters of the Malayan Races Liberation Army", offering to negotiate with the Government to end the Emergency. The Government rejected this offer to end the Emergency by negotiation on the grounds that the Communists could not be trusted to keep any agreement and because this peace-feeler illustrated that the Communists were on the verge of defeat. In the Federation only the Labour Party and the National Association of Perak criticized the government for rejecting the Communist offer to talk "peace".[43] Although the Alliance did not directly attack the Government's decision, it campaigned even more vigorously for the amnesty proposals, claiming that the Communists had given evidence that they would respond to an amnesty so that the Emergency could be brought to a speedy conclusion. This claim seemed plausible and undoubtedly contributed to the support given the Alliance at the polls.

Results of the Federal Elections

During the course of the electioneering, the Alliance had called upon the voters to elect all 52 Alliance candidates as a means of assuring the independence of Malaya. Other parties claimed that this was evidence of the authoritarian tendencies within the Alliance, since it sought to overwhelm all its opposition. Almost no one except the most ardent partisan believed that the Alliance could come close to making a clean sweep of all the seats, yet nearly everyone expected an Alliance victory by a substantial margin. After the close of the polls on July 27, it became apparent from the first returns that the Alliance had engineered a landslide victory that threatened to put every constituency in its column.

When the votes were finally counted the Alliance had won 51 seats, one of them being returned on nomination day when no opponent entered against the Alliance candidate. The lone seat lost by the Alliance was won by the Pan-Malayan Islamic Party by the narrow margin of 450 votes in the Krian "rice bowl" district of Perak where the electorate was 93 per cent Malay.[44] Being the sole Alliance opponent who won a seat, this PMIP member, Tuan Haji Ahmad, was immediately dubbed "Mr. Opposition" by the local press. The Alliance polled over 81 per cent of the total electorate, or four times the vote polled by all opposition candidates, and 10 times the vote polled by Party Negara (which contested only 30 of the 52 seats). Even the venerable Dato Onn bin Ja'afar was only able to capture 22·4 per cent of the votes in his home constituency of Johore Bahru.[45]

Although 32 members of the Legislative Council were not elected by popular vote, the Alliance was able to count on 19 additional votes from non-elected members,[46] thus assuring it of a majority of approximately 70 in a Council of 98. With this handsome majority the Alliance, under the leadership of Tunku Abdul Rahman, undertook to form the first elected government of Malaya and assume responsibility for determining the policies which would pave the way for Malayan independence. The federal elections marked the conclusion of one phase and the beginning of another in the development of Malayan politics. At this juncture, the politics of elections was displaced by the politics attending the formation of the new government and its program for Malayan independence. The defeated political parties turned their energies to the task of forming a coherent and effective opposition to the government of the day, even though they were largely unrepresented on the Legislative Council.

[1] Usha Mahajani, *The Role of Indian Minorities in Burma and Malaya*, (Bombay: Vora & Co., 1960), pp. 245–246 and 262–263.

[2] For example, see *Straits Times*, March 26, 1954, p. 4; July 29, 1954, p. 6; July 30, 1954, p. 6.

[3] *Singapore Standard*, October 12, 1954, p. 1. An Indian woman had been included on the UMNO-MCA ticket in the first Kuala Lumpur elections in February 1952, but she was defeated.

[4] Quoted in *Straits Times*, January 30, 1954, p. 4.

[5] *Straits Times*, January 2, 1955, p. 1; January 3, 1955, p. 7.

[6] A letter from Nehru to the president of the Malayan Indian Association, Mr. G. V. Thaver, supporting communal cooperation did not end the dispute, particularly since many Indians resented the name of Nehru being injected into questions which were peculiar to Malaya. See *Straits Times*, January 22, 1955, p. 1.

[7] *Singapore Standard*, October 12, 1954, p. 1. In 1950 P. Ramani formed the Federation of Indian Organizations (FIO) with a view to uniting all Indian organizations within a single federation. However, the rivalry between the Malayan Indian Association and the Malayan Indian Congress prompted the latter to withdraw from the FIO leaving the FIO largely in the hands of the MIA.

[8] *Malay Mail*, April 9, 1953, p. 3; April 11, 1955, p. 1. See also "*Resolusi2 Yang Telah Diambil Dalam Congress Pemuda Yang Bersidang Pada 8, 9, 10 April, 1955 di Kuala Lumpur*", (mimeographed, n.d.), pp. 1–3.

[9] *Utusan Melayu*, April 13, 1955, as quoted in *Weekly Digest of the Non-English Press*, No. 15, 1955, (Singapore Public Relations Office), p. 22.

[10] *Utusan Melayu*, April 21, 1955, as quoted in *Weekly Digest of the Non-English Press*, No. 16, 1955, (Singapore Public Relations Office), p. 31.

11 Dato Onn's participation in the Malay Nationalist Front was interpreted by some political observers as his complete capitulation to Malay communalism in politics. Whatever his motives, it spelled the end of any significant non-Malay support for Party Negara.

12 This organization was founded with the name Pan-Malayan Islamic Association, but later changed its name to Pan-Malayan Islamic Party (PMIP) at the insistence of the Registrar of Societies. The party was an outgrowth of the Malayan Muslim Party formed in Perak in 1948.

13 *Straits Times*, January 9, 1955, p. 1; February 22, 1955, p. 5.

14 *Straits Times*, May 4, 1955, p. 8; *Singapore Standard*, May 10, 1955, p. 5.

15 *Straits Times*, June 17, 1955, p. 5.

16 In August, the Alliance swept aside all opposition in the critical town council elections in Ipoh, Taiping and Telok Anson; in October, it captured all elected seats in the Johore State elections, and later in the month it gained another victory in the Trengganu State elections, which were marred by irregularities and malpractices in the campaigning and polling. In December the Alliance swept municipal elections in Kuala Lumpur, Malacca, Penang, Klang, and Port Swettenham, but lost to the Labour Party and the Radical Party in Butterworth and Seremban. In February 1955, the Alliance won all 14 elected seats in the Penang Settlement Council elections. See *Straits Times*, June 17, 1955, p. 5; August 17, 1954, p. 2; October 12, 1954, p. 1; October 31, 1954, p. 1; November 1, 1954, pp. 1 and 6; February 21, 1955, p. 4; *Singapore Standard*, December 5, 1954, p. 1.

17 *Singapore Standard*, January 23, 1955, p. 1. The Negara manifesto promised: to secure independence by 1960 under a constitution to be drafted by a Constituent Assembly; to preserve the "functions and privileges" of the Malay Rulers; to promote a more diversified economy that would "retain and further secure external capital assistance"; to inaugurate a Planning Commision; to ensure the creation of a Permanent Civil Service free from the "corrupting influences of political power and patronage"; to speed the Malayanization of administration; to avoid further increases in direct taxation in order to attract foreign capital; to "curtail government expenditure"; to enact a "single Nationality Law"; to enact "suitable legislation to provide security to the Malays against the risks of becoming a back number in their own country, and also regulate by suitable machinery, such as a quota system, the immigration of the nationals of other countries"; to "accelerate the pace of Progress, so that in a reasonably short time [everyone] . . . will have secured . . . rights as human beings under the U.N. Charter of Human Rights"; to initiate free compulsory education up to the Secondary School standard; to make Malay the National Language and English a second language; to conserve the Chinese and Indian culture by giving appropriate encouragements to the study of their language and literature; to expand health and medical facilities; to promote good housing; to "proceed gradually to a system of comprehensive Social Security"; to remedy the monopoly in the transport industry which is detrimental to the Malays; to improve the conditions for padi cultivation; to initiate state financial aid to the peasants through Land Banks; to uplift the economic and social status of women, and to encourage youth movements as a means of creating a new nation. See *Negara*, Vol. II, no. 1 (June 15, 1955), pp. 6–8.

18 *Legislative Council Debates, 30th and 31st March 1955*, Federation of Malaya, 151.

19 At one point Eurasians became incensed at some derogatory remarks made by Dato Onn in one of his speeches. Since many Eurasians had been supporting the party, Dato Onn quickly explained that he was referring to prewar Eurasians. See *Straits Times*, February 13, 1955, p. 1.

20 *Straits Times*, February 14, 1955, p. 1.

21 *Straits Times*, June 9, 1955, p. 5; June 18, 1955, pp. 1 and 5.

[22] *Singapore Standard*, May 10, 1955, p. 5.

[23] *Straits Times*, June 16, 1955, p. 5.

[24] *Malay Mail*, June 22, 1955, p. 7.

[25] *Legislative Council Debates, 4th and 5th May 1955*, Federation of Malaya, 405–433, 445–486.

[26] *Singapore Standard*, May 8, 1955, p. 1.

[27] *Straits Times*, October 18, 1954, p. 1.

[28] *Sunday Times*, June 5, 1955, pp. 1 and 11.

[29] The two were Haji Abdullah Abbas and Inche Idris bin Hakim, both of Kedah. See *Straits Times*, June 17, 1955, p. 5; June 14, 1955, p. 7.

[30] *Straits Times*, October 18, 1954, p. 5.

[31] *Straits Times*, February 15, 1955, p. 7.

[32] One of those resigning was Leong Chee-cheong, the president of the Federation of Selangor Chinese Guilds and Associations. See *Straits Times*, February 22, 1955, p. 5.

[33] *Singapore Standard*, June 14, 1955, p. 8.

[34] *Singapore Standard*, March 6, 1955, p. 1.

[35] *Tamil Murasu*, March 7, 1955, as quoted in *Weekly Digest of the Non-English Press*, No. 10, 1955, (Singapore Public Relations Office), p. 24.

[36] *Straits Times*, July 14, 1955, p. 5.

[37] *Menuju Kearah Kemerdekaan*, (Kuala Lumpur: Alliance National Council, n.d.).

[38] See *Straits Times*, January 26, 1955, p. 1; July 10, 1955, p. 9.

[39] *Menuju Kearah Kemerdekaan, op. cit.*, pp. 36–38.

[40] *Straits Times*, October 21, 1954, p. 6.

[41] *Straits Times*, January 7, 1955, p. 1.

[42] *Straits Times*, January 18, 1955, p. 1.

[43] *Straits Times*, June 24, 1955, p. 1; June 25, 1955, p. 7.

[44] *Straits Times*, June 16, 1955, p. 2.

[45] *Straits Times*, July 29, 1955, p. 7; July 30, 1955, p. 1.

[46] Five members were appointed to the "reserved seats" by the High Commissioner on the advice of Tunku Abdul Rahman who became the Chief Minister of the new Government. This was the "extra-constitutional" arrangement which had been agreed upon by the High Commissioner during the crisis of June 1954, when the Alliance staged its mass boycott. The Alliance was able to count on additional votes from the following members: the five Government officials; two Mentris Besar who were Alliance supporters; two members of the All-Malaya Chinese Mining Association; two members of the Associated Chinese Chambers of Commerce; one representative from each Settlement Council in Malacca and Penang; and one member nominated by the Rubber Producers Council. See *Straits Times*, July 30, 1955, p. 1.

12 The Merdeka Constitution

Merdeka is the Malay word for "freedom". In recent years the word has been used so frequently and enthusiastically that it is now a part of the daily vocabulary of all Malayans regardless of their mother tongue. Indeed, it has even been incorporated into the English legal vocabulary in Malaya and in treaties between the United Kingdom and Malaya. The Indonesian nationalist movement used it as a slogan for their revolution against the Dutch. However, in Malaya the word achieved a more evolutionary association as a result of its use by the most respected and law-abiding of the indigenous political leaders. The anticipation of elections to the Federal Legislative Council spurred local politicians to campaign on the *merdeka* theme. The competition of the election campaign stimulated both political interest and the desire for swift attainment of independence.

The overwhelming victory of the Alliance in the elections of July 1955 can be attributed to a large extent to their ability to identify themselves more successfully than their opponents with the slogan *merdeka*. The Alliance election platform had demanded self-government within two years, and the establishment of an "independent commission" to draft a constitution for the attainment of independence within four years. After securing control of the Government, the Alliance, under the leadership of Tunku Abdul Rahman, proceeded to give top priority to the fulfilment of their *merdeka* pledge. During the first talks between the Chief Minister and the High Commissioner about the formation of the new Government, Tunku Abdul Rahman indicated his party's dissatisfaction with the existing constitution, especially the provisions giving the High Commissioner "reserved powers" over the Legislative Council. Furthermore, he expressed the intention of his party to seek a revision of the Federation Agreement in order to introduce internal self-government and a fully-elected Legislative Council.[1]

When the Colonial Secretary, Mr. A. Lennox-Boyd, visited Malaya a month after the elections, the Alliance Government informed him of its desire to send a delegation to London to discuss constitutional reform.[2] At the inauguration of the newly elected Legislative Council, Tunku Abdul Rahman reiterated the Alliance request for negotiations between an Alliance delegation and Whitehall to consider the terms of reference for a review of the constitution by an "independent commission".[3] Meanwhile, Mr. Lennox-Boyd had discussed this proposal with the Malay Rulers, who indicated their willingness to consider the problem of further revision of the Federation Agreement. However, the Rulers were unwilling to have negotiations conducted by a Malayan delegation composed only of Alliance members.[4] When the Colonial Office indicated that the way was clear to begin negotiations, the issue of the composition of the Malayan delegation had not yet been resolved. The Rulers proposed a seven-man delegation of four representatives of the Rulers, two from the Alliance, and the Attorney General as an advisor. The Alliance Government backed down from its demand for an exclusive Alliance delegation, but refused to participate as a minority on the Malayan delegation. Ultimately, agreement was reached on an eight-member delegation, four representing the Rulers and four representing the Alliance Government.[5]

Ever since the formation of the Alliance, its leaders had exhibited political antagonism toward the Malay Rulers. Evidence of the continued suspicion of the political motives of the Rulers is contained in a speech delivered by Tunku Abdul Rahman in the Legislative Council after the Alliance victory at the polls. In this speech he expressed the concern of his Government over the possible frustration, by the Rulers, of Alliance plans for self-government, and he warned them that if "they cannot bring themselves to agree with us, the path will be rugged, and the going stormy and difficult".[6]

A speech delivered by the Sultan of Johore on the occasion of his diamond jubilee in September 1955, caused increased antagonism between the Alliance and the Rulers.[7] This stimulated speculation that the Rulers Conference might not assent to all the constitutional proposals of the Alliance. Before the "*Merdeka* Mission" departed for London, the Rulers, meeting in a session of the Rulers Conference, sought a guarantee from the Alliance that their status as constitutional heads of state would be upheld. In return the Rulers promised to back certain Alliance proposals for self-government.[8] Apparently, most of the major points of issue between the Alliance and the Rulers were resolved before the delegation departed for London.

The *merdeka* talks extended from January 18 to February 8, 1956, between the Malayan delegation, the Colonial Secretary, the High Commissioner, and the United Kingdom Minister of State. A number of advisors aided the delegation as it split into sub-committees to discuss technical details. The Malayan delegation was advised by three prominent members of the Labour Party who were known for their interest in colonial affairs, Lord Ogmore, Woodrow Wyatt and Douglas Jay.[9]

Throughout the talks there seemed to be very few points of contention. The major efforts of the conference were devoted to technical problems of administration during the transition to independence. Seventeen of the twenty pages of the report of the conference cover administrative questions concerning defense and internal security, public services, and problems of finance and economics. The final three pages contain constitutional provisions in anticipation of independence.

A number of the administrative and financial agreements prepared at the conference were significant. However, for the most part they were detailed and technical, and their specific provisions need not be examined here. The five major agreements which concern constitutional development are summarized below.

1. Members of the Executive Council other than the Chief Secretary and the Attorney-General shall be appointed by the High Commissioner after consultation with the Chief Minister.

2. The following Nominated Officials in the ministry are to be replaced by Unofficials selected on the advice of the Chief Minister:
The Financial Secretary
The Minister for Economic Affairs
The Secretary for Defence.

3. The Chief Secretary's responsibilities will be confined to matters relating to the Public Service, to administrative work involved in constitutional changes, and to matters of external affairs.

4. The British Advisers to the Malay Rulers are to be withdrawn.

5. An independent Constitutional Commission should be appointed as soon as possible to draft a constitution providing for full self-government and independence within the Commonwealth by August 1957, if possible.[10]

The first three agreements provided the means whereby the elected government could assume full responsibility for finance, economic affairs and internal defense and security. In this last phase before independence, only the limited responsibilities of the Chief Secretary for administration and external affairs were beyond the immediate supervision of the Chief Minister, and even in those matters the Chief Secretary was required to answer to the Legislative Council.[11] The agreement to arrange for the withdrawal of the British Advisers to the Malay Rulers had several motives behind it. The British Advisers were continuing symbols of a departing colonial administration. They were also blamed by the Alliance for much of the political opposition to the Alliance by the Rulers. Perhaps most important, the Rulers could not be restricted to the functions of constitutional monarchs until their independent advisors were replaced by the political leaders of the party in power in the State Legislative Assemblies. The British Advisers were both a thorn in the political flank of the Alliance and a source of influence over the Rulers which was incompatible with their proposed roles as constitutional monarchs.

The provision for an independent Constitutional Commission was accompanied by a further agreement setting forth the "terms of reference" for the preparation of the new constitution. These terms of reference were not made public until they were approved by the Conference of Rulers, and the Chairman of the Commission had been appointed. Included in the terms of reference were the following provisions: the establishment of a strong central government, with the States and Settlements enjoying a measure of autonomy; "a common nationality for the whole of the Federation"; and "the safeguarding of the special position of the Malays and the legitimate interests of other communities".[12]

The Reid Commission

At the London Conference it was agreed that the Chairman and one other member of the Constitutional Commission should be nominated by the United Kingdom, and that Australia, Pakistan, India and Canada should each nominate one member. The five members of the Commission were Sir Ivor Jennings from the United Kingdom, Sir William McKell from Australia, Mr. B. Malik from India, Mr. Justice Abdul Hamid from Pakistan, and the Chairman, Lord Reid from the United Kingdom. The Canadian Government was unable to find a representative of sufficient caliber and did not make a nomination.[13]

The Commission began the first of a total of 118 sessions in late June. By October, when the Commission left Malaya, it had held hearings in all the States and Settlements and had compiled a large volume of evidence, including 131 written memoranda from individuals and organizations. After the Commission had collected all the evidence which it considered adequate to its task, it left Malaya and reconvened in Rome to prepare its Report.

The most important evidence presented to the Reid Commission was provided by the Alliance Party and the Alliance Government. The Commission gave their views top priority because of the overwhelming elected majority enjoyed by the Alliance in both federal and state councils, and because the Alliance comprised the three major communal organizations in Malaya—the United Malays National Organization, the Malayan Chinese Association, and the Malayan Indian Congress. The recommendations of the Alliance Political Committee were preceded by five months of negotiations and discussions between the three communal associations affiliated under the Alliance banner.[14] On the most controversial issues—those involving communal interests—the Alliance proposals represented compromises already agreed upon by leaders of the respective communal organizations in the Alliance. Consequently, the Reid Commission was able to avoid the responsibility for working out solutions to many highly emotional communal issues by accepting the compromises already agreed upon within the political structure of the Alliance. Nevertheless, the Commission had to resolve many other political issues and create in precise legal form a comprehensive constitutional document. The representations of other political groups and associations were not ignored, but their influence in most cases was slight.

As soon as the Reid Report[15] was made public, political organizations began to align themselves either for or against its provisions. Because the Report incorporated so many of the Alliance recommendations, the most vociferous critics were the anti-Alliance parties. The ultra-communal political leaders were disappointed that their political demands were not incorporated into the Reid Report. The flurry of criticisms that followed its publication prompted the Alliance Government to rally to the defense of the Reid proposals, and the Chief Minister, Tunku Abdul Rahman, called upon the various communal leaders not to make demands that could not be reconciled with the interests of other communities. In some respects, the Tunku's support of the Reid Report as "the best compromise under the circumstances" revealed not only his awareness of the pressures of communalism in Malayan politics, but also his concern over internal communal divisions within his own party, composed as it was of three communal associations.

In spite of the initial Alliance Government support of the Reid draft constitution, it was unwilling to give a blanket endorsement to all the features of the Report. In the first place, the Report had deviated from the Alliance recommendations submitted to the Commission during its hearings. On most issues the Commission had accepted the proposals contained in the Alliance memoranda, but it added a number of significant innovations. On several issues the Commission had followed the suggestions of the Rulers, or submitted proposals designed to adjust the political interest not fully represented by the Alliance Party.

Malay opinion was quick to react against the Reid proposals relating to special privileges for Malays. The Commission expressed itself as being opposed in principle to special privileges for the Malays, but recognized the temporary need for special consideration to be given to the Malays. The proposals, therefore, did not include any provisions for Malay special rights in the draft constitution, preferring to leave the matter up to the appropriate state and federal legislatures. While the Malays were highly critical of these omissions, the Alliance Government's misgivings were not expressed for some time, since it had proposed the Commission as the appropriate method for drafting a constitution for Malaya. Yet the political reaction of the Malays made itself felt both outside and within the Alliance. The Chief Minister, Tunku Abdul Rahman, found himself hard-pressed to defend the Reid Report before meetings of the United Malays National Organization, of which he was president. He was more than anxious to allay the misgivings of the Malay elements in the Alliance by assuring them that while the Report had overlooked provisions for the Malays, the Alliance would remedy these defects.[16] Although he was given a vote of confidence by UMNO, his leadership of that organization was not reaffirmed without expressions of criticism. It is worth noting that many Chinese were also disappointed with the Reid Report relating to citizenship and the special status of the Chinese language. However, the more extreme communal elements among the Chinese were not in control of the Malayan Chinese Association. The Alliance remained more sensitive to Malay criticisms of the Report, particularly since the Malay voters outnumbered all the others.

Following the publication of the Report, the government prepared to review the findings of the Commission by means of an eleven member Working Committee consisting of four representatives of the Rulers, four representatives of the Alliance Government, and the High Commissioner, the Chief Secretary and the Attorney General representing Her Majesty's Government. The Working Committee was selected before the Commission had completed its task, and when the Report was ready, it was submitted to this Committee, before being considered by the Conference of Rulers and the

Legislative Council. The Working Committee began deliberations on the Reid Report in March 1957, and by May 1 it had completed its recommendations for the revision of that document. A few remaining unresolved issues were then taken up in new negotiations in London between representatives of the Alliance, the Rulers and the Colonial Office.[17] These negotiations culminated in an agreement on a draft constitution which ultimately was adopted as the Constitution for an independent Malaya.

To examine the Reid Report in its entirety, and then analyze the final constitutional document would be a duplication of effort since the two are very similar. These documents will be examined together by topics. In this way the final document will receive primary emphasis, but some attention will also be given to the more important political and constitutional issues which were raised during the extended negotiations for the "Merdeka Constitution".

Citizenship

On the very difficult problem of citizenship, the Reid Commission proposed that all persons born in Malaya after independence should be citizens. Non-citizens might attain citizenship by fulfilling the following requirements: (a) residing five to eight years in Malaya (depending on place of residence at the time of independence), (b) taking an oath of allegiance, (c) renouncing foreign citizenship, and (d) passing an elementary examination in the Malay language (subject to exception for one year after independence). Naturalized citizenship might be lost as a result of acts of disloyalty to the Federation or by taking advantage of foreign citizenship.[18] Although the proposal to create Malayan citizenship on the principle of *jus soli* was highly controversial, all the above recommendations of the Commission were incorporated into the final constitution primarily because they had the backing of the Alliance, which had previously worked out similar proposals in a delicate compromise between the demands of the Malays, the Chinese and the Indians.

A special problem of citizenship developed over the status of the large number of residents of Malaya, particularly in the Settlements, who were British subjects, and consequently enjoyed the privileges accorded to citizens of "the United Kingdom and Colonies". Unlike the Malay States, the two Settlements of Penang and Malacca were under the sovereignty of the British Crown, a co-participant in the Federation Agreement of 1948. Before that time the Settlements were under the direct authority of the Crown. The citizenship of the residents of Penang and Malacca thus depended upon the laws of the Federation and the United Kingdom. Few residents in these two Settlements had availed themselves of the rights of either Federal citizenship or those afforded a "citizen of the United Kingdom and Colonies". Yet many persons residing in these territories were jealous of their rights as "subjects of the Queen" and they insisted upon the perpetuation of their dual status. The Reid proposals had sought to meet these demands by making Federal citizenship synonymous with Commonwealth citizenship.[19] But doubt was raised whether citizens of other Commonwealth countries would not also be able to retain their citizenship upon acquiring Malayan Federal citizenship. If this had been permitted Indians, Pakistanis, Ceylonese, and citizens of the "United Kingdom and Colonies" might retain their dual citizenship outside Malaya, but the Chinese from China and the Malaysians from Indonesia would be prohibited from retaining dual citizenship. The Reid proposals had specifically prohibited the exercise of the rights of citizenship in a "foreign country", but it still provided for Commonwealth citizenship, which apparently meant that Commonwealth citizenship was not to be classified as "foreign".

The legal consequences of Commonwealth citizenship are hard to determine, but the political rationale behind the category is obvious. Residents of Malaya who were subjects of the Queen or citizens of India, Pakistan, or Ceylon could become Federal citizens without renouncing their previous citizenship. Indeed, they might enjoy any special privileges as "Commonwealth citizens" which other Commonwealth countries might extend. However, in answer to those who criticized or feared divided loyalty, the Report, with some inconsistency, called for undivided loyalty to the country of residence.

For several important political reasons, the Alliance had made opposition to dual citizenship a cardinal feature of its political dogma. In this way it hoped to avoid the complications of foreign political controversies and any communal identification with the countries from which the various Malayan communities originated. Moreover, the Alliance considered the principle of exclusive nationality to be an important factor in developing in Malaya a nationalism unencumbered by the competition of loyalty to states outside Malaya. The Reid Commission proposals for the creation of both Malayan Federal citizenship and Commonwealth citizenship appeared to be directly contrary to previous Alliance pronouncements. After the publication of the Report, Tunku Abdul Rahman announced on several occasions that the Alliance Government would not accept any compromise which would admit the principle of dual nationality.[20] However, the Alliance was ultimately forced to accede to a compromise on the issue of Commonwealth citizenship because of political pressure and the legal complications involving a large proportion of the inhabitants of Penang and Malacca.

The ultimate compromise on the issue of citizenship retained the principle of Commonwealth citizenship, but defined it in such a way as to avoid any separate legal consequences from Malayan citizenship either in Malaya or abroad. It was defined as a status held in common with citizens of all other Commonwealth countries. To meet the problem posed by the status of the "subjects of the Queen" in the former Settlements, a provision was added whereby citizens of the "United Kingdom and Colonies" might register as Malayan citizens within a period of one year after independence.[21] In return for their support of the Commonwealth citizenship proposals, the Alliance successfully demanded that the oath of allegiance required of citizens include the specific renunciation of loyalty to all foreign nations and states.[22] Retained from the Reid draft were the provisions for the termination of citizenship upon acts of disloyalty or by voluntarily taking advantage of foreign citizenship. However, the final form of the Constitution does not carry this penalty for the exercise of Commonwealth citizenship, provided the rights so exercised are available to all other Commonwealth citizens.[23]

In summary, we may note that the highly explosive issue of citizenship was settled by creating, in effect, a single nationality with provisions to enable all persons in Malaya to qualify for citizenship, either by birth or by fulfilling requirements of residence, language and oath of loyalty. The implications of these provisions were clear. The proportion of citizens from the non-Malay communities would steadily rise and in time the Malays, who were a numerical minority in Malaya, might also become a minority at the polls. It was a major concession by the Malays to agree to such liberal citizenship requirements. The United Malays National Organization was persuaded to accept these provisions on the understanding that the Constitution would contain other sections which would give to the Malays special privileges.

Malay Special Privileges

Ever since the first British administration in Malaya, it had been government policy to give the Malays certain privileges on the assumption that they alone were indigenous to Malaya and needed both political and economic protection. Under the Federation Agreement of 1948, Malay privileges continued in four main areas of public policy: the system of Malay reservations, reserving certain lands for Malays only; the operation of quotas within the public services reserving a certain portion for Malays; the operation of quotas for licenses and permits for certain businesses, chiefly those related to road transport; and special quotas for public scholarship and educational grants.

The Alliance Government decided to continue these traditional policies, and in the terms of reference to the Reid Commission instructed it to provide means for "safeguarding the special position of the Malays". However, these same terms of reference also called for the creation of "a common nationality". The Commission expressed some difficulty in reconciling these two principles. Special rights to one community precludes equality before the law and creates separate rights for two classes of citizens. The instruction to create "a common nationality" is incompatible with a permanent granting of special privileges to some citizens on the basis of race. Although the Commission expressed a preference for equality, it also realized that the Malays would suffer if these special privileges were suddenly withdrawn. Consequently, it proposed that the existing Malay privileges should be continued "for a substantial period, but that in due course the present preferences should be reduced and should ultimately cease".[24] In pursuance of this objective, the Commission included in its draft a prohibition against increasing the total area in a State allocated to Malay reservations. Special quotas giving preference to Malays might be changed by the simple process of ordinary legislation, while the reduction or dissolution of Malay Reservations would, according to the Reid Proposals, require a two-thirds majority in the appropriate State legislature.[25]

The most criticized parts of the Reid Report were those bearing on the special privileges for the Malays. Both the Alliance and the Rulers responded to this criticism by carrying "the case for the Malays" to the London Conference. Because the Reid Report had provided for the continuation of the Malay privileges existing under the Federation Agreement, most of the objection was directed at the provisions for their termination. The Reid Report recommendation that Malay privileges should be reviewed within fifteen years with a view toward the eventual abolition of these preferential rights[26] was deleted in the final draft to avoid the implication that Malay special rights were to be abandoned at some future date. Moreover, the Paramount Ruler,[27] as a Malay, was given "the special responsibility of safeguarding the special position of the Malays and the legitimate interests of other communities".[28] The same responsibility was entrusted to the Rulers or Governors for the protection of Malay rights within each State. However as constitutional rulers, they were enjoined to act on the advice of the Prime Minister and Cabinet or the Chief Minister or Mentri Besar in their respective States.

An additional concession to the Malays' demand for special rights was made in regard to Malay Reservations. The Reid restriction on increasing the existing total areas within Malay Reservations in any State was deleted and replaced by the proviso that the States might retain or increase the land within the Malay Reservations until the area represented fifty per cent of the total area available for general private land use. Similarly, the new States of Penang and Malacca, not being "Malay States" were given the right to institute the system of Malay Reservations on the same terms as all other States in the Federation.[29]

The final constitution provided an added guarantee of Malay privileges by requiring the approval of the Rulers Conference on any legislation or administrative act changing the status of Malay privileges. Furthermore, amendments to the legal status of Malay Reservations was made especially difficult by the requirement of an enactment passed by a two-thirds vote in the State Legislature and a similar resolution passed by a two-thirds vote in each House of Parliament.[30] Land policy pertaining to Malay Reservations was thus placed in the anomalous position of being more difficult to amend than the Constitution itself, which could be amended by a two-thirds vote in each House of Parliament. In view of the Malay domination of state governments and the preponderance of power they enjoyed in the Senate and the House, the likelihood of the reduction of Malay Reservations became inconceivable. The system of Malay Reservations thus became enshrined in the present constitution as a permanent feature of land policy, to the detriment of the non-Malay communities.

Two other additions made in the final draft Constitution had a bearing on the privileged position of the Malays, though these additions were not classified as special privileges. The first involved religion, and the second language.

Following the practice under the Federation Agreement, the majority of the Reid Commission had not proposed a revision of the system whereby the Ruler of each State was established as the head of the Muslim religion for that State. The Malays represented through the Alliance sought to make Islam the official religion in the Federation, besides retaining the practice of each Ruler being the head of the Muslim religion for his own State. Such a provision was added to the Constitution as well as one conferring upon the Paramount Ruler responsibility for the Muslim religion in the two non-Malay States of Penang and Malacca. The provisions making Islam the official religion of Malaya were accompanied by articles to the effect that "every person has a right to profess and practice his religion" and may propagate it, except that "state law may control or restrict the propagation of any religious doctrine or belief among persons professing the Muslim religion".[31]

In many of the newly independent nations of the world that were formerly under colonial rule, the question of national language has become a political problem that has created internal dissension and stimulated the emotions of communalism. Malaya is no exception. The Reid Commission proposed to deal with this question by making Malay the national language, subject to the provision that for a period of ten years or more, as determined by Parliament, English might be used for official purposes, and both the Chinese and Indian languages would be permitted in Parliament and the State Legislatures. The Merdeka Constitution contained three changes from these proposals. First, no person shall be prohibited from using or learning any language. Secondly, "Federal and State Governments shall have the right to preserve and sustain the use and study of the language of any community", and thirdly, the national language is Malay, but English may also be used in any legislature or court for a period of at least ten years after Merdeka Day. No other languages may be used in legislative proceedings.[32]

It can be seen from the revisions made to the Reid Report that the labors of the Working Committee and the subsequent London negotiations resulted in some very substantial concessions to the Malays on the issues of special privileges, religion and languages. Some have questioned whether these concessions will really strengthen the position of the Malays in the long run. In any event, these decisions were made part of the "fundamental law of the land" and will be extremely difficult to revise as long as the country remains committed to the "rule of law" as established under the present Constitution.

The Position and Power of the Rulers

Although there was no serious agitation for the abolition of the Malay Rulers, the Reid Commission still had to devise a formula whereby the nine Malay Rulers could fit into a democratic, parliamentary, federal system composed of eleven states. The Reid Commission proposed that a single, constitutional monarch be elected for the Federation by the Conference of Rulers from among their number on the basis of seniority, for a term of five years.[33] After serving a term as Paramount Ruler, a Ruler would lose his seniority for purposes of election. This system created a rotation of the office of Paramount

Ruler among all the nine Malay Rulers who are not minors and do not withdraw their name from candidacy at the time of election. The Conference of Rulers was given the discretion to vote against the Ruler with the greatest seniority if the members believed that he was unsuitable for the office of Paramount Ruler. The next in order of seniority would then be considered for the office. These proposals of the Reid Commission were incorporated into the final constitution with no significant revision.[34]

The constitution drafted by the Reid Commission relegated the Rulers to the position of constitutional and ceremonial heads of state, having almost no functions that might be separated from the responsibility of elected ministers, both State and Federal. The notable exception was the provision that the Paramount Ruler might dissolve or refuse to dissolve Parliament at his own discretion, and he was free to exercise his own judgment in selecting a Prime Minister who would be likely to command the support of the House. The Reid draft continued the Conference of Rulers as a body, but gave it only one significant function—that of electing the Paramount Ruler for the five-year term of office.

The Rulers were understandably apprehensive over these proposals to divest them of nearly all substantive authority. Their objections were voiced in the Working Committee sessions and later at the London Conference. Accordingly, the final constitution which emerged from this conference gave the Rulers a number of functions which would not impair the responsibility of elected government, but could be justified from the point of view of upholding the Constitution or of protecting the special position of the Malays and of the Muslim religion.

Certain categories of legislation, under the *Merdeka* Constitution, required the consent of the Conference of Rulers acting at the discretion of the individual Rulers. These included the following matters: election or removal of the Paramount Ruler and the Deputy Paramount Ruler; advising on appointments; consenting to laws altering State boundaries or affecting the "privileges, position, honours and dignities of Their Highnesses and Governors",[35] and the appointments of the Chief Justice, Judges of the Supreme Court, the Auditor-General, and the members of the quasi-judicial Election Commission and Public Services Commission. The two Governors of Penang and Malacca were added to the membership of the Rulers Conference for all functions except that of electing a Paramount Ruler.[36]

On matters affecting the "special position of the Malays or the legitimate interests of other communities", the consent of the Rulers Conference was also required. But when Malay special interests were to be considered, the Rulers were not permitted to exercise their independent judgment. On this matter the Constitution required that each Ruler or Governor be accompanied in the Rulers Conference by his Mentri Besar, Chief Minister or Prime Minister, and the Rulers were to be bound by the advice of their State Executive Councils, while the Paramount Ruler was similarly bound by the advice of his Cabinet. Thus, for all practical purposes, the issue of Malay rights was subject to approval by the ministers of ten of the States and the

Federal Government, with each of ten States having one vote, while the vote of the remaining eleventh State was cast by the Paramount Ruler on the advice of the Prime Minister.

The Rulers Conference was also given the right to deliberate on any questions of national policy not requiring their approval, but when it met in this capacity, each Ruler or Governor was to be accompanied by his Mentri Besar, Chief Minister, or Prime Minister, and was subject to his minister's advice.[37]

In summary, it may be noted that the Rulers Conference was given three separate functions: first, some legislation required the consent of the Rulers acting on their own discretion; secondly, revision of Malay privileges required the consent of the Rulers acting on their minister's discretion; and thirdly, the Rulers Conference might be used as the vehicle for discussion of national policy by the State and Federal ministers acting through their respective Rulers or Governors.

Parliament

The Reid proposals for the composition and election of a national parliament were received with very little criticism, and they were incorporated into the final constitution. Parliament was to be composed of a wholly-elected House of Representatives and an appointed Senate. The House was given primary legislative authority in the tradition of British parliamentary institutions. The maximum term of office of the House was set at five years, with the possibility of dissolution earlier by the Paramount Ruler. The membership of the House was fixed at one hundred except for the first election after independence, when the Constitution called for the election of one hundred and four members from the then existing fifty-two electoral constituencies. The Constitution provided for redistricting by a permanent Election Commission which was responsible for reapportionment into one hundred constituencies determined on the basis of population, the means of communication and the distribution of the different racial communities.[38]

The Constitution called for an initial Senate membership of 33, 22 members to be elected by the State Legislative Assemblies and 16 nominated by the Paramount Ruler on the advice of his ministers. Parliament by an ordinary enactment might, (*a*) increase the number of Senators elected by each State from two to three, (*b*) decrease the number nominated by the Paramount Ruler, or (*c*) provide direct popular election of Senators. The Senator's term of office was fixed at six years, with one half of their number being elected or appointed every three years.[39]

The powers of the Senate were largely confined to a limited delay of bills. An ordinary bill may be delayed by the Senate for one year, but the period of delay of a money bill was reduced to 21 days. The real power of the Senate was exercised in the matter of an amendment to the Constitution, which required a two-thirds majority in both House and Senate, with no provision for the House to overrule the Senate. Because 22 members of the Senate were to be appointed by the State Legislative Assemblies, the Senate was supposed to represent the views of the States providing them with a bulwark of "states rights" against unwarranted encroachment of federal power. An impasse creating a constitutional crisis would be difficult to break by means of the power of creating additional seats in the Senate. Over the objection of a Senate majority, this process would take a year, and the additional seats would be elected by the State Assemblies or directly by popular election. Any changes made by Parliament, under the terms of the Constitution, could only result in increasing the proportion of Senate members elected by the States. Because of the Alliance's ability to control the election and nomination of Senators, the Senate became little more than a "rubber stamp" for bills emanating from the lower house. If an effective two- or multi-party system emerges, the Senate could eventually develop a character quite distinctive from the House of Representatives. Whether the Senate will become the champion of "states rights" or merely the refuge of tired statesmen remains to be seen.

Federalism and the Power of the States

A federal system of government is frequently plagued by continuous controversy over the distribution of power. Aligned on one side are those favouring strong, centralized government able to pursue, without hindrance, coherent national plans. On the other side are those who favor decentralization in order to stimulate local responsibility and enable the adaptation of policy to the peculiar circumstances of each particular area. In Malaya these traditional protagonists have been facing each other since the early days of the British administration. The need for uniformity of policy prompted the formation of the first federal system in Malaya—the Federated Malay States—dating from 1895 and including only four of the nine Malay States.[40] In a previous chapter reference was made to the ill-fated Malayan Union of 1946 which had to be abandoned, partly because of the inappropriate application of a unitary form of government to Malaya. The federal compromise incorporated in the subsequent Federation Agreement proved more compatible with the political climate of Malaya.

As has been noted earlier, the Federation Agreement of 1948 provided for highly centralized legislative powers residing in the Federal Government, and greatly decentralized administrative powers exercised by the State Governments in execution of both Federal and State legislation. The Reid Commission considered this division of authority between the Federal and State Governments to be unsound from the point of view of democratically responsible government, and proposed a fundamental revision of the federal structure to enable legislative power and executive responsibility to emanate from the same source of authority. Three lists of subjects were drafted to divide powers and responsibilities between the Federal and State Governments. The first list defined federal subjects, the second state subjects, and the third concurrent subjects upon which both Federal and State Governments might legislate. The use of defined powers for both federal and state governments follows the pattern of federal division of powers employed in India and Australia. As in most federal systems, a "supremacy clause" was included to establish the higher legal status of federal powers. A "residual powers" clause allocated all undefined subjects to the States, partly on the assumption that the Federal Government is the creature of the States from which ultimate authority is derived.

The major subjects allocated to the Federal and State Governments in the Reid Report include the following.[41]

Federal List	State List	Concurrent List
Defence	Land Laws and licenses	Social welfare
External affairs		Scholarships
Internal affairs	Muslim law, religion and Malay custom	Protection of wild animals
Civil and criminal law		
Federal citizenship, naturalization and aliens	Agriculture	Town and country planning
State and Federal elections	Local government	Vagrancy
	Local services	Drainage and irrigation
Finance, trade, commerce and industry	State works and water	
	State government	Rehabilitation of mining land
Shipping		
Communications		
Federal works and power		
Surveys		
Education		
Medicine and health		
Labor and social security		
Welfare of aborigines		
Censorship and publications		

Flexibility was provided within the federal system through the power of delegation whereby federal powers could be delegated to the States or state powers to the Federation through agreements made by executive action. In addition, the Federal Parliament was given power to pass model legislation on state subjects, but this legislation required adoption by the State, either with or without amendments, before the legislation became part of the law of that state. Thereby, Parliament was able to set a standard of uniform legislation which the States might adopt if they desired.

Government finance has always presented special problems of federal-state relations in Malaya. Federal revenues are derived mostly from import and export duties and income tax, while the bulk of state revenues comes from land. The state revenues have almost never been sufficient to meet state expenditures. Under the Federation Agreement deficit was made up by federal funds which were transferred to the States by allocations and grants. As an example, in 1956 between 60 per cent and 83 per cent of state funds were obtained from federal allocations. Federal grants to the States brought the States under even greater federal control than might be assumed from a strict legal reading of the division of powers enunciated in the Federation Agreement.[42]

Through the power of the purse, the Federation maintained a tight reign on state finances, and thereby helped to create uniformity in state administration. Clearly, this practice was causing a weakening of the federal system which, by its terms of reference, the Reid Commission was called upon to uphold. Consequently, the Commission sought to find the means for making the States independent of direct federal supervision through the power of the purse. The Commission might have proposed that some independent taxing authority be transferred to the State List of powers. Instead, it proposed to give the States a more precise share of federal funds to be determined for a five-year period, rather than a year-to-year allocation. Moreover, it suggested that a defined "formula" be used for the allocation of federal revenues—one which might be determined by the population and the mileage of the state road system. It was also proposed that certain percentages of duties collected, say on tin, be automatically remitted by the Federation to the State of origin or destination as the case may be. One of the largest of state expenditures under the Federation Agreement had been for education. By transferring this responsibility to the Federal List, the Commission believed that the States would be strengthened *vis-a-vis* the Federal Government by their having to rely less upon federal funds. Nevertheless, the Reid Commission candidly stated that the federal system must rely upon funds forthcoming from federal revenues for the substantial support of all levels of government. On the other hand, the Commission pointed out that if the States were to have an independent existence and be given the authority to both legislate and administer on certain designated matters, they should also have independent sources of income not subject to the discretion of the Federal Government.[43]

Although the Reid formula was taken as the basis for the division of authority between the Federation and the States, a number of important revisions appear in the final Constitution. The Reid decision to guarantee certain Federal revenues to the States was incorporated into the new Constitution, but certain minor amendments were made in the formula for calculating federal revenues due to the States as a matter of right. The calculations were to be made on the basis of a capitation grant, a road grant and the guarantee of certain taxes and fees collected by the Federation from sources within each State.[44] To provide coordination and national planning, the Reid Commission proposed a National Finance Council composed of Federal and State representatives. The Federal Government would be required to consult this Council on matters relating to auditing of accounts and financial accounting procedures. This proposal was incorporated into the final Constitution with inconsequential amendments.

Land policy is another issue that was the subject of contention between those favoring state powers and those favoring federal powers. The Malay States were traditionally responsible for the administration of land laws, although the responsibility for legislation on matters of land had at various times been exercised by both the States and the Federation. Under the Federation Agreement, land legislation was within the legislative competence of the Federation, but the States both administered the land laws and obtained all revenues from land licenses and quit rents (the equivalent of a property tax). A certain standard of uniformity in the land laws was deemed to be essential to land utilization, particularly in view of the importance of land policy to the rubber and tin industries—the cornerstones of Malaya's economy.[45] The Reid Report abandoned this somewhat irrational division between authority and responsibility for land policy, in favor of a system which gave to the States sole responsibility for both land legislation and administration. The Report also proposed that the admitted need for uniformity of land laws in the different States might be accomplished by federal enactment, after consultation with the States, of a uniform National Land Code, which each State would be free to adopt or amend as the circumstances dictated.[46]

On matters of land and local government, the Working Committee disagreed with the Reid Commission on the ground that the Federation Agreement provisions for ensuring uniformity of land legislation and a common land policy should be preserved both in the interests of the States and for the well-being of the country as a whole. Accordingly, the new Constitution gave the Federation power to make laws on matters relating to land and local government "for the purpose of ensuring uniformity of law and policy". However, executive authority over and responsibility for these matters could not be conferred upon the Federation without the approval of the Legislative Assemblies of the respective States.[47]

Because of the joint Federal-State responsibility for land, the Working Committee provided for a separate organ of government to consider and formulate national policy in regard to all matters relating to land, such as land utilization and control, mining, agriculture and forestry. This body, the National Land Council, was to be composed of one representative of each of the eleven States and no more than ten representatives of the Federal Government. The Constitution stated that "the Federal and State Governments shall follow the policy so formulated", but it appeared that this was a statement of obligation that would be difficult to enforce through legal action. However, since the Federation was given the overriding power to enact uniform legislation on matters relating to land, it appeared highly unlikely that the National Land Council would not reflect the view of the Federation Government of the day, since that government may appoint ten of the possible twenty-one members on the Council.

To provide some perspective in regard to the changes made in Malaya's federal system, let us briefly summarize the stages in the development of this important constitutional issue. The federal system in operat on from 1948 to

185

1957 was a hybrid political creature in comparison with most other federal systems, in that legislative powers were centralized in an almost unitary manner in the Federal Government, while the States were given the largest share of responsibility for administration. In 1956 the Reid Commission recommended the more traditional division of powers so that the government competent to legislate on a matter would also have responsibility for the administration of its legislation. To implement this recommendation, the Reid Commission proposed a list of federal and state powers combining legislative authority with executive responsibility. When the Reid proposals were considered by the Working Committee and after the subsequent London negotiations, the decision was made to retain in the new constitution the features which permit the Federation, for purposes of uniformity, to legislate on matters within the competence of the States. Thus, on matters of land and local government, legislative authority rested with both Federal and State Governments (with Federal legislation superseding State enactments), and the responsibility for administration of these two subjects rested entirely with the States (except for the capital city of Kuala Lumpur which came under the direct authority of the Federal Government).

The separation of legislative and administrative responsibility for land and local government violated the principles which the Reid Commission considered to be essential for the operation of a responsible democratic federal system. However, conflicts and confusion over the channels of responsibility were expected to be reconciled through informal arrangements and agreements between the States and the Federal Government. The very existence of the National Land Council and the National Finance Council bore witness to the admitted need for Federal-State harmony on policies relating to finance, land and local government. If the consultation and deliberation of these bodies did not result in substantial agreement between the States and the Federation, the new federal structure could aggravate controversies on such issues through the competing and overlapping delineation of Federal-State responsibilities. But such an eventuality was unlikely so long as the Alliance retained preponderant power in both Federal and State Governments.[48]

Civil Rights and Judicial Review

In a democracy having a written constitution, individual rights and liberties may be left to Parliament to determine and protect, or they may be carefully defined and inserted into the constitution as a fundamental statement of law that is supreme above ordinary legislation. The latter form was selected by the Reid Commission which explained its choice as follows:

A Federal constitution defines and guarantees the rights of the Federation and the States: it is usual and in our opinion right that it should also define and guarantee certain fundamental individual rights which are generally regarded as essential conditions for a free and democratic way of life . . . The guarantee afforded by the Constitution is the supremacy of the law and the power and duty of the Courts to enforce these rights and to annul any attempt to subvert any of them whether by legislative or administrative action or otherwise.[49]

The usual provisions guaranteeing personal liberty, freedom of speech and assembly, freedom of religion, equality before the law and rights to property were included by the Reid Commission in a section on fundamental liberties. The Commission did express difficulty in reconciling the principles of equality before the law with its responsibility, set forth in the terms of reference, for the "safeguarding of the special position of the Malays". It may be recalled that the Commission avoided the obvious contradiction between these two principles by leaving Malay "special rights" to the processes of ordinary legislation. No suggestion was made that the Malay "special rights" secured by ordinary legislative enactments might violate the principles enunciated in the constitutional section on fundamental liberties.

The Reid draft constitution incorporated the principle of judicial review over all constitutional questions. The Commission considered judicial review to be essential in a federal system if the autonomy of the States was to be maintained against Federal encroachment. Similarly, they expressed the opinion that the inclusion of fundamental liberties in the Constitution required a legal procedure by which infringements might be challenged by private action in the ordinary courts.[50] Rather than vest the responsibility of constitutional interpretation in a separate Constitutional Court or *ad hoc* Interpretation Tribunal, the Reid constitution placed this responsibility on the ordinary courts.

It was proposed that the judiciary should remain essentially the same as that under the Federation Agreement. Following the practice of Canada, Australia and New Zealand, the Commission proposed that appeals to Her Majesty's Privy Council should be retained, particularly on constitutional matters, since the Privy Council has had considerable experience with other federal constitutions. A legal difficulty was encountered in that after independence the Paramount Ruler would become the "fountain of justice", while appeal to the Privy Council is an appeal to the British Crown and requires an Order-in-Council under the seal of the Crown. To surmount this difficulty imposed by the legal fictions of monarchy, the Commission proposed changes in the legislation of the United Kingdom to permit the Judicial Committee of the Privy Council to accept appeals directly from the Supreme Court of Malaya without invoking a petition to the Crown. The judgment of the Judicial Committee would then be transmitted to the Supreme Court in Malaya which would be bound to enforce it, but in the name of the Paramount Ruler.[51]

The Alliance Government did not accept the arguments supporting judicial review as expounded by the Reid Commission. Rather, it expressed preference for parliamentary supremacy, and its views dominated the Working Committee which reviewed the Reid Report. Accordingly, the constitutional draft was amended to remove some constitutional questions from the purview of the Courts.

Under the *Merdeka* Constitution, the Supreme Court could interpret both federal and state constitutions in cases appearing in any court. However, the Court was denied the right to invalidate an act of Parliament on the grounds of a constitutional limitation of legislative authority involving the following questions: whether a law creates unreasonable restrictions on the right of a citizen to move freely or reside in any part of the Federation; or whether a law imposes unnecessary restrictions on the right of free speech, the right of peaceable assembly or the right to form associations. Other "fundamental liberties" such as freedom of religion, right to equal protection of the laws, and prohibition against discrimination on the basis of religion and race were qualified in the Constitution by permissible exceptions. Under its Emergency Powers, Parliament was given unlimited power to infringe upon the rights of personal liberty, guarantees against banishment of citizens, or freedom of speech, and with these powers Parliament could also legislate in matters exclusively reserved for the States.[52] Thus, the preservation of certain fundamental liberties and the maintenance of the federal system rested to a large extent upon the self-restraint of Parliament. While the Court could play an important role, it was subject to parliamentary supremacy on most issues involving the preservation of constitutional rule.

After the revisions of the Working Committee were made public, the English press in Malaya, joined by some vernacular papers, voiced strong criticism of the abandonment of the principle of judicial review. Some leaders of Malaya's minority communities looked with favor upon judicial guarantees for civil and political rights. Some Malays were also fearful that the rights of the States might be subverted by the Federal Government. Although the new constitution embodied the principle of parliamentary supremacy, this issue was to be revived once again with the formation of the more inclusive Malaysian Federation.[53]

Ratification of the Merdeka Constitution

The first step in the ratification of the new Constitution occurred on June 27, 1957, when the Rulers Conference gave their formal consent to the Constitution. Later the Alliance National Council, composed of the top political leaders from its three communal parties, reviewed the constitutional draft for the final time and made preparations to defend it in the Legislative Council debates which preceded its ratification.[54]

The Legislative Council debates give evidence of an exceptional degree of support for the new Constitution. However, there would have been more criticism had it not been for the party discipline of the Alliance and the general recognition that the compromises in the Constitution could not be re-argued and re-fought at that late date. Although the debate at the first reading lasted almost eleven hours, with some fifty speakers participating, only one member voiced serious criticisms of the new Constitution.[55] The debate at the second reading aired the issue of the function of the courts in protecting fundamental rights and liberties. Two members rose to criticize the amendments to the original Reid draft constitution which removed individual civil rights from the jurisdiction of the courts.[56]

Although few of the communal leaders were entirely satisfied with all features of the Constitution, they demonstrated an amazing spirit of unity in the Legislative Council and freely expressed their gratitude to the British Government and the colonial officials for aid and advice rendered in drafting the Constitution. On August 15 the Legislative Council ratified the draft Constitution by unanimous acclamation.

The Transfer of Power

August 31, 1957, had been selected by the Alliance Government in January, 1956 as the target date for *merdeka*. The necessary preliminary negotiations and work of the Reid Commission had been accelerated to make possible the attainment of independence on or before that date. After the ratification of the new Constitution only two weeks before *Merdeka* Day, the greatest attention of the government was devoted to transitional measures not already agreed upon, and preparation for the ceremonial pageantry to accompany the attainment of independence.

The official ceremonies proclaiming Malaya's independence took place on the evening of August 31. In attendance were representatives of most of the non-Communist Western and Asian nations. The Duke of Gloucester represented the Queen in the final transfer of sovereignty, placing Malaya within the ranks of the independent nations of the Commonwealth.

The *merdeka* ceremonies marked the end of British rule in Malaya, which had dated from 1786 when a treaty with the Sultan of Kedah ceded the Island of Penang to the British East India Company. *Merdeka* had brought to a close a period of 171 years of British rule, interrupted only by the four years of the Japanese occupation. The prewar constitutional structure of Malaya had followed the traditional pattern of colonial government, and in that era the forms of government and administration had remained fairly static. In contrast, the postwar years were marked by vigorous political activity and constitutional experimentation. In the short period of slightly over a decade, Malaya had moved by gradual stages from a colonial regime to that of a fully independent state in the community of nations.

[1] *Straits Times*, August 1, 1955, pp. 1 and 7; August 2, 1955, pp. 1 and 7.

[2] *Malay Mail*, August 20, 1955, p. 1; *Straits Times*, August 23, 1955, pp. 1 and 2.

[3] *Legislative Council Debates, 30th and 31st August 1955*, Federation of Malaya, 34–41.

[4] *Straits Times*, September 3, 1955, p. 7.

[5] *Straits Times*, October 20, 1955, p. 1; November 9, 1955, p. 1.

[6] *Legislative Council Debates, 3rd December 1955*, Federation of Malaya, 77.

7 Sir Ibrahim's speech from the throne marked the climax of celebrations commemorating his sixtieth year as a ruling monarch. The Mentri Besar of Johore was not consulted on the contents of the speech, which contained statements suggesting that independence would lead to disaster and Communist rule. At the next meeting of the Johore State Council, the Alliance majority passed a resolution censuring the Sultan for his remarks, and calling upon him to consult with the Mentri Besar before making political speeches. This prolonged dispute between the Alliance and the Sultan of Johore threatened to disrupt the impending deliberations on constitutional revision. Note *Sunday Times*, September 18, 1955, pp. 1 and 11; *Straits Times*, September 19, 1955, p. 1; *Malay Mail*, December 17, 1955, p. 1.

8 *Straits Times*, December 22, 1955, p. 1; December 23, 1955, pp. 1 and 4.

9 *Straits Times*, January 17, 1956, p. 1.

10 *Self-Government for the Federation of Malaya, Report of the Constitution Conference London, January-February 1956* (Kuala Lumpur: Government Press, 1956).

11 *Ibid.*, p. 2. These measures were implemented in March 1956, after approval by the Rulers Conference and the Legislative Council.

12 *Federation of Malaya Information Services*, Bulletin No. 6072/56, pp. 1–2.

13 *Straits Times*, July 18, 1956, p. 5.

14 For reports on some of the negotiations see *Straits Times*, August 23, 1956, p. 7; August 24, 1956, p. 8; August 27, 1956, p. 1.

15 The proposals of the Reid Commission will be examined later in conjunction with an account of the constitution as finally adopted.

16 *Federation of Malaya Constitutional Proposals*, Council Paper No. 41 of 1957, Federation of Malaya; *Straits Times*, February 8, 1957, p. 7; February 25, 1957, p. 7; March 29, 1957, pp. 1 and 9; July 1, 1957, pp. 1 and 7; *Sunday Times*, June 30, 1957, pp. 1 and 5.

17 The unresolved issues, as reported unofficially in the papers, had been narrowed to the following: the status of Penang and Malacca upon the withdrawal of the sovereignty of the Crown; the question of appeals to the Privy Council; some legal technicalities concerning the revoking of the Federation Agreement; the extent of autonomous power for the States; financial rights of the States; and control of land by the States. See *Straits Times*, May 2, 1957, pp. 1 and 7; May 9, 1957, pp. 1 and 9.

18 *Report of the Federation of Malaya Constitutional Commission, Appendices II, III, and IV*, Kuala Lumpur: Government Press, 1957, pp. 128–133, Articles 14–23.

19 *Report of the Federation of Malaya Constitutional Commission* (Kuala Lumpur: Government Press, 1957), p. 87.

20 *Straits Times*, April 5, 1957, p. 4; May 9, 1957, pp. 1 and 7.

21 *Federation of Malaya Constitutional Proposals, Annexe I, II, and III*, Council Paper No. 41 of 1957, Federation of Malaya, p. 90, Article 170.

22 *Straits Times*, May 11, 1957, p. 6.

23 *Constitutional Proposals, Annexe I, II, and III, op. cit.*, pp. 6–14, Articles 14–31.

24 *Report of the Constitutional Commission, op. cit.*, p. 72.

25 *Report of the Constitutional Commission, Appendices II, III and IV, op. cit.*, pp. 150–151, Article 82.

26 *Ibid.*, p. 183, Article 157.

27 This is the title given to the Ruler selected as the constitutional monarch for the entire Federation.

28 *Constitutional Proposals, Annexe I, II, and III, op. cit.*, p. 74, Article 153.

29 *Constitutional Proposals, op. cit.*, p. 18.

30 *Constitutional Proposals, Annexe I, II, & III, op. cit.*, p. 40, Article 89.

31 *Ibid.*, p. 5, Article 11.

32 *Ibid.*, pp. 73–74, Article 152.

33 The Malay title is *Yang di-Pertuan Agong*; the English title is Paramount Ruler.

34 *Constitutional Proposals, Annexe I, II, and III, op. c t.*, pp. 96–98, Third Schedule.
 When the first Paramount Ruler was elected, the senior Ruler was the Sultan of Johore, who withdrew his name for reasons of health. The next in seniority was the Sultan of Pahang, who had just become involved in a scandal by secretly marrying a young dancing girl from a very common background. To comply with the Muslim limitation of four wives, he had to divorce one of his previous wives to marry this girl. For some time after the marriage his previous four wives had not been informed which one was divorced. In view of this unfavorable publicity attending his marital involvement, the Conference of Rulers considered him unsuitable for Paramount Ruler. The third in order of seniority was the Ruler of Negri Sembilan, who thus became Malaya's first Paramount Ruler.

35 *Constitutional Proposals, Annexe I, II, and III, op. cit.*, pp. 17–18, Article 38.

36 *Constitutional Proposals, op. cit.*, p. 6.

37 *Constitutional Proposals, Annexe I, II, and III, op. cit.*, p. 17, Article 38, (3).

38 *Ibid.*, p. 22, Article 46, pp. 53–55, Articles 113–117. *The Constitution (Amendment) Act, 1962* fixed the size of the House at 104 and transferred to Parliament the responsibility for reapportionment after receiving recommendations of the Election Commission. See *Federation of Malaya Government Gazette, 1962*, L. N. 164.

39 *Malayan Constitutional Documents*, 2nd ed. Vol. 1 (Federation of Malaya: Government Printer, 1962), pp. 53–54, Art. 45. After the formation of the Federation of Malaysia the appointed membership of the Senate was increased to 22. The Malay term for the Senate is Dewan Negara, while the House of Representatives is called Dewan Ra'ayat.

40 Rupert Emerson, *Malaysia—A Study in Direct and Indirect Rule*, (New York: The Macmillan Co., 1937), pp. 136–137.

41 *Report of the Constitutional Commission, Appendices II, III and IV, op. cit.*, pp. 204–209, Sixth Schedule.

42 *Report of the Constitutional Commission, op. cit.*, p. 56.

43 *Ibid.*, pp. 59–65.

44 The capitation grant was calculated at $15 per person for the first 50,000 population; $10 per person for the next 200,000 population; and $4 per person for the remaining population. The road grant was calculated by multiplying the average maintenance cost per mile of road in the Federation with the total road mileage (at a set standard) within each State. In addition, each State was to receive not less than 10 per cent of the export duty on tin produced within it, on such terms and conditions as may be determined by Parliament. Note *Report of the Constitutional Commission, op. cit., pp.* 13–14.

[45] Even with land a subject of Federal legislative power, many of the land laws dated from the prewar era. Thus the former Federated Malay States had essentially uniform land enactments, while the former Unfederated Malay States retained many land enactments that were not uniform.

[46] *Report of the Constitutional Commission, op. cit.*, pp. 35–40.

[47] *Constitutional Proposals, Annexe I, II and III, op. cit.*, pp. 32–33, Article 76.
There are several phrases in this article which the Federal Government could employ to justify legislation on almost any topic. These could become the focal point for controversy between the Federation and the States over constitutional interpretation.

[48] For an explanation of the role of the Senate in the federal system see above, pp. 181–182.

[49] *Report of the Constitutional Commission, op. cit.*, p. 70.

[50] *Ibid.*, p. 52.

[51] *Ibid.*, pp. 54–55.

[52] *Constitution of the Federation of Malaya*, Articles 5–13, 129–130, and 149–151. See also L. A. Sheridan (ed.), *Malaya and Singapore, The Borneo Territories, the Development of their Laws and Constitutions*, (London: Stevens & Sons, 1961), pp. 55–66.

[53] The events leading to the formation of the Malaysian Federation are examined in Chapter 16. The creation of Malaysia revived the issue of judicial review in a more complicated form, because the Borneo States and Singapore were not completely satisfied that their special status and guarantees in the new federal system would be fully assured if these guarantees were to depend upon the shifting tides of parliamentary majorities. Later events demonstrated that their fears were well-founded.

[54] Before the final constitutional draft was transmitted to the Federal Legislative Council, it became the subject of dissension at the annual general assembly of UMNO. In spite of the added concessions to placate Malay objections to the Reid Report, the support of the Malays in UMNO for the final draft was not enthusiastic. However, the UMNO general assembly did finally give unanimous approval for the Constitution, considering it to be the best that could be obtained under the circumstances.

[55] The critic was S. M. Yong, who was nominated MCA member and a legal advisor to the Federation of Chinese Guilds and Associations. He represented a dissident element that had been within the MCA and had refused to accede to some of the Alliance concessions to the demands of the Malays represented through UMNO. His objections to the new Constitution were mostly directed at the citizenship provisions and the Malay special rights, which he considered to be unfair to the Chinese. See *Legislative Council Debates, 10th July, 1957*, Federation of Malaya, 2878–2886.

[56] S. M. Yong and K. L. Devaser were the two members voicing their objections to the absence of judicial review. The latter was a past-president of the MIC. See *Legislative Council Debates, 15th August 1957*, Federation of Malaya, 3142–3178.

13 The Alliance Government

After the Alliance came to power, policies for many difficult problems had to be worked out gradually by the Alliance partners. The election manifesto was very vague on many issues, and even where it was fairly precise, specific programs of action had to be formulated. The preceding chapter has examined the implementation of the Alliance promise to secure Malayan independence. This one will examine some of the internal politics of the Alliance coalition.

Communalism

In one form or another, communalism had been a recurring issue that was particularly difficult for the Alliance Government. In part, this may be ascribed to the peculiar structure of the Alliance, composed as it was of communal political associations which took communal stands on political issues, but were generally willing to compromise their position to preserve the unity of the Alliance. Thus, within the Alliance communal politics were intense, but the Alliance policies, once decided upon, were put forth and defended as a non-communal approach to national issues.[1]

Communal pressures within the Alliance became particularly acute during the period when the *Merdeka* Constitution was being drafted. The party was caught up in the midst of these disputes because the Alliance Government drafted the terms of reference for the Reid Commission, and its recommendations became the primary basis for both the Reid Report draft constitution and for the final *Merdeka* Constitution. On such sensitive communal issues as the national language or languages, citizenship, Malay "special rights" and education policy, communal demands threatened the unity of the Alliance. Local branches of the member parties began passing resolutions demanding that the Constitution contain certain provisions beneficial to their community. For a time it appeared that the Alliance partners would present conflicting demands to the Reid Commission. To forestall such a development, the top leadership of the Alliance announced that only one memorandum would be submitted to the Reid Commission by the Alliance. Although no memoranda were to be permitted from the affiliated parties, local branches of each Alliance party were invited to submit their views to the general secretary of their party for submission to the Alliance National Council, which assumed the delicate task of drafting the unified memorandum for submission to the Reid Commission.

This formula did little to preserve the unity of the Alliance, because branch organizations began to organize public mass meetings to formulate their demands for submission to the Alliance National Council. Consequently, Chinese were attending mass meetings sponsored by MCA branches, Malays were attending mass meetings sponsored by UMNO branches, and Indians were attending MIC-sponsored mass meetings. To arrest these developments, the Alliance leaders attempted to control the activities of the affiliated party branches while communal issues were being discussed and resolved by the Alliance leaders. Party discipline was subject to severe strains during the period of more than three months of negotiations preliminary to the drafting of the Alliance memorandum to the Reid Commission.

Even after the constitutional debates had come to an end, the major political battles were still along communal lines and were largely fought out within the Alliance. Political agitation within each of the three communal parties was primarily directed at the top Alliance leaders, who had to work out and defend the party's compromise program. Consequently, some tension developed between the UMNO, MCA and MIC leaders and their branch organizations in the states and at the local level. The former had to keep the Alliance in balance and defend the decisions of the Alliance National Council, while the latter felt obliged to defend the communal interests of their constituents with all the vigor at their command. When communal compromise proved difficult, branch organs and outspoken communal critics were more likely to ignore party discipline and defy their more restrained national leaders. In time of crisis, the strongest proponents of communal demands did, on occasion, break away from their party to join an opposition party, or to form another communal political association free from the restraints imposed by the Alliance upon its member associations. Usually, however, the lower organs of the member parties toed the line, but with rumblings of discontent. The way in which the explosive communal issues were resolved by the Alliance was both its secret of success and its ever-present threat of disaster.

The dynamics of politics within the Alliance can best be understood by viewing some of the political factions and examining some of the political activities associated with each constituent party.

The Alliance and UMNO

Because UMNO was founded during the upsurge of Malay political consciousness that accompanied the Malayan Union, the party attracted support from nearly all the elements that compose the Malay community. Most important, however, was the cooption of the traditional Malay leadership elites that were part of the "court circles" at the state levels. UMNO's critics, particularly in the first few years of its existence, characterized these traditional elites as "bureaucratic, reactionary and feudalistic". In fact, they were usually more modern, more tolerant, and less tradition-bound than the subelites in Malay society, represented by the Malay teachers in the kampong schools, the religious teachers, and the Islamic clergy. The explanation can be found in the education which the Malay aristocracy received, nearly always in

English schools, often followed by study abroad. Although more cautious about upsetting traditional patterns of authority, these established Malay leaders were more exposed to the modern world, more cosmopolitan and tolerant, and generally more western and progressive in outlook than the sub-elites.

By contrast, UMNO also recruited the lesser elites and the common Malays who were not associated with the "court circles" and not necessarily dedicated to the preservation of the prerogatives of their traditional leaders. A few of these were attracted to leftist, anti-aristocratic protest movements that have at times been flavored with ideas of social or political revolution. And yet, by and large, Malays in the secondary leadership strata were quite conservative and tradition-bound, while exhibiting a strong sense of Malay communal nationalism.

The small segment of radical leftist Malay opinion, inspired in part by political currents from Indonesia, could also be found within UMNO. At first glance, these radical leftist elements appeared to be liberated from the fetters of tradition and not greatly motivated by Malay chauvinism. On closer analysis, these Malay radicals had much in common with the conservative tradition-bound sub-elites. The former hoped to promote and protect Malay interests through policies that would give the Malays privileged economic and political position in the country, while preserving the Malays' traditional social and religious patterns. The former also hoped to promote Malay interests, but through "non-racial" economic controls and expropriation that would, in practice, be directed against the more wealthy non-Malay communities with the aim of raising the economic position of the "ordinary people" (*ra'ayat*), which by definition means the peasant Malays. On racial issues, the most noticeable difference was in the political language being employed. The conservative orthodox-Muslim Malays were much more willing to make direct communal appeals, while the left-oriented Malays disguised their objectives in the semi-Marxist terminology of class conflicts, but in practice directed their attack almost exclusively against the non-Malay "capitalists". Both these wings exhibited marked "anti-Western" and "anti-foreign" sentiments.

It is not easy to classify UMNO leaders according to their membership of various factions. As practical politicians, many of them had cultivated the political art of "being all things to all people". However, it should be noted that a large proportion of the top leadership of the party was drawn from the ranks of the traditional elites of Malay society, including the Prime Minister, the Deputy Prime Minister, and a majority of the Malay members of the Cabinet.[2] While the traditional-communal Malay chauvinists and the Malay radical leftists were to be found within UMNO, they were the main critics of the top UMNO leadership, and were largely denied higher office within the party. Until 1963, the outstanding exception was Abdul Aziz bin Ishak, who for many years was Minister of Agriculture and Cooperatives until his removal from the Cabinet and his ultimate resignation from UMNO.[3] Although characterized as a "left-wing Malay", he was removed because of

195

economic policies which would have promoted Malay cooperatives by eliminating the Chinese from certain businesses after revoking their licenses. The conservative-traditional elements were scattered through the party at the state level and in its ancilliary organizations. At the top level, the President of UMNO Youth, Dato Sardon bin Haji Jubir, was said to be most representative of the UMNO right wing, although this may have been an unfair characterization.[4]

Some of the factional divisions in UMNO were the result of powerful Malay interest groups which worked through UMNO to promote their more specific objectives. One of the most active interest groups operating in and out of UMNO politics was the Federation of Malay School Teachers' Associations (FMSTA). This organization, claiming a membership of 10,000 Malay teachers[5] became involved in an extended fight to promote Malay education, particularly at the secondary level. Chafing at the rather restricted job opportunities for the Malay-educated, the FMSTA became a leading force in Malay chauvinism, demanding exclusive use of the national language (Malay) in government, the rapid expansion of the Malay-media school system, and equal status and pay for Malay school teachers compared with the higher-quality English and Chinese-medium schools. At stake were more and better jobs for both Malay teachers and the large number of Malays who had only attended Malay schools. The issues involved cut across UMNO factional divisions, but the FMSTA had its strongest supporters among the younger Malays who were more keenly conscious of job competition and opportunities Although ably represented by a number of UMNO stalwarts, its demands were not all met by the Alliance Government. To back up its demands the FMSTA called for a mass boycott of UMNO, and staged rallies and demonstrations against the government. In Kota Bahru demonstrations degenerated into student riots.[6] Both the Pan-Malayan Islamic Party and Party Negara tried to capitalize on this Malay discontent which was most intense on the East Coast where Malay educational and employment opportunities were dismal. Later, Tunku Abdul Rahman tried to come to some understanding with the FMSTA to win back its support for the 1959 elections.[7] However, the election results suggest that the FMSTA members contributed more to the strength of the Pan-Malayan Islamic Party and Party Negara than to the Alliance. In any event, the FMSTA was but one of a number of Malay organizations that were willing to play a dual political game both within UMNO and within rival Malay parties.

The organization and constitution of UMNO was a matter of recurring dispute. The party was composed of a heirarchy of branch, division, state and national organs. There existed a continuous tug between the national and state party leaders on the extent of central direction over lower party bodies. The pressures for decentralization were greatest when the national leaders had to work out difficult compromises among the Alliance partners over issues, or even more difficult, over candidate selection. At these times, the national party leadership was most anxious to strengthen party discipline and centralize the party apparatus. In 1955 the State Executive Committee gained extensive powers over state affairs, which stimulated the growth of separate state machines and, in some states, resulted in prolonged factional fights over the control of the State Executive Committee. In 1959 the party high command attempted to change the UMNO constitution to strengthen central control, but key state organizations successfully blocked most of the proposed amendments. The selection of candidates for the Alliance ticket in 1959 caused much turmoil within the party, particularly in constituencies where MCA or MIC candidates were selected to run. The extreme bickering and factionalism within UMNO at the lower levels during 1959 must have been an object lesson to the party, since a new constitution was adopted in 1960 which eliminated the State Executive Committees and replaced them with "State Liaison Committees" having minimal authority over the lower organs of the party. The Supreme Executive Council was given full powers to determine policies, select candidates, supervise the lower organs, and settle party disputes. Regional boards were set up to deal with matters of party discipline, with ultimate appeal to the Supreme Executive Council.[8]

Three auxiliary organizations were founded by UMNO. The most important was UMNO Youth, which attracted a large membership from among the Malay-educated youth, and represented a substantial force in UMNO politics. The leader of the UMNO Youth, Inche Sardon bin Haji Jubir, was a Cabinet Minister and was known to have a very large national following within UMNO. For a time he was even mentioned as a possible successor to Tunku Abdul Rahman. A second UMNO auxiliary was Kaum Ibu (Women's Movement). It developed as a political extension of the Women's Institutes which the Government sponsored during the Emergency to promote social welfare projects among the Malay women living in the rural *kampongs*. Kaum Ibu grew in political importance, but Malay women never became an active independent force in Malay politics. Even so, Kaum Ibu helped to get the women's vote out for UMNO, and its leaders raised their voices for women's rights on such issues as reform of Muslim marriage and divorce laws, control of prostitution, and equal pay and equal educational opportunities for women.[9] The Ulama Section (Religious Leaders Section) was another functional arm of UMNO. It was designed to enlist the political support of the Malays through the influence in Malay society enjoyed by the established Muslim religious leaders. The first attempt to organize the *ulama* in a separate body was made in 1950 in one division in Selangor.[10] However, nothing was done on a wider scale until July 1959 when the competition of the Pan-Malayan Islamic Party for the Muslim vote became more than obvious.[11] The Ulama Section gave added emphasis to the promises contained in the UMNO Constitution to safeguard, preserve and promote Islam in Malaya. Its effectiveness in combating the appeal of the PMIP among the devout orthodox Muslims is difficult to assess, but it did provide a vehicle for the representation of Muslim religious leaders within the councils of UMNO. As such, this organization tended to be associated with the more brazenly communal factions in UMNO.

Because UMNO was designed to be the political expression of Malay opinion, it consistently advanced the "case for the Malays" in the intra-Alliance negotiations on public policy. Preceding the formulation of the *Merdeka* Constitution the more extreme communal elements within UMNO concentrated their attention on three major topics: definition of citizenship, Malay "special rights", and educational policy. On the first topic, the communal Malays were very much opposed to citizenship based on the principle of *jus soli* because they feared that very shortly Chinese and Indian voters would outnumber the Malay voters. On the second topic, these Malays wanted a wide number of "special rights" and preferential privileges for Malays in regard to guaranteed representation in government, guaranteed quotas for government employment, commercial license preferences, and preferential land policies. On the third topic, they wanted an educational policy which would make Malay the universal and sole official language of Malaya, and which would propagate the culture and religion of the Malays among the other communities, as well as providing easier access to the public service and opening many more jobs for Malays.

The Alliance policies which emerged after prolonged negotiations among the affiliated partners involved a complex of compromises. The UMNO leaders reluctantly accepted the principle of *jus soli* in return for the acceptance by the Malayan Chinese Association of an educational policy which would make Malay compulsory in all schools and would gradually develop a unified "Malayan" curriculum for the different language-media school systems.[12] The MCA and the MIC also tacitly agreed to a continuation of the four-to-one ratio between Malays and non-Malays recruited for the Malayan Civil Service.[13] In addition, they consented to support Malay as the national language, although other languages were not to be suppressed and English was to be accepted as an official language until 1967 or later. In return, there was an understanding that the Alliance would pursue liberal economic policies which would permit the non-Malays to pursue their economic activities without fear of confiscation or discriminatory taxation.[14]

When the Reid Commission rejected the idea of constitutional guarantees of "special rights" for the Malays, UMNO leaders became disturbed because this went counter to the fundamental understanding worked out among the Alliance partners. Tunku Abdul Rahman was hard pressed by the ultra-communal faction to explain his stand on the alleged "anti-Malay" bias of the Reid Report. A number of "closed door" meetings were held between the national and state UMNO leaders prior to the convening of an UMNO General Assembly in late March 1957. The Tunku received a unanimous vote of confidence after announcing that four major changes would be made in the Reid Commission draft constitution, all of which had been the result of intra-Alliance negotiations: the Paramount Ruler would be given responsibility for safeguarding Malay "special rights"; Islam would become the state religion; Malay would become the only national language; and there would be no provision for dual citizenship.[15]

With the incorporation of these basic compromises into the Constitution, political argument on these issues became somewhat restricted since it was obvious to nearly all factions in the Alliance that Pandora's box would be opened if any major constitutional revision affecting these communal compromises were to be proposed. Within UMNO there were many who chafed at the communal compromises to which their party had become committed. Yet, when dissatisfaction was aired in public, the grievance was nearly always over the interpretation or implementation of the basic Alliance compromises. In 1959, when some of the most militant Malay communalists in UMNO began to engage in loose talk about major constitutional revision beyond the Alliance compromises, the ultra-communal factions in the MCA became alarmed and more militant than ever before. A constitutional and political crisis ensued which might have plunged the country into major racial-communal clashes. As Tunku Abdul Rahman was able to meet successfully the challenge of the militant Chinese chauvinists, he regained favor and prestige in the eyes of the Malays, including those who had been most critical of him for his moderate and compromising stand on communal issues.

The Alliance and the Malayan Chinese Association

The Malayan Chinese Association attempted to become the authoritative spokesman for Chinese interests in Malaya. However, it was seldom able to speak for a majority of the Chinese. This was true partly because the Chinese are a heterogeneous community and were divided over so many political issues. The MCA also had to compete with many other Chinese organizations, such as the Chinese guilds, clan associations, and the large number of Chinese-organized trade unions. Furthermore, the MCA leadership was drawn from one rather small segment of the Chinese community, the western-educated Chinese in business or professional life. Consequently, the political effectiveness of the MCA depended to a large extent upon its ability to win the cooperation of the leaders of other Chinese organizations for the political objectives of the MCA. Where there was general agreement among the Chinese on a political issue, it was comparatively easy to get prominent Chinese leaders to cooperate with and through the MCA. But as a partner of the Alliance, the MCA was not able to espouse Chinese political views without also considering what effect these views might have on the other two communal partners in the Alliance. The national leaders of the MCA had some of the same difficulties as the national leaders of UMNO—both had to defend complex inter-communal compromises against the determined opposition of strong communal factions in the local branches of their respective parties. The tasks of balancing these interests and defending the compromises was perhaps more difficult for the leaders of the MCA, if for no other reason than that the Chinese often got the short end of the communal bargaining simply because they carried less electoral weight than the Malays.

A number of factional struggles developed within the MCA after 1955. In the early days of the party, men closely associated with Tan Cheng-lock and the Chinese Chambers of Commerce held the major leadership positions of the MCA. In the top circles were such names as Colonel H. S. Lee of Selangor, Leong Yew-koh and T. H. Tan of Perak, Wong Pow-nee in Penang, and Tan

Siew-sin, of Malacca, the son of Tan Cheng-lock. It was this group which forged the understanding with the top UMNO leaders which made the Alliance a reality. While Tan Cheng-lock was an important factor in this equation, he was nevertheless, in 1955, an old and frail man, and was increasingly limited in his ability to play an active leadership role. Nonetheless, he was a living symbol of Alliance unity and communal understanding between the Malays and Chinese, even though he had not, in fact, been the architect of the original temporary Alliance agreement which had been negotiated for the 1952 Kuala Lumpur municipal elections.

Within this original circle of MCA leaders, struggles for power between personalities occasionally developed, which may have concealed some political differences within the party. For example, in 1955 Colonel H. S. Lee, then Finance Minister in the Government and Vice-President of the MCA, was defeated for re-election as president of the Selangor MCA by a former subordinate in the party, Ong Yoke-lin, then Minister for Posts and Telecommunications.[16] The press interpreted this as a defeat for the Kuomintang element in the Selangor MCA because of Colonel Lee's former association with the KMT.[17] It is difficult to determine whether major policy issues were at stake in this election. However, it does indicate that upheavals were going on within the party, perhaps because younger men with different ideas were taking a more active part in MCA politics.

As the MCA attempted to expand its political following, new leaders were brought into the party, often coopted from the other Chinese organizations. Except for its leaders, this newer element was largely Chinese-educated, and was undoubtedly more representative of the bulk of the Chinese community. The foremost spokesman for these Chinese were Lau Pak-khuan and Tan Kee-gak.[18] Although not fully in sympathy with the outlook of the MCA leadership, this new blood was willing to utilize the party to represent its point of view, which was distinctly more communal and less concerned about Alliance harmony than Tan Cheng-lock and his followers. Having one foot within the MCA and the other outside it, these more openly communal members subjected the MCA to internal stress. When the Reid Commission was preparing to hold hearings on constitutional proposals, the more communal Chinese wanted the MCA to present a separate memorandum to the Commission stating the "Chinese point of view". Tan Cheng-lock openly invited all Chinese to mobilize their opinion and express it through the MCA.[19] Among others, Chinese guilds and cultural-fraternal associations were invited to attend meetings to consider Chinese representations to the Reid Commission. Within a short time it became apparent that the Chinese guilds were not going to be content with any MCA memorandum that would be watered down in the process of Alliance negotiations. In particular, the Chinese guilds were willing to force the hand of the MCA leadership by launching a major public campaign in favor of *jus soli* as the basis for citizenship even before the Alliance position could be agreed upon. The MCA leaders were fearful that the unity of the Alliance might be threatened by a Chinese ultimatum on this issue.

When the Alliance leaders decided not to permit its three parties to submit separate representations to the Reid Commission, the Chinese guilds became even more independent of the MCA and began to prepare a memorandum of their own for the Commission. It became clear that the Chinese guilds led by Lau Pak-khuan were directly challenging the MCA claims to the leadership of the Chinese. In April, 1956, a move was made to form a "Federation of Chinese Guilds and Organizations" which was to be a thinly veiled political rival to the MCA. Although the proposal was rejected at a mass meeting in Kuala Lumpur,[20] the Chinese guilds and Chinese Chambers of Commerce which supported this proposal continued to act independently of the MCA. Later, one thousand delegates from six hundred Chinese associations assembled to draft resolutions in apparent open defiance of both the Alliance and the MCA. Many of those in attendance were members of the dissident communal factions within the MCA. Resolutions passed at this meeting called for nationality by right of birth; citizenship rights after five years' residence; no language test for citizenship; and the adoption of Chinese as an official language in Malaya.[21]

When the Reid Report was made public in February, 1957, the newly formed Federation of Chinese Guilds and Associations decided to send a delegation to London to attempt to get the British Government to espouse the cause of the Chinese in the final negotiations on the Constitution. The Malayan Chinese Association issued a very strong statement denouncing the trip to London by the delegation from the Chinese guilds as a "foolhardy attempt to divide the Chinese against the Chinese, or to set the Chinese at variance with the other races". The statement went on to accuse the guilds of "wavering in their loyalty" between Malaya and Formosa.[22] Nevertheless, the guild delegation headed by Lau Pak-khuan continued to London where it obtained from the Colonial Secretary the promise that their proposals would be given careful consideration and be incorporated in the final constitution "if possible".[23]

It was obvious that the Malayan Chinese Association could command no respect in the Alliance if it could not have some control over its membership, both while negotiations were in progress and after agreement had been reached. The open defiance of the ultra-communal faction in the MCA made party discipline a crucial issue for the continuing political effectiveness of the MCA. Restraint and caution had, nonetheless, to be used, because the more militant Chinese communalists did indeed enjoy the support and encouragement of the bulk of the Chinese population. Faced with this dilemma, the MCA finally suspended five MCA members who had been most closely associated with the guild delegation to London. Heading the list was Lau Pak-khuan.[24]

The factional split in the MCA that was so apparent during the negotiations for the *Merdeka* Constitution continued to characterize MCA politics for a number of years afterwards. This fundamental division stimulated the rise of a third faction which could see the merit in maintaining the Alliance and keeping on good terms with UMNO. However, it was also sympathetic to the political demands being put forward by the more communal wing, and believed that the MCA could make a much more forceful stand in intra-Alliance politics. This new group began to emerge as a separate entity around 1957. It was led by Dr. Lim Chong-eu, Alliance Whip in Parliament, and was buttressed by the influx of young intellectual western-educated Chinese in Kuala Lumpur, Penang and Ipoh. On the whole, this new blood was motivated by left-wing and socialist political ideals. Although this middle group was not large in itself, it quickly attracted the support of the critics of the existing MCA leadership, and within a comparatively short time it was able to capture the national leadership positions of the MCA. Their success set off a chain of events which subsequently led to one of the most serious political crises since independence. That account must be postponed until attention is given to some of the issues which precipitated the crisis.

The MCA and Educational Policies

In the process of negotiations within the Alliance, the agreement on citizenship was tied to an acceptance of a "Malayan" educational policy for all schools as proposed by a Committee on Education under the chairmanship of Abdul Razak, the Minister for Education. The essential features of this report (popularly known as the "Razak Plan") are as follows: the separate language-medium school systems were to remain; Malay and English were to be compulsory subjects in all schools; all schools were to be made eligible for government grants-in-aid provided they conformed to the educational policy; the content, subject matter and syllabuses in all schools were to be common, even though the medium of instruction would be in different languages. The Razak Plan called for one unified professional teaching service on a unified salary scale with rights and freedom of transfer from one employer to another.[25]

The object of this policy was to develop a common curriculum which would promote a "Malayan outlook" among all the racial communities without sacrificing each community's desire to preserve its own language and cultural identity. "Malayanization" was the term used to refer to the objective of the government's school policy. It represented a compromise between policies of fusion and separation between the racial communities.

For the Chinese schools, this policy meant that the Government was pledged to counter the Chinese nationalistic orientation of the Chinese-medium schools by replacing subjects having a strong bias for China with subjects related to Malaya. The requirement for compulsory teaching of Malay and English in all schools meant that students whose home language was Malay or English would become bi-lingual, while other students would become tri-lingual. In actual practice, under this policy, most Chinese students attending Chinese-medium schools were forced to become quadri-lingual, because nearly all Chinese schools used as the medium of instruction the Chinese national language of *Kuo-Yu*,[26] which no Southeast Asian Chinese normally speak as a mother tongue.

The Razak Plan generated a wave of opposition among the defenders of the Chinese-medium schools. Leading the attack were two organizations most closely identified with the operation of Chinese schools, namely, the United Chinese School Teachers Associations (UCSTA), and the All-Malaya Chinese Schools Management Association (AMCSMA). The mounting bitterness and discontent among the Chinese made it imperative that the MCA play an active role in resolving some of the issues of Chinese education. Accordingly, a "Central Education Committee" was formed under the aegis of the MCA to study the consequences of the Razak Plan for the Chinese schools. This committee called a conference of Chinese educators in February, 1957, which attracted some 200 delegates. This conference "rejected" as "unacceptable" the Alliance Government's education policy as applied to Chinese schools, and appointed a delegation to approach the Government to secure a revision of the proposed Razak Plan.[27] Apparently, however, since the Razak Plan was part of the compromise by which the principle of *jus soli* was to be embodied into the Constitution, a major attack on the Alliance education program involved risks which elected Chinese political leaders were unwilling to take at that time.[28] After three hours' debate in the Legislative Council, the Razak Plan passed without any dissenting votes.[29]

The enactment of the Razak Plan only intensified the increasingly hostile criticism which emanated from a wide variety of Chinese organizations taking up "the cause of Chinese education". The MCA joined in the chorus of protest by sponsoring various conferences and committees to study the problems of Chinese education, and to agitate for alteration of the Government's policies. Under the continuous prodding of the MCA, the Alliance Government finally promised to establish a committee to review the Razak Plan after the August 1959 elections.[30] However, the leading organizations opposing government policy were not convinced that a nine-man government committee headed by Razak and having only three Chinese members would come up with a satisfactory revision of education policy. In April 1959 a large conference of Chinese educationists was held, at which top officials of the MCA were in conspicuous attendance. A set of fifteen demands were drafted for submission to the Federal Government.[31] These added up to a rejection of the "pro-Malay" features of the Razak Plan. They considered Government terms for grants-in-aid to be highly discriminatory against the Chinese education system. They were opposed to the practice of holding promotion examinations in the schools and entrance examinations for Government service only in Malay and English. The government reasoned that these were the two officially recognized languages, and that all educational institutions were required under the Razak Plan to teach these two languages. The Chinese viewed this policy as gross discrimination against graduates from Chinese schools restricting their educational future and clearly limiting their ability to qualify for government positions. Moreover, the shortage of trained language teachers made it impossible for Malay and English to be adequately taught in all Chinese schools—a responsibility which the Chinese felt rested with the Government.

Political Upheaval in the MCA

In the political maneuvering over education policy, the MCA found itself facing in two directions. On one side, it was part of the Alliance Government and officially identified with Alliance policies. Yet frequently MCA leaders, egged on by the Chinese press, cooperated with Chinese communal organizations in attempts to pressure the Government, and even encouraged them to resist government policies.[32] The MCA leaders dared not let the Chinese guilds steal the political initiative nor undermine the political weight and influence of the MCA among the Chinese, for then the MCA would not have been in a position to secure from the Alliance any major concessions for the Chinese. Consequently, it had to counteract the political activity of the Chinese guilds and enforce greater discipline over its members, which was a very risky form of political surgery.

Within the MCA the dissident factions were large but were not in control of the party. These militant communal chauvinists might have withdrawn from the party to form a common political front with the rising tide of Chinese groups which were attracted to the banner of the Federation of Chinese Guilds and Associations. Sensing this decampment, a third "middle road" faction in the MCA began, instead, to recruit new MCA members from these communal organizations in sufficient numbers to tip the balance in their favor, in the hope that the MCA might be made into a more effective political vehicle for the communally conscious Chinese. Alarmed by this development, Tunku Abdul Rahman announced that the Kuomintang was engaged in an organized effort "to infiltrate into Chinese organizations such as the MCA".[33] Some MCA officials echoed this statement in an attempt to pin the Kuomintang label on the troublesome faction, because it would have been foolhardy to engage in a public attack on the Chinese guilds. This label was plausible enough to the outsider since some of the rebels in the MCA had been known for their Kuomintang sympathies. Furthermore, in Selangor where the first signs of political upheaval were clearly evident, the faction challenging the authority of the national MCA leaders secured some support from Colonel H. S. Lee, who was still smarting from his previous defeat in the state organization at the hands of Ong Yoke-lin. In probable reference to Colonel Lee and the Chinese guilds, top MCA officials in Selangor stated that "Kuomintang diehards and stooges" were seeking to undermine the MCA prior to discussions on the new constitution.[34] By employing the Kuomintang label for the communalist factions in the MCA, the Alliance leaders indirectly accused them of being "un-Malayan" and of being alien in their politics.

The political maneuvers of the newer "middle" faction of the MCA during early 1958 must have been quite successful in bringing in new members and winning over the rank and file in the party,[35] if subsequent events are to be taken as evidence. At the next session of the MCA General Committee, the venerable Tan Cheng-lock was removed from the presidency of the MCA in favor of Dr. Lim Chong-eu, the Alliance whip in the Legislative Council. The vote was 89 for Dr. Lim against Tan Cheng-lock's 67. As a gesture of good-will Tan Cheng-lock was elected honorary life president of MCA. Nonetheless, he was visibly disappointed over his rejection by the party he had founded.[36] The new president was generally believed to be more in touch with Chinese opinion, and somewhat more communal in sympathy, yet as Alliance whip he had been able to work with the other parties in the Alliance. Before his election he indicated he would give greater priority to Chinese interests and the achievement of unity among the Chinese, but not at the expense of abandoning the Alliance.[37] Tunku Abdul Rahman was obviously disturbed by the results of the election, but he expressed the hope that the new MCA leaders would continue the close cooperation with UMNO and the MIC. Promises to that effect by Dr. Lim allayed some misgivings, but uncertainty and distrust remained, partly because Dr. Lim and Tunku Abdul Rahman were not close personal friends, and neither made a move to remedy that situation. When political struggles became intensified, there was no reservoir of goodwill to draw upon, which might have been built up through close personal contact between the leading figures in each party. Instead, relations between UMNO and the MCA became increasingly formalized, at a time when new stresses were developing within the Alliance which threatened to divide it against itself on the eve of the 1959 elections.

The victory of the new leadership of the MCA did not heal its internal divisons. One of the first major acts of Dr. Lim and his associates was to prepare a major reorganization which would strengthen the central organs of the party. The proposed reorganization was ostensibly designed to bring new unity to the party. However, other motives were readily apparent. The new leaders had captured the central offices, but did not control a number of state organizations which continued to support the Tan-Ong faction. A major motive for the reorganization was to gain full control of the party and to prevent the Tan-Ong faction from making a political comeback.[38]

As a first step, disciplinary action was dropped against all "rebel" MCA members who had been among the leaders of the Chinese guild delegation to London.[39] Secondly, a major constitutional revision of the MCA was prepared by the new Central Working Committee. Among the most important proposed amendments were the following: restricting membership to citizens only; permitting the affiliation within the MCA of other Chinese organizations having similar political and social interests; strengthening of the Central Executive Committee, which was to be chosen at the "absolute discretion" of the President; transferring from the state branches to the Federal head-quarters of the party all funds in excess of M$5,000; giving to the Central Working Committee the absolute power to nominate candidates for federal election; giving the Central Working Committee the power to discipline, expel or fine a member for breach of party discipline; and, prohibiting resort to a court of law to contest the legality of a decision of the Central Working Committee.[40]

The proposal to force members to become Federal citizens within a certain time or face the threat of expulsion was prompted, in part, by the Federal constitutional provision that the Malay language test for citizenship did not go into effect until August 31, 1958. The MCA hoped to put pressure on its members to become citizens (and voters) before this discriminatory provision against the non-Malays went into effect. The proposal to permit the affiliation of other Chinese organizations would have allowed the Chinese guilds to become incorporated into the MCA. This would have strengthened the communal Chinese wing of the MCA, especially if a proportionate vote were given to the Chinese guilds with their membership of over 100,000 as compared to an existing MCA membership of about 50,000.

Included in the proposed MCA constitution was a statement of objectives which called for the union of Singapore with the Federation. Although the Alliance had avoided the issue of the merger of Singapore with the Federation in 1955, Tunku Abdul Rahman came out against any immediate moves to prepare the way for incorporating Singapore into the Federation. Many political considerations were involved. The addition of Singapore to the Federation would bring the population of the Chinese up to that of the Malays and make the Malays into a minority "in their own country". Further, the growth of the radical left-wing Chinese-dominated People's Action Party in Singapore caused the Tunku to view the political developments there with misgivings.[41]

The proposed MCA constitution was vigorously opposed by the recently defeated wing of the party, particularly since Dr. Lim and his cohorts were relying so heavily upon the political support of the Chinese guilds. His maneuvering to isolate the more moderate faction created bitter dissention in the party. Furthermore, it was obvious that he was trying to strengthen the MCA as a prelude to an intensified attack on the existing Alliance agreements, which were already under attack by him.[42]

The controversial amendments to the MCA constitution were to be considered at a full convention of the Central General Committee on November 2, 1958, but the Tan-Ong faction successfully obtained a postponment until an accurate Chinese translation of the amendments could be circulated to all state branches.[43] The proposals were finally considered by the Committee on November 30, and after several hours of heated debate, they were passed by a vote of 75 to 50 with one abstention. A legal dispute ensued, since amendments to the MCA constitution required a three-fifths majority, which was obtained only if the abstaining vote was not counted in the total. Dr. Lim, as President and presiding officer, ruled that the amendments had obtained the required majority.[44] Tan Siew-sin and Ong Yoke-lin refused to recognize the legality of the new constitution and led a boycott by the Selangor, Malacca and Pahang branches against the new constitution. The critics of Dr. Lim were vindicated when the Registrar of Societies rejected the new constitution of the MCA on the grounds that it failed to secure the necessary majority and that it violated the law by providing for affiliation with a foreign political party (the Singapore MCA).[45]

After the rejection of their new constitution, the leaders of the MCA attempted to work out a compromise to avoid another major crisis within the association. In early March, the broad outlines of an agreement were worked out between the major factions in the party.[46] Several weeks later a redrafted constitution was passed unanimously by the Central General Committee. The constitution was not to go into effect for six months (after the general elections). Political organizations with the "same objectives" as the MCA could apply for affiliation.[47] Deleted from the earlier draft was the section providing for transfer of state branch funds to the central headquarters. State divisions were assured the right to nominate candidates for election, and if vetoed by the MCA Central Committee, they would have the right to make another nomination.[48] On the basis of these compromises, the Malayan Chinese Association gave outward evidence of having achieved a new degree of unity in preparation for the general elections of August 1959.

The Alliance and the Malayan Indian Congress

The Malayan Indian Congress had always been the junior partner in the Alliance. It joined almost three years after the other two partners. Its lesser size and political weight was recognized in its representation on the major governing organs of the Alliance.[49] When the seats on the Alliance ticket were distributed in 1955, only two MIC candidates were selected out of a total of 52 contested. No MIC official was included in the Alliance delegation which departed for London in January 1956 to demand independence for Malaya.[50] In the 1959 state elections 14 MIC candidates were selected to run on the Alliance ticket which numbered 277 candidates. Seven of the MIC candidates were elected, a proportion which was considerably less than the overall performance of the Alliance.

In the inter-Alliance negotiations, the ability of each member to deliver to votes was an important calculation in the compromises that were reached. It was very difficult to determine how many Indian votes were attracted by the MIC.[51] Few Indians could get really enthusiastic about the MIC because it had not been in a position to extract from the Alliance significant concessions for specifically Indian interests. Nevertheless, its influence was significant on a number of occasions, particularly in helping to adjust differences that developed between UMNO and the MCA. To many Indians the MIC appeared to be just "tagging along", asking for Indian support but not espousing Indian political demands with the same vigor shown by the other two parties in the Alliance. For this reason the MIC found it difficult to count upon a large and consistent following among the Indians.[52] Furthermore, the MIC was not able to develop roots among the lower class Indian laborers. Although in some districts it had attracted nearly all the Indian vote, in others it had lost it to opposition parties. This was largely dependent upon the type of opposition being offered the Alliance, and whether one of the opposition parties happened to be fielding an Indian candidate. Since non-Indians were not permitted to join as full members of the MIC, the party did not become a vehicle for political action for the Ceylonese or Eurasian communities, which had much in common with the political objectives and outlook of the Indians.[53]

Of the three parties in the Alliance, the MIC was outwardly the least communal. As a small minority, the Indian community would have been greatly harmed by any excesses of communalism by the Chinese or the Malays. Thus it sought to protect Indian interests by promoting inter-communal compromises that would temper excessive communal demands by either the Malays or the Chinese. Yet the MIC was subject to internal division between those who sought close identity with the Alliance, and those who wanted the MIC to take political stands independent of the Alliance in a more open fight for Indian interests. An editorial in the *Straits Times* explained the reasons for the factional split within the Malayan Indian Congress.

> A major cause of instability is that Congress has become the battleground for two schools of thought. The president regards the MIC as an Indian organization wedded to the national purposes of the Alliance Government. This implies the subordination of communal interests where they conflict with the Government's national purposes. It means more than not recognizing any Indian interest outside the national framework. It calls for active opposition to any Indian interest which is not in harmony. As long as the MIC is a component of the Alliance Government, loyalty to Government policies and priority for national interests in fact must remain the prime consideration.
>
> This is what the second faction has refused to see. This group treats the MIC as an organization independent of the Alliance and the Government. Many of the criticisms it has levelled imply that the MIC representative in the Government has behaved as an Alliance spokesman and has not imposed the MIC viewpoint on its partners. It may not have been stated as bluntly as this, but that unquestionably is the underlying assumption. This group has found the Alliance partnership a restraint rather than a source of strength.[54]

After joining the Alliance the leadership of the MIC remained consistent in upholding the principle of "collective responsibility" within the Alliance. Even more important, the President of the MIC, V. T. Sambanthan, developed a close personal association with Tunku Abdul Rahman. To a large extent the political position of the MIC and its top leaders depended upon the mutual understanding and support these two gentlemen gave each other. Because of the MIC leaders' heavy reliance upon political support from Tunku Abdul Rahman, challengers and disgruntled elements periodically tried to attack or undermine this mutual dependence. The opposition to V. T. Sambanthan's leadership tended to originate from urban centers in areas where there were clusters of lower-class Indian laborers. These critics tended to be both more communal and more left. Indeed, militant Indian communal nationalism often went hand-in-hand with leftist dogmas. It is understandable that this combined appeal was attractive to the Indian urban laboring classes. The major centers of anti-Sambanthan factions were Ipoh and Kuala Lumpur, with a few other pockets located in Province Wellesley, Negri Sembilan and Kuantan. In 1958 the former president of MIC, K. L. Devaser tried to unseat Sambanthan, relying in large measure upon support from these areas.[55]

The attraction of the Peoples Progressive Party, with its fairly high proportion of Indians and Ceylonese in the top echelon, created recurring problems for the MIC in Ipoh. During 1956 a faction demanded the resignation of Sambanthan from his post as Minister for Labour. The leader in the attack, A. K. S. Maniam, charged that Sambanthan was neglecting his duties as MIC President.[56] The dispute is said to have originated over the failure of the MIC to take a strong stand on behalf of *jus soli* and against Malay special rights during the constitutional negotiations. Further rumblings of revolt developed after Perak MIC demanded three seats on the Alliance slate in the state elections in 1959, but received only two seats. The Alliance promise to appoint a Perak Indian to the Senate helped to assuage some of the bitterness, but defections and behind-the-scenes support for the PPP continued. One of the leaders of the anti-Sambanthan faction in Ipoh, A. E. Mohamed Ismail, later in 1959 made an unsuccessful bid to unseat Sambanthan as the President of the MIC.[57]

Kuala Lumpur was another source of continuing trouble for the party leaders. The Bungsar Ward, which has a high proportion of Indian laborers, many of them working on the railways, was particularly unruly. The fiery, dynamic Socialist Front leader, V. David, had developed a strong following among the Indians in Kuala Lumpur, and charges were made that local MIC officials contributed to his victory in the 1957 Kuala Lumpur municipal council elections. The inability of the MIC to deliver Indian votes in wards with heavy Indian population led to a period of extreme friction between Selangor UMNO and Selangor MIC, during which the MIC was temporarily suspended from participation in the Alliance at the local level.[58] Only strong disciplinary action by President Sambanthan against the more militant and communal elements in the MIC made it possible to heal the breach between UMNO and MIC. The hard feelings in UMNO subsided only after the expulsion of K. Gurupatham, President of Bungsar MIC, K. Annamalai,[59] and A. Tharmalingam, Secretary of the Selangor Branch. Another leader in the anti-Sambanthan faction was K. R. Dass, the Secretary of MIC Youth. He later resigned from the party after it became apparent that the more communal Indians in the MIC were going to be subjected to party discipline and had no chance of unseating the Sambanthan faction. By May 1958, the anti-Sambanthan faction in Selangor could only muster 27 votes in support of K. L. Devaser for Selangor MIC President, as against the 88 votes polled by Sambanthan's right-hand man, V. Manickasavasagam.[60]

Much of the unrest in the MIC was due to the passive role which the MIC had to play as the weak third partner in the Alliance. Yet the Indian community produced more than its proportionate share of politically ambitious politicians. Thus, except for a few of the entrenched leaders in the party, the politically ambitious and younger politicians were bound to become disillusioned or fall to fighting among themselves over the very few positions of political power available through the MIC.

Just as UMNO and the MCA have had fights over their party constitutions, so also did the MIC. In 1958, attempts to give the national leadership greater control over the party met with strong resistance from the recalcitrant branches. In accordance with Alliance policy, a proposal was made to restrict membership in the MIC to federal citizens. This stirred up a hornets' nest of protest, and the amendment was later watered down to apply only to the office-holders in the MIC. Even so, the amendment was postponed for about a year before it was finally passed. Similar moves to strengthen financial control over the party was resisted by some state organizations. But after 1958 the party came increasingly under the control of the national MIC leaders working hand-in-hand with the Alliance National Council.

Problems of Strengthening the Alliance

Every time a communal faction became active in one of the Alliance parties, the Alliance was weakened. Direct action against those obstructing or undermining the decisions of the Alliance National Council was difficult since any breach of "party" discipline within the Alliance was the responsibility of the leaders of each affiliated party. If the member party leaders were unable or unwilling to exercise adequate party discipline over dissident factions, there was little the Alliance could do except berate the leaders of the party concerned, and threaten that party with expulsion from the Alliance. Thus, in 1958, when members of the Malayan Indian Congress defied the Alliance in Selangor, UMNO demanded that strong disciplinary measures be taken by the MIC against its wayward members. When (in the eyes of UMNO) insufficient discipline was applied by the MIC, UMNO, in effect, refused to be "allied" with the MIC in Selangor. This unsatisfactory state of affairs continued for nearly eight months, until there was a reconciliation after a number of top MIC officials in Selangor had been purged by the MIC high command.[61]

The UMNO-MIC dispute in Selangor pointed up the need to increase the powers of the Alliance *vis-a-vis* the member parties and their recalcitrant communal factions entrenched in some local branches. A step in this direction was made in November 1957, when the Alliance was registered as a political party independent of its member parties. In May 1958 a new draft constitution was prepared to strengthen the national organs of the party. This draft constitution was first ratified as a June meeting of the UMNO General Assembly. The strong communal factions in UMNO vigorously opposed the new Alliance constitution and proposed many amendments designed to diminish the representation of the MCA and the MIC or to give UMNO a veto power over the decisions of the Alliance National Council. However, all the major amendments were defeated and a motion to defer consideration of the constitution was rejected 56 to 39. After a dramatic walk-out by 13 Penang delegates, the slightly revised draft was passed by an overwhelming vote.[62] This draft was later ratified by the Malayan Chinese Association and the Malayan Indian Congress.

The new Alliance constitution continued the representation on the Alliance National Council as before: UMNO, 16; MCA, 16; and MIC, 6. However, Chinese representation on the Alliance Executive Council was reduced by one, with six seats for UMNO, five for the MCA, and three for the MIC. The constitution required that the chairman of both bodies must be an UMNO representative.[63] The decisions of both bodies had to have the unanimous agreement of all three member parties (but not the unanimity of all the individual representatives). The Alliance National Council was given full power to select Alliance candidates for federal office, and the Executive Council was given the authority to expel any individual from the Alliance (and its member party) by a simple majority vote, subject to appeal to the National Council. This controversial provision was designed to give the Alliance direct party discipline over the membership of all three affiliated parties. According to the Alliance constitution, members of the Alliance had to be federal citizens.[64] This provision was designed to force members of the MCA and the MIC to register as citizens, if eligible, or to be expelled from the party. We have seen that the MCA attempted to comply with this provision and proposed to amend its own constitution to make membership contingent upon federal citizenship, but this had to be abandoned because it would have split the party and enforcement would have been difficult. Thus, for a while, federal citizenship appeared to be a requirement only for persons holding high party positions or for the selection of party candidates.

Despite attempts to strengthen the Alliance, it still remained only what the three member parties were willing to make of it. When cooperation and conciliation were not forthcoming from any of the three parties, the Alliance faced new crises that threatened to bring it to an end. What party discipline the Alliance had in theory could be exercised in practice only against a few renegades, but not against any major factional divisions.

Prime Minister Tunku Abdul Rahman was aware of the potential discord which might develop within the Alliance. Further, he was very sensitive to the political inroads being made at the state level by some of the opposition parties. Consequently, at a meeting of the general assembly of the United Malays National Organization in February, he announced his intention of resigning as Prime Minister to devote full time to strengthening the Alliance in preparation for the August general elections. He proposed to overhaul the election machinery of the Alliance and work for closer liaison between the three partners in the Alliance.[65] Although the former Deputy Prime Minister, Dato Abdul Razak, was sworn in as Prime Minister on April 16, the Tunku was still recognized as the leader of the Alliance. The Tunku undoubtedly sensed the political pressures building up within the Alliance, and he hoped to head off any open splits which might bring the Alliance to defeat in the August elections. He stated, "The real danger facing the Alliance is not from the opposition. I do not fear their challenges. The real danger is from the Alliance itself."[66]

The July Crisis

These dangers became evident during the crisis of July 1959. The Alliance was faced with the necessity of preparing a slate of candidates for the general elections. Before the Alliance National Council met to allocate the seats on the Alliance ticket, the Malayan Chinese Association Central Working Committee met and decided to nominate 40 MCA members to run on the Alliance ticket. However, leading members of the Alliance National Council had already agreed informally to allocate the 104 federal constituencies[67] in the following way: 74 to UMNO, 28 to the MCA, and 2 to the MIC. The Malayan Chinese Association had had slightly less than half the representation of UMNO on the Alliance ticket in the 1955 elections, and since then the percentage of Chinese in the electorate had increased from approximately 11·2 per cent in 1955 to an estimated 35·6 per cent in 1959 as a result of the registration of Chinese under the new citizenship laws.[68] Consequently, the MCA wanted a proportionate increase in representation on the Alliance ticket in 1959. However, two major considerations appeared to the leaders of the Alliance to justify the smaller number of seats for the MCA. First, the MCA was way over-represented in 1955, with only about one-ninth of the voters being Chinese at that time. Secondly, the Alliance had just suffered some major defeats at the hands of the Pan-Malayan Islamic Party in the state elections in Trengganu and Kelantan. They felt that the Alliance could not afford to lose any more of the Malay electorate to the ultra-communal Pan-Malayan Islamic Party, and they feared that this would be the result if the Alliance gave too big a proportion of its ticket to Chinese candidates.

The Alliance-MCA dispute heightened when Dr. Lim, MCA president, made public a letter to Tunku Abdul Rahman asking for 40 seats in terms that appeared to be tantamount to an ultimatum. The letter began:

> The fear of Malayans of other racial origins—Chinese, Indians, Eurasians—is simply one of fear of Malay communalism . . . the fear still remains and it is kept alive by the provision of the constitution, which allows amendment of the constitution with a two-thirds majority.[69]

Besides the demand for 40 seats on the Alliance ticket, three other "requests" were made. First, MCA candidates should be selected by the MCA, not the Alliance National Council. Second, the manifesto should promise to uphold the present constitution (against increasing Malay clamor for "pro-Malay" amendments). Third, the manifesto should promise to review education policy. This letter was followed by a press statement by the MCA publicity chief.

> If we do not succeed in getting what we think is fair the MCA general committee will decide on July 12 whether we fight under the Alliance banner or on our own. . . . The MCA will stand absolutely firm on the issue of Chinese education and the allocation of seats for the MCA. . . .

As a compromise . . . we are prepared to accept 35 seats—nothing less.[70]

Riled by this "ultimatum", Tunku Abdul Rahman replied by a letter which was also made public. This letter called the bluff of the MCA by suggesting that they could either follow the Alliance under his leadership or they could withdraw from the Alliance.

Your action in presenting me with an ultimatum (which is the only deduction I can make of your action) at this late hour is really a stab in the back to me, and has given me a feeling of great disappointment in my friends, the present leaders of the MCA.

It is obvious that your intention is to break from the Alliance and it offers me and others in the Alliance no room for discussion. . . .

I, therefore, see that no useful purpose will be served by our Alliance National meeting fixed with your group this evening. Undeterred, we will fight the elections as the Alliance with MIC and those members of the MCA who do not support your stand. . . . [71]

This letter must have stunned the MCA, for Dr. Lim admitted that the MCA was not prepared to fight the election on its own.

At the height of the crisis, Tan Cheng-lock emerged from semi-retirement to use his prestige to help resolve the crisis.[72] After consulting with the principals in the dispute, they issued a statement, part of which is reproduced below.

Unfortunately, after the MCA central working committee meeting held on July 9, contents of secret documents were released to the Press and the MCA practically sent a public ultimatum to the Alliance. . . .

I must confess that I was tricked into signing this letter without the contents thereof being disclosed. . . .

In a plural society such as ours, any tendency towards extreme communalism can have only one ultimate end, that is, racial conflict, if not bloodshed.

The Alliance has proved during these years that it is the only party capable of uniting the diverse races in our country into a single united nation.

To smash it up now, as the MCA president apparently intends to do, would cause untold misery. . . .

At this critical hour in our history I therefore appeal to all right-thinking persons to support the Alliance, its policies and its leader, Tengku Abdul Rahman . . . .[73]

At an emergency meeting of the UMNO General Assembly on July 12, Tunku Abdul Rahman laid down his terms for admitting the MCA back into the Alliance. "We cannot end this crisis if he [Dr. Lim] does not withdraw the threatening letter and expel those irresponsible members who created the crisis."[74] Later in the day, Tunku Abdul Rahman and Dr. Lim reached an agreement to settle the crisis. These terms were announced by Dr. Lim to an emergency meeting of the MCA Central Working Committee.

> It is most likely we will be allocated 32 seats. . . .
>
> [Nomination of candidates] will be made by the Tengku alone because of the shortness of time. But before finalising the list I will, to some extent, be consulted. . . .
>
> [The education] clause will not be included in the manifesto. The government will implement it by administrative directive as soon as possible.[75]

In a very turbulent meeting, the MCA Central Working Committee voted to accede to these "terms" by a vote of 89 to 60. The opposition within the MCA objected to giving the Tunku a "blank check" and criticized those who did not want to stand firmly for "justified demands from the Chinese".[76]

The defeated ultra-communal faction was removed from effective participation in the Alliance, since it was clear that Tunku Abdul Rahman would not nominate to the Alliance ticket any MCA members who had precipitated the crisis. A wave of resignations from the MCA followed the return of the MCA into the Alliance. The resignation list was headed by Yong Pung-how, MCA Publicity Director who released the controversial letter, and Too Joon-hing, the MCA Secretary General and former Assistant Minister for Education. When Mr. Yong resigned he stated, "the MCA has outlived its usefulness and is no longer able to carry out even the main objects for which it was formed. . . . The Tengku may not be a dictator but he has got himself into such a powerful position that he is practically in the position of a dictator."[77] Within a few days the press reported that over thirty MCA officials at the state and national level had resigned. Five of them also announced that they would contest the elections as independents.[78]

Immediately after the crisis, it was uncertain what would become of Dr. Lim, who had espoused the ultra-communal cause, but had taken a more moderate position when the Alliance was threatened. With the virtual capitulation of the MCA to Tunku Abdul Rahman, he said his position as MCA leader was "completely untenable . . . I definitely cannot stand as a candidate. I would be a hypocrite. . . ."[79] The Alliance ticket as drawn up by the Tunku was revealed to the public on the eve of filing day—three days after the crisis. Dr. Lim's name was conspicuously absent from the Alliance ticket. The government also announced that Colonel H. S. Lee, Minister of Finance, would not be a candidate "for medical reasons".[80]

Dr. Lim resigned as president of the MCA and announced that he was leaving Malaya for eight months for medical treatment in Britain, and a "long leave". At the next meeting of the MCA Central Working Committee, Dr. Cheah Toon-lok was elected the new Acting President of the MCA. He was a Kedah State Assemblyman, and relatively unknown at the federal level. He had the merit of being a very vigorous individual, and one who was not closely associated with either faction of the MCA, nor was he entangled in the controversies of the crisis between the Alliance and the MCA. He came from Kedah to Kuala Lumpur at the height of the crisis to try to resolve the dispute and apparently played a part in saving the Alliance from disintegration and disaster.[81] He was therefore a natural choice to lead the MCA in the difficult task of re-establishing harmony with the other parties in the Alliance.

The resolution of the July crisis undoubtedly made the Alliance more centralized and coherent, since only those closely identified with Tunku Abdul Rahman were nominated, and the opposition to his leadership was thoroughly discredited. The opposition parties' hope for a fracture of the Alliance did not materialize, but their campaigning did aggravate the communal divisions within the Alliance. The communal opposition parties were able to pick up support from some of the disgruntled communal factions in the Alliance. The issues that precipitated the crisis in the Alliance were by no means solved. But the clear assertion of Tunku Abdul Rahman's leadership over the Alliance helped to sharpen the distinction between the Alliance Government and its opposition.

After the Crisis

The Alliance that survived the July crisis was not and could never again be the Alliance of the earlier period. Not only had there been an exodus of the strident communalists from the MCA, but similar defections of communal elements from the other two Alliance parties in the earlier disputes helped to make the Alliance more unified. Tunku Abdul Rahman had always been the dominant personality and "balance wheel" of the Alliance, but after the crisis his role as the "court of last resort" in communal conflicts became more clearly and willingly recognized. And, for the elections, it was he that settled all the unresolved questions over candidates and over the contents of the Alliance manifesto.[82]

It is difficult to judge whether the Alliance suffered greatly from the crisis. Undoubtedly, many Chinese who might have supported the Alliance had Chinese demands been met, either cast their votes for one of the opposition parties, or did not vote. On the other hand, many Chinese who were not happy with Alliance policies, preferred the Alliance to the obvious consequences of greatly intensified communal politics. The decisive way in which Tunku Abdul Rahman met the challenge of Dr. Lim and the chauvinist wing of the MCA must have attracted some additional support from the Malays, partially offsetting the loss of Chinese votes. However, the political turmoil and confusion within the Alliance probably did shake public confidence somewhat. One piece of evidence which might be taken as a measure of the loss of support for the Alliance is the percentage difference in the votes cast in the state elections [83] and the federal elections. The Alliance polled 55 per cent of the votes for the state assemblies. In the federal elections it received only 51 per cent, a difference which is slight, but may be of some significance.[84]

A greater degree of inter-party harmony appeared to prevail within the Alliance after the 1959 political conflicts. The political leaders who remained loyal to the Alliance through the crisis had greater trust and respect for each other. Following the crisis, the Alliance worked more as a political party than as a temporary and unstable coalition. Furthermore, both the MCA and UMNO reorganized their constitutional structure the following year to increase the degree of party discipline and centralize the control of the national leadership over the party, so that revolt within the parties could be nipped in the bud. The new UMNO constitution of 1960 practically eliminated the state organizations, while placing party discipline and the selection of candidates within the power of the national leadership.[85] Similarly, in November 1959, the MCA passed a revised version of the disputed constitution which had been proposed a year earlier.[86] However, the tightened powers of control and party discipline were back in the hands of the Ong-Tan faction which had the personal confidence and support of the Tunku, and were dedicated to exercise that authority to uphold the integrity of the Alliance.

After 1959 the government followed a more determined and openly recognized policy of catering to Malay opinion. Large investments were put into the rural development program, which had as its primary objective the raising of the standard of living of the rural Malay population. Although not entirely ignoring the rural non-Malays, the program was designed and administered in such a way that the Malays received a disproportionately large share of the benefits. The Federal Land Development Authority (FLDA)

TABLE 8
Selective comparison of public investments, first and second five year plan

Sector	Approximate Actual 1956–60	Plan target 1961–65
Drainage and irrigation	38·3 (millions)	100·0
Land development	16·7	191·0
Cooperative credit	n.a.	20·0
Agricultural research and extension work	2·4	20·0
Animal husbandry	1·7	10·0
Roads and bridges	95·2	190·0
Rural industry	n.a.	10·0
Education	60·9	260·0

opened up vast new areas of land, built roads to the new areas, cleared the land and planted crops, including high-yielding rubber, and settled families on these lands under very favorable terms, providing them with a monthly allotment until the crops became productive, which, in the case of rubber, is about seven years. The usual allotment for each family was seven acres of rubber and three acres for other crops. The plans called for the opening up of 250,000 acres of new land and the settlement of 40,000 families in the period from 1961 through 1965. The increased expenditure on both rural development and education was illustrated by some of the figures on page 216 taken from the Second Five Year Plan.[87]

During 1961, the government announced that 1967 was the target date to make Malay the sole official language to be used in full in government. This promised to be a boost for the Malays by opening up more employment opportunities for them. Of course, it was also hoped that by that year the non-Malay population would be well on the way to mastering the "National Language" which was considered to be an essential requirement for building a Malayan nation. In any case, the non-Malays were having to make an effort to learn the language in order that they would not be at a great disadvantage after 1967.

Perhaps the most important feature of Government policy was in the field of education. In accordance with the promise made before the 1959 elections, the Government set up a committee to review the Razak Plan. This committee, under the chairmanship of Inche Abdul Rahman bin Haji Talib, presented its report by August 1960. In brief, it approved of the general objectives of the Razak Plan but proposed a number of changes which were one step farther along in the process of unifying Malaya's educational system. It proposed to stop all subsidies for schools not fully converting to "national type" schools, *i.e.* those schools which followed government standards as to subject matter, texts, curriculum and the selection of staff. The Talib Report called for promotion and school-leaving examinations to be held only in the nation's official languages (English and Malay).[88] English and Malay were to be required subjects in all schools. Although Chinese language and literature were still to be taught in Chinese schools, the number of hours devoted to it were to be limited and, increasingly, Chinese schools were to be brought into line with the requirements of "national type" schools. To placate the Chinese, the Alliance held out the promise of free primary education in Chinese schools after 1962.[89] In addition, the usual "school-leaving" age was to be raised from about 13 years to 15 years. Post-primary technical and vocational schools offering a three-year course were to be set up to cater to the needs of the 70 per cent of the primary students who failed to pass the examination for the secondary (academic) schools.[90]

The Talib proposals were a bitter pill for the Chinese educationists to swallow. In the early stages of discussions on the Report, the Malayan Chinese Association maintained close liaison with the Chinese educators. However, when the United Chinese School Teachers Association began sponsoring protest meetings, the MCA did not attend and was very careful to avoid being identified with the protest movement. Later a government committee was formed "to explain the education report to the Chinese". But this did not prevent the Chinese educators from publicly condemning and rejecting the Talib Report. The new education policy was finally passed in October 1961,[91] under circumstances that would suggest that the militant Chinese communalists were becoming more resigned to political defeats on this issue.

The government's increasing dependence on Malay opinion was also noticeable in other aspects of its educational policy. Malays were given very privileged opportunities to secure better education. Malay secondary schools were being built for the first time, and special "removed classes" were being established to make it easier for students from Malay schools to qualify for secondary education in the English-media secondary schools. Any Malay who could qualify for entrance to the University of Malaya was assured of an automatic scholarship which included not only tuition and fees, but a very handsome monthly allowance. Some similar scholarships were available to the non-Malays, but the number was less and there was stiff competition for the scholarship provided under the non-Malay entrance and scholarship quotas.

All of these programs were designed "to raise the economic and educational standards of the Malays" in a massive "boot-strap" operation. Whether these programs have been effective remains subject to debate. It is clear nonetheless that the Alliance recognized the political necessity of its actions and had the fairly complete support of all the three member parties within it[1]

As the Alliance Government followed a more consistent and openly pro-Malay bias, the Malayan Chinese Association found it difficult to retain or recover its dominant political position among the Chinese. In 1961, the MCA began a major campaign to recruit wider support in Penang, Johore and Perak, apparently appealing to the Chinese to make the MCA more effective so that its hand could be strengthened in the internal negotiations within the Alliance. Even though the MCA had to defend the many "pro-Malay" policies of the government, it won back substantial Chinese support because it provided the only significant access to the government that the Chinese enjoyed. The politically astute Chinese realized this important fact.

The Alliance was successful in maintaining its rather delicate political balance on economic and communal issues. All the while, the opposition parties were trying to dislodge the Alliance from its commanding political position, hoping that it would lose its political equilibrium or become more vulnerable to a direct political assault.

[1] The long process of give-and-take negotiations between the three partners in the Alliance became more difficult after it came to power. Responsibility for Alliance policies no longer rested with the Alliance Council, but with the new Cabinet composed of Alliance members of the Legislative Council. Decisions of the Alliance National Council required the unanimous approval of all member-parties, but this was not true of Cabinet decisions. On occasion the members of the Alliance Council publicly voiced objection to the fact that they were not consulted on matters of government policy and on matters of patronage appointments. See *Constitution and Rules of the Alliance Party*, (as amended May 20, (1958), p. 6, (para. 16); *Straits Times*, June 5, 1957, p. 7.

[2] Tunku Abdul Rahman is a prince of the Kedah royal family, while the Deputy Prime Minister, Dato Abdul Razak is the grandson of one of Pahang's four major territorial Chiefs. For some background on other UMNO leaders see Daniel E. Moore, "The United Malays National Organization and the 1959 Malayan Elections", (unpublished dissertation, University of California, 1960), pp. 65–144.

[3] A government servant before the war, Abdul Aziz bin Ishak became president of the Malay Youth Action League in 1946 and attended the founding meetings of

UMNO which he joined in 1948. In 1952 he followed Dato Onn out of UMNO and ran on the IMP ticket in the Kuala Lumpur municipal elections. For a number of years he was the editor of the Federation edition of the most influential Malay daily, *Utusan Melayu*. He rejoined UMNO in about 1953 and after being elected to Parliament in 1955 became the Minister of Agriculture and Cooperatives, a post he held until late 1962 when he was dismissed and ultimately expelled from the party. He continued to hold his seat in Parliament and later attempted to form his own party, the National Convention Party, which followed a radical, anti-Western line in an attempt to appeal to the Malay peasants.

4 Many of the terms usually applied to political struggles in the West give a false impression of the nature of the political contest. Words like "conservative", "liberal" "progressive", "radical", and "left-wing" lose much of their meaning in a multi-communal society in the transitional stage of economic and political development. For example, all factions within UMNO (and within the Malay community) practiced a "selective conservatism", mixed with a liberal dose of "selective radicalism". In a period of extreme flux, even the inherent conservative is in favor of *some* radical changes, and the inherent radical is anxious to stabilize *some* change or even to revert to a real or imagined past on *some* issues. Consequently, the extreme wings as well as the center dominant faction in UMNO have all been called "conservative" with obvious justification. Furthermore, politics within UMNO is much more complicated than any simple division between two or three different factions. Much of UMNO politics involved personal cliques and rivalries which can develop in any party where there is a vigorous contest for power and office.

5 *Straits Times*, February 1, 1958, pp. 1 and 6. Associated with the FMSTA were the following organizations: Malay Otherwise-Trained Teachers' Union, Union of Malay Teachers in Non-Malay Vernacular Schools, Religious School Teachers Association, and Ra'ayat School Teachers Association.

6 *Sunday Times*, February 2, 1958, pp. 1 and 11; *Straits Times*, February 3, 1958, p. 6; March 31, 1958, p. 1.

7 *Straits Times*, June 14, 1958, p. 7.

8 The Selangor and Malacca state organizations opposed these amendments. See *Malay Mail*, April 18, 1960, p. 2; *Undang² Tuboh Pertubohan Kebangsaan Melayu Bersatu* (The Constitution United Malays National Organization), (Kuala Lumpur: Life Printers, 1960).

9 Both UMNO Youth and Kaum Ibu have guaranteed representation in the Divisional Executive Committees and in the UMNO General Assembly.

10 *Straits Times*, May 17, 1950, p. 17.

11 Moore, *op. cit.*, pp. 59–60.

12 See *Straits Times*, June 20, 1956, p. 1; June 21, 1956, p. 8.

13 Government policy in Malaya has always given preference to the Malays for the higher civil service posts. The four to one ratio was established for the MCS in 1952. (See *Federation of Malaya, Legislative Council Debates, 19th November 1952*, pp. 473–474.) Before that the MCS was confined to British and Malays. This ratio does not extend to the great majority of the public service which is not within the MCS, but even so, preference is nonetheless given to qualified Malay candidates for non-MCS positions. After *merdeka*, a three to one ratio was established for the higher administrative positions in the Ministry of External Affairs and the Malayan foreign service.

14 One occasionally would hear rumors to the effect that the Alliance had agreed in principle that Malay "special rights" are inherently unjust, but were temporarily necessary to raise the economic and educational position of the Malays. Officials sometimes hinted that the Malay "special rights" would be reviewed as the economic

position of the Malays improved. On that basis, non-Malays seemed willing to tolerate these discriminatory policies for the time being. 1970 and 1972 were both mentioned as tentative dates for the termination of some Malay "special rights". However, it seems doubtful that the three Alliance partners ever came to any firm agreement on this issue.

15 *Straits Times*, March 29, 1957, pp. 1, 2 and 9. These overt expressions of UMNO unanimity were marred by the walk-out from the UMNO General Assembly of nine delegates from Negri Sembilan. Dissatisfied with the concessions to the non-Malays, some elements in UMNO actively promoted the convening of a second "Malay National Congress" to bring together "all sections of the Malays" to determine a unified stand for the Malays in regard to the Reid Report. The Malay press was quite attracted to this proposal. UMNO refused to support such a congress since it would have meant by-passing the Alliance and would have identified UMNO with a rigid communal stand. Despite UMNO opposition, the second "Malay National Congress" was convened in May 1957 under the guidance of Dato Onn and Dr. Burhanuddin who used it as a platform for appealing to the ultra-communal Malays, some of whom defected from UMNO. See *Utusan Melayu*, April 2, 10, 12, and 17, 1957, and the *Straits Times* for the same period.

16 *Straits Times* December 19, 1955, p. 7.

17 Hau Shik Lee is a Malayan Chinese whose father was a tin miner in Perak. He received a B.A. from Cambridge University and later became a leading spokesman of Chinese mining interests in Malaya. During the war he went to India and became a liaison officer in the Chinese Nationalist Army.

18 Lau Pak-khuan had been president of the National Association of Perak, and later became president of the Perak MCA and the Perak CCC. However, his political power rested primarily upon his leadership of the Chinese guilds in the state. Tan Kee-gak was associated with the Malacca CCC and in 1959, helped to form the Malayan Party, under the banner of which he was elected to Parliament.

19 *Straits Times*, March 22, 1956, p. 4.

20 *Sunday Times*, April 22, 1956, p. 1.

21 *Straits Times*, April 28, 1956, p. 7. The demands of the Chinese on the issues of nationality and citizenship were partially met when the Alliance National Council agreed to support the principle that all persons born in Malaya after independence should automatically be citizens. On most other communal issues the demands of the Chinese guilds differed substantially from the Alliance proposals.

22 *Straits Times*, April 17, 1957, pp. 1 and 9.

23 *Straits Budget*, July 4, 1957, p. 17. During the final stages of revision of the Reid proposals, the Chinese guilds had almost no influence, since the final draft was revised according to the Alliance formula.

24 *Sunday Times*, May 5, 1957, p. 1; *Straits Times*, October 28, 1957, p. 1. Expulsion orders were also issued for Yap Mau-tatt, former Executive-Secretary of the MCA, Leong Chee-cheong, President of Selangor Association of Chinese Guilds, and Cho Yew-fai, Selangor MCA working committee member.

25 Dato Abdul Razak (Chairman), *Report of the Education Committee, 1956*, Council Paper No. 21 of 1956, Federation of Malaya.

26 This dialect is the "Mandarin of public life" and was used for centuries as the language of officialdom in China.

27 *Straits Times*, February 4, 1957, p. 1; February 25, 1957, p. 2.

28 The Constitution had not yet been ratified, and communal Malays were in the process of mounting a vicious attack on the *jus soli* principle.

29 *Federation of Malaya, Legislative Council Debates, 7th March 1957,* 2529–2567.

30 *Straits Times,* January 28, 1959, p. 9; July 21, 1959, pp. 1 and 14.

31 *Straits Times,* April 29, 1959, p. 6.

32 The Peoples Progressive Party capitalized on the compromised position of the MCA by taking up the cause of Chinese education and cooperating without hesitation with the UCSTA and the AMCSMA.

33 *Sunday Times,* June 30, 1957, p. 1.

34 Tan Cheng-lock, who was off in Malacca, contradicted this statement by announcing that he knew of no "Kuomintang plot". The difficulty with this scapegoat label was vividly demonstrated when the Alliance, while attacking "Kuomintang subversion", retained H.S. Lee as Minister of Finance after a warning that he should cut his ties and renounce his associations with "Kuomintang elements". This was a blunt warning to him not to throw in his lot with the communalist rebels or the Chinese guilds—a warning he apparently did not heed.

35 In July 1957, Tan Siew-sin reported that M$50,000 had been spent by "KMT diehards" and "disgruntled MCA members" to win control of the Selangor state MCA organization. Subsequent events indicate similar campaigns were under way in some other states. By this time, Tan Cheng-lock was no longer able to play the dominant leadership role demanded in the MCA. Increasingly these responsibilities were assumed by his son, Tan Siew-sin and by Ong Yoke-lin. See *Straits Times,* July 3, 1957, p. 7.

36 *Straits Times,* March 24, 1958, pp. 1, 2 and 5; March 25, 1958, pp. 1 and 7. Also defeated for major committee assignments were Ong Yoke-lin, former Secretary General, and Tan Siew-sin, former Chairman of the publicity Committee.

37 *Straits Times,* March 13, 1958, p. 6; March 14, 1958, p. 4.

38 Most of the MCA members in the Federal Legislative Council were identified with the moderates, who were in firm control of the MCA branches in Selangor and Malacca, but had lost control in Perak.

39 *Straits Times,* April 3, 1958, p. 7.

40 *Straits Times,* November 27, 1958, p. 6; November 29, 1958, p. 8; December 1, 1958, pp. 1 and 7.

41 The People's Action Party assumed power in the Singapore Municipal Council in December, 1957, and won a 43 to 8 majority in the Singapore Legislative Assembly in May 1959. Some Malays favored merger as a means of "rescuing" a Malay minority in Singapore, but most were opposed to merger until they had strengthened their political position in the Federation, and then only under terms which would have minimized the political impact of the large Chinese majority in Singapore. Chinese clamor for merger with Singapore undoubtedly encouraged some ultra-communal Malays to consider, once again, the possibility of union with Indonesia as an answer to the potential political challenge of the Chinese.

42 Besides calling for merger with Singapore, Dr. Lim demanded that Chinese be made an official language, that the Chinese "way of life, our language and our schools" be preserved, and that the Chinese be treated with complete equality—apparently meaning the end of Malay "special rights".

43 *Straits Times,* November 3, 1958, p. 2.

44 *Straits Times,* December 1, 1958, pp. 1 and 7.

45 All societies, political and otherwise, were required to register their constitutions and list their officers with the Registrar of Societies. This provision was designed to secure compliance with the law and to combat the menace of secret societies. See *Straits Times,* January 15, 1959, pp. 1 and 7.

[46] *Straits Times*, March 14, 1959, p. 5.

[47] This wording was designed to exclude the affiliation of any Chinese guilds seeking to pursue an independent political course while being affiliated with the MCA.

[48] *Straits Times*, March 23, 1959, pp. 1 and 7; March 25, 1959, p. 8.

[49] In 1955 the MIC had 8 seats on the National Council, while UMNO and MCA commanded 16 seats apiece. In 1958, the MIC representation on the National Council was reduced to 6 seats. See *Constitution and Rules of the Alliance Party (as amended 20th May, 1958)*, (Kuala Lumpur: Printcraft Ltd., n. d.).

[50] Considerable criticism developed within the MIC for this omission. See *Tamil Murasu*, November 3, 1955, as quoted in *Weekly Digest of the Non-English Press*, No. 44, 1955, (Singapore Public Relations Office), p. 36.

[51] Statistics were not released by the Election Commission or the Department of Statistics on the racial composition of each constituency or the racial composition of the registered electorate. However, it has been reported that the registered electorate in 1955 was divided as follows: Malays 84·2 per cent; Chinese, 11·2 per cent; Indians, 3·9 per cent and others, 0·7 per cent. See K. J. Ratnam, *Communalism and the Political Process in Malaya*, (Singapore: University of Malaya Press, 1965), p. 187.

[52] Party membership for 1958 was estimated by Daniel Moore to be somewhere between 48,000 to 80,000 members. See Moore, *op. cit.*, p. 236.

[53] The Ceylonese seemed to be cynical about the Alliance as a result of their exclusion from full membership. They circulated what was claimed to be an explanation of the real nature of the Alliance according to the initials of its three parties. UMNO is said to stand for "U May Not Oppose!"; MCA is a shortened form of "Money Commands All"; and MIC stands for "May I Come in?"

[54] *Straits Times*, February 19, 1958, p. 6.

[55] K. L. Devaser suffered a decisive defeat, getting only 1,540 votes to Sambanthan's 15,353. See Moore, *op. cit.*, p. 244.

[56] *Straits Times*, April 20, 1956, p. 7. An account of the Peoples Progressive Party is presented in the next chapter, pp. 235–237.

[57] *Straits Times*, October 3, 1959, p. 13.

[58] *Sunday Times*, January 5, 1958, p. 1.

[59] Subsequently, Mr. Annamalai became a PPP candidate.

[60] *Straits Times*, May 19, 1958, p. 7.

[61] *Straits Times*, August 20, 1958, p. 4.

[62] *Sunday Times*, June 8, 1958, pp. 1 and 8; *Straits Times*, June 9, 1958, pp. 1 and 7; *Utusan Melayu*, June 10 and 14, 1958; *Semenanjong*, June 14, 1958, as quoted in *Weekly Digest of the Non-English Press*, No. 24, 1958, (Singapore Public Relations Office), pp. 20–23.

[63] These positions are held by Tunku Abdul Rahman.

[64] *Straits Times*, June 9, 1958, p. 7.

[65] *Straits Times*, February 10, 1959, pp. 1 and 7; February 11, 1959, pp. 1 and 9.

[66] *Straits Times*, February 12, 1959, pp. 1 and 7.

67 Article 46 of the Constitution of Malaya reads: "The House of Representatives shall consist of one hundred elected members except that the first House of Representatives shall consist of one hundred and four." This provision was designed to facilitate election from 52 constituencies until the Electoral Commission could be formed to more carefully redistrict to 100 constituencies. However, later the number was fixed at 104 constituencies.

68 *Straits Times*, June 29, 1959, p. 5. The estimates on the ethnic distribution of the electorate were published in *Straits Times*, August 19, 1959, p. 1.

69 Appearing first in *China Press*, July 8, 1959, reproduced in *Straits Times*, July 10, 1959, p. 16.

70 *Loc. cit.*

71 *Straits Times*, July 11, 1959, p. 14.

72 Tan Cheng-lock had earlier supported Lim Chong-eu by means of a letter he wrote in longhand to the MCA Central Working Committee. It stated:
Dear Members,
    Dr. Chong Yew has been to see me and has come and consulted me over the two points on which he had written to Tunku Abdul Rahman, *viz.* that we must have at least ⅓ of the seats for the MCA and also that we must stand firm over the issue of Chinese education.
    I agree with him and I sincerely advise all of you to stand firm on these two points for the sake of the Malayan Chinese as well as for other Malayans.
                                    Yours sincerely,
                                    (signed) Tan Cheng Lock
See *Straits Times*, July 11, 1959, p. 14.

73 *Loc. cit.*

74 *Straits Times*, July 13, 1959, p. 2.

75 *Ibid.*, p. 12.

76 *Ibid.*, pp. 1, 7 and 12.

77 *Straits Times*, July 14, 1959, p. 1.

78 *Straits Times*, July 16, 1959, p. 1; July 17, 1959, p. 1; July 18, 1959, p. 1; *Sunday Times*, July 19, 1959, p. 4. Just after the crisis Lau Pak-khuan and the Chinese guilds of Perak announced that they were reconsidering their earlier decision to support the Alliance in the elections. See *Straits Times*, July 18, 1959, p. 14.

79 *Straits Times*, July 15, 1959, p. 16; July 16, 1959, p. 1.

80 Col. H. S. Lee was later appointed to the Senate.

81 *Sunday Times*, August 2, 1959, p. 1, *Straits Times*, August 3, 1959, p. 6. The crisis was clearly a sobering experience for Dr. Lim as well as for others who believed that the Chinese could get their way by taking a stronger and more daring political stance. In retrospect, Dr. Lim explained that he did not authorize the release to the press of the letter which undermined his authority and made negotiations impossible. He went on to explain, "In the MCA there are two camps—those who feel that relations with all communities must be placed first, and others who want priority for Chinese interests. My duty as MCA president is to bring these two camps together." See *Straits Times*, July 15, p. 16. This statement does not explain, however, how he viewed his responsibility to the Alliance.

82 The crisis had forced the postponement of the formulation and publication of the Alliance manifesto. When it was finally published in the last week of the campaign, it received very little attention since the Government was willing to stand on its record, and the general themes of the Alliance program were well publicized earlier. See *What the Alliance Offers You, 1959 Parliamentary Election Manifesto*, (Kuala Lumpur: Alliance Headquarters, n.d.).

83 Seven state elections occurred before the crisis was resolved, while three were held afterwards.

84 The results of the 1959 elections are analyzed in some detail in: Smith, T. E., "The Malayan Elections of 1959", *Pacific Affairs*, Vol. 33, No. 1, (March 1960), pp. 38–47; McGee, T. G., "The Malayan Elections of 1959, A Study in Electorial Geography", *The Journal of Tropical Geography*, Vol. 16, (October 1962), pp. 70–99. See also *Report on the Parliamentary and State Election, 1959*, (Federation of Malaya, Government Press, 1960).

85 See above, pp. 196–197.

86 *Straits Times*, November 7, 1959, p. 5. See above, pp. 206–207.

87 Second Five-Year Plan, 1961–1965 (Federation of Malaya, Government Press 1961) pp. 28–31. The expenditures of these massive sums on rural development was charged with political significance. Not only was it an appeal for the Malay vote, but the program was administered with one eye on election results. Massive injections of public investment were made in key constituencies. Where the PMIP controlled the state government, very little national investment in rural development took place, in part because the PMIP refused to cooperate with the Federal Government. The FLDA projects were not exclusively for Malays which the PMIP insisted upon. This PMIP-Alliance controversy over land policy enabled the Alliance to hold out to the electorate the promise of large rural development schemes which were denied so long as the voters supported a PMIP state administration.

88 Control of content and subject matter was partly accomplished through the screening process of the school examinations which were conducted by the Ministry of Education.

89 This proposal necessitated a large increase in expenditure for Chinese schools, benefitting some 350,000 Chinese who would thereby obtain free primary education.

90 *Report of the Education Review Committee, 1960*, (Talib Report), (Federation of Malaya, Government Press, 1960).

91 *Federation of Malaya, Parliamentary Debates, Dewan Ra'ayat*, Vol. III, no. 19 (October 19, 1961), 1927–2009; Vol. III, no. 20 (October 20, 1961), 2029–2127; *Federation of Malaya, Parliamentary Debates, Dewan Negara*, Vol. III, no. 5 (October 23, 1961), 319–337.

14 The Challenge of the Opposition

The Alliance gained an overwhelming victory in the first federal elections in 1955, winning 81·7 per cent of the total vote cast and capturing all but one of the elected seats in the Federal Legislative Council. Nevertheless, the opposition parties could not be ignored, partly because of instability within the Alliance, and partly because of uncertain political trends within Malaya. The Malayan electorate had not developed firmly entrenched voting habits to assure the Alliance of continued success at the next election. If the experience of Singapore provided a guide to political trends in Malaya, it demonstrated that each victorious political party would be supplanted at the next general election by a new party formed from a coalition of more radical opposition elements. With this in mind, the Alliance was alert to the activities of all the various opposition parties, and many government policies were drafted to undercut the political appeal of these parties.

Although the next federal elections were not held until August 1959, the Alliance did not have the political stage entirely to itself during these four years. The controversies over the *Merdeka* Constitution evoked vigorous opposition from many quarters. Similarly, the complicated issues which the Alliance Government faced in the first term of office gave the opposition parties plenty of opportunity to gather political ammunition. However, the big problem for the opposition parties was not in finding issues, but in building a political coalition strong enough to draw more votes than the Alliance. The challenge of the opposition depended upon the combination of two factors, the first being the strength and appeal of the individual opposition parties, and the second their ability to compromise on their differences for the sake of victory at the polls.

In the 1959 parliamentary elections, the Alliance percentages dropped to a bare majority of 51·8 per cent. Nonetheless, it still won 74 out of 104 seats, primarily because the opposition parties were divided against each other. The strongest opposition party was able to capture only 13 seats. The difficulties encountered by these parties in their attempts to challenge the commanding position of the Alliance continued in the period after 1959, even though there was a change in political climate and the issues of the *Merdeka* Constitution were to be replaced by the issues related to the formation of the Federation of Malaysia. Essentially the task of the opposition was to forge a coherent, unified and broad-based coalition which would command majorities in Malaya's single-member-district constituencies. Such an opposition appeared to be almost as remote as it was for the first parliamentary elections. To understand the difficulties they have faced, it is necessary to examine the strength, leadership, and appeal of the more significant opposition parties.

The Pan-Malayan Islamic Party

The most successful challenge to Alliance supremacy at the polls came from the Pan-Malayan Islamic Party. This party represented a combination of ultra-communal Malay sentiment reinforced by pan-Islamic religio-political ideals. Its origin can be traced back to early 1948, when a Malayan Muslim Party was officially launched by Islamic religious leaders and *ulamas* (Muslim theologians) at a meeting of the *Majlis Agama Tertinggi* (Supreme Religious Council).[1] The Malayan Muslim Party had very little national impact on politics and contested no important elections until after it was reorganized as the Pan-Malayan Islamic Party (Persatuan Aislam Sa-Melayu).[2]

In its formative period, the PMIP relied heavily upon the support of students and teachers in the religious *pondok* schools, where young Malays are instructed in the religious tenets of Islam. On at least one occasion the PMIP sponsored a Muslim Youth Congress to help organize and direct the political energies of these people, many of whom were frustrated by political developments and inadequate job opportunities for the graduates of the Muslim schools. Some of the party's leaders were recruited among the faculty and students at the Malayan Muslim College at Klang. In its activities the PMIP was aided by a number of Islamic organizations such as the All-Malaya Muslim Missionary Society. Critics of the PMIP have claimed that Muslim religious leaders and *imams* used the mosques to propagate the political views of the PMIP and were using *zakat*[3] tax money to promote the program of the PMIP,[4] despite rules prohibiting such activities.

For a year or so, the PMIP (then called AMIA) worked through UMNO to further its political objectives. In 1953 it participated in the Alliance-sponsored "National Convention". However, it found it impossible to accept the Alliance demand for *jus soli*. Consequently, it withdrew its political support for UMNO and began pursuing an independent political course.

The PMIP was a relative latecomer in entering the race for the 1955 federal elections. Until just before the elections, the Alliance considered Party Negara to be the only serious challenger. However, within a short period of time, the PMIP developed a substantial following in Perak, where the Alliance was weakened by the split in UMNO which had resulted in the formation of the National Association of Perak under the leadership of Dato Panglima Gantang. The more openly communal Malay sub-elites were confused by the political maneuvers of the traditional Malay leaders in Perak, and began to look around for a more dependable vehicle for the promotion of their communal demands. For good reason, a number of small Malay communal parties flourished in the wake of the factional fights between UMNO on the one hand, and the NAP and Party Negara on the other.[5] As election day approached, many of these small parties threw their support to the PMIP, which became a catalyst suddenly binding together the latent and often leaderless communal elements that were looking for a way to protest against the "alien threat" and the concessions the Alliance had made to the non-Malay communities. The PMIP ultimately fielded a slate of eleven candidates who contested the "rice bowl" districts of Perak, Kedah, Province Wellesley, Trengganu and Selangor. When the votes were counted, one PMIP candidate was elected, preventing an otherwise clean sweep by the Alliance. He won in the Krian constituency where the Malay electorate was estimated to be 93 per cent.[6]

Although the PMIP was able to draw strong support in the rural Malay coastal districts, it suffered from its inability to attract Malays in other parts of the country. It did not have a nationally prominent figure as its leader to appeal to the more educated and sophisticated urban Malay. The lone PMIP member in the Legislative Council was colorless and ineffective. In December 1956, at the party's annual conference, this situation was remedied by the election of Dr. Burhanuddin as its new president. Under his vigorous leadership the party began an extensive campaign to extend the base of its support and win voters away from UMNO and the Alliance. He played upon the two themes of Malay chauvinist nationalism and the political obligations of the state to preserve and promote the Muslim religion. While he did not openly endorse the concept of the political union of Muslim countries in a vast pan-Muslim state, he was very sympathetic to the idea of close ties with other states where Islam was the dominant religion. In his first address as PMIP president he said, "Historically and geographically, there is a need for the future independent Malaya to have a specially close tie with Indonesia—closer than those with other neighboring countries."[7]

When Dr. Burhanuddin was president of the Malay Nationalist Party he appeared to be more willing to divorce religion from politics. However, after becoming president of the PMIP and discovering the powerful political appeal of Islam, he identified his party with the political principles of Islam and the traditional parochialism and racial-cultural chauvinism of the peasant Malays. Yet Dr. Burhanuddin and the PMIP exhibited some ambivalence in their identification with traditionalism and the prejudices of the rural peasant Malay. For one thing, the Malay communal nationalist who was attracted to the PMIP was not satisfied with the traditional patterns of Malay life and wanted to break some of the bonds of tradition and custom which were believed to be responsible for the Malays' economic plight. By stressing the exclusive religious and racial-cultural identity of the Malays, many of these traditionalist versus reformist issues could be avoided within the party. It is significant to note that Dr. Burhanuddin became more of a Malay communalist than he was in 1946. The following quotations from one of his speeches at a PMIP rally illustrate this change of emphasis.

First and foremost it should be emphasized that Malaya belongs to the Malays and they are the masters in this country.

It is to the Malays as the rightful owners that this country should be returned.

227

The Malays should not be asked to pay for the mistake of the imperialists in bringing non-Malays into the country.

This does not mean that we must push non-Malays out, but there must be a distinction between the aliens and the masters.[8]

Under Dr. Burhanuddin's direction, the PMIP began a systematic campaign to win over the support of Malays who could be roused on communal and religious issues. During the protracted negotiations and debate over the *Merdeka* Constitution, the PMIP attacked the Alliance for its communal compromises and for "abandoning the Malays". It campaigned in favor of very restrictive citizenship laws which would have required at least fifteen years of residence as a first step to naturalization of the non-Malays. On repeated occasions the party demanded that the constitution include a statement that "Malaya belongs to the Malays" and sought to have Malayan citizenship defined as "Melayu" citizenship, to emphasize the essential Malay characteristics expected from those seeking citizenship. The party also proposed to make the former Straits Settlements of Malacca and Penang into "Malay States" so that the system of Malay "special privileges" would be extended to these states, complete with the selection of Malay Rulers to assure that the "special position of the Malays" would be fully protected.[9] Dr. Burhanuddin attacked what he called Malaya's "open-door" immigration policy, charging that the immigration of non-Malays furthered British interests and promoted continued imperialist rule.[10] The PMIP was particularly upset when the Reid Commission recommended against making Islam the state religion. It appears that the potential PMIP appeal on this issue contributed in no small measure to the Alliance decision to demand a change from the Reid recommendations in the final constitution—a demand which was later endorsed by the Council of Rulers despite an earlier decision of the Rulers against having any state religion for the Federation as a whole.[11]

On the East Coast the PMIP mushroomed almost overnight into a formidable political power. In contrast to UMNO, the PMIP enlisted the support of sub-elites in Malay society that were disturbed by political developments and resentful of the poor job opportunities available to those Malays who had only attended Malay schools. Spearheaded by Malay teachers and students from the Muslim religious schools and the Malay primary schools, the party reached out to the ordinary Malays in their scattered villages. Closely associated with the PMIP in this campaign was the Federation of Malay School Teachers Association which had its center of activities at Kota Bharu in Kelantan.[12] The religious-communal appeal was particularly effective when the PMIP could also focus attention upon the economic, professional and educational liabilities which the Malay faced when he determined to break away from his traditional occupations of peasant and fisherman.

Much of the appeal of the PMIP has been the result of Malay concern with education and language issues. The party repeatedly insisted that Malay be the sole official language in government as soon as possible, and it agitated for a greatly expanded Malay educational system. Both policies would open new job opportunities for those who have had their education in the Muslim religious schools or in Malay-media government schools.[13] These proposals were nakedly "bread and butter" propositions, particularly appealing to those ambitious Malay sub-elites who looked to the immediate future with a sense of frustration and despair.[14] It is not surprising therefore, that in the 1959 elections the PMIP made tremendous gains among the East Coast electorate which has the heaviest percentage of Malays and is more isolated from the mainstream of Malayan life.

The PMIP viewed its educational policies both as a tool to raise the status of the Malays and as a method of building a new society that would be fundamentally Malay in character. In 1959 Dr. Burhanuddin announced that his party was dedicated to the principle of promoting the teaching of Islam until a "single Muslim society" could be created.[15] He appeared to hint at the day when all the people of Malaya would embrace Islam and thereby accept Malay patterns of life, religion and culture.[16] This was in accord with the traditional Muslim view of the role of the state in furthering the teachings of Islam and discouraging the non-Islamic religions in the areas under Muslim rule.

Within the PMIP there was a strong attraction for schemes to unite Malaya with neighboring areas in such a way as to strengthen the political position of the Malays or rescue Malay minorities in neighboring states. In the PMIP strongholds of Kelantan and Trengganu, the party took up the cause of the Pattani Malays living in the southern provinces of Thailand. It alleged that the Thai Government's education and language policies discriminated against Malays and that Thai officials were unsympathetic and uncooperative in cases that should have been governed by Muslim jurisprudence and practice. On numerous occasions, PMIP leaders proposed the annexation to Malaya of the Pattani districts of southern Thailand—a demand which on several occasions complicated Malayan-Thai relations.

Of much greater significance, however, was the movement within the PMIP which sought to create a grandiose empire of Malay ethnic stock in Southeast Asia. Some of the leaders of the party were associated with political parties in Indonesia, and were attracted to ideas of some form of political union between Malaya and Indonesia.[18] At the annual conference of the PMIP in 1959, the party was split over a motion to incorporate North Borneo, Brunei and Sarawak into the Federation of Malaya. Dr. Burhanuddin and the party's central executive committee opposed the resolution. A compromise was adopted calling for independence from British rule for the Borneo territories.[19] The following year at the annual convention of his party Dr. Burhanuddin spoke out very strongly in favor of *Melayu Raya*, likening it to the pan-Arab nationalism in the Middle East, reminding his listeners that the three million Malays in Malaya were not the only Malays, and proposing that Malay nationalism should unite the Malays wherever they might be. He attacked the Federal Government's policy of close relations with the United Kingdom and the western bloc, claiming that Malaya was indirectly tied to SEATO which he believed stood in the way of and delayed the eventual establishment of *Melayu Raya*.[20] Although the party was somewhat divided on the question of the merger of Singapore with Malaya, Dr. Burhanuddin increasingly made it clear that the answer to merger lay in the creation of the much larger *Melayu Raya* which could more easily absorb the racial and political impact of Singapore's Chinese majorities. In this way he hoped not to abandon the Malay minority in Singapore, but he did not encourage their demands for rapid or immediate incorporation of Singapore into the Federation of Malaya.

When the Malayan Government began to promote the idea of the Malaysian Federation to embrace Malaya, Singapore and the Borneo territories in a larger union, the PMIP suffered from internal dissensions. Many of its members looked with favor upon both merger with Singapore and the wider union with the British protected states of Borneo, as had earlier been proposed at the PMIP annual conference in 1957, but had been opposed by the party leaders. Finally, after five months of silence, the PMIP came out in opposition to the government's proposals, fearing the entry of Singapore into the larger federation without the simultaneous inclusion of Indonesia and the Philippines in the union. However, the party was cautious and did not take an unequivocal stand. It announced that it "would accept Malaysia on condition that it would safeguard the interests of the Malays".[21] When viewed against its other proposals, it must be assumed that the PMIP believed that this was possible only through the creation of *Melayu Raya*, which would include Malaya, Singapore, the Borneo states, Indonesia and perhaps the Philippines.[22]

Because the party was dedicated to uphold Muslim political and religious ideals, some of the religious differences within Islam were fought out in the councils of the PMIP.[23] The basic contest was between the traditional, conservative, orthodox *ulamas*,[24] and the modernist-reformist element in Islam inspired in part by the movement centered at Al'Azhar University in Cairo. The latter attempted to re-interpret Islam in light of modern science, technology and historical research. The orthodox *ulamas* tried to follow a literal interpretation of the *Koran*. Consequently, they generally opposed policies which would allow Muslims to obtain any interest on investments, they opposed the use of proceeds from state-run lotteries for Muslim welfare, schools and mosques, and they opposed the consumption of alchoholic beverages, especially at government and official functions. The orthodox element was also much more likely to favor strict enforcement of the *khalwat* law[25] including its provisions against non-Muslims. On these issues the modernist-reformist elements were more lenient and sometimes tried to avoid the literal application of the *Koran* or the *hadith*[26] through re-interpretation or through some subterfuge which upheld the strict letter of Muslim law, but avoided some of its harsher consequences. Among the latter faction were found the most active proponents of the pan-Islamic ideal, taking as their example the pan-Arab and pan-Muslim views of Colonel Nasser and the United Arab Republic. Neither of these factions was noticeably more tolerant than the other toward non-Muslims, but the reformist element was rather more cosmopolitan in outlook and had the better-educated, more sophisticated leadership. This element was in a definite minority, both within Islam and within the PMIP, but the movement has been growing.[27] It maintained ties with similar modernist Islamic elements in Indonesia, where the reform movement was comparatively stronger. Where Dr. Burhanuddin stood on these issues is difficult to determine, but his previous association with the Malay Nationalist Party would suggest that he tended to entertain more secular reformist views. However, since the party built much of its power by exploiting the religious identification of the Malays, it could hardly be expected to champion reformist currents in Islam without the serious possibility of losing a large part of its support, because the Malays, on religious matters, are overwhelmingly nurtured in and disciples of the tradition-bound orthodox practices and doctrines of Islam.

In the 1959 state elections, which preceded the federal elections of that year, the PMIP won control of the state governments in Kelantan and Trengganu by capturing 41 out of a total of 53 seats at stake in those two states. In other states, the PMIP had scattered support, primarily in Pahang, Perak, Selangor and Kedah, but was only able to elect one other state assemblyman in the Krian district of Perak. In the federal elections later in the year, the PMIP won 13 out of the 14 parliamentary seats in Trengganu and Kelantan, but was unable to win anywhere else, although it did come close in one district in Kedah and two districts in Perak.[28] PMIP supremacy in Kelantan and Trengganu gave that party the largest number of seats of any opposition in Parliament, and the largest number of state assembly seats won by the opposition parties. However, over the next two years, political events in these same states undermined the apparent PMIP stranglehold of Malaya's Northeast Coast.

Internal fissures and personal feuding developed within the party even before its victories in the 1959 elections. The bitterest struggle occurred in Trengganu where a number of divisions of the PMIP challenged the state party leader, Ustaz Ahmad Azam bin Napiah. The first significant public airing of differences arose over the selection of party candidates for the parliamentary elections.[29] The struggle for power was intensified after the PMIP took office and government positions had to be distributed among the party leaders.[30] After a protracted struggle, Ahmad Azam demanded that the national leadership of the PMIP give him sufficient authority to deal decisively with his opponents in the party. Dr. Burhanuddin rejected this demand and Ahmad Azam thereupon resigned his position as head of the PMIP in Trengganu.[31]

After Ahmad Azam's resignation the PMIP lost its clear majority, having only 12 seats (including the Speaker), as against 7 for the Alliance, 4 for Party Negara and one independent (Ahmad Azam). In the Legislative Assembly Ahmad Azam voted against key government measures, but abstained on "no confidence" votes to allow a tie which was broken by the PMIP Speaker.[32] Because of the deadlock, the PMIP Government attempted to carry on without convening the Legislative Assembly, which did not meet for seven months. When the Assembly finally convened, the PMIP Government fell on a "no confidence" motion, at which time 2 PMIP members and all 4 Party Negara members joined the Alliance Party. Two other PMIP members abstained on the crucial vote.[33] The six assemblymen that joined the Alliance enabled that party to form a new government without the necessity of holding new elections.[34] With a 13 to 11 majority, the Alliance obtained a working majority which enabled it to operate the state government for the period until the next general elections.

The Alliance victory in Trengganu was made possible largely through the internecine feuds within the PMIP followed by the deadlock and incompetence which characterized its rule. Perhaps just as important, however, was the ability of the Alliance to undermine PMIP support by promising massive federal money for economic development in the backward and distressed rural areas of the East Coast. Some federal funds were made available to the PMIP state governments, but the PMIP was at a disadvantage in that it had to accept the federal money in accordance with policies determined by the Alliance Government and the National Land Council.[35] Without the power and influence of the Federal Government, it is doubtful whether the Alliance could have succeeded in nearly doubling its strength in the State Assembly of Trengganu merely by attracting members from rival parties. Similar economic and political pressures were applied by the Alliance in Kelantan, although there the PMIP retained its control of the state government. In the Kelantan local council elections of 1961, however, the PMIP won only 14 seats while the Alliance took 51 seats. In Trengganu the Alliance won 32 local council seats, Party Negara 4 seats and the PMIP captured only one seat.[36] These statistics indicate the great loss of support for the PMIP in those areas where previously it had gained its most striking victories. Nevertheless the party had exceptional vitality and could easily recover from these reverses, depending on the temper of communal feelings among the Malays and the emergence of new political issues which might arouse new communal or religious passions.

Party Negara

In 1955 Party Negara had hoped to be the opposition party in the Legislative Council and party officials had confidently expressed their conviction that they would win close to a dozen seats in the legislature. Instead, Party Negara emerged from the contest a defeated and broken party. Not one Negara candidate was elected to the federal legislature, and 13 out of its slate of 30 lost their election deposits. Following these devastating defeats Dato Onn made a great effort to rebuild the party. In many areas of supposed strength, the party existed more on paper than in active branches. Throughout its history, the party was so closely tied to the personal leadership of Dato Onn that almost no other supporting leadership emerged with contact at the grass roots. The energy of Dato Onn could never overcome this basic defect of the party.

A parliamentary by-election in 1957 gave Dato Onn another opportunity to try for a parliamentary seat, this time in Batu Pahat, Johore, where he had been a District Officer years before. Once again, however, he suffered defeat, succumbing to the Alliance candidate by a vote of 12,179 to 5,614.[37] As the party sustained one loss after another, the big names associated with the party began drifting away from its folds. In part, this was because of the new tactics of the party based upon a very conservative brand of strident Malay chauvinism which it was hoped would win over the Malay electorate. Heah Joo-seang, who had been elected Vice President of the party in 1955, eventually became associated with the MCA and the Alliance.[38] Dato Clough Thuraisingham, who had been the first Minister of Education and a leading figure in the party, retired from active politics after 1955 in circumstances that indicated his disgust with the turn of events. Dato Nik Ahmad Kamil also left Party Negara and was recruited by the Alliance Government to be the High Commissioner for Malaya, first in Australia and then in the United Kingdom. Later he was made Ambassador to the United States.

With the approach of the 1959 elections Dato Onn engaged in an untiring campaign to prepare his party for the contest. His main attention was devoted to the East Coast states and Johore. The Negara manifesto was not significantly changed from that of 1955.[39] However, Dato Onn made the problems of Malay education one of the major issues in his electioneering. He tried to cash in on the dissatisfaction of the Malay teachers and students over the failure of the government to begin a massive program for Malay-medium secondary schools. The party continued to attack the constitutional provisions for citizenship, and it heaped ridicule upon the constitutional arrangements for a "rotating King", just as it had in 1957 when it joined with other Malay communal parties in the "Malay Congress" to mount a unified attack against the "anti-Malay" provisions of the Reid Commission's proposals. The party sought the conservative Muslim vote by charging the Alliance with violating Muslim law in a number of ways. In particular it criticized the government for donating profits from welfare lotteries to Muslim institutions,[40] and rumors spread that Tunku Abdul Rahman did not abide by all the Muslim dietary restrictions.

In the state elections of 1959, Party Negara contested 79 seats in the states of Johore, Kedah, Negri Sembilan, Penang, Kelantan and Trengganu.[41] It polled 14·9 per cent in the state constituencies it contested, but received only 4·3 per cent of the total vote in the state elections. The party won only 4 assembly seats, all of them in Trengganu. In the parliamentary election, the party contested 6 seats in Johore, 1 seat in Negri Sembilan and 1 seat in Trengganu, getting 22·2 per cent of the vote in the constituencies it contested. The only Negara candidate to win a seat in Parliament was Dato Onn, who ran in Kuala Trengganu Selatan. The fact that all the Negara seats in the state elections were won in the vicinity where Dato Onn campaigned for his parliamentary seat attests to the personal appeal and prestige he enjoyed among the Malays. In January 1962 Dato Onn died,[42] and his seat was re-captured by the Alliance in a by-election. For all practical purposes, his death marked the end of Party Negara. It is somewhat ironic that Dato Onn's party was conceived as a non-communal answer to UMNO but ended as a communal goad to UMNO. Ultimately most of his political heirs re-united with the "mother party" once he was no longer there to lead the diminishing ranks of those who gave their political loyalty directly to him.

The National Association of Perak

In 1955 the National Association of Perak represented many of the same interests as Party Negara. Both parties claimed to be "non-communal", which was true insofar as membership was open to all races. Likewise, both parties were closely identified with the conservative Malays in the "court circle" and the higher civil servants in the state administration.

The political influence of the National Association of Perak probably reached its peak shortly after it was founded in 1953. The party has found it very difficult to develop a substantial following among the common people of any race. The party appears to have been a product of the personal following attracted by its founder, Dato Panglima Bukit Gantang.[43] As the party suffered reverses, that following gradually drifted away to the camps of the major contenders on the political scene.

Because of the shifting balance of political power in Perak, the NAP tried to use its weight to bargain with other parties for alliances in most of its election efforts. Party Negara and the NAP joined forces in the 1955 elections. Although they did not field a joint slate, they did not contest the same districts, and each party threw its support to the other where it had no candidate. The NAP polled a slightly higher proportion of the votes in constituencies it contested than did Party Negara. However, the NAP still suffered an overwhelming defeat, getting only 14·1 per cent of the vote where it fielded candidates.[44] Four months later, in the Perak State Council elections, the NAP experienced an even more devastating blow with five of its eleven candidates losing their election deposits.[45]

In the Perak town and rural council elections of 1955 the NAP joined with the Peoples Progressive Party and by this means was able to get one seat on the Ipoh Town Council.[46] This union continued into 1957 when the NAP gave its support to the leader of the PPP, D. R. Seenivasagam, who successfully contested a federal by-election in the Ipoh-Menglembu constituency.[47] The agreement between the NAP and the PPP ceased shortly afterwards, apparently due to difficulties in choosing a slate for the 1958 town council elections in Perak. The weakness of the NAP was demonstrated when the party fielded its own slate in Ipoh and all its candidates lost their deposits.

In July 1958 a new president was elected to lead the virtually defunct party. He was a cousin of the Sultan of Perak.[48] However the leadership of the party changed hands once again after the defeats in the 1958 Ipoh elections. Both the incoming president and the vice-president were Chinese and the party shifted its appeal somewhat to give more attention to the demands of the

Chinese in Perak. By this time the PPP enjoyed the overwhelming support of the Chinese and Indian voters around Ipoh and in the Kinta Valley. The new NAP leaders hoped to recover some of their losses by opening negotiations for joining the Alliance in the 1959 federal elections. As a consequence, the vice-president of the NAP, Leong Kee-nyean, was placed on the Alliance ticket in Kampar and emerged the victor over the PPP candidate by a narrow margin. Paradoxically, that triumph was the final gasp of the NAP since it ceased having an independent existence as a political party in anything but name after 1959.

The Peoples Progressive Party

Another regional political party having Perak as its locus of activity was the Perak Progressive Party.[49] In the 1955 federal elections it contested only two seats, and both candidates lost their deposits.[50] However, the leader of the Perak Progressive Party, Mr. D. R. Seenivasagam, had won a seat on the Ipoh Town Council the year before by joining his party with the Alliance. He later used that vantage point to direct a continuing political attack against it. Soon he became identified in the public eye as one of the most dynamic and effective critics of the Government. As Mr. Seenivasagam began to attract the attention of the press and the public elsewhere in Malaya, the party began to push plans for expansion beyond the borders of Perak. The ambitions of the party were reflected in its change of name in the latter part of 1956 from Perak Progressive Party to Peoples Progressive Party.

When Leong Yew-koh became Governor of Malacca in 1957, a federal by-election was held in the Ipoh-Menglembu district to fill his vacant seat. Mr. Seenivasagam had his greatest strength there, so he welcomed this opportunity to run for federal office once again. In a hard-fought election, he emerged the victor,[51] and became the second elected member of Parliament to be counted among "the opposition". In Parliament he quickly assumed the role of champion of the "underdog" and became a formidable advocate for the mounting number of non-Malays who had developed grievances against the Government for its policies. Quite often the four members nominated to represent the trade unions supported his stand in Parliament.

From its inception the Peoples Progressive Party adroitly combined the issues of political, legal and racial equalitarianism with a selective dose of "socialist" economics. Although the party claimed to be "non-communal", it followed a political line that appealed mainly to Chinese and Indians, but was repugnant to most Malays. Its greatest support has resulted from its forceful espousal of non-Malay communal interests in such issues as education, citizenship, Malay "special rights", language policies, immigration and land use.[52] Although the two dominant figures in the party were Ceylonese, and the core of the party in its early years was Indian, mass support came from the large Chinese population in and around Ipoh. The more intensely communal Chinese found it very valuable to have a non-Chinese be such a willing and able advocate for their cause. A majority of the party's candidates[53] and the overwhelming bulk of the party's lesser functionaries were Chinese.

In the first few years of its existence the party was casting about for issues that would lure large numbers of voters. In 1957 Chinese opposition to the Razak Plan and the government's education policies became so intense that civil disorders broke out in Penang, Ipoh and Kuala Lumpur. By taking advantage of this issue, D. R. Seenivasagam was able to win his first smashing victory against his MCA opponent who had to defend the communal compromises worked out by the Alliance. The PPP worked very closely with the Federation of Chinese Guilds in Ipoh and with the Federation of Chinese Teachers Associations in their attempts to force a change of policy, and in their subsequent attempts to unseat the MCA leadership and sabotage the Alliance. Throughout this period the PPP openly supported the Guilds' demands on education, citizenship and "multi-lingualism".

The Alliance has charged that the PPP flirted with Communist elements and resorted to "strong-arm" tactics to maintain its political power. It is true that the party tended to de-emphasize the menace of Communism to Malaya. It was also one of the first to come out in favor of reaching an agreement with the Malayan Communist Party to end the guerrilla fighting. When negotiations between the government and the MCP failed, the PPP hinted that the Emergency had not been ended because of blunders and inflexibility on the part of the government. It suggested that there should be a clear distinction made between Communism and the lawless acts of the guerrillas.[54] Similarly, the PPP persistently attacked the Emergency Regulations and its sequel, the Internal Security Act of 1960, especially those provisions which permitted the authorities to detain persons without a court trial. It has also claimed that these laws have been used to stifle freedom of speech and intimidate the opposition parties. Some of its critics have accused the PPP of being sympathetic to Communism and infiltrated by Communists, but the party's leaders have strongly denounced these allegations. They claim to have been successful in preventing Communist infiltration.[55]

Within the Peoples Progressive Party the reins of power had been held by D. R. Seenivasagam, sided by his elder brother, S. P. Seenivasagam. Their father was a well-known lawyer in Ipoh and the sons both studied law in London. Both have political talents, but D. R. in particular has had charismatic powers over the Ipoh electorate. Although quite well-to-do and making no attempt to conceal the fact, he commanded the loyalty and affection of many thousands of lower-class laborers through his apparently genuine concern for their plight and his willingness to perform favors, give free legal aid, and provide other services in the manner of some American politicians. The personalized character of the PPP made it difficult for the party to expand beyond the Ipoh area. However, it developed a following in Penang and Selangor, and made moves to enlist support in Malacca and Johore. The party recruited dissidents from the Alliance, the most notable being K. Annamalai, the rebel member of the MIC, who later ran as a PPP candidate to Parliament from Sungei Siput and was defeated. Similarly, some

PPP members transferred their support to the Alliance after intra-party fights and amid charges that the PPP was run by a "pocket dictator".[56]

As a minor party on the political scene, the PPP has been under pressure to combine with other opposition parties to challenge Alliance supremacy. In the 1957 by-election it secured the support of Party Negara. In 1958 it entered into negotiations with the Labour Party, Party Ra'ayat and the Socialist Youth League to form a "United Socialist Front" but agreement failed,[57] as did similar overtures to Party Negara in 1959. Apart from policy and personality differences, the problem of making common cause with the PPP was complicated by its insistence on preserving its monopoly position around Ipoh while it asked for a division of the electoral slate in other areas.

The Peoples Progressive Party manifesto for the 1959 elections was quite similar to its pronouncement four years earlier.[58] It was more openly equalitarian in its message than the Socialist Front with which it shared the left wing of the policital spectrum. Animosity between the two became rather intense after they fought each other in Penang during the 1959 elections. In the state elections the PPP put up 16 candidates in Perak, 11 in Penang and 4 in Selangor. Only 8 were elected, all of them in Perak. There the PPP polled 23·4 per cent, but it gained only 5·7 per cent in Penang and 3·9 per cent in Selangor. In the Federal elections 15 candidates ran on the PPP ticket in the four states of Perak, Selangor, Penang and Johore. Four were elected, all from contiguous constituencies around Ipoh. The party polled 26·9 per cent of the vote in Perak, but only 4 per cent in Selangor, 2·9 per cent in Penang and 1 per cent in Johore.[59]

In Parliament the PPP often engaged in bitter exchanges with the Pan-Malayan Islamic Party, since the two were at opposite poles on communal issues. Although the Alliance had no love and little respect for the PPP, it had enjoyed being relieved of some responsibility for responding to some of the communal demagogy of the PMIP, since the PPP was more than willing to step into the fray. When the Chinese Communist troops attacked India, the Alliance saw this as an opportunity to undermine the PPP because of its joint Indian-Chinese composition. D. R. Seenivasagam criticized the Government for not offering its services as a neutral "third party" to end the dispute between China and India and announcing his party's neutrality on the issue.[60] This position was not popular with most Indians who praised Malaya's full support for India and the Prime Minister's sponsorship of the "Save Democracy Fund" for those who wished to contribute money to the Indian Government for strengthening its defences. However, the PPP stand was probably wise in view of its heavy dependence on the Chinese vote.

Because of the difficulty the PPP experienced in developing political allies in Malaya, it seemed likely that with the creation of the Malaysian Federation the PPP would make a move to find political allies in Singapore and perhaps in the Borneo states. There is evidence that the PPP did make overtures to the Peoples Action Party in Singapore, with which it had much in common on the major political issues of the day, but a formal political alliance did not materialize.

The Labour Party of Malaya

In the 1955 elections the Labour Party of Malaya nominated only four candidates, one in Penang and the other three in the tin-producing districts of Perak and Selangor. In these four districts the Labour candidates polled only 9.3 per cent of the vote. The strongest showing by a Labour candidate was in Penang where the Labour Party polled 26·7 per cent.[61] This rather poor showing of the Labour Party may be partly attributed to the fact that the party had been formed only a short time before the elections,[62] and in reality was little more than a coalition of several small separate parties that were not even prepared to contest local elections.

After 1955 the Labour Party began steadily increasing its following in the key states of Penang, Perak, Selangor, Johore and Malacca. A number of major unions contributed to its growing strength. As a leftist alternative to the Alliance the party gained both support and stature. However, it suffered from a series of debilitating revolts and internal feuds. For example, in the latter part of 1955 the Selangor division of the Labour Party dissolved the Kuala Lumpur branch of the party for insubordination and breach of party discipline. The National Executive of the party appointed a committee to inquire into the dispute, but the Selangor division leaders refused to appear and did not concur with the findings of the committee. Thereupon the National Executive suspended the Selangor division of the party for "unconstitutional conduct". In return the leaders of the Selangor division got the cooperation of representatives from five other state divisions to "suspend" the National Executive. The "rebels", led by the Selangor Labour Party chairman, Tan Tuan-boon, then proceeded to hold a "rump" annual conference of the party, and as a gesture of disdain for the "suspended" parent organization, proceeded to elect the president of the Labour Party, Mr. D. S. Ramanathan, as one of the three vice-presidents of the "rump" faction of the party. Both groups claimed to be the Labour Party of Malaya.[63] More than a year went by before this division of the Labour Party was patched up. The strife appears to have been less over differences in policy than over the clash of personalities and localized party cliques.

The Labour Party claims to be a genuine socialist party, and from time to time it has made vague pronouncements calling for nationalizing industry, mining and rubber estates.[64] These general theoretical objectives are admittedly not to be secured in the near future. On the more immediate issues, the Labour Party took up a posture that tried to adapt Fabian Socialism to the Malayan environment. Its 1955 manifesto[65] avoided commitment on most communal issues and made no direct reference to racial or communal problems. It gave the impression that its leaders thought that those issues were too dangerous to raise and, conveniently, communal differences could be blamed upon British "divide and rule" tactics. However, by 1956 the party took a stand on several issues that were then at the heart of communal politics. It stood for the recognition of Chinese and Indian as official languages, and in the George Town City Council attempted to introduce "multi-lingualism" (English, Malay, Chinese and Indian) in its proceedings. It favored easy citizenship requirements based on the principle of *jus soli*.[66] It favored legal and political equality for all citizens, but by 1963 was willing to tolerate Malay "special privileges" if treated only as a transitional measure to raise the economic position of the Malays.[67] These policies reflected the Labour Party's overwhelming Chinese and Indian composition. The majority of its members and leaders were Chinese, but in most states Indians shared the key positions and Indians constituted an important source of support for the party. Efforts to recruit Malays from urban areas into the party met with little success.

The Labour Party became an outspoken critic of the Government's policy toward Communism. It proposed in 1957 that all persons detained for political reasons be released.[68] Also, it called for an end to the Emergency through negotiation with the Communists, and could see no reason why the Malayan Communist Party should not be permitted to emerge from the jungle and become a legally recognized party. Resolutions of the party also called for the withdrawal of all foreign troops from Malaya, hinting that the foreign troops may have been the cause of the Emergency. Like the Peoples Progressive Party, the Labour Party consistently favored Malayan recognition of the Communist government of the Peoples Republic of China.[69]

Some people in Malaya were of the opinion that the Labour Party was Communist dominated, but this is clearly an exaggeration. The party may have been naïve when it came to the threat from the Communist quarter, but its leaders would have been among the first to object to a one-party dictatorship of a Communist regime. However, the Malayan Communist Party, during its "united front" tactics, adopted policies that were quite similar to many of those taken by the Labour Party. Consequently, the Labour Party was a primary target for the infiltration tactics of the MCP. One Communist-controlled political front, the Socialist Youth League, attempted to join forces with the Labour Party and sought to place its members in the Labour Party at all levels. When this pattern of Communist infiltration was publicly revealed after the sensational arrests of alleged Communist agents in 1958 and 1959, Mr. Ramanathan, then president of the Labour Party, announced his determination to expel any Communists from his party.[70]

Party Ra'ayat

After the 1955 federal elections, a new party appeared on the political scene. It was founded by the former president of Angkatan Pemuda Insaf, Ahmad Boestamam, who had been released in June 1955 after seven years' detention.[71] Apparently he began to re-establish his political contacts, and made known his intention to form a new party. Within a few months he announced, "Former members of the API have responded to the move to form this party."[72] In December 1955, the party was formally launched with the name of Party Ra'ayat, which in Malay means "Peoples Party".[73]

Party Ra'ayat was formed in ample time to participate in the political deliberations over the *Merdeka* Constitution. At first the party prepared a petition to submit to the Reid Commission and gave this petition wide publicity. But when the time came to present its views, Party Ra'ayat decided to boycott the Reid Commission on the grounds that the Commission was composed of "foreigners" and was limited by too narrow terms of reference.[74]

Ahmad Boestamam has described his party as an "agrarian socialist" party. However, Malayan politics do not follow patterns which fit the usual socialist categories, and the party's rudimentary ideology has not provided ready answers to the pressing issues of Malayan politics. On some of the immediate political issues of the day, Party Ra'ayat took the following stands: it favored granting citizenship "to all locally domiciled people owing undivided loyalty to Malaya", but was opposed to the principle of *jus soli*; it called for "no discrimination against any race or religion in commerce, education and culture"; it proposed international mediation as a means for securing peace with the Malayan Communist Party; it demanded abolishment of the Emergency Regulations; and it favored halting foreign investments in Malaya.[75]

Although Boestamam has claimed that Party Ra'ayat is non-communal, it has appealed rather narrowly to the radical Malays who, before 1948, were attracted to the Malay Nationalist Party or its more radical affiliate, Angkatan Pemuda Insaf. Boestamam's Party Ra'ayat deliberately avoided any formal association with Dr. Burhanuddin (former president of the Malay Nationalist Party), partly because it wanted to avoid the commitment to the extreme communal stand taken by Dr. Burhanuddin when he was leader of the Malay National Front in 1955 and later when he became leader of the Pan-Malayan Islamic Party. Yet Party Ra'ayat supported Malay "special rights" as necessary "so long as Capitalism exists to exploit the Malays".[76] Its non-communal guise did not conceal the fact that Party Ra'ayat lined up on the distinctly "Malay" side on nearly all communal issues.

Ahmed Boestaman has been accused of willingly giving support to the Malayan Communist Party. However, it is highly unlikely that he is a Communist or has any genuine desire to see the Communists assume command in Malaya. Nonetheless, he appears to have been influenced by Marxist theories of class struggle, and the Leninist interpretation of colonialism. This may partly explain his desire to de-emphasize communal issues as "a small matter",[77] stressing instead political struggle in terms of "class war" and "imperialist exploitation". He thus tended to be receptive to certain aspects of Communist propaganda and made political proposals that were in harmony with the short-term objectives of the Communist Party's "united front" program.[78] Consequently, Party Ra'ayat was selected by the MCP as a major target for infiltration,[79] but there has been little evidence made public of successful Communist infiltration into Party Ra'ayat. No doubt, one of the major obstacles has been the fact that the Communist Party had so few Malay members that can be used to infiltrate an essentially Malay political party.

In February 1963 Boestamam was arrested under the extraordinary powers of the Internal Security Act. The Government claims that Boestamam made the following statement shortly after his detention:

> I am prepared to cooperate with the Communists to achieve my long-term plan to unite Indonesia, the Philippines, the Borneo territories, South Thailand, Malaya and Singapore into a greater Malaysia state.
>
> We are fighting the Alliance so why not cooperate with everybody, be they Communists or any other political party.
>
> Once in power I shall leave them alone if they do not oppose me. . . .
>
> In other words, I shall use the Communists, but I shall not be indebted to them. . . .
>
> If my party comes into power it will recognise the MCP, provided they cooperate constitutionally.
>
> If my party comes into power I shall repeal the Internal Security Act. But if the Communists or anybody else acts unconstitutionally I shall introduce another Bill to cover not only the more important points of the Internal Security Act, but also to broaden the scope to cover all my political enemies.[80]

Whether he actually willingly made this statement or not, it appears to this writer to be a fairly accurate summary of his political objectives.

A Coalition of Opposition Parties—The Malay Congress

As long as the Alliance remained intact, the only chance for the opposition parties to exercise political power was through some sort of coalition. However, the opposition parties had more divergent political views among themselves than did the partners in the Alliance. Furthermore, several of the opposition parties were led by men who were temperamentally opposed to compromising any major segment of their political credo. Rather than building a coherent and united opposition, it appears that many of these opposition leaders were counting instead upon the "inevitable" break-up of the Alliance Party. Although the Alliance suffered from internal strains, it did not disintegrate, and it became increasingly obvious that victory at the polls could not be secured by default.

The first substantial attempt to build an opposition coalition after the first federal elections was made in 1957. The initiative was taken by an ex-official of the United Malays National Organization who had objected to UMNO's compromising on the Reid Report. After unsuccessfully challenging the leadership of Tunku Abdul Rahman, he resigned from UMNO and helped to plan the convening of the Malay Congress in the capitol.[81] Party Negara, Party Ra'ayat, the Pan-Malayan Islamic Party and the Peninsular Malays Union were invited to participate in this Malay Congress.[82] Dato Onn and Dr. Burhanuddin were the dominant figures in the conference, and they helped to prepare a set of political demands to be presented to the Alliance Government concerning the Reid Commission constitutional proposals. The resolutions of the Malay Congress reflected the "pro-Malay" communal point of view of Party Negara and the PMIP, the two parties controlling the Congress.

Ahmad Boestamam's Party Ra'ayat was cautious about becoming wholly indentified with some of the more extreme communal demands of the Malay Congress. Its delegation refused to sit on the committee drafting resolutions, and later the entire Ra'ayat delegation walked out of the plenary sessions of the Malay Congress, accusing it of being too communal.

Because the Alliance Government refused to consider the demands of the Malay Congress, Dr. Burhanuddin and Dato Onn travelled to London to press for the views of the Malay Congress.[84] In Malaya the Congress threatened to organize mass demonstrations against the new constitution and to encourage all Malays to go into mourning, much as had been done in 1946 by the United Malays National Organization when it successfully challenged the Malayan Union constitution. However, this threat never materialized, primarily because Malay opinion was not as unified as it had been in 1946. Furthermore, the Alliance concessions to Malay criticism of the Reid Proposals stole some of the wind from the sails of the Malay Congress.

Like previous anti-Alliance conferences, the Malay Congress did not result in a unified opposition coalition. Indeed, several important opposition parties were not invited because their political views were too much at variance with those of the Malay politicians convening the Malay Congress, and even those parties attending were unwilling to build a lasting unified political front among themselves at the expense of compromising their differences.

A Coalition of Opposition Parties—The Socialist Front

A more serious attempt to create the nucleus for a major opposition coalition was made during the early months of 1957. In February six opposition parties met to discuss the creation of an anti-Alliance front.[85] Nothing came of these discussions until after the Malay-oriented parties formed their short-lived Malay Congress. Later, in June, extensive negotiations continued between the Labour Party, Party Ra'ayat, the Peoples Progressive Party and the Socialist Youth League, but only the Labour Party and Party Ra'ayat finally agreed to join forces to form the Malayan Peoples Socialist Front, which was formally launched on August 31, 1957, the date of Malayan independence. At its inaugural meeting Ahmad Boestamam of Party Ra'ayat was elected president and Mr. D. S. Ramanathan of the Labour Party became vice-president.[86]

In order to combine political forces, the Labour Party and Party Ra'ayat had to find a political platform that would be acceptable to both parties. They both claimed to be socialist, so great stress could be laid on that ill-defined political term that has such widespread appeal for most Asians. Both favored the immediate merger of Singapore with Malaya (but for slightly different reasons). Both liked to characterize their program as "anti-colonial and nationalist". Both considered themselves champions of the "exploited common people", and both had been severe critics of the defense treaty with the United Kingdom, under the terms of which Commonwealth troops helped Malayan forces in the anti-guerrilla operations. The difficulty in reaching agreement between them turned on communal issues: Party Ra'ayat favored Malay interests, while the Labour Party favored Chinese and Indian interests. One way out was to ignore the more communal issues. But before the two could collaborate, the Labour Party had to renounce its previous stand against the Malay Rulers and against Malay "special rights". The Labour Party admitted that it was wrong in seeking to have a republic headed by a president, and it promised neither to question the status of the Malay Rulers under the *Merdeka* Constitution nor to challenge the existing special privileges of the Malays.[87] In return, Party Ra'ayat tacitly consented that equal treatment for all citizens would be possible sometime in the indefinite future. On other communal issues, it was agreed that Malay should be the only official language, but that Chinese and Tamil should continue as "languages of convenience". Similarly, the Socialist Front promised to support Malay national schools along with Chinese and Tamil schools.[88] The Socialist Front also pledged to recognize Communist China and to promote closer ties with Afro-Asian countries (which some have interpreted to mean closer political ties with Indonesia).[89]

In general, both parties tried to dismiss communal issues as unimportant, on the argument that special privileges were of little real value to the Malays. The Socialist Front has also argued that communal divisions are being artificially stimulated by the Alliance to prevent the masses from realizing the basic conflict of class interests. This interpretation had some appeal for a substantial number of Malay intellectuals who found that traditional Malay leaders stood in the way of their economic and political ambitions. With some justification they felt that religious and racial feelings were artificially exploited for conservative objectives.

The Socialist Front leaders had hopes that other opposition parties might be induced to join the Front. Special efforts were made to persuade the Peoples Progressive Party to become a member at the time the Front was formed. Later, in November 1957, just after D. R. Seenivasagam won a seat in Parliament in the Ipoh by-election, further overtures were made.[90] There followed a period of uncertainty and vacillation in the relations between the PPP and the Socialist Front. For example, D. R. Seenivasagam was invited to speak to a Socialist Front conference in Malacca, but at the last moment the invitation was withdrawn with the explanation that those who made the arrangements were "unaware that the PPP's constitution was not in line with Socialist aims".[91] The real explanation for this blunder is more likely to be found in the running dispute between the Labour Party and the PPP in Penang at that time. The PPP was attempting to organize branches in "Labour districts" and was also brash enough to suggest a "common front" with Labour, to fight the Alliance where Labour had hopes of single-handed victory. As could be expected, Mr. Seenivasagam felt insulted and maligned when the invitation was withdrawn. The prospects for a three-way coalition to fight the Alliance in the federal elections were seriously damaged by this incident.[92] In fact, the Socialist Front were not able to embrace any more opposition parties before the big test of the 1959 federal elections.[93]

The election statistics for 1959 clearly demonstrate that the Labour Party was the dominant force behind the Socialist Front. Altogether, the Socialist Front fielded 108 candidates scattered in all eleven states in the state elections. However, only 16 were elected in only four states, and then only from areas where Chinese and Indian voters were concentrated.[94] In the federal elections the Socialist Front fielded 30 candidates, 8 of whom were elected, 5 from Selangor and 3 from Penang.[95] Party Ra'ayat's inability to attract the Malay vote was demonstrated by the fact that all 22 SF candidates in Kelantan and Perlis lost their deposits in the state election. The pattern was repeated in all other states in the districts where Malays constitute most of the electorate. It is possible that Party Ra'ayat had some significant support from the urban Malays, but, if so, that support is concealed in the statistics because of the mixed racial composition of urban areas.

The Labour Party has attempted to give strength to Party Ra'ayat, in the hope that an increasing number of Malay voters would be persuaded to abandon the Alliance, or even to shift from the PMIP to the Socialist Front. With this objective in mind, the Labour Party played down its Chinese and Indian bias, and in 1959 even elected the radical Malay politician Ishak bin Haji Mohamed to replace D. S. Ramanathan as party president.[96] Similarly, Ahmad Boestamam, president of Party Ra'ayat was selected as president of the Socialist Front. In both cases their selection appears to have been motivated by a desire to attract more Malay voters, rather than to transfer power to a cluster of Malay leaders.

Active leadership in the Socialist Front was largely the monopoly of those who had been key figures in important trade unions, nearly all of whom were Chinese or Indians. There was, however, a remarkable variety in the background of the top leadership. The party had both a small professional and western-educated elite and a rather poorly educated indigenous leadership which emerged from the rough-and-tumble political environment of some of the larger unions. At times the better educated and more sophisticated leaders appeared to be under pressure from within the party to make more exaggerated and irresponsible statements than they really cared to make. On the, whole the party was better equipped to assume the reigns of government than any other opposition party, because it had been able to recruit more of the educated, trained and professional people than other opposition parties. Nonetheless, its support from these sources remained small.

The structure of the Socialist Front coalition resulted in both internal divisions and periodic defections. At times the disputes within the party must be attributed to personalities and the clash of rival factions. However, some rather fundamental differences, especially on communal issues, exacerbated the natural rivalries within the party. Although the Socialist Front tried to avoid or play down communal issues, occasionally the party was forced to take a stand. One such crisis occurred in 1960 over education policy and the party's reaction to the Talib Report. In general, it may be said that the

Labour Party "wing" favored "multi-lingualism" and continued support for Chinese, Indian and English-medium education, even after 1967 (when Malay "special rights" were to come up for review), while the Party Ra'ayat "wing" favored Malay as the sole official and national language, and proposed to establish Malay as the sole medium of instruction in primary and secondary schools by 1967. During the height of the argument within the party, Ahmad Boestamam announced his resignation as party president. Finally, the issues were resolved and agreement was reached on a short compromise statement explaining the party's stand on education policy.[98] On the basis of this agreement Ahmad Boestamam continued to serve as Socialist Front president.

On other communal issues the Socialist Front exhibited similar internal divisions or inconsistencies. For example, in 1960 it backed a PPP motion regretting that the royal speech explaining the Government's policy contained no reference "to the democratic claim for equal rights of all citizens of this country".[99] Later, in 1962, the Socialist Front Conference agreed to support Malay "special rights" while belittling their effect and suggesting that these rights did not aid the "masses". A party spokesman explained that Malay "special rights" were necessary as a transitional measure to help the Malays.[100] How long these measures would be needed was subject to varied interpretation within the party. On the whole, the party was quite successful in skirting, avoiding or finding incomplete compromises on the major communal issues that have arisen in Malayan politics.

The Socialist Front claimed that it was prevented from becoming the strongest party because of the use and threatened use of the Government's emergency powers under the Internal Security Act. Through the years a few members of the Socialist Front were detained without trial with the explanation that they were giving aid and support to the Communist Party. Whether these charges were accurate or not depends on whom one is inclined to believe. Nevertheless, it is clear that the Socialist Front was a target for infiltration by the Malayan Communist Party, and it seems likely that the Communist Party had some success in its efforts. At the same time, it is obvious that arrests of *bone fide* Communists within the Socialist Front had a very deleterious effect upon the party. It is also possible that arrests were made where there was little or no evidence to justify such action. On the other hand, it seems probable that the effect of the occasional arrests under the emergency powers has been greatly exaggerated by the Socialist Front in an attempt to gain sympathy and overcome some of the unfortunate publicity that followed in the wake of these arrests.[101] In the long run, it appeared that the use of the Government's extraordinary powers had much less to do with the party's fortunes than the problem of working out a coherent alternative to the Alliance Government that would also command the support of a majority of Malaya's voters.

The Malayan Party

The Malayan Party was founded in 1956,[102] partly in response to the dissatisfaction among the Chinese in Malacca with certain provisions in the

Reid Report concerning the status of the former Straits Settlements in independent Malaya. A few key individuals in the Malacca Chinese Chamber of Commerce and the Federation of Chinese Guilds became the moving force behind the Malayan Party. The president of the party, Tan Kee-gak, was one of the four members on the Chinese guild delegation which was sent to London to seek constitutional alterations easing citizenship requirements and giving equal status to all citizens. He was also president of the Malacca Chinese Chamber of Commerce and had been a founder-member of the Malayan Chinese Association. Associated with him were Leon D'Cruz, an Indian with a Portuguese name, originally from Trivandrum, South India, and Humphrey Ball, a British lawyer who had been legal advisor to the Chinese delegation to London.[103]

Large numbers of Chinese and Indians in Malacca wished to preserve their status of equality as "subjects of the Crown" which they enjoyed by virtue of being permanent residents in a former Crown colony. The Malayan Party espoused this cause and won the widespread support of the more conservative non-Malays in Malacca.[104] To preserve the legal rights of the citizens of Malacca, the Malayan Party tried to invoke the 133-year-old Treaty of Holland (1824), which stated that Malacca would never be transferred to another power, and if abandoned it would revert to the Netherlands.[105] Needless to say, this argument for the preservation in the *Merdeka* Constitution of equal status for the Malacca citizens (and by implication sovereign status for Malacca), carried little weight with Whitehall or the Alliance Government.

The Malayan Party became a vitriolic critic of the policies of the Alliance, particularly on constitutional matters and on the issues of Chinese education. To a large extent it became the political mouthpiece for the Chinese guilds and the Chinese Chambers of Commerce. Some of the rebel members of the Malayan Chinese Association were recruited by the party, particularly after the crisis within the MCA when the more outspoken communal elements were defeated and purged from the Alliance. In his speeches Tan Kee-gak accused the MCA of being a traitor to the Chinese because of its membership in the Alliance and its support of the "anti-Chinese" policies of the Alliance Government.[106] Despite its appeal to discontented Chinese communal interests, the party paraded under a banner of "non-communalism" on the argument that full legal and political equality was not a communal issue. The party based much of its campaigning on this issue of political and legal equality for all persons in Malaya. Its leaders explained that the party's basic platform was the United Nations Declaration of Human Rights, and they said that they envisaged a Malaya that was a "multi-racial Socialist, property-owning democracy" somewhat similar to the political and economic system found in Switzerland.[107]

The initial successes of the Malayan Party were in the Malacca Municipal Council elections of 1957, at which time the party captured four out of six contested seats. Two years later in the state elections the entire six-member Malayan Party slate was defeated.[108] In the federal election of that year, the party concentrated all its resources on one campaign to elect its leader, Tan Kee-gak, who successfully ran in the Malacca Town area after a stormy campaign involving public arguments with Tan Siew-sin.[109]

After 1959 the Malayan Party appeared to be trying to consolidate its communal and sectional support around Malacca, and made very little effort to become a nation-wide party. It cooperated with the Peoples Progressive Party in speaking for Chinese interests, but it avoided any formal link with the PPP. With the formation of the Malaysian Federation, the Malayan Party found political allies from among the members of Parliament representing Singapore.

The United Democratic Party

After 1959 two small splinter parties appeared on the political scene. Both were the creatures of divisions within the Alliance, and both were led by a dominant figure who suffered the humiliation of party discipline while a member of the inner councils of the Alliance Party. One of these parties was the United Democratic Party led by Lim Chong-eu. The other was the National Convention Party led by Abdul Aziz bin Ishak. Each party deserves separate consideration.

It may be recalled that the more communal elements in the MCA succeeded in wresting control from the moderates in 1958. Tan Cheng-lock was defeated for re-election to the presidency of the MCA by Dr. Lim Chong-eu who was backed by the more strident communal wing of the MCA. The ensuing internal tension within the Alliance reached a climax when the allocation of seats on the Alliance ticket had to be decided for the 1959 elections. The political victory of Tunku Abdul Rahman in the "July Crisis" forced Dr. Lim Chong-eu to resign as president of the MCA and returned control of the party to the moderate Tan-Ong faction.[110]

At first Dr. Lim announced his retirement from active politics because of "poor health". His decision, in 1961, to resign from the MCA sparked rumors that he was about to found a new party to challenge the MCA.[111] Later in the year a close political affiliate of Dr. Lim, Too Joon-hing, won a seat in Parliament for Telok Anson, Perak, in a by-election campaign based primarily on the issues of Chinese education.[112] Finally, in April 1962 Dr. Lim Chong-eu and Too Joon-hing announced their intention to form a new "non-communal" party to challenge the Alliance.

The United Democratic Party was formally launched at a meeting in the Seremban Town Hall on April 21, 1962. D. R. Seenivasagam of the Peoples Progressive Party gave his endorsement and promised to cooperate with the new party. In an interview with a reporter, Dr. Lim admitted that the main reason for founding the party was to oppose the Government's education policies.[113] From Dr. Lim's speeches it was obvious that he hoped that the prospect of a Malaysian Federation to embrace Malaya, Singapore and the Borneo states would result in a reconsideration of many of the communal compromises which were incorporated into the *Merdeka* Constitution. His demand that "Malaysia should not be a mere extension of the Federation of

Malaya"[114] should be viewed in this light. He expressed the hope that the UDP might create a new political alignment in view of the changed environment arising from the proposals for the Federation of Malaysia.[115]

The claim that the UDP was "non-communal" was true only in so far as the party welcomed the support of non-Chinese voters and attempted to include a few Malays in party posts and as its candidates. A former leader of Party Negara, Haji Abdul Hamid bin Haji Ishak, was even selected as titular president of the UDP to bolster the "non-communal" image of the party, but the leadership remained with Dr. Lim and a small core of Chinese politicians associated with him. The appeal of the party was almost exclusively to the Chinese who had earlier been aroused by the issues of Chinese education.

A major problem for the United Democratic Party was that other opposition parties had already capitalized on Chinese discontent with the Alliance, and they had become fairly well entrenched in most areas where Chinese majorities could be constructed. The Socialist Front controlled George Town, the Peoples Progressive Party had its strength in Ipoh and the Malayan Party was anchored in Malacca. As a start, the UDP recruited two independent members of Parliament who had been elected as independents. One was Too Joon-hing, who had won a parliamentary by-election in Telok Anson in 1961. The other was Chin See-yin, who was elected to Parliament from Seremban in 1959, and who with nine other independents won control of the Seremban Town Council in 1961. However, the prospects of a local base for the party were jeopardized in April 1963 when Mr. Chin resigned from the UDP in a dispute over the leadership of the party and over the action of Dr. Lim in making temporary alliances of convenience with Malay communal parties.[116]

Although the UDP was willing to cooperate with other opposition parties, its tactics made it unpopular with their leaders. In areas where the opposition parties had strength, the UDP split the vote and the Alliance benefited. In areas where the opposition parties had little strength, the UDP joined forces with one or more of the other parties, but to no avail. In the Penang local elections of 1963 the UDP won only one seat in George Town, but in doing so nearly unseated the Socialist Front from its control of the city. Throughout Malaya the UDP made a poor showing in local council polls during 1963, even where it was allied with the Socialist Front or the PPP. Its weakness was most evident in the defeat of Too Joon-hing who contested a Perak State Assembly seat from Telok Anson.[117] By 1964 the hoped for "realignment of Malayan politics" had not been accomplished by the United Democratic Party.

The National Convention Party

The newest party on the Malayan scene was also a product of disputes within the Alliance. For a number of years a left-wing faction within UMNO had been critical of the Alliance for its conservatism, its concessions to non-Malays, and its pro-Western political and economic orientation. Abdul Aziz bin Ishak was the most influential representative of this faction.[118] In 1955 he became the first elected Minister of Agriculture and Co-operatives, and with exceptional vigor and imagination he undertook the task of improving the economic conditions for the Malay peasantry. He believed that the cooperative movement held the key to successful Malay competition with non-Malays in the field of agriculture, trade and industry.[119] Under his guidance the Ministry initiated a variety of ambitious programs designed to improve the standard of living for the rural Malays engaged in both agriculture and fishing. These services provided by the Ministry of Agriculture helped to build a significant political following for Inche Aziz among important segments of the Malay community. The core of that following was among the membership of the 3,000 cooperatives founded through the efforts of the Ministry.

With increasing regularity the flamboyant and ambitious character of Inche Aziz clashed with other members of the Cabinet. In 1962 friction within the Cabinet became public after Inche Aziz' proposal to construct a cooperative urea fertilizer plant was rejected by the Cabinet as too costly and impractical.[120] He had earlier toured the country enlisting support for his plans for large-scale industrial cooperatives which would be operated exclusively by the Malays with Government support in order to help the Malays break the non-Malay control of credit, marketing and industry. Consequently, the urea plant, regardless of its economic viability, became symbolic of the hope of many left-wing Malays that the cooperative movement provided the means by which the Malays could challenge the economic superiority of the non-Malays.

After the proposal for the urea plant was rejected by the Prime Minister, Inche Aziz continued to campaign among his supporters to organize pressure on the Government to force it to reconsider its decision.[121] After several months of open friction, Tunku Abdul Rahman announced a cabinet reshuffle that, among other changes, shifted Inche Aziz to the Ministry of Health and replaced him with Dato Haji Sardon bin Haji Jubir, the leader of UMNO Youth.[122] Inche Aziz countered by announcing that he would resign from the Cabinet rather than switch portfolios. To avoid a crisis, Inche Aziz was temporarily allowed to remain as Minister of Agriculture. However, at the next UMNO General Assembly he was defeated in a bid for re-election to his position as one of its three vice-presidents.[123] Finally, in October 1963, the Prime Minister asked Inche Aziz to resign from the Cabinet.[124]

For several months Abdul Aziz bin Ishak remained a member of UMNO and continued to serve as an Alliance Member of Parliament. However, because he became increasingly critical of the Government, he was expelled from UMNO within a few months.[125] By July, Inche Aziz had launched a new party with the support of several UMNO members who had been part of his political machine in Selangor and had resigned from UMNO earlier in the year.[126]

The objectives of Inche Aziz' National Convention Party were somewhat concealed in the broad manifesto drafted at its founding meeting. Nonetheless, it was fairly obvious that this new party hoped to reconstitute the political power of the Malay left-wing. Inche Aziz attacked the rich Chinese, aliens and foreign capitalists, and made a strong appeal for support among the peasant Malays. On a number of issues the similarity of his program with the policies of Indonesia was striking, including his anti-Malaysia stand, his virulent attacks on Western influences and "neo-colonialism", and his professed faith in *gotong royong*.[127]

Inche Aziz is a Malay communal nationalist who was dissatisfied with many of the communal compromises of the Alliance. But after the formation of the NCP he avoided precise commitment on nearly all communal issues, probably in order to keep the door open for political alliances that crossed communal lines. In trying to build political alliances he gave speeches at rallies sponsored by the Socialist Front and the United Democratic Party, despite earlier attacks on these parties for their "Chinese communalism".

A Selangor Assembly by-election provided the first test of strength for the NCP. Its candidate polled 1,919 to the 3,699 votes for the victorious Alliance candidate.[128] It appears that even in Selangor most of the UMNO supporters remained loyal to the Alliance. However, in time the NCP hoped to become the center of a left-coalition that could challenge the Alliance by shifting its focus from communal issues to economic issues. Since the National Convention Party represented a veiled Malay communal reaction to the Alliance, and the communal calculus continued to be given high priority, the prospects for a non-communal left coalition remained rather bleak.

Observations on the 1959 Elections

Before the national elections of 1959, a number of local elections provided all parties with the opportunity to test their strength with the electorate. By 1957, with the Alliance losing 19 out of 37 contests in the December town council elections, it was apparent that the Alliance majority had diminished in key areas. The Labour Party, the Peoples Progressive Party and the Malayan Party all demonstrated the ability to win in urban areas where their strength was centered.[129] A year later in the town council elections the Alliance won 42 out of 54 contested seats, but the Peoples Progressive Party, the new Socialist Front and the Malayan Party continued to make important gains in Ipoh, Penang, Seremban and Malacca.[130]

The state legislative assembly elections of 1959 revealed that the Alliance still enjoyed widespread support, but the opposition parties were gaining strength in key localities. In the Perak state election, the Alliance was unable to crack the Ipoh stronghold of the Peoples Progressive Party, although the Alliance won all but one of the remainder of the seats in the state.[131] In Penang, the Alliance won only 17 out of 24 seats, with the Socialist Front winning the other 7 seats.[132] But the real challenge to Alliance supremacy came in the state elections in Trengganu and Kelantan where the Malay electorate was responding to the communal campaigning of the Pan-Malayan Islamic Party and Party Negara. Capturing 13 out of 24 seats, the PMIP secured control of the state government in Trengganu, while the Alliance won

7 seats and Party Negara 4 seats.[133] In the Kelantan elections, the PMIP scored an even more devastating and surprising victory. Out of 30 seats it captured 28, with the Alliance winning only 2.[134] In the remaining 7 states the Alliance won easily. Out of 164 seats at stake, the Alliance captured 150, the Socialist Front 9, the Malayan Party 1, and 4 seats were won by independent candidates.[135]

TABLE 9
Seats won in selected local authority elections

	Party Alliance	Lab/SF	NAP	PPP	Ind.	MP
George Town						
1956	7	5			3	
1957	5	8			2	
1961	1	14				
Ipoh						
1956	11			1		
1957	9		1	2		
1961	2			16		
Seremban						
1956	7	5				
1957	7	5				
1961	4	2			9	
Johore Bahru						
1956	10					
1957	10					
1961	10	4				
Taiping						
1956	9					
1957	7	2				
1961	13				2	
Malacca						
1957	2					4
1958	6	1				5
1961	5	5				2

Sensing that the Alliance might be in trouble, Tunku Abdul Rahman temporarily resigned as Prime Minister to devote himself full time to the job of strengthening the Alliance.[136] In part, this meant dealing with the internal revolts weakening the Alliance. But just as important, he was able to embark on a vigorous personal electioneering campaign in areas where the Alliance was losing support to the PMIP and Party Negara. He hoped to win back the Malay voters by face-to-face contacts, particularly in the remote rural villages. His prestige and personal popularity as the "Father of *Merdeka*" was used to good advantage in the campaigning.

It was generally recognized that the parliamentary elections of 1959 were almost as important as the first national elections of 1955. The year 1959 marked the beginning of the full implementation of the *Merdeka* Constitution with the replacement of the Federal Legislative Council by a fully elected lower house (Dewan Ra'ayat) and the creation of the new upper house (Dewan Negara).[137] Furthermore, this election provided the first opportunity for the electorate to judge the performance in office of an elected national government.

The registered electorate in 1959 was approximately double that of 1955, partly due to the large number of persons who had qualified for citizenship in the intervening years. The number of Chinese voters had increased nearly seven times since 1955. The electorate was divided according to race approxi-

TABLE 10
Seats won in parliamentary and state elections 1959

| | Party Alliance | | MP | | Negara | | PMIP | | PPP | | SF | | Ind. | |
	S	P	S	P	S	P	S	P	S	P	S	P	S	P
State														
Kedah	24	12												
Perlis	12	2												
Malacca	20	3	1											
Perak	31	15					1		8	4				1
Selangor	23	9									3	5	2	
Negri Sembilan	20	4									3		1	2
Penang	17	5									7	3		
Johore	28	16									3		1	
Trengganu	7	1			4	1	13	4						
Kelantan	2	1					28	9						
Pahang	23	6											1	
Total	207	74	0	1	4	1	42	13	8	4	16	8	5	3

mately as follows: 1,217,000 Malays (56·8 per cent); 764,000 Chinese (35·6 per cent); 159,000 Indians (7·4 per cent); and 4,000 others (0·2 per cent).[138] These new electors added to the uncertainty of the elections and contributed to their significance.

On August 18, 2,110,495 voters cast their votes—over twice as many votes as had been cast at the first federal elections. Again the Alliance emerged the victor, but with greatly diminished percentages than those of 1955. It controlled 74 seats, while the opposition parties won 30 seats.[139] The election returns give evidence of continued popular support of the Alliance, but its overall majority dropped from 81·7 per cent in 1955 to 51·5 per cent in 1959. The Alliance showed that it had the ability to win in most of the rural and small-town areas of Malaya, except along the East Coast. Also, it was able to win 24 of the 40 constituencies where the Chinese electorate constituted a majority.[140] The Alliance had trouble in the urban areas where there had been political turmoil over Chinese education policies, and where there was a large Chinese or Indian laboring class population. It also lost the vote of many of the Chinese-populated "new villages", which were formed under the government's resettlement programs in the years between 1950 and 1955. The

Alliance failed to gain a majority of the vote in the predominantly urban constituencies, although it did poll more votes than any single opposition party even in the urban areas.[141] The added support given to the Alliance in rural constituencies meant that the electoral system which gives "weightage" to rural areas, plus the failure to re-district before the 1959 elections tended to exaggerate the Alliance representation in Parliament beyond the normal exaggeration of representation in a single-member-district system of election.

Independent candidates have had the ability to win a fairly high proportion of the seats in local elections. However, the trend has been for the voters to become more and more attracted to one of the established political parties.

TABLE 11
Comparison of state and federal elections 1955 and 1959

Percentage of valid votes by parties on federation basis

Party		Overall		In constituencies contested		
	Federal 1955	State 1959	Federal 1959	Federal 1955	State 1959	Federal 1959
Alliance	81·7	55·5	51·8	81·7	55·5	51·8
PMIP	4·1	20·7	21·3	17·6	29·4	36·4
Socialist Front	—	9·7	12·9	—	21·7	34·9
Party Negara	7·9	4·3	2·1	12·8	14·9	22·2
PPP	0·1	5·7	6·2	4·6	30·8	32·2
Malayan Party	—	0·5	0·9	—	32·1	41·5
Labour Party	0·5	—	—	9.3	—	—
NAP	2·1	—	—	14·1	—	—
Perak Malay League	0·5	—	—	11·9	—	—
Independent	2·2	3·6	4·8	5·8	15·1	20·4

Sources: T. E. Smith, *Report on the First Election of Members to the Legislative Council of the Federation of Malaya*, (Kuala Lumpur: Government Press, 1955) pp. 68–76; *Report on the Parliamentary and State Elections 1959* (Kuala Lumpur: Government Press 1960) p. 12.

This trend was evident in the parliamentary elections since only 3 of the 29 independent candidates secured a seat in Parliament. Even in local council elections there was an increasing tendency for independents to become affiliated with an established party either before or after election.

Support for the opposition parties appeared to have been increasing fairly steadily from 1956 to 1961. Fragmentary and impressionistic evidence seemed to indicate that the opposition parties reached a plateau in popular support in about 1961. If they were to replace the Alliance through the electoral process they needed to forge a wide coalition among themselves, but this had proved to be extremely difficult. Without an effective wider union of opposition parties, the period of Alliance supremacy of Malayan politics appeared to be assured, even if the Alliance popularity had slipped to less than half of the electorate. However, the creation of the Malaysian Federation in 1963 greatly altered the political picture for the next parliamentary elections by the addition of 55 seats in Parliament for Singapore, Sarawak and Sabah. An examination of the political impact of the Malaysian Federation must be postponed to a later chapter.

1 Significantly, this body met at Semanggol in the heart of the Krian"rice bowl" district of Perak which is one of the most traditional, conservative rural Malay districts in the country. See *Times of Malaya & Straits Echo*, March 20, 1948, p. 6.

2 For several years the party was called the All-Malaya Islamic Association, (or the Pan-Malayan Islamic Association), but the name was changed in 1955 when the Registrar of Societies insisted that a party must be so labeled in order to contest elections.

3 *Zakat* is an "alms tax" that is collected by religious authorities from all Muslims to support poor relief and Muslim welfare projects.

4 In 1956 the PMIP came out in opposition to the ban on political discussion and political instruction in the mosques. See *Straits Budget*, May 31, 1956, p. 12.

5 A great variety of small Malay parties were in existence at the time, most of which gave some support to the PMIP. These included the Muslim League (which had previously been in alliance with UMNO during the Penang elections of 1953), the Malay League (which had joined and then dissolved into UMNO in 1946, but was later revived about 1954 after a personal and factional split in the NAP), *Semangat Permuda Melayu, Semangat Permuda Islam* (which had close ties with Dato Onn), *Barisan Kebangsaan Melayu*, the Peninsular Malays Union, *Perikatan Melayu Perak*, and *Persatuan Persetiaan Malayu Kelantan*.

6 Although this candidtae won only 42·9 per cent of the vote, a three-cornered fight gave him the plurality. The other PMIP candidates polled considerably less, ranging from 27·5 per cent to 6 per cent of the votes cast. See T. E. Smith, *Report on the First Election of Members to the Legislative Council of the Federation of Malaya*, (Kuala Lumpur: Government Press, 1955), pp. 68–76.

7 *Straits Times*, December 27, 1956, p. 8.

8 *Straits Budget*, March 28, 1957, p. 9. These views may be contrasted with the constitutional proposals of the Malay Nationalist Party when Dr. Burhanuddin was its chairman. These proposals called for citizenship for all born in Malaya, no religious implications in Malayan citizenship, and a Bill of Rights conferring equal rights upon all citizens.

9 See *Straits Budget*, July 26, 1956, p. 13; July 19, 1956, p. 17.

10 *Straits Budget*, August 5, 1959, p. 14.

11 In May 1957 the PMIP joined with Party Negara, the Peninsular Malays Union and Party Ra'ayat to sponsor the "Malay Congress" which became the major political expression of communal Malay dissappointment with the Reid Commission. Ahmad Boestamam, leading the Party Ra'ayat delegation, later withdrew his party from the "Malay Congress", charging that it was "too communal". See *Straits Budget*, May 9, 1957, pp. 13, 15 and 17; *Straits Times*, May 6, 1957, p. 7. See below pp. 241–242.

12 Some of the activities of the FMSTA are described earlier in connection with Alliance educational policies. See p. 196.

13 In 1960 the PMIP issued a special memorandum on education explaining its demands. It made the following proposals: (*a*) Malay should be the medium of instruction in all primary and secondary schools by 1965; (*b*) special classes of one year duration should be set up for Malay students who failed to secure places in secondary schools; (*c*) financial aid should be stopped in those schools where Malay is not taught; (*d*) the Language Institute should not be used to develop languages other than Malay before 1965 at the earliest; (*e*) English may be taught as a subject in national schools; (*f*) Muslim religious teachers should be provided for schools that did not have such teachers; (*g*) "the Federal School Inspectorate should give leadership to teachers and not merely to find out mistakes"; (*h*) free primary

education should be introduced and; (*i*) increased government financial assistance should be given to non-government Islamic schools. In short, the PMIP demanded the end of all government support for all but the Malay medium school system, and asked for special help for Malay students who still might not be able to qualify for entrance to Malay medium secondary schools. See *Straits Budget*, March 30, 1960, p. 8.

14 The West Coast Malays were less discontented because of better educational facilities, more job opportunities, and because it was easier for the more ambitious to transfer to the English-media school system for primary or secondary education, which opened the door to better and more responsible jobs, particularly within government service.

15 *Straits Budget*, August 5, 1959, p. 14.

16 On a much smaller scale, PMIP leaders have been laying plans to coax or cajole Malaya's 45,000 aborigines into becoming Muslim and accepting both Malay customs and Malay political leadership. For a variety of reasons, most aborigines detest the Malays. Their conversion to Islam could be accomplished only by greatly increasing the subtle but persistent pressures of the Aborigines Department to Muslimize these jungle people. Such a policy would meet with the determined, and perhaps even violent, resistance of these forgotten and often exploited people.

17 All orthodox schools of Muslim jurisprudence agree that non-believers may not be permitted to erect new places of worship in towns or villages, although there is some disagreement as to whether this allows restoration of dilapidated or over-aged churches, synogogues or temples. Similarly, non-Muslim mission work is proscribed. In essence, orthodox Muslim law allows non-believers to practice their religion in private, but not to propagate it, and makes it difficult to transmit their religion from one generation to the next. Apparently, Dr. Burhanuddin was attracted to this traditional view of the role of the state in promoting Islam and discouraging the continued existence of rival religions. For a partial explanation of Muslim law on this subject, see Reuben Levy, *The Social Structure of Islam*, Cambridge University Press, 1962), pp. 184–185.

18 It is generally believed that Dr. Burhanuddin was inspired by President Sukarno of Indonesia and maintained some contact through the years with Sukarno's Partai Nasionalis Indonesia (PARTINDO). However, some elements within the PMIP also had ties with *Darul Islam*, a fanatical, staunchly orthodox Islamic party that participated in the rebellion against the Indonesian Republic. Note *Straits Budget*, December 3, 1958, p. 9.

19 Dr. Burhanuddin's objection to this resolution is significant evidence supporting the view that his real objective was a much wider political union embracing Malaya, the Borneo territories, the Philippines and Indonesia. See *Straits Budget*, August 29, 1957, p. 17.

20 *Straits Budget*, December 31, 1958, p. 16.

21 *Straits Budget*, October 25, 1961, p. 5.

22 Dr. Burhanuddin participated in the Malaysia Solidarity Consultative Committee which drew up the first proposals for the Federation of Malaysia, and he attached his name to that report. However, he later claimed that his signature only indicated his attendance at the meetings and not his approval of the Report. Later, under his direction, the PMIP sponsored a resolution in the Federal Parliament calling for the inclusion of Indonesia and the Philippines in the proposed Federation of Malaysia. Note Department of Information, Federation of Malaya, *Malaysia*, No. 2 (April 1962), pp. 7–16; Federation of Malaya, *Parliamentary Debates, Dewan Ra'ayat, May 2nd, 1962*, (Vol. IV, No. 6), 699–740.

23 Party members refrain from discussing their differences on this subject with outsiders, especially those who are not Muslim, in the belief that Islam should present a unified image to the general public.

24 *Ulamas* are Muslim religious instructors and mosque elders, most of whom in Malaya suffer from poor education obtained in sub-standard religious schools.

25 The *khalwat* law, otherwise known as the "proximity law", makes it an offense for any Muslim to be in "suspicious proximity" to a member of the opposite sex if the two are not married. Depending on the attitude of the religious authorities and the *kathis* in the Muslim courts, it can even apply to holding hands in public or strolling unchaperoned after dark. The Muslim male is almost never punished when his partner is non-Muslim, but when the female is Muslim, attempts have been made to punish both partners under Muslim law. Practically every state has a *khalwat* law (sometimes called *bersunyi-sunyian*). See for example State of Trengganu, *Administration of Islamic Law Enactment, 1955*, No. 4 of 1955, Sect. 135–136, pp. 48–49.

26 The *hadith* is the report and account of the Prophet's conduct, desicions and sayings. Next to the *Koran* it is the most important source of Muslim jurisprudence.

27 In Malaya strong currents of modern reformism emanated from the Malayan Muslim College at Klang, while most of the *kathis* and Muslim Religious Councils had a strong bias towards the orthodox fundamentalist views.

28 Federation of Malaya, *Report on the Parliamentary and State Elections 1959* (Government Press, 1960), Appendix A, p. 9. The PMIP manifesto for the 1959 elections promised to accomplish the following: to revise the Constitution to "restore Malay sovereignty"; to abolish the remnants of colonialism; to give just treatment for all and freedom of "worship, politics and thought"; to require that only Malays can hold the positions of Mentris Besar, ministers and the head of the Armed Forces; to "ban wild dances and strip tease"; to make Malay the language of administration without delay; to "not encourage the spread of English"; to provide the country with Islamic economic rules; to combat monopoly and aid small industries; and to "enforce the unification of teaching in schools which use Malay as the medium of instruction". See *Sunday Times*, August 16, 1959, p. 5.

29 *Straits Budget*, July 29, 1959, p. 11.

30 Ustaz Ahmad Azam's faction was weakened by the failure of the party to select one of his candidates as the new Speaker of the Trengganu State Assembly. Later the new Speaker, Inche Taib Sabree, did not remain above political strife in the party and occasionally made unfavorable comments on the performance of the PMIP state government. The new Mentri Besar, Inche Daud bin Samad, was also the object of criticism since he had been elected on the PMIP ticket even though he remained a member of Party Ra'ayat. The attack against Ustza Ahmad Azam's leadership of the Trengganu PMIP sas directed by Inche Wan Hussain Azmi bin Wan Kadir. At one time, three of the six PMIP sub-branches in the state passed votes of "no confidence" against Ahmad Azam.

31 Among other things, Ahmad Azam sought to reform the PMIP State Executive Council and remove the Speaker of the Assembly from his position. See *Straits Budget*, July 27, 1960, p. 8.

32 This intolerable situation forced the PMIP Mentri Besar to seek a coalition with Party Negara, but that party was uncooperative. Internal feuding continued when others in the PMIP tried to unseat the Speaker because of the latter's alleged dealings with Party Negara, supposedly contributing to the severe defeats of the PMIP in local elections in 1961. See *Straits Budget*, August 17, 1960, p. 7; July 26, 1961, p. 4; Federation of Malaya, Election Commission, *Local Authority Elections 1961 Results and Statistic of Voting*, (mimeographed, 1961), Appendix A.

33 *Straits Budget*, November 8, 1961, p. 13.

34 The Sultan supported the Alliance by refusing to dissolve the Assembly. The new Mentri Besar, Inche Ibrahim Fikri bin Mohamed, was the former director and editor of *Utusan Melayu*, the foremost Malay language newspaper in the country.

[35] PMIP policies called for rural development and economic aid for "Malays only". Federal requirements demanded that all Malayans were to benefit from rural development schemes, even though in practice the programs have been administered so that economic aid is extended to "Malays mostly". This issue was bitterly debated between the PMIP and the Alliance.

[36] *Local Authority Elections 1961, op. cit.,* Appendix A.

[37] *Straits Times,* December 13, 1957, p. 8; December 16, 1957, p. 1.

[38] Note *Straits Budget,* March 7, 1957, p. 8.

[39] See above p. 159

[40] Orthodox Muslim authorities have ruled that proceeds from lotteries are *haram* (tainted) since the *Koran* proscribes gambling. See *Koran,* Chapter 5, Verse 90. The Federal Government got around these objections by having lottery profits go directly to the general fund. Federal money is appropriated for Muslim purposes in such a way that it cannot be said that the money comes specifically from the lottery fund.

[41] The following table illustrates how Party Negara fared in the state elections of 1959:

State	Seats Contested	Seats at Stake	Won by Negara	Percentage of Total Vote
Johore	23	31	0	15·4
Kedah	4	24	0	1·9
Kelantan	21	30	0	5·2
Negri Sembilan	4	24	0	4·0
Penang	3	23	0	·8
Trengganu	20	24	4	16·3
Selangor	4	28	0	2·0

Report on the Parliamentary and State Elections, 1959, op. cit., pp. 13–23.

[42] *Straits Times,* January 20, 1962, p. 1.

[43] He was Mentri Besar in Perak from 1948 to 1957, and in 1956 he was selected by the Malay Rulers to head their delegation to the constitutional conference in London. His death in 1959 marked the end of an era in Perak politics. See *Straits Times,* April 17, 1959, p. 9.

[44] Calculated from *First Election of Members, op. cit.,* pp. 68–76.

[45] *Sunday Times,* November 13, 1955, p. 1; *Straits Times,* November 14, 1955, p. 1.

[46] Daniel E. Moore "The United Malays National Organization and the 1959 Malayan Elections", (unpublished dissertation, University of California, 1960), p. 258. The NAP Ipoh Councillor later defected to the PPP when the PPP-NAP alliance floundered.

[47] The by-election was necessary to fill the seat vacated by Leong Yew-koh when he was appointed Governor of Malacca. The defeated Alliance candidate was Yap Yin-fah who was the leader of the MCA in Perak. *Sunday Times,* November 24, 1967, p. 1.

[48] His name was Rajah Hanif Shah bin Rajah Abdul Rahman. Five months later he was replaced by Foong Seong. See *Straits Budget,* July, 23, 1958, p. 14.

I

49 For a brief account of the origins of the PPP see above pp. 235–237.

50 *First Election of Members, op. cit., pp.* 68–76.

51 *Sunday Times*, November 24, 1957, p. 1.

52 The PPP manifesto in 1955 contained some of the following pledges: to secure fundamental rights, including equality before the law, prohibition of racial discrimination, equality of opportunity, freedom of speech, no deprivation of life or liberty "except by due process of law" and trial by jury, and freedom "to profess, practise and propagate religion"; to promote welfare based on social, economic and political justice; to "have a written Constitution guaranteeing fundamental rights capable of being enforced by Courts of law"; to repeal the non-essential parts of the Emergency Regulations; to recognize Malay as the national language, English and Malay as official languages and "multi-lingualism" for a period of ten years; to promote the educational and economic interests of the Malays and protect them from exploitation; to pass "humane and equitable" immigration laws; to establish a National Health Scheme with free medical treatment for all; to provide free compulsory education up to "University standard"; to impose an excess profits tax on tin and rubber companies; to Malayanize the public service without discrimination based on race; and to encourage the labor movement. See *Perak Progressive Party, Federal Elections 1955 Manifesto, Onward to Freedom,* (Ipoh: Mercantile Press, 1955).

53 In the state elections of 1959, 24 out of 39 PPP candidates were Chinese, and practically all the others were Indians or Ceylonese. In the federal elections of that year the ratio was 9 Chinese and 11 non-Chinese. In its early days, the PPP was able to attract a few left-wing Malays who were disgruntled with the established leaders of the Malay community. For example, D. R. Seenivasagam's only running mate in the 1955 elections was Zaharie M. Hassan, a Malay who was one of the founders of the MNP and who was a writer for a small radical Malay weekly called *Suara Ra'ayat*. He got only 273 votes and has since drifted into political oblivion.

54 *Straits Budget*, September 22, 1955, p. 13; January 26, 1956, p. 11. The party also came out in favor of recognizing Communist China. See *Straits Budget*, September 24, 1958, p. 7.

55 Since both the MCP and the PPP have tried to exploit Chinese communalism, especially as it related to the problems of Chinese education, it is highly probable that some Communists lent their support to the PPP in some of its political activities. But no evidence has been made public to suggest that Communists obtained positions of power within the party, and no prominent members of the PPP have been detained by the police. Certainly, the party's manifesto is strong evidence in support of the view that class warfare and the "dictatorship of the proletariate" is completely repugnant to its leaders. In 1958 the leadership of the party in effect repudiated doctrinaire Marxism by publicly rejecting the concept that "the workers are downtrodden", that "labour and capital are opposed", and that "only socially minded people can save workers". *Straits Times*, November 3, 1958, p. 5.

56 *Straits Budget*, May 18, 1960, p. 7.

57 *Straits Budget*, July 4, 1957, pp. 4 and 15; *Straits Times*, November 3, 1958, p. 5; October 28, 1958, p. 7.

58 The 1959 PPP manifesto contained 28 points. It demanded amendments to the Constitution to guarantee equal rights and privileges for all, "multilingualism". and "only one class of citizenship". It condemned the Razak Report and demanded compulsory education within two years, the medium of instruction to be in the mother tongue with Malay language as a compulsory subject, all teachers "to be treated equally", and the removal of the ban on student travel between Singapore and the Federation. It called for Malay as the "national language" and

Malay, Chinese, Tamil and English as official languages. It promised to raise taxes on companies and on higher personal incomes. In foreign policy it opposed involvement in "power blocs". It condemned the "present immigration policy", and demanded that the Emergency Regulations be repealed and all persons under detention be tried or released. It promised free medical services for all under a health insurance scheme, and demanded minimum wage legislation. *Straits Times*, August 6, 1959, p. 2.

[59] Elected to Parliament were the two Seenivasagam brothers, Khong Koh-yat and Chan Swee-ho. *Report on the Parliamentary and State Elections, 1959, op. cit.*, pp. 9–12, 55–56.

[60] See for example *Straits Budget*, December 12, 1961, p. 12; *Malayan Times*, December 6, 1962, p. 3.

[61] Calculated from *First Election of Members, op. cit.*, pp. 68–76.

[62] See above, pp. 157–158.

[63] See *Straits Budget*, December 22, 1955, p. 12; *Straits Times*, March 23, 1956, p. 4; April 30, 1956, p. 4; May 5, 1956, p. 4; July 26, 1956, p. 8; August 1, 1956, p. 5; August 3, 1956, p. 6; *Sunday Times*, August 12, 1956, p. 4.

[64] One of the first policy statements of the party contained such a suggestion. See The Pan-Malayan Labour Party, *Towards a New Malaya*, (Butterworth: Phoenix Press, 1952), pp. 6–7.

[65] The 1955 manifesto of the Labour Party contained some of the following: It envisaged a society of "free and equal people" cooperating to bring about "an equitable distribution of the national income" under "a system of planned economy". It called for land distribution, promised a long list of economic and social "rights" for all, and endorsed the *Universal Declaration of Human Rights*. It attacked the continued existence of colonial rule, the denial of the franchise to "a substantial proportion of the population", and the "Puritanian Rulers" who work with the British and "mislead the Malay ra'ayats". It demanded a "single nationality for the whole of Malaya including Singapore". It decried the Emergency Regulations as an abuse of power and a denial of democracy. "Though the Labour Party regards the activities of Communism as dangerous to the growth of democratic institutions, we feel that we cannot defend a democratic way of life if under the Colonial regime we are deprived of the very institutions we are called upon to defend". It explained its decision to contest the elections as "the only way we can show up the defects of the system. . . ." It proposed a 16 point "Programme for Progress".

1. Create a union of Malaya and Singapore with common nationality for all who have been residents for 10 years.
2. Demand immediate self-government.
3. Repeal or revise the Emergency Regulations in conformity with basic concepts of democratic justice.
4. Malayanize the public service.
5. Enact social and labor legislation including unemployment insurance, minimum wage, abolition of contract labor, equal pay for men and women.
6. Establish a planned economy.
7. Free peasants by land distribution, cooperatives, agricultural banks, collective farming and mechanization.
8. Control land values and rent.
9. Revise the tax structure in accordance with ability to pay.
10. Encourage local industry.
11. Create a Central Banking Authority.
12. Provide free compulsory primary education for all.
13. Create a Malayan Army.
14. Promote Youth Organizations.
15. Establish a National Housing Trust.
16. Create a National Health Scheme.

This is a summary of *Manifesto of the Labour Party of Malaya*, (mimeographed, n.d. [1955?]).

66 *Straits Times*, June 21, 1956, p. 9; August 6, 1956, p. 4; *Straits Budget*, June 27, 1957, p. 10; May 14, 1958, p. 6.

67 *Straits Times*, February 11, 1963, p. 5.

68 *Straits Times*, August 7, 1957, p. 6.

69 For example see *Straits Times*, August 25, 1957, p. 4.

70 He also accused the Government of becoming suddenly alarmed about Communist subversion to discredit the opposition parties. *Straits Budget*, April 8, 1959, p. 6.

71 It may be recalled that API was an organization of Malay revolutionary activists seeking to promote Malayan independence through violent tactics, and having strong affinities for Indonesia. See above, pp. 91–92.

72 *Straits Times*, November, 10, 1955, p. 9.

73 In romanized Malay the name may be spelled Ra'ayat, Raayat, or Rakyat. This name has a more "Malay" connotation than the translation "people" because it was earlier used to refer to the traditional subjects of the Malay Sultans.

74 *Straits Budget*, July 19, 1956, p. 5.

75 *Straits Budget*, May 24, 1956, p. 17; *Straits Times*, May 19, 1956, p. 5; November 5, 1956, p. 7; November 13, 1956, p. 4.

76 From notes taken by the author during one of Boestamam's speeches.

77 *Straits Budget*, May 24, 1956, p. 17.

78 For example, Party Ra'ayat's proposal for "international mediation" of the guerrilla war was practically identical with the proposal made by the MCP the month before and sent to the Eighth Chinese Communist Party Congress in Peking. See *Straits Budget*, November 8, 1956, p. 3; *New China News Agency*, Peking, in English Morse to Europe, September 20, 1956, 1352 GMT, as reported in a document which permits quotation but does not permit citation of source.

79 *The Communist Threat to the Federation of Malaya*, Council Paper No. 23 of 1959, Federation of Malaya, p. 20.

80 *Straits Times*, March 13, 1963, p. 16.

81 The convenor of the Malay Congress was Tuan Haji Yahaya bin Sheikh Ahmad. This Congress was very similar to previous attempts to build a "pro-Malay", anti-Alliance coalition. Such a coalition had been the primary objective of the All-Malaya National Congress (March 1954), the All-Malaya Malay Youth Congress (April 1955), and the Malay Nationalist Front (May 1955).

82 *Straits Times*, April 24, 1957, p. 5; May 6, 1957, p. 7.

83 *Straits Budget*, May 9, 1957, pp. 13, 15 and 17.

84 *Straits Times*, May 23, 1957, p. 11.

85 Represented at the discussions were Party Ra'ayat, the Pan-Malayan Islamic Party, the Labour Party, the National Association of Perak, the Peoples Progressive Party and *Pertubohan Bumi Putera* (the Malay League). See *Straits Times*, February 15, 1957, p. 4. An earlier attempt to create a Socialist Front had been made in 1956 by Boestamam, but these preliminary talks had revealed fundamental disagreements on the issues of Malay "special rights" and the position of the Malay Sultans. See *Straits Times*, September 26, 1956, p. 7.

86 *Straits Times*, July 1, 1957, pp. 4 and 5; September 3, 1957, p. 1; *Straits Budget*, July 4, 1957, p. 4. In February 1958 the first "National Congress" of the Socialist Front was convened in Kuala Lumpur. Besides the delegates from the Labour Party and Party Ra'ayat, there were observer-representatives from the Peoples Progressive Party, the Socialist Youth League, and a Singapore party, the Workers Party (founded by the former Singapore Chief Minister, David Marshall). A twelve-member "Central Council" was created to direct the Socialist Front, in much the same way that the Alliance was directed by its "National Council". Party Ra'ayat was represented by Ahmad Boestamam, Karam Singh, Ahmad Daud, Nazar Nong, Tajuddin Kahar and Ja'afar Tan, and the Labour Party was represented by D. S. Ramanathan, Tan Phock-kin, See Toh-fatt, Ng Thow-lin, Yong Kong-ying, and Lim Kean-siew. *Straits Times*, February 1, 1958, p, 7; February 4, 1958, p. 6; *Sunday Times*, February 2, 1958, p. 4.

87 See *Straits Times*, February 4, 1958, p. 6.

88 Moore, *op. cit.*, p. 266.

89 The Socialist Front manifesto for 1959 avoided most communal issues, emphasizing instead "Three Stages to a Socialist Malaya". In the first stage it proposed that "national capitalists must be organized and recruited to work under a planned system and to take over from foreign interests wherever and whenever possible". In the second stage "these national capitalists must be absorbed into a planned socialist economy under the direction of a Socialist Government and national enterprises must be set up". The third stage would involve direct control of national enterprises combined with legislation providing for rent control and security of land tenure. It also promised legislation to prevent fragmentation of land holdings, to provide more land to farmers and new villagers, and to enforce compulsory replanting and reinvestment in the plantation industry. Among other things the manifesto promised to end "easy divorces,' and establish equal rights for women. See *Straits Times*, August 10, 1959, p. 7; August 11, 1959, p. 2. Behind the scenes, communal issues proved to be difficult for the Socialist Front. In particular, differences arose over language issues, special rights, education policy, political symbols, and political allies. The latter problem involved the party's relations with the Socialist Youth League, the Peoples Progressive Party, Party Ra'ayat in Brunei and the Partai Nasionalis Indonesia.

90 *Straits Times*, November 25, 1957, p. 1.

91 *Straits Budget*, September 3, 1958, p. 10; *Straits Times*, November 3, 1958, p. 5.

92 The antagonism between the PPP and the Socialist Front carried over to the federal election, since the PPP, although not contesting the constituency where Ahmad Boestamam was running, instructed its members to vote against him and support an independent candidate. Note *Straits Budget*, September 3, 1958, pp. 10 and 14; August 19, 1959, p. 5.

93 In Pahang the Socialist Front is reported to have had a local temporary agreement with the PMIP not to sap each other's strength with three-way election contests. The state's six constituencies were divided equally among the Socialist Front and the PMIP, and members of each party were instructed to vote for the other party if their party did not nominate a candidate in that district. See *Straits Times*, August 3, 1959, p. 14.

94 In the state elections the SF won 7 seats in Penang, 3 in Selangor, 3 in Negri Sembilan, and 3 in Johore. The main centers of strength were in Penang, Kuala Lumpur, Serembam, and in the larger "new villages" in Selangor, Negri Sembilan and Johore.

95 The Socialist Front obtained 9·7 per cent of the total vote in the state elections and 12·9 per cent in the parliamentary elections. *Report on the Parliamentary and State Elections, 1959, op. cit.*, pp. 12 and 32–57.

96 *Straits Times*, October 19, 1959, p. 7. Ishak bin Haji Mohamed was a founder of *Kesatuan Melayu Muda* and had been active in Malay politics since 1937, keeping in close contacts with political movements in Indonesia. After the war he became a charter-member and later president of the Malay Nationalist Party. He was detained under the Emergency Regulations in 1948 and released in 1953, returning to active politics several years later. In 1959 he ran as the SF candidate in his home district of Temerloh, Pahang, but lost despite the electoral agreement with the PMIP. In 1961 Ishak was named as "National Chairman" of the Socialist Front.

97 D. S. Ramanathan was president of the National Union of Teachers; V. David was a founder and Secretary-General of the National Union of Factory and General Workers and a member of the Malayan Trade Union Congress; Ooi Thiam-siew was closely associated with the MTUC; and Karam Singh helped to organize Indian estate laborers. Lim Kean-siew, the most dynamic of the party's spokesmen in Parliament, was not a union leader, but has been a legal advisor to a host of unions. A similar background is to be found with many other important figures in the party.

98 The compromsie agreement stated that Malay should be "the only national language" and it should be enriched and more widely propagated. "Those secondary schools which, after 1967, use the national language ɛs the medium of instruction should also teach English, Chinese and Tamil as subjects, particularly the last two. . . . The Front is not against the setting up of independent schools of any language." It supported government subsidies for Chinese and Tamil schools until 1967, "when the issue will be reviewed by Parliament". What was left unsaid, particularly in regard to English schools, was as significant as what was included in this policy statement of the Socialist Front. See *Straits Budget*, September 28, 1960, pp. 3 and 6.

99 *Malay Mail*, April 22, 1960, p. 7.

100 *Straits Budget*, May 23, 1962, p. 6; *Straits Times*, February 11, 1963, p. 5.

101 The most sensational arrest of a Socialist Front member was in 1963 when its president, Ahmad Boestamam, was accused, not of supporting the Communist Party, but of supporting the 1962 revolt in Brunei and of developing underground contacts with Indonesia to wreck the Malaysian Federation. This issue will be covered in greater detail in the chapter on the Federation of Malaysia.

102 *Straits Times*, October 29, 1956, p. 5.

103 See Moore, *op. cit.*, p. 286; J. Victor Morais (ed.), *The Who's Who in Malaysia, 1963*, (Kuala Lumpur: Solai Press, 1963), p. 68.

104 In Penang, Heah Joo-seang of the Straits Chinese British Association was agitating for the same objectives. However, the Malayan Party sought to avoid the implication that they owed a continuing loyalty to the British Crown, such as was implied by critics of the SCBA. See *Straits Budget*, April 25, 1957, p. 12.

105 *Straits Budget*, May 16, 1957, p. 14.

106 *Straits Times*, December 2, 1958, pp. 1 and 7.

107 See Moore, *op. cit.*, p. 286; *Straits Times*, August 8, 1959, p. 1.

108 The party ran five candidates in the Malacca Town area and permitted an independent in Selangor to use the party label to contest Kuala Selangor.

109 See Moore, *op. cit.*, p. 288.

110 See above. pp. 204–207, 212–215.

111 *Straits Budget*, February 1, 1961, p. 4; April 5, 1961, p. 3.

112 Too Joon-hing was a former Secretary-General of the MCA who had also been subject to Alliance discipline for his uncompromising stand on communal issues. In the Telok Anson election it was reported that Mr. Too received the support of the Peoples Progressive Party. His victory made Mr. Too the second ex-MCA member in Parliament since Chin See-yin had successfully contested the Seremban constituency as an independent after being eliminated from the Alliance ticket in 1959.

113 *Straits Times*, April 23, 1962, p. 5. The stated objectives of the UDP as agreed upon by its leaders, but not published at the time were:
"To fight for the rights of non-Malays, expecially in education based on a more reasonable policy than the Razak Report.
While recognising Malay as the national language, multi-lingualism should be allowed in all councils.
To fight for fair distribution of land, and equal employment in the administration and the defence of the country."
See *Straits Times*, April 19, 1963, p. 5.

114 *Sunday Times*, April 22, 1962, p. 5.

115 Dr. Lim had earlier been on a tour of the Borneo states trying to make the UDP into a common political organ for Chinese interests throughout Malaysia. He claimed to have the support of the Sarawak United Peoples Party and the North Borneo United Party, but these parties did not send representatives to the founding meeting of the UDP.

116 *Straits Times*, April 19, 1963, p. 5.

117 *Straits Times*, June 24, 1963, p. 8.

118 In 1946 Abdul Aziz bin Ishak was president of *Gerakan Angkatan Pemuda Melayu* (GERAM). Two years later he joined UMNO, only to leave it in 1951 to join Dato Onn's Independence of Malaya Party. In the first municipal council elections in Kuala Lumpur he was an unsuccessful IMP candidate. He rejoined UMNO in 1952 and was later elected to the Federal Legislative Council in 1955. From 1958 to 1962 he was one of the three vice-presidents of UMNO. He was the editor of *Utusan Melayu* in the years from 1948 to 1951. His brother is Yusof bin Ishak, who was the Yang di-Pertuan Negara (Head of State) for Singapore.

119 At one time Inche Aziz suggested that the Soviet system of agriculture might be adapted for Malaya. See *Straits Times*, March 21, 1958, p. 9.

120 *Straits Times*, April 20, 1962, p. 1.

121 For example see *Straits Times*, April 28, 1962, p. 17.

122 *Straits Times*, July 16, 1962, p. 1.

123 *Straits Budget*, August 29, 1962, p. 16.

124 *Straits Times*, October 2, 1962, pp. 1 and 20; October 11, 1962, pp. 1 and 18. Rumors circulated to the effect that the MCA demanded the removal of Inche Aziz from the Cabinet because he tried to promote Malay cooperatives by revoking business licenses of competing Chinese traders and businessmen. However, there were other probable reasons, including his defiance of Cabinet decisions, and the threat posed by the independent political machine he was said to be constructing from the membership of the more than 3,000 cooperatives his ministry had sponsored. Inche Aziz later explained that he was removed because of differences with Tan Siew-sin and because he opposed government policies toward Indonesia. The Alliance Government accused Inche Aziz of mismanagement and of wasting "millions of dollars" in hastily conceived schemes to promote cooperatives. See *Straits Times*, January 28, 1963, pp. 1 and 16; January 29, 1963, pp. 1 and 14; January 30, 1963, pp. 1 and 14.

125 *Straits Times*, February 13, 1963, p. 9. After his removal from the Cabinet, Inche Aziz approached the opposition parties to find a basis for cooperation. He was then elected "Chairman of the Joint Opposition Parties". In a statement to the press he deplored "the manner and methods employed by the Alliance in dealing with the concept of Malaysia . . . and . . . the use of the powers of arbitary arrest by the Federation Government". See *Straits Times*, March 12, p. 18.

126 *Straits Times*, July 15, 1963, p. 5.

127 *Gotong royong* is a policy of village economic development based on the "self help" principle as developed in Indonesia.

128 *Straits Times*, September 9, 1963, p. 8.

129 *Straits Times*, December 9, 1957, p. 7; *Straits Budget*, December 18, 1957, p. 3.

130 *Straits Times*, December 8, 1958, pp. 1 and 4. See also Table 9, p. 251.

131 *Straits Times*, May 29, 1959, pp. 1 and 16.

132 *Straits Times*, June 8, 1959, p. 2.

133 *Sunday Times*, June 21, 1959, pp. 1 and 5; *Straits Times*, June 22, 1959, pp. 1 and 14.

134 *Straits Times*, June 25, 1959, pp. 1 and 16; June 26, 1959, pp. 1 and 16.

135 *Federation of Malaya Election Commission Report*, Kuala Lumpur, 25 August, 1959, pp. 1–4.

136 *Straits Times*, April 17, 1959, pp. 1 and 9.

137 The Constitution provided for a lower house of 104 members in the first Parliament to permit the permanent Election Commission to reapportion the constituencies for a 100-member House. In 1962 the Constitution was amended to fix the size of the Dewan Ra'ayat at 104 and to revoke the authority given to the Election Commission to reapportion the constituencies. This responsibility was transferred directly to Parliament. See *Constitution (Amendment) Act, 1962 (Government Gazette of the Federation of Malaya, 1962*, L.N. 164). With the creation of Malaysia the membership of the lower house was expanded by 55 seats to 159.

138 Calculated from figures in *Straits Times*, August 19, 1959, p. 1. Of the population over 21 years of age, it has been estimated that 81 per cent of the Malays were enrolled in the electorate in 1959, as compared with 66 per cent for the Chinese and 46 per cent for the Indians. See T. E. McGee, "The Malayan Elections of 1959, A Study in Electoral Geography", *The Journal of Tropical Geography*, Vol. 16 (October 1962), p. 74.

139 *Election Commission Report, op. cit.*, pp. 1–4. The voting was postponed in one constituency for six weeks after a PMIP candidate was disqualified at the last moment. See *Straits Budget*, October 7, 1959, p. 16.

140 *Straits Times*, August 21, 1959, p. 8.

141 For an analysis of the rural and urban voting patterns see T. E. McGee, *op. cit.*, pp. 80–88.

15 The Communist Challenge

The vexing problems posed by the Communist insurgency loomed large in the election campaigning of 1955. A number of vital issues would face an elected government once it assumed office. Would the Communists end their war when a popularly elected government assumed office or after the attainment of independence? Could a satisfactory negotiated peace be achieved? Should the military operations be stepped up? Could the Government wage a more effective counter-insurgency campaign with different tactics? While the answers to these questions were difficult and elusive, the questions could not be ignored, particularly since the financial drain on the Malayan Government had been very heavy and had retarded investment in vital economic and social welfare projects.[1] Furthermore, the public was weary of the war and was hopeful that it would soon terminate so that the stringent Emergency Regulations could be revoked and the country could look forward to a period of peace and prosperity.

In their election campaign of 1955 the Alliance played on the theme that the Communist insurgency could be ended by a combination of perseverence against terrorism and leniency toward the individual guerrilla. In its platform the Alliance made the following proposals concerning the Emergency:

> The Alliance considers that an effort should be made to end the Emergency—by offering general amnesty, and, if that fails, by mobilizing all our resources and seeking all foreign aid to increase the vigor and intensity of the fight against the terrorists. . . .
> The Alliance is of the considered opinion that $50 million a year will be a fair share for the Federation to meet the cost of fighting the Emergency, and that the rest of the total expenditure should be borne by all other nations interested in fighting world communism. A special appeal should be addressed to Britain and the United States for help in greater measure.[2]

Shortly after taking office, the new Alliance Government announced an amnesty to all persons who had committed any offense connected with the Emergency.

> Those of you who come in and surrender will not be prosecuted. . . .
> Those who show that they genuinely intend to be loyal to the Government of Malaya and to give up their Communist activities

will be helped to regain their normal position in society and be reunited with their families.

As regards the remainder, restrictions will have to be placed on their liberty, but if any of them wish to go to China their request will be given due consideration.[3]

Civilians were asked to aid in the surrender of Communists, and certain "safe areas" were officially designated where the Communists could surrender without fear of being shot by Security Forces. While no general cease-fire was declared, Security Forces were instructed to shoot at suspected guerrillas only after a call demanding their surrender had proved futile. Obviously, military operations against the guerrillas became more difficult since the guerrillas, if discovered, were thus given a few free moments to escape into the heavy jungle when they chose not to surrender.

The amnesty proved disappointing to the Alliance, since only seven Communists surrendered in the first two weeks.[4] Furthermore, the Communists stepped up their attacks and utilized the "safe areas" to replenish their supplies by intimidating the local populace without fear of effective military operations. Even mass "amnesty rallies" staged by the Alliance in villages throughout the country did little to increase the surrender rate. However, the amnesty did apparently encourage the Communist high command to send the following letter to Tunku Abdul Rahman:

> In response to the Malayan peoples' struggle for a Peoples' democratic independent Malaya, the Federation Government had to announce the amnesty on the 8th instant.
>
> This shows that the Federation Government intends to end the Malayan war by political means.
>
> However, methods stated in the announcement are unjust and unrealistic.
>
> Here we wish to reiterate that we are in favour of an immediate discussion between the parties at war to reach a fair decision so that the questions of cease-fire, a satisfactory solution to end the emergency, and a peaceful and independent Malaya can be settled at an early date. . . .
>
> In view of this we shall in the near future be sending our representative to the Alliance headquarters in Kuala Lumpur to arrange with the Alliance leaders a meeting between Tengku Abdul Rahman and Dato Sir Cheng-lock Tan and Comrade Chin Peng.[5]

Tunku Abdul Rahman made immediate plans to arrange for a meeting with Chin Peng "to clarify the amnesty declaration".[6] After more than two weeks' delay, additional letters were received from the Communist high command.[7] However, the arrangements for a meeting proceeded so slowly that it appeared that the Communists were either stalling or had changed their minds after the public pronouncements by the Tunku that his terms to the Communists were not subject to negotiation, but that he would be glad to explain them and listen to the Communists' views. Eventually, Chen Tien, Communist propaganda chief, emerged from the jungle to negotiate the arrangements for the proposed meeting and to issue propaganda statements to the press explaining the position of the Malayan Communist Party.[8]

The Baling Talks

The meeting with the Communists finally took place on December 28 and 29 in the small mountain village of Baling, close to the Siamese border. Chin Peng led the Communist delegation which included Chen Tien, propaganda chief, and Abdul Rashid bin Mydin, a Malay who joined the Communist Party during the Japanese occupation and who, after the war, was a founder member of the banned Malay Nationalist Party. The other delegation was made up of Tunku Abdul Rahman (Federation Chief Minister), David Marshall (Singapore Chief Minister) and Tan Cheng-lock (President of the Malayan Chinese Association) in addition to several aides and secretaries.

The talks revolved around two subjects: the amnesty terms, and whether the Alliance leaders could speak for the Government of Malaya. On the first issue, Chin Peng objected to the terms of the amnesty which would not permit the Communist Party to emerge as a legal political party. He also vehemently rejected the idea that the Communists would have their loyalty investigated by the police prior to being released from detention to resume normal life. Chin Peng told his adversaries:

> The principle of investigation of our loyalty implies surrender. We will never accept surrender at any time and will continue the struggle to the last man.[9]

The Communists claimed to be fighting only "British colonialism and imperialism" and that they were seeking independence, and were thus similar to the Alliance in their objectives. Quite a point was made of the fact that the Alliance Government had not yet secured independence for Malaya and at that time did not have control of internal security and the local armed forces, and thus could not speak authoritatively for a government which was still "colonial".[10] Since the Communists claimed to be fighting only the "British imperialists," David Marshall got the Communist delegation to confirm their position in writing. The statement was released immediately to the press. It reads:

> As soon as the elected Government of the Federation obtains control of internal security and local armed forces we will end the hostilities, lay down our arms and disband our forces. It does not amount to acceptance of the present amnesty terms.[11]

Very quickly a deadlock was reached in the discussions and the meeting broke up after Tunku Abdul Rahman announced that the amnesty would be withdrawn shortly since the Communists were not willing to accept it. However, the door was left open for further meetings. At the conclusion of the talks, Mr. Marshall told Chin Peng,

> If ever in the future there is the chance that you can sink your pride for the welfare of the people of Malaya, the Tengku and I will not stand on our dignity and would be glad to meet you again.[12]

Although the Baling meeting did not bring the Communist guerrilla war to an end, it cannot be viewed as a complete failure. The stand of the Communists made it clear to the Malayan public that they would never renounce their ultimate objective of a Communist Peoples' Republic of Malaya. They might have agreed to call off their immediate terrorist activities, but only if they were permitted to retain their disciplined party organization which could resume "the revolution" when, in their view, such a tactic would be more likely to realize their ultimate objectives. The reasons for the Communist "peace feelers" are clearly stated in a Malayan Communist Party document which was drafted just before the Baling meeting by the Vice-Secretary General of the Party, Yeong Kuo.

> Undoubtedly, our tactics today are to join with the Tunku in a common effort to get rid of the colonial rule of the British Imperialists. After there is a state of peace we can then immediately win over more support of the broad masses of the people and go a step further by overthrowing the Tunku's bourgeoisie dictatorship and changing it into a joint dictatorship of all races and strata.[13]

After Baling, both the Alliance Government and the Communists knew where the other stood, and the Government was able to decide upon a clear line of action against the Communists.

The Surrender Campaign and Peace Feelers

On February 8 the amnesty was withdrawn. The results had been disappointing since the surrender rate had been lower than before the amnesty.[14] With great determination the Tunku began to lay plans for stepping up military action and psychological warfare against the Communists. By March the Alliance had secured complete internal self-government and the Tunku called upon Chin Peng to honor his "pledge" to "lay down arms and disband. . . . forces" when the Alliance secured control of internal defense and local forces.[15] At the same time new surrender terms were announced which were designed to induce the individual Communist guerrilla to give up the "senseless fighting".

Those of you who have genuinely given up the struggle against the Government of the people will be helped to regain your freedom and be re-united with your families. If you prefer, you will be repatriated to China.[16]

Later the Tunku offered to give every Communist guerrilla who wished to return to China free passage and M$600 to help him get established there. These terms were revised again after Malayan independence to overcome some of the psychological obstacles to "surrender"—a term which was abandoned in favor of "those wishing to leave the jungle". The revised terms also promised not to investigate or interrogate those who would not foreswear Communism and who wished to return to China.[17]

Ultimately, however, the major successes against the Communist guerrillas came not because of amnesty surrenders, but because of continued military operations and greater cooperation from a public which may have been severely disappointed over the Communists' failure to accept the amnesty terms.[18]

The Communists' claim to be fighting for Malayan independence had an increasingly hollow ring as *Merdeka* Day approached. They were caught in a "Stalinist dead end", unwilling to accept "surrender terms" but seeking a way out of their guerrilla war so that their party would continue as a political force, pursuing the same objectives, but following different tactics.

During 1956 the Communists tried to mount a propaganda campaign showing how their "policy of peace" was being thwarted by the unreasonable stand of the Malayan Government.[19] Also, in an effort to make the MCP appear to be more representative of Malayan nationalism, a Malay, Musa bin Ahmad, was elevated to the Chairmanship of the Party—a purely titular position. In September 1956 a message outlining MCP objectives was sent to the Eighth Chinese Communist Party Congress meeting in Peking. Radio Peking's report of this message deserves to be quoted.

The letter said that . . . the Malayan authorities had not been able to see through the colonialist scheme of "making Malayans fight Malayans" and had tried to use military force to coerce the Malayan Communist Party into unconditional surrender. . . .

"We warmly hope that the people of all countries will extend to us sympathy and support for the restoration of peace in our country. We also welcome well-intentioned international mediation which will contribute to the restoration of peace. . ."[20]

Needless to say, Chin Peng's idea of what constituted "well-intentioned mediation" differed from that of the Malayan Government.

Although these "peace" overtures of the MCP were having no apparent effect on the Malayan Government, Chin Peng still hoped to be able to negotiate a settlement which would extricate the Communist Party from its predicament and enable it to emerge as a legal party. In March 1957 an indirect offer was made to the Malayan Government to reopen "peace negotiations". Letters from the MCP Central Committee were sent to several Chinese communal organizations listing three terms for ending the guerrilla war.

> Members of the MCP [are] to be given the privileges enjoyed by citizens:
> They should have freedom to participate in elections and also stand as candidates; and
> A guarantee [must be given] that political as well as armed members of the MCP should not be punished.[21]

This offer was summarily rejected by the Tunku who refused to liberalize the terms offered at Baling.

Just after Malayan independence in August 1957, the Communists made one last bid to secure reconsideration of the Baling terms. The following letter, dated October 12, was not mailed for three weeks, probably due to the time of transit by courier from the deep jungle:

> The Honourable Prime Minister, Federation of Malaya.
> With due respect I wish to inform you that I am prepared to meet you again for a talk with the object of obtaining a just and fair agreement in order to end this war.
> In this matter it is expected that this time agreement will be reached to our mutual satisfaction.
>
> > Yours faithfully,
> > [signed] Chin Peng
> > Secretary-General
> > Malayan Communist Party[22]

Tunku Abdul Rahman made the following public announcement shortly after receipt of the letter:

> From the text of the letter, I can only infer that Chin Peng has accepted the principle of surrendering and that he has asked for a preliminary talk between my representatives and his representatives to discuss arrangements for surrender.
> I agree to a preliminary meeting and shall therefore await a message from Chin Peng announcing the name of his representative and proposing the time and place where contact can be made with him.[23]

After receipt of the letter from Chin Peng, the Government also released a document giving extracts from captured MCP documents showing how the Communists planned to pursue their same objectives through front groups promoting open and legal activities.[24]

The Government's reaction to Chin Peng's letter was hardly what the Communists had hoped for. More than a month passed before another message came from Chin Peng:

It is generally known that the aim of the armed revolt organised by my party was to oust the colonial power and to fight for Malayan independence.

It is not our intention to treat the elected government as our enemy. It is also clear that the question of surrender by us to the elected government does not arise.

The Communist Party's object is to end the Emergency by reaching a fair and just agreement.

To talk of surrender on your Government's unreasonable terms is unfair and unjust.[25]

The letter went on to propose a preliminary meeting of representatives, but warned that the negotiations "would not be concerned with surrender". The Tunku's answer speaks for itself:

I cannot see any possibility of coming to terms with him unless and until he is willing to surrender.

There will never be any peace in Malaya if the shooting war is to end on Chin Peng's terms.

It follows that there will be no security for the people here.

Now it is obvious that the goal of the Malayan Communist Party is to spread Communist politics with the ultimate aim of overthrowing the democratic Government and setting up a Communist state.

I will not tolerate this for the responsibility of the Alliance Government is to safeguard the security of this new nation and her people.[26]

With this last exchange, the Communists apparently became convinced that the Alliance Government would have to be treated as the implacable foe of the Malayan Communist Party. It took some time for Communist policy to adjust to this fact.

Communist Strategy and Tactics

So long as the Chinese Communist Party acknowledged the ideological leadership of the Soviet Union, the Malayan Communist Party looked to Moscow for guidance in mapping its strategy and tactics. When the Cominform enunciated the hard line in 1947 and indicated that conditions were opportune for launching armed revolution in former colonial areas, the Malayan Communist Party responded by initiating its "war of national liberation". By 1951 the MCP had begun to realize that it could not win its war unaided, and acknowledged that it had placed too much reliance on terrorism.[27] Although Chin Peng probably was looking for a convenient way to end the war, no such opportunity presented itself. Besides such a move would have been out of harmony with the hard line which Moscow continued to proclaim until after Stalin's death in 1953.

The tactical line of International Communism became more moderate following the Korean Truce and the Geneva Conference of 1954. In both Europe and Asia, Communist diplomatic moves indicated that both China and Russia found the risks and costs of militant and expansionist policies to be too great, and were therefore willing to stabilize the East-West conflict with partial or temporary settlements. For the Malayan Communist Party, the settlement at Geneva meant that it could no longer count on the imminent expansion of Communist power from China into Southeast Asia. Thus, the MCP realized it would have to rely on its own unaided efforts and resources for survival, at least for a few more years, and perhaps much longer. The morale of the guerrilla forces suffered accordingly.

Meanwhile, a new line of "peaceful co-existence" was being formulated by the Kremlin. At the now famous Twentieth Party Congress of the CPSU in February 1956, Nikita Khrushchev suggested that less violent tactics might be utilized to achieve Communist goals in the new states of Asia and Africa. In the Report of the Central Committee he stated:

> And it is not true that we regard violence and civil war as the only way to remake society.
> . . . in present-day conditions the working class in many capitalist countries has a genuine opportunity to unite the overwhelmingly majority of the people under its leadership. . . . In these conditions, the working class, uniting around itself the working peasantry, the intellectuals and all patriotic forces, and firmly rebuffing opportunist elements incapable of renouncing a policy of collaboration with the capitalists and landlords, has an opportunity to defeat the reactionary, antipopular forces, to win a firm majority in parliament and turn the parliament from an agency of bourgeois democracy into an instrument of genuinely popular will. (Applause.) In such a case this institution, traditional in many highly developed capitalist countries, may become an agency of genuine democracy, of democracy for the working people.[28]

While this interpretation of Marxist-Leninist scriptures did not eschew violent revolution, it did suggest that a variety of tactics could be used depending on the circumstances in each country. In the peace overtures and the Baling Talks, the Malayan Communist Party had already experimented with less militant tactics, but found that the Malayan Government would not allow the Communists to emerge from the jungle as an organized force. While the MCP leaders undoubtedly would have preferred to pursue open legal tactics, now legitimized by Khrushchev, such options were not open to them. However, the new tactics could be utilized by front organizations even while the top leadership of the party remained exiled in the deep jungles along the Siamese border. Consequently, the MCP attempted to enhance its political position by de-emphasizing its dedication to terrorism and violent revolution and concentrating instead on the formation of front groups to capitalize on popular causes. A party directive of 1956 explains the new tactics:

> If we do not make use of open and legal activities, we would have to restrict our movement within the narrow scope of secret activities. This would cause us to be separated from the masses and plunge us into a position of isolation and danger. . . .
> The purpose of making use of open and legal activities is to maintain the social position and professional standing of the comrades. Whenever there are parties or organisations which can be utilised, irrespective of whether they are neutral, backward or reactionary, or whether they are political or non-political, ways should be found to infiltrate into them. Make use of the programmes, postulates, policies, regulations, etc., of these parties and organisations which are favourable to the improvement of the masses' living conditions to lead the masses into launching open struggles. Where there are no parties or organisations to exploit, ways should be devised to set up legal organisations which are appropriate to the masses' degree of wakefulness and acceptance. . . .
> No matter what places we are in, we should always make more friends by posing as members of the masses working hard in the service of the interests of the masses. In this way we gradually establish and elevate our position in the open and step by step extend our contact with the masses and enlarge the scope of our service to the masses.[29]

Since infiltration tactics of legal organizations had been utilized by the MCP during all its history, the "new line" involved little more than assigning greater priority to these activities. Singled out for infiltration were those organizations pursuing political objectives which the Communists hoped to exploit to build a mass following of sympathizers. In these tactics, the Communists concentrated on three types of organizations: Chinese student associations, labor unions and "left-wing" political parties. Their activities in each of these three areas will be considered separately.

Communist Tactics and the Schools

The unrest in Chinese schools resulting from Government education policy in both Malaya and Singapore made it easy for Communists to sponsor, or operate within, a number of Chinese youth organizations. In the guise of promoting "Chinese culture" and "student democratic movements" Communists organized students into highly disciplined groups where they were indoctrinated with Communist slogans and ideology. The following are some excerpts from instructions given party organizers in the years between 1951 and 1956:

Town organisations must train up working personnel, particularly young cultural working personnel, to send out to operate in the rural areas. To this end it is very necessary for the Party to be active among Middle School Students [the seventh through the eleventh year of schooling], and this aspect of our work must be completed satisfactorily.[30]

. . . students and children are generally the potential force of our revolutionary power. They are pure in heart and can easily accept the teaching of the Party.[31]

We are to set up lawful public organisations acceptable to the masses, such as old boys [alumni] associations, basket ball teams, theatrical clubs, singing clubs and literary societies.

We should encourage the students to voice their demands. For example, if they are not pleased with the school administration, or with the conduct of a teacher, we must urge them to oppose the school authority or the teacher.[32]

The work of winning over the school children is very important and must not be overlooked. Especially in circumstances where the enemy is stronger than we are, the work of winning support from school children and organising them to struggle is more important than military activities.[33]

The Communist Party's preoccupation with youth had more immediate objectives than the political indoctrination of the next generation. School students can dramatize issues, make demands, publicize the Communist propaganda line, and demonstrate against the Government. The more militant and politically tested students can be recruited as party cadres. Government action against Communists in the front organizations was difficult since the Communists, for their own safety, avoided keeping any party records, and were careful to conceal the command and authority system of their organization.

In front organizations, Communists attempted to utilize indoctrination techniques according to the principle of *Hsueh Hsih*, which loosely translated means "study for action". However it has a more specific meaning in the lexicon of the Chinese Communist Party. Mao Tse-tung initiated the *Hsueh Hsih* campaign in 1938 to foster ideological conformity of the rank and file with party doctrine. He explains:

Generally speaking all those members of the Communist Party who are qualified to *Hsueh Hsih* must study the theory of Marx, Engels, Lenin and Stalin, the history of our nation and the circumstances and trends of the present movement. . . .

It is impossible for a party to lead a great revolutionary movement to victory if it has no knowledge of revolutionary theory, no knowledge of history and no profound understanding of the actual movement.[34]

A publication of the Communist-infiltrated Singapore Chinese Middle Schools Students' Union explains the aim of the study cell groups:

The theory is expounded that *Hsueh-Hsih* groups should be organised and popularised as against individual *Hsueh-Hsih*. The main aim is again to enforce uniformity within the *Hsueh-Hsih* groups and carry out criticism and self-criticism within the group.[35]

Individual and collective "self-criticism" is but one of the techniques employed to enforce "democratic centralism" which ensures that a front organized according to these Communist principles will have an authoritarian command system. Collective study, collective recreation, collective work and finally collective discipline are all designed to make the students into a mobilized force beyond the influence or control of their families or school authorities.

These tactics were quite successful in building a network of organizations in Chinese-media schools in both Malaya and Singapore. It is likely that Communist cells and front groups had been organized in a majority of Chinese schools by 1955. While schools in the "new villages" were particularly vulnerable to Communist influence, security restrictions then in effect greatly restricted student activities, thus making it more difficult for the party to use these groups for promoting its objectives. However, in the cities, surveillance of student activities was more difficult, and hence the tasks of indoctrination and of inciting anti-government demonstrations or riots were greatly simplified.

Singapore became the center of Communist subversion tactics since it was easy to conceal the party's presence while exploiting Chinese communal issues among its large Chinese population. The Singapore Chinese Middle Schools Students' Union (SCMSSU) became the most important Communist front for student activities. A number of ancillary clubs were formed under the guidance and leadership of the SCMSSU, and similar student unions were established in the major cities of Malaya. After a series of disorders and riots involving Chinese students, the Singapore Government banned the SCMSSU in September 1956. After that, the leaders of the SCMSSU shifted their organizational activities to Nanyang University. By 1958 a Nanyang University Students' Union (NUSU) was formed under a constitution carefully designed to ensure pro-Communist monopoly on its Executive Committee. Through NUSU initiative various subsidiary societies were founded, including the Political Science Society, the Social Science Research Society, the History and Geography Society and the NU Dramatic Research Society. The NUSU and several of these affiliated societies established their own journals, under the guise of which the Communist propaganda line could be disseminated.[36] To retain the graduating membership of the NUSU in its political and organizational structure, the NUSU founded the Nanyang University Guild of Graduates in 1959. According to a Government white paper, the NUSU and its cluster of related societies were under the secret direction of Lim Oon-kiat, who was a key member of the MCP organization in Singapore.[37]

At recurring intervals, Chinese students became involved in mass demonstrations or rioting. In May 1954 students at a number of Chinese schools in

Singapore staged protests against the National Service Act and the National Registration system, which required everyone to register for an identity card and subjected able-bodied men between the ages of 18 and 20 to possible compulsory service in the military forces.[38] Communist activists found it easy to mobilize student demonstrations against these measures, since students were faced with the prospect of being forced to fight for a government they opposed. Following these disorders, the Singapore Government closed eight Chinese schools, and allowed them to reopen only on condition that school authorities maintain effective discipline.

Much more serious rioting occurred in November 1956 when Chinese students and pro-Communist union members joined forces to defy and attempt to undermine the Labour Front Government in Singapore.[39] Chinese school students were agitated over the following grievances: the Singapore Government had recently banned the pro-Communist Singapore Chinese Middle Schools Students' Union; it had also taken strong disciplinary measures against student agitators in Chinese schools; and it had prevented certain publications from Communist China from being used in the schools. The militantly chauvinist Chinese school students were convinced that the government was anti-Chinese and that education policies designed to make the school curriculum more "Malaysia-centered" were in fact an attack on "Chinese culture".

Similar disorders erupted in Penang later in the month, and again the following April. Chinese students objected to disciplinary action by school officials and to the increasing government control and supervision of Chinese schools. During the April disorders students carried banners written with blood proclaiming: "Unity is Strength", "We seek human rights","Protect our Chinese education", "Loving Chinese culture is no crime".[40]

Because of fear that growing student unrest in the Federation was being promoted from Singapore, the Federation Government restricted the travel of Chinese students between Singapore and Malaya. In a move to reduce the number of older student agitators who were believed to be Communist-influenced, the Federation Minister of Education announced that within a year all government-aided schools would enforce maximum age limits for each class, so that students four years over the normal age would require special permission to continue their schooling. Coming during a period of intense controversy over the government's Chinese education policies, this announcement sparked extensive Chinese student demonstrations or riots in many cities. The most serious disorders occurred in Penang, Kuala Lumpur, Ipoh and Seremban.[41]

While many Chinese organizations were involved in the political controversies over Chinese education, the hand of the Communist Party was evident in its distinctive methods of operating through fronts and secret student societies that organized "cultural events" to disseminate the Communist propaganda line. The turmoil over education policies and over issues involving the cultural and racial identity of the Chinese provided the MCP with favorable opportunities to gain converts and sympathizers, while undermining the governments in Singapore and the Federation. Increasing government supervision of Chinese schools does not seem to have been entirely successful in eliminating the Communist hold over a significant minority of militant activities in the Chinese schools.

Communist Tactics and Labor Unions

When the Malayan Communist Party went underground in 1948, it controlled between 45 and 60 per cent of the existing labor unions in Singapore and Malaya. In the early stages of the Emergency, firm government action broke the Communist control of the labor union movement. Thus the two key central Communist labor-union organizations, the Singapore Federation of Trade Unions and the Pan-Malayan Federation of Trade Unions, went out of existence in 1948 because they could not or would not comply with the trade-union registration laws. The known Communist leaders of other trade unions were either detained or they joined the guerrilla forces in the jungles.[42]

In a move to re-establish its position of leadership in the trade union movement, the MCP singled out labor unions as prime targets for infiltration. In line with a Peking directive, the MCP drafted the following instructions to party members shortly after the failure of the Baling talks:

> Push ahead with the open and legal trade union work. Form new yellow trade unions and mobilise the masses into joining yellow unions which are already in existence. Create activities for the open and legal organisations.
>
> Operatives in the Labour movement must first be proficient in their own occupation in order to establish prestige among the masses. Secondly, they must unite and contact the masses to carry out various forms of open and lawful activities for the benefit of the workers and lead the masses forward to strive hard for their personal interests, national independence and democratic freedom. . .
>
> We are to convert the workers' struggle into a struggle to be led by the Party. Therefore unmask the true colours of the "yellow" Union's running dogs. While carrying out the struggle make an effort to enhance the Party's prestige. The struggle must be carried out in the name of the "yellow" Union so as to shield the Party's identity. . . It is the Party which should play the leading role. We can select some of the office-bearers of the "yellow" Union to suit our purposes.
>
> While conducting struggles for raising the standard of living we must see to it that the influence of the Party is increased as well. Only in these ways can we fulfil our Party duties.[43]

Although the authorities were aware of the new tactics, counter-measures were difficult, especially when Communists and their sympathizers restricted their activities to the legitimate demands of labor. The major obstacle the

Communists had to contend with was the determination of genuine union leaders to keep their unions free of Communist influence, a determination caused in part, no doubt, by fear of government restrictions or reprisals against their unions. For its part, the Alliance Government became exceedingly suspicious of the activities of labor unions, and Tunku Abdul Rahman issued repeated warnings to the unions about Communist subversion.

If the evidence of the Malayan Government is to be believed, Communists were able to operate within some unions. One of these was the Pan-Malayan Rubber Workers Union. It claimed a membership of about 10,000 workers, mostly in rubber processing plants. In June 1956, the Registrar of Trade Unions refused to register the PMRWU on the grounds that it was likely to be used for unlawful purposes. The PMRWU appealed to the courts which upheld the discretionary authority of the Registrar.[44]

The National Union of Factory and General Workers was also accused of having Communist ties. Within the Malayan Trade Union Congress it consistently proposed a more militant anti-government line, and the union also became noted for the great number of strikes which it initiated, some of which were "lightening strikes" with demands being presented after the surprise strike had been called. Some officials of the union were arrested for propagating "Communist subversive doctrines" and for possession of Communist literature, including some books which exalted the life of the guerrilla soldier.[45]

Five months later, the Federation Government banned the NUFGW, claiming that it followed a political line similar to that of the Malayan Communist Party. As evidence the Minister of Defence cited the following directive to the union branch officers from the NUFGW General Secretary, Mr. V. David:

> ... point out to the rank and file members that through militant trade unions only the emancipation of the working class could take place. Tell the workers to be prepared for a working class revolution. A working class revolution could only bring a change in the political, economical and social life of the toiling masses.[46]

Two weeks later Mr. David was arrested. A government announcement explained:

> David has repeatedly demonstrated, by his words and actions that he is acting in support of the Malayan Communist Party's policy to gain control of the trade union movement so that it can be used to further the party's aims to create a Communist state in the Federation.
>
> He has maintained frequent contacts with the known Communists of the Middle Road group in Singapore.
>
> In his position as general secretary of the N.U.F.G.W. he has been responsible for encouraging the subversive activities of the union, to the members of which he has not hesitated to advocate the use of violence.[47]

Although Mr. David may have cooperated with the Communists, the Federation Government did not make public any concrete evidence of his alleged Communist ties, and after six weeks' "preventive detention", he was released on a good behaviour conditional bond.[48]

Defenders of the union charge that the government's actions against the union were motivated by a desire to harass and intimidate legitimate political opposition, particularly since the General Secretary of the NUFGW, V. David, was also one of the key figures in the Socialist Front. That the Communists made an effort in infiltrate the NUFGW is obvious, and it is probable that these efforts were not entirely in vain. But the case against V. David was not as obvious and was never presented in court.

Due to government vigilance and the caution exercised by most union leaders in Malaya, no trade union in the Federation was infiltrated to the point where the Communists could consider it to be a reliable front for its operations. The same cannot be said of the unions in Singapore. Among its large Chinese working population were many who became agitated over the same issues and ideological loyalties as activated the students in the Chinese high schools. Therefore the political climate among the trade unions in Singapore was more radical and the Communists found it easier to recruit allies and supporters in their "united front" tactical campaign.

When the Communist Party began to place higher priority on infiltration tactics, special attention was given to union leaders who had been closely affiliated with the Communists before 1948. A small clique of former Malayan Democratic Union activists were recruited into the Communist-sponsored Singapore Peoples' Anti-British League, or into small private Marxist study groups. The arrest of John Eber and some other members of the ABL provided a warning to pro-Communists that the British authorities were determined to act decisively against those found to be collaborating with the Communist Party.[49] Even so, the Communists made headway in gaining the sympathy and cooperation of many unionists who viewed the Communist struggle as an anti-colonial liberation movement. By the time the Communist Party officially adopted the "united front" tactical line in 1955, it had a small but effective cadre scattered through most of the larger Singapore trade unions.

The Singapore Trade Union Congress became a major target for Communist infiltration. Until about 1956, Communists made substantial progress toward their objective of capturing the STUC. However, the riots against the Labour Front Government in that year and the next brought Communist agitators into the open prematurely, and many of the key figures in the cadre organization were detained or deported by the Singapore authorities. Subsequently, the Communist Party admitted its tactical errors in over-playing its hand in those years.[50]

After the Peoples Action Party victory at the polls in June 1959, the newly elected-Singapore Government secured the release of those who had been detained in the riots against the previous government. Because the Communist Party had infiltrated many of its supporters into the PAP, it assumed that the government would become more lenient toward its activities and therefore it became more bold in its campaign to make the trade union movement a bastion of Communist strength. Yet, despite the apparently more favorable circumstances for the Communist Party, it faced two obstacles not encountered before. First, Malaya had achieved its independence, but, at the Baling talks, the Communist Party refused to give up its armed struggle. This caused a number of English-educated pro-Communists to doubt the Communists' loyalty to Malayan nationalism, and they also became increasingly concerned over the dangers inherent in the party's espousal of militant Chinese communalism.[51] Secondly, the Communists now had to compete with the PAP for the loyalty of trade unions, many of which had formed the core of support for the PAP at its inception. Having been closely associated with the Communist organization in Singapore, the leaders of the PAP had first-hand experience both of Communist tactics and with the leading cadres who engaged in "open front" activities for the Communist high command.[52] Therefore the PAP leaders were better prepared to compete with Communists for the control of the labor union movement. Nonetheless, the pro-Communists gained control of the General Employees Union and the Singapore Shop and Factory Workers Union, and using them as a base for their activities, gradually expanded their support in many other unions.[53] In time an internal power struggle developed within the Singapore Trade Union Congress between a pro-Communist wing, led by Lim Chin-siong and Fong Swee-suan, and a pro-PAP non-Communist wing led by the General Secretary of the STUC, C. V. Devan Nair.

In 1961 the Communist Party made a desperate bid to capture both the PAP and the Singapore Trade Union Congress, but was unable to seize control of either. Instead, both the PAP and the STUC suffered the defection of their pro-Communist wings and the formation of rival pro-Communist organizations. The defecting pro-Communist unions formed the Singapore Association of Trade Unions (SATU) at the same time that pro-Communists broke with the PAP to found the Barisan Sosialis political party.[54] While the Communists had in SATU a more pliable open front organization within which to operate, it became increasingly difficult to conceal their presence and their activities.

Communist Political Tactics

From 1955 to 1957 the immediate objective of the Malayan Communist Party was to negotiate a settlement of the guerrilla war which would enable it to play a major role in the politics of an independent Malaya. When no such settlement could be secured from the Malayan Government, the party leaders were forced to make a fundamental reassessment of policies toward the Alliance Government in an attempt to discredit it and force its collapse. To justify its continued struggle, the MCP refused to recognize Malaya's independence,[55] attacking in particular the Treaty of Defence and Mutual Assistance between Malaya and Britain. The diplomatic recognition of

Malaya by the Soviet Union, and Malaya's admission to the United Nations without a Soviet veto must have proved somewhat embarrassing to the Malayan Communist Party. However, by this time, the MCP was far more closely identified with the Chinese Communist Party and its militant doctrines concerning the necessity of pursuing "wars of national liberation" against neo-colonialism. Quite apart from its ethnic and political ties with China, the MCP found that the Peking line helped to legitimize the guerrilla war which it wanted to terminate, but could not. National ties and necessity thus combined to bring the MCP into the Peking camp even before the Sino-Soviet rift became formally acknowledged in the Communist world.

With Malaya's independence, the Communist Party drafted a new program which made no mention of "revolution" or "struggle". Instead, it was a very mild statement of dedication to inter-racial Malayan nationalism. It proclaimed the following objectives:

1. Strengthen and safeguard the independent status of our country; pursue an independent and self-determined foreign policy of peace and neutrality; establish diplomatic relations with all countries; oppose war and uphold peace; refrain from joining any military bloc; unite and cooperate with Afro-Asian countries; strive for the reunification of Singapore with the Federation of Malaya.

2. Foster unity and mutual support among the Malays, Chinese and Indians, etc. with the Malays as the pivot; protect the legitimate rights and interests of the various nationalities in the country.

3. Safeguard the democratic rights and liberties of the people; release all patriotic prisoners; extend legal status to all political parties and public organizations which pledge loyalty to the Malayan fatherland.

4. Protect and develop national industries, agriculture and commerce; improve and develop culture; enforce universal education and ameliorate the living conditions of the people.

5. Terminate the war; repeal the Emergency Regulations and restore internal peace.[56]

This manifesto was probably designed more for foreign audiences than for Malayan, since the party's supporters were being recruited through the exploitation of militant Chinese communal chauvinism rather than appeals to Malayan nationalism "with the Malays as the pivot". In any event, this program could not be widely distributed in Malaya or Singapore, but was published abroad. Of greater significance were the operational directives given to the party cadres prior to the 1959 parliamentary elections. The full text of the document appears below:

Concerning next year's Federal general elections.

Our attitude is to support the general elections, but our basic principle is:

1. To bring about the downfall of the Alliance in the general elections for the victory of the political parties of the socialist front, such as Party Rakyat, the Labour Party, the People's Socialist Youth League.

2. The overall method is to make good use of the election campaign period to call on the masses' executives and active elements of the public to carry out large-scale propaganda openly and constitutionally by using their legal status.

Through the influence of the organised masses, we can approach their relatives and appeal to them to vote in favour of those candidates who are regarded by us as progressive elements.

We may also use the students' defiance of the education policy and urge their guardians not to vote for the Alliance.

When possible, we may assemble all the masses' executives to take part in the propaganda campaigns organised by the progressive parties' candidates and appeal to the public to cast a blank vote or abandon their voting right when, in their constituency, only Alliance candidates, and none from other political parties, are contesting.

3. We will appeal to the public to boycott all open election rallies organised by the Alliance candidates, or instigate the children and students to create disturbances and boo them at the scene.

Any sort of annoyance will serve the purpose. We may even tip the public to use the transport facilities provided by the Alliance to go and cast their votes in favour of the candidates of the other political parties.

During the election campaign, our verbal propaganda is to disclose that the Alliance has been bluffing the people by making all kinds of pledges and the havoc that it has made since it came into power.

The continuation of the Emergency is of particular importance. The public should be given to know that their democratic rights have been robbed clean by the Alliance and that the peace talks were abandoned.

This copy of directives is to be destroyed by fire immediately after perusal.[57]

While this document identified the two parties in the Socialist Front as the prime targets for infiltration and "united front" tactics, it seemed to imply that the Communists were willing to join forces with any opposition party having a chance to unseat Alliance Members of Parliament. The Alliance was not averse to making political capital out of this document, and on occasion attempted to implicate left-wing parties such as the Socialist Front and the Peoples Progressive Party with the Malayan Communist

Party.[58] On two occasions prior to the 1959 elections, the police staged a major round-up of persons suspected of being Communist agents or supporters. Nearly all the detained persons were believed to be affiliated with one or more of three Communist front organizations the Selangor National Independence League, the Socialist Youth League, and the Malayan Races Liberation League. The government claimed to have evidence that members of these organizations "visited jungle camps for instruction in subversive methods". While these were probably the cadres who were expected to infiltrate the opposition parties, it is of some significance that, of the over 225 persons detained, only about 15 were identified as members of the Labour Party and several others were members of Party Ra'ayat.[59] However, one of the fifteen was Chairman of the Selangor division of the Labour Party.

Spokesmen for the Socialist Front accused the Alliance Government of using the word "subversive" to detain and intimidate the opposition. They also claimed that the Communists were infiltrating the Alliance. While the government may have had a variety of motives for staging the detentions, it appears that they were not designed to silence or immobilize the opposition parties, particularly since the opposition leaders were not detained, and were more vociferous than ever. It is more likely that the police had obtained new information on the structure and operations of the Communist Party from surrendered guerrillas.[60]

Evidence presently available, indicates that the Communists had rather limited success in infiltrating political parties in Malaya, and apparently had very slight ability to influence the outcome of the 1959 elections. In fact, the "united front" tactics may have weakened those parties singled out for infiltration, besides complicating the task of forming a political coalition with a sufficiently broad base to challenge the Alliance.

By 1959 Communist fortunes were at a low ebb. Military operations of eleven years' duration, the resettlement and "new village" programs, the amnesty and surrender campaigns, and finally the achievement of Malayan independence, all contributed to the Communist Party's military defeat.[61] Even many hard-core Communists could see no hope of victory and decided to surrender. Others joined Chin Peng in retreat to the most inaccessible dense jungle along the Perak-Thai border. Attempts by Security Forces to pursue the remaining guerrillas proved quite futile in such vast areas of dense jungle. Because the Communist guerrilla forces avoided all military operations, they appeared to pose little threat to Malaya's security. Consequently, the Federal Government avoided making the large expenditures which would have been required to eliminate the remaining guerrilla forces.[62]

In recognition of the Communist retreat and isolation, one area after another was declared to be "white" and most Emergency restrictions were lifted.[63] Finally, the Emergency was officially terminated on July 31, 1960 and Parliament repealed the Emergency Regulations.[64]

Meanwhile, Chin Peng and his comrades were playing a waiting game, hoping that, in time, changes in the international or domestic scene would occur which would give them a new opportunity to seize power in Malaya.

They found solace and inspiration in the example of Mao Tse-tung who retreated to interior areas with a small force, and after more than twenty years was rewarded with ultimate victory in China. Events in Vietnam after 1960 may also have bolstered Communist morale. But of more immediate importance to the Communists were the developments in Singapore, where the environment was much more favorable for the successful implementation of "united front" tactics. Consequently, Communists in Malaya primarily looked to Singapore for salvation once it became clear that victory could not be secured by guerrilla warfare.

Communist Political Tactics in Singapore

Shortly after the founding of the Peoples Action Party in November 1954, Singapore Communists were instructed to infiltrate that party and develop it as an instrument for furtherance of Communist objectives. A concerted campaign was undertaken to ensure the election of Communist sympathizers to positions of authority in the PAP. Under Lee Kuan-yew's leadership, the party seemed to welcome Communist support while seeking to prevent the party's capture by the pro-Communists operating within it. At one point he even announced that the PAP did not differ from the Communists in the "ultimate objectives" of "building a socialist Malaya", but did contend that the PAP differed on the question of methods to be employed.[65] For two years the struggle for control of the PAP was concealed in the behind-the-scenes politics of the party, but in 1957 the pro-Communist faction became more bold. They expected to elect nine out of the twelve positions on the PAP Central Executive Committee, yet retain Lee Kuan-yew as General Secretary and Dr. Toh Chin-chye as Chairman of the party. By this move, it was hoped that the non-Communist leaders would have their powers circumscribed, while continuing to provide a front for Communist-inspired political activity within the party. Assisted by their fraudulent use of PAP membership cards for admission to the 1957 annual party conference, the pro-Communist faction succeeded in electing six of the twelve-member Executive Committee, but Lee Kuan-yew and Dr. Toh Chin-chye refused to assume office without majority backing on the committee. This forced the pro-Communist faction to fill the six major party offices from among their own number.[66] Lee Kuan-yew's tactic may have anticipated subsequent events. Ten days after the PAP changed leadership, the Singapore Government arrested forty suspected Communists, including twenty PAP members, five of whom were on the PAP Central Executive Committee. Seven of the arrested PAP members were charged with having ties with the MCP, while the remainder were accused of allowing themselves to be used by the Communists.[67] These arrests enabled the non-Communist faction to regain control of the PAP. After T. T. Rajah resigned for "health reasons", Lee Kuan-yew resumed leadership of the party once again.[68]

The pro-Communist faction was not purged from the PAP despite government arrests, and the Communists continued to utilize the party for its "open front" tactics even though the PAP leaders remained free from Communist control. As far as the Communists were concerned, this made the PAP undependable as a vehicle for political action. Therefore, the Communist cadres began working through other parties on a selective basis when PAP policies or candidates seemed to work at cross purposes with Communist objectives. Thus, in the 1957 Singapore City Council elections the Communists supported the Workers Party; in the 1959 general elections, the Communists worked through the PAP, but supported Party Ra'ayat (Singapore) candidates in four constituencies; and in two by-elections in 1961 the Communist organization successfully supported PAP opponents. Yet, as long as the PAP provided a haven for pro-Communist activities and its political power was rising, the Communists and their sympathizers remained relatively quiescent within the party.

In 1959 the Peoples Action Party won a decisive victory at the polls, capturing 43 out of 51 seats in the Singapore Legislative Assembly. Lee Kuan-yew immediately arranged for the release of eight leading PAP members who had challenged his leadership of the party and had later been detained by the previous Labour Front Government.[69] While it appeared that Communist sympathizers had gained access to government power through participation in the PAP Government, in fact Lee Kuan-yew kept the pro-Communists in check, giving them very few government positions, and then only non-critical ones.[70] Attempts were made also to persuade leading members of the Communist cadre system to renounce their Communist ties. The released detainees were obliged to sign a statement highly critical of the Malayan Communist Party's continuation of the guerrilla war, and were also required to pay lip service to the party's program of building an independent "non-Communist socialist" state by merging with Malaya. Several leading Communist cadres were weaned from the MCP and joined forces with Lee Kuan-yew. However, at the same time, the Communists were methodically cultivating grass-roots support within the PAP for an eventual second attempt to capture the party from its "non-Communist" and more moderate English-educated multi-communal leadership. That showdown did not come, however, until 1961 when the issues associated with the Federation of Malaysia proposals brought the PAP and the Communists into open conflict.

Communist Strategy

The "open front" tactical maneuvers of the Communist Party described above were designed to secure a number of limited objectives as part of a wider strategy. An attempt was made to build a new organizational structure for the party and to remobilize the mass support it had lost or abandoned in 1948 when its leaders entered the jungles of Malaya. Even more important, the Communists hoped to make Singapore a "safe haven" for their political activities. Consequently, they were most sensitive to issues related to the exercise of internal security powers in Singapore.[71] From their actions in the years from 1955 to 1963, it is possible to reconstruct in rough outlines the Communist strategy. It was based on the following calculations.

Communist victory in Malaya could not be achieved by force of arms or by elections without substantial outside assistance. If the party could negotiate "peace terms" permitting it to engage in open political campaigning and recruitment of supporters, its political position would be strengthened, particularly through political alliances ("united front" tactics) with opposition parties. Ultimately, however, Communist success depended upon assistance from "progressive forces" outside Malaya. With proper tactics, the Communists had a good chance to bring Singapore under Communist or pro-Communist control. If Singapore did not succumb, additional support could be obtained from Indonesia, especially from its Communist Party. If the PKI came to dominate Indonesian politics, that would help even more to tip the political scales in favor of the Communists in Singapore. With a pro-Communist Singapore Government, British influence in the area could then be eliminated and Malaya (and the Borneo states) could be subverted with impunity. Agitation for the merger of Singapore and Malaya could begin *after* Singapore came under effective Communist control. Such agitation for union would mask the political campaign to subvert and defeat the "reactionary" Alliance Government.

This strategy depended upon the formation of the widest possible "united front" composed of all opponents, both domestic and foreign, of the Alliance and PAP Governments to assist in their revolutionary overthrow. Apparently, the task of recruiting such a "united front" was given to the Malayan National Liberation League (MNLL), which differed from the Malayan Communist Party only in name. Later, when political tensions were high in Malaya, Singapore and abroad over the proposals to form the Federation of Malaysia, the MNLL issued the following appeal:

> To all patriotic political parties and organizations opposing "Malaysia", whether functioning publicly or secretly, whether in Malaya or overseas, and to all compatriots at home or abroad, the Malayan National Liberation League makes this fervent appeal:
>
> Although there are differences in political views among ourselves, nevertheless, let us join our forces and form a strong united front. Let us crush "Malaysia" and fight for our country's true independence, democracy, peace, and the reunification of Singapore with the Malay Peninsula.
>
> . . . we are willing to hold talks with all patriotic political parties and individuals opposing "Malaysia" whether in Malaya or overseas, and, through adequate consultations, to reach agreement with them in accordance with the principle of seeking concord while preserving differences.[72]

As we shall see, the proposals to create the Federation of Malaysia were designed in part to counteract Communist strategy. However, the disputes raised by these proposals also gave the Communists new opportunities to "fish in troubled waters" and enlist support from among the disappointed and the desperate both within Malaysia and abroad.

1 The Federal Government's counter-insurgency expenditures totalled M$203 million in 1953 and M$169 million in 1954. These expenditures were partly offset by direct grants from the United Kindgom of M$51·4m in 1954 and M$62·5m for 1955. See "The High Commissioner's Speech", *Federation of Malaya, Legislative Council Debates*, November 17, 1954, 3–6. In 1954 it cost the Government about M$183,000 for each Communist guerrilla killed, captured or wounded. The costs of the Emergency to Malaya's economy as a whole are impossible to calculate, but obviously they were far greater than the counter-insurgency costs borne by the government.

2 *Alliance Platform for the Federal Elections* (Kuala Lumpur: Alliance National Council, 1955), p. 24.

3 *Straits Times*, September 9, 1955, p. 1.

4 *Straits Times*, September 22, 1955, p. 1.

5 *Straits Times*, September 29, 1955, p. 7.

6 *Straits Times*, September 30, 1955, p. 1.

7 *Straits Times*, October 15, 1955, p. 1.

8 *Straits Times*, November 18, 1955, pp. 1 and 2.

9 *Straits Times*, December 30, 1955, p. 2.

10 The Baling Talks took place on the eve of the departure of the Malayan delegation to the London Conference which determined the procedure for the drafting of the *Merdeka* Constitution.

11 *Straits Times*, December 30, 1955, p. 1. Also note *Report by the Chief Minister of the Federation of Malaya on the Baling Talks*, Federation of Malaya, Council Paper No. 25 of 1956, pp. 1–13.
   Apparently the original Chinese version of the press release was more ambiguous than the English translation, and allowed more leeway for interpreting the phrase "lay down our arms". Did it mean "to cease open hostilities" or "to surrender arms to the government forces"?

12 *Straits Times*, December 30, 1955, p. 2.

13 Federation of Malaya, *The Communist Threat to the Federation of Malaya*, Council Paper No. 23 of 1959, p. 17. This MCP document, from which the above quotation is taken was found the following year when Security Forces killed Yeong Kuo.

14 *Straits Times*, February 8, 1956, pp. 1 and 8.

15 *Straits Times*, February 23, 1956, p. 1.

16 *Straits Times*, March 16, 1956, p. 1.

17 *Straits Times*, September 4, 1957, p. 1.

18 The amnesty and surrender campaigns combined with the demonstrated position of strength of the Malayan Government undoubtedly contributed to the demoralization of the Communist guerrilla forces. Sir Robert Thompson lays considerable stress on the importance of a surrender campaign as part of counter-insurgency operations, but gives no evidence to show how it influenced the outcome of the guerrilla war in Malaya. See Sir Robert Thompson, *Defeating Communist Insurgency* (New York: Frederick A Praeger, 1966), pp. 90–102.

19 For example see *Straits Times*, April 24, 1956, p. 1; April 26, 1956, p. 1; April 27, 1956, p. 6; May 12, 1956, p. 4.

20 *New China News Agency*, Peking, in English Morse to Europe, September 20, 1956, 1352 GMT, as reported in a document which permits quotation but does not permit citation of source.

21 *Straits Times*, March 23, 1957, p. 1.

22 *Straits Times*, November 9, 1957, p. 1.

23 *Loc. cit.*

24 Federation of Malaya, *The Danger and Where It Lies*, (Kuala Lumpur: Government Press, 1957). Note also *Straits Budget*, November 13, 1957, p. 15.

25 *Sunday Times*, December 22, 1957, p. 1.

26 *Loc. cit.*

27 A secret document of the MCP dated September 1951 called for a reduction of terrorist attacks on the civilian population and stated that greater efforts should be made to strengthen "urban organization" i.e. legal front groups. See Harry Miller, *Menace in Malaya*, (London: George G. Harrap & Co., 1954), pp. 213–214.

28 N. S. Khrushchev, "Report of the Central Committee of the Communist Party of the Soviet Union to the 20th Party Congress", in Leo Gruliow, (ed.), *Current Soviet Policies—II, The Documentary Record of the 20th Communist Party Congress and Its Aftermath*, (New York: Frederick A. Praeger, 1957), p. 38.

29 *The Communist Threat to the Federation of Malaya, op. cit.*, p. 19.

30 "The Party's Urgent Tasks" (1951) as reproduced in *Singapore Chinese Middle School Students' Union* (Singapore Legislative Assembly, Paper no. 53 of 1956), p. 1.

31 *Singapore Standard*, February 14, 1955, p. 1, quoting an MCP document of 1954.

32 *Straits Times*, February 14, 1955, p. 4.

33 *Singapore Chinese Middle School Students' Union, op. cit.*, p. 1, quoting an MCP document of June 1956.

34 *Ibid.*, p. 9. See also Peter S. H. Tang, *The Training of Party Cadres in Communist China*, (Washington, D.C.: Research Institute on the Sino-Soviet Bloc, 1961), pp. 5–17.

35 *Singapore Chinese Middle School Students' Union, op. cit.*, p. 10.

36 *The University Tribune* was the official publication of the NUSU. It was banned in 1959 by the Federation of Malaya, but continued to be circulated in Singapore.

37 *Communism in the Nanyang University*, (Kuala Lumpur: Government Printer, 1964). The Communists also attempted to infiltrate the Pan-Malayan Students' Federation, but had less success, probably because the leadership of that organization remained in the hands of the English-educated. However, some students broke away from the PMSF in 1956 charging that it was promoting Communist-inspired causes. See *Straits Budget*, November 1, 1956, p. 6.

38 *Straits Times*, May 13, 1954, pp. 1 and 7; May 14, pp. 1 and 7.

39 In the November riots, seven persons were killed and over sixty persons were injured. *Straits Budget*, November 1, 1956, pp. 11–13.

40 *Straits Times*, April 4, 1957, pp. 1 and 7; April 5, 1957, pp. 1 and 7. Penang also suffered riots in January 1957, but they were apparently not directly connected with the disorders in the Chinese schools, but developed when rumors of communal clashes spread at a Chinese celebration and quickly touched off serious Sino-Malay rioting. See *Straits Times*, January 4, 1957, pp. 1 and 7; January 5, 1957, pp. 1 and 7.

41 *Straits Times*, November 15, 1957, pp. 1 and 9; November 18, 1957, pp. 1 and 2; November 22, 1957, pp. 1 and 9; *Sunday Times*, November 17, 1957, pp. 1 and 4.

42 *Colonial Annual Reports—Malaya, 1948.* (London: His Majesty's Stationery Office, 1949) pp. 12–13.

43 *The Communist Threat to the Federation of Malaya, op. cit.*, p. 28.

44 *Straits Budget*, June 27, 1957, p. 11.

45 *Straits Times*, October 31, 1957, pp. 1 and 9; November 29, 1957, p. 1; *The Communist Threat to the Federation of Malaya, op. cit.*, p. 30.

46 *Straits Times*, April 24, 1958, p. 7; *Legislative Council Debates, May 1, 1958*, Federation of Malaya, 4721.

47 *Straits Times*, May 14, 1958, p. 1; *Sunday Times*, May 18, 1958, p. 1.

48 *Straits Times*, June 27, 1958, p. 1.

49 Some time after the Eber arrests in January 1951, the Anti-British League was disbanded as a Communist front, partly because the Communists found that they could work more effectively through other organizations.

50 The Communist Party made an evaluation of its tactics in the years before 1959 and circulated them in a document entitled, "Summary of Experiences of the Anti-Persecution Struggle".

51 See Lee Kuan Yew, *The Battle for Merger*, (Singapore: Government Printing Office, 1961), pp. 3–39 and 131–138.

52 The highest Communist organization in Singapore was the Singapore Town Committee. It remained cleverly concealed from police surveillance, but the "open front" cadres of the party were much easier to identify, particularly by the inner circle of left-wing trade union and political figures who had close and continuous contact with these cadres. The Singapore Town Committee was decimated by police raids during 1951 but some members of the inner organization fled to the Indonesian islands just south of Singapore, and from there continued to direct Communist activities in Singapore.

53 The Singapore Shop and Factory Workers Union grew from 200 members in 1954 to 50,000 members in 1957. It was dissolved by order of the Singapore Government in February 1957. Shortly afterwards the Singapore Trade Union Working Committee was formed to become the coordinating committee and provide leadership for the pro-Communist wing of the STUC. Unions affiliated with the STUWC were popularly known as the "Middle Road" unions since a good share of these unions had their offices along Middle Road. See *Straits Budget*, February 21, 1957, p. 11; August 29, 1957, pp. 14–15.

54 Pro-Communists and non-Communists in the PAP and the STUC divided over the issues associated with the formation of the Federation of Malaysia. The nature of the contest and the issues are examined in the next chapter.

55 Spokesmen for the MCP announced in Indonesia that the party would not recognize Malaya's independence. See *Straits Budget*, September 18, 1957, p. 9.

56 Frances L. Starner, "Communism in Malaysia, a Multifront Struggle", in Robert A. Scalapino (ed.), *The Communist Revolution in Asia*, (Englewood Cliffs, N.J.: Prentice Hall, 1965), p. 239.

57 These directives were formulated by the MCP at top level strategy meetings held in a jungle hide-out in Perak during May and June 1958. The document was dated June 1, 1958 and was recovered on June 28 when the Security Forces stumbled

K

onto the camp. Only one Communist of lesser rank was killed in the encounter, but a coded copy of the directive was found and was deciphered with the aid of a code book. See *Straits Budget*, July 30, 1958, p. 19; *Straits Times*, August 9, 1958, pp. 1 and 7.

58 For example note *Legislative Council Debates, 30th July 1958*, Federation of Malaya, 4880–4922.

59 Over 100 persons were detained in October, 1958 and 125 additional persons were picked up in February, 1959. See *Straits Times*, October 2, 1958, pp. 1 and 8; February 26, 1959, pp. 1 and 8; February 27, 1959, pp. 1 and 9.

60 In Johore and Southern Perak the guerrilla forces had been crumbling during 1958. The second most important Communist in Malaya, Hor Lung (Head of the South Malayan Bureau of the MCP), surrendered and helped to negotiate the surrender of 160 other guerrillas. Thus, much detailed information was obtained, and it undoubtedly helped the government to identify the Communist agents in civilian life. See *Straits Times*, August 27, 1958, pp. 1 and 7.

61 The Federal Government released the following casualty figures for the eleven years of the Emergency: "terrorists eliminated", 11,609; Security Forces killed, 1,345; Security Forces wounded, 1,685; Security Forces missing, 26; civilians killed, 2,473; civilians wounded, 1,385; civilians missing, 810. See *Straits Budget*, April 27, 1960, p. 11.

62 By 1960 the Federal Government estimated the Communist forces to be down to about 700 from a high of about 10,000. There were practically no "eliminations" of Communist guerrillas after 1960, but some probably returned to "civilian life". By 1964 the number in the jungle was estimated to be around 500 to 600 men.

63 When an area was designated as "white" it indicated the absence of active Communist guerrillas, and the Emergency Regulations were greatly relaxed in the area. By August 31, 1959, 13,226 square miles of the Federation had been declared "white areas".

64 When the Emergency Regulations were repealed, Parliament passed an amendment to Article 149 of the Malayan Constitution which expanded the authority of Parliament to enact legislation against subversion and to maintain public security without regard to the civil rights guarantees of due process of law, of prohibition of banishment and freedom of movement, and of freedom of speech, assembly and association. Pursuant to this amended article, the *Internal Security Act, 1960*, (No. 18 of 1960), was enacted, under which act the government has continued to exercise extraordinary powers, including the power of preventive detention without public trial in the regular courts.

65 *Straits Budget*, August 8, 1957, p. 13.

66 T. T. Rajah became General Secretary and Tan Chong-kin was elected Chairman of the PAP. These two were the only English-educated among the new officers, and were probably elected to "front" in place of Lee and Dr. Toh. See *Straits Budget*, August 22, 1957, p. 5. The pro-Communist faction was led by Lim Chin-joo, the brother of Lim Chin-siong, who was then in prison.

67 Three of the seven PAP members were later deported—a penalty which could only be applied to non-citizens born outside Malaya or Singapore. The Singapore Government released a White Paper presenting evidence of Communist infiltration of the PAP. Substantial portions were reproduced in *Straits Budget*, August 29, 1957, pp. 14–15. The October 1957 issue of the official magazine of the PAP, *Petir*, also presents an account of how "left-wing adventurers" attempted to capture the PAP. See also *Singapore Legislative Assembly Debate*, October 9, 1958.

68 *Straits Budget*, October 16, 1957, p. 12.

69 *Straits Budget*, June 10, 1959, p. 18.

70 For example, Lim Chin-siong (later identified by Lee as the leading "open front" Communist cadre) was made a political secretary in the Ministry of Finance, but given few responsibilities and access to no classified information. See Lee Kuan Yew, *op. cit.*, pp. 31–33.

71 Under Singapore's 1958 constitution, matters of internal security were the responsibility of the Singapore Internal Security Council which was composed of British, Malayan and Singapore representatives. Thus, any two governments could together control the action of the Council and exercise the extraordinary powers of preventive detention under the *Preservation of Public Security Ordinance, 1958*. The Singapore Government could act on its own against "criminals" with extraordinary powers under the provisions of the *Criminal Law (Temporary) Amendment Bill, 1958*.

72 "Manifesto of the Malayan National Liberation League," March 15, 1965, in *Peking Review*, Vol. 8, no. 27 (July 2, 1965), pp. 18–19. The Malayan Government referred to this organization as the "Malayan Races Liberation League", perhaps to discount its nationalist pretensions.

16 The Federation of Malaysia

In May 1961, the Prime Minister of Malaya, Tunku Abdul Rahman set into motion political forces which later transformed the map of Southeast Asia and greatly affected its political environment.[1] In a speech before the Foreign Correspondents Association of Southeast Asia he said that Malaya "should have an understanding with Britain and the peoples of the territories of Singapore, North Borneo, Brunei and Sarawak. It is premature for me to say now how this closer understanding can be brought about but it is inevitable that we should look ahead to this objective . . . "[2]

What made this statement so sensational was not that the idea of a Greater Malaysia was so new. Indeed, the idea (in different forms) has captured the imagination of many Malay and Indonesian nationalists for years, and during the war this sentiment was encouraged by the Japanese who hoped to channel the force of nationalism in Southeast Asia against Japan's enemies. But in the period after the war very few people in authority mentioned the idea of a larger political union because such proposals were either politically dangerous or impractical in that period of political change and ferment. Even the proposals for union between Singapore and the Federation of Malaya were spurned by the Malayan Government because of the unstable political situation in Singapore and the fear that Singapore's Chinese population would "upset the racial balance" in the Federation.[3] Under these circumstances, the possibility of a wider union seemed remote. In Malaya such thoughts were expressed in public by only a few of the more radical Malay politicians who occasionally referred to the idea of *Melayu Raya*—generally defined as a Malaysian Empire embracing all the peoples of Malay ethnic stock and modelled after the Indonesian Republic, which would presumably become its center.

Why Malaysia?

What, then, were the circumstances in 1961 which prompted the Malayan Government to reverse its apparent long-standing opposition to political union with other nearby territories? A major factor in the decision was the problem of Singapore. Politics on that island had been extremely unstable and volatile. Since the introduction of elections in 1948 there had been a continuing trend toward the left with radical Chinese elements increasingly dominating the political scene. In this environment the Communists developed a highly effective *modus operandi* which helped to conceal their activity while they built up their political support in a host of front organizations. In view of Malaya's fourteen-year war against Communist guerrillas, the Malayan Government was concerned about the situation in Singapore, but felt that it could be handled by the British as long as they were in control. In 1958, when Singapore was given internal self-government, internal security and external defense became the combined responsibilities of the United Kingdom, the Singapore Government and the Federation of Malaya acting through an organ set up by treaty—the Singapore Internal Security Council. Under this form of limited self-government foreign relations remained in the hands of the United Kingdom, and security matters in the hands of the United Kingdom and Malaya when they acted jointly. However, this constitution of Singapore was transitional and automatically expired in 1963.

The Malayan Government began to see the possibility of Singapore demanding and gaining independence. Tunku Abdul Rahman candidly expressed some of his thoughts on Malaysia in a speech to publicity officers in his own party.

> The most important point is that the constitution of Singapore will come to an end in 1963 and with it two issues will be faced: firstly, whether Singapore becomes independent; and, secondly, whether Singapore should merge with the Federation of Malaya.
>
> It is impossible to grant independence to Singapore because of the danger of it going communist, and if it goes communist it would with the help of the communist powers try to overrun the whole of Malaya.
>
> We can fight them with the help of our British and American friends, but the inevitable result will be catastrophic, with suffering, misery and distress facing the people of Malaya and perhaps disasters never before experienced in this country.
>
> The resultant losses would be so tremendous that the gains would not be noticed. Therefore to prevent this most unhappy and disastrous state of affairs occurring, the only course open to us would be to accept Singapore as a member of the Federation of Malaysia.[4]

In private conversation, Malayan government officials often referred to "the lesson of Cuba" in explaining their concern over the possible political developments in Singapore.

Despite the fears of the possible course of events if Singapore became independent, it would have been difficult to bring about such a union because the existing racial and political balance in Malaya would be upset. But by bringing the British-protected Borneo states into the union, a communal ratio fairly similar to that prevailing in Malaya could be retained. A glance at the population statistics will demonstrate one reason why the Borneo states were so important as a counterbalance to Singapore's left-leaning Chinese majorities.

The proposals for Malaysia might have been put off for a short time, but it was felt that the initiative had to be seized before political developments made federation impossible. In Singapore, the Communists were making a serious bid to topple the government, while in the Borneo territories, pressures were building up for independence. There was also a general fear that Indonesia might have designs upon the Borneo states after her dispute with the Dutch over West Irian was resolved. Any of these developments would have made negotiations for Malaysia extremely difficult, if not impossible.

TABLE 12

Estimated population by racial-ethnic groups December 31, 1964[a]

	Malaysians[b]	Chinese	Indians	Others	Total
Malaya	3,963,549	2,918,340	884,025	153,141	7,919,055
	50·05%	36·85%	11·16%	1·93%	
Singapore	262,400	1,383,000	152,100	46,700	1,844,200
	14·22%	74·99%	8·25%	2·53%	
Sarawak	547,923	262,615	2,712	6,558	819,808
	66·83%	32·03%	0·33%	0·8%	
Sabah (North Borneo)	341,974[c]	116,525[c]	3,546[c]	44,583[c]	506,628[d]
	67·5%	23·00%	0·7%	8·8%	
Brunei	71,306[e]	26,260[e]	—[e]	3,434[e]	101,000[e]
	70·6%	26·00%		3·4%	
Total	5,187,152	4,706,740	1,042,383	254,416	11,190,691
	46·35%	42·06%	9·31%	2·27%	
Total minus Brunei	5,115,846	4,680,480	1,042,383	250,982	11,089,691
	46·13%	42·2%	9·4%	2·26%	
Total minus Brunei and Singapore	4,853,446	3,297,480	890,283	204,282	9,245,491
	52·49%	35·67%	9·63%	2·21%	

Notes:

a "Malaysian Population Statistics, Estimated Population by Race and Sex as at 31st December, 1964", (mimeographed), Department of Statistics, Malaysia 1965.

b The category "Malaysians" includes Malays, indigenous Malaysian peoples and Indonesians, except that Sarawak and Sabah count Indonesians as "others".

c Sabah estimates based on percentage ethnic distribution as reported in North Borneo Census 1960 and *North Borneo Annual Report 1961*, p. 14.

d Estimated by Department of Statistics, Malaysia as at June 30th, 1964.

e Total estimate for Brunei, 1964, is made by The World Almanac 1965. The ethnic distribution for Brunei is estimated on the basis of percentages at time of 1960 Census as reported in Brunei Report on the Census of Population Taken on 10th August, 1960, (Kuching, Sarawak: Government Printing Office, 1961) p. 82. Brunei Census counts Indians as "others".

Although these were the basic calculations of the Malayan Government in proposing the Malaysian Federation, it is by no means certain that the initial move was made by Tunku Abdul Rahman. Because of the obvious advantages accruing to Great Britain from the Malaysian Federation, the opponents of Malaysia have charged that the idea originated with the British. In fact, such a union had been considered as a possibility by both the British authorities and the Malayan Government for many years.[5] It makes very little difference precisely who took the initiative in suggesting that the time was opportune in May 1961. Certainly, Tunku Abdul Rahman was persuaded to make the move then, and he did so after calculating the advantages and risks to Malaya.

The Political Situation in Singapore

Because of the importance of Singapore in the Malaysia scheme, some attention must be given to political developments on that strategic island. Communal issues, while partially submerged, played a most significant part in the course of Singapore politics. Not only does the Chinese community in Singapore comprise 75 per cent of the population, but it had become much more organized and politically active under the stimulus and direction provided by the large militant left-wing unions Many among the Chinese educated and the Chinese working classes were persuaded that "Chinese culture" was being threatened, and that the "genuine" Chinese were being discriminated against by government policies, particularly towards Chinese education and unions. Various attempts by the government to combat the Communist infiltration of Chinese schools and trade unions appeared to the ultra-communal Chinese to be directed against the demands of the Chinese community, since the Malayan Communist Party and the militant Chinese communalists were attracted to each other.[6] Consequently, political success came to politicians who responded to Chinese demands and used the rhetoric of "socialism" and an "anti-colonial" invective. However, once in power, these leaders had to deal with the complex economic and social problems, most of which could not be solved through the application of socialist or nationalist formulas. The frustration of the public become apparent at each successive election with the defeat of the party in power.

In 1959 the left-wing Peoples Action Party (PAP) led by Lee Kuan-yew swept into office by winning 43 out of 51 seats in the Legislative Assembly. The results of this election presaged a more lenient policy toward the Malayan Communist Party, as well as greater concessions to the communal demands of the Chinese. Yet, the new PAP Government proved later to be more moderate than it had appeared from its previous militant campaigning. While the responsibilities of office may have had a sobering effect, probably the greatest factor promoting moderation was the fundamental question of a merger with Malaya. The PAP, in its election platform, had pledged itself to work for Singapore's independence through some form of union with Malaya. It had come to the conclusion that it would be unrealistic and economically disastrous to make Singapore an independent sovereign state. But the previous rejections by Malaya of merger proposals presented a major barrier. To overcome the fears of Kuala Lumpur, Lee Kuan-yew had to play down Chinese communalism in Singapore politics and take a more cautious approach on political issues which might antagonize the Federation of Malaya.

Reaction in Singapore to Merger Proposals

Unfortunately the PAP from its very inception suffered from a factional division on a number of issues, one of the most important being that of party attitude and policy toward the illegal Malayan Communist Party. Lee Kuan-yew proclaimed a "non-Communist policy" (which he carefully defined as not being an anti-Communist policy). But others in the party were much more sympathetic to the Communist cause and were willing to allow the party to become a vehicle for Communist political action. The pro-Communist and ultra-communal Chinese elements within the PAP resisted Lee Kuan-yew's moderation and after 1957 made periodic attempts to oust him from the leadership of the party. In 1960 the conflict broke into the open when the former PAP mayor of Singapore, Ong Eng-guan, challenged Lee's leadership.[7] After a protracted struggle, Ong and two other assemblymen were expelled from the party, only to form a rival party called the United People's Party, whose policiy had much in common with the Communist tactical line.

A by-election in July 1961, proved to be even more damaging to the PAP, coming as it did just after Abdul Rahman's speech proposing Malaysia. The primary contest was between the PAP (whose candidate was the president of the Singapore Trade Union Congress) and the Workers Party (whose candidate was David Marshall, the controversial former Chief Minister). The debate centered around the question of union with Malaya. The PAP campaigned on behalf of "independence through merger", while Marshall called for "independence before merger". The contest took on new dimensions when another split developed within the PAP ranks.[8]

David Marshall's narrow victory in the by-election proved to be a minor blow to the PAP compared with the action of thirteen PAP assemblymen who "crossed the floor" to join the opposition[9] and form a new party on the extreme left of the political spectrum, the Barisan Sosialis. Thus in the course of three months, the government had its voting strength reduced from 43 seats to a bare majority of 27 in the 51-member Assembly. More than anything else, this defection was the result of opposition to the PAP's policy toward union with Malaya.

In a series of twelve radio talks in the following weeks, Lee Kuan-yew made dramatic revelations about Communist activities in Singapore. He blamed the Communists for the defections from the PAP, largely because of their opposition to PAP policy on the merger question.

On June 9, we announced our programme that in the 1963 constitutional talks we would ask for independence through merger with or without Borneo territories. This was how the fight started. . . .

The thing they [the Communists] fear most is that security will be in the hands of a Pan-Malayan government which they will not be able to intimidate or control. . . .

The most important reason why the Communists prefer a Singapore still under British control to a Singapore that is part of Malaya, is that with the British in control, their struggle for a Communist Malaya can be camouflaged as an anti-colonial struggle.[10]

Although Lee Kuan-yew may have exaggerated the role of the Malayan Communist Party in the by-election defeats, it is clear that the MCP, with its formidable power, had been trying to thwart a Malaysian Federation by every means at its command.

In Singapore, much of the early debate over merger reflected a genuine fear that too many concessions would have to be made to overcome Malaya's long-standing opposition to union with Singapore. The issues became more clearly defined after August 1961 when Lee Kuan-yew met with Tunku Abdul Rahman for three days to draw up a preliminary agreement for merger.[11] The most important features of this agreement provided that Singapore would be guaranteed its free port status, be given special autonomy in education and labor policies, and be allowed to retain a very large proportion of its revenues (about 75 per cent) for these additional responsibilities. Because of the greater autonomy and lesser financial obligations proposed for Singapore, it was agreed that Singapore be given only fifteen seats in the Federal House of Representatives—three or four less than proportionate for its population (if calculated with Malaya's representational formula which gives "weightage" to land areas).

The Singapore Legislative Assembly was to become a State Assembly with no authority over defense, external affairs or internal security. Because of the differing citizenship laws in Singapore and the Federation, it was agreed that all Singapore citizens would become "nationals" of the larger Federation, and would enjoy equal rights with Federation citizens, except that Singapore citizens would be eligible to vote only in Singapore unless they could qualify under the much more restrictive Malayan Federal citizenship laws.[12]

The political debate in Singapore never developed into a direct fight for and against merger. Rather, the attack was directed against the provisions of the merger agreement. The Barisan Sosialis and the United People's Party of the extreme left directed their major attack upon the "unequal citizenship" provisions. They claimed that they were for "genuine merger", which was never defined precisely but apparently meant that Singapore would have full proportionate representation, special autonomy in various fields including labor, education, and internal security, and the full right of Singapore citizens to engage in political activity throughout Malaya without the fear of restriction from Malaya's internal security laws. They also suggested that

Malaya would have to abandon its traditional "special rights" for Malays in order to effectuate "genuine merger" without "second class citizenship" for the Singapore Chinese.

The Malaysia Referendum

After the initial public debate on the terms published in the White Paper, the controversy shifted to the question of whether the voters still supported the PAP Government. After a direct challenge from David Marshall, Lee Kuan-yew agreed to submit the merger issue to the voters, even though consti-tutionally, a referendum could have no legal effect. The debate then turned entirely to the question of how the referendum should be conducted, and what choices would be presented to the voters.[13] Despite widespread criticism, the PAP was determined to control the wording of the choices presented to the voters so that the PAP Government's merger proposals would be more likely to secure approval at the polls.[14]

In accordance with Singapore's compulsory voting laws, all eligible citizens were required to cast a ballot. There was no opportunity on the referendum ballot to reject merger altogether, on the argument that "all parties accepted the idea of some form of merger". Similarly, all blank or spoiled ballots were to be counted as supporting the government's White Paper proposals of Alternative A (on the argument that the "undecided voter is willing to let the government decide").

Nearly all the opposition parties in Singapore criticized the arbitrary way in which the issues were presented to the voters, and for the same reason, one more PAP assemblyman defected to the opposition in protest. The Barisan Sosialis and the United People's Party exhorted the voters to cast blank votes in opposition to the "sell-out plots" of the "British-sponsored Malaysia plan". David Marshall of the Workers Party ultimately agreed to support the White Paper proposals, but somewhat inconsistently advised the voters to cast blank votes in protest over the "undemocratic" referendum choices.[15] The threat by Tunku Abdul Rahman that the causeway between Singapore and Malaya might be closed if Singapore rejected merger also entered into the battle for votes.[16]

The Singapore electorate responded to the referendum as follows:

Alternative A	397,626 (71·1%)
Alternative B	9,422 (1·7%)
Alternative C	7,911 (1·4%)
Blank votes	144,077 (25·8%)

The PAP hailed these results as an evidence of overwhelming support for its merger policies. Because of the nature of the referendum any interpretation is subject to dispute. However, the figures seem to indicate that the voters were fairly satisfied with the White Paper formula for merger. It would be safe to assume that the pro-Communist element in the electorate cast blank ballots. How many others also cast blank ballots can never be known. The results were clearly a political set-back for the Barisan Sosialis and the United People's Party, both of which campaigned vigorously for casting a blank ballot.

After the Singapore referendum an uneasy lull in political agitation settled over the island as the Communists and extremists tried to assess the situation and plan for their next moves in the power struggle which was also spreading to the Borneo states amd was already beginning to involve major foreign powers.

Political Awakening in Borneo

Political agitation had begun in the three Borneo states before Malaysia was proposed. But, without doubt, the Malaysia issues subsequently became the primary reason for the proliferation of parties and the sudden flash of political activity which spread like wildfire to engulf even the primitive people in remote jungle areas.

With the exception of Brunei (which is given separate consideration later) the first legal party appeared in Sarawak in June 1959. This party, the Sarawak United People's Party (SUPP), grew very quickly, attracting members from nearly all races, but its leadership and the bulk of the membership were Chinese. Because of the party's strong Chinese bias and because of its increasing militant Chinese inspired nationalism, the SUPP became the object of a major campaign of infiltration by the small but highly organized Communist Party which in embryonic form had existed under a variety of names and guises since the Japanese occupation.[17] The rather alarming growth and militant posture of SUPP, particularly involving the issues of government policies toward Chinese education, labor controls, and Chinese land-holding, prompted the formation of rival parties representing diverse non-Chinese elements in the population. The Government of Sarawak developed misgivings about the future should the Communists succeed in expanding their power by using SUPP as a cover for their political activities. Government officials privately encouraged the formation of rival political parties and began to consider ways to give Sarawak her promised independence without turning the country over to the highly organized Sarawak United People's Party and its political parasite, the Communist Party. Consequently, the idea of a Malaysian Federation began to be considered as an answer to possible political deterioration (from the official and native viewpoint) in Sarawak.[18]

At first Tunku Abdul Rahman's "Mighty Malaysia" plan met with the opposition of the "front running" political leaders in all three states, who promptly agreed to form a "united front" to oppose Malaysia[19] possibly partly because they hoped to inherit political power in their respective states by holding out for complete independence. A "goodwill tour" by the Tunku to Brunei and Sarawak in July, 1961 added fuel to the anti-Malaysia sentiment because a number of his statements were both patronizing and undiplomatic, and revealed the lack of knowledge and understanding of the Malayan

Government of the sensitive issues involved in Borneo politics. But after a bad start, some anti-Malaysia spokesmen were wooed and most of the important political leaders in Sarawak and North Borneo agreed to participate in negotiations to draft proposals for merger.

The regional meeting of the Commonwealth Parliamentary Association, meeting on July 28, passed a resolution (proposed by Donald Stephens, formerly one of the most outspoken critics of Malaysia) which called for a "Malaysia Solidarity Consultative Committee" to collect views and make proposals for the creation of a Malaysian Federation. Shortly afterwards, delegates from among the members of the legislatures of the five states were appointed to this semi-official committee, which, by February, had unanimously agreed on the first set of general recommendations for Malaysia.[20]

After the negotiations began in earnest between political leaders in Borneo and Malaya, all three Borneo states experienced a period of political jockeying by nearly all elements in the population. In both Sarawak and North Borneo most of the top political leaders were either opposed to, or very critical of Malaysia at one time or another, depending on the issues being considered in the Malaysia negotiations. But eventually almost all the leaders agreed to support Malaysia, even though some were unhappy about certain issues or "second-best" compromises. Ultimately, the only parties (with the exception of the Communist Party which was illegal) in all three states that opposed Malaysia were Party Rakyat (Brunei) and SUPP. The latter had earlier approved in principle the idea of Malaysia, and its chairman had agreed to the "Consultative Committee" recommendations.

The issues raised in the constitutional talks had a tendency to fragment and proliferate political parties. In most cases, political parties, as they were being formed, claimed to be non-communal. The first parties in Sarawak were a little more non-communal than those that were formed later. But, as the more communal parties developed, the older parties tended to lose their minority members who were from other racial and tribal groups. Thus, in Sarawak (although this was denied by many party leaders) SUPP was largely lower-class and Chinese-educated Chinese, the Sarawak Chinese Association was upper-class and English-educated Chinese, Party Negara Sarawak (PANAS) was largely Malay as was BARJASA (Barisan Ra'ayat Jati Sarawak), the Sarawak National Party (SNAP) was largely Land Dyak and Iban (Sea Dyak), and Pesaka (Party Pesaka Anak Sarawak) was almost completely Iban, Kayan and Kenyah (primarily in the Third Division).

North Borneo followed a similar pattern, except that political parties developed later and the communal structure of the parties were more openly admitted right from the very beginning. The first and strongest party, the United National Kadazan Organization (UNKO), restricted its membership to Dusun peoples, the Borneo Utara National Party was almost exclusively Chinese, the United Sabah National Organization (USNO) was largely Brunei Malay, Bajau and Sulut, representing the larger Muslim communities. The United National Pasok Momogun Organization was largely Dusun and

Murut, with a smattering of Chinese who, for a while, tried to exploit the anti-Malaysia sentiment of the natives in the Interior Residency.

While there developed among the native peoples a surprising degree of political concern, there was little political understanding. They were aware that important events were taking place and decisions were being made that would affect them, but, in general, most of the common people seemed to be confused by events and the competing claims of rival parties. Consequently, they tended to fall back on tribal loyalties and follow their traditional communal leaders. One would often hear the statement, "We don't understand political affairs, but we know we must stand united behind our tribal leader." Therefore, nearly all the key political figures were traditional leaders of an ethnic-cultural community, and they enjoyed great power and a free hand to negotiate favorable terms for their people. Consequently, each political party tended to be dominated by one central and rather autocratic indigenous leader. Although most of these leaders lacked education, they were experienced in practical politics (Borneo-style) and they appeared to have developed considerable skill in the arts of negotiation and compromise, both in internal politics and in the protracted negotiations with Malaya.

Malaysia Terms for North Borneo and Sarawak

After the preliminary negotiations within the "Malaysia Solidarity Consultative Committee", the Malayan Government and the United Kingdom agreed to appoint a commission of experts headed by Lord Cobbold to conduct hearings and make proposals for constitutional changes.[21] Its recommendations[22] differed little from those of the earlier committee. Later in the year an Inter-governmental Committee was given the task of drafting the precise administrative and constitutional formulae for the Malaysian Federation.[23]

The terms worked out by these three bodies were quite favorable to Sarawak and North Borneo. North Borneo was given sixteen seats in the national House of Representatives and Sarawak twenty-four seats.[24] The Borneo states were promised special "safeguards" and "guarantees" which gave them a high degree of autonomy in certain areas, and a special status in the new Federation. Both states were given authority to exercise immigration and deportation control, even against Malaysian citizens from other states. A number of other "federal powers" in the Malayan constitution were not applied to Sarawak and North Borneo. Even though Malay was recognized as the "National Language", English was continued as the primary medium of instruction in Borneo schools and English was retained as the official language for state government until the State Legislature decided otherwise. While it was agreed that Islam was to be the official religion for the entire Federation, the Malayan constitutional provisions restricting the propagation of non-Muslim religions among Muslims were not to apply to these two states, and whenever the Federal Government gave financial aid to Muslim religious or educational institutions, a proportionate sum of tax money would be returned to the North Borneo and Sarawak Governments. The indigenous peoples of Sarawak and North Borneo were promised special privileges similar to those guaranteed to the Malays in the Federation of Malaya, *i.e.* special quotas for admission to the public service, for scholarships and for certain licenses, and privileged rights of ownership and use of land in large areas reserved for "natives". The two states were guaranteed federal revenues through a complicated system of earmarked taxes and guaranteed sums for economic development. Federal taxes and duties were to be applied gradually over a number of years. A separate Federal Public Service for North Borneo and Sarawak was promised so as to retain the services of expatriate officers for a number of years and permit the absorption of existing departments into the Federal Public Service. Certain parts of the Malaysia constitution would require state consent to be amended and a limited system of judicial review on constitutional interpretation was made the responsibility of a newly constituted Supreme Court of Malaysia.[25]

Politics and Elections in North Borneo and Sarawak

Although there was much uncertainty over Malaysia in North Borneo and Sarawak toward the end of 1962, the Brunei revolt and threats of intervention by Indonesia and the Philippines helped to crystalize Borneo opinion in favor of the new Federation.[26] The pro-Malaysia elements began to coalesce and various political alliances were created with the help and encouragement of Malayan political leaders who spent much time explaining how Malaya's ruling Alliance Party was the creature of a political union between three communal parties.

In North Borneo all political parties joined to form the pro-Malaysia Sabah Alliance. Unlike the Malayan Alliance, however, the parties in the Sabah Alliance contested against each other in local elections when they could not agree on candidates. Thus the Sabah Alliance began primarily as a union of political parties for negotiating favorable terms for North Borneo's admission into Malaysia, and later became a vehicle for resolving internal political issues.

The first elections in North Borneo were held in the early part of 1963, beginning at the local level. Popular franchise was employed to elect local councils, but election to the Legislative Council was by means of electoral colleges chosen by local councils.[27] Following the local elections the Sabah Alliance met to decide on distribution of seats among member parties for the State Legislature and for Parliament according to a rough ratio of seats won by each party in the local elections [28] The selection of candidates was left up to each constituent party according to the agreed allocation of seats. Complete Alliance domination of the political process meant that the electoral colleges and the Legislative Council merely ratified the distribution of elected seats as worked out within the Alliance. Table 13, below gives the seats won by each party in local elections as of July 1963, and the distribution of seats by the Sabah Alliance for the Legislative Council and for the Malaysian Parliament.

The lack of opposition to the Sabah Alliance was brought about by the desire of all parties to unite in favor of Malaysia and avoid any political controversies that might give Indonesia or the Philippines a chance to capitalize on political division within the country. There was some indication that without foreign threats, some elements in the Sabah Alliance would probably have broken away to form an opposition party.[29] As it developed, political opposition was expressed within the Sabah Alliance, thus avoiding excessive public involvement in the debate.

TABLE 13
Political party representation in North Borneo 1963

	USNO	UNKO	BUNAP	PM	Independent
Elected Local Councils	53	39	27	12	6
North Borneo Legislative Assembly	8	5	4	1	—
Parliament, House of Representatives	6	5	4	1	—
Parliament, Senate	1	1	1	1	—

Notes: Local elections had been held in all but three of the most remote districts of North Borneo by July, 1963. These figures do not include the local councils elected after that date. The following abbreviations are used in the table: United Sabah National Organization (USNO), United National Kadazan Organization (UNKO), Borneo Utara National Party (BUNAP), and United National Pasok Momogun Organization (PM).

Source: North Borneo News and Sabah Times, May 18, 1963, p. 1; June 25, 1963, p. 1; July 13, 1963, p. 6; July 18, 1963, p. 1.

In Sarawak five parties united to form the pro-Malaysia Sarawak Alliance, leaving only the Sarawak United Peoples Party (SUPP) lined up against Malaysia.[30] Within a short while severe strains developed within the Sarawak Alliance because it attempted to field a single slate of candidates in the first elections in order to face the challenge posed by SUPP. Since no party had tested its national strength at the polls, distribution of seats on the Alliance ticket had to be based in large measure upon party membership. Extremely competitive membership campaigns and exaggerated membership lists complicated relations between the five Alliance parties. When the Sarawak Alliance first met to determine the division of seats on the Alliance ticket, the five parties claimed a total membership of about 300,000, a figure which approximated the total eligible electorate of the state. The obviously exaggerated claims led to prolonged and acrimonious arguments over nominations and ultimately led to the withdrawal of Party Negara Sarawak (PANAS) from the Alliance.[31]

The electoral system of Sarawak was similar to that of North Borneo, utilizing a "three-tiered" indirect election process. The electorate voted directly for district and municipal councils, which chose representatives for the Divisional Advisory Councils. Each Divisional Advisory Council selected a certain number of members to sit in Sarawak's Council Negri (Legislative Assembly), the number depending on the apportionment of seats in the Council for that district.[32] While this system speeded up the process of establishing elected councils at all levels of government, it also tended to exaggerate the representation of the dominant party at both divisional and state levels.

In the crucial local and municipal council elections in Sarawak of June 1963, the following number of seats were captured by each party: Alliance 138, SUPP 116, PANAS 59 and Independents 116. Because of the defection of PANAS from the Alliance on the issue of nominations to the Alliance ticket, and because of the large number of independents elected, it was not certain that the Alliance could gain control of the Council Negri. The political picture became even more confused when PANAS, which was Malay-oriented and pro-Malaysia, negotiated a coalition agreement with the Chinese-oriented, anti-Malaysia SUPP.[33] This SUPP-PANAS coalition was not based upon agreement on policy, but was an arrangement to assure that both parties would have adequate representation in the higher levels of government when the indirect elections to the District Advisory Councils and the Council Negri were held. By this maneuver the SUPP-PANAS coalition almost captured the Council Negri, but after some frantic behind-the-scenes maneuvering, the Alliance was able to win the support of enough independents to capture 19 out of the 36 elected seats on the Council Negri and form a coalition government with 7 independents.

TABLE 14
Elections to Council Negri Sarawak by divisions 1963

	Alliance	Independents	SUPP	PANAS
1st Division	—	2	5	3
2nd Division	6	—	—	—
3rd Division	11	—	—	—
4th Division	2	4*	—	—
5th Division	—	3*	—	—

* Indicates members supporting Alliance coalition

Source: Sarawak Tribune, July 16, 1963, pp. 1 and 3.

Some friction developed over the distribution of government posts among the Alliance leaders. Ultimately Stephen Kalong Ningkan, an Iban and leader of Sarawak National Party was selected to be the Chief Minister. The Chairman of the Sarawak Alliance and leader of Pesaka, Temenggong Jugah anak Barieng was prominently mentioned for the post of Governor of Sarawak. However, under the Malaysia Constitution the choice was to be made by the Paramount Ruler of Malaya and the Queen of England acting on the advice of their governments. The Malayan Government objected to an Iban Christian as Governor, particularly since the Chief Minister was also an Iban, so Temenggong Jugah was not made Sarawak's first Governor. Instead the position of Governor was filled by Dato Abang Haji Openg, who was president of the Sarawak Muslim Council (Majlis Islam Sarawak) and a traditional Malay leader who had served in the government under Rajah

Vyner Brooke.[34] As a consolation, Temenggong Jugah was given a newly created position on the Federal Cabinet of Malaysia, that of Minister for Sarawak Affairs.[35]

As a generalization, it can be said that the Sarawak Alliance Government was based on a multi-racial and multi-party coalition with its core strength being the two largest native-oriented parties, Party Pesaka Anak Sarawak (PAPAS) and the Sarawak National Party (SNAP). The new government did not represent a substantial break in policy from that of the colonial administration, which attempted to balance the competing claims of Sarawak's racial groups, but tended to assume that the government must give priority to the needs and interests of the native tribal peoples. The Sarawak Alliance Government, being dependent upon a core of native support, followed the same priorities with perhaps rather more zeal.

The opposition was badly divided. PANAS looked to Malaya for political support for its pro-Malay and pro-Muslim objectives and moves were made to ally it with the United Malays National Organization to strengthen its position in Sarawak. Despite its agreement with SUPP, PANAS favored Malaysia and strongly opposed the demands of the more militant Chinese chauvinists in SUPP. As the prospects for Malaysia became greater, the top leaders of SUPP appeared to be more resigned to the new federation. They avoided being placed in uncompromising opposition to the union, even though militant Chinese extremists within SUPP flirted with the Communist underground in an attempt to disrupt the formation of Malaysia and undermine the elected government of Sarawak.

The Brunei Revolt

Brunei is a unique, paradoxical, miniature state run by a benevolent, but autocratic Sultan, dedicated to public service who has, for good reasons, commanded the affection of the majority of his people. His rule has been aided by the large revenues which derive from the oil concessions which the Brunei Shell Petroleum Company secured over forty years ago. Although distrustful of democracy, the Sultan promulgated a new constitution in 1959, providing for elections by 1961 and the establishment of a legislature of sixteen elected and seventeen appointed members. While the promised elections did not materialize until 1962 and the Sultan still retained ultimate powers, it was generally accepted that Brunei would shortly make the transition to a democratic constitutional monarchy.

The ensuing political developments cannot be understood without reference to a young man with boundless political ambition, A. M. Azahari. Born on Labuan Island in about 1928 to a Malay mother and an Arab father who was a businessman, he came to Brunei at an early age. During the war he was sent by the Japanese on a scholarship to Indonesia where he studied veterinary science and later joined the Indonesian army to fight in the revolution against the Dutch. He returned to Brunei in about 1952 and began to organize a political party to follow the example of Indonesia. Charged with organizing an unlawful assembly, he was jailed for six months.[36] After a further period abroad, he returned to Brunei to operate a printing firm which he obtained through the assistance of the Sultan. On January 22, 1956, he founded Brunei Party Rakyat, which was duly registered as Brunei's first political party. A tireless political organizer and a spellbinding speaker, he developed a mass following over the next few years, relying upon the enthusiastic support of many Malay young people and union members.[37]

A. M. Azahari and his associates began laying plans for the restoration of the Brunei Sultanate over the neighboring territories of Sarawak and North Borneo — lands that were nominally under Brunei's authority a century ago. They also toyed with the idea of a *Melayu Raya* to include Indonesia and perhaps the Philippines. However, as a first step, their energies were directed to uniting the three Borneo states within the Brunei Sultanate. Brunei has a preponderant Malay majority with Brunei Malays and Indonesians dominating the political scene.[38] A reconstituted Brunei Sultanate would assure Malay political superiority, even though the Malays comprise only 5·5 per cent of the population of North Borneo and 17·3 per cent in Sarawak. Since the non-Malay indigenous peoples of Sarawak and North Borneo remembered the history of the previous Brunei Sultanate as a period of Malay domination and political oppression, they were very suspicious of anything which might bring Malay domination once again, whether from the Malays in Brunei or those in Malaya.

Azahari's plans never received the Sultan's approval, probably because the Sultan could see the difficulties in extending a claim over territories where the British were still in control, and where violent resistance to such a move would be likely to develop from a great majority of the local people. However, Azahari did not let the Sultan's cautious approach stand in his way. He hoped the Sultan would support him after his party gained power, either through elections or by revolution.

The slow constitutional developments in Brunei and the resistance of entrenched conservative elements around the Sultan prompted Azahari and his compatriots to prepare for revolution.[39] He also attempted to expand his political organization to Sarawak and North Borneo by making political alliances and by courting or founding a few radical-nationalist Malay political organizations. Thus, in Sarawak he had close liaison with the remnants of *Gerakan Pemuda Melayu* and *Persatuan Pemuda Melayu*—two small fanatical nationalist organisations which in 1949 engineered the murder of Sir Duncan Stewart, the second colonial governor of Sarawak, and which, at the time, had also tried to persuade the Sultan of Brunei to reclaim Sarawak,[40] ceded a century earlier to the "White Rajah" James Brooke. In 1962, the small "non-political" society, *Barisan Pemuda*, provided a focus for these Malay nationalist elements in Sarawak who were both pro-Indonesian and who were attracted by Azahari's promises of Malay domination of the area. Undoubtedly, Azahari counted upon the material and physical support of these Malays for a revolutionary force in Sarawak.

He also made contact with the left-wing, Chinese-dominated Sarawak

United People's Party. The extreme anti-Chinese statements he made in Brunei to the Malay crowds were discounted with explanations that he was really anti-capitalist, and that the Chinese in Brunei were all "capitalist businessmen". It was on this basis that an anti-Malaysia united front was created with SUPP, even though it was apparent to both parties that their opposition to Malaysia was for contradictory objectives.

In North Borneo, Azahari encouraged his followers among the Malays to found two organizations modeled on Party Rakyat, *Angkatan Ra'ayat Anak Sabah* (ARAS) and *Angkatan Desa Bersatu*. Registration of these organizations was pending when the revolution started, at which time they were promptly made illegal.[41]

In Singapore and Malaya Azahari also made extensive political contacts in the hope of obtaining substantial support. If the Malayan and Singapore Governments' evidence is correct, some Barisan Sosialis leaders had prior knowledge of the Brunei revolution and promised their support. Similarly, Ahmad Boestamam of Party Ra'ayat Malaya had foreknowledge of the affair and proceeded to organize an underground organization having ties with the Indonesian Communist Party, presumably to give material aid to the rebellion[42]

Of most value to Azahari was the support he was able to secure in foreign states where the Malaysian Federation was viewed with some hostility. On one of his numerous trips to Indonesia, he was given secret promises of financial and material assistance from some Indonesian political leaders. Among other things, a base was set up in Malinau, in Indonesian Borneo, to train and arm the nucleus of a secret guerrilla army called *Tentera Nasional Kalimantan Utara* (Northern Borneo National Army).[43] A significant number of young militant Brunei Malays trekked through the jungles of Sarawak and North Borneo (the easiest route) to get arms and training at this base. Others were armed and trained in Brunei.

Because of Philippine opposition to Malaysia, Azahari led several Rakyat delegations to Manila. Apparently the Philippine Government refused to make any official commitments, but Azahari did receive a sympathetic hearing from high officials and obtained the cooperation of Nicasio Osmena (a moving force behind the Philippine claim to North Borneo) who later acted as his host, legal advisor and spokesman in the period following the outbreak of hostilities.[44] From the Philippines he obtained substantial sums of money for his cause.

The Party Rakyat revolution is said to have been planned to follow an anti-Malaysia resolution to be debated at the December meeting of the Brunei Legislative Council. The Sultan was to be captured and persuaded (or forced) to proclaim the independence of the three Borneo states and the formation of the new "Unitary State of Kalimantan Utara" (Northern Borneo). At the last minute, the meeting of the legislature was postponed, but the plan for revolt continued anyway. Azahari had already left Brunei for Manila where he joined Zaini. The revolt began during the night of December 7, but Sultan Saifuddin was not captured.[45] In a radio broadcast the next day, the Sultan declared a state of emergency, banned Party Ra'ayat and denounced the rebels as traitors. Earlier he had made a request to the British Commissioner-General in Southeast Asia, Lord Selkirk, for military assistance against the rebels under the terms of the treaty providing for the British protectorate over Brunei.

Safe in Manila, Azahari proclaimed himself "Prime Minister of Kalimantan Utara".[46] He announced to the press, "The Sultan is in our hands and supports the revolution. We have half a battalion protecting him. If we have to retreat we have arranged a hideout for him." To achieve the objective of restoring the Brunei Sultanate, the revolution had to be carried out in the Sultan's name.[47] Azahari promised a scorched-earth policy and destruction of the oil wells if the British forces intervened, but nonetheless appeared to be conciliatory, apparently hoping to negotiate terms with the British. The revolution was not so much anti-British, anti-Sultan, or anti-court clique; rather it was against anyone opposing Brunei's recovery of Sarawak and North Borneo. The rebels themselves, although zealous, were never very clear about their objectives.

Without communications with Brunei, Azahari made periodic announcements about developments according to his revolutionary timetable, revealing, in part, what he expected would happen. At one time, he announced that the capitals of Sarawak and North Borneo were being besieged. However, the revolution proclaimed in Sarawak and North Borneo never materialized except for small pockets of trouble-makers close to Brunei's borders, almost all of which were in the scattered villages around Brunei Bay, part of which forms the coastline of Sarawak and North Borneo. With few exceptions, the rebels were Brunei Malays and Kedayans, a small Muslim native group that had for years been treated as second-class citizens of Brunei.[48]

Within five days British troops flown in from Singapore had racaptured all the towns taken by the rebel forces, and in short order re-established the government's authority. Although the rebels fled to thick jungle along the coast, the military quickly depleted the guerrilla ranks, until by April only a few score remained.

Malaysian Politics and the Brunei Revolt

The opponents of Malaysia in Malaya, Singapore and Sarawak tried to exploit the rebellion for their own objectives (which in nearly every case were quite different from those of Party Rakyat). The Sarawak United People's Party meekly denounced the revolt, but proceeded with arrangements to present to the United Nations an anti-Malaysia memorandum that had been drafted jointly by SUPP and Party Rakyat (Brunei). The very similar Barisan Sosialis Party of Singapore expressed full support for the revolt against "neo-colonialism". In Malaya, the Socialist Front professed a qualified encouragement for the revolt, because one party in that "front", Party Ra'ayat Malaya, had very close ties with the Brunei Party Rakyat. Having strong Indonesian sympathies, the Pan-Malayan Islamic Party, caught in a dilemma, first stated its support for the revolt, but later claimed to be neutral in regard to the revolution and the ensuing controversy between Malaya and Indonesia.

The two governments of Malaya and Singapore feared that some opposition parties and anti-Malaysian elements might seize the opportunity to create a crisis situation. In February, the Internal Security Council approved the emergency detention of 113 persons in Singapore who were believed to be working with the Communist Party or Brunei Party Rakyat to obstruct Malaysia. In Malaya, the leader of Party Ra'ayat Malaya, Ahmad Boestamam, was also put under detention for similar reasons. Rather surprisingly, there was very little public outcry aginst these detentions. While this may be attributed to the fear of additional emergency measures, it was also apparent that support for Malaysia was growing and that many who were still opposed were becoming resigned to the assumption that Malaysia would become a reality. Far from being able to exploit the Brunei revolt, it appeared that the anti-Malaysia parties suffered greatly from their apparent complicity with the revolt. Consequently, the Malayan and Singapore Governments seemed to be more firmly in charge of the situation in mid-1963 than they were in the last months of 1962.

1 This chapter is a revised and expanded version of an article by the author entitled "Malaysia—A New Federation in Southeast Asia" appearing in *Pacific Affairs*, Vol. XXXVI, no. 2, (Summer, 1963), pp. 138–159.

2 Department of Information, Federation of Malaya, *Malaysia*, No. 2 (April, 1962), p. 6.

3 Singapore's first Chief Minister, David Marshall, made the first moves to negotiate a merger agreement in 1955 before Malayan independence. Similar feelers by Singapore's next Chief Minister, Lim Yew-hock, were also politely rejected after Malayan independence.

4 The complete text of this speech is reproduced in *Malayan Times*, September 25, 1962, pp. 6–7.

5 During the Japanese occupation the Colonial Office examined the possibility of union between Malaya and the Borneo states, but such a union was rejected as impractical after the war. The leaders of the Alliance Party, now ruling Malaya, considered the idea of eventual union with the Borneo states even before Malaya became independent in 1957, but all such discussions were secret. The first serious discussions of the Malaysia proposals were reported to have taken place in July, 1960, followed by another meeting between Duncan Sandys (Minister of State for Commonwealth Relations), Lee Kuan-yew and Tunku Abdul Rahman in December, 1960. See *Malayan Times*, June, 21, 1962, p. 5.

6 It was difficult in practice to distinguish between Chinese communalists and the Communists because of the Malayan Communist Party decision some years earlier to use Chinese communal nationalism to rebuild its political following.

7 *Straits Budget*, June 29, 1960, p. 9.

8 *Straits Times*, July 15, 1961, pp. 1 and 20. For a more complete account of Singapore politics during this period see Milton E. Osborne, *Singapore and Malaysia*, (Cornell University, Ithaca, N.Y.: Southeast Asia Program, Data Paper No. 53, 1964); C. Paul Bradley, "Leftist Fissures in Singapore Politics", *Western Political Quarterly*, Vol. 18, no. 2, Part 1 (June, 1965), pp. 292–308; Michael Leifer, "Politics in Singapore", *Journal of Commonwealth Political Studies*, Vol. 2, no. 2, (May, 1964), pp. 102–119.

9 *Straits Times*, July 21, 1961, p. 1.

10 Lee Kuan-yew, *The Battle for Merger* (Singapore: Government Printing Office, n.d.), pp. 37, 43 and 45.

11 *Memorandum Setting Out Heads of Agreement For a Merger Between the Federation of Malaya and Singapore*, Cmd. 33 of 1961, Singapore Legislative Assembly. More detailed merger terms were revealed to the Singapore Legislative Assembly by Lee Kuan-yew on April 5, 1963. At that time the only significant matter that remained to be worked out was the respective financial responsibilities of the Singapore and Federal Governments. See *Straits Times*, April 6, 1963, pp. 8–9.

12 Shortly after the agreement with Singapore had been negotiated, Tunku Abdul Rahman and Prime Minister Harold Macmillan, meeting in London, agreed to extend the 1957 Anglo-Malayan Defense and Mutual Assistance Treaty to include the Singapore bases. The British forces were to remain there, but, according to the Tunku, Malayan approval would be required if the bases were to be used for SEATO operations, since Malaya was not a member of SEATO.

13 *Report of the Select Committee on the Singapore National Referendum Bill*, No. 7 of 1962, Singapore Legislative Assembly.

14 The following choices appeared on the ballot:
Alternative A (symbol—Singapore flag): Merger with reserve powers, notable autonomy over labour and education; automatic conversion of Singapore citizenship to Malaysian citizenship; 15 seats in central parliament; retention of multilingualism.
Alternative B (symbol—Penang flag): Merger as a state within the Federation; application of present Federation labour and education policies; only persons born in Singapore and some citizens by descent will automatically become Federation of Malaysia citizens; parliamentary representation in proportion to number of citizens eligible under stricter Federation citizenship laws; only English and Malay to be used in state legislature
Alternative C (symbol—flag with shields of Sarawak and North Borneo): Merger on terms no less favourable than the Borneo territories

15 *Malayan Times*, August 20, 1962.

16 This threat was repeated on a number of occasions in March and April. See for example, *Straits Times*, April 16, 1962, p. 1.

17 The government referred to the Communist Party as the Clandestine Communist Organization (CCO) partly because of the confusing variety of organizations which the Communists formed to cloak their activities. See *The Danger Within* (Kuching: Government Printing Office, 1963).

18 With good reason, it is commonly supposed that the Sarawak Government, acting through the Colonial Office, played a significant role in initiating the preliminary secret discussions about Malaysia prior to the Tunku's first public pronouncement in May, 1961. The previous proposal of the Governors of Sarawak and North Borneo, made in 1957, for a "Borneo Federation" was quietly dropped in favor of the larger union with Malaya.

19 The Anti-Malaysia United Front was formed by Ong Kee-hui of SUPP, A. M. Azahari of Brunei Party Rakyat, and Donald Stevens, who later formed the United National Kadazan Organization of North Borneo. See *Straits Times*, July 10, 1961, p. 1.

20 Department of Information, Federation of Malaya, *Malaysia*, no. 2 (April, 1962), pp. 7–16.

21 *Straits Times*, November 27, 1961, pp. 1 and 20. The Commissions terms of reference did not include Brunei, because it was not a colony and preferred to negotiate directly with the United Kingdom and Malaya.

22 *Report of the Commission of Enquiry, North Borneo and Sarawak* (Federation of Malaya: Government Printer, 1962).

23 *Malaysia Report of the Inter-governmental Committee, 1962* (Federation of Malaya: Government Printer, 1963).

24 The average population per parliamentary constituency was as follows: Malaya, 60,372; Singapore, 96,394; North Borneo, 28,401 and Sarawak, 31,022.

25 *Malaysia Report of the Inter-governmental Committee, op. cit.*, pp. 5–45.

26 There is no evidence of popular support for the union of North Borneo with the Philippines as was being demanded by Manila. Indeed, the continued high incidence of attacks and plundering by Filipino pirates left a residue of fear and hate in North Borneo that could not be easily erased.

27 Colony of North Borneo, *The Local Elections Ordinance, 1962* (no. 2 of 1962); "Indirect Elections to Legislative Council," *Colony of North Borneo Government Gazette Extraordinary*, Vol. XVIII, no. 31. Also see below pp. 373–381.

28 *North Borneo News and Sabah Times*, May 18 1963, p. 1. At the same time the Sabah Alliance agreed that the Head of State for North Borneo was to be Dato Mustapha bin Dato Harun, the leader of USNO, while Donald Stephens, the leader of UNKO was selected as Chief Minister designate. After incorporation into Malaysia, North Borneo officially changed its name to Sabah.

29 An abortive attempt was made to form an opposition Socialist Party by one wing of the Borneo Utara National Party, but party discipline was sufficient to prevent any opposition party from gaining a foothold in North Borneo. See *Sabah Times*, October 17, 1963, pp. 1 and 8; October 21, 1963, pp. 1 and 7.

30 The following parties joined the Alliance: Party Pesaka Anak Sarawak (PAPAS), Sarawak National Party (SNAP), Sarawak Chinese Association (SCA), Barisan Ra'ayat Jati Sarawak (BARJASA), Party Negara Sarawak (PANAS). *Sarawak Tribune*, October 23, 1962, p. 1. Also see below pp. 381–387.

31 *Sarawak Tribune*, April 17, 1963, p. 1.

32 Divisional apportionment of seats in the Council Negri was as follows: First Division, 10 members; Second Division, 6 members; Third Division, 11 members; Fourth Division, 6 members; Fifth Division, 3 members.

33 *Sarawak Tribune*, July 2, 1963, p. 1.

34 *Sarawak Tribune*, September 14, 1963, pp. 1 and 3.

35 In the elections for Sarawak's representation to the Malaysian Parliament, the Council Negri agreed to divide the 24 seats among the parties as follows: Alliance 17, SUPP 3, PANAS 3, and Independents 1. The choice of individuals was left to each party except that the Council Negri voted for the Independent to be represented in the Malaysian Parliament. *Sarawak Tribune*, October 23, 1963, pp. 1 and 12.

36 The year was probably 1953, but there is some discrepancy in the reports of his personal acquaintants. The documentary evidence is not at present available to the author. For a fairly good, but not completely accurate, profile of Azahari, see *Borneo Bulletin*, December 29, 1962, p. 14.

37 The Borneo United Labour Front, a labor union led by H. Laksamana, became an important source of political power for Party Rakyat.

38 Chinese, Indians and some of the non-Malay indigenous peoples of Borneo were denied the right to acquire citizenship or voting privileges in Brunei.

39 Azahari's lieutenant, Zaini Haji Ahmad, went to the London School of Economics on a scholarship given by the Sultan. In London he spent his time making a blueprint for revolution by a "careful analysis" of successful and unsuccessful revolutions. These preparations, including the training of guerrillas in Brunei, were known to many people for months before the revolution, and an item about these preparations even appeared in a local paper nearly a year before. Few people, including government officials, took these developments seriously. Rather, people joked about "grown men playing soldiers" when men were seen parading in public places with wooden guns.

40 The Party Rakyat version of this event was broadcast in English on April 5, 1963, over "Voice of Freedom Fighters Kalimantan Utara", from a station probably located near Djakarta.

41 *Colony of North Borneo Government Gazette Extraordinary*, Vol. XVIII, no. 10, (February 27, 1963), pp. 94–98.

42 See *Malayan Times*, February 3, 1963, p. 1; February 4, 1963, p. 6; February 14, 1963, p. 1; and *Straits Times*, March 13, 1963, p. 1.

43 From a statement made by the Prime Minister, Tunku Abdul Rahman, to Parliament on December 11, 1962. Department of Information, PEN. 12/62/119 (in English), pp. 2–3.

44 Just before the revolution, Zaini, Azhari's right-hand man, announced that the Philippines had agreed to drop their claim to North Borneo if a Borneo Federation were formed. Whether this promise was a fabrication cannot be determined, but at least it was not denied. See *Borneo Bulletin*, December 8, 1962, p. 1.

45 The Sultan succeeded in fleeing to the police station in Brunei Town where he was protected by loyal police. Azahari misled his followers into believing that the Sultan really supported the revolution and that Indonesian aid would be on the way in a matter of hours. His deceptions and the people's veneration of the Sultan saved the Sultan's life, as it also made it easier for the British planes carrying troops to land in Brunei, since the rebel troops were convinced they were Indonesian.

46 Captured Ra'ayat rebels subsequently reported that secretly Ahmad Boestamam was appointed "Prime Minister of Malaya and Singapore" and Stephen Yong of SUPP was appointed "Chief Minister of Sarawak".

47 The Rakyat version of the revolution, broadcast on April 10, 1963, from its station in Indonesia, still maintained that, "At 8.00 a.m. of the same day, His Highness the Sultan came down from his palace and read the Proclamation of Independence of the Unitary State of Kalimantan Utara in front of hundreds of thousands of people." The author found no witness to this event in Brunei Town which has a population of 9,057 with about 15,000 more living in the environs.

48 Tom Harrisson, Curator of the Sarawak Museum, wrote for the British forces in Brunei a small handbook in which he explains some of the anthropological and social reasons for the Kedayans' support for the revolution. See Tom Harrisson, *Background to a Revolt*, (Brunei: Light Press, 1963). For a more complete account of the Brunei revolt see Arnold C. Brackman, *Southeast Asia's Second Front* (New York: Frederick A. Praeger, 1966), pp. 133–156.

17 Malaysia under attack

The prospect of a Federation of Malaysia had obvious international implications, which did not go unnoticed in the capitals of the major powers and in neighboring states. The Soviet Union and Communist China were both fearful that Malaysia would inhibit the growth of Communist movements in Southeast Asia. Both powers saw the Malayan Government as being anti-Communist in the extreme and, therefore, according to Communist logic, the Malayan Government was a "lackey of imperialism and twentieth century neo-colonialism". The Communist-organized World Federation of Democratic Youth, meeting in Warsaw in August 1962, passed a resolution on Malaysia which reads in part as follows·

> Faced with the ever-growing strength of the anti-colonialist movement the British imperialists are making use of native hands, particularly of those governing circles of the Federation of Malaya, which always were loyal servants of the British imperialists. . . .
>
> In reality they are trying to reach still further with their hands soaked in the blood of the massacred people of the Federation of Malaya to these other territories.[1]

It was apparent from the broadcasts beamed by Moscow and Peking to Southeast Asia that both powers hoped to simulate Indonesian hostility to Malaya and to the formation of the Malaysian Federation.[2] Although the objectives of Indonesian policy remained obscure, Malayan officials knew that Indonesian leaders did not like Malaysia. At the official level, Indonesia did not express its objections before the Brunei revolt. Sukarno's statement that Indonesia did not have any more territorial claims after the settlement of the West Irian dispute was received in Malaya with both relief and skepticism.[3]

Indonesia's Anti-Malaysia Policy

Despite Indonesia's public posture of official non-involvement, developments in Indonesia during 1962 were increasingly disturbing to Malayan leaders. The Indonesian Communist Party (PKI), which supported Sukarno's government and had been admitted into its inner circles, was, of course, espousing the Communist line with regard to Malaysia. A PKI resolution of December 1961 denounced the Federation of Malaysia as "a form of neo-colonialism" designed "to suppress the democratic and patriotic movement of the peoples in these five countries. . . ."[4] Then followed a PKI propaganda campaign of increasing intensity calling for government policy that would bring the defeat of the proposed union.

After the Brunei revolt, Indonesia became more openly committed to a policy of opposition to Malaysia. The week following the revolution both Sukarno and the Indonesian Parliament came out officially in support of the Brunei rebels.[5] From Manila, Azahari boasted that 100,000 Indonesian volunteers were ready to fight for the revolution, a threat which was repeated time and again by high officials in Djakarta. After Azahari's presence in Manila became an embarrassment to the Philippine Government, he moved to Indonesia[6] where he set up a skeleton government-in-exile, which operated a radio station that nightly broadcast violent propaganda and threats against Malaya and Britain.[7]

In January, 1963, Indonesian Prime Minister Subandrio announced that Indonesia was pursuing a policy of "confrontation" against Malaya. What was meant was unclear at the time, but as it developed in the early stages it involved a break in diplomatic relations, threatening talk about massive intervention in Borneo by "volunteers", attacks on Malayan fishing boats in international waters to capture the vessels and to murder, intimidate or kidnap the fishermen, and complicated diplomatic maneuvers designed to isolate Malaya in international affairs.

One of the first diplomatic struggles over Malaysia took place at the Afro-Asian Solidarity Conference held in Tanganyika in February, 1963. Because of the way the conference was organized the pro-Communist elements dominated the proceedings. The joint Malayan-Singapore delegation was never seated by the conference, nor given a chance to be heard on Malaysia or on any other issue. On the other hand, two delegates representing Azahari's shadow government of "Kalimantan Utara" were seated.[9] Two anti-Malaysia resolutions were passed without debate, providing grist for Communist Chinese and Indonesian propaganda machines.[10]

The Philippine Involvement

The prospect of a Malaysian Federation also engendered opposition from the Philippines. Although Malaya and the Philippines had been on friendly terms and, together with Thailand, had formed the Association of Southeast Asia (ASA), tension suddenly mounted in June, 1962, when the Philippine Government claimed sovereignty over North Borneo.

The forerunners of the British North Borneo Company obtained title to North Borneo in 1877 from the Sultan of Brunei in return for an annual cash payment. However, because the land was also claimed by the Sultan of Sulu, the Company negotiated a second treaty with the Sultan of Salu to "reinsure" its title to North Borneo. The Philippine claim was based upon the Arabic wording of the latter deed issued in 1878. The Philippines argued that North Borneo was not ceded, but was a leasehold from the Sulu Sultanate, which subsequently became absorbed into the Philippines.[11] The last Sultan of Sulu died in 1936, but his heirs formed the Kiram Corporation to press for a cash settlement from the British Government which assumed direct authority over North Borneo in 1946, thus terminating the administration of the British North Borneo Company. Under the guidance of Nicasio Osmena, son of former President Sergio Osmena, the Kiram Corporation was reported to have sold stock to officials in the Philippine Government as part of a campaign to persuade the Philippines to collect through diplomatic channels what was originally a private claim. This claim was later transferred to the Philippine Government in order to strengthen its hand in negotiations with Britain, Malaya or Malaysia.[12]

Although officially the Philippine Government claimed sovereignty to North Borneo, it seems improbable that it really expected to annex that state. Rather, the claim appeared to be an attempt to extract a maximum financial settlement and perhaps some economic concessions in North Borneo for Philippine businessmen who held stock in the Kiram Corporation.[13] Both the British and the Malayan Government refused to give any recognition to this claim, which they maintained had no legal basis. Furthermore, these claims met with the universal condemnation of all political leaders in North Borneo, and there was no evidence of any significant sentiment in North Borneo favoring the union of that state with the Philippines.

The Manila Conference

Indonesian and Philippine objections to Malaysia led to a complicated series of diplomatic maneuvers prior to Malaysia's inauguation, which was initially set for August 31, 1963. The Philippines was trying to extract from Malaya or Britain a favorable settlement to its claim to North Borneo. Indonesia's demands were much less precise, but Indonesia based much of its early criticism of Malaysia on the charge that the people of the Borneo states were not given an opportunity in a plebiscite to vote on the Malaysia proposals.

Prospects for peaceful settlement of the points at issue seemed brighter after Tunku Abdul Rahman flew to Tokyo to confer with President Sukarno. Following their talks,t he two leaders issued a statement reaffirming their faith in the 1959 "Treaty of Friendship" between Malaya and Indonesia, and promised to settle their differences "as envisaged in the Treaty of Friendship". They also agreed to a meeting of ministers of Indonesia, the Philippines and Malaya "which they hoped would lead to a meeting of Heads of Governments. . . ."[14]

After a preliminary foreign ministers' conference, the Heads of Government met at the Manila Conference for a full week from July 30 to August 5, 1963. Despite severe differences, President Sukarno, President Macapagal and Tunku Abdul Rahman finally agreed to the following conditions for a settlement of the Malaysia dispute:

Indonesia and the Philippines stated that they would welcome the formation of Malaysia provided the support of the people of the Borneo territories is ascertained by an independent and impartial authority, the Secretary-General of the United Nations or his representative.[15]

Malaya agreed to ask the Secretary General or his representative to head an international commission to ascertain whether the elections which had recently been held in Sarawak and North Borneo accurately indicated the wishes of the majority of the populations of those territories to enter the Federation of Malaysia. All three governments were to be permitted to send observers to witness the work of the United Nations commission. In its undertakings, the UN team was asked to determine whether in the elections, Malaysia was the main issue, whether the elections were free and properly conducted, and whether they were affected by the inability of qualified voters to cast ballots because of imprisonment for political activity or absence from the territory.[16] Because of the time it would take to complete this task, it was understood that the formation of Malaysia would be postponed until after the UN Secretary General could complete his report, and would only then take place if the findings showed that Malaysia had the support of the Borneo peoples.[17]

The Philippines made it clear that its position on the inclusion of North Borneo in the Federation of Malaysia is subject to the final outcome of the Philippine claim to North Borneo.[18]

. . . the three Heads of Government decided to request the British Government to agree to seek a just and expeditious solution to the dispute between the British Government and the Philippine Government concerning Sabah (North Borneo) . . .[19]

[It was] further agreed that foreign bases—temporary in nature—should not be allowed to be used directly or indirectly to subvert the national independence of any of the three countries. In accordance with the principle enunciated in the Bandung Declaration, the three countries will abstain from the use of arrangements of collective defence to serve the particular interests of any of the big powers.[20]

The three leaders also approved a proposal to establish a "Confederation of nations of Malay origin" comprised of the three states and to be called Maphilindo. Jointly they pledged cooperation through Maphilindo "to maintain fraternal relations" and to "combine their efforts in the common struggle against colonialism and imperialism in all their forms and manifestations and for the eradication of the vestiges thereof in the region . . . and in the world. . . ."[21]

The Manila Agreements caused some dismay in Malaya and Singapore, particularly among the Chinese who saw Maphilindo as an attempt to forge a political union of "Malay stock" peoples to ensure their political supremacy over the non-Malay communities in Southeast Asia. British officials were apprehensive about the implications of the agreement of foreign bases, and the apparent admission that the elections in Sarawak and North Borneo may not have been representative of popular opinion. Sukarno returned to Indonesia claiming a diplomatic victory. He appeared confident that the United Nations investigating team would find fault with the Borneo elections, and that British and American military forces would shortly be subjected to intense pressure from Maphilindo to abandon their bases in Singapore, Malaya, the Borneo states and the Philippines. Some of Indonesia's political jargon had been incorporated into the agreements, and he had secured approval for the first step toward hisl ong-held dream of *Indonesia Raya*.[22] Therefore, the Manila Conference was seen by Djakarta as a very successful maneuver to block the formation of Malaysia and as an important stepping stone to the establishment of Indonesian military and political supremacy in Southeast Asia.[23]

No sooner had the Manila Agreements been signed than there were rumblings of trouble ahead. Prime Minister Lee Kuan-yew of Singapore asserted that Singapore was not bound by the terms of the Manila Conference, and that Singapore would insist upon independence on August 31 under the terms of the London Agreement regardless of the delay or fate of Malaysia.[24] All the while, Indonesia gave no evidence that its "confrontation" policy had been abandoned or relaxed as a result of the Manila Conference. Instead, Indonesian guerrilla attacks were intensified in Sarawak and North Borneo in a move clearly designed to impress the UN fact-finding team with the extent of opposition to Malaysia. When the nine-member neutral nation UN commission was being formed under U Thant's direction, Indonesia demanded the right to transport thirty observers in Indonesian aircraft into Sarawak and North Borneo. The British authorities refused to permit more than four observers and four clerical assistants from each of the three countries to accompany the United Nations fact-finding team. Thereupon, Indonesia boycotted the proceedings of the commission, claiming a violation of the Manila Agreements, and setting the stage for Indonesian rejection of U Thant's report if he found that the people of North Borneo and Sarawak did, in fact, support Malaysia.

The United Nations Mission to Sabah and Sarawak conducted its survey from August 16 to September 5. U Thant's report, based on the findings of that mission, was released on September 14. After examining all the charges levelled against the elections in Sabah and Sarawak, the UN Secretary-General in his report concluded, ". . . there is no doubt about the wishes of a sizeable majority of the peoples of these territories to join in the Federation of Malaysia".[25]

Even before the report was made public, both Indonesia and the Philippines began discrediting the survey, apparently in anticipation of its findings, and charged that the agreements reached at Tokyo and Manila had been broken by Malaya. Their main criticizm was directed against the preparations for Malaysia which continued while the survey was being conducted. The Malayan Government's proclamation of August 29 announcing "that

Malaysia shall come into existance on September 16",[26] was the subject of their strongest protests. U Thant, in his report, rebuked Malaya for this announcement because it led to "confusion, and even resentment" among the other parties to the Manila Agreements.

Two days after the Secretary-General made public his findings, Malaysia was officially inaugurated.[27] Indonesia and the Philippines refusing to recognize the new federation, immediately broke off diplomatic relations with Malaya, and the Malaysia dispute entered a more dangerous phase.

Indonesia's "Crush Malaysia" Campaign

Indonesian troops under the guise of "volunteers" had been making periodic attacks along the borders of Sarawak and Sabah as early as April, 1963. These attacks became much more severe and frequent after Malaysia came into being. In time, the operations were expanded to Malaya and Singapore, where Indonesian-armed saboteurs landed to engage in numerous acts of terrorism mostly by indiscriminate bombings of public places. In Indonesia, the government-sponsored political movement known as Front Nasional arranged mass rallies and demonstrations to stir up public sentiment and secure the enlistment of volunteers in support of Sukarno's new "crush Malaysia" campaign. Some anti-Malaysia rallies triggered mob attacks, led by the Communist agitators, against Malaysian and British properties. One such attack culminated in the complete destruction of the British Embassy in Djakarta.

In time, the violent tactics of Indonesia became somewhat of an embarrassment to the Philippines which disavowed the use of force as a method of solving its differences with Malaysia. In an attempt to consolidate their opposition to Malaysia, President Sukarno flew to Manila to meet with President Macapagal. After five days of negotiations, the two leaders agreed to reassert their support for Maphilindo on the understanding that Malaysia would be welcomed as a partner "after freeing itself of British domination".[28] Indonesia agreed not to ask the Philippines to join its "confrontation" against Malaysia and promised not to bring in any "third party" into its confrontation campaign. Indonesia also expressed official support for the Philippine claim to Sabah, thus, by implication, renouncing its earlier support for the claims to Sabah being advanced by A. M. Azahari's exile "Government of Kalimantan Utara".

The Philippine Government was evidently fearful that Indonesia might start major hostilities and, in so doing, become overly committed to military and diplomatic assistance from Communist China. Philippine membership in SEATO and its defense pacts with the United States made it rather difficult for that country to join Indonesia in attacking similar defence arrangements between Malaysia and Great Britain. Because of these fundamental differences, Indonesia's concession to the Philippines on the claim to Sabah provided the key to their limited agreement jointly resisting Malaysia.

Robert Kennedy's Peace Mission

As Indonesian attacks on Malaysia came closer to open warfare, a number of states in alarm sought to initiate attempts at mediation in the dispute.[29] The most publicized peace effort was that made on behalf of the United States by Robert Kennedy who flew to Tokyo in mid-January to meet President Sukarno. The *New York Times* reported that Mr. Kennedy warned Sukarno that American aid to Indonesia would be discontinued if guerrilla operations continued. On the other hand, support for the Maphilindo confederation was promised if Indonesia would seek a peaceful settlement of the Malaysia dispute through a new tripartite conference.[30] Sukarno agreed that the conflict should be solved by direct consultations, but no understanding was reached on possible terms of settlement.[31]

Travelling on to Kuala Lumpur, Mr. Kennedy encouraged Malaysia to attend the proposed new peace talks.[32] Tunku Abdul Rahman agreed to a new series of three-power conferences on the condition that Malaysia received assurance that her integrity and sovereignty would be respected. The Tunku made it clear that cessation of military hostilities on the part of Indonesia was an essential precondition to peace negotiations with Indonesia Finally, under prodding from Robert Kennedy, President Sukarno agreed to a cease fire between Indonesian forces and Malaysia.[33]

The Bangkok Conference

As preparations were being made for a preliminary foreign ministers conference, a new dispute arose over the "cease fire". Indonesia had ordered guerrillas operating in Malaysia to "hold their positions and keep their guns in their hands", while it also insisted that the "cease-fire" orders did not apply to the "Kalimantan Utara" guerrillas since they were "not under Indonesia's command". Meanwhile, Malaysian authorities were broadcasting appeals to the guerrillas to withdraw to Indonesia or turn over their arms.[34]

The cease-fire terms became the primary issue when the ministers of the three countries finally met in Bangkok.[35] Although outwardly amicable, the talks were largely deadlocked because of Indonesia's insistence that the cease-fire was dependent upon settlement of political questions first.[36] Nonetheless, the three parties reaffirmed adherence to the Manila Agreements. In the discussions each state claimed it had adhered to those agreements and charged that it had become the victim of violations. The final communique announced that an interim cease-fire would be observed, and that U Thant was being asked to appoint Thailand as a neutral party to supervise the cease-fire.[37] However, since the conditions for the cease-fire were not agreed upon, and Indonesia refused to withdraw her armed forces from Malaysian territory, Malaysia attached a reservation to the final communiqué stating that the presence of Indonesian forces in Malaysia would "provoke incidents" and make the cease-fire ineffective.[38] Shortly afterwards, the Malaysian Government ordered its armed forces to disarm Indonesian terrorists in Malaysia and "send them back across the border".

While the Bangkok ministerial talks were under way, Tunku Abdul Rahman and President Macapagal met in Cambodia to discuss the Philippine claim to Sabah.[39] It was apparent that Malaysia was willing to make significant concessions in return for Philippine support against Indonesia's "crush Malaysia" campaign. Although the talks were cordial, and the two states appeared to be near agreement on the resumption of diplomatic relations, the continued Malaysian-Indonesian dispute over cease-fire terms prompted Manila to postpone any further moves toward rapprochement until Malaysia and Indonesia were closer to settling their differences. Apparently, President Macapagal did not want to buy a compromise settlement of the Sabah claim at the expense of alienating Indonesia.

Within a few weeks after the Bangkok ministerial meeting, relations between Indonesia and Malaysia reached a new low. Malaysia resumed its anti-guerrilla operations, while Indonesia continued to supply and reinforce its guerrilla units in Borneo. All the while, guerrillas continued to make their surprise attacks along the borders.

To counter the deteriorating trend of events, a second tripartite ministerial meeting was hastily convened in Bangkok on March 3 and 4. However, this time the talks quickly collapsed when Malaysia refused to accept the Indonesian demand for a "political settlement" before a withdrawal of guerrilla forces. Following these talks, Tunku Abdul Rahman announced that Malaysia would take whatever measures were necessary to insure its integrity. In effect, this amounted to a repudiation of the cease-fire agreement.[40] Sukarno, who had never called off or suspended his "crush Malaysia" policy, began talking about the plans for Indonesia's "revolutionary offensive".[41]

The Tokyo Summit Meeting

Intensified hostilities during March and April prompted a number of nations to redouble their efforts to reopen diplomatic negotiations. Among the most active were Japan, Thailand, the Philippines and Pakistan. However, the status of Indonesian guerrillas continued to be the major stumbling block to a new summit meeting which was being proposed for Tokyo. Malaysia insisted upon the guerrillas withdrawal before talks, while Indonesia would not depart from its demands for a "political settlement" prior to guerrilla withdrawal. After many false starts, a compromise was worked out whereby Indonesia made a token withdrawal of thirty-two guerrillas from Sarawak the day before a new "summit meeting" convened in Tokyo.[42]

At the Tokyo meetings, President Macapagal took the lead in proposing to President Sukarno and Tunku Abdul Rahman that their differences be turned over to a four-nation Afro-Asian commission. While this proposal was tentatively accepted in principle, the talks deadlocked once again over the issue of whether guerrilla activities were to cease while a solution was being sought by the proposed Afro-Asian commission. President Sukarno insisted that withdrawal of guerrilla forces from Malaysia would be dependent upon what progress such a commission might make toward a "political settlement".[43] Since he never revealed what kind of "political settlement" he had in mind, he appeared to be saying that Indonesian attacks would continue until the proposed commission had forced Malaysia to accept a political settlement which was in harmony with Indonesia's as yet unspecified objectives.

Malaysia's Case at the United Nations.

Failure at the Tokyo Summit Meeting served to make Indonesia more brazen in the pursuit of its "crush Malaysia" campaign. More guerrillas were thrown into the contest in Sabah and Sarawak. By mid-August small bands of guerrillas were being landed on the west coast of Johore, bringing Malaya under direct military attack for the first time.[44] This was followed, on September 2, by an air drop of about one hundred heavily armed paratroopers from the Indonesian Air Force transports. The landing was in Johore near the town of Labis. Following this attack, Malaysia appealed to the United Nations Security Council for an urgent meeting to consider action to counter Indonesian aggression.[45]

Malaysia's case against Indonesia was heard by the Security Council from September 9 to 17. Dr. Ismail, Minister of Home Affairs, represented Malaysia, giving a fairly extensive account of the military attacks and incidents staged by Indonesia against Malaysia. In answer, the Indonesian representative, Dr. Sudjarwo, admitted that the guerrillas were Indonesian but explained that the attacks should be viewed as part of a wider movement against "the remnants of colonialism".

I, for one, regret that we should oppose each other here in this world body, since our two peoples are so close, racially as well as culturally, and indeed we can be called brothers within the same family, the family of the great Malay race. We speak the same language, possess the same cultural heritage, inhabit the same home area in South East Asia.

It was colonialism and imperialism which separated our peoples, artificially dividing our great family into differing units—thereby causing if not opposition, almost complete estrangement. . . In reality, the deep conflict between the new emerging revolutionary forces of freedom and national self-assertion in the new emerging countries—especially in Asia and Africa, and probably also in Latin America—and the old dominating forces still exists. It even takes an acute form in many parts of the world, and certainly does so—as my President, Dr. Sukarno, recently stated—in South East Asia, where new emerging revolutionary forces meet strong opposition from the old established forces of the world. . . .[46]

L

Dr. Sudjarwo defended Indonesian support of guerrilla forces by reference to alleged provocations that had occurred when Indonesia faced revolts in its outer islands. Rejecting the argument that Indonesia had violated the rules of international law, he stated,

> . . . legal arguments, particularly when they are based on the so-called international law of the world of the colonial Powers, cannot be applied to stop this struggle.[47]

Disclaiming the argument that one nation was attacking another, he explained,

> It is a people's fight for freedom against colonialism and neo-colonialism, against "Malaysia" as a political notion. For the volunteers, national boundaries do not exist. Their boundaries are political ones.[48]

He also justified the attacks on the basis of Indonesia's revolutionary doctrines as expounded by President Sukarno.[49]

After considerable behind-the-scenes consultations, Norway submitted a compromise draft resolution to the Security Council requesting the parties to avoid the recurrence of all incidents, "to refrain from all threat or use of force", and recommending that the governments resume their talks which were broken off at the Tokyo meetings. This rather mild resolution was opposed by Indonesia as being "one-sided" and because it implied the recognition of Malaysia. On the final vote in the Security Council, the resolution was supported by nine votes to two, with Czechoslovakia and the Soviet Union casting negative votes, which in the case of the latter meant that the resolution failed due to a big power veto.[50]

Malaysia's appeal to the Security Council may have helped to win diplomatic support for Malaysia, but it had little noticeable effect upon Indonesian policy toward her neighbor. Additional attempts were made to land guerrillas and saboteurs in Malaya and Singapore, and border attacks in Sarawak and Sabah continued unabated.

Indonesia Withdraws from the United Nations

Because of the Russian veto, Indonesia could find some comfort from the fact that the Security Council failed to intervene in the Malaysia dispute. However, Indonesia was placed on the defensive in the UN and became hypersensitive to other UN activities related to the Malaysia controversy. For example, Indonesia took strong exception to U Thant's annual report in which he appealed to the "statesmen of the area to solve this difficult question peacefully. . ." and referred with approval to the earlier conclusions of his fact-finding team that Malaysia "may be regarded as the result of the freely expressed wishes of the territory's peoples acting with full knowledge of the change in their status . . ."[51] Piqued by U Thant's report, Sukarno retorted, "To hell with U Thant and his statement".[52] In public speeches,

Sukarno bitterly attacked the Secretary-General and had harsh words for the United Nations as well, which, he said, should be "retooled" since it no longer represented the world's balance of power which was shifting to the *Nefos*—a coined word meaning "New Emerging Forces".

Even more galling to Sukarno was the election of Malaysia to one of the Security Council seats for a half term of one year.[53] As soon as Malaysia assumed its seat in the Security Council, Indonesia carried out its earlier threats and withdrew from the United Nations. Attacking the United Nations for its neo-colonial bias, Sukarno called for a new United Nations made up of the "New Emerging Forces". He apparently had hopes that the Afro-Asian Conference, which was scheduled to open in Algeria in March, could be persuaded to support a new revolutionary world organization of the *Nefos*. Much to Indonesia's disappointment, only Communist China and Albania seemed to react favorably to these proposals. Likewise, Indonesia expected some diplomatic support from the Afro-Asian Conference, but the conference had to be cancelled due to the surprise revolution in Algeria that toppled the Ben Bella regime.

The Tactics of Confrontation

In the contest with Malaysia, Indonesia's tactics tended to follow a distinctive pattern. The approximate sequence was as follows: hunt for an issue to oppose Malaysia; demand negotiations; make limited demands without commitment concerning ultimate objectives; if negotiations lead to agreements, raise new issues. Because military and economic pressure was being used in an attempt to prevent the formation of Malaysia, Indonesia pursued a policy of "fight and talk". Of course such tactics undermined moves for pacific settlement, since the fighting did not end even after agreements had been reached.[54] It was precisely for this reason that Malaysia insisted upon the cessation of hostilities and the withdrawal of guerrillas as a condition for diplomatic negotiations.

The reasons given by Indonesia for opposition to Malaysia were revised as the dispute dragged on. At first, Malaysia was allegedly opposed because there had been no plebiscite in Borneo and because the federation was not supported by the people. Then, after the report of U Thant, Indonesia objected to the preparations being made for the formation of Malaysia while the United Nations team had been preparing its report. When British and Malayan forces were being sent to Borneo to counter Indonesian guerrilla attacks, Indonesia objected to Malaysia's dependence upon foreign military assistance and charged that Malaysia was engaged in the colonial encirclement of Indonesia. When the cease-fire was agreed upon in January, 1964, as a result of Robert Kennedy's efforts, there was ample opportunity to claim violations and argue over the terms of the cease-fire or its implementations.

The Motives Behind Confrontation

Since Indonesian tactics concealed their motives, what, then, were the real reasons for Indonesia's objections to Malaysia? Unfortunately, there is no simple answer. The confrontation policy received wide support in Indonesia, but for a variety of contradictory reasons. Furthermore, it appears that Indonesian objectives shifted somewhat during the dispute. Confrontation developed a momentum and *raison d'etre* of its own which, in time, made it increasingly difficult to abandon, particularly without a significant "victory" or a face-saving formula that could be disguised as a "victory".

Expansionist motives have always been present in Indonesia, but they became increasingly important as the "confrontation" policy became translated into a national crusade involving mass action organizations.[55] Of course, expansionist objectives were not sold to the Indonesian public in terms that suggested Indonesian imperialism. Instead, the Indonesian people were led to believe that colonial powers had prevented the national unification of the peoples of Malaysian-Indonesian stock, and thus, Indonesia had been denied its natural geo-political and ethnic boundaries. Rather than arguing conquest and annexation of disputed territories, the Indonesian propaganda machine talked of encouraging "liberation movements" against neo-colonialism—which by definition condemned all who stood in the way of Indonesia's revolutionary goals". The old ideas of *Indonesia Raya*, which in 1945 had been vigorously espoused by Sukarno, Mohammed Yamin and others,[56] provided the ideological justification for a campaign depicting Malaysia as an "artificial entity" standing in the way of Indonesia's national unification. From this perspective, the conflict with Malaysia was viewed more as a revolutionary civil war than as a conflict between two sovereign states.

In the official Indonesian view, Malaysia was not truly independent: Malayan independence was not won in a violent revolution; Malaysia continued to rely on British protection through a defense treaty, and the "capitalist system" and western influence persisted in Malaysia. An essential feature of this view of Malaysia was the assumption that, given a free choice, the people of Malaysia (or at least the indigenous people) would reject their government and enthusiastically seek some form of union with the Indonesian Republic. Any evidence to the contrary, such as that uncovered by U Thant's team, had to be categorically rejected as a fabrication in order to sustain Sukarno's view of Indonesia's "manifest destiny" in Southeast Asia.

Besides expansionist objectives, other motives for Indonesian actions can be traced to a series of irritations which plagued relations between Indonesia and the states entering the Malaysian Federation. In 1948 and after, Malaya and Singapore were used as a sanctuary by the PRRI rebels who challenged the authority of the Indonesian Government and threatened to divide the country.[57] Similarly, the failure or inability of Malayan and British officials to prevent black-marketeering and smuggling involving Indonesian trade was a constant source of irritation since these activities resulted in a heavy drain on Indonesian government revenues, dependent as they were upon tariff duties and exchange controls. In 1960 the efforts of Tunku Abdul Rahman to act as a mediator in Indonesia's dispute with the Netherlands over West Irian produced further strain. The Tunku proposed Indonesian administration of the disputed area, but under UN trusteeship. Indonesia rejected the proposal, but finally, under pressure from the United States, accepted slightly modified terms for settlement of the West Irian dispute. Malaya was condemned for not giving full support to Indonesia.

When Malaysia was in the planning stage, Indonesia took umbrage at the failure of Malaya and Britain to consult Indonesia on the impending changes. President Sukarno had been very insistent upon asserting Indonesia's place in the world. His assertive diplomacy, his preoccupation with staging international conferences, and his frequent trips to foreign capitals were all designed to demonstrate that Indonesia was cutting a wide swath in international affairs. Consequently, he was hypersensitive to slights which might belittle the claim that Indonesia was the "third most powerful country in the world". Indonesia increasingly assumed that with the retreat of colonialism, it must claim a "sphere of influence" in Southeast Asia commensurate with its power.[58] Whether intended or not, the formation of Malaysia without Indonesia's active participation was viewed both as an insult to her prestige and power, and as an unfriendly move designed to limit the area of Indonesian influence.

Domestic Factors in Indonesian Policy Toward Malaysia

Considerations of domestic politics played a significant role in the formulation of Indonesian policies toward Malaysia. Indonesian politics tended, after 1958, to revolve around the competition between the army on one side and the Indonesian Communist Party (PKI) on the other, with Sukarno and his supporters in the bureaucracy acting as a balancing agent between these two primary centers of power.[59] Each faction in Indonesian politics gave support to the "crush Malaysia" campaign in order to strengthen its position on the domestic political scene.

The army emerged as a dominant political force in Indonesia after 1957, primarily as a result of its successful suppression of rebellion. The victory of the units of the army committed to defend Sukarno's regime gave it a very strong position in the government—a position which was reinforced by decrees of martial law, transferring to the military many of the powers of civil government. A very large proportion of the national budget and large sums of foreign military aid from both the West and the Soviet Union [60] helped to build the army into a formidable military and political force, which then became an effective instrument of national unification and administration. So long as a crisis situation existed, or could be prolonged, the army could make its claims against national revenues and could utilize the powers of martial law over the civil bureaucracy and over troublesome political parties.[61]

In 1958 the crisis was internal rebellion. By 1959 the crisis had shifted to the dispute with the Dutch over West Irian. In mid-1962 the Dutch finally agreed to turn over West Irian to Indonesian administration under a UN trusteeship. The justification for crisis rule had suddenly evaporated. The army faced the prospects of demobilization, of diversion into "civic action" (public works construction projects) of cuts in military budget, and of the termination of martial law. By May, 1963, martial law had been lifted, and many of the restrictions placed by the army upon its primary rival, the PKI, were no longer in force.

Because of Indonesia's rapidly disintegrating economy, the government made an attempt in mid-1963 to shift priorities to meet the very severe economic problems facing the country. However, the failure of the economic stabilization program made it relatively easy for the army to seize upon the Malaysia issue as the new crisis which called for a return to old priorities and which would help restore the army's position of power and militant national leadership.[62] The enemy was still colonialism. It was just in a different guise.[63]

The Indonesian Communist Party (PKI) also had its reasons for backing a militant policy toward Malaysia. As a result of its cultivation of Sukarno's favor, the party enjoyed a privileged position of immunity from excessive political repression by the army. Sukarno's political formula of a government based on "Nasakom" (national unity through the cooperation of nationalist, religious and Communist parties), meant that the Communists were represented in the government. However, they were denied the more important positions of real power.[64] Thus, quite apart from Communist strategy and ideology in international politics, it was in the interest of the Communist Party to "radicalize" Indonesian politics so that it could sustain the momentum of its revolutionary fervor and continue to capitalize on the growing discontent and frustration without directly challenging the government which it officially supported.

Considering Malaya's well-established anti-Communist posture, it was not surprising that the PKI took an official stand opposing Malaysia a full year before the Indonesian Government began a similar policy.[65] By helping to shift the focus of politics to a foreign threat, the PKI was able to use "confrontation" to legitimize many of its activities, including those which amounted to pressuring the government into new lines of action. Thus, political initiative moved perceptibly to the Communist Party.[66] Sukarno's slogans were mouthed within the context of Communist ideology so as to build up greater enthusiasm for the party based upon an appeal to militant nationalism. Armed with a new cause, the PKI gained greater freedom of action to stage mass demonstrations in the name of national unity and anti-imperialism. The Communists helped to scuttle the government's well-intentioned economic reform, which if successful, would have diminished the revolutionary appeal of the party. Increasingly intense anti-British and anti-American mass demonstrations staged by the Communists tended to force the hand of the government in its dealings with western powers. Since national unity and loyalty were measured by outward professions of support for Sukarno and his "Political Manifesto" (*Manipol*), the PKI became the mainstay in the Front Nasional "unity chorus" and thereby "proved" its loyalty through energetic support of the government's "confrontation" policy. Even so, the PKI continued to criticize economic mismanagement, corruption and bureaucratic stagnation as "subversion from above" but blamed it upon the army or the civil service rather than upon Sukarno or his Government. There can be no doubt that D.N. Aidit hoped his party would one day fall heir to power in an enlarged Indonesia. In the meantime, the party concentrated on expanding its already formidable base of support among the workers and peasants, and was temporarily quite willing to play the role of the "tail" that had developed a singular ability to "wag the dog".[67]

Sukarno too, had his reasons for opposing Malaysia. Although his motives remain obscure, it appears that for a while Sukarno genuinely wanted to get on with the task of meeting Indonesia's economic problems. But, when political attention shifted to domestic questions, the measures necessary for economic reform threatened the domestic *status quo* to such an extent that dangerous internal conflicts seemed imminent. Caught in a potential power struggle between the Communists and the army, he was hard pressed to find areas of agreement and compromise between them. Since they both supported the anti-Malaysia campaign even before he became committed to it as a national crusade, this issue had the effect of subduing and postponing internal domestic strife. It must have seemed fortuitous to Sukarno that the Malaysia issue could so easily be seized upon to extricate his government from its precarious position.

If this interpretation is correct, the attack against Malaysia was not created as an artificial issue to unify the country, but followed from a genuine extension of Indonesian nationalism as idealized in the concept of *Indonesia Raya*. Malaysia would have been opposed by Indonesia in one way or the other. However, the intensity and tenacity of that opposition derives in large measure from the circumstances of domestic politics within Indonesia.

Although the army, the Communists and Sukarno all supported the campaign against Malaysia, it must be noted that there were important differences in their view of the struggle. The army view of politics, both domestic and international, was permeated with overtones of racialism having a decidedly anti-Chinese bias. The army developed into an important vehicle for the propagation of Indonesian nationalism based upon an idealized ethnic unity of Indonesian-Malay stock peoples—the *Indonesia Raya* idea. For the army, "confrontation" was a fight to free Malaysia from inevitable Chinese control and restore Malay-Indonesian hegemony in insular Southeast Asia. Because of this racial-communal perspective, the army generally avoided cooperating with Chinese from Malaya, some of whom were quite eager to fight Malaysia from within.[68]

The Communist view of the struggle with Malaysia followed from typical Marxian analysis. Malaysia was seen as a country ruled by feudal Malays and the Chinese bourgeoisie, propped up through their ties with western capitalists. Malaya's long war against Communist insurrection and the country's defense arrangements with Britain were taken as evidence of the persistence of bourgeois-capitalism and neo-colonialism in Malaysia. There was no doubt that the PKI hoped that "confrontation" would help to spark a Communist revolution in Malaysia.

Sukarno's view of the conflict appears to have been very similar to that of the army, except that Sukarno seems to have been slightly more sophisticated in his realization of the inherent dangers of conflict defined along racial lines. He was aware that undiluted racial-communal nationalism would make Indonesia more prone to dangerous outbreaks of communal violence. Furthermore, an important source of disaffection within Malaysia could not be tapped if the conflict were racially defined. In addition, relations with Communist China would have become strained at the very time when Communist Chinese diplomatic and economic support was most needed. President Sukarno had the advantage of being able to play on both communal and Marxist class interpretation of the conflict with Malaysia, thereby obtaining much greater support both at home and abroad than would otherwise have been the case.

To sum up, Indonesian motivation for the anti-Malaysia campaign stemmed from a paradox. The army and the Communists came to opposite conclusions about the nature of the conflict and about the likely course of the future, but for that reason, they could support the same policy of opposition to Malaysia. In over-simplified form, the army feared that the Malaysian Government would fall under the control of the Chinese Communists and their sympathizers, while the PKI feared that the Malaysian Government would not do so, but would remain pro-capitalist, pro-western and anti-Communist.[69]

1 *Straits Budget*, September 19, 1962, pp. 5–6.

2 The following excerpt from Radio Moscow's Indonesian language broadcast on August 9, 1962 was typical of its propaganda line toward the proposals for the Malaysian Federation:
   "With Malaysia set up, the colonialists and their allies will intensify their activities against the liberation movements in Asia. . .
   "The colonialists have had previous experience in using Singapore for this purpose. It was previously the seat of SEATO which organized the rebellion in Indonesia. [Sic] It was from Singapore that the Indonesian rebels were supplied with arms and ammunition."

3 In a letter to the *New York Times*, Foreign Minister Subandrio wrote as follows: "Of course, the people there [in the Borneo states] are ethnologically and geographically very close to the others living in the Indonesian territory. Still, we do not show any objection toward this Malayan policy of merger. On the contrary, we wish the Malayan Government well if it can succeed with this plan." *New York Times*, November 17, 1961, p. 34.

4 *Straits Times*, January 24, 1962.

5 *Borneo Bulletin*, December 22, 1962, p. 1.

6 After it was clear the revolution had failed, Zaini Haji Ahmad asked for asylum in Hong Kong and then later agreed to return to Brunei, placing himself at the mercy of the Sultan.

7 Paradoxically, the radio signal was strong in Singapore, but very weak in Brunei.

8 *Straits Times*, January 22, 1963, p. 1.

9 These "delegates" were, in fact, Indonesians from Djakarta.

10 The Malayan-Singapore delegation reported that the attack against Malaysia was led by Indonesia and Communist China. On the other hand, the Russian delegates made no speeches against Malaysia and indicated their willingness to seat the Malayan-Singapore delegation.

11 For an explanation of the case made by the Philippines see Martin Meadows, "The Philippine Claim to North Borneo", *Political Science Quarterly*, Vol. 77, no. 3 (September, 1962), pp. 321–335. Because this article concentrates on the arguments of the Philippines, it presents a very distorted picture of the strength of the claim. If the Philippine arguments are to be accepted, then Brunei could put forth an even more valid claim (which is precisely what Azahari was attempting to do). The best history of North Borneo covering the early period of British expansion is that of K. G. Tregonning, *A History of Modern Sabah*, (Singapore: University of Malaya Press, 1965).

12 Nicasio Osmena approached the Malayan Government late in 1962 and is said to have asked for £10,000,000 in a private settlement of the claim on the understanding that the Philippine Government would then abandon its diplomatic pressure. Rumors in diplomatic circles suggest that a similar offer was later made to the Indonesian Government for the purchase of this claim.

13 Several Filipino businessmen associated with the Kiram Corporation had investments in North Borneo and were trying to get exclusive concessions for some time, but without success, since it was contrary to government policy.

14 *Joint Statement Issued After Tokyo Meeting*, published as Appendix XII in *Malaysia/Indonesia Relations*, (Kuala Lumpur: Government Printing Office, 1963), p. 44.

15 *Tripartite Summit Meeting—Manila Accord*, published as Appendix XIV in *Malaysia/Indonesia Relations, op. cit.*, pp. 47–49.

16 *Tripartite Summit Meeting—Joint Statement*, published as Appendix XV in *Malaysia/Indonesia Relations, op. cit.*, pp. 50–52.

17 *New York Times*, August 5, 1963, pp. 1 and 2.

18 *Tripartite Summit Meeting—Manila Accord, op. cit.*, p. 48.

19 *Tripartite Summit Meeting—Joint Statement, op. cit.*, p. 51.

20 *Ibid.*, p. 51.

21 *Tripartite Summit Meeting—Manila Declaration, op. cit.*, p. 45.

22 In 1945, when Sukarno was a member of the committee which negotiated with the Japanese for Indonesian independence, he made a strong plea for the inclusion of all peoples of "Indonesian ethnic stock" as was being proposed by Mohammed Yamin. The following statements indicate Sukarno's views at that time: ". . . I have on one occasion in my life dreamt of a Pan-Indonesia, which will include not only Malaya and Papua (New Guinea) but also the Philippines. . . . when I look at the islands situated between Asia and Australia and between the Pacific and the Indian Oceans, I understand that they are meant to form a single entity. For that reason I shall support those who advocate that independent Indonesia should extend to Malaya and Papua." See *Background to Indonesia's Policy Towards Malaysia*, (Kuala Lumpur: Department of Information, 1963), pp. 20–22.

23 Indonesian Foreign Minister Subandrio had proposed that the control of British military bases in the event of war should be surrendered to Maphilindo, rather than be subject to the jurisdiction of Malaya or Malaysia. *New York Times*, August 4, 1963, p. 20.

24 *Straits Budget*, August 14, 1963, p. 16.

25 U Thant, "Mission to Sarawak and Sabah, Secretary-General's Conclusions", *United Nations Review*, Vol. 10, no. 9 (October, 1963), p. 15.

26 *Straits Budget*, September 11, 1963, p. 18.

27 *Straits Times*, September 16, 1963.

28 *Straits Times*, January 10, 1964, p. 1.

29 At the Colombo Conference in November the foreign ministers of Malaysia, Thailand, Indonesia and the Philippines met to explore the possibility of new diplomatic negotiations. Thai Foreign Minister, Thanat Khoman, assumed the role of principal mediator. However, continued Indonesian attacks in Borneo hampered such moves. *Straits Times*, November 9, 1963, p. 1; November 11, 1963, p. 1; November 13, p. 1.

30 *New York Times*, January 17, 1964, p. 42.

31 *Straits Times*, January 18, 1964, pp. 1 and 20.

32 *Straits Times*, January 21, 1964, p. 1; January 22, p. 1.

33 *Straits Times*, January 24, 1964, p. 1.

34 *Straits Times*, February 1, 1964, pp. 1 and 24; February 4, 1964, pp. 1 and 20.

35 Malaysia was represented by Deputy Prime Minister Abdul Razak, Indonesia by Foreign Minister Subandrio and the Philippines by Foreign Minister Salvador Lopez. *Straits Times*, February 7, 1964, pp. 1 and 20; February 8, 1964, pp. 1 and 24; February 10, 1964, pp. 1 and 24.

36 *Straits Times*, February 8, 1964, p. 24.

37 U Thant refused to appoint Thailand to supervise a cease-fire since the governments had not proposed any form of United Nations control or supervision of the Thai mission. Instead, the Secretary-General offered his "good offices" if they were needed and desired, and "took note" of the role Thailand was expected to play. *Straits Times*, February 14, 1964, p. 1.

38 *Straits Times*, February 11, 1964, p. 1.

39 *Straits Times*, February 11, 1964, p. 1; February 12, 1964, p. 1.

40 *Straits Times*, March 5, 1964, p. 1.

41 *Straits Times*, March 10, 1964, p. 1. In preparation for expected Indonesian attacks in force, the Malaysian Government announced on March 11 that eligible men between the ages of 21 and 29 were to be subject to compulsory military service. Both Malaysian and British military forces were being rapidly strengthened, and strong units of the British navy arrived for duty in the area.

42 *New York Times*, June 16, 1964, p. 2; June 19, 1964, p. 8.

43 *New York Times*, June 20, 1964, p. 3; June 21, 1964, p. 1.

44 *Straits Budget*, August 26, 1964, p. 8.

45 At the time of the Security Council sessions, Malaysia had evidence of only one air drop, which was believed to have consisted of about thirty paratroopers. Later, captured guerrillas revealed that a second parachute force landed in Johore on the same evening.

46 *Malaysia's Case in the United Nations Security Council*, (Kuala Lumpur: Ministry of External Affairs, 1964), p. 8.

47 *Ibid.*, *op. cit.*, p. 12.

48 *Ibid.*, p. 24.

49 Indonesia espoused the doctrine that it must actively promote "revolutionary wars of national liberation". On this issue it took a stand that was nearly identical with the doctrines espoused by Communist China and Cuba.

[50] *Malaysia's Case, op. cit.*, p. 80.

[51] *Introduction to the Annual Report of the Secretary-General on the Work of the Organization, 16 June, 1963–June 15, 1964*, United Nations, General Assembly Official Records: Nineteenth Session, Supplement No. 1A (A/5801/Add. 1), pp. 8–9.

[52] *Straits Times*, November 27, pp. 1 and 24.

[53] Malaysia's election to the Security Council had been agreed upon the year before when an election deadlock was broken by a compromise arrangement which divided a two-year term on the Security Council between Malaysia and Czechoslovakia.

[54] In a newspaper interview prior to the Manila Conference, the author stated that Indonesian objections to Malaysia had little to do with a plebiscite and that the Manila Conference might create a façade of unity but not much more than that for some time. The Indonesian Consulate-General issued a press release condemning the author for his views. Yet, not many months later Sukarno was quoted as saying in a public speech, "The tactics may change 24 times a day, but the objectives remain the same—confrontation and the crushing of Malaysia." See *Malay Mail*, July 17, 1963, p. 1; *Straits Times*, July 18, 1963, p. 16, February 3, 1964, p. 1.

[55] For a more complete analysis of expansionist motives in Indonesia see Bernard K. Gordon, "Potential for Indonesian Expansionism", *Pacific Affairs*, Vol. XXXVI, no. 4 (Winter 1963–1964), pp. 378–393.

[56] See *supra* footnote 22, p. 329.

[57] The Permentah Revolusione Republic Indonesia (PRRI) rebellion was based primarily in Sumatra and Sulawesi. It began in 1958 but quickly deteriorated into guerrilla action which was not brought under control until 1961. See Herbert Feith and Daniel S. Lev "The End of the Indonesian Rebellion", *Pacific Affairs*, Vol. XXXVI, no. 1 (Spring 1963), pp. 32–46.

[58] The Maphilindo Confederation was vigorously supported because it was hoped that through it, Indonesia, as the largest and most powerful member of the confederation, could effectively exercise its weight within this "sphere of influence".

[59] See Herbert Feith, "Dynamics of Guided Democracy," in Ruth T. McVey (ed.), *Indonesia* (New Haven, Conn.: Human Relations Area Files Press, 1963), pp. 309–409.

[60] Between 1955 and 1963 Indonesia had obtained a total of US$1,032·3m. in loans from the USSR and East European countries, of which US$450m. were for arms purchases. Substantial military assistance was also obtained from other countries. See Donald Hindley, "Foreign Aid to Indonesia and Its Political Implications", *Pacific Affairs*, XXXVI, no. 2 (Summer 1963), pp. 107–119.

[61] See Daniel S. Lev, "The Political Role of the Army in Indonesia," *Pacific Affairs*, XXXVI, no. 4 (Winter 1963–64), pp. 349–364.

[62] See Justus M. van der Kroef, "Indonesian Communism and the Changing Balance of Power", *Pacific Affairs*, Vol. XXXVII, no. 4 (Winter 1964–1965), pp. 364–365.

[63] In a speech at Djakarta Dr. Subandrio explained the shift in priorities. "President Sukarno is now trying to revive the iron spirit of the people, to give them confidence. . . We are neglecting our wealth purposely because we are concentrating on nation-building. Because of the natural wealth of Indonesia, we can afford not to give priority to economic problems." *Straits Times*, December 6, 1963, p. 1.

[64] See Donald Hindley, "President Sukarno and the Communists: the Politics of Domestication", *American Political Science Review*, Vol. 56, no. 4 (December, 1962), pp. 915–926.

65 *Supra*, pp. 313–314.

66 See van der Kroef, *op. cit.*, pp. 357–383 for a very comprehensive analysis of the changed power position of the PKI after Indonesia embarked upon its anti-Malaysia policy. A similar analysis may be found in chapter 7 of Justus M. van der Kroef, *The Communist Party of Indonesia*, (Vancouver, Canada: University of British Columbia Publications Centre, 1965), pp. 267–294.

67 The anti-Malaysia policy of the PKI produced a side effect of helping to heal the fissures within the party, even though the party became more firmly committed to Peking's "hard" line in international affairs. See van der Kroef, "Indonesian Communism and the Changing Balance of Power", *op. cit.*, pp. 362–363 and 375–383.

68 For some examples see *Indonesian Intentions Toward Malaysia*, (Kuala Lumpur: Government Press, 1964), pp. 32–48.

69 Some aspects of this paradox were analyzed in Donald Hindley, "Indonesia's Confrontation With Malaysia: A Search for Motives", *Asian Survey*, Vol. IV, no. 6 (June, 1964), pp. 904–913.

18 The Internal Challenge to Malaysia

If one were to judge from the speeches and celebrations marking "Malaysia Day", the threats to the new federation all seemed to emanate from abroad. Nonetheless, in the back of the minds of Malaysia's political leaders there must have been some apprehension about how the union would operate in practice and how stable it would be during its infancy. The tensions within Malaysia were such that compromise and accommodation clearly would be a slow and bitter process, particularly since some of the most difficult problems of governmental and political integration had yet to be resolved.

Among the more serious of the problems facing the union were the following: the political threat posed by the anti-Malaysia opposition parties; the threatened resurgence of communal hostilities over alterations in the *status quo*; the formulation of economic policies for a "common market"; the extension of federal authority and government services into Singapore and the Borneo states; and the creation of a pan-Malaysian party system. While these problems were being worked out, new political alignments would obviously develop which might generate political instability or fracture the union.

Singapore Elections of 1963

The most immediate internal threat to Malaysia seemed to arise from the activities of the formidable anti-Malaysia opposition in Singapore. The Barisan Sosialis and the United People's Party had, with covert Communist support, waged a long and bitter campaign to break up Malaysia before it was formed, and had never conceded that the new state might be accepted even on a trial basis.

In July, 1963, Prime Minister Lee Kuan-yew promised that elections would be held for the Singapore Legislative Assembly some time after Malaysia came into being. It was clear that this was to be a test of support for Malaysia. In preparation for this contest, Lee Kuan-yew visited every election constituency to explain the advantages expected to accrue from Malaysia and to promise additional government services to deprived communities. These tours were not billed as election campaigning, since the date for the elections were not announced until September 4th, with the election set for September 21.[1]

The decision for an early election was probably based on the following considerations: the PAP had lost its working majority of one seat when its Minister of Labour died, thus making it dependent upon the unpredictable support of UMNO and Singapore People's Alliance votes; the PAP had gained a head start over rivals in its campaigning and was more confident of support after the successful negotiations for Malaysia, while the Barisan Sosialis was politically on the defensive, not having found a positive alternative to Malaysia, and suffering from the handicap of having many of its key leaders still being held in detention.[2]

A decision of the Malayan Alliance to enter the Singapore elections complicated the picture and made cooperation between Singapore and Kuala Lumpur increasingly difficult. The Singapore Alliance had been formed in June through the union of the Singapore People's Alliance and the Singapore branches of the Malayan Chinese Association and UMNO.[3] Many old political foes of the PAP, who had been active in the defunct Progressive Party and the Labour Front, now joined the Alliance in an effort to construct a pro-Malaysia force less radical than the PAP and more in harmony with the Malayan Alliance. The Singapore Alliance challenge forced the PAP to fight on two fronts and raised the possibility of a split pro-Malaysia vote paving the

TABLE 15
Party distribution in Singapore Legislative Assembly before and after September 1963 elections.

	Seats in previous Assembly	Seats won in 1963	Percentage of total vote 1963	Appointed parliamentary seats
People's Action Party	25	37	47%	12
Barisan Sosialis	14	13	33%	3
United People's Party	3	1	7%	—
Singapore Alliance:			8%	—
Singapore People's Alliance	4			
UMNO	3			
Malayan Chinese Association	—			
Workers Party	1		—	—
Independents	1		4%*	—

* Includes both independents and minor party vote.

Note: The complete results of the Singapore elections of 1963 are reproduced in Milton E. Osborne, *Singapore and Malaysia* (Ithaca, New York: Southeast Asia Program, Cornell University 1964) pp. 95–112.

way for a Barisan Sosialis victory. However, when the votes were tallied, the PAP emerged the victor commanding a majority of thirty-seven seats in the fifty-one member Legislative Assembly. The electorate appeared to have concluded that the principal contest was between the PAP and the Barisan Sosialis, for all minor parties and independents lost support. While the PAP lost much of its 1959 "left wing" support to the Barisan Sosialis and the UPP, it gained almost an equal amount from the disintegration of moderate parties, which, in Singapore, appear as "right wing". The PAP lost three seats as a result of Alliance competition splitting the pro-Malaysia vote, but gained seven seats as a result of a split "left wing" vote between the Barisan Sosialis and the UPP.[4]

Besides renewing its mandate, the new People's Action Party Government gained the right to appoint twelve of Singapore's fifteen-member delegation in the Federal Parliament. All nine PAP cabinet ministers were appointed to seats in Parliament in addition to three other PAP Legislative Assembly members.[5] The three remaining Parliamentary seats went to the Barisan Sosialis.

After the Singapore elections, the Federal Government determined to exercise its new authority to crack down on centers of pro-Communist and anti-Malaysian activity. Communist cadres had been assiduously cultivating support at Nanyang University and had converted a number of student organizations into vehicles for propagating the Communist line and organizing militant Chinese chauvinists to adopt militant tactics against Malaysia. To halt these activities, the Federal Government used its powers of preventive detention to make 23 arrests at Nanyang University of persons suspected of Communist affiliations. Included were three individuals who had been Barisan candidates in the 1963 elections.[6] Nine months later another group of 51 Nanyang University students was also arrested.

The Singapore Association of Trade Unions (SATU) was another center of pro-Communist activities. A mainstay in the political structure of the Barisan Sosialis, this federation of unions called a general strike for October 8, supposedly in protests against government interference in union affairs. All sides recognized that it was a political strike against the government for its crackdown on Communist cadres, their associates and their front organizations. Again, federal authorities acted with dispatch and the strike fizzled out. Fourteen strike leaders were arrested, including SATU President S. T. Bani and two other Barisan Legislative Assembly members.[7]

Malayan Elections of 1964

In Malaya the Alliance Government's term of office did not expire until August, 1964. Even so, the Federal Government decided to hold state and federal elections on April 25th.[8] Several motives are suggested for the earlier date. The Alliance had won several decisive by-election victories over the past year, demonstrating that it continued to command overwhelming strength at the polls.[9] Indonesia's propaganda against Malaysia was playing on the theme that Malaysia was established without popular support. It was felt that a decisive Alliance victory would provide irrefutable evidence that Malaysia was endorsed by the public and was not a "neo-colonial plot" as charged by Indonesia. The election would also force the anti-Malaysia opposition parties to choose between supporting Malaysia as a *fait accompli* or giving the appearance of rendering aid and comfort to Malaysia's foreign attackers. It is uncertain whether the Alliance expected elections during that period of foreign crisis would make the opposition more moderate, or more radical and tend to force them into league with Malaysia's attackers abroad. In any event, the opposition parties were vulnerable.

As soon as the elections were announced, the opposition parties began negotiations to pool their strength. However, the construction of a united front of opposition parties was even more difficult than in previous elections because of sharp communal differences and because of their conflicting reasons for opposing Malaysia. After several weeks, Abdul Aziz bin Ishak announced that his National Convention Party was joining Party Ra'ayat and the Labour Party in an enlarged Socialist Front.[10] A wider union of opposition parties failed to materialize.

In its campaign the Socialist Front continued to criticize Malaysia for "the way it was formed" but was unwilling or unable to present any specific alternatives to Malaysia. The Alliance Government was blamed for alienating Indonesia and causing "confrontation". A Socialist Front peace plan was proposed, calling for a Borneo cease-fire, the withdrawal of British and Indonesian troops, the release of all political detainees, and a referendum in Borneo "to ascertain the true wishes of the peoples".[11]

The attitude of the United Democratic Party toward Malaysia gradually shifted. Whereas it had opposed Malaysia before it was formed, during the election it opposed Indonesian "confrontation" and criticized the "timing of Malaysia" and the "hasty manner in which it was set up".[12] By implication, these defects in the implementation of Malaysia, rather than its legal and political arrangements, had caused the troubles with Indonesia.

The Pan-Malayan Islamic Party appeared to shy away from the Malaysia issue, for in its manifesto it avoided any stand on Malaysia, concentrating instead on these promises: to establish an Islamic state in which Islamic teachings would be "a guide for state administration"; to extend Malay special rights by requiring that certain state offices must be held by Malay Muslims; to provide more scholarships and build more religious schools; and to expand government services to fishermen and padi planters, and in rural areas.[13] PMIP candidates tried to discount the existence of any foreign threat to Malaysia, while they also tried to avoid being identified as sympathizers of Indonesia's "crush Malaysia" campaign. They appeared to have a difficult time answering the continuing accusations against their loyalty,[14] and thus preferred to concentrate on very concrete Malay grievances at the state and local level.

Of the opposition parties in Malaya, the Peoples Progressive Party was unique in that it took a very militant anti-Indonesian posture and carefully avoided any ties with other opposition parties which equivocated on that issue.[15] It attacked the Socialist Front and the PMIP with as much vigor as it did the Alliance, accusing the SF of being pro-Communist and accusing both the SF and the PMIP of willingness to "sell the country" to Indonesia.[16] When charged with failure to promote peace, the PPP warned its supporters of Sukarno's anti-Chinese policies, emphasizing that confrontation was to be preferred to a peace established on the basis of Maphilindo.[17]

The Malayan elections were complicated by the role played by the Peoples Action Party. The PAP had never been brought into the Alliance structure either at the state level or in the "Malaysian Grand Alliance". Instead, the party had kept free of such political ties, and as a consequence had had to contend with an Alliance challenge to its power in the Singapore elections.

When the first Malaysian Parliament met in November, 1963, Lee Kuan-yew explained the position of his party as being that of a "friend, loyal opposition and critic".[18] While promising to support the Alliance Government on national issues, the PAP treated the Alliance as a friendly adversary—that is, as both a partner in Malaysia and as a political opponent. What this meant became clearer when the PAP Deputy Prime Minister, Dr. Toh Chin-chye, announced that the party would field candidates in the Malayan elections in a "token role".[19]

Only nine PAP candidates ran for parliamentary seats. Yet the impact on the Malayan scene was far greater than suggested by the small number of seats contested. The PAP selected the urban and predominantly Chinese constituencies to test its electoral strength, thus challenging the Alliance where MCA candidates appeared on the ticket.[20] Most of these constituencies were also contested by the Socialist Front, the United Democratic Party or the Peoples Progressive Party.

Making no election agreements with the opposition parties, the PAP concentrated its attack upon the Socialist Front and upon the Malayan Chinese Association. The former was said to be pro-Communist and "running dogs of Sukarno".[21] The latter was charged with "corruption, greed and ineptitude". Although the PAP claimed to be the spokesman for "urban people of Malaysia of all races",[22] its appeal was directed almost exclusively to the Chinese voter, to whom it said in effect, "Chinese politicians in the past have failed you, but the PAP, with its power base in Singapore, will be able to be a much more effective advocate for your interests in the tough political negotiations with the UMNO-dominated Alliance Government." Lee Kuan-yew freely admitted that his objective was to defeat the MCA and make UMNO "take stock of the new position".[23] Although Tunku Abdul Rahman staunchly defended the MCA and criticized the PAP for is communalism, the PAP still claimed that it would be a far better partner in the Alliance Government than the Malayan Chinese Association. The following quotations from Lee Kuan-yew's campaign speeches show how he hoped to "save" Tunku Abdul Rahman from his "incompetent MCA friends".

> Half the problems Malaysia faces have been created by his old friends who skilfully and cynically exploit his personal loyalities. We have repeatedly said that we want the Tengku to win the elections and we want to help him to implement a more intelligent economic and social policy in the urban areas.[24]

> The MCA had become too feeble. It is now too flimsy a facade and can make no contribution.

> We do not expect any immediate change, for that is not the nature of the Tengku But if the towns show decisively that they want a social revolution, it is also in the Tengku's nature to take heed of popular feelings and make adjustments accordingly.[25]

Although the PAP carefully avoided attacking UMNO, its policy of raising communal issues disguised behind an appeal to "urban areas" and its apparent attempt to force its way into the Alliance, generated a strong antipathy on the part of UMNO. Abdul Razak, Dr. Ismail, Tan Siew-sin and Syed Ja'afar Albar assumed the primary responsibility for the Alliance campaign. In answer to the PAP, they called upon all Malay voters to reject the PAP so as to preserve UMNO-MCA unity and avoid the dangers of communalism in Malaya.[26] They also warned the Chinese voters that "their survival in the country could not be guaranteed if parties other than the Alliance came into power".[27]

Prior to the polling date Indonesian agents engineered a number of incidents designed to influence the outcome of the elections in favor of the anti-Malaysia parties.[28] However, terrorism may have produced an opposite effect, for, after the votes were counted, the Alliance had once again gained a decisive victory, improving on its 1959 record.

TABLE 16
Comparison of parliamentary and state elections in Malaya 1959 and 1964

	1959			1964			
	Parliament		State	Parliament			State
	Seats won	% Total vote	Seats won	Seats contested	Seats won	% Total vote	Seats won
Alliance	74	51·8%	207	104	89	58·3%	240
PMIP	13	21·3%	42	54	9	14·2%	25
Party Negara	1	2·1%	4	4	—	0·4%	—
Socialist Front	8	12·9%	16	63	2	16·0%	8
PPP	4	6·2%	8	8	2	3·5%	5
Malayan Party	1	0·9%	—	—	—	—	—
United Democratic Party	—	—	—	27	1	4·4%	4
PAP	—	—	—	11	1	2·1%	—
Independents	3	4·8%	5	8	—	0·7%	—

Source: Pilehan Raya Parliamen dan Negeri 1964 (Kuala Lumpur: Jabatan Penerangan Malaysia 1964) pp. 1–5.

By adding the Parliamentary seats from Singapore, Sarawak and Sabah, the Alliance commanded a majority of 123 seats out of a total membership of 159 in the House of Representatives (Dewan Ra'ayat). Only 14 seats were held by opposition parties which were definitely opposed to Malaysia.

Among the prominent members of the opposition who failed to secure election were Ahmad Boestamam, (SF), V. David (SF), Ishak bin Haji Mohammed (SF) and Abdul Aziz bin Ishak (NCP). The two victorious Socialist Front MPs were Lim Kean-siew and Dr. Tan Chee-khoon, both of whom were comparative "moderates" in their party.[29] Dr. Lim Chong-eu won the only seat for the UDP, while the PPP's parliamentary membership was reduced to the two Seenivasagam brothers. The PMIP retained the state of Kelantan as their stronghold, winning 8 of the 10 seats from that state. All the PMIP MPs from Trengganu, including PMIP President Dr. Burhanuddin, failed to run for re-election in 1964.[30] Two weeks after the election the PMIP lost another stalwart when its Vice President, Zulkiflee bin Mohammad, was killed in an automobile accident.

TABLE 17

Party distribution in House of Representatives 1964

	The Government	123
Alliance (Malaya)	89	
Alliance (Sarawak)	18	
Alliance (Sabah)	16	
	The Opposition	36
People's Action Party	13	
Pan-Malayan Islamic Party	9	
Party Negara Sarawak	3	
Sarawak United People's Party	3	
Barisan Sosialis	3	
Socialist Front	2	
People's Progressive Party	2	
United Democratic Party	1	

Source: Pilehan Raya Parliamen dan Negeri 1964 (Kuala Lumpur: Jabatan Penerangan Malaysia, 1964) p. 39.

Plotting with Indonesia

Beginning about 1960 a number of Indonesian officials in the diplomatic corps secretly began laying the foundations for a pro-Indonesian underground in Malaya and Singapore. These efforts were the work of a group of Javanese army officers directed by the former Consulate-General of Indonesia to Singapore, Brigadier Djatikusumo.[31] The recruitment of "West Irian Volunteers" to help Indonesia "liberate" that area from Dutch rule provided a good cover to contact radical Malay political organizations and enabled the Indonesian army to form the nucleus of a pro-Indonesian guerrilla force. In Malaya and Singapore over 4,700 "West Irian Volunteers" were recruited, but only 88 were selected for training in Indonesia. In addition to military instruction, these recruits were indoctrinated in "Guided Democracy", "Panchasila", and *Indonesia Raya*. The training began in July, 1962, only a few months before the West Irian dispute was settled. To avoid suspicions about Indonesia's intentions, the volunteers returned to Malaya and Singapore by the end of December, 1962, shortly after the Brunei rebellion. However, before their return, 28 volunteers formed a secret revolutionary organization called APREMA[32] and made a blood oath to overthrow the Malaysian Government by revolution.[33]

When "confrontation" began in early 1963, Indonesian officials intensified their efforts to use Malayan and Singapore political organizations to undermine Malaysia. Top party leaders of Party Ra'ayat Singapore, the Peninsular Malays Union, and Party Ra'ayat of Malaya established secret liaison with

Indonesian agents. Ibrahim bin Haji Jaacob and his KMM (*Kesatuan Melayu Merdeka*) became a key link in the system. His contacts with Malay political leaders were valuable, while the KMM provided a front of "Malay exiles" in the name of which Indonesian "volunteers" could assist the "revolution in Malaya and Singapore".[34] Bong Kahar, President of the PMU was a key figure in a network which recruited radical Malays for an Indonesian-supported revolutionary movement.[35]

As Malaysia came closer to reality, guerrilla training bases were set up on one of the Rhio islands only ten miles from Singapore. About 27 guerrillas were being trained by the Indonesian army at that base when Malaysia was proclaimed. The following day, a Nasional Republik Malaya was proclaimed on the Rhio islands with Ahmad Boestamam named as its Prime Minister.[36] Sergeant-Major Samsuddin Nur bin Nurut, who commanded the guerrilla training base, was made a "Major-General" in the *Tentera Republik Nasional Malaya* (Armed Forces of the National Republic of Malaya).[37] This small group of dissidents from Malaya and Singapore was useful to Indonesia for it was the basis for the claim that the attacks against Malaysia were a part of a popular uprising against "neo-Colonialism" within Malaysia.

Because the outcome of the Malayan elections of 1964 would have a direct bearing on the future of Malaysia, Indonesian agents offered assistance to anti-Malaysia parties, particularly those that were noted for their extreme Malay communalist and pro-Indonesian views. According to a government white paper, Indonesian agents gave the following sums to political parties for campaign expenses: Party Ra'ayat Malaya, M$145,000; PMIP, M$105,000; Party Ra'ayat Singapore, M$15,000; National Convention Party, M$6,000; Labour Party, M$5,000.[38]

While the Malayan elections may have demonstrated the extent of popular support for Malayasia, it also had the effect of demoralising some of the opposition parties and may have made their leaders even more willing to accept offers of political assistance from abroad. In any case, Indonesian subversion of political parties became even more widespread during 1965.

Indonesia's immediate objective was to get pro-Indonesian political leaders to flee the country and form a "Malayan Government-in-Exile". The Nasional Republik Malaya was no more than a shadow and no active Malayan politician had openly joined it, although Ahmad Boestamam's name was used to give it a fragile claim to legitimacy. To achieve this objective, Indonesian agents began a series of surreptitious contacts with certain leaders of opposition parties to sound them out on possible cooperation with this venture. According to a government white paper,[39] this, in brief, is what happened.

Abdul Aziz bin Ishak (Chairman of the NCP) and Hasnul bin Abdul Hadi (Chairman of the SF) went to Cairo in October to represent the Socialist Front at the Cairo Conference of Non-Aligned Nations. They were not able to gain admission to the conference, but while there they met an Indonesian who arranged for a meeting with General Djatikusumo, the former Indonesian Consulate-General of Singapore. Following this meeting, Indonesian agents met Abdul Aziz at Jeddah, Karachi and New Delhi in repeated attempts to try to persuade him not to return to Malaysia, but to take a long tour at Indonesian expense and to join an exile Malayan government. The Indonesian offer was rejected and the two Socialist Front representatives returned to Malaysia.

Meanwhile, in Malaya, an Indonesian revolutionary organization received instructions to try to persuade Abdul Aziz and several other Malay political leaders to leave the country.[40] In January, 1965, a series of discussions took place, arranged through the initiative of these agents. The participants finally agreed to form a "National Front" which would send representatives to the Afro-Asian Conference scheduled in Algiers for June, 1965. A "Malayan Government in Exile" would then be proclaimed and it would direct the armed struggle against the Malaysian Government. Involved in this plot were the following political figures: Abdul Aziz bin Ishak, former Minister of Agriculture and Chairman of the NCP; Dr. Burhanuddin, President of the PMIP; Ishak bin Haji Mohammed, former Chairman of the Socialist Front; Dato Raja Abu Hanifa, Vice-President of the PMIP; Hasnul bin Abdul Hadi, Chairman of the Socialist Front; Tajuddin Kahar, Secretary-General of Party Ra'ayat Malaya and Dato Kampo Radjo, Secretary-General of the NCP and SF Treasurer. For some time the Malayan authorities had been intercepting the secret messages to and from Indonesia, and before final arrangements could be made for the inconspicuous departure of these individuals, they were arrested.[41]

Two weeks later the Socialist Front staged a rally in the capital to protest against the arrests. The demonstrations quickly degenerated into rioting as militant Chinese joined by a few Malay extremists began ransacking the United States Information Service library, shouting anti-Malaysia slogans and fighting with police who attempted to restore order. The police arrested 166 people for rioting, including a Barisan Sosialis MP from Singapore and V. David, the Socialist Front Leader who lost his seat in the 1964 elections.[42]

Although the Indonesian-inspired plot against Malaysia was foiled by the pre-emptive arrests of the conspirators, the events nonetheless had their tragic effects. Much of the political opposition was left leaderless and ineffective in its role as a parliamentary opposition. The frustrations and defeats suffered by opposition leaders made them more than willing to resort to revolutionary tactics with foreign assistance. Faced with revolutionary plots and treason, the Federal Government retaliated by the exercise of its extraordinary powers under the Internal Security Act. On both sides, there seemed to be a recognition that political contests were not being waged according to the rules of parliamentary constitutional democracy.[43] Public consensus concerning the nature of legitimacy appeared to be decaying.

PAP versus Alliance—The Expanding Struggle

Malaysia's continued existence depended upon more than security measures against foreign attack and subversion. Even more important, in the long run, was the question of how the constituent units in the federation were to be integrated into a single national entity. The central issue involved the role of Singapore in the new union. However, because the PAP represented Singapore, its place in the new federation was clouded by the partisan competition that developed between the Alliance and the PAP. Many reasons may be found for the progressive estrangement between Singapore's PAP Government and the central Malaysian Government. At stake were personal ambitions economic questions, communalism, political ideology and questions of federal power versus state autonomy. All these issues were interrelated and mutually reinforcing, tending to produce a "multiplier effect" upon normal conflicts within the political system.

In the early stages of the contest, the main irritant appeared to develop from the competition between the PAP and the MCA for the support of the Chinese electorate. The PAP focused their attacks upon Tan Siew-sin, MCA president, who was believed to be the moving force behind the Alliance decision to contest the 1963 Singapore elections.[44] In the Malayan elections the following year, it was the PAP that expanded its operations to Malaya to challenge the MCA for the moderate pro-Malaysia Chinese vote. It may be noted that in both the Singapore and the Malayan elections the political contest was limited. The PAP did not attack the Alliance as a whole, it avoided criticism of UMNO and it expressed support for Tunku Abdul Rahman while it waged the contest against the MCA candidates on the Alliance ticket. Federal ministers, including Prime Minister Tunku Abdul Rahman, gave their full support to the MCA as a constituent partner of the Alliance, but the PAP was not treated as an implacable foe.

That conflict is contagious is an axiom of politics, and the course of events after the 1964 Malayan elections amply demonstrate that axiom. During July and September communal passions in Singapore erupted into serious racial riots. These disorders were a by-product of the intense competition between the PAP and the Alliance. The PAP had defeated all UMNO candidates in the 1963 elections, partly as a result of promises to improve the housing and working conditions of the urban Malays. To meet these promises, it began a number of projects of slum clearance and low cost housing in the largest concentrations of Malay urban slums.

Meanwhile, the Alliance sent the Secretary-General of UMNO, Syed Ja'afar Albar, to Singapore to rebuild UMNO after its total defeat in the Singapore elections.[45] To regain Malay support, he began playing on the theme that the PAP was a "Chinese party" hostile to Malay interests. Through his efforts, a campaign was organized to demand Malay special rights and privileges in Singapore along the lines of those enjoyed by Malays across the causeway. When the PAP invited 114 Malay organizations to send representatives to meet with the PAP Minister of Social Affairs, Othman bin Wok (who was a Malay), to discuss programs to assist Singapore Malays, militant communalist UMNO agitators organized a mass protest rally of about 12,000 Malays and formed an "Action Committee" to press for Malay demands. Malays who cooperated with the PAP-sponsored Malay convention were branded as "traitors" by the "Action Committee".[46] Instead, Malays were exhorted to demand Malay special rights, Malay job quotas, Malay scholarship stipends, Malay land reservations, and exclusive Malay occupancy at special reduced rates in certain government-built housing projects.[47]

When Lee Kuan-yew met with representatives of some Malay organizations he told them that the PAP would not introduce Malay special rights or Malay quotas, but did promise to improve the condition of the Malays in Singapore through more jobs, better education opportunities and better housing (but not allocated on the basis of Malay quotas or exclusive Malay privileges). On the day of the PAP-sponsored Malay convention, two people were killed, but the worst rioting began two days later. An incident during a procession of Malays celebrating the Prophet Mohammed's birthday triggered off pitched battles between pro-Indonesian Malay extremist gangs and pro-Communist Chinese extremists. During the disorders 22 persons were killed, about 200 injured, and over 1,130 arrested.[48] Five weeks later, the same areas erupted in racial rioting once again, with 8 killed and about 60 injured.[49] The PAP blamed Syed Albar, Malay "ultras" in UMNO, pro-Indonesians, and the Malay paper *Utusan Melayu* for stirring up Malay communal passions. An "Action Committee" leaflet circulated in the streets the day before the July riots had warned that the Chinese were planning to kill Malays, and then proposed, "Before Malay blood flows in Singapore, it is best to flood the state with Chinese blood."[50] Since the "Action Committee" had many members who were known for their pro-Indonesian sympathies, Lee Kuan-yew suggested that the riots were planned beforehand, "probably with Indonesian cooperation".[51] The Malay press, however, blamed the PAP and its Singapore Work Brigade for starting the riots, while from Kuala Lumpur, the Alliance Government seemed to imply that the riots were jointly engineered by Communists and Indonesian agents seeking to wreck Malaysia.

While Indonesian agents and Communists may have tried to exploit the situation, they did not create the riots, but they may have played a part in triggering off the riots later in September.[52] A more immediate cause was the political contest being waged between Singapore's PAP Government and Malaysia's Alliance Government. At this stage it was impolitic for either side to accuse the other openly of complicity in the disorders. The English press avoided practically all mention of the causes of the rioting, thus cloaking the events in an air of mystery.

After each outbreak, the city was placed under strict curfew while government-sponsored "goodwill committees" tried to reduce communal tensions and restore peace. Even the peace efforts were colored by the Alliance-PAP competition, with the Alliance accusing the Singapore Government of forming "goodwill committees" from members drawn from only one party. Finally, Tunku Abdul Rahman intervened to appoint "peace committees" to replace the "goodwill committees" which had been formed on the initiative of the Singapore Government.[53] Far more was at stake than who represented the Malays of Singapore. Ultimately, both sides came to view the contest as a question of whether Singapore's or Malaya's approach to communal issues would become the pattern for all the states in Malaysia. Or, put more bluntly, who was the genuine non-communal leader—Tunku Abdul Rahman or Lee Kuan-yew?

Fearful of the consequences of escalated political conflict, the Alliance and the PAP agreed in late September to a two-year political truce "during which all sides will avoid sensitive issues" and keep party branches at the *status quo*.[54] Lee Kuan-yew hoped that the Tunku would restrain UMNO from capitalizing on Malay racial grievances in its bid to recoup its position in Singapore politics.[55] However, the terms of the truce were vague and did not deter the Alliance from pursuing its program of political reconstruction in Singapore nor prevent the PAP from continuing its operations in Malaya. Consequently, when Khir Johari announced that the Singapore Alliance was to be strengthened and reorganized in order to displace the PAP in the 1967 elections,[56] the political in-fighting broke out with renewed intensity.

This time, the primary protagonists were UMNO and the PAP. Khir Johari (Minister of Agriculture and Chairman of Singapore UMNO), Syed Ja'afar Albar (UMNO Secretary-General), and Senu bin Abdul Rahman (Minister of Information and Broadcasting) exchanged epithets with the PAP team of Prime Minister Lee Kuan-yew, Deputy Prime Minister Dr. Toh Chin-chye, Minister of Labour Jek Yeun-thong and Minister of Culture S. Rajaratnam. The UMNO spokesmen attacked the PAP for failure to support the Federal Government in time of foreign crisis and for failure to meet legitimate Malay demands in Singapore, while the PAP criticized UMNO for harboring and encouraging "ultras"—defined as Malay communal extremists who want a "Malay Malaysia" instead of "Malaysia in its present form".

A number of "bread and butter" issues between Singapore and the central government added new fuel to existing fires. The Federal Government and Singapore had yet to work out the details for the progressive implementation of the common market and for Singapore's promised loans for economic development in the Borneo states.[57] With rising unemployment and the slump in Singapore's entrepôt trade resulting from "confrontation", the PAP negotiators expected from the Alliance ministers a more lenient and understanding attitude toward Singapore's problems. However, "confrontation" had also necessitated a sharp increase in federal expenditure for defense and the Alliance Government expected Singapore to shoulder a larger share of the burden for this new expenditure. Under these circumstances implementation of financial arrangements for Malaysia became progressively more difficult as the positions of the two governments hardened.

Other economic issues widened the breach. To limit foreign competition and preserve its foreign exchange Britain severely reduced the quota on textiles imported from Malaysia. Singapore textile producers complained that the Federal Government had not protested with sufficient vigor and had failed to protect Singapore industry by applying retaliatory sanctions against British goods. On its own initiative the Singapore Government banned the import of some British goods and imposed a license import system for other products from Britain. After a full year of unpleasantness, this three-way dispute between Singapore, Britain and the Federal Government was finally resolved in May, 1965, with a compromise agreement.[58]

In November, 1964, Tan Siew-sin had revealed to Parliament the Government's new tax program designed to raise new revenues for the mounting costs of defense and development. Besides moving to equalize the income tax in all parts of Malaysia, the Federal Government imposed new duties and a series of new taxes on business and industry.[59] Although chambers of commerce throughout Malaysia were active in protesting the new legislation, the greatest resistance developed in Singapore because the tax changes appeared to shift the financial burden to Singapore since that island state had the largest concentration of business and industrial enterprise. Caught in this storm, the PAP Government was subjected to intense pressure from both left and right in Singapore to stand up to the Federal Government in its negotiations over financial arrangements.[60] Prime Minister Lee criticized the taxes and encouraged the mobilization of public opinion to "help bring changes in policy in the Central Government",[61] but avoided making a direct assault on the Federal Government for its new fiscal measures. Nonetheless, for the Alliance, the PAP appeared to be mobilizing mass support in Singapore and elsewhere to defeat or undermine the Federal Government's economic programs. Limited cooperation between the two governments gradually degenerated into intransigence and deadlock.

The Malaysian Solidarity Convention

In the eyes of the PAP, the Alliance Government was engaged in a prolonged struggle to dislodge the PAP from its power base in Singapore so as to bring Singapore under its political control, or, failing that, to neutralize effectively the political and economic impact of Singapore upon the rest of Malaysia. No Singapore minister had been brought into the Federal Cabinet and the PAP had never been included in the power structure of the Alliance Government. Instead, cooperation depended upon a process of semi-formalized negotiations between the governments. As the political contest between the PAP and the Alliance became escalated, negotiations between the governments tended to end in stalemate.

Two years later it was revealed that Britain's Prime Minister Sir Alec Douglas-Home had suggested to Tunku Abdul Rahman that a PAP-Alliance coalition government would be an appropriate way to "consolidate Malaysia after communal riots. . . ." Similar suggestions had come from the PAP earlier. Mr. Lee and the Tunku met on September 25, 1964, to discuss this question, but the Tunku rejected the proposal on the grounds that he could not secure UMNO approval for at least two years. Reporting on these talks, Lee Kuan-yew stated:

> I listed up my complaints about the dual-faced policy of UMNO.
> (A) The top leaders reaching reasonable agreement and political truce with us whilst the secondary leaders kept up a shriek of hate in

Utusan Melayu and Malayan Merdeka which circulate in the kampongs

I told him that any future agreement must be in writing and made known to all, including the secondary leaders, and this shriek in the Malay press must stop.

Otherwise any political accommodation is meaningless. . . .

The most significant remark he made was "we must decide whether you are going to work with us or fight us" [62]

Tun Abdul Razak, writing in an UMNO publication about these discussions, made the following assertion:

Lee Kuan Yew urged the Tengku and I to take the PAP into the Alliance Government.

It was said that only in this way communal harmony could be ensured. We rejected his request outright.[63]

As has so often happened in Malayan politics, a decision of monumental importance for the future of Malaya and Malaysia was made in utmost secrecy and apparently with very little debate or public evaluation of the alternatives. This decision represented a major turning point in Malaysian politics as later events have since revealed.

It was against this background that the PAP began its aggressive campaign to assert its political power by means of a fundamental political realignment on a pan-Malaysian basis. Changing his tactics, Lee Kuan-yew began openly criticizing the Federal Government and the Alliance for having come under the domination of "ultras" in UMNO who wanted to revert to a Malay-controlled Malaysia. Stressing that the Malays comprised only 39 per cent of the population of Malaysia, while the non-Malayas formed 61 per cent of the total population,[64] Lee promised to fight for a "Malaysian Malaysia" as opposed to the "Malay Malaysia" being imposed by the Federal Government. Although he carefully explained that he was not opposed to Malay special rights, Lee Kuan-yew left no doubt that he intended to mobilize political support throughout Malaysia to end what he claimed to be the monopoly of political power in the Federal Government. Once again the usual accusations of Malayan politics were exchanged. Each disputant accused the other of communalism while claiming to practice non-communalism. For the PAP, non-communalism was conceived to consist of equality for all regardless of race and national origin. For the Alliance, non-communalism meant communal harmony achieved through consensus and cooperation among the Alliance partners.

The PAP assault against the political power of the Malays shifted from verbal criticism to political action when PAP Deputy Prime Minister Dr. Toh Chin-chye announced the formation of a united opposition front.[65] Five parties, the People's Action Party, the Sarawak United People's Party, the United Democratic Party, the People's Progressive Party, and Machinda of Sarawak,[66] met in Singapore to form the "Malaysian Solidarity Convention" and jointly pledged "to build a Malaysian Malaysia". All these parties were known for their preponderant Chinese composition, and all but the PAP had been outspoken critics of Malaysia.

What had begun as a friendly test of strength between the Alliance and the PAP in the Singapore and Malayan elections, had, by mid-1965, become an undisguised effort to mobilize all non-Malays, with the promise of "equal rights for all" and the end of a "Malay Malaysia", in a bid to seize the reigns of government from the Alliance. When Lee Kuan-yew was criticized for harboring ambitions to become the Prime Minister of Malaysia, Rajaratnam proudly asserted that this, indeed, was the PAP objective.[67]

Political Realignment and Communal Tension

A mood of increased militancy was discernible among the more communal Malays who became alarmed by the possibility of a fundamental political realignment. Within UMNO they began to press harder for measures that would reinforce their position in government. For example, a number of top UMNO officials were successful in their demands that they be given a more important role on policy-making within the government. Likewise, some UMNO branches proposed constitutional amendments to provide for uniform administration throughout Malaysia—a move designed to eliminate administrative autonomy in troublesome states controlled by opposition parties.[68] Malay politicians stepped up their agitation for speedier implementation of the decision to make Malay the sole national language. The leading spokesman for this group even proposed that the government abandon English-medium instruction in primary schools.[69]

If Lee Kuan-yew's statements were correct, Malay papers, led by *Utusan Melayu*, helped to generate Malay communalism by articles based on the theme "that to be a co-owner of Malaysia, the people should be converted into Muslims and adjust their way of life similar to that of the Malays".[70] The implication was clear—those who failed to come up to these standards were not Malaysians and should therefore have no claim to political rights.

The communal debate on both sides was carried on via radio and television. Since the PAP Government administered radio and television broadcasting from Singapore, their programs gave emphasis to PAP pronouncements, while broadcasts from transmitters in Malaya publicized the statements made by the Alliance leaders. The public arguments developed into personal mud-slinging.[71] Some of the more alarmist elements in the Alliance began to moot the question of whether Lee Kuan-yew and other PAP leaders should be detained under the emergency powers of the Internal Security Act. Presumably Lee would have been charged with inciting racial strife. Tunku Abdul Rahman was criticized in Alliance circles for being too soft on the PAP. The PMIP lent its political weight to the alarmist Malays in UMNO to make the same indictment in a much less diplomatic way.[72]

When Parliament convened during the last week in May, the PAP and UMNO continued their churlish debate. Following the speech from the throne by the Yang di-Pertuan Agong, the Malaysian Solidarity Convention, led by the PAP, moved to censure the Federal Government for its failure to include in the speech a promise to progress toward a "Malaysian Malaysia".[73] In the debate which followed, Lee Kuan-yew accused the government of undermining the Constitution and of having unconstitutional intentions to end democracy if the Alliance should lose its public support. Speeches from the government benches denied the accusations and instead accused the PAP of playing a dangerous game of arousing communal passions in the pursuit of political ambition. Acrimonious and intemperate remarks were made from both sides of the floor.

At one point in the debates, Lee responded to suggestions that Singapore should get out of Malaysia by saying, ". . . we have not the slightest intention of secession".[74] Yet only a few days later he issued an ominous warning that if the government were to use unconstitutional methods to stop a "Malaysian Malaysia", then Singapore would consider "alternative constitutional arrangements". He went on to mention Sabah, Sarawak, Malacca and Penang as states which might get together with Singapore to form a "Malaysian Malaysia".[75] Lee's statements provide convincing evidence that he was confident a stable non-Malay majority could be formed to end Alliance rule. He seemed to believe that this eventuality could be prevented only by unconstitutional rule by force. As a political gambler, Lee seemed determined to force this new political realignment regardless of the effect on communal harmony, political stability or the prospects for democracy's survival. No doubt, the accumulated "grievances and wrongs" believed to have been committed against the PAP and its Singapore government were considered to constitute adequate reason for taking such risks.

[1] *Straits Times*, September 4, 1963, p. 1. The sudden postponement of the Malaysia date following the Manila Conference almost upset the sequence of events which were planned by the PAP Government. This may explain why Singapore declared *de facto* independence on August 31 and announced that it would temporarily exercise federal powers until it joined Malaysia. This caused strained relations with Kuala Lumpur and probably forced the Malaysia date to be hastened thus greatly antagonising Indonesia and compromising U Thant's Borneo inquiry. See above pp. 316–318.

[2] Over 100 anti-Malaysia party members, most of whom were associated with the Barisan Sosialis or the UPP, were detained by the action of the Internal Security Council in February, 1963, because of their alleged complicity with the abortive Brunei revolt. See above pp. 305–309.

[3] *Straits Times*, June 26, 1963, p. 11.

[4] Michael Leifer, "Politics in Singapore", *Journal of Commonwealth Political Studies*, Vol. 2, no. 2 (May, 1964), p. 116. This evaluation is based on the assumption that the Malaysia issue was the only question of concern to the voters. Such an assumption, of course, over-simplifies the nature of the contest, but is, nonetheless, of some value for purposes of analysis.

[5] *Straits Budget*, October 23, 1963, pp. 15–16.

[6] *Communism in the Nanyang University* (Kuala Lumpur: Government Press, 1964), pp. 5–21. *Straits Times*, September 27, 1963, pp. 1 and 20. The Singapore Government ordered the dissolution of five organizations because of Communist affiliations. *Straits Times*, October 4, 1963, pp. 1 and 20.

7 The arrested were accused of planning acts of violence against the government. *Straits Times*, October 9, 1963, pp. 1 and 19. Earlier the Singapore Government had frozen SATU bank accounts when it discovered that the funds were being used to finance Barisan's anti-Malaysia campaign during the Singapore elections. The Singapore Government charged that this campaign was Communist-directed.

8 *Straits Times*, March 3, 1964, pp. 1 and 20.

9 In the Muar parliamentary by-election of December, 1963, the Alliance defeated the PMIP by 17,104 votes to 2,497 votes. *Straits Times*, December 30, 1963, p. 13. There had been similar victories in previous by-elections at Port Swettenham and Kampar, and in the local council elections during June and July, 1963, the Alliance captured 411 out of 579 seats. See *Straits Times*, August 6, 1963, p. 16.

10 *Straits Times*, March 17, 1964, pp. 1 and 20.

11 *Straits Budget*, April 29, 1964, p. 14.

12 *Straits Times*, March 23, 1964, p. 5; April 10, 1964, p. 8.

13 *Straits Budget*, April 29, 1964, p. 9.

14 The Alliance claimed that the PMIP was "secretly trying to form an underground movement to overthrow the Government". Dr. Burhanuddin dismissed the charge as malicious, saying, "I am completely unaware of the secret movement. . . . Our struggle is to enable the Malay race to unite after gaining independence from the Dutch, British and the Americans." *Straits Times*, April 8, 1964, p. 18.

15 At its 1963 annual conference, the PPP condemned Indonesia, but it also criticized certain features of the Malaysia proposals, including the failure to provide for a referendum in the Borneo states. See *Sunday Times* (Singapore), March 10, 1963, p. 1.

16 *Straits Times*, March 16, 1964, p. 10; *Straits Budget*, April 15, 1964, p. 14; April 29, 1964, p. 8.

17 See *Straits Budget*, April 1, 1964, p. 16.

18 *Straits Budget*, November 6, 1963, p. 15.

19 *Straits Times*, March 2, 1964, pp. 1 and 4.

20 Two PAP candidates withdrew from the contest (although their names remained on the ballot) when they discovered that their Alliance opponent was an UMNO candidate.

21 *Straits Times*, March 25, 1964, pp. 1 and 11.

22 *Straits Times*, March 28, 1964, p. 9.

23 *Straits Times*, March 25, 1964, p. 11.

24 *Straits Times*, March 30, 1964, pp. 1 and 4.

25 *Straits Times*, April 13, 1964, p. 20.

26 For example, see *Straits Times*, March 31, 1964, p. 13; April 6, 1964, pp. 1 and 4; April 13, 1964, pp. 1 and 20.

27 *Straits Times*, April 8, 1964, p. 5.

28 In the two months before election day about a dozen bombs exploded in Singapore killing about ten people, boats were attacked in Malayan waters, and mysterious parachutes were found on jungle fringes. Several Indonesian arms caches were discovered and some lesser PMIP and Party Ra'ayat officials were arrested and charged with being accomplices in an Indonesian infiltration plot.

29 The post-election statement of Lim Kean-siew suggested a willingness to shift the party line on the Malaysian issue. He said, "The elections have shown that the people have accepted the Alliance policy of Malaysia. The Socialist Front as a democratic organisation accept the people's choice. . . . We take this opportunity to reiterate that we are loyal, and not pro-Soekarno. We will definitely co-operate with the Alliance Government on all matters of national interest and security." *Straits Budget*, May 6, 1964, p. 6.

30 Dr. Burhanuddin became ineligible for re-election because of his conviction for violation of the Companies Ordinance as a result of his activities as a director of the Malay-German Shipping Company. See *Straits Times*, February 20, 1964, p. 7.

31 As far as can be determined, Indonesian agents who organized espionage and conspiratorial "fifth column" groups were from the army or navy, and, in most cases, had played an active role in suppressing the PRRI rebellion in Sumatra and Sulawesi.

32 *Angkatan Pemuda Revolusione Malaysia* is the full name. It may be translated as Organization of Malaysian Revolutionary Youth.

33 Two earlier Malay extremist strong-arm groups were organized in Singapore about 1960. One was Hang Tuah (the name of a hero in Malay literature); the other was ARTIS (*Angkatan Revolusi Tentera Islam Singapure* or Singapore Islamic Revolutionary Armed Forces). Both were affiliated in some way with the PMU. The Indonesian Consulate-General in Singapore secretly gave money to ARTIS and probably also to Hang Tuah. In January, 1961, the Singapore Police uncovered an ARTIS plot to foment racial rioting against the Chinese. See *Straits Budget*, January 18, 1961, pp. 14–16; *Indonesian Intentions Towards Malaysia* (Kuala Lumpur: Government Press, 1964), pp. 10 and 17–18.

34 Ahmad Boestamam had arranged with the KMM to send four of his Party Ra'ayat members for underground training in Indonesia. This arrangement was discovered by Malayan authorities who arrested him in February, 1963. See above, p. 309.

35 *Indonesian Intentions Towards Malaysia, op. cit.*, pp. 32–34.

36 Boestamam was still in prison in Malaya.

37 *Straits Budget*, May 6, 1964, p. 8.

38 In the case of the Labour Party, the money went to the Malay titular head of the party, Ishak bin Haji Mohammed, probably to insure that only radical Malay candidates on the SF ticket would be aided. It is doubtful whether this financial assistance altered the election results in any significant way. *A Plot Exposed*, Cmd. 12 of 1965, Federation of Malaysia, pp. 4–5.

39 *A Plot Exposed, op. cit.*

40 An Indonesian intelligence officer, R. M. Soenita, recruited Hussain Yaacob to head the organization. The latter was a Patani Malay who was a reporter for the Malay paper *Utusan Melayu*. Another key individual in the organization was Dato Raja Abu Hanifah, Vice-President of the PMIP. *Ibid.*, pp. 1–3.

41 *Straits Times*, January 28, 1965, pp. 1 and 4; January 30, 1965, pp. 1 and 24.

42 *Straits Times*, February 15, 1965, pp. 1 and 16. Following these disorders, Dr. Lim Chong-eu made a slashing attack on the Socialist Front, blaming it for the riots and, in effect, promising the support of the United Democratic Party for Malaysia and the central government. See *Straits Times*, February 17, 1965, p. 7.

43 In defense of the government, it should be noted that, despite the evidence of widespread conspiracy, no political party was declared illegal. Rather, action was taken only against individuals based on their own activities.

44 Federal Minister of Finance Tan Siew-sin had been the primary protagonist against the PAP in the protracted and bitter negotiations between the Singapore and Malayan Governments over financial arrangements for Malaysia. Singapore's Finance Minister, Dr. Goh Keng-swee is a cousin of Tan Siew-sin, and family rivalries antedating Malaysia made agreement and cooperation even more difficult to achieve.

45 In the 1959 elections UMNO had won three seats from predominantly Malay constituencies. For a good account of the problems facing the Malay community in Singapore see Willard A. Hanna, "The Malays' Singapore" (Part I–V) *American Universities Field Staff*, Vol. 14, nos. 2–6 (1966).

46 The Singapore Malay National Action Committee consisted of 23 members from UMNO, the PMIP and the Peninsular Malays Union. One member of the committee had earlier been identified by the Federal Government as a paid agent of Indonesia. See Willard A. Hanna, "The Separation of Singapore from Malaysia", *American Universities Field Staff*, Vol. 13, no. 21 (1965), p. 13.

47 *Ibid.*, pp. 12–14; Michael Leifer, "Singapore in Malaysia: The Politics of Federation", *Journal of Southeast Asian History*, Vol. 6, no. 2 (September, 1965), pp. 63–65.

48 *Straits Budget*, July 29, 1964, pp. 9 and 17.

49 *Straits Budget*, September 9, 1964, pp. 17 and 20.

50 Michael Leifer, "Singapore in Malaysia", *op. cit.*, p. 65.

51 *New York Times*, July 22, 1964, p. 3.

52 The September riots erupted when a Chinese trishaw rider was murdered in a Malay section of town. There is some evidence that Indonesian agents paid local gangsters to commit the crime in the expectation that additional Sino-Malay riots would occur. See Hanna, *op. cit.*, p. 13. Chinese troublemakers agitated over the July arrests at Nanyang University took a lead in some of the rioting, partly to undermine the authority of both the Federal Government and the Singapore Government.

53 *Straits Budget*, September 30, 1964, pp. 8–9.

54 *Straits Budget*, November 4, 1964, pp. 13, 17 and 19. Tunku Abdul Rahman later explained that the truce only applied to "communal issues". *Straits Times*, October 29, 1964, pp. 1 and 20.

55 Lee Kuan-yew continually seemed to be offering Tunku Abdul Rahman his unsolicited advice and assistance, thus tending to undermine cooperation which otherwise might have been possible. The following statement is but one example: "Singapore has seen Chinese extremists and chauvinists, and we have been able to put them down. . . . Now that the Tengku has returned, we will help him to handle the extremists and chauvinists in Malaya." *Straits Budget*, August 19, 1964, p. 18.

56 *Straits Times*, October 26, 1964, pp. 1 and 24.

57 See Osborne, *op. cit.*, pp. 50–61.

58 See *Straits Budget*, September 2, 1964, pp. 3 and 19; *Straits Times*, May 18, 1965, pp. 1 and 18; May 19, 1965, p. 8.

59 The new taxes included: a business and professional turnover tax of $\frac{1}{2}$ per cent on gross earnings; a 2 per cent tax on the total payroll of trades and businesses; a capital gains tax of from 5 per cent to 20 per cent on assets held for less than ten years; and a special profits tax on tin mining. *Straits Times*, November 26, 1964, pp. 1 and 22.

60 Since Malaysia had been sold to Singapore largely on the basis of its economic benefits, the Barisan Sosialis now claimed that their view of Malaysia had been correct all along—namely that Singapore would suffer economic losses and political domination at the hands of a hostile government in Kuala Lumpur.

61 *Straits Times*, December 14, 1964, p. 24.

62 *Straits Times*, July 29, 1966, p. 20.

63 *Straits Times*, July 28, 1966, p. 20.

64 *Straits Times*, February 18, 1965, p. 9.

65 *Straits Times*, April 28, 1965, pp. 1 and 20.

66 *Straits Times*, May 10, 1965, pp. 1 and 20. Machinda was formed in 1964 as a splinter off of Party Negara Sarawak (PANAS) when the latter did not live up to its earlier claims of being pan-communal. Although Machinda is a composite word for "Malay, Chinese, Indian, and Dayak", it was founded by a Chinese and remained almost completely a Chinese party. The Socialist Front's absence from the convention was due to the opposition of Party Ra'ayat in the SF, as well as the lingering animosities which had resulted from the PAP challenge to the SF in Penang during the 1964 elections.

67 *Straits Times*, June 9, 1965, p. 7.

68 *Straits Budget*, September 9, 1964, p. 16; *Straits Times*, May 14, 1965, pp. 1 and 22.

69 The proposal was made by Syed Nasir bin Ismail who was the director of the Dewan Bahasa dan Pustaka (Language and Literature Agency). See *Straits Times*, June 15, 1965, p. 11.

70 *Straits Times*, June 14, 1965, pp. 1 and 6.

71 Lee Kuan-yew sued UMNO Secretary-General Syed Ja'afar Albar and the editor of *Utusan Melayu* for statements they were alleged to have made accusing Lee of being an "agent of Indonesia" and "an agent of the Communists". *Straits Times*, April 28, 1965, p. 1.

72 Note *Straits Times*, May 17, 1965, p. 5.

73 The censure motion expressed "regrets that the Address by His Majesty did not reassure the nation that Malaysia will continue to progress in accord with its democratic constitution to a Malaysian Malaysia; on the contrary, the Address had added to the doubts over the intentions of the present Alliance Government and to the measures it will adopt when faced with a loss of majority popular support." *Straits Times*, May 28, 1965, p. 6.

74 *Ibid.*

75 *Straits Times*, June 1, 1965, pp. 1 and 22.

19 Political Realignment: Partition and Peace

While Tunku Abdul Rahman was in London to attend the June 1965 meeting of the Commonwealth Prime Ministers Conference, he became ill and had to remain in hospital for about a month. During the period of enforced inactivity he devoted his time to a consideration of the implications of the political hostility and deadlock that had developed between the PAP and the Alliance. He later explained to Parliament the alternatives as he saw them:

> I gave it plenty of thought while lying in bed in London and also when convalescing before my return to this country.
>
> I conveyed my thoughts to my friend and colleague, Tun Abdul Razak, who had sought to find an understanding with the leaders of Singapore, but, I am afraid, to no avail.
>
> It appeared that as soon as one issue was resolved another cropped up. Where a patch was made here, a tear appeared elsewhere, and where one hole was plugged, other leaks appeared.
>
> So it does seem completely impossible to arrive at a solution whereby we can hope to pull along together and to work together in the interest and common good of Malaysia.
>
> We tried everything possible to avoid the separation of Singapore from the rest of Malaysia. In the end we found that there were only two courses of action open to us.
>
> No. 1 was to take repressive measures against the Singapore Government for the behaviour of some of its leaders;
>
> No. 2 was to sever all connections with a State Government that had ceased to give even a measure of loyalty to the Central Governement. . .
>
> It was clear some action had to be taken. It is odious for us to take repressive measures against the Singapore Government, for such action is repulsive to our concept of parliamentary democracy.
>
> Even then it would not have solved the problem before us because, as I said just now, there is not one problem but many, and one that gave us the most concern was the communal issue.
>
> This is the matter which concerns me most, because the peace and happiness of the people in this country depend on goodwill and understanding of the various races for one another.
>
> Without it this nation will break up, with consequential disaster which we have seen and read about happening elsewhere.
>
> We feel that this repressive action against a few would not therefore

solve the problem because the seed of this contempt, fear and hatred has been sown in Singapore, and even if we try to prevent its growth, I feel that after a time it will sprout up in a more virulent form. . . .

Things are getting worse every day. Irresponsible utterances are made by both sides which, reading between the lines, is tantamount to challenge, and if trouble were to break out innocent people will be sacrificed at the altar of belligerent, heartless and irresponsible troublemakers of this country.

So I believe that the second course of action which we are taking—the breakaway—is the best and the right one, sad as it may be.

We had pledged to form Malaysia with Singapore, but having given it a trial we found that if we persisted in going on with it, in the long run, there would be more trouble to Malaysia than Singapore is worth to us.[1]

The decision to expel Singapore from Malaysia was made by the Prime Minister on July 25, while he was still convalescing in London. The PAP leaders were informed and, to avoid unrest, both parties agreed to strict secrecy while the separation agreement and the constitutional amendment was being prepared for parliamentary approval. After the Tunku returned to Malaya a final attempt at reconciliation was made, but to no avail. For two weeks only a few selected PAP and Alliance ministers were aware of the decision to separate Singapore. The Alliance Members of Parliament were not told until half an hour before the parliamentary sessions began.[2] At 10 a.m. on August 9, 1965, the Dewan Ra'ayat (House of Representatives) was called to order. At the same hour simultaneous announcements were made from Singapore and Kuala Lumpur to the press and over the radio that Singapore was seceding from the Federation. Two hours later the Constitutional Amendment Bill was approved unanimously in the Dewan Ra'ayat by a vote of 126 to nothing. Later the same day, the Dewan Negara (Senate) unanimously passed the amendment after about two hours of debates.[3]

During the parliamentary debates, the United Democratic Party, the Sarawak United People's Party and the People's Progressive Party made quite similar comments, warning that there would probably be increased repression for those who continued to support the "Malayasian Malaysia" concept. They also criticized the Alliance Government for secrecy and haste, which made Parliament a "rubber stamp", and blamed it for failing to solve communal problems. While not opposing the amendment, they called for new general elections and a plebiscite on the "new Malaysia".

The Pan-Malayan Islamic Party accused the Alliance of following the same basic concept of a "Malaysian Malaysia" as was being expounded by the PAP. It demanded that the Alliance Government and UMNO change its policies to place the interests of the indigenous people first. Reminding the Alliance that the PMIP had opposed the formation of Malaysia with Singapore, it expressed the hope that Indonesia's "confrontation" would cease and that the Maphilindo concept would be revived. One PMIP speaker complained of the money being spent on Sarawak, and addressing the

Sarawak MPs, said, "If you have any intention of leaving Malaysia, too, you can do it now."[4]

By prior agreement the PAP members from Singapore were absent from Parliament. However, Devan Nair, the sole PAP member elected from Malaya, spoke for his party, saying:

> . . . Singapore has been put in a situation where it has no choice but to accept the ultimatum presented to it by the Central Government.
>
> I know Singapore does not want to leave Malaysia because the present Singapore Government leaders believe in the unity of Singapore and Malaya.
>
> This has been the basic belief of the PAP leaders from the time the party was founded. It still is and I think it will always be their belief.
>
> It is a belief in a Malaysian Malaysia, a multi-racial, non-communal and tolerant Malaysia.
>
> Singapore was ejected because it has refused to postulate unity on the basis of a communal Malaysia. There was no other reason.
>
> In this, the Alliance extremists, the opponents of a Malaysian Malaysia, are greviously wrong and this they will discover soon. . . .
>
> I do not believe for one moment that the ejection of Singapore will bring peace and harmony.
>
> On the contrary, I forsee mutual disaster for both Singapore and Malaysia which can benefit others who may bring about a reunification of a kind which most of us who believe in a free society may find hard to accept.[5]

Nearly all the key figures in the drama viewed the break as a painful expedient which was temporarily necessary for political stability and domestic tranquillity. Many of them expressed their belief and hope that renunification would be achieved at some indeterminate date in the future. This view was expressed in the letter which Tunku Abdul Rahman received from the PAP in response to his proposal for Singapore's separation from Malaysia. On behalf of the PAP Government, Dr. Toh wrote as follows:

> It has come as a blow to us that the peace and security of Malaysia can only be served by the expulsion of Singapore from Malaysia.
>
> If this is the price for peace in Malaya and Singapore, then we must accept it, however agonising our inner feelings may be.
>
> Although lasting unification of Singapore and Malaya has not been achieved this time, nevertheless it is my profound belief that future generations will succeed where we have failed.[6]

After Partition

Singapore's separation from Malaysia was designed to end the escalating political troubles between the two governments, reduce tensions and thereby promote political stability in both states. At best, it was a "time-buying" tactic which postponed difficult issues for a few years in the hope that political adjustments would be easier at a later date. Yet, the realities of politics in Malaysia and Singapore made it difficult to terminate the contest merely by making Singapore an independent state and issuing pious pronouncements about non-intervention in the domestic affairs of "foreign" states. Subsequent events demonstrated that political competition continued (albeit in a milder form) and that the political situation in each state was greatly influenced by events in the other. Several post-partition developments may be cited in illustration.

With Singapore's independence, the Malaysian Government sought to prevent Singapore parties from operating in Malaysia. The Malaysian Registrar of Societies ruled that the PAP was illegal in Malaysia since it had become a "foreign" party.[7] Mr. C. V. Devan Nair, the PAP Member of Parliament representing the Bungsar constituency in Selangor, responded by forming a "new" party—the Democratic Action Party, which, while legally independent of the PAP, was admittedly designed to be its Malaysian equivalent.[8] Similarly, in Singapore, both the MCA and UMNO formally renounced any ties with their Malaysian parent organizations. Yet, legal fictions contained in party constitutions could not obscure the fact that political loyalties and party systems extended in both directions across the causeway.

In a similar vein, public criticism and verbal attacks were not limited by international boundaries. The leaders of both Singapore and Malaysia engaged in an extended post-mortem on the former union with both sides trying to pin the blame for its failure on the other. Lee Kuan-yew, in explaining the PAP *demarche* over Malaysia, made numerous critical and disparaging remarks about the Malaysian Government and its policies. His comments elicited a formal diplomatic protest from Malaysia charging the Prime Minister of Singapore with making "mischievous and uncalled for remarks, which will inevitably lead to the creation of distrust, disharmony and even conflict among the people" and calling upon Singapore to "cease forthwith . . . interference in the domestic affairs of Malaysia".[9] Singapore's reply, while promising not to incite racial feelings, in turn accused Ministers of the Malaysian Government of making statements and publishing articles which were highly inflammatory and likely to lead to racial and religious conflicts in Singapore. It concluded, "friendly relations can only be established if responsibilities and courtesies are reciprocal . . ."[10] However, these diplomatic notes did not halt the fairly steady barrage of epithets being hurled from both ends of the causeway.[11]

In the short run, Singapore's departure from Malaysia probably did contribute to greater political stability in both states. However, such political surgery also created a host of new problems. Almost immediately, both Singapore and Malaysia began erecting economic barriers in the form of tariffs, financial controls, licenses, immigration restrictions and work permits for "aliens". For Singapore, abandonment of the Common Market meant a much greater threat to its economic position since it could no longer be assured of free access to a pan-Malaysian market for its trade and industry. If Singapore was to meet its serious unemployment problem resulting from a rapidly expanding population, its economic growth had to be substantial. Indonesia's "confrontation" with its economic boycott of Malaysia was already having detrimental effects upon Singapore's economy before the split. With independence, Singapore's economic isolation became even more severe and the economic prospects looked more bleak. Because of the economic pinch on both sides of the causeway, in September Singapore and Malaysia agreed to lift the quota trade restrictions which had virtually halted trade between the two states in a wide variety of restricted items.[12] This agreement helped to restore closer economic ties between them and was hailed in some quarters as a step toward the creation of a new Common Market. Nonetheless, Singapore and Malaysia continued to engage in what promised to be a long drawn out competition for industry, foreign investments and markets. Prime Minister Lee Kuan-yew frankly admitted the severity of the economic challenge. "This is a lesson in survival. Take a deep breath . . . We have really got to pull ourselves up by the bootstraps," he said in a speech explaining his government's belt-tightening policies.[13]

To overcome its political and economic isolation, Singapore embarked upon an independent course in international affairs. During the first weeks after the separation, Singapore seemed to have high hopes that it could restore relations with Indonesia and regain its former trade with that nation. Although Indonesia's Foreign Minister Dr. Subandrio expressed delight that Singapore had split off from Malaysia, Indonesia did not respond to the overtures for a *rapprochement*. Instead, the trade boycott continued, and Indonesian-supported terrorists persisted in their activities designed to overthrow the Singapore Government.[14] By the end of the year the Singapore Government attempted to circumvent the economic boycott by constructing facilities for a "barter trade center" on a small island twelve miles south of Singapore in the hope that some unofficial trade could be established with Indonesian merchants (or smugglers) from nearby islands.

In its diplomatic realignment, the PAP Government attempted to develop friendly ties with Communist China, the Soviet Union and other states which never recognized Malaysia. However, Singapore moved cautiously in this direction because it realized the necessity of retaining good relations with Malaysia, Britain and the Commonwealth countries. Although the Singapore Government was eager to assert its independence, it did not want the British to abandon their military and naval bases on the island. Lee Kuan-yew recognized that British forces provided security against the potentially aggressive designs of Indonesia Furthermore, the military bases provided thousands of jobs for local citizens and contributed about £63 million annually to the economy of Singapore.[15] Shortly after independence, Singapore negotiated treaties with Britain and Malaysia providing for British retention of the Singapore bases, and for cooperation in the joint defense of Malaysia and Singapore. One part of the agreement provided for a Singapore regiment to be sent to Borneo to assist in the defense against Indonesian attacks.[16]

In its foreign relations Singapore was caught on the horns of a dilemma. On the one hand it needed British assistance and Malaysia's good will. On the other, it hoped to find new markets and new friends among Communist and militantly anti-western Asian states. It is against the background of this dilemma that Lee Kuan-yew's slashing attacks on the United States and his revelations about the improper activities of American CIA agents must be viewed.[17] By making the United States a "whipping boy", Lee could demonstrate Singapore's independence and become more acceptable in the eyes of the Communist world and the non-aligned Afro-Asian states. At the same time, such an attack did not complicate relations with Britain or Malaysia.

Malaysia Without Singapore

The exclusion of Singapore from Malaysia had not been without cost to Malaysia. Singapore had been the hub of the Malaysian economic and transportation system. Singapore was now free to pursue economic and diplomatic policies detrimental to Malaysia. Malaysia no longer collected the large revenues from Singapore's economy, and Singapore's promised financial assistance to Borneo for economic development now had to be obtained from other sources if the programs were not to be abandoned. Since the Borneo states had entered Malaysia on the promise of economic development, any substantial re-allocation of public funds threatened to raise many new political issues among the states remaining in Malaysia. Thus, while Singapore's withdrawal from Malaysia was designed to preserve the political balance within both Malaya and Singapore, it tended to change the political balance within Malaysia as a whole, and to aggravate political disputes over the distribution of the more limited public resources.

In the smaller Malaysia, Malaya now exercised unchallenged economic and political power. Quite naturally, an atmosphere of concern and anxiety characterized the mood of public opinion in Sabah and Sarawak. Not only was there resentment over the failure of Tunku Abdul Rahman to consult with any Borneo leader concerning Singapore's expulsion, but the move jeopardized the economic development programs in the Borneo states and raised the possibility of increasing domination from Kuala Lumpur. Clearly, the Borneo states were no longer so important in the political balance of Malaysia. The more astute political leaders were quick to realize the significance of the changed environment. Generally, the Chinese in Borneo disapproved of the partition; the Malays supported the move; the non-Muslim interior natives were anxious and concerned about their more vulnerable political position.

Shortly after the break with Singapore, Prime Minister Tunku Abdul Rahman announced that he and Deputy Prime Minister Abdul Razak would undertake visits to Sabah and Sarawak "to explain the circumstances leading to Singapore's separation from Malaysia".[18] It was no secret that some effort had to be made to assuage the feelings of the dominant political groups in the Borneo states. Official quarters became apprehensive over the possibility that Singapore's departure from Malaysia might spark new secessionist moves in Borneo, perhaps even within the political family of the Sabah and Sarawak Alliance. However, after a short period of hesitation and uncertainty, the Chief Ministers of Sabah and Sarawak announced their full support for the Central Government and pledged to remain within Malaysia.[19] On the surface, relative political calm was maintained. But behind-the-scenes, there was evidence of intense political activity as various factions reappraised the implications of the partition.[20]

Meanwhile, in Malaya the political scene resumed many of the characteristics of the pre-Malaysian period. Yet, a return to the *status quo ante* was impossible because of the after effects of the struggle with Singapore and the continuing necessity of including the Borneo states in the calculus of power. Consequently, Malayan politics after partition still had a Peoples Action Party (now renamed Democratic Action Party) and a Malaysian Solidarity Convention to voice the equalitarian demands and special interests of the more aggressive non-Malay communal interests. But these were essentially the same elements which had earlier participated in non-Malay protest movements and who had failed in their attempts to dislodge the Alliance coalition from power. Thus, the new party and an opposition action front did not substantially alter the political balance from that in the pre-Malaysian period, even if it did bring experienced and vigorous leadership into the ranks of the opposition. The non-Malay opposition leaders could hardly be sanguine about their chances for political success in the new environment. Their opportunity had been foreclosed by the political amputation of Singapore. A new sense of frustration and despair increased the temptation of some of them to engage in irresponsible attacks on the government, since they knew full well that they would not be put to the test of performance in office.

The political system of Malaysia in its pruned form thus reinforced the one-party dominance of the Alliance. Consequently, the significant political process was once again internalized within the Alliance structure. Constituent factions within the Alliance system were once again more willing to pursue their rival claims since the outside challengers had been reduced to relative impotence by the partition. It is more than mere coincidence that MCA branches began to press for "a more liberal policy" toward Chinese education and the measures to implement Malay as the national language, while communally militant UMNO branches made moves to have more strict citizenship laws and increase the tempo of conversion to Malay as the sole official language.[21] As usual, the more militant participants in the intra-Alliance contest raised problems of party discipline, when, in their zeal, they made their demands public and attempted open mobilization of support for their positions. Once again, the Tunku performed the role of compromiser between the communalist wings of the Alliance, although not without some comments (which he later retracted) that disgruntled elements in UMNO were plotting his downfall.[22]

Indonesian Realignment

Malaysia's political adjustment to Singapore's expulsion from the union had only just begun when the larger political scene in Southeast Asia suddenly began to change. Indonesia became locked in a deadly internal power struggle which consumed her energies for some time and resulted in a political upheaval which had profound repercussions throughout Southeast Asia. We must briefly review these events to show how they affected the prospect for peace between Indonesia and Malaysia.

During the latter part of 1965 the Indonesian political system had reached a state of impasse and near paralysis. The country suffered from economic stagnation, galloping inflation, mounting political frustration, and a receptiveness to the strident revolutionary doctrines being propagated by Peking to guide Communists abroad. All these problems, and many more, combined with Sukarno's uncertain health, intensified the internal political contest between Indonesia's Communist Party and its Army. Each side began making preparations for an ultimate showdown. Rumors about plots and counter-plots, designed to eliminate rivals or capture the government, provided one indicator of this escalating behind-the-scenes contest. Intrigue and conspiracy were not new to Indonesian politics. Yet, this time the stakes were higher and the participants were thus willing to be more ruthless than before.

Fragmentary evidence suggests that an anti-Army cabal was formed, determined to find a way to break the political deadlock and bring about a significant shift to the left in Indonesian politics.[23] Involved in the conspiracy were Foreign Minister Subandrio, Air Vice Marshall Omar Dhani, Central Banking Minister Jusuf Muda Dalam and a few military officers who chaffed under the Army's command system. In retrospect, the most important figure in the cabal was D. N. Aidit, the leader of *Partai Kommunis Indonesia*, and a member of Sukarno's cabinet. Each of the principal figures in the plot committed, in a rather limited and uncoordinated way, the resources of the organizations they headed. Thus the Air Force provided some weapons and training for Communists in the PKI's para-military youth organization, *Pemuda Rakyat*. Some dissident military commanders were willing to commit a battalion or two of their troops for the showdown with the Army High Command. Present evidence indicates that Sukarno was partly aware of these developments, and gave his tacit approval, if only by his silence and inaction. If the plotters succeeded in their goals, Sukarno could claim credit and retain leadership under conditions more to his liking; if they failed, he could deny complicity in the plot to ensure his political survival.

On the night of September 30, 1965 six of the highest ranking generals in the Indonesian Army were murdered by armed units of *Pemuda Rakyat*. However, Defense Minister Nasution escaped from the assassins and was able to make his way to Army Headquarters in Djakarta to help organize the Army's counter atatck. The following day troops loyal to the Army command, led by General Suharto, quickly dispersed the forces of *Pemuda Rakyat* and those units of Sukarno's palace guard who acted for the plotters in their attempt to seize the city and neutralize the political power of the Army leaders. Some twelve hours after the coup was crushed by the Army, the official PKI newspaper *Harian Rakyat* appeared on the streets with an endorsement of the "September 30th Movement".

While the PKI had not been fully mobilized for the crisis, nor were its entire resources committed to support the coup, the Army quickly identified its principal protagonist as the moving force behind the treacherous attack and accused the Communists of attempting to overthrow Sukarno's government. To justify its massive campaign against Indonesian Communists, the Army capitalized on the public outrage over the brutal assassinations of the six Army generals. A mounting wave of violence and terror spread across Indonesia as the Army methodically pursued Communist leaders and their supporters. D. N. Aidit was captured in November 21 near Solo in Central Java and was killed the following day. Local military commanders used the crisis an as occasion to settle old political grievances with the Communists, and either executed thousands who were believed to be supporters of the PKI, or incited anti-Communist militant orthodox Muslim youths to massacre thousands of confused and innocent peasant supporters of the Communist Party. The orgy of mass killings and communal violence lasted from mid-November to mid-January.[24] By all accounts the slaughter was excessive, and while the total will probably never be known, the figure certainly exceeded 100,000 and may have been as high as 900,000.

The abortive "September 30th Movement" left Sukarno in an exposed position, being implicated in the plot, yet having to accommodate himself to the preponderant power of the Army. Since the anti-Communist purge was justified as punishment for what was alleged to be a revolutionary attempt to overthrow the legitimate government of Sukarno, Army commanders were hesitant to seize full control. At least for a time, the Army needed Sukarno's prestige as a nationalist hero and "Father of Indonesia" to legitimize its rule. Consequently, Indonesian politics were characterized by an extended test of strength and will between the Army and Sukarno. By February 1966, Sukarno succeeded in having General Nasution removed as Minister of Defense.[25] Yet, for Sukarno, this was a Pyrrhic victory, since Nasution's successor, General Suharto, was a more astute politician and soon forced Sukarno to accede to Army demands. After a series of anti-Sukarno student riots in Jakarta, Suharto presented to Sukarno what was, in effect, an ultimatum: if a suitable cabinet was not formed, the Army would not assume responsibility for any violence which might follow. On March 27, Sukarno, having little choice in the matter, finally consented to appoint a new cabinet under the leadership of General Suharto.[26] While Sukarno was not removed from the picture, the new cabinet reflected the supremacy of the Army, anti-Communist moderates, and westernized intellectuals.

Determined to set Indonesia on a new course the new regime pursued more pragmatic policies than had been characteristic during Sukarno's heyday. With the Communists out of the picture, "confrontation" became anachronistic. No longer was it necessary to hunt for "national solidarity" issues. Besides, "confrontation" had contributed in large measure to Indonesia's economic bankruptcy. At the time of the formation of the new cabinet General Suharto expressed a desire to reach a negotiated peace settlement with Malaysia.[27] By April, Indonesia's new Foreign Minister, Adam Malik, proposed peace negotiations with Singapore, but, sensitive of Malaysian fears and opinion, Lee Kuan-yew indicated that no agreement would be possible which might prejudice the interests or security of Malaysia. The issue with Malaysia had to be resolved first.

After a flurry of behind-the-scenes diplomatic activity, the Indonesian Government finally issued a statement on May 15 expressing the hope for a peace settlement with Malaysia on the basis of the Manila Agreements of 1963.[28] This overture was welcomed by Tunku Abdul Rahman, and official contacts were soon established to make arrangements for formal negotiations. Ironically, a preliminary Indonesian military mission from the "Crush Malaysia Command" (Kogam) arrived in Kuala Lumpur on May 27 and reportedly engaged in very amicable talks with Malaysian officials. Two days later formal negotiations opened in Bangkok between the two Foreign Ministers, Abdul Razak and Adam Malik. Terms for settling the dispute were agreed to on June 1, but they were not made public pending the approval of the two governments.[29]

While both sides indicated that "confrontation" was over and that outstanding issues would be settled by negotiation, the ratification of the Bangkok Agreement was delayed for several months. The secrecy over terms and the delay over ratification were caused by Sukarno's attitudes and his anomalous political position. It was no secret that Sukarno did not approve of the peace overtures,[30] and wished to continue "confrontation". While he no longer had a free hand to determine Indonesia's foreign policy, if he was to remain in the office of President, even if only in a titular role, he represented an obstacle which had to be overcome. The terms of the Bangkok Agreement were not made public because of the difficulty in securing Sukarno's approval, and because the new leadership desired not to antagonize him unnecessarily by exposing the titular position which the new government was trying to force upon him. For over two months, Sukarno engaged in a rear-guard action against the policies of the Army-dominated cabinet. To bring Sukarno into line, Indonesia's Provisional People's Consultative. Congress was convened in June under the Chairmanship of General Nasutium and on July 5, Sukarno was stripped of his title: "President for Life". While Sukarno retained his position as president, his power to issue decrees was revoked, and General Suharto was given full authority to form a new cabinet.[31] The Congress also passed a resolution in favor of resolving the dispute with Malaysia on the basis of the 1963 Manila Agreement. When Sukarno later announced that Confrontation was not over and that "We are opposed to Malaysia because it is a neo-colonialist project",[32] Suharto hastened to explain that those were the personal opinions of Sukarno and not those of the ruling Presidium. Finally, without Sukarno's approval, the Bangkok Agreement was ratified in Jakarta on August 11, 1966 by Abdul Razak and Adam Malik.

The Indonesian-Malaysia treaty of peace contained three provisions. First, Malaysia promised "to afford the people of Sabah and Sarawak. . . an opportunity to reaffirm, as soon as practicable, in a free and democratic manner through general elections, their previous decision about their status in Malaysia". Secondly, "diplomatic relations between the two countries shall be established immediately . . ." Thirdly, "hostile acts between the two countries shall cease forthwith"[33]. It may be noted that no referendum was promised for the Borneo states. Instead, the Indonesians were willing to accept a promise to hold general elections according to the normal processes of Malaysia's existing laws. While the preamble of the treaty mentions the "spirit of the Manila Agreement" it left in doubt the exact status of that document.

Following the ratification of the peace treaty, Indonesia and Malaysia formed a joint committee to deal with common problems of defense and security.[34] A series of agreements covering such issues as trade, exchange controls, diplomatic relations, communications and border security were made over the following weeks. Of particular concern to the Malaysian Government was the problem posed by the continued existence of guerrilla units in Sabah and Sarawak. The Indonesians agreed to cooperate to secure the surrender of "incursionists", but this had a limited effect since both the Communists of Sarawak and Azahari's *Tentera Nasional Kalimantan Utara* (TNKU) organization appeared determined to continue their guerrilla activities, even though Indonesian support was no longer forthcoming.[35]

Political Consequences of Indonesian-Malaysian Peace

Ever since the Army victory over the Indonesian Communist Party, Communists in Malaysia and Singapore had realized that their hopes for victory had been dashed and that they were in a more exposed political position. Indonesia's new leaders no longer assisted Malaysian or Singapore Communists and denied to them the use of Indonesian soil as a safe haven or a base for their operations. Instead, the Indonesian Army arrested the top officers of the Malayan National Liberation League, which had operated out of Djakarta.[36] From Peking efforts were made to breathe new life into the Malayan National Liberation League. The activities of a delegation of representatives of the MNLL to Peking were given prominent space in news reports from China. After it became apparent that the MNLL organization in Indonesia had been thoroughly decimated, the leader of the visiting delegation to Peking, P. V. Sarma, was elevated to the leadership of the revived MNLL.[37] Whether this reconstituted MNLL would operate out of Peking as a "paper front" or attempt to reestablish a base for active operations against Malaysia was unclear. In either case, the effectiveness of the new organization was likely to be minimal, particularly after Malaysia and Indonesia settled their dispute, since the two governments agreed to cooperate in their fight to eliminate Communism from their respective areas.

It was hardly coincidental that on the eve of the signing of the Indonesian-Malaysian Peace Pact, Communist guerrillas on the Thai border ambushed a joint Malaysian-Thai military patrol.[38] This was the first major guerrilla incident in more than seven years. Chin Peng probably decided to step up Communist guerrilla activities to bolster sagging morale by demonstrating to Communists in Malaysia and Singapore that the guerrilla arm of their party still had some life. Although the Communists still commanded substantial strength in Singapore and Sarawak, in both places their strength was being sapped and their activities severely curtailed by effective government counter-measures. The collapse of Communism in Indonesia forced Malaysia's Communists to look to the north for rescue from their plight. Their hopes for an ultimate Communist victory now depended upon the outcome of the struggle in Vietnam and upon the success of the Communist guerrilla war which was being fomented in Thailand. However, without discernable Communist advances on either front, the Communists in Malaysia faced a bleak and unpromising future.

The end of Confrontation also involved a fundamental shift in relations between Kuala Lumpur and Singapore. From Singapore, the *rapprochement* between Malaysia and Indonesia was viewed with some misgivings and apprehension. Many in Singapore feared that the peace moves were designed as a prelude to a campaign to isolate Singapore on the basis of a racial-communal division of Southeast Asia. These fears were stimulated by the expanding number of Malay and Indonesian politicians who talked openly of Malay racial alignment as the basis for uniting the two countries. For example, General Suharto stated in an interview with Bernard Krisher that:

> Our intention is to build up a greater Maphilindo, which means we would like to unite with the Malay race and other friendly neighboring countries.[39]

Similar views were being aired by Malay communalist politicians in the Federation. The Alliance Minister of Information and Broadcasting, Inche Senu bin Abdul Rahman, openly mocked Singapore, stating that its position was like that of Israel in the Arab world, and accused Singapore of relying upon Israeli advisors.[40] Singapore's growing anxieties were not allayed by the rather cryptic statement in a radio broadcast by Tunku Abdul Rahman that "in the conduct of our foreign affairs, we may have to change a little".[41]

Even before Indonesia and Malaysia began direct peace negotiations, Lee Kuan-yew undertook an extended six weeks tour of Asian and European capitals. His object was to strengthen Singapore's diplomatic ties with states outside Southeast Asia. In London, talks centered on the issue of future arrangements for the military bases in Singapore. Both Britain and Malaysia exercised rights to utilize these bases on the condition that a Malaysian veto could prevent their use for any active operations not related to the direct defense of Malaysian territory. We may assume that Singapores would have preferred to exercise this veto, and now looked upon the presence of British troops as more than a mere economic asset. If she did become beleaguered, the British military commitment to Singapore might help to deter Singapore's neighbors from rash acts. After his return from London, Prime Minister Lee candidly admitted, "It is my duty to see that Singapore is not isolated. What else do you think I have been travelling for?"[42] Later in September Lee traveled to New Delhi and proposed to Prime Minister Indira Gandhi that India should prepare to exercise a "guardian role" in Southeast Asia when the British "policeman role" came to an end after ten more years. When asked if he was concerned about Communist expansionism he replied that the integrity of the whole region needed to be protected from "whoever wants to destroy us—whether it is Communism of whatever variety or plain straightforward imperialism or expansionism".[43] No formal action was taken on these proposals, but from across the causeway the more vocal Malay communal politicians mounted a chorus of intense opposition to Lee's suggestions.

The Malaysian-Indonesian *rapprochement* also had an impact on domestic politics. In both Malaysia and Singapore Malay communalists became less cautious in pressing their demands. Singapore's leaders feared renewed racial clashes might be triggered by Malay communal extremists in a rash attempt to bring Singapore under Malay control, probably through creating the conditions which might lead to some form of intervention from abroad. These fears were not completely unfounded, for in July and August the Singapore police arrested key members of two affiliated Malay extremist underground organizations. Seven Malays were charged with precipitating racial clashes and planning for the violent overthrow of the Singapore Government.[44]

In Malaysia, the ultra-communal Malay opposition parties became less vitriolic in their criticism of the Alliance Government after Singapore's exit from the union, partly because Malay communal interests within the Alliance were exercising greater influence over government policies. The end of "confrontation" made the Federal Government increasingly sensitive to Malay demands and caused a growing anxiety among the non-Malays, including many who were active within the political structure of the Alliance. Non-Malays feared that the moderate communal policies of the Alliance might soon be abandoned, especially if Tunku Abdul Rahman (who was recognized to be a restraining influence against excesses of Malay communalism) were to retire from active leadership of the country. Mindful of these apprehensions, the Tunku went to pains to explain that he had no intention of retiring. He also promised that if he were no longer able to continue in office, his successor, Tun Abdul Razak, would carry on "with no change in policy toward the non-Malays".[45] Such assurances were made because of widespread belief that Abdul Razak was appreciably more pro-Malay on policy issues than the Tunku. Those who expressed such views were accused by the Tunku of engaging in a malicious campaign to smear Abdul Razak by calling him "anti-Chinese". In a number of speeches, the Tunku exhorted non-Malays to support his appointed successor, to be loyal to the country, to accept the national language, and to cooperate with the Malays. In one such speech he added a rather ominous comment: "If the country is destroyed, it will not be the fault of the Malays".[46] Hidden behind this statement was the implicit recognition that the Malays had privileged access to the political system, were the principal beneficiaries of government policies, and were therefore quite naturally the principal base of support for both Malaysia and the Alliance Government.

The Supremacy of the Alliance System

In surveying their accomplishments since coming to power, the Alliance leaders had reason for confidence and pride. The Alliance structure had survived the vicissitudes of sixteen turbulent and critical years in Malaya's political history. The party had compiled an impressive record of meeting numerous challenges to its authority and of being able to shape the political environment to suit its objectives. In every federal election since the first one in 1955 the Alliance had won decisive majorities. Within two years of assuming office it gained for Malaya its independence on the basis of a constitution which had been drafted under its close supervision and control. Less than three years after independence, the Alliance Government had achieved a decisive military victory in a long and costly Communist guerrilla war. That victory made it possible to divert extensive human and material resources to social welfare and economic development programs designed to raise the standard of living for substantial numbers of economically deprived citizens of the country.

As the Federation of Malaya was a creature of the Alliance, so too was its successor, the Federation of Malaysia. While the new union required considerable bargaining with Britain, Singapore and the Borneo states, the Alliance Government retained the final say on the terms for union, since the new states were to be integrated into the basic political and constitutional structure of Malaya. Once it became apparent to Malaysia's leaders that Singapore would not accommodate itself to this basic structure, the decision was made to expel Singapore from the Federation. Just as Singapore had come into Malaysia on conditions largely defined by the Alliance, so too was its exit engineered on conditions dictated by the Alliance.

For a while after 1963, it appeared that the turmoil which accompanied the formation of Malaysia might prove to be the undoing of the Alliance. Indonesia's intense hostility to the new federation was soon translated into hostile and provocative acts. Yet, with substantial foreign assistance, the Alliance Government was able to mobilize Malaysia's resources to resist these harassments and the insurgent movements which were spawned from abroad. In time, Indonesia underwent a paroxysm of self-destruction. From that struggle emerged new leaders who were willing to abandon "confrontation", and acknowledge the legitimacy of Malaysia's Alliance Government. Thus, by a combination of fortuitous circumstances and the skilful exercise of its powers, the Alliance had created a political environment favorable to its continued dominance of Malaysian politics.

As the tenth anniversary of Malayan independence approached, the Malaysian Government was able to give higher priorities to those domestic programs designed to build a new Malaysian nation. Since its inception, the Alliance had been committed to the task of creating a unified nation based on the promise that the country's basic Malay character must be carefully preserved and promoted. The adoption of Malay as the sole national language on August 31, 1967, and massive government programs to raise the standard of living of the Malays represented only two aspects of that basic commitment. The political realignment resulting from Singapore's expulsion from Malaysia and the *rapprochement* with Indonesia gave the Alliance a freer hand to pursue these long-term political objectives. Those who in the past had rejected the Alliance vision of Malaysia's national identity continued to oppose the pro-Malay bias of government policies. Yet, the political supremacy of the Alliance, made attempts to put Malaysia on a substantially different course even more futile than before.

1 *Straits Times*, August 10, 1965, pp. 10–11.

2 *Sunday Times*, August 15, 1965, p. 2.

3 *Straits Times*, August 10, 1965, p. 13.

4 *Ibid.*, p. 15.

5 *Straits Times*, August 10, 1965, p. 14. The last paragraph in the quotation appears to be a cryptic reference to Indonesia.

6 *Straits Times*, August 11, 1965, p. 22.

7 *Straits Times*, September 10, 1965, p. 7.

8 *Straits Times*, October 11, 1965, p. 5.

9 *Straits Times*, September 17, 1965, p. 20.

10 *Straits Times*, September 18, 1965, pp. 1 and 18. Singapore's note took strong exception to the extreme Malay communal statements made by Syed Nasir, Director of Dewan Bahasa, and Ali Haji Ahmad, Deputy Head of the UMNO Youth Movement.

11 For example, Lee Kuan-yew charged that the Alliance Government was "bogged down by corruption", that it wished to preserve a "medieval feudal society", and that it was implicated in the two racial riots which rocked Singapore during 1964. See *Straits Times*, October 19, 1965, p. 18. This speech touched off a second exchange of diplomatic notes protesting against political statements made by officials of the other state.

12 *Straits Times*, September 29, 1965, p. 1; September 30, 1965, pp. 1 and 22.

13 *Straits Times*, October 19, 1965, p. 18.

14 During the last week of August, 1965, the police arrested twenty leaders of an Indonesian-backed organization called the People's Revolutionary Party of Singapore. It was led by Sim Siew-lin, an official of the Malayan Communist Party's "Singapore Town Committee" who escaped to Indonesia when the police uncovered the latter organization in 1962. The PRPS was directed by a small group of exiled MCP leaders operating from Jakarta in cooperation with the PKI and with the assistance of the Indonesian authorities. The organization planned for the assassination of Singapore's Ministers and was responsible for planting the bomb in front of the American Consulate in Singapore on August 1. See *Straits Times*, August 27, 1965, pp. 1 and 24; August 28, pp. 1 and 22.

15 *Christian Science Monitor*, August 12, 1965, p. 6.

16 Speculation abroad that Britain might abandon its bases in Singapore may have prompted the new Defence Minister, Dr. Goh Keng-swee to announce that Singapore would obtain "international tenders" from other powers who would be willing to take over the bases if Britain should withdraw. He claimed that at least four countries were interested in operating the bases, but he did not name the countries. See *Straits Times*, September 3, 1965, p. 24. It would appear that Dr. Goh's threat was directed primarily towards London.

17 On a television broadcast Lee Kuan-yew revealed that in 1960 a CIA agent had been caught trying to buy secret information from a Singapore Special Branch Officer. The U.S. Government (at the time of the Eisenhower administration) offered Lee and his party M$10 million to stay silent, but Lee instead demanded M$100 million as a "gift" to Singapore for development purposes. The negotiations continued until the Kennedy administration withdrew the offer of any money to keep the incident secret. Immediately following these public allegations by Lee, a spokesman for the U.S. State Department issued a denial, whereupon Lee made public a letter of apology sent to him by Secretary of State Dean Rusk in April, 1961. Lee also ventilated a private grievance against the United States. He had asked the American Ambassador that arrangements be made to bring a certain American medical specialist to Singapore to treat "someone very dear to me". Lee became irritated when he was informed that the specialist was not free to fly to Singapore at that time, and, instead, the proposal was made that the patient could be flown to the specialist. See *Straits Times*, September 1, 1965, pp. 1 and 20; September 2, 1965, pp. 1 and 18; September 3, 1965, pp. 1 and 24.

18 *Straits Times*, August 14, 1965, pp. 1 and 22.

19 *Straits Times*, August 13, 1965, pp. 1 and 18.

20 The political situation in Sabah and Sarawak is examined in greater detail in Chapter 20.

21 Carrying the banner on one side was MCA Youth, on the other side, UMNO Youth. Outside the Alliance the MCA position was supported by 52 Chinese associations and guilds, while the UMNO position had a variety of backers, including the National Language Action Front. See *Straits Times*, August 18, 1965, p. 7; September 16, 1965, p. 10.

22 A 20-man "Alliance Action Committee" was appointed to help resolve internal disputes within the Alliance and help to enforce party discipline. That such a committee was necessary is indicative of the increased tensions within the party following Singapore's exit from Malaysia. See *Straits Times*, September 2, 1965, p. 18; November 18, 1965, p. 6.

23 For an excellent account of the political upheaval in Indonesia see the four articles by Seymour Topping appearing in *New York Times*, August 22, 1966, pp. 1 and 2; August 23, 1966, pp. 1 and 2; August 24, 1966, pp. 1 and 16; August 25, 1966, pp. 1 and 4.

[24] Indonesian society, particularly in Java, tends to be divided into two religio-cultural traditions. In the *abangan* tradition the pre-Muslim, animist and Hindu elements of culture and traditional *adat* law are preserved, while many of the obligations of Islam are ignored or substantially modified. The *santri* tradition is represented by more orthodox Muslims who wish to purge Indonesian culture of its syncretic animism and vestiges of Hindu law and beliefs. The rural peasants of Central Java are essentially in the *abangan* tradition, while urban and entre-preneurial Indonesians have tended to be associated with the *santri* tradition. The PKI drew its strength from the *abangan*, thus the purge of the Communist Party represented a thinly disguised form of religio-communal violence perpetrated by the *santri* against the *abangan*. This basic division in Indonesian society is described and analyzed in Clifford Geertz, *The Religion of Java* (New York: The Free Press, 1960).

[25] *Straits Times*, February 22, 1966, pp. 1 and 16.

[26] *Straits Times*, March 28, 1966, pp. 1 and 4; March 29, 1966, pp. 1 and 18.

[27] *Straits Times*, March 31, 1966, p. 1.

[28] Suharto later admitted that even before the September 30 coup attempt the Army had already made secret contacts with the Malaysian Government to consider peace terms. *Straits Times*, August 3, 1966, p. 1. See also *The Times* (London), May 16, 1966, p. 8.

[29] *Straits Times*, June 2, 1966, p. 1.

[30] Adam Malik openly admitted that Sukarno was "furious" over the moves to begin peace negotiations. See *Straits Budget*, June 1, 1966, p. 5.

[31] Later it was agreed to let Sukarno "participate" in the formation of the new cabinet in order to preserve the fiction that Sukarno was still ruling the country.

[32] *Straits Times*, July 29, 1966, p. 1.

[33] *Straits Times*, August 12, 1966, p. 1.

[34] *Straits Times*, August 17, 1966, p. 1.

[35] See *Straits Times*, September 13, 1966, p. 1 and 20; September 14, 1966, pp. 1 and 20; September 29, 1966, pp. 1 and 20.

[36] *Straits Times*, January 1, 1966, p. 1. Among those arrested were Eu Chooi-yip, the former Secretary-General of the Malayan Democratic Union, and Ibrahim Mohamed, a former Communist guerrilla and officer in the Communist organized Johore Rubber Workers' Union.

[37] *Peking Review*, IX, no. 2 (January 7, 1966), p. 23; *Peking Review*, IX, no. 4 (January 21, 1966) pp. 3–4; *News From Hsinhua News Agency*, February 2, 1966, p. 37.

[38] *Straits Times*, August 9, 1966, p. 1.

[39] Bernard Krisher, "A Talk With General Suharto", *Newsweek*, September 5, 1966, p. 43.

[40] *Straits Times*, July 30, 1966, p. 24. This was before the June War in the Middle East in 1967 when the Arabs were optimistic about their chances of imposing an "Arab solution" on the "Palestine Problem".

[41] *Straits Times*, September 1, 1966, p. 1.

[42] *Straits Budget*, June 8, 1966, p. 16.

[43] *Straits Times*, September 5, 1966, p. 1. See also *Straits Times*, September 3, 1966, p. 1.

[44] Singapore UMNO became rather agitated over these arrests since two of the detained men were UMNO members. The two underground organizations were: *Pasokan Gerak Chepat Bumiputra Singapura* (Swift Indigenous League of Singapore) and *Gerakan Permuda Islam Singapura* (Singapore Islamic Youth Movement). See *Straits Times*, July 27, 1966, pp. 1 and 20; August 4, 1966, p. 9.

[45] *Straits Budget*, February 9, 1966, pp. 8 and 10.

[46] *Straits Times*, July 15, 1966, p. 1.

20 Eastern Malaysia:
The Politics of Federalism

The separation of Singapore created a substantially different political environment in Malaysia. The dominant position of the Alliance Government was assured in the political system of the pruned union, since the opposition to its rule had come from a coalition of forces led by Singapore's Peoples Action Party. With Singapore out of the union, the pro-Malay policies of the Alliance were not likely to be successfully challenged, since Malaya contained over 85 per cent of the population in the federation and enjoyed even greater political power through its near monopoly of wealth, education and public office. At the same time as security became less of a problem for Malaysia, spokesmen for regional and local interest proved more bold in asserting their demands. The conditions which had brought peace to Malaysia also had created the basis for increasing political frustration and a sense of political grievance within the two states of Eastern Malaysia.

Regional Issues and Grievances

The sudden expulsion of Singapore from Malaysia without prior warning created a mood of anxiety and concern in Sarawak and Sabah.[1] Tunku Abdul Rahman's failure to consult any Borneo leader before his precipitous action created much resentment. These states had joined Malaysia on the assumption that Singapore would be in the union and would help to finance the large economic development programs which were promised to them as an inducement for joining the union. Now in the smaller Malaysia they faced the prospect of reduced economic benefits and increasing political domination from Kuala Lumpur. Astute political leaders were quick to realize that they had lost some of their room for political maneuver. Now, Kuala Lumpur could, if it wished, ignore them with impunity on the major issues of politics. This mood of anxiety and concern intensified after Malaysia came to terms with Indonesia and domestic pressure increased to impose Malaya's political pattern upon Eastern Malaysia.

The states of Eastern Malaysia have been particularly sensitive to the following political issues: Malaysianization of the civil service, conversion to the national language, the status of Islam, special rights and privileges for Malays or indigenous people, and economic development programs. Each of these issues deserves some explanation.

The Malaysianization of the civil service was a difficult problem in Sarawak and Sabah since these states did not have enough educated people to assume all the jobs in the civil service which were performed by colonial officials. Those who wanted to "Borneanize" the civil service in the two states tried to retain the colonial expatriate officers until local candidates could be found to take their place. The Federal Government, on the other hand, insisted on speeding up the process of removing expatriate colonial officers and replacing them with those from Malaya who had the education and training to assume these positions. Thus, a fast pace of conversion improved employment opportunities for Malayan elites, while a more leisurely pace was more advantageous to those in the Borneo states who had hopes of gaining an education and eventually securing government employment.

The language issue was also ticklish, since only a small minority of the population in Sabah and Sarawak are Malay, even though both states have a majority of indigenous people who speak Malay-root languages. Nearly all the educated elites used English either as a first language or as a second. Apart from Malay elites, few had proficiency in Malay equal to their knowledge of English. In a way, the language issue was tied in with the Malaysianization issue, since the adoption of Malay as the official language for the Borneo states not only involved the imposition of a minority language on these states, but also erected an added obstacle for many of those in Borneo who had an education and could hope to compete for the available positions in the civil service.

Muslims account for approximately 23·4 per cent of the population of Sarawak and 37·9 per cent in Sabah. When Malaysia was formed, special provisions were included for these states to limit the effect of Islam as the official religion of Malaysia. For example, federal financial aid to Muslim institutions was prohibited in these states unless approved by the Yang di-Pertua Negara (Governor) of that state. Federal funds, which in other states were allocated for the support of Islam, were to be donated instead to general social welfare purposes. Likewise, state laws restricting non-Muslim religious proselytizing of Muslims required a two-thirds majority in the state Legislative Assembly.[2] These special provisions were designed to insulate the Borneo states from the pattern of state-mosque relations prevailing in Malaya. However, because of pressure from Kuala Lumpur these constitutional guarantees for Sabah and Sarawak were having only a limited effect. Substantial funds from government-operated lotteries had gone for the support of Islam in both states and there had been agitation to pass state ordinances patterned on state laws in Malaya which protect and promote Islam.[3] The Federal Government's ten-year residence limitation imposed on expatriate missionaries was also interpreted by many as a measure designed to restrict Christian mission work among interior natives.

In Sabah and Sarawak the tribal natives enjoyed certain privileges, particularly in the administration of native land laws. The Malays in Sabah and Sarawak understandably would have liked Malaya's system of Malay "special privileges" extended to them. The indigenous tribal people, who are far more numerous than the Malays, also sought to have some of these privileges extended to them, but without giving up the privileges they already enjoyed. The non-indigenous people, of course, opposed all such privileges as discriminatory and basically undemocratic. The nature of these issues provided the opportunity for the formation of cross-communal coalitions based on the distribution of benefits to one community or another.

On all these issues, the Federal Government had been pressing for the Borneo states to come into line with the policies of peninsular Malaysia, on the argument that nation-building demanded uniform policies throughout the federation. Because of the political divisions within Sabah and Sarawak, the Federal Government found it easy to intervene in local political disputes in these states to tip the balance in favor of those who were more sympathetic to its policies on the national level. Consequently, the constitutional guarantee of local autonomy for these states was rather drastically and subtly undermined by a process of political intervention from Kuala Lumpur. Such intervention was facilitated by the large economic development funds which could be withheld or dispensed to secure state cooperation and compliance. Likewise, federal powers over such matters as federal patronage, internal security, trade, commerce, labor and emergency powers were all part of the arsenal of political weapons available to the Federal Government in case of disputes with Borneo political leaders who were vocal in demanding "states rights".

An examination of political developments in the states of Eastern Malaysia will illustrate in greater detail the nature of these tensions and conflicts.

Politics in Sabah

Politically Sabah was the most retarded of the states in Malaysia. Enlightened colonial rule, an expending economy, lack of political agitation, and fear of inflaming communal animosities all contributed to the government's cautious approach for introducing democratic institutions. However, after Malaysia was proposed, popular participation in politics became more imperative, and, in any event, could not be delayed any longer even if the colonial authorities had desired it, which they did not. Political parties began to form in 1961 and the first elections were held in December of the following year, while negotiations were still in progress for the terms of Sabah's entry into Malaysia.

Just as in Malaya, the Sabah party system formed along enthic-communal lines. The Dusuns (who now preferred the name Kadazan) were recruited by the United National Kadazan Organization (UNKO) which was founded by Donald Stephens, a Jesselton business man, who was half Kadazan and half Australian by birth. The bulk of the support for this party came from the non-Muslim native peoples in the West Coast and Interior Residencies. In general, the Kadazans were difficult to mobilize for political action because of their isolated settlement patterns and localized tribal loyalties. Consequently, the voting strength of UNKO was not proportionate to the population which the party claimed to represent.

For several years UNKO competed with another party which sought the support of tribal natives, causing further dissipation of their electoral strength. The rival party was the United National Pasok Momogun Organization (PM), which was led by the traditional Murut chief G. S. Sundang of the Keningau area. This party's support was concentrated among the Muruts of the Keningau valley and along the Padas River. While G. S. Sundang favored the continuation of British colonial administration, at least until his more backward interior peoples had achieved a higher economic and educational level, he was finally persuaded to support Malaysia. During 1964 G. S. Sundang and Donald Stephens agreed to merge their two parties to form the United Pasokmomogun Kadazan Organization (UPKO).[4] The circumstances which prompted this union will be described later.

Strictly speaking, there are almost no Malays in Sabah. However, there are a number of peoples who are Muslim, who are physically similar to the Malays, and who share the same basic cultural tradition as the Malays. These include the Bruneis, Bajaus, Sulus, Illanuns, Kedayans and several lesser groups. For the most part, these people live along the coasts and devote their energies to rice cultivation and fishing. These "Malay-type" peoples have been represented by the United Sabah National Organization (USNO), led by the traditional Sulu chief from the Kudat area, Dato Mustapha bin Dato Harun. Under his forceful leadership, this party was quite successful in mobilizing Sabah's Muslim population for effective participation in politics.

The Chinese of Sabah, who comprise 23 per cent of the state's population were rather slow to unite for political action, and hence somewhat weaker than their numbers would indicate. In 1962 there were two Chinese-based parties, the United Party operating out of Sandakan and the Democratic Party, which had its strength in the Jesselton Area. Prior to the 1962 elections, these two parties merged to form the Borneo Utara National Party (BUNAP). When North Borneo changed its name to Sabah upon its entrance into Malaysia, the party changed its name to Sabah Nationalist Party (SANAP). Later a merger was effected with the Sabah Chinese Association (SCA), after which the SCA became the major political party representing the Chinese.[5]

Sabah's Indian community, comprising 0·7 per cent of the population, has been politically insignificant. Yet, it was represented by the Sabah Indian Congress, which successfully claimed the right to be included in inter-communal political negotiations.

When political parties were being organized in Sabah, pressures for political unity were quite intense. The reasons are not hard to find. During the negotiations for Malaysia, division would have weakened Sabah's bargaining position. Later, after Indonesia's *Konfrontasi* attacks on Malaysia, political divisions risked Indonesian exploitation of political differences. Consequently, all of Sabah's active political parties joined a Sabah Alliance which was formed in mid-1962, and patterned after the Alliance coalition in Malaya. Yet, because of the lack of an identifiable political opposition, the Sabah

Alliance did not operate as a unified party organization. For Sabah's first elections, the member parties were unable to agree on a common ticket, and thus they contested against each other for public support, ostensibly on the same party program. As a result the Sabah Alliance became primarily a mechanism for post-election negotiations where the demands of each party were balanced against each party's strength as reflected at the polls. Public debate on sensitive communal issues were avoided, so that Sabah politics, as reported in the press, appeared to be "issueless" and "unreal".

TABLE 18
Distribution of party seats within the Sabah Alliance

	USNO	UNKO	PM	BUNAP (SCA)	Independent	Others
Directly elected seats to local authorities 1962–63	53	39	12	27	6	—
Legislative Assembly 1963	8	5	1	4	—	—
Cabinet 1963	2[a]	2	1	2	—	—
Parliamentary seats 1963	6	5	1	1	—	—
		UPKO				
Legislative Assembly 1964	15	12		8	—	1[b]
Cabinet 1964	3	3		2	—	1[c]
Cabinet 1965	3	3		3	—	—

Notes:

[a] Later in the year the Cabinet was expanded by one to give USNO three seats.

[b] This seat was awarded to the Sabah Indian Congress.

[c] By agreement, the Federal Government nominated a "non party" person for one Cabinet seat in June 1964.

Under the multiple indirect election system then in effect, district councils and town boards, were directly elected by popular vote in the period from December, 1962, to April, 1963. These bodies elected members to "electoral colleges" which in turn elected members to the Sabah Assembly and to the Malaysian Parliament.[6] The Alliance carefully manipulated the whole electoral process through negotiated agreements among its member parties on the basis of their performance in the local authority elections. These agreements also covered the distribution of offices in the Sabah Government. Donald Stephens (leader of UPKO) became Sabah's Chief Minister, while his primary rival, Dato Mustapha of USNO became the Yang di-Pertua Negara (Head of State). Ultimately, the stability of the Alliance depended on the ability and willingness of these two individuals to work out political agreements acceptable to their respective parties.

Land policy was one of the first contentious issues faced by the Sabah Alliance. From 1952 Sabah began phasing out the long-term timber concessions granted under company rule, and instead issued an increasing number of annual licenses to smaller operators.[7] Because Donald Stephens hoped to open up new agricultural land for interior natives, he proposed instead to revive the system of long-term timber concessions to the larger companies which had the capital to operate in interior areas and would agree to log specified areas which could be converted to agricultural land after being cleared. The money from these concessions was to be used to sponsor economic development projects for all the state, but with high priority for the more backward interior areas. Many natives in these areas would be employed as laborers and also be encouraged to share in timber profits through participation in government-sponsored cooperatives. These proposals were resisted by Chinese timber operators who benefited from the piecemeal approach of the annual licenses, which were usually secured for more profitable timber lands along the coast and major rivers. Together the "timber lobby" in the SCA, and USNO, which wanted development projects for coastal areas, forced Donald Stephens to abandon his proposals designed to improve the economic condition of interior natives. Instead, annual licenses were continued, and used to "buy" the political support of certain Chinese interests. Annual timber licenses became a sordid aspect of Sabah politics, since many politicians invested in timber companies and actively influenced the process of awarding these lucrative annual licenses. The "honest graft" of the annual timber license system was practised while Donald Stephens was Chief Minister, but was utilized much more effectively for political purposes and private profit by his successors.[8]

Other issues challenged the unity of the Sabah Alliance. Donald Stephens had played a prominent role in negotiating the terms for Sabah's participation in Malaysia. Later, as Chief Minister he was in no mood to see the concessions to state autonomy forgotten or eroded, and was thus insistent upon a strict interpretation, not only of the *Malaysia Agreement*, but also of the earlier *Report of the Inter-governmental Committee*[9] which had set forth in greater detail, but with less legal precision, the "safeguards" and "guarantees" which were promised to the states of Sarawak and Sabah as a condition of entry into Malaysia. These guarantees had been included in the *Malaysia Agreement* primarily to placate the fears of non-Malays and many interior natives that Malaysia might mean Malay-Muslim political domination. As defenders of "native rights" Donald Stephens and his supporters attached great importance to what came to be known as the "20 points". To draw public attention to these "guarantees" a public monument commemorating the "20 points" was erected while he was Chief Minister.[10] However, Dato Mustapha and his USNO followers opposed many of the "20 points", particularly those which restricted governments upport for Islam, guaranteed the continued use of English, delayed the introduction of Malay as the national language, and gave Sabah control over immigration from Malaysia and abroad.

Beginning in 1964 the Sabah Alliance suffered from a series of crises. The first was precipitated by the necessity of choosing a new slate of Alliance candidates for an expanded State Assembly to be elected by the same electoral colleges as had chosen the first assembly. Deadlock developed when USNO demanded that it control the post of Chief Minister. The dispute was referred to Tunku Abdul Rahman who proposed a solution which allowed Stephens to remain Chief Minister but gave USNO greater weight in the Cabinet.[11] Before the year was out another controversy arose when Chief Minister Stephens, under pressure to Malaysianize civil service positions held by expatriates, appointed to the post of State Secretary Mr. John Dusing, who was a Kadazan and was believed to be sympathetic to UPKO's demands for substantial state autonomy. Dato Mustapha as titular head of state (Yang di-Pertua Negara) refused to confirm the appointment.

While no reason was given at first, later Mustapha argued that he had accepted the post as titular head of state only on the understanding that he could continue to exercise "political leadership", and therefore claimed the right to reject the appointment. For this reason, a constitutional dispute arose over the question of the powers of the Chief Minister and the Yang di-Pertua Negara. Could the Yang di-Pertua Negara as titular head of state "veto" an appointment made by the Chief Minister? Did the Chief Minister have an obligation to secure the approval of all his colleagues in the cabinet? These questions were never presented to a court of law for authoritative determination. Instead of taking the issue to the courts, the disputants were finally persuaded to submit their conflict once again to the mediation of Tunku Abdul Rahman. Under extreme pressure, Donald Stephens finally signed a "peace pact" based on a formula proposed by the Tunku.[12] By this formula, Donald Stephens was removed as Chief Minister and instead joined the Federal Cabinet as minister without portfolio. With federal assistance a "Malay-Chinese" political coalition was forged between USNO and the SCA, based in large measure on patronage, and agreement on timber license policies favoring Chinese interests. UPKO as representative of the interior natives was effectively isolated from position of power and its leader, Donald Stephens, was thus removed from the Sabah political scene. This was the situation which prevailed when Singapore was expelled from Malaysia.

Within a week of Singapore's exit from Malaysia, UPKO's National Council issued a policy statement which expressed "grave concern" over the Central Government's future relations with Sabah, claiming that "Sabah had every right to be consulted before such a far-reaching decision was taken".[13] UPKO called for the renegotiation of terms for Sabah's participation in Malaysia, and Donald Stephens hinted that a new referendum on Malaysia might be appropriate.

Dismayed by the demands being voiced by UPKO, the federal authorities began a series of moves to placate critics and undermine UPKO's political support. A number of federal ministers, led by the Prime Minister, made a series of "goodwill" tours to Sabah and Sarawak, using these occasions to announce development projects for maximum political effect. Meanwhile, Donald Stephens was forced to resign his post in the Federal Cabinet. Tunku

Abdul Rhaman explained: "If any member of the Cabinet cannot adhere to policy, he can leave, and that is what he has done".[14]

Within the Sabah Alliance, moves were made to discipline UPKO. USNO demanded that UPKO "dissolve itself" and that UPKO members might then apply for membership in USNO. Such a move was proposed as "the only way to bring about native unity".[15] When UPKO rejected this proposal, it was presented with an ultimatum: Donald Stephens and UPKO Secretary-General Peter Mojuntin must resign from all leadership positions in the party or UPKO would be expelled from the Sabah Alliance. Kuala Lumpur's support of this "ultimatum" contributed to its coercive effect. Donald Stephens explained his decision:

> Our party leaders were disappointed but I persuaded them that we should try to stay in the Alliance and make it work. I agreed to be the scapegoat, the sacrifice. I felt that if the UPKO were to leave the Alliance at that time, when Confrontation was still at its peak, differences in the state could reach a dangerous stage.[16]

On the surface, the Sabah Alliance was preserved, yet, within UPKO there was a great deal of resentment.

TABLE 19
Inter-party contests in Sabah Legislative Assembly elections 1967

	USNO	UPKO	SCA/Alliance*
UPKO	21		
SCA/Alliance*	0	2	
Independent	6	7	5

* When an SCA candidate had no UPKO opponent he stood as an Alliance candidate; otherwise he contested as an SCA candidate.

Throughout 1966 USNO and UPKO squabbled over appointments, over development projects, over federal officials assisting USNO recruiting, and over interpretation of the "20 points". As the date for elections approached (about two years after they were first promised), Donald Stephens abandoned his "political retirement" to resume the presidency of UPKO after making a ritualistic public pledge of loyalty to Tunku Abdul Rahman. Within the Sabah Alliance agreement was achieved on a minimal platform,[17] but an irreconcilable deadlock developed on the allocation of seats. The dominant USNO-SCA coalition was willing to allocate to UPKO only 8 seats while claiming 18 for USNO and 6 for SCA. UPKO demanded a 13:13:6 ratio. Under the circumstance, Donald Stephens announced that UPKO would engage in "friendly contests" so that it could prove its electoral strength justified its demands. Dato (now Tun) Mustapha retorted that "there would be nothing friendly" about the elections.[18]

By all accounts, the ensuing election campaign was sharply contested with both sides appealing to racial and religious prejudices. Malayan officials from UMNO and the MCA arrived to help USNO and the SCA. Although claiming its rights as a full member of the Alliance, UPKO issued a Policy Statement which went far beyond the platitudes of the Sabah Alliance platform. Since that statement was an indictment of the incumbent leadership of the Sabah Government, it defined the central issues in the campaign.[19]

The election results vindicated UPKO's earlier demands for representation on the Alliance ticket. It gained the largest number of votes cast for any party, and won the 13 seats it had claimed, even against the combined opposition of USNO and the SCA. However, its very success complicated the problem of reconstituting the Alliance coalition after the election since USNO, the SCA and the Federal Government were more determined than ever to prevent UPKO from gaining a position in the Sabah Government from which it could upset the political balance or expand the base of its support.

TABLE 20
Results of Sabah Legislative Assembly elections 1967

	Seats won	Seats contested	Percentage of total valid votes	Total votes in all contested districts
USNO	14	23	40·75%	64,638
UPKO	13	25	40·83%	64,767
SCA/Alliance	4	6	9·41%	14,924
Independents	1	13*	9·02%	14,306

* A total of 26 Independents contested these 13 seats.

Source: Calculated from "Sabah State Legislative Assembly General Elections 1967", (mimeographed report of Sabah State Supervisor of Elections).

Appointed Chief Minister designate by the new Yang di-Pertua Negara, Tun Mustapha played the key role in defining the terms for UPKO's continued participation in the Sabah Alliance. In the post election negotiations, UPKO was informed that it must accept a subordinate role in the government, and prove its intentions of "good behavior" by a pledge of complete loyalty to Mustapha's Government. Before more precise terms were defined, Mustapha appointed a "temporary" Cabinet of two SCA members and three USNO members. Tunku Abdul Rahman approved of Mustapha's decision to form a Government without UPKO. When UPKO's requests for further negotiations were consistently rebuffed, its National Council met and decided that it had no option but to withdraw from the Sabah Alliance and become an opposition party.[20] Federal officials sought unsuccessfully to conciliate the dispute, after which both sides engaged in ritualistic behavior designed to blame the other for the breach.

379

In Parliament UPKO issued a detailed indictment of the Federal Government and the USNO-SCA dominated Sabah Government for violating, ignoring or circumventing the "20 points", while Donald Stephens demanded some "new guarantees to guarantee the guarantees".[21] The Federal Government replied that it had been very generous with Sabah, had tried to safeguard the "20 points", but also had a responsibility to build an integrated Malaysian nation. The implication was clear: it viewed guarantees of state autonomy as inimical to its nation-building responsibilities. In response to the charge that these issues had not been debated during the preceding elections, UPKO asked for a referendum under United Nations auspices to determine whether the public was concerned about "the new form of colonialism" from Malaya and the "surrender of rights" to the center. The demand for a referendum under international auspices was one thing the Federal Government was not willing to tolerate. Deputy Premier Abdul Razak issued warnings that UPKO's political tactics could endanger security, the clear implication being that the government might use its emergency powers under the Internal Security Act to deal with "disloyal" critics.[22]

To strengthen its position UPKO began exploring possible political alliances in other states. During July and August formal talks were held with the Sarawak Nationalist Party (SNAP) to coordinate strategy for resisting "federal encroachment" upon states rights.[23] Meanwhile, Tun Mustapha made efforts to entice key UPKO members to defect to the Sabah Alliance by offers of cabinet posts.[24] By December these tactics succeeded in persuading two UPKO assemblymen to defect. Concerned about erosion of its strength UPKO began behind-the-scenes negotiations to explore whether it might rejoin the Alliance. Soon after, UPKO made a dramatic announcement that its National Council unanimously decided to "dissolve" the party and advise its members to join USNO,[25] "in order to preserve the unity of the *bumiputera*" (literally "sons of the soil", i.e. indigenous people of both the tribal and Malay types). The pro-government press hailed the "good sense" of Donald Stephens, and interpreted the move as form of political capitulation. The motives still remain unclear, but it appears that UPKO may have come to the following calculations: UPKO could regain access to the Sabah Government, share in the distribution of offices and prevent further defections from its ranks; the absorption of UPKO by USNO would substantially change the latter and undermine its pro-federal orientation; once again in the Sabah Alliance, tribal native leaders could join forces with the SCA on many key issues; failure to accept UPKO members in USNO would place the onus on the latter for opposing "bumiputera unity". It is significant that Tun Mustapha, who had originally made the "UPKO must dissolve" demand in June 1967, was singularly unenthusiastic about UPKO's apparent capitulation. Yet, in January the unification of the two parties was formally pronounced.

The re-admission of the "UPKO faction" to the Alliance suggested that an attempt would be made to restrict public involvement in vital political issues. Instead, critical conflicts were to be internalized within the Sabah Alliance structure once again, mostly because of the fear that widespread political mobilization might lead to communal violence or serious political instability. Despite UPKO's apparent demise and the assertion of federal supremacy in Sabah, states rights sentiment remained strong, and may indeed have increased.

Politics in Sarawak

Just as in Sabah, federal-state relations were a central issue of Sarawak politics, with the Federal Government throwing its support to those within the state most likely to favor its "nation-building" policies. The complicated political configuration of Sarawak provided federal authorities with ample opportunity to play a decisive role in the coalition alignments which characterized Sarawak politics.

While the Sarawak party system developed along ethnic lines, it was complicated by the fact that each major community was represented by at least two political parties. Thus, the Malay community was represented by *Barisan Ra'ayat Jati Sarawak* (BARJASA) and by Party Negara Sarawak (PANAS). Until 1967 the two were unable to unite because of regional differences and political divisions within the Malay community dating from the dispute over the issue of the cession of the Brooke Sultanate to the British Crown in 1946. The native tribal peoples were also recruited into two parties which had not been able to unite because of tribal differences, personal rivalries and disputes over political alliances. *Party Pesaka Anak Sarawak* (Pesaka) was led by the traditional Paramount Chief of the Rejang River, Temenggong Jugah, and drew its major support from the Ibans of that area. The Sarawak Nationalist Party (SNAP) led by Stephen Kalong Ningkan had its main support from Ibans and Land Dayaks in Sarawak's First, Second and Fourth Divisions. The dominant Chinese party was the Sarawak United Peoples Party (SUPP) which was Sarawak's oldest and most formidable party but had been suffering from internal division between a pro-Communist and a more moderate non-Communist wing. Because of Communist infiltration of the party, SUPP had been subject to harassment by government authorities but had not been outlawed. The leadership of the party had been retained by the moderates, but some party branches had at times fallen under the control of Communists operating through a host of front organizations, which for the purposes of simplicity, the Sarawak Government called the Clandestine Communist Organization (CCO). A small number of conservative and westernized Chinese formed the Sarawak Chinese Association (SCA) patterned after the Malayan Chinese Association. Machinda was another party claiming to be non-communal, but in practice its supporters were primarily natives and Chinese.

Prior to the 1963 elections five parties joined to form the Sarawak Alliance.[26] In its formative years its history was punctuated by a series of crises arising from shifting alignments among the five parties. Until 1966 the SCA was fairly consistently aligned with SNAP, but the four other parties avoided more permanent alignments. In this situation, any three parties could isolate a fourth, and the isolated party could threaten retaliation by joining the Opposition. This political configuration may be illustrated as follows:

Malay parties	Native parties		Chinese parties	
BARJASA	Pesaka		Machinda*	The legal Opposition
PANAS	SNAP ⟷ SCA		SUPP	
The Alliance Government			↑↓	
			CCO	The illegal Opposition
				The Opposition

⟷ indicates mutual political support
* Machinda had both Chinese and Dayak members

In such circumstances as these, political disputes over issues were usually accompanied by a contest over political alliances, with the Federal Government playing a significant role in the negotiation of intra-Alliance agreements in the attempt to isolate proponents of state autonomy. A brief review of political events will illustrate the pattern of federal involvement in state politics.

During 1965 a political crisis developed within the Sarawak Alliance over land reform legislation proposed by the Chief Minister, Stephen Kalong Ningkan of SNAP. While the legislation had been under consideration for almost three years[27] the decision to implement the proposals came as a surprise to those who hoped they would be forgotten. The basic question was whether the system of native land rights should be amended to allow greater land use by the immigrant communities. Under previous laws, the Chinese could only own land in very limited areas designated as "Mixed Zones", while Malays and natives had exclusive rights to own land in "Native Areas". In addition, the interior tribal natives had customary rights over "Native Customary Land". Chief Minister Ningkan's land reform bills would have changed these laws by giving the interior natives right to acquire full title to "Native Customary Land", including the right to sell their land to whomever they wished. Consequently, the proposed reforms were advantageous to interior tribal natives who would gain title to large tracts of potentially valuable jungle land. The Chinese who suffered from severe land shortage also supported the legislation since they would be allowed to buy land from natives and no longer be confined to the restricted "Mixed Zones".

Within the Sarawak Alliance the Malay parties joined forces to make a determined attack on Mr. Ningkan and his land reform bills. While not in complete agreement, they wished to see Sarawak adopt laws which would restrict land ownership by the Chinese, perhaps by a system of "Native Reservations" patterned after Malaya's system of "Malay Reservations".[28] Their problem was to convince the tribal natives that they could benefit more from exclusive "Native Reservations" than from obtaining free title to lands where they enjoyed customary rights. In short, this meant forging a Malay-native coalition to fight against a potential native-Chinese coalition. Since Chief Minister Ningkan had committed his party (SNAP) in support of these bills, moves were made to form a three-way coalition within the Sarawak Alliance to oust Mr. Ningkan from his post as Chief Minister. This Malay-native coalition was to include BARJASA, PANAS and Pesaka, and was to be called the "Native Alliance". Before the union could be consummated Mr. Ningkan withdrew the land bills, whereupon Temenggong Jugah of Pesaka refused to join the anti-Ningkan cabal and withdrew his support from the proposed "Native Alliance". The crisis was quickly, but temporarily, resolved, with a political settlement which among other conditions stated that:

> There was no justification in the proposition of a Sarawak Native Alliance as it would cause disunity in the State . . .[29]

During the 1965 troubles, Chief Minister Ningkan took care to emphasize that disputes should be settled in Sarawak without intervention from Kuala Lumpur. While he had been actively cooperating with the Federal Government, particularly on matters of economic development, he was not in sympathy with some federal policies. For example, he did not believe that Malaya's communal policies were necessarily appropriate for Sarawak. He resisted efforts to speed up Malayanization of the Sarawak civil service, preferring instead to "Borneanize" the state administration. Likewise, he resisted increasing pressures to accept Malay as the sole official language for Sarawak in 1967 so as to harmonize with the timetable established for West Malaysia. Perhaps even more galling to Kuala Lumpur was his statement that he favored Iban and Chinese as official languages for Sarawak, along with Malay and English.[30] He also objected to federal funds being given for support of Islam and firmly supported the "special position" of Sarawak as defined in the *Malaysia Agreements* and the "20 points" of the IGC Report.

While the Malayan Alliance leaders tried to influence the outcome of the Sarawak dispute in 1965, that crisis was settled without decisive intervention by Kuala Lumpur. Such was not to be the case one year later. During the interval relations between Kuching and Kuala Lumpur had become strained, making the latter more determined to engineer the overthrow of the Ningkan government. When Tunku Abdul Rahman visited Sarawak in February 1966 he tried to revive the idea of a "Native Alliance", this time under the guise of a "United Malaysian National Organization" for Sarawak. Behind-the-scenes efforts continued for several months in an effort to forge a three-party "UMNO type" coalition to topple Ningkan's Government, but such a union was difficult to construct. Pesaka, while keeping on good terms with Kuala

Lumpur, was suspicious of a Malay-native union, hoping instead to create a unified native movement by absorbing SNAP or providing the leadership for a Pesaka-SNAP merger. Although a Malay party, PANAS had a strong sense of local loyalty and resented political directives from Kuala Lumpur. Furthermore, since it represented many of the more educated Malays from the Kuching area, its members expected to benefit from Ningkan's program of "Borneanizing" the civil service. Only BARJASA seemed to be enthusiastic supporters of Kuala Lumpur's proposed realignment.

When Ningkan got wind of the efforts being made by BARJASA Secretary-General Inche Abdul Taib bin Mahmud to undermine his government from within, he dismissed Inche Taib from the Sarawak Cabinet. This action precipitated a crisis between the pro-Ningkan forces and the pro-Kuala Lumpur forces. From the point of view of the Federal Government, the test of strength came prematurely, for only BARJASA and Pesaka joined the revolt, while Ningkan retained the support of his own party (SNAP) along with PANAS and the SCA.[31] The next day an entourage of BARJASA and Pesaka officials flew to Kuala Lumpur, and later produced a letter which expressed "no confidence" in Ningkan. On the basis of this letter, signed by 21 members of the Council Negri, Tunku Abdul Rahman demanded that Ningkan resign. Ningkan refused to do so since the opposition parties had no desire to bring down his government on this issue, and thus with their votes he was confident of gaining 21 of the 42 votes in the Council Negri, plus the Speaker's casting vote. Consequently, BARJASA and Pesaka boycotted the Council Negri sessions, preferring instead to invite direct federal intervention. After discussions in Kuala Lumpur, the Malaysian Alliance National Council (not the Sarawak Alliance Council) nominated Tawi Sli (a Pesaka member and an Iban) as the new Chief Minister. Later the Governor of Sarawak, Tun Abang Haji Openg, was persuaded by federal authorities to dismiss Ningkan and install Tawi Sli in his place on the basis of the "no confidence letter" signed by half of the Council Negri members, excluding the Speaker.[32]

Tawi Sli, with the support of BARJASA and Pesaka, tried to gain a majority in the Council Negri by using the offices at his disposal to induce individual members of PANAS, SNAP and SCA to join his government. At first the latter three parties maintained their unity in opposition to him, but after individual defections, PANAS and SCA finally agreed to cooperate with the new government. All parties suffered from disciplinary problems during this period as some sought to get on the "winning side", while others objected to Kuala Lumpur's heavy hand and highly irregular tactics. No moves were made to accommodate SNAP within the Alliance, so in July it withdrew charging that it had been expelled from the Sarawak Alliance.[33]

Meanwhile, Mr. Ningkan brought suit against Governor Openg and Tawi Sli for violation of the constitution. The High Court in Borneo, meeting in Kuching, finally upheld the contention of Mr. Ningkan that he had been deprived of office unconstitutionally, and declared that Ningkan continued to be the lawful Chief Minister since he had not suffered a vote of no confidence in the Council Negri, nor had he been given the opportunity of resolving the crisis by resigning or by dissolution of the Council Negri. The Court explained that the "no confidence letter" (which had not even been shown to Mr. Ningkan) did not give the Governor "implied powers" to improvise constitutional "stop gaps" as was argued by the defense.[34]

By the time that Ningkan resumed the office of Chief Minister, his three-party coalition had disintegrated and he could no longer count on majority support in the Council Negri. Consequently, he announced: "It is my bounden duty to request the Governor for immediate general elections. Let the people decide whom they want to be their representatives in the Council Negri and Parliament."[35] However, Tunku Abdul Rahman, away in London at the time, opposed Ningkan's decision, insisting, "There is no need to have general elections."[36] Abdul Razak explained that Sarawak's three-tiered election system was not suitable especially "because non-citizens could participate".[37] The Tunku demanded a special meeting of the Council Negri be called to depose Ningkan, and another "no confidence letter" was sent to the Governor containing 25 signatures of Council Negri members. But Ningkan remained adamant. He was determined to dissolve the Council and call for general elections. This was one action that Kuala Lumpur would not countenance, so it determined to play its trump card.

On the argument that the political situation in Sarawak was being exploited by Communists and subversive elements, Malaysia's King (Yang di-Pertuan Agong) declared a "State of Emergency" on September 14, thus activating the Emergency Powers of Parliament under clause 150 of *The Federal Constitution of Malaysia*, whereby all state powers were transferred to Federal authority. The Malaysian Parliament was hastily called into emergency session so that it could amend *The Sarawak Constitution* under these Emergency Powers. The bill gave the Governor, "subject to his absolute discretion", powers to convene the Council Negri, to suspend any Standing Orders of the Council, to "give any special directions which he may consider necessary" to the Speaker and to remove the Speaker and appoint another in his place if he should fail to comply with the Governor's orders. The Governor was also given "absolute discretion" to dismiss the Chief Minister and members of the Supreme Council after a vote of no confidence.[38] In conjunction with the constitution amendment bill, the Federal Government published a Parliamentary White Paper on the Communist threat to Sarawak.[39] While substantial evidence of Communist activities was revealed in this document, the Federal Government failed to present convincing evidence either that the Communists were behind the political difficulties in Sarawak, or that the Communists had suddenly become such a severe threat to the security of the country that the Federal Government needed to take extraordinary measures to postpone general elections until later under more favorable conditions, as decided and defined by the Alliance Government.

When Parliament convened, the four SNAP Members of Parliament from Sarawak joined the opposition benches to condemn the "undemocratic" and "unconstitutional" tactics of the Federal Government. Before the vote was taken, the entire Parliamentary Opposition, twenty members in all, walked out of Parliament, so the constitutional amendment was passed 118 to nil.[40] Later in the week, the Sarawak Council Negri was convened by order of the Governor. A no confidence motion against Ningkan was passed. Tawi Sli was installed as Chief Minister of Sarawak once again, and Tunku Abdul Rahman expressed his satisfaction, explaining, "We must have somebody responsible as Chief Minister who will try to make himself a Malaysian and not perpetuate colonial rule."[41]

With the return to office of Tawi Sli, the new Sarawak Alliance was based on the two Malay parties, BARJASA and PANAS, plus one native party (Pesaka) and one Chinese party (SCA). With this alignment, Pesaka now became the keystone of the Sarawak Alliance, because without its cooperation, the Government would fall. The political loyalties of Sarawak's natives became even more important than before. Would the interior natives support Pesaka in the Sarawak Alliance or SNAP as an opposition party? It soon became apparent that SNAP was making inroads into Pesaka's base of support among the natives. SNAP branches were springing up in Pesaka areas, and in Januray 1967 SNAP won a decisive by-election at Kapit, the home district of Pesaka's leader, Temenggong Jugah. It won another by-election at Lawas in the Fifth Division two months later, and emerged the victor in two more by-elections at Limbang in December. Earlier in the year Party Machinda had decided to dissolve and urged its followers to join SNAP.

Behind the scenes, federal authorities, concerned about the stability of the Alliance, had been exerting pressure upon the two Malay parties to unite, as a step in the direction of a "Malay-native" party. Finally BARJASA and PANAS were persuaded to merge to form Party Bumiputera.[42] While this union supposedly strengthened the Sarawak Alliance, it also increased Malay influence within it and thus made cooperation with Pesaka and the SCA more difficult. To avoid a fracture in the Sarawak Alliance, member parties agreed upon a moratorium on certain sensitive issues, particularly those relating to land policy.

When Pesaka began to see its political support being lost to SNAP, it was forced to take a more militant stand within the Alliance on behalf of native interests. Temenggong Jugah made a series of public accusations against Party Bumiputera leaders and certain federal ministers for their "pro-Malay bias", and charged that the Sarawak Government was ignoring the Ibans. He demanded that the offending ministers be dropped from the Sarawak Cabinet.[43] Rumors circulated that Pesaka might join SNAP in a coalition of native parties to bring down the Government. Under the circumstances it was difficult to discipline Jugah as the Federal Government had done when Donald Stephens had stepped out of line in Sabah. Jugah certainly appreciated the leverage which Pesaka exercised within the Sarawak Alliance, and pressed ahead with his demands. Finally, after consultations in Kuala Lumpur, Inche Abdul Mahmud,[44] Secretary-General of Party Bumiputera, was removed from the Sarawak Cabinet and replaced by a more moderate spokesman for his party. This concession to native demands was sufficient to preserve the Sarawak Alliance at least for some time.

Although Governor Openg promised that direct general elections would be held in August or September 1967, the Federal Government was fearful that the Sarawak Alliance might fail to gain a majority, or might fracture if forced to face the electorate. Consequently, preparations for elections proceeded at a snail's pace, forcing indefinite postponement of the date.[45] Meanwhile, all parties made feverish preparations for elections which would be called only when Kuala Lumpur became more confident of its political support.

The Federal Government faced many difficulties in its relations with both Sabah and Sarawak. It was dedicated to make Malaysia into a viable political system by building a unified nation from its disparate states. In Kuala Lumpur's view, Malaysia must be a multi-communal and multi-racial country, but also one which recognized its basic Malay linguistic, ethnic and cultural character. It was the latter assumption which, when challenged by Singapore, led to the expulsion of that state. While the costs of integrating Singapore into Malaysia were believed to be too great, in the case of Sabah and Sarawak, Kuala Lumpur was more confident of success. On several occasions federal spokesmen stated that "no state may break away from Malaysia", and warned that vigorous measures would be taken against advocates of state autonomy who were "anti-Malaysia". On the one hand, federal authorities tried to be conciliatory toward all communal interests and accommodating to some local demands. On the other hand, Kuala Lumpur was insistent that these states cooperate with the Federal Government's nation-building policies. Consequently, the Federal Government felt obliged to intervene in local politics to insure the supremacy of those who cooperated with Kuala Lumpur and thought "Malaysia first". While the Federal Government no doubt wished to preserve democracy, it attached much greater importance to the preservation of the union.

[1] Substantial parts of this chapter are taken from the following article: Gordon P. Means, "Eastern Malaysia: The Politics of Federalism", *Asian Survey*, Vol. VIII, no. 4 (April 1968), pp. 289–308.

[2] See: *Malaysia, Agreement concluded between the Federation of Malaya, United Kingdom of Great Britain and Northern Ireland, North Borneo, Sarawak and Singapore*, (Federation of Malaya: Government Press, 1963), Art. 64–65.

[3] See: Gordon P. Means, "Religion, State and Ideology in Malaya and Malaysia", in M. M. Thomas & M. Abel (eds.), *Religion, State and Ideologies in East Asia*, (Bangalore, India: East Asia Christian Conference, 1965).

[4] *Sabah Times*, June 14, 1964, p. 1.

[5] The Liberal Party and the Social Democratic Party were two other small Chinese parties which were never absorbed in the process of political consolidation among Chinese organizations in Sabah.

[6] Robert O. Tilman, "The Alliance Pattern in Malaysian Politics: Bornean Variations on a Theme", *The South Atlantic Quarterly*, Vol. LXIII, no. 1 (Winter 1964), pp. 60–74.

[7] See: M. H. Baker, *North Borneo, The First Ten Years, 1946–1956*, (Singapore: Malaya Publishing House, 1962), pp. 90–99.

[8] For a revealing account of the politics of the timber license system see *Sabah Times*, June 15, 1967, p. 12.

[9] *Malaysia Report of the Inter-governmental Committee, 1962*, (Federation of Malaya: Government Printer, 1963), pp. 5–45.

[10] *Sabah Times*, May 7, 1964, p. 7.

[11] *Sabah Times*, June 13, 1964, p. 1. Fearing political instability and possible exploitation by anti-Malaysia elements, Donald Stephens' request for direct elections "as soon as possible" was rejected by the Tunku as "impossible".

[12] Political offices were redistributed as follows: Chief Minister, Peter Loh (SCA); Deputy Chief Minister, G. S. Sundang (UPKO); a "non-party" member of the cabinet previously appointed by Kuala Lumpur "joined" UPKO to balance party representation on the Cabinet. *Sabah Times*, December 10, 1964, pp. 1 and 24; December 19, 1964, p. 1.

[13] *Straits Budget*, August 25, 1965, p. 6. No Borneo politician was consulted or even knew that Singapore was to be expelled until the day that the articles of separation were rushed through Parliament in a short two-hour period on August 9, 1965.

[14] *Straits Times*, August 23, 1965, p. 1.

[15] At the time, the public was unaware of these maneuvers within the Alliance. See *Sabah Times*, June 20, 1967, p. 2.

[16] *Ibid.*, p. 2.

[17] The Sabah Alliance platform affirmed "unshakable faith in Malaysia", promised that the Philippine claim to Sabah would be rejected, and that economic development and welfare programs would be expanded in cooperation with the Malaysian Government to "fulfil the needs and aspirations of various communities" and to "promote the economic and social well-being of the natives". *Peace, Justice & Prosperity*; *What the Sabah Alliance Party Offers You: Manifesto of the Sabah Alliance Party, 1967* (Jesselton: Sabah Alliance Headquarters, 1967).

[18] *Straits Budget*, March 15, 1967, p. 20.

[19] The UPKO statement expressed anxiety over: one-party control, loss of state control of immigration, loss of loans from Singapore, loss of rights permitting continued use of English, loss of full religious freedom, and premature imposition of federal "tax parity" before 1974. It promised to Sabahanize the civil service, and the Federal Secretariate, protect native land titles, and establish special privileges for natives who were "behind" and needed assistance. *Sabah Times*, April 7, 1967, pp. 1 and 12.

[20] *Sabah Times*, May 17, 1967, p. 1.

[21] *Sabah Times*, June 20, 1967, p. 2.

[22] An USNO firebrand had earlier suggested the possibility of "firing squads" for UPKO leaders for their anti-national activities. *Sabah Times*, June 22, 1967, p. 1; July 18, 1967, pp. 1 and 12; July 22, 1967, p. 1.

[23] *Sabah Times*, July 10, 1967, p. 1; August 18, 1967, p. 1; *Sarawak Tribune*, August 21, 1967, p. 1.

[24] UPKO charged that the enticements included monetary "bribes" from SCA business men and sharing in profits from timber license awards.

[25] *Straits Times*, December 11, 1967, pp. 1 and 4.

26 The original members were: BARJASA, PANAS, Pesaka, SNAP, and SCA. PANAS left the fold in 1963 in a dispute over the distribution of seats, but was re-admitted to the Sarawak Alliance the following year. For an account of the Sarawak elections in 1963 see: Robert O. Tilman, "Elections in Sarawak", *Asian Survey*, Vol. III, no. 10 (October 1963), pp. 507–517.

27 See Government of Sarawak, *Report of the Land Committee, 1962*, (Kuching, Sarawak: Government Printer, 1963).

28 See International Bank for Reconstruction and Development, *The Economic Development of Malaya*, (Baltimore: Johns Hopkins Press, 1955), pp. 306–316.

29 *Sarawak Tribune*, May 25, 1965, p. 1.

30 *Sarawak Tribune*, May 12, 1965, p. 7. Later Ningkan, who is an Iban Dayak, asserted that Tunku Abdul Rahman told him "that there is no such language as the Dayak language". *Sarawak Tribune*, July 4, 1966, p. 8. Ningkan's political views are expressed in a number of press releases, radio broadcasts and letters. See *The Times*, (London), October 8, 1966, p. 9; *Sarawak Tribune*, July 1, 1966, p. 1; July 5, 1966, p. 8; August 22, 1966, p. 1; August 27, 1966, p. 1.

31 *Sarawak Tribune*, June 13, 1966, p. 1; June 14, 1966, p. 1. Just prior to the crisis, PANAS had made an agreement to merge with a Melanu political party called Tugau United Peoples Party (TUPP). These two parties united on a common platform opposing the extension of Malaya's UMNO to Sarawak. Politically the Melanaus are a strategic community in Sarawak, since they are sometimes classi-fied as Malays, and sometimes as "natives". They live on the coast between the Rejang and Baram rivers, are physically very like the Malays, but only about one-third of their number are Muslim, the remainder being divided about equally between animist and Christian. See Tom Harrisson (ed.), *The Peoples of Sarawak*, (Kuching, Sarawak: Government Printing Office, 1959), pp. 85–94.

32 *Sarawak Tribune*, June 18, 1966, p. 1; *Sunday Tribune* (Sarawak), June 19, 1966, p. 1.

33 *Sarawak Tribune*, July 4, 1966, p. 1; August 27, 1966, p. 1.

34 The full judgement of the High Court was reproduced in *Straits Times*, September 8, 1966, pp. 12–13.

35 *Straits Times*, September 8, 1966, p. 1.

36 *Straits Times*, September 9, 1966, p. 1.

37 *Straits Times*, September 15, 1966, p. 1. Ningkan charged that Radio Malaysia refused to broadcast reports on the High Court decision, denied him the use of its facilities, even while Chief Minister, and failed to broadcast any of his statements.

38 These amendments to the Sarawak Constitution, imposed by Parliament, were temporary in that they were to cease having effect six months after the date the Emergency was proclaimed. See *Emergency (Federal Constitution and Constitution of Sarawak) Bill, 1966*, (Kuala Lumpur: Government Press, 1966); Malaysia, *The Federal Constitution together with Sections 73 to 96 of the Malaysia Act*, No. 26 of 1963 (Kuala Lumpur: Attorney-General's Chambers, 1964), Article 150, pp. 94–95.

39 *Communist Threat to Sarawak*, (Kuala Lumpur: Government Press, 1966). A month later a second white paper on the Communist threat was published. See *The Militant Communist Threat to West Malaysia*, (Kuala Lumpur: Jabatan Chetak Kerajaan, 1966).

40 *Straits Times*, September 20, 1966, pp. 1 and 18.

41 *Straits Times*, September 26, 1966, p. 1. The last part of this statement was an oblique reference to the Malaysianization issue.

42 *Sarawak Tribune*, December 20, 1966, p. 1.

43 *Sarawak Tribune*, October 9, 1967, p. 1. Because Chief Minister Tawi Sli was hesitant to push the issue, the public witnessed the curious spectacle of Party Pesaka threatening disciplinary action against its own Chief Minister for failure to follow party directives.

44 *Sarawak Tribune*, November 24, 1967, pp. 1 and 2. Inche Taib had been BARJASA Secretary-General and was a key figure behind the anti-Ningkan maneuvers of 1966.

45 The Constituency Delimitation Report was made public in May 1967, but had yet to be approved by Parliament some nine months later. The Malaysia-Indonesia peace pact of August 1966 had provided for general elections in Sabah and Sarawak "as soon as practicable". In the case of Sarawak, that pledge was conveniently ignored.

21 An Interpretation of Malaysian Politics

During the colonial period, the political process was monopolized by the bureaucracy. Politics were not open to public view, and except for a few native leaders who were appointed by colonial authorities to "advisory councils", public policy was made with the absolute minimum of public involvement. The system depended upon public apathy, a general level of social contentment, and a passive acceptance of the principles of "benevolent bureaucratic authoritarianism". The traditional political patterns of China, India and of the Malay sultanates all contributed to the basic environment which made it possible for a colonial bureaucracy to rule so effectively and with so little public involvement or opposition.

In the period of transition from colonial rule to national independence, public attitudes changed and apathy was replaced by increasing public involvement in the political process. In Malaya, the development of political parties was largely a product of the rising tide of nationalism and the rigors of the Japanese occupation, both of which challenged traditional attitudes toward government. As political activity began, some groups in society were mobilized for political action relatively fast and effectively, while others were slow to make their political weight felt. Creation of a stable political balance is extremely difficult even for the most able politicians in a situation like this, with first one group and then another entering the political arena and demanding to be counted. Although the personal qualities of individuals within the emerging elites may be an important contributing factor to political instability, the Malayan experience suggests that such non-synchronous mobilization of publics for political action was a major cause of chaotic and volatile politics.

The year 1946 provides a excellent case in point. At the end of the war militant Chinese leftist leaders who had been associated with the anti-Japanese resistance movement were the most active and dominant force in politics. A small urbanized and western-educated elite, mostly of Chinese, Indian and Eurasian ethnic origin were also trying to recruit political support. The returning British civil and military administrators felt compelled to make substantial concessions to the demands of these early political activists. Thus, the 1946 proposals for the Malayan Union constitution were based on the implicit assumption that the left-wing Chinese and western-educated non-Malay elites would be the dominant forces in Malayan politics for many years. Whitehall's colonial authorities thought that the equalitarian and moderately liberal Malayan Union proposals would be an acceptable and logical "next step" in Malaya's constitutional development toward eventual self-government. Yet, just as the Malayan Union constitution was being inaugurated, the largest element in Malayan society suddenly stirred from what seemed to be eternal lethargy to emerge as the major force on the political scene. Dato Onn utilized the existing structure of authority in Malay society, from the Malay Rulers down to the *kampong* headman in the Malay village, to build a mass party having both excellent leadership and roots reaching to the isolated Malay village. The surprisingly rapid political mobilization of large segments of Malay society by UMNO so upset the political balance in Malaya that negotiations had to begin almost immediately for the replacement of the Malayan Union constitution by another which was to give greater concessions to Malay interests.

Subsequent crises in Malayan politics may also have been the result of new segments of society entering the political arena. However, in time, the number of actors moving on and off the political stage became proportionately smaller. For example, the "July Crisis" of 1959 apparently was partly the result of a greater participation in politics by the Chinese, who were taking advantage of an expanded franchise. However, since the Chinese community had already been partially mobilized for political action, the upsurge of Chinese political activity in 1959 did not involve large enough segments of society to destroy the political equilibrium.

Non-synchronous mobilization of publics for political action creates great instability in the first stages of the transitional period from colonial rule. The more intensive mobilization, or re-mobilization, of publics that occurs later on in the transitional period creates a phenomenon that might be characterized as a "second shock" which is much less severe in its effects on political stability.

One may view the history of the development of political parties as an account of the successive mobilization of publics. In time, the recruitment of non-activists becomes exceedingly difficult since those who are more responsive to politics have already been mobilized and therefore much greater effort is required to mobilize a much smaller number of inactivists. There is a "law of diminishing returns" in politics as well as in economics. As this happens, the political process commences to revolve around the problems of political alignment and re-alignment in the tasks of constructing winning majorities. When this stage is reached, the chances for political stability become much greater.

The Negative Response

Political developments in Malaya suggest that each segment of society became politically active largely as a negative response to some policies or events that affected it adversely, or threatened to do so. Politics in the transitional period seemed to consist of a series of negative reactions from first one element in society and then another. The political activity of one group became the primary stimulus for the countervailing political reaction of other segments of society which were threatened by the upsurge of political action of rival interests.

Numerous illustrations of this principle of negative response may be found in Malayan politics. The Communists were able to build up a following primarily in response to the brutal, anti-Chinese policies of the Japanese military regime. The mobilization of the non-Malay left-wing was primarily a reaction against the re-constitution of British rule in Malaya. With the exception of radical Malay elements who were inspired by Indonesian politics to resist British rule, nearly all segments of Malay society became politically conscious in the fight against the Malayan Union constitution which threatened to undermine the Malay special privileges of the prewar era. Similarly, the non-Communist communal Chinese elements became significantly more active in politics in a reaction against the "pro-Malay" Federation of Malaya Agreement, which, to most Chinese, appeared to threaten their political and economic future in Malaya. Later, when government policies threatened the identity of the Chinese community with "Malayanization" policies as applied to citizenship, immigration, official languages, and schools, the diverse and often conflicting segments of Chinese society became unified in opposition to these common threats. However, when the policies were modified in political compromise, or the threats appeared to be less serious than imagined, the Chinese community tended to fragment and the intensity of political involvement waned. The events leading up to and following the "July Crisis" of 1959 illustrate this process at work.

In summary, the development of the Malayan political system appears to have been a product of a "chain reaction" of negative responses toward political developments. Each politically-activated segment of society tended to trigger the political mobilization of its rival and competitive elements in Malayan society.

Politics Without Power

One of the most crucial periods in political development is that between the time when the tempo of politics begins to pick up as more and more segments of society enter the political fray, and the time when elections are introduced. During this period, political activity has no institutionalized means of expression, and there is no general consensus as to what constitutes the "fair rules" of political activity. Furthermore, the radical elements which are among the first to become politically active, frequently pride themselves on their perfection of extremist tactics. Indeed, they often place so much emphasis on the tactic and techniques of "revolutionary" politics that they tend to make these the primary basis for their political appeal, and in so doing avoid many of the very crucial issues which a government in power would have to face.

Without the institutionalized methods of political expression provided by the processes of representative government, politics becomes a process of extra-legal and illegal maneuvers. The political groups can be distinguished by their techniques. Some restrict their activity to "lobbying" government authorities or staging passive demonstrations. Others resort to activist and socially disruptive tactics, such as the use of political strikes, hartals, mass demonstrations, and wholesale resignations from public office, while the most militant begin to experiment with strong-arm tactics and the use of violence and intimidation to achieve their aims.

It is difficult to point to any group in Malaya that consistently gave whole-hearted cooperation to the colonial authorities in the attempt to make the transition to independence a smooth one. Rather, there was often a degree of competition among political groups in their attempts to stage militant demonstrations in opposition to policies or proposed action of the government. Much of the militant political activity during this period was generated by the essentially negative character of politics. Political passions were aroused relatively easily by leaders who found something to crusade against. Since the government was the center of political power, nearly all political expression was directed against it, and "anti-colonialism" and "anti-imperialism" became the universal slogans of politics.

When the Malayan Communist Party decided to switch from militant demonstrations to active revolution, all political parties were forced to make a fundamental decision as to whether they should join in the attempt to overthrow the government. Although the Communist leaders tried to utilize Malayan nationalist sentiment to bring popular support to their rebellion, almost no political groups, other than Communist fronts, joined in support of their revolution. The outbreak of the Communist revolt in June 1948, had a chastening effect upon political activity, since political groups which did not join in support of the guerrillas were placed in a position where they could not talk in terms of securing their objectives by means of revolution. Those groups that wavered as to whether they would lend support to the revolution of the Malayan Communist Party were shortly dissolved, either through the action of the government or by the party leaders as an expression of their frustration with the turn of events.

In the transition to independence, nationalism became very important as a factor in politics. Indigenous elites and "power-seekers" could see that their future depended upon the termination of colonial rule, and they were eager to hasten the process by the generation of strong nationalist and anti-colonial sentiments. In the earlier stages of political mobilization, nationalist leaders were preoccupied with the task of challenging and overturning the political system. To avoid divisive dissentions in their ranks, they gave merely perfunctory attention to the equally important task of building a broad-based consensus for an alternative form of government.

The near univeral appeal to nationalism by all political groups helped to conceal their differences. In fact, under the banner of nationalism, the most unusual and divergent political groups came together to form a temporary "national front", which purported to represent Malayan nationalism. The following list of "national fronts" illustrates how short-lived they were: The All-Malaya Council of Joint Action, PUTERA, the National Conference, the National Convention, the All-Malaya National Congress, and the Malay Nationalist Front. The AMCJA was the most unusual of these "national fronts" since it contained both extreme right and left elements under its banner. Yet none of these "national fronts" represented a cross-section of all the important segments of Malayan society. Even the passionate slogans of nationalism proved incapable of concealing the fundamental political divisions which existed in Malayan politics.

The illusory unity created by nationalism was evident in the proliferation of political parties during the period before the first elections. Each divergent element in society, as it became politically conscious, usually organized for some form of political action. Before elections provided effective avenues to power, political parties were, for all practical purposes, indistinguishable from militant pressure groups; in fact, most political parties were the offspring of the larger interest groups. Parties which were founded to attract a broader base of support often split asunder when issues or personal rivalries over party leadership generated factional feuds. For example, personality conflicts were particularly intense within several parties formed in Perak, and led to the formation of the Perak Progressive Party and the National Association of Perak.

The Effect of Elections

The first elections, even on the local level, have a great impact upon politics. They provide institutionalized means of political expression and a vehicle for political power, no matter how slight that power may be. Also, they provide the first opportunity for self-styled leaders to test their popular support. If a single-member district electoral system is adopted, the road to political power depends upon winning a plurality of the votes, which entails the creation of a wide coalition of often conflicting interests.

To effect such a coalition is a particularly difficult task in countries such as Malaya, where politics have been badly fragmented into many diverse political parties. Prior to the first elections, several attempts were made to form broad coalitions to compete in Malaya's single-member district electoral system.

During 1949 and 1950 the Communities Liaison Committee provided a forum where leading political figures could discuss communal problems and suggest possible compromises. If this committee had functioned smoothly, it might have provided the leadership for a broad political agreement between the most powerful communal organizations in the country. Although personal and communal animosities brought this committee to an early demise, this experiment in intercommunal cooperation apparently did have an impact on the thinking of communal leaders who saw more clearly the necessity of building political support that extended beyond communal boundaries. Dato Onn bin Ja'afar, who had founded the United Malays National Organization and was the leading spokesman for postwar Malay nationalism, began to act less and less like a spokesman for one ethnic community. He tried to persuade his party to expand its base of support by opening its membership to non-Malays and by avoiding political postures which were likely to antagonize most non-Malays. When the party refused to follow his lead in this tactic,

Dato Onn attempted to create a new party which would have a core of Malay support, but which would also enlist moderate nationalists from other ethnic communities. The Independence of Malaya Party was to be such a party.

However, Dato Onn's tactics had three serious defects. First, in abandoning UMNO he lost his power base, and the Malays failed to support the new party to the degree he expected. Secondly, the non-Malays were generally unconvinced that Dato Onn had been genuinely converted from Malay communalism to "non-communalism", so he recruited very few non-Malays for his new party. Thirdly, the IMP provided the incentive for the two largest communal organizations, the United Malays National Organization and the Malayan Chinese Association, to seek a temporary agreement to neutralize the political impact of the IMP. The success of this temporary agreement ultimately led to the formation of the Alliance as an effective and lasting political partnership. Although Dato Onn's tactic led to disastrous defeat for his new party, paradoxically, it did in the end promote the formation of that genuine broad-based electoral coalition extending across communal lines that he had hoped for. The IMP professed to be following a "non-communal" approach to politics, while the Alliance extolled the virtues of a "multi-communal" approach to politics. The net result might have been much the same, except that the Alliance had the advantage of relying on the existing strength of established communal associations. Alliance victories in the first elections helped to attract additional supporters, and made it the prime target of all other political parties which were faced with the increasingly difficult task of forging an equally broad and formidable coalition. Despite the centrifugal forces generated within it, the Alliance coalition remained intact, partly as a result of the rewards of elective office.

Competitive appeals to nationalism and opposition to the departing colonial regime were common features of all the early election campaigns. As the first federal election approached in 1955, each party tried to prove its dedication to Malayan nationalism by vigorous demands for expediting Malayan independence. Several parties advanced their announced target dates for independence in an attempt to outbid their rivals. In many respects, the nationalism and anti-colonialism of this transitional period of political development was a symptom of the difficulty of forging a broad-based coalition in a plural society, seriously divided on many of the most important issues facing the country. Nationalism and anti-colonialism were surrogates for a broad political consensus on fundamental questions.

As nationalism became more intensified with the introduction of elections, it became more difficult for the colonial administrators to prepare Malaya for independence at a leisurely pace. Once released by the electoral process, competitive politics tended to develop a "snowball" effect which rapidly threatened the ability of the colonial authorities to determine the sequence and the content of constitutional reform leading to Malayan independence. The pressure of intensified political activity forced the British to agree to Malayan independence sooner than seemed desirable or possible prior to the first elections. Fortunately, the broad-based Alliance coalition which emerged from these first elections also provided a power base to which the British could transfer their authority with some reasonable expectation of political stability.

Those political leaders who had been selected by the British authorities to share in the responsibilities of government as a preparation for self-government were in most cases repudiated by the electorate in the first elections. The "Member System" experiment in a partial cabinet government of native politicians was not particularly successful since association with the British in higher administrative posts became a stigma which was a serious liability once elections became the test of political success. Although the British might have exercised better judgement in selecting local leaders who would have been more likely to win the first elections, it is dubious whether the more representative and astute political leaders would have been too cooperative in such appointed positions. With great difficulty the British were able to persuade two Alliance leaders to accept portfolios in the government in late 1953, but within a little more than half a year both of them withdrew from the government when the Alliance decided to stage its boycott in protest against the system of elections passed by the Legislative Council.[1] Any attempt by colonial authorities to transfer the mantle of governmental authority to leaders of their own choosing was bound to be resented, and native politicians who did not have the confidence of the British were quick to suspect or imagine that such an attempt was being made. This illustrates but one of the difficulties that was encountered in the preparations for a gradual transition to independence.

The nationalist sentiment that was generated with the first elections appeared to aid the Alliance above all other parties. Through its obstructionist tactics, it had become identified in the public eye with the demand for a speedy, yet orderly, transition to independence. As the strongest party, the Alliance began to campaign on the argument that independence would be jeopardized or postponed if it did not obtain an overwhelming mandate. The weaker parties were thus placed in the difficult position of appearing to obstruct independence by competing with the Alliance. Because of this, the anti-colonial and nationalist focus of politics tended to favor the strongest party and contribute to one-party dominance in the developmental stages of Malayan politics.

Power and Responsibility

After the first elected government assumed full responsibility, politics underwent a marked change. The processes of compromise and adjustment continued from the previous period, but the issues which were largely avoided or glossed over in the election campaigns now had to be resolved. In office the Alliance was forced to make difficult decisions on the most troublesome issues and then obtain a consensus within it own ranks to supplant the rather shallow unity of ill-defined nationalism generated by anti-colonial slogans. In a relatively short time, fundamental decisions were made in secret negotiations by the ruling coalition which was none too stable, and under constant attack from a bevy of opposition parties. The task was made easier, no doubt, by the rewards of office which were shared among the Alliance partners. In terms of long-range impact on Malayan politics, this initial period after the Alliance assumed office was probably the most vital period in the transition from the closed politics of colonial rule to the more open politics of national independence.

After the Alliance assumed control of the government, its tone and posture shifted. A short time before, it had staged mass demonstrations to impress the colonial authorities and had provoked a constitutional crisis to demonstrate its nationalism and advance its demands for constitutional reform. In office, the Alliance became much less militant, and worked in close cooperation with the colonial authorities. It had become more concerned with making a smooth transition from self-government to complete independence, than with generating anti-colonial passions. Furthermore, the Alliance leadership apparently became more appreciative of the problems previously faced by the colonial regime. On several occasions Tunku Abdul Rahman went out of his way to praise the British, explaining to the public the dangers involved in cutting ties with Britain or of releasing colonial administrators from government service before adequately trained Malayans could be found to take their place. In short, responsibilities of office made the Alliance more conservative, cautious, and a more vigorous defender of the processes of law and order. This change may be attributed partly to the cooperation accorded the Alliance by the colonial authorities, and partly to the fact that the Alliance was primarily responsible for the provisions of the new Merdeka Constitution. It is obvious that those who have a stake in a political system and who have been its principal architects will become its strongest defenders.

Because the Alliance was fairly successful in working out balanced and acceptable compromises on most of the intractable issues facing the nation, it did not have to resort to artificial devices to divert attention from domestic divisions or serious disorders. After it took office, the new government contributed to and greatly benefited from the economic prosperity Malaya experienced. Had a severe recession or economic collapse occurred, it is questionable whether popular democracy could have survived. Failure to meet economic or political problems would have spelled disaster. In place of open competitive politics there would probably have been an intensification of xenophobic nationalism to justify some system of "benevolent authoritarianism" or "guided democracy".

The Process of Political Stabilization

Initially, introduction of democratic processes to countries emerging from colonial rule inevitably results in political confusion. Maximum uncertainty about the political future is combined with exaggerated hopes for success on the part of those entering the political contest for the first time. Without previous power or tested political allies, most political parties tend to be irresponsible and inconsistent. Elections may be necessary as a first step toward political stabilization after the end of a colonial regime, but the first elections can hardly be said to be a true test of the democratic mandate.

As a test of the democratic process, the second national elections are more important than the first, since it is only then that the delicate compromises and adjustments worked out by the elected government are subjected to the test of public support. A government seeking re-election has a record of performance against which the public may judge political leadership. Consequently, the electoral mandate, becomes more meaningful and those who have experienced the problems of government first hand will exercise a salutory effect on political campaigning. In a country like Malaya, where the social structure makes it difficult for leaders to secure the wholehearted support of a communal electorate for complicated intercommunal compromises, the second national elections are particularly indicative of both political stability and cleavage.

The results of the second elections revealed the dangerous political cleavage between the Malay and the non-Malay communities, but the Alliance Government still retained the confidence of the majority of the electorate. The Alliance polled 81·7 per cent of the votes in 1955, 51·8 per cent in 1959 and 58·3 per cent in 1964. The continuing strength of the Alliance gave some indication of the extent of public consensus on the fundamental compromises worked out by the Alliance on sensitive economic and communal issues. Election statistics revealed a fairly high degree of continuity and consistency from 1959 to 1964, suggesting that Malayan party politics was becoming more stabilized and that the parties had cultivated a rather large core of dependable support among the voters. The average Malayan voter appeared to understand the function of a political party and was fairly willing to commit himself to the support of a party, even though he may not have cared to be a partisan activist. The transient shifting voter will always remain the key factor in politics so long as open elections determine who is to hold public office, but a much smaller percentage of the Malayan electorate appeared to be in this category in 1964 than in 1954.

An Analysis of Party Competition

The whole structure of Malayan politics has been determined by the competition generated between the parties. To simplify the analysis, we may begin by examining the configuration of Malayan society based on communal and economic divisions. These are the two great issues of Malayan politics. In Malaya, communal differences very nearly divide the population into two equal parts since about one half of Malaya's inhabitants are Malay. Although the non-Malays consist of Chinese, Indians, Ceylonese, Eurasians and others, these communities are fairly united on communal issues by their common opposition to Malay special rights and privileges. While there are moderates and extremists on both sides, communalism creates a rather clean cleavage in society, with the moderates accepting the necessity for compromise, but still tending to line up on one side or the other on communal issues. If a circle is used to represent the "political universe" of Malaya, the communal cleavage may be represented by Figure 1.

Politics and economics are linked together in any society, but especially so in a country engaged in a massive program of economic development through government action. Consequently, the economic stakes of politics are much higher than in a tradition-bound society. In Malaya "pocket book" issues divide the electorate, but in a much different way than communal issues. If communal cleavage is in a vertical plane, economic cleavage is in a horizontal plane, and might be illustrated by Figure 2. However, the economic cleavage does not split Malayan society into two nearly equal and clearly divided sides. Although reliable statistics on income distribution in Malaya are not available, a correlation of individual income with the percentiles in order of the size of individual income would probably look something like Figure 3. On the economic scale there is a continuum with no sharp division between upper and lower income groups. Arbitrary categories can be established for analytical purposes. For example, the shaded section of the percentile scale represents the percentiles that would probably fall in the "middle income" groups, and would have some middle class characteristics on economic issues, taking a moderate position between the extreme economic demands made by either the destitute or the well-to-do.

Because the income distribution is not the same for Malays and non-Malays, the economic cleavages cannot be depicted as being at right angles to the axis of communal cleavage. The Malays have smaller percentages in the middle and upper income brackets than the non-Malays.[2] Figure 4 represents the approximate configuration of Malayan society on the basis of the two basic issues of communalism and economics. The communal cleavage is quite sharp and distinct, while the economic cleavage is graduated, and does not cut across the communal axis at right angles.

All the more important Malayan political parties have been forced to take some stands on economic and communal issues. Consequently, it is possible to consider their approximate locations on the model of Malayan political society represented by Figure 4.

The Alliance, in itself a coalition of communal political associations, makes a wide appeal to voters of all races, and thus straddles the communal axis. By its policies, it takes a moderate position on communal issues, but definitely leans toward the Malay position by supporting Malay special privileges, at least for the present as "temporary" measures needed to improve the position of the Malays. On the economic issues, the Alliance gains fairly high support of middle and upper income groups, but it has also initiated expensive rural development programs to raise the standard of living, especially for the poor rural peasant Malays. Although it is difficult to represent diagrammatically the extent of Alliance support, the party tends to have a political center of gravity that is slightly pro-Malay and with a greater proportion of its support coming from above average income groups. Because of the competition of other parties, the Alliance has not always been able to win as broadbased support as it would like to have.

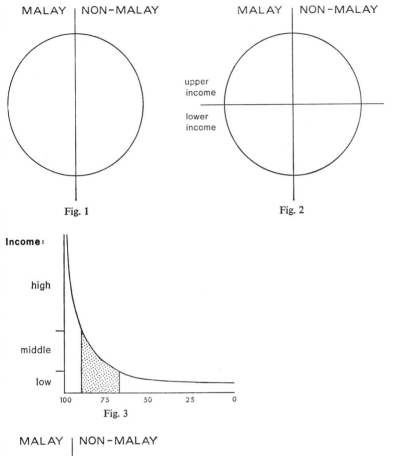

Fig. 1

Fig. 2

Income:

Fig. 3

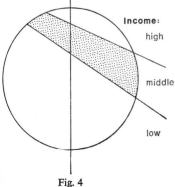

Fig. 4

401

The approximate appeal of the Alliance and of other major parties is represented in graphic form in Figure 5.

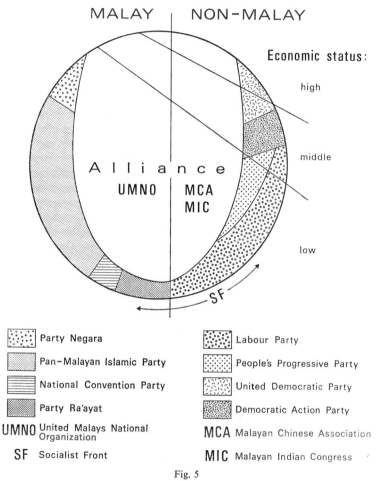

Fig. 5

Figure 5 illustrates how the Alliance has dominated the center of Malayan politics, while the opposition parties have tended to be arrayed on the periphery of the political stage.[3] One can see why it has been so difficult for the opposition parties to combine their forces to provide a coherent and responsible alternative to the Alliance. The Socialist Front appeared to have the best chance of becoming the core of the opposition, since it linked the two main wings of opposition to the Alliance. However, a wider coalition bridging the communal axis would have had to be based on an intensification of economic issues at the expense of communal ones. While the Socialist Front has tried to follow such a strategy, it was unable to mobilize sufficient Malay support, and probably would have been unable to do so even if it had assumed a more "pro-Malay" bias. Coalition with the PMIP was impossible since Malay leaders in that party were unwilling to push asides communal issues in the interest of opposition unity. Consequently, the opposition has been severely weakened and immobilized by communalism, while the Alliance has exploited the communal cleavage to insure its continued domination of Malayan politics. Even if the Alliance had lost the majority support it probably would have continued to enjoy a majority in Parliament because Malay and non-Malay opposition parties were incapable of effective cooperation even in the matter of limited agreements to avoid triangular contests during elections.

The Bias of the Malayan Political System

Because the axes of economic cleavage and communal cleavage do not cross each other at right angles, practically any economic issue raises side issues of communalism, and conversely, communal issues involve economic questions. For example, a program to aid the economically destitute, or to increase the tax burdens of the higher income groups is bound to aid larger proportion of Malays than non-Malays. For this reason, communalism was partially disguised in Malayan politics under the cover of "non-communal" issues, such as taxation, social welfare, education, foreign policy, religious questions, and a host of other matters.

The political party system has, however, helped to mitigate communalism. A good share of the credit for the supression of extreme communalism must be given to the Alliance, which until mid-1965 had successfully resolved the major communal conflicts through compromises worked out in secret negotiating sessions among its three member parties. Only those opposition parties that have no hope of winning national majorities could afford to make brazen appeals to communal passions. Most opposition parties hoped to displace the Alliance by building a broad base of support from more than one racial group, and therefore approached communal issues with caution. Nevertheless, all parties made communal calculations on practically all issues of politics, and their appeal for communal support has at times been very thinly disguised. Even though the nature of the Malayan political system has tended to mitigate extreme communalism by its combination with other issues of politics, the dominant cleavage in Malayan politics remains communal.

The Malayan public has been warned time and again about the dangers of communal conflict, and on occasions communal rioting and disorders have occurred to provide a suitable object-lesson on the perils of communal strife. Consequently, there is considerable evidence to indicate that a large segment of the Malayan public will pursue communal objectives only until the point is reached where communalism threatens domestic tranquility or political stability. While some militants are unmindful of the consequenses of extreme communalism, they are restrained in part by the more moderate and cautious dattitues of large numbers among all the ethnic communities.[4]

Because of the complicated intertwining of issues, it has become quite difficult to raise new questions for public consideration or to re-examine old policies. The Alliance has worked out the major compromises on the great issues, and dominates Malayan politics by its defense of these compromises. To avoid re-opening all the divisive issues of the past, the Alliance partners are warned against "rocking the boat" by making new political demands or by raising new issues for public debate. Some Alliance compromises have even involved a moratorium on the discussion of certain issues until a fixed future date. Similarly, the opposition parties often seem even more rigidly committed to old issues and dogmas. If new questions do arise, such as happened with the creation of Malaysia, the opposition parties seemed to suffer from excessive rigidity or a near paralysis of decision. Thus, rather than engaging in a competition for new ideas and exploring new ways to meet Malaysia's complex problems, Malayan parties resembled wrestlers who become locked in the same hold throughout a match. In part, this may be due to the fundamental communal cleavage which makes it difficult to raise issues that may upset the communal balance, threaten political stability, or even lead to communal violence.

The Political Consequences of Malaysia

After the 1959 elections, a period of reasonable political stability persisted until the time of Tunku Abdul Rahman's dramatic May 1961 proposal to form Malaysia. It is obvious that the Malayan Government, before embarking upon the venture of trying to win the support of Singapore and the Borneo states for Malaysia, had given some attention to the consequences of such a union for Malayan politics. For Malaya, the big problem was Singapore. The Malayan Government feared that if Singapore became an independent state, it might prove a source of many troubles and perhaps become a base for foreign intrigue or intervention against Malaya. As we now know, Malaya's answer was to bring Singapore into a wider union under circumstances that would be economically favorable to Singapore, while giving the Federation sufficient authority to deal with internal subversion and potential threats to domestic order. The Borneo states, which were also facing an uncertain future, conveniently provided a large native population to balance against Singapore's Chinese majorities. While these were not the only calculations in the Malaysia proposals, they were of primary importance to Malaya insofar as domestic politics was concerned. It was assumed that such a combination of states in a wider federation (with the help of a little gerrymandering) would be able to keep the same communal balance as Malaya, and, therefore, Malaysia would have minimal political impact on Malayan politics.

As finally constituted, the Malaysian Federation did have a communal distribution somewhat similar to that of Malaya, *provided* all "Malaysian" stock peoples are grouped together. However, many of the indigenous

404

peoples of Borneo differ significantly from the Malays in their religion, language, political views and social organization. A number of important Malay leaders either chose to ignore or were not aware of the differences between the Borneo peoples and the peninsular Malays. In fact, in the early stages of negotiations for Malaysia, Tunku Abdul Rahman unnecessarily generated additional opposition in the Borneo states when he chose to state the case for joining Malaysia in terms of the common "Malay" heritage shared by the indigenous peoples of both Borneo and Malaya. Traditionally,

TABLE 21
Ethnic distribution on a percentage basis for Malaya and Malaysia

	Federation of Malaya		Federation of Malaysia (including Singapore)	
	1957 census	1964 estimates	1957 census	1964 estimates
Malaysians	49·8%	50·0%	46·5%	46·1%
Chinese	37·1%	36·9%	42·0%	42·2%
Indians	11·1%	11·2%	9·3%	9·4%
Others	2·0%	1·9%	2·2%	2·3%

the interior natives of Borneo have strong anti-Malay feelings because of their long history of conflicts with Brunei Malays who ruled the coastal areas and extorted tribute from the inland tribal peoples. Consequently, it was a serious mistake to assume that the Borneo natives could all be counted as "Malays" for the purpose of preserving Malaya's communal balance in the new federation. Indeed, it may be more appropriate to think of politics in the new Malaysian Federation in terms of four, instead of three, major ethnic communities—the Malays, the Chinese, the Indians, and "non-Malay indigenous tribal peoples". For census purposes, the last category is imprecise, and depends on the definition one uses for "Malay". Is the distinction to be based on religion, custom, language, or political attitudes? Since the

TABLE 22
Ethnic and tribal distribution in Malaya and Malaysia, 1964 by percentages[5]

	Malaya	Malaysia (with Singapore)	Malaysia (without Singapore)
Malays and Muslim tribal people	49·2%	40·6%	45·9%
Non-Muslim tribal people	0·8%	5·5%	6·6%
Chinese	36·9%	42·2%	35·7%
Indians	11·2%	9·4%	9·6%
Others	1·9%	2·3%	2·2%

concept of the Malay community is so tied up with religion, that is perhaps the most easily identified and politically meaningful dividing line between the different Malaysian peoples in Borneo. If religion is used as the only basis for division between the "Malay-type" people in Borneo and the native tribal peoples, then the Federation of Malaysia was substantially different from Malaya's communal distribution.

In the campaign to sell the idea of the Malaysian Federation political differences within the new union were glossed over as "unity" became the watchword. Following the example and pattern of Malayan politics, pro-Malaysia "Alliance" coalitions were formed in Sabah and Sarawak to capture elective office and smooth over or suppress internal divisions. These developments contributed to the impression that a single party system was being extended throughout Malaysia. Yet, despite semantic and organizational similarities, the Sabah Alliance and the Sarawak Alliance were fundamentally different from the Malayan Alliance. In both Borneo states, the Alliance was essentially a multi-party coalition in which parties representing the non-Muslim native peoples were the dominant force, while in Malaya, the Malays represented by UMNO were the basic source of Alliance strength.

Because the political equilibrium of Malayan politics was different from that of Singapore or the Borneo states, Malaya's politicians were subject to strong temptations to intervene in the local politics of the new states joining the union. Such involvement was easy to justify as a desirable and necessary part of the process of nation-building. Whatever rationalizations or explanations might be used, the net result was the intensification of conflict between the Federal Government, controlled by the Malayan Alliance, and certain state governments, controlled by locally based parties which were either in the opposition, or if in the Malaysian Alliance, still mounted a form of covert or passive resistance to the political authority of the Federal Government. Under such circumstances, the new union suffered from severe problems of political accommodation and integration.

These frictions were most intense in the case of Singapore, since the Federal Government had very limited capabilities of influencing Singapore politics, except in a rather negative way, through "dire warnings" and threats of coercion. In the purely political sphere, the PAP had greater capabilities than the Federal authorities since the Alliance was totally ineffective in the Singapore elections of September 1963, while the PAP did pose a greater threat to the Alliance when the former entered the 1964 parliamentary elections. In its early stages, the Alliance-PAP competition was tempered by the support of both parties for Malaysia. Yet, the contest was crucial since its outcome would determine whether political realignment would occur in Singapore or Malaya. The Malaysian Solidarity Convention became the primary vehicle for those who wished to engineer a political realignment in Malaya. Whether it might have succeeded or not can never be known since Singapore's expulsion from Malaysia abruptly terminated the contest in such a way that the issue could not be resolved by normal political means. It is somewhat ironic that the Alliance feared the free operation of the political system which it had created. That the Malaysia Solidarity Convention helped to trigger off the events which completely negated its stated objectives is, in retrospect, equally ironic.

The constitutional arrangements for Malaysia had been designed to minimize the political consequences of union, but the rapid expansion of party competition, first across the causeway and ultimately spreading to all parts of Malaysia, forced the pace of political integration. The processes of conflict resolution and accommodation were unable to keep pace with the competitive demands being raised. As unresolved issues accumulated, the political system became overloaded. Political apoplexy ensued. By then, the alternatives appeared to be narrowed to partition or coercion on a large scale accompanied by civil disorders.

To a large extent, Singapore's expulsion from Malaysia was the result of failures of political leadership. In the Malaysian political system, Parliament has played a minor role (if any at all) in the process of working out compromises on the crucial issues of politics. Rather this function has been performed by the Alliance National Council, with Prime Minister Tunku Abdul Rahman being an "eminently fair court of last resort" particularly and Kuala Lumpur, the PAP had no effective access to the decision making on sensitive communal issues. However, in the dispute between Singapore process within the Federal Government since it had no representation in the Alliance or on the Federal Cabinet. Consequently, the Alliance National Council could not resolve the conflict since it had become a party to the dispute. Furthermore, it became all too apparent that the Alliance leadership of the Federal Government remained too closely identified with Malayan interests and was committed to maintaining the political balance in Malaya at the expense of the overall needs of the wider Malaysian Federation. When Tunku Abdul Rahman came under direct political attack from the PAP, he could no longer perform the function of "impartial" political mediator. No institutional arrangements existed which could be substituted for this vital function, except the laborious process of semi-formal "diplomatic" negotiations, which, as so often happens, led to stalemate.

Singapore's leaders must also share some of the blame for Singapore's expulsion from Malaysia. First, the PAP leaders launched an undisguised assault on the MCA in a bid to split the Alliance. When that objective failed to materialize, they shifted to a direct offensive against UMNO for allegedly "harboring Malay communalists", following which they began their campaign against the Federal Government. Finally, Tunku Abdul Rahman came into their line of fire. By progressive stages, the avenues of political communication were being closed, as mutual respect and tolerance were destroyed. Rather than devote their energies to working out mutually acceptable compromises, one issue at a time, Singapore's leaders were willing to intensify politics by raising many new controversial issues at the very time when it was apparent that the political system had become overloaded with seemingly irreconcilable demands. As the political contest became intensified, it appeared to be a struggle for political survival between two completely incompatible foes. In reality, however, the policy differences between the Alliance and the PAP-led Malaysian Solidarity Convention were not nearly as great as indicated by the temper of the political dialogue. Certainly, equally difficult issues had been resolved before in Malayan politics. But when each party viewed the contest in terms of ultimate victory or defeat, accommodation and compromise on even the smallest issue became practically impossible since each dispute was taken to be only a skirmish in a larger fight for political victory or extinction.

The Politics of Partition

Both the formation of Malaysia and the expulsion of Singapore were motivated, in large measure, by a desire on the part of Kuala Lumpur to control politics through manipulation of political boundaries. A variety of ties and common problems could be found to justify various configurations of political union, but it appears that calculations of political power were foremost. In the creation of the new union, those in positions of power had a substantial advantage, for they negotiated the constitutional terms, and they became the "boundary-makers". Therefore, to a certain extent, Malaysia was the product of political gerrymandering by the ruling parties in each of the constituent states. Conversely, when the political balance seemed to jeopardize the ruling party in the federation, rather than make political adjustments within the system, emergency political surgery was performed instead.

Singapore's independence has certainly not irrevocably settled the basic issues of its political future. Key political figures in both Malaysia and Singapore exhibited widely divergent attitudes toward the possibility of eventual reunion of the two states. Most PAP leaders expressed the hope that Singapore would be reunited with Malaysia within a decade or two. Within the Alliance, prominent members of both the MCA and UMNO voiced similar hopes,[6] even though Tunku Abdul Rahman rather pointedly tried to close the issue by saying that Singapore would never be welcomed back into Malaysia.[7] Yet, the issue is not so easily disposed of since boundary manipulation is a game which can be played by many politicians and for a variety of objectives. With the defeat of the Communists in Indonesia and the commencement of friendly relations between Djakarta and Kuala Lumpur, Malaysia has been much less concerned with political developments in Singapore, since it has been erecting "containment" barriers around Singapore. If Singapore were to seek entrance to Malaysia under present circumstances it would have to accept far less favorable terms than those negotiated in 1963. Even so, the issue of merger will probably be raised again when the present generation of leaders in Singapore and Malaysia passes from the scene. The next time, however, the agitation for merger may come from the Malay communal extremists who want to bring Singapore under Malay control, perhaps as a capstone to the edifice of a *Melayu Raya*.

Political Tensions in Malaysia After Partition

Singapore's exodus may make it easier to develop a sense of national identity within Malaysia. Yet the partition also highlights a major problem of developing national loyalties that can transcend communal and regional allegiances. Such loyalties will not develop if substantial elements of the public feel that they are denied access to power or feel that the Federal Government is insensitive to their needs. The Alliance Government has been reasonably successful in representing the major interests in Malayan society and in working out acceptable compromises between their competing demands. Consequently, it has developed loyal and dependable support within Malaya, but its support in the Borneo territories has been much less secure. While the Alliance Government has made an effort to recruit leaders from Borneo to share office and participate in the decision-making processes of government, it has frequently been more concerned with finding "collaborators" than with sharing authority with people who genuinely represent the local interests of these two states.[8] After Singapore's departure from Malaysia, Malaya's dominance over the union became more complete and the Federal Government was thus more willing to act decisively in case of conflicts of interest with the Borneo states.

The political supremacy of the Alliance and its high-handed treatment of Singapore has caused a substantial number of articulate citizens in Sarawak and Sabah to view the Malaysian Government as an "alien" administration having more concern with the interests of Malaya and the Malays than with Malaysia as a whole. Since no opinion surveys have been taken in Borneo, it is impossible to determine how widespread these attitudes have become. What is clear is that those who entertained these views can now point to events occurring after Malaysia was formed to demonstrate that their suspicions were well-founded.

While the Malaysia Agreement contained "guarantees" of substantial state autonomy for Sarawak and Sabah, the Federal Government was not in sympathy with some of the concessions which had been given to these states as an inducement for them to join the union. Kuala Lumpur's periodic intervention in the politics of Sarawak and Sabah may be viewed as an attempt to circumvent by political means what had earlier been granted in the form of legal and constitutional guarantees. After the disastrous experience with Singapore, the Federal Government became more determined than ever to apply unyielding pressure against those who espoused separatist or autonomous demands. Cloaked in the mantle of Malaysian nationalism, the argument was both self-righteous and logical: the Federal Government has responsibilities for the whole union. If there is potential instability in some of the constituent states, the Federal Government has a responsibility to intervene. Since political stability and economic development depend upon harmony and cooperation between federal and state authorities, why should the states not be brought into line with national policies and objectives? If large sums of federal money are spent in the states, the states have an obligation to comply with federal policies. If Malaysia is to become a single unified nation, the advocates of state autonomy are "anti-national", and should be dealt with accordingly.

While federal authorities expressed these views with some consistency, they tried to avoid antagonizing those who have become distrustful of the policies and motives of the Federal Government. As large federal development programs give Sabah and Sarawak a greater stake in the Malaysian economy, and as greater efforts are made to promote a wider sense of Malaysian nationalism, these attitudes may change. However, since these same issues were behind the estrangement between Singapore and Malaysia, we may assume that they will present a continuing threat to the present union for some years to come.

With Singapore's expulsion, the Alliance obtained insurance against political challenges to its authority. The Malays once again became the largest ethnic community,[9] and the pro-Malay bias of the Alliance could more easily be defended and justified. Public policies on sensitive communal issues would continue to be worked out in secret negotiations within the Alliance structure where its Malay leadership exercised careful control and direction of the whole process. Thus, communal accommodation was to be only on terms acceptable to the top echelon of UMNO. In this way, access to the political system was denied to all non-Malays except those who agreed to the following conditions: they must cooperate with UMNO by participating in the Alliance; they must be cautiously solicitous of Malay opinion on sensitive communal issues; and they must be careful not to criticize or oppose in public the patronizing "non-communal" leadership of the Alliance Government.

In the recast Malaysia the political power of the Malays is considerably enhanced. Political wisdom dictates that non-Malays in Malaysia avoid public expressions which would reflect their fear that the Alliance will become even more pro-Malay than before. Meanwhile, the more communally-minded Malays have been pressing the government to give higher priority to policies which will favor the Malays and assert in more unequivocal terms the basic Malay character of Malaysia. While it is uncertain how the Alliance will change its stand on communal issues, there is ample evidence to suggest that the Alliance is more sensitive to demands of Malay communal extremists, and has trimmed its political sails accordingly. For example, previously, talk of uniting all Malays in a union of *Melayu Raya* was deliberately discouraged by the Alliance as a subversive political doctrine, but after the treaty with Indonesia, high government officials engage in public discussions on ways to promote the union of all the Malay peoples of Southeast Asia. For many, the Maphilindo proposal is seen as a first step in this direction. In line with these objectives, Malaysia and Indonesia agreed to standardize and unify their two national languages so as to create a common language to be called Malindo.[10] An increasing pro-Malay bias has also been discernible in economic development and education policies. Mounting pressure by the Federal Government to bring the states into conformity with its pro-Malay national policies led to a number of political incidents during which Kuala Lumpur acted decisively to impose a settlement upon recalcitrant local politicians in Sarawak and Sabah.

The year 1967 was a critical one in Malaysian politics, since on August 31, Malay became the sole national language. Ultra-communal Malays expected to retain all Malay privileges and have the added advantages of enforced use of Malay in government and education. While non-Malays have been exhorted to learn and use the National Language, many have not done so, and one gets the impression that the Malays expect and hope that the non-Malays will not become too proficient in the use of the language. If Malay is to be the key for access to jobs and political power, then the Malays expect to have a decisive advantage for many years to come. At present Romanized script (*rumi*) is used to write the National Language, but already there is a mounting cry to adopt the far more difficult Arabic script (*jawi*). If *jawi* is adopted as the official script for the National Language, then the language barrier will become even more difficult for non-Malays to surmount.

At the time of Malaya's independence in 1957, non-Malays were persuaded to accept Malay as the sole national language within ten years on the assumption that Malay special rights were temporary and presumably might be terminated or gradually eliminated after 1967. While no promises were given, non-Malays were told that Malay special rights were needed to raise the economic and educational level of the Malays so that Malays could enjoy "economic parity" with the non-Malay communities. For this reason, there is an implied promise that practically all communal issues will eventually be thrown back into the political arena once again for re-negotiation. From past experience, one may assume that, if this implied promise is to be kept, communal passions will become particularly intense and that the political system will be subject to very severe tensions while new compromises are worked out on these delicate and irascible issues. With the increased political supremacy of the Malays the reduction of Malay special rights and privileges would require an act of self-denial of enormous proportions on the part of the Malays. Human nature being what it is, we may assume that the pressures for change will be in the other direction.

Democracy in Malaysia

One of the most serious consequences of Malaysia has been its effect upon the political opposition. In general, the constitutional arrangements re-inforced the position of the dominant political party or coalition in each state. As a result, the opposition parties, regardless of their policy objectives, tended to look upon the new federation with trepidation or outright hostility. The tendency toward one-party dominance was re-inforced and the opposition parties, already located at the extremes of the political spectrum, were more inclined to desperate and irresponsible responses. Under these circumstances, it is little wonder that most opposition parties have exhibited considerable contempt for the democratic process, particularly that represented by Malaysia's Parliament. Boycotts, mass demonstrations, politically inspired rioting, conspiracy with foreign powers and ultimately armed insurgency provide alternative tactics which become increasingly attractive for dispossessed and disillusioned "permanent political minorities". Such attitudes were clearly evident in the actions of the top leaders of the PMIP, the National Convention Party and Party Ra'ayat when they decided to leave Malaya secretly in order to form an Indonesian-sponsored "Malaysian Government in Exile".[11]

Important features of the democratic process are displayed in the functioning of the Malaysian Parliament. Following British parliamentary practices, the government has complete control over all bills,[12] and a substantial measure of control over motions and over the time allotted for debate. Although Parliamentary rules provide for a number of select and standing committees,[13] most bills are considered by the Committee of the Whole only a few days after being introduced. Consequently, the opposition parties have only a short time to study the government's proposals, and there is usually insufficient time for debate or discussion on the details of the legislation. Frequently, the more important the legislation, the greater has been the haste in pushing it through Parliament without prior notice. The opposition parties neither have the expertise nor the time to prepare informed and responsible criticism of the more complex legislation such as the budget. Parliamentary surveillance of the executive is very cursory, and the opposition parties are denied access to some information which would enable them to be more effective in revealing malfeasance or misfeasance of office. Therefore, parliamentary debate tends to take on the flavor of campaign oratory with its exchange of acrimony and epithets.

Under these circumstances, the outward forms of democratic procedure are followed, but there appears to be cynicism about the functions of Parliament on both sides of the House. To the government, the opposition seems ill-informed, malicious and destructive. It is a great temptation for the government to harrass the opposition through the use of police powers, and to exercise its control of parliamentary proceedings to limit criticism on certain sensitive issues.

Under the Malaysian Constitution there are few institutional restraints on the exercise of power by the Federal Government so long as it commands a decisive majority in Parliament. While the Constitution enumerates a number of "fundamental rights" these may be limited or suspended by an ordinary legislative enactment.[14] Consequently, if democracy and individual liberty are to be preserved, it depends upon the self-restraint of the Federal Government. While the Alliance professes to be dedicated to the principles of constitutionalism and democracy, its detractors say this is only because it has not yet faced a serious challenge from a constitutional opposition. Whichever interpretation is more nearly correct is difficult to determine since the Alliance Government has not been put into a position where it has had to make a clear cut choice between defending democracy and staying in power by undemocratic means. However, it has not been above "tampering with the rules" for partisan political advantage.

For the most part, the Alliance Government has not had to rely upon "Constitution tampering" tactics since it possesses extensive persuasive and coercive powers which have been quite effective in perpetuating its rule and securing compliance with its objectives. The Federal Government operates and controls all radio broadcasting facilities, and has denied the use of these facilities to its critics except under very limited and restricted conditions.[15] Restrictions have been placed on the freedom of the press through press licensing and publication import restrictions laws, as well as by the possible use of extraordinary police powers.[16] While Malaysia has no laws providing for prior censorship, penalties are applied to the importation or publication of materials expressing certain views or doctrines. For example, Communist literature is prohibited, as well as religious literature which expresses contempt for Islam or propagates "unorthodox" Muslim doctrines. On other issues, the law is vague, and much depends upon the discretion of the authorities who have broad powers to punish the critic

Except under extreme provocation or in the midst of political crisis, the Government has avoided the more overt exercise of its authority to silence or punish critics. However, threats of the use of extraordinary powers against members of opposition parties if they go "too far" have been fairly frequent. While it had been the practice to let the Minister of Interior issue such warnings, in later years Tunku Abdul Rahman was also willing to threaten opponents of his government with severe penalties. For example, during the Sarawak crisis he stated that talk about Sarawak withdrawing from Malaysia was "treachery" and then added:

> Whoever talks of or takes any step which reveal that they have the subversive and treacherous intention, then we shall take the action against them as we did against the communists.
> I like to see if we can make an example of these traitors.[17]

Later when similar warnings were made, he stated:

> . . . there are still subversive elements in our midst whose only aim is to try and destroy our happiness and to do all they can to mar our natural unity.[18]

At times his speeches have seemed to imply that a subversive is anyone who, by criticism, weakens national unity. These warnings and threats, for whatever reason they may be made, constitute a symptom of ambivalent attitudes toward the operation of free democratic processes.

In politics the art of persuasion ultimately depends on the ability to provide tangible benefits to supporters. Malaysia's dynamic economic growth has placed the Alliance Government in a very strong political position. While general economic growth has received a very high priority in Government policies, the Government has also been quite adept at allocating its resources so that its supporters are more likely to receive a greater share of the benefits. Government jobs, scholarships, contracts and development projects can and frequently have been awarded with some consideration to the mobilization of political support for the Alliance. In Malaysia's federal system, the Federal Government provides the bulk of the funds spent by the states. It is no mere coincidence that when opposition parties have controlled state governments, the Federal Government has been less generous with its funds, arguing that the cuts were necessary because of mal-administration and waste by state authorities. The allocation of federal funds has been cleverly employed to secure state compliance with federal policies and to improve the political fortunes of the state Alliance organization. When federal authorities have intervened in state politics, a settlement according to a "federal formula" is usually accompanied by announcements of new federal expenditures for local development projects.[19] In response to one such announcement, an opposition politician asked, "Are these simply arbitrary amounts of taxpayers' money, handed out to us—like sweets to children—by a Father Christmas in a songkok?"[20]

The Social Foundations of Politics

In most Western democracies, pluralism is primarily a product of functional specialization and diversification within society. In such modern urban-centered societies, social and group structures are characterized by complex overlapping membership and loyalty patterns. With a social structure of this sort, each political issue is likely to generate the mobilization of a unique configuration of political forces, so that the axis of conflict on one issue tends to bisect the axes of conflct of other issues. Compromise and adjustment may be effected, since all issues are not fought along the same axis and "enemies" in one contest become "allies" in the next. Furthermore, with overlapping membership and loyalty systems, the individual citizen is likely to give his support to a political party on a very limited and contingent basis. Substantial numbers of citizens are willing to change their support from one party to another in response to slight shifts of position by political parties because of their contingent loyalties and the cross-pressures which arise out of their identification with diverse and frequently conflicting interest groups. With no sharp social, economic or ethnic-cultural cleavages in society, party success depends upon competing actively for wide popular support among nearly all elements of the population. Consequently, where the social structure reflects great functional pluralism, democracy is facilitated, for overlapping loyalties tend to reduce the intensity of political conflict and political change can occur through shifting loyalties of voters.

By contrast, Malaysian society, similar to that of many emerging nations, is composed of multiple communal structures which are a product of diverse ethnic and cultural-linguistic traditions. Society is not as functionally diversified as that found in the West. But more important, what functional diversification has developed tends to be confined within communal compartments. Each community tends to dominate or monopolize certain skills professions and economic activities required for the maintenance of the total social order. The communal structure of society exhibits some features of a caste system, in that certain functions are performed by groups traditionally acknowledged to have ascriptive rights (and perhaps duties) to provide certain services, and are generally believed to have "natural abilities" or skills which are inherited as an ethnic trait.[21] This form of "communal pluralism" (as opposed to functional pluralism) intensifies conflict since the boundaries of functional and economic interest groups tend to coincide with cultural-ethnic divisions in society. Therefore, few overlapping loyalties bridge the fundamental cleavages along communal lines. Such a social structure gives the political system a far more rigid and inflexible character than the more diffuse and diversified pluralism of modern industrial societies.

A party system based on communal politics tends to acquire the rigid character of the social structure. Formed along communal lines, the parties reinforce communal barriers, and hence inhibit or prevent the shift of voter allegiances from one party to another. So long as democratic institutional forms are followed, the allocation of power within society is determined essentially by two kinds of activities: (1) through the formation of inter-communal coalitions; or (2) through manipulating the "rules of the game" by shifting political boundaries or tampering with the constitution. In the first method, politics is essentially a game of intrigue and behind-the-scenes bargaining played by a small number of charismatic leaders who represent, in a rather autocratic way, the communal organizations which they head. Those who are in office can preserve existing inter-communal coalitions by skillful use of the persuasive, distributive and coercive powers at their command. If that fails, and some new inter-communal political alignment shows promise of success, those in office have a more powerful weapon in their political arsenal. Opposition can be effectively undercut by alteration of the "rules of the game" in the form of boundary adjustment or constitutional amendment. Under such conditions, politics acquires a rigidity which makes it difficult to achieve changes in the allocation of power since those who have power can control the political environment to perpetuate their supremacy. Therefore, the rigidity of the communal structure of society provides little nourishment for the growth of a truly viable democratic system in which political change and the allocation of power depends upon the shifting loyalties of voters.

Perhaps the most vexing of the predicaments of transitional politics is this: nation-building depends upon firm and decisive political leadership to integrate and unify a polymorphic society. To the degree that the leadership succeeds in this task, it creates the political base for its monopoly of power. Such a monopoly of power undermines the democratic process in a most deceptive and insidious way since the forms of democracy may be retained without its substance. It is obvious that a responsible and effective opposition is a *sine qua non* of a functioning democratic system. Yet, such a unified and responsible opposition seems unlikely to emerge in large measure because of the communal social structure. Instead, the opposition tends to fragment, form at the extremes of the political spectrum, and respond in a negative way to sustain common political institutions, particularly if those institutions are to be patterned on the democratic model. So long as power is hopelessly monopolized by a ruling party or coalition, opposition will tend to be expressed by means of anomic actions which threaten the orderly processes of the democratic system.

We have seen that under circumstances of political stress, democracy and constitutional order are subject to serious threats from at least two quarters: first, from opposition parties willing to employ any tactics, including those which threaten the basic fabric of society:—communal rioting, insurgency and the reliance upon foreign support, all in the pursuit of political power heretofore denied at the polls; and second, from a government that could become so preoccupied with meeting these crises that it might decide that democracy and constitutional processes are luxuries which can no longer be tolerated during such a national emergency. Even in an established and stable country the distinction between a "loyal opposition" and a "disloyal opposition" is difficult to make with precision. In a country only just beginning the process of nation-building such a distinction is even more obscure and, in any case, too subtle to be appreciated by most of the population who have yet to think in terms of loyalty to the political entity which is Malaysia.

Ultimately democracy will be on firm ground only after power is shifted from one party to another as a consequence of free and meaningful elections. The opposition will then have a significant stake in making the democratic process function effectively so that it may once again assume power in an orderly way. Furthermore, significant numbers of the opposition leaders will have had experience in elective office and will be much better equipped to perform the functions of providing responsible criticism and a realistic alternative to the Government of the day. Experience in public office provides a practical education in the limits of power and the complexities of translating political ideals into workable public programs. In a like manner, past performance in office becomes a most important yardstick to hold against future promises, thus providing an effective check on irresponsible opposition. The legitimacy of the constitutional system will then be much more secure, since consensus about the "rules of the game" will be more widely shared throughout society.

The rather dismal prospects for a competitive party system must not be allowed to overshadow the progress Malaysia has made toward establishing basic democratic institutions at a time when increasing numbers of newly independent states in Asia and Africa are succumbing to "benevolent authoritarianism" or military rule. By contrast, in Malaysia, free and honest elections to Parliament, state assemblies, and local councils have been held regularly, even during emergency situations. An independent judiciary continues to function effectively to provide impartial justice. The domestic press, although somewhat cautious because of government licensing, does provide a source of independent information and criticism which helps to keep the government responsive to public opinion.

Patterns of Leadership

During the two decades after the war, both Malaysia and Singapore turned to the English-educated for political leadership. While they may have possessed certain skills for operating the basic institutions of government, they found it difficult to mobilize any mass popular support to back their claims. By and large, the English-educated had lost contact with their ethnic communities. Some of them made a valiant effort to re-establish contacts with their own community, particularly when they decided to enter politics. A few were able to do so successfully, usually by becoming champions of the interests of the community of their own ethnic origin. Even so, the English-educated stood apart from the basic communal structure of traditional society.

The role of the English-educated has been a critical one in the operation of the political system. The communal barriers of society are less formidable and less important for them than for the remainder of society. This has been true even for those who have become outspoken advocates for one ethnic-cultural community. With the progressive mass mobilization of the population after the war, deep communal fissures in society were exposed. Yet, because the English-educated elites were more likely to have continuous and meaningful contacts with each other regardless of communal origins and because they shared much in common among themselves, they provided the main links by which a communally fragmented society was held together. It was they who were largely responsible for working out the major communal compromises which preserved the peace. They also provided the main channels of inter-communal communication, and gave far more than ordinary intellectual and professional services for society. A fractured society was being insecurely bound together at the top by its very small English-speaking westernized elite.[22]

Malaysia's present leaders have largely come from the ranks of the English-educated. These "founding fathers" have dedicated themselves to the task of making their country into a free and functioning democracy, within which multi-cultural traditions can be preserved while political unity and social harmony are promoted. There was no revolutionary break in government when colonial rule was terminated since those who came to power were the bearers of western ideas and traditions imparted by the English. However, in the years after independence, a new second-generation political elite has been gradually becoming more assertive. The latter seek a greater voice in government and are demanding that the older leaders relinquish some of their powers. Because of the predominant political power of the Malays, most of the second generation (and now second level) elites who will shortly inherit power are Malays who received their education in Malay vernacular schools. For them English is likely to be a second language rather than the first. While they may be able to speak English quite adequately, they are not members of an English-speaking elite community. Because these vernacular-educated elites suffer from the same communal compartmentalization which afflicts society as a whole, they will not be able to bridge the communal fissures in the same way as have the English-educated. Furthermore, the vernacular elites, both Malay and non-Malay, are more intensely communal in their outlook, so that communal conflicts are likely to become much more

o

intense as they assume more power in the political system. This transfer of political power will be greatly accelerated now that Malay has become the sole official language of the country.

The English-educated will not be completely displaced by Malay vernacular elites in the forseeable future, but their role will undergo substantial transformation. English education will undoubtedly continue to be the primary avenue for access to advanced education, and from there to the professions and highly skilled occupations. While Malaysia's intellectuals and professionals will still be recruited from the ranks of the English-educated, political leadership will no longer be theirs. They may still be able to provide the most important "connectors" between society's "communal compartments" but this will have to be done, not at the apex of the political system, but at some lesser level. The future role of the English-educated may also be complicated by a progressive estrangement or alienation from those who will later inherit political power.

An examination of trends in the formation of elites must not ignore the changes which are also taking place in the lower levels of the social order. Malaysia's steady pace of economic development is having important consequences on the communal structure of society. As more and more people find a place in the modern industrial and commercial sectors of the economy, they are brought into closer contact with people of other ethnic communities. Furthermore, the functional diversification of those who adopt modern urban styles of life gradually make the cultural-ethnic cleavages in society of less importance. In the long run, the processes of modernization may prove capable of building a unified nation far more effectively than nationalist symbols such as the enforced use of a single language. In the meantime, however, Malaysia will have to endure serious growing pains before a more homogenous society emerges.

The future is always clouded with uncertainty, even when all the indicators point in the same direction. Conflicting trends make the future an even more "impenetrable blank". Yet we may speculate on the broad outlines of likely future developments.

While the processes of economic growth and modernization seem to be leading to the displacement of the communal compartmentalization of society, the processes of politics appear to be leading in the other direction. In the race between these two conflicting trends, the impact of political changes will probably be more immediate and of greater short term significance. For this reason, it is likely that communal tensions and cleavages in Malaysian society will become even more pronounced over the next decade as the vernacular Malay elites undertake to reconstruct Malaysian society according to their image of what it should be. Those who will assume political leadership during this period have proclaimed their intention to preserve democracy and promote social harmony within Malaysia. However, if communal tensions become much more severe as a result of government policies which force the pace of change and ignore the demands of substantial segments of the population, the future prospects for democracy will not be bright. We can only ask the question which more perceptive Malaysians are asking themselves: will the good intentions of the next generation of leaders be matched with equal wisdom and insight into the requirements for social harmony and a democratic polity?

[1] See above, pp. 60–63, 147–149.

[2] Estimated average income per adult male by race in 1957 was as follows: Malays, M$1,463; Chinese, M$3,223; Indians, M$2,013. The average annual income per head by race for 1957 was estimated to be as follows: Malays, M$367; Chinese, M$837; Indians, M$669. For further figures and estimates on the racial distribution of national income see T. H. Silcock and E. K. Fisk (eds.), *The Political Economy of Independent Malaya*, (Berkeley: University of California Press, 1963), pp. 276–281.

[3] This model cannot accurately depict the complex distribution of support for each party. It is rather designed for the purpose of visualizing the approximate position of each party on the two axes of conflict; communal and economic. Neither does the diagram take into account the higher proportion of Malays who are qualified to vote, nor does it depict the "weightage" given in the representation system to rural areas where the Malays predominate. Both factors give the political system a more pro-Malay bias than is indicated in this diagram.

[4] Several students of history at the University of Malaya, in studying communalism, concluded that as soon as an issue was publicly labeled as "communal" by responsible public figures, the public became quite hesitant to pursue their militant communal demands. However, communal conflict did become quite serious on several occasions before the issues were denounced as "communal" by leading political figures.

[5] These percentages do not reflect the relative political power of each communal group. Inequities in the representation system distorted the distribution of political power by exaggerating rural representation at the expense of urban areas and by the partial disenfranchisement of the non-Malays. Likewise, in the Federation of Malaysia, Singapore was under-represented, while Sarawak and Sabah were grossly over-represented. These factors tended to increase the political power of the Malays and Borneo tribal peoples at the expense of the Chinese and Indian population. Furthermore, the two and three-tiered system of election in effect until 1967 in Sabah and Sarawak placed the non-Malay Borneo tribal peoples in a somewhat stronger political position than is indicated by their percentage in the total population of Malaysia.

[6] Among those who have expressed a desire for the eventual reunification of Malaysia and Singapore are: Tan Siew-sin, Mohamed Khir Johari, and Lim Yew-hock.

[7] *Straits Times*, August 21, 1965, pp. 1 and 18.

[8] If substantial numbers of Borneans were brought into the political structure of the Alliance or recruited into the civil service, it would have a side effect of increasing political tensions within the Alliance, not only because of the problems of making accommodation to regional demands, but also because aspiring power-seekers in Malaya would discover that the Alliance would have to fill a disproportionate number of new openings in the party and in government service with Borneans and non-Malays before a balanced and equitable ratio was achieved. The issue is academic, since Sabah and Sarawak have so few educated elites who can compete for positions available in Borneo let alone in the Federal Government.

[9] See Table 22, page 405.

[10] *Straits Times*, September 8, 1966, p. 20; September 24, 1966, p. 5; September 28, 1966, p. 18.

11 See above, pp. 339–341.

12 Parliament of the Federation of Malaya, *Standing Orders of the Dewan Ra'ayat, 1959*, (Kuala Lumpur: Government Printer, 1960), para. 48–49.

13 *Ibid.*, para. 54–60 and 76–88 (as amended).

14 While the Courts have the power to declare an act of Parliament or a State Legislature invalid on the grounds of contravening the Constitution, these powers of judicial review do not apply to acts infringing the "fundamental liberties" guaranteed in the Constitution.

15 During the Sarawak Crisis, Radio Malaysia refused to broadcast any statements of Stephen Kalong Ningkan because he opposed the Federal Government, even though the High Court had ruled that he was the legal Chief Minister of Sarawak. See above pp. 384–387.

16 An editor of one of Malaysia's daily papers explained to the author his understanding of limits of press freedom which applied to his paper. He said, "We may 'nudge' the Government in a friendly way, but we dare not 'needle' the Government."

17 When viewed against the Alliance Government's expulsion of Singapore, this statement has an ironic ring. If the argument is taken seriously, it means that any proposals for the withdrawal of a state from Malaysia is treacherous unless it is made by the Alliance Government, in which case, of course, it is not treachery but an act of loyalty to the national interest. See *Sarawak Tribune*, July 6, 1966, p. 8.

18 *Straits Times*, January 12, 1967, p. 1.

19 As an example, under the First Malaysia Plan covering the period from 1966–1970 the expenditures of the Sarawak Government were expected to be M$465m, of which about M$401·5m was to be spent on social services and economic development. Of the total expenditure, the Federal Government agreed to provide M$396m. In the aftermath of the Sarawak Crisis this sum was increased slightly by "gifts" and by special arrangements for federal loans to the state.

20 This statement was made by the Secretary-General of SUPP, Stephen K. T. Yong. See *Sarawak Tribune*, May 23, 1966, p. 6.

21 Under such a system, role allocation in the society combines both ascriptive and achievement criteria. Professor Fred Riggs has examined this phenomenon at some length in various writings in which he develops his theory of a "prismatic society". He uses the term "fused" to refer to traditional society within which one finds a comparatively low degree of functional and institutional specialization and ascriptive norms are used to allocate roles. Transitional society is "prismatic" in the sense that the fused social patterns are being broken up, but elements of traditional society continue to persist. The term "refracted" is employed to describe the essential characteristics of modern urban society, with its emphasis upon achievement norms and the high degree of functional specialization of the basic institutional structures of society.

22 In many respects these were also the functions which the British performed during the colonial era.

Bibliography

BOOKS

Ali, S. Husin — *Social Stratification in Kampong Bagan.* Singapore: Monographs of the Malaysian Branch Royal Asiatic Society, 1964.

Allen, Sir Richard — *Malaysia: Prospect and Retrospect.* London: Oxford University Press, 1968.

Ardizzone, Michael — *A Nation is Born.* London: The Falcon Press, 1946.

Baker, Michael — *North Borneo, The First Ten Years.* Singapore: Malaya Publishing House, 1962.

Baring-Gould, S., and Bampfylde, C. A. — *A History of Sarawak under its Two White Rajahs.* London: Henry Sotheran & Co., 1909.

Bartlett, Vernon — *Report from Malaya.* London: Dereck Verschoyle, 1954.

Bastin, John, and Winks, Robin W. (eds.) — *Malaysia, Selected Historical Readings.* Kuala Lumpur: Oxford University Press, 1966.

Blythe, W. L. — *Historical Sketch of Chinese Labour in Malaya.* Singapore: Government Printing Office, 1953. (Reprint from Journal Vol. XX, Part I, June 1947, Malayan Branch, Royal Asiatic Society).

Blythe, Wilfred — *The Impact of Chinese Secret Societies in Malaya.* London: Oxford University Press, 1969.

Brackman, Arnold C. — *Southeast Asia's Second Front.* New York: Frederick A. Praeger, 1966.

Braddell, Roland St. John — *The Law of the Straits Settlements. A Commentary,* 2nd ed., Singapore: Kelly and Walsh, Ltd., 1931.

Brimmell, J. H. — *Communism in South East Asia.* London: Oxford University Press, 1959.

Cady, John F., Barnett, Patricia G., and Jenkins, Shirley — *The Development of Self-Rule and Independence in Burma, Malaya, and the Philippines.* New York: American Institute of Pacific Relations, 1948.

Chapman, F. Spencer — *The Jungle is Neutral.* New York: W. W. Norton & Co., 1949.

Coedes, G. — *The Making of South East Asia.* Berkeley: University of California Press, 1966.

Comber, Leon — *Chinese Ancestor Worship in Malaya.* Singapore: Donald Moore, 1954.

——— — *Chinese Secret Societies in Malaya.* Locust Valley, N.Y.: Published for the Association for Asian Studies by J. J. Augustin, 1959.

Conservative Commonwealth Council — *Colonial Rule.* London: Conservative Political Centre, 1955.

BIBLIOGRAPHY

Coupland, Sir R.	*Raffles of Singapore*. London: Collins, 1946.
Crabb, C. H.	*Malaya's Eurasians—An Opinion*. Singapore: Eastern Universities Press, 1960.
Dobby, E. H. G.	*Malaya and Southeast Asia*. London: University of London Press, 1947.
——	*Monsoon Asia*. London: University of London Press, 1961.
——	*South-East Asia*. London: University of London Press, 1950.
Douglas, William O.	*North from Malaya*. New York: Doubleday & Co., 1953.
Dow, Maynard Weston	*Nation Building in Southeast Asia*. Boulder, Colorado: Pruett Press, 1966.
Emerson, Rupert	*Malaysia: A Study in Direct and Indirect Rule*. New York: The Macmillan Co., 1937.
——	*Representative Government in South East Asia*. Cambridge: Harvard University Press, 1955.
Fatimi, S. Q.	*Islam Comes to Malaysia*. Singapore: Malaysian Sociological Research Institute, 1963.
Firth, Raymond	*Malay Fishermen: Their Peasant Economy*. London: Kegan Paul, Trench, Trubner & Co., Ltd., 1946.
Fisher, Charles A.	*South-East Asia, A Social, Economic and Political Geography*, 2nd ed., London: Methuen & Co., 1966.
Gamba, Charles	*The Origins of Trade Unionism in Malaya*. Singapore: Eastern Universities Press, 1962.
Ginsburg, Norton S., et al.	*Area Handbook on Malaya*. Preliminary Edition. Chicago: University of Chicago, for the Human Relations Area files, 1955.
Gordon, Bernard K.	*The Dimensions of Conflict in Southeast Asia*. Englewood Cliffs, New Jersey: Prentice Hall, 1966.
Groves, Harry E.	*The Constitution of Malaysia*. Singapore: Malaysia Publications, 1964.
Gullick, J. M.	*Indigenous Political Systems of Western Malaya*. London: The Athlone Press, 1958.
Hake, H. B. Egmont	*The New Malaya and You*. London: Lindsay Drummond, 1945.
Hall, D. G. E.	*A History of South-East Asia*. New York: St. Martin's Press, 1955.
Hanna, Willard A.	*The Formation of Malaysia: New Factor in World Politics*. New York: American Universities Field Staff, 1964.
Hanrahan, Gene Z.	*The Communist Struggle in Malaya*. New York: Institute of Pacific Relations, 1954.
Harrison, Brian	*South-East Asia—A Short History* 2nd ed. London: Macmillan & Co., 1964.
Harrisson, Tom (ed.)	*The Peoples of Sarawak*. Kuching, Sarawak: Government Printing Office, 1959.
Hawkins, Gerald, and Gibson-Hill, C. A.	*Malaya*. Singapore: Government Printing Office, 1953.
Hickling, R. H.	*An Introduction to the Federal Constitution*. Federation of Malaya: Information Services, n.d. (1960).

Holland, William L. (ed.)	*Asian Nationalism and the West.* New York: Macmillan Co., 1953.
Ho Seng Ong	*Education for Unity in Malaya.* Penang: Malayan Teachers' Union, 1952.
——	*Methodist Schools in Malaysia.* Petaling Jaya, Malaysia: Methodist Board of Education, 1965.
Hyde, Douglas	*Confrontation in the East.* London: The Bodley Head, 1965.
Ibrahim, Ahmad	*Islamic Law in Malaya.* Singapore: Malaysian Sociological Research Institute, 1965.
International Bank for Reconstruction and Development	*The Economic Development of Malaya.* Baltimore: Johns Hopkins Press, 1955.
Irwin, Graham	*Nineteenth-Century Borneo—A Study in Diplomatic Rivalry.* Singapore: Donald Moore, 1955.
Jackson, R. N.	*Immigrant Labour and the Development of Malaya, 1786–1920.* Federation of Malaya: Government Press, 1961.
Jones, S. W.	*Public Administration in Malaya.* London: Royal Institute of International Affairs, 1953.
Josey, Alex	*Trade Unionism in Malaya.* Singapore: Donald Moore, 1954.
Kennedy, Captain Malcolm	*A History of Communism in East Asia.* New York: Frederick A. Praeger, 1957.
Kennedy, J.	*A History of Malaya.* London: Macmillan & Co., 1962.
Kondapi, C.	*Indians Overseas, 1838–1949.* New Delhi: Indian Council of World Affairs, 1951.
Landon, K. P.	*Southeast Asia, Crossroads of Religion.* Chicago: University of Chicago Press, 1948.
Lee Kuan Yew	*The Battle for Merger.* Singapore: Government Printing Office, 1961.
Levy, Reuben	*The Social Structure of Islam.* Cambridge: Cambridge University Press, 1962.
Lim Tay Boh	*The Co-operative Movement in Malaya.* Cambridge: Cambridge University Press, 1950.
Low, N. I., and Cheng, H. M.	*This Singapore.* Singapore: Ngai Seong Press, 1948.
Mahajani, Usha	*The Role of Indian Minorities in Burma and Malaya.* Bombay: Vora & Co., 1960.
Markandan, Paul	*The Problem of the New Villages of Malaya.* Singapore: Donald Moore, 1954.
Mason, Fredric	*The Schools of Malaya.* Singapore: Donald Moore, 1954.
Meek, C. K.	*Land Law and Custom in the Colonies.* London: Oxford University Press, 1949.
Middlebrook, S. M., and Pinnick, A. W.	*How Malaya is Governed* 2nd ed. London: Longmans Green & Co., 1949.

423

BIBLIOGRAPHY

Miller, Harry —— ——	*Menace in Malaya*. London: George G. Harrap & Co., 1954. *Prince and Premier*. London: George G. Harrap & Co., 1959. *The Story of Malaysia*. London: Faber and Faber, 1965.
Mills, Lennox A., *et al* ——	*The New World of Southeast Asia*. Minneapolis: The University of Minnesota Press, 1950. *British Rule in Eastern Asia*. London: Oxford University Press, 1942.
Milne, R. S.	*Government and Politics in Malaysia*. Boston: Houghton Mifflin, 1967.
Mohammad Yunus Hamidi	*Sejarah Pergerakan Politik Melayu Semenanjong*. Kuala Lumpur: Pustaka Antara, n.d. (1961?).
Morais, J. Victor (ed.) —— (ed.)	*The Leaders of Malaya and Who's Who, 1956*. Kuala Lumpur: The Economy Printers, 1956. *The Who's Who in Malaysia*, 1963. Kuala Lumpur: Solai Press, n.d.
Onraet, Rene	*Singapore: A Police Background*. London: Dorothy Crisp & Co., n.d.
Osborne, Milton E.	*Singapore and Malaysia*. Cornell University, Ithaca, N.Y.: Southeast Asia Program, Data Paper No. 53, 1964.
Owen, Frank	*The Fall of Singapore*. London: Michael Joseph, 1960.
Parkinson, C. Northcote —— ——ᴛ	*A Short History of Malaya*. Singapore: Donald Moore, 1954. *Britain in the Far East*. Singapore: Donald Moore, 1955. *British Intervention in Malaya 1867–1877*. Singapore: University of Malaya Press, 1960.
Parmer, J. Norman	*Colonial Labor Policy and Administration, A History of Labor in the Rubber Plantation Industry, c. 1910–1941*. New York: Association for Asian Studies, 1960.
Peet, G. L. ——	*Malayan Exile*. Singapore: Straits Times Press, 1936. *Political Questions of Malaya*. Cambridge: Cambridge University Press, 1949.
Percival, A. E.	*The War in Malaya*. London: Eyre & Spottiswoode, 1949.
Pillai, P. P. (ed.)	*Labour in South-East Asia: A Symposium*. New Delhi: Indian Council of World Affairs, 1947.
Public Relations Office	*Malaya*. Singapore: Public Relations Office, 1954.
Purcell, Victor —— —— —— —— —— —— ——	*The Chinese in Malaya*. London: Oxford University Press, 1948. *The Chinese in Modern Malaya*. Singapore: Donald Moore, 1956. *The Chinese in Southeast Asia*. London: Oxford University Press, 1951. *The Colonial Period in Southeast Asia*. New York: Institute of Pacific Relations, 1953. *Malaya: Communist or Free?* London: Victor Gollancz, 1954. *Malaya, Outline of a Colony*. London: Thomas Nelson, 1946. *Malaysia*. New York: Walker & Co., 1965. *Problems of Chinese Education*. London: Kegan Paul, 1936.
Pye, Lucian W.	*Guerrilla Communism in Malaya*. Princeton, New Jersey: Princeton University Press, 1956.
Raghavan, Nedyam.	*India and Malaya: A Study*. Bombay: Orient Longmans, Ltd., 1954.

Raja Singam, S. D.	*India and Malaya through the Ages.* Singapore, 1954.
Ratnam, K. J., and Milne, R. S.	*The Malayan Parliamentary Election of 1964.* Singapore: University of Malaya Press, 1967.
Ratnam, K. J.	*Communalism and the Political Process in Malaya.* Singapore: University of Malaya Press, 1965.
Rees-Williams, David *et al.*	*Three Reports on the Malayan Problem.* New York: Institute of Pacific Relations, 1949.
Robinson, J. B. Perry	*Transformation in Malaya.* London: Secker & Warburg, 1956.
Roff, William R.	*The Origins of Malay Nationalism.* New Haven: Yale University Press, 1967.
Runciman, Steven	*The White Rajahs—A History of Sarawak from 1841 to 1946.* Cambridge: Cambridge University Press, 1960.
Ryan, N. J.	*The Making of Modern Malaya, A History From Earliest Times to Independence,* 2nd ed. Kuala Lumpur: Oxford University Press, 1965.
Scalapino, Robert A. (ed.)	*The Communist Revolution in Asia.* Englewood Cliffs, N. J.: Prentice Hall, 1965.
Scott, James C.	*Political Ideology in Malaysia.* New Haven: Yale University Press, 1968.
Sheppard, M. C. ff.	*Historic Malaya, An Outline History.* 2nd rev. ed. Singapore: Eastern Universities Press, 1959.
Sheridan, L. A. and Groves, Harry E.	*The Constitution of Malaysia.* Dobbs Ferry, New York: Oceana Publications, 1967.
Sheridan, L. A. (ed.)	*Malaya and Singapore, The Borneo Territories, The Development of their Laws and Constitutions.* London: Stevens & Sons, 1961.
Silcock, T. H. —— and Fisk, E. K. (eds.)	*The Economy of Malaya.* Singapore: Donald Moore, 1954. *The Political Economy of Independent Malaya.* Berkeley: University of California Press, 1960.
Smith, T. E.	*The Background to Malaysia.* London: Oxford University Press, 1963.
Swettenham, Sir Frank ——	*British Malaya,* 3rd ed. rev. London: George Allen & Unwin, 1948. *The Real Malay.* The Bodley Head: John Lane, 1899 .
Tan Cheng Lock	*Malayan Problems.* Singapore: Tannsco, 1947.
Taylor, W. C.	*Local Government in Malaya.* Alor Star: The Kedah Government Press, 1949.
Thayer, Philip W.	*Southeast Asia in the Coming World.* Baltimore: The Johns Hopkins Press, 1954.
Thomas, M. M. and Abel, M. (eds.)	*Religion, State and Ideologies in East Asia.* Bangalore, India: East Asia Christian Conference, 1965.
Thompson, Sir Robert	*Defeating Communist Insurgency.* New York: Frederick A. Praeger, 1966.
Thompson, Virginia	*Labor Problems in Southeast Asia.* New Haven: Yale University Press, 1947.

BIBLIOGRAPHY

Thompson, Virginia and Adloff,	*The Left Wing in Southeast Asia*. Stanford, California: Stanford University Press, 1955.
Richard ———	*Minority Problems in Southeast Asia*. Stanford, California: Stanford University Press, 1955.
Tilman, Robert O.	*Bureaucratic Transition in Malaya*. Durham, North Carolina: Duke University Commonwealth-Studies Center, 1964.
Tregonning, K. G.	*The British in Malaya, The First Forty Years, 1786–1826*. Tucson, Arizona: University of Arizona Press, 1965.
———	*Malaysia*. Melbourne: F. W. Cheshire, 1964.
———	*North Borneo*. London: Her Majesty's Stationery Office, 1960.
——— (ed.)	*Papers on Malayan History*. Singapore: Journal of Southeast Asia History, 1962.
———	*Under Charter Company Rule*. Singapore: University of Malaya Press, 1958.
———	*A History of Modern Malaya*. Singapore: Eastern Universities Press (for the University of London Press), 1964.
———	*A History of Modern Sabah (North Borneo 1881–1963)*. Singapore: University of Malaya Press, 1965.
Tweedie, M. W. F.	*Prehistoric Malaya*. Singapore: Donald Moore, 1955.
Wang, Gungwu (ed.)	*Malaysia—A Survey*. New York: Frederick A. Praeger, 1964.
Wheatley, Paul	*Impressions of the Malay Peninsula in Ancient Times*. Singapore: Eastern Universities Press, 1964.
Wheeler, L. Richmond	*The Modern Malay*. London: George Allen & Unwin, 1928.
Wilkinson, R. J.	*A History of the Peninsular Malays, with Chapters on Perak and Selangor*, 3rd ed. Singapore: Kelly & Walsh, 1923.
Williams-Hunt, P. D. R.	*An Introduction to the Malayan Aborigines*. Kuala Lumpur: Government Press, 1952.
Winstedt, Sir R. O.	*Britain and Malaya*. London: Longmans, Green and Co., 1944.
———	*A History of Malaya*. London: Luzak and Company, 1935.
———	*Malaya and its History*. London: Hutchinson's University Library, 1953.
———	*The Malays: A Cultural History*, 3rd ed. rev. London: Routledge & Kegan Paul Ltd., 1953.
Wynne, W. L.	*Triad and Tabut*. Singapore: Government Printing Office, 1941.

CONSTITUTIONAL DOCUMENTS

British Military Administration	*Statement of Policy for the Future Constitution of the Malayan Union and the Colony of Singapore*. Singapore: Department of Publicity and Printing of the British Military Administration, 1946.
Colony of Singapore	*Papers on Financial Arrangements Submitted by the Federation of Malaya and Singapore for Consideration by the Inter-Governmental Committee and Related Documents*. Misc. 4 of 1963.
The Federation of Malaya	*The Federation of Malaya Agreement 1948*. Kuala Lumpur: Government Press, (reprinted) 1952.

426

—— *Federation of Malaya Constitutional Proposals 1957.* Kuala Lumpur: Government Press, 1957.

—— *Federation of Malaya Constitutional Proposals, Annexe I, II, and III.* Kuala Lumpur: Government Press, 1957.

—— *Malayan Constitutional Documents,* 2nd ed. Vols. I & II. Kuala Lumpur: Government Press, 1962.

—— *Malaysia, Agreement concluded between the Federation of Malaya, United Kingdom of Great Britain and North Ireland, North Borneo, Sarawak and Singapore.* Kuala Lumpur: Government Press, 1963.

—— *Malaysia Report of the Inter-governmental Committee, 1962.* Kuala Lumpur: Government Printer, 1963.

—— *Report of the Commission of Enquiry, North Borneo and Sarawak* (Cobbold Commission). Kuala Lumpur: Government Printer, 1962.

—— *Report of the Federation of Malaya Constitutional Commission 1957* (Reid Report). Kuala Lumpur: Government Press, 1957.

—— *Report of the Federation of Malaya Constitutional Commission, Appendixes II, III, and IV.* Kuala Lumpur: Government Press, 1957.

—— *Self-Government for the Federation of Malaya, Report of the Constitution Conference,* London, January–February, 1956. Kuala Lumpur: Government Press, 1956.

Federation of Malaysia   *The Federal Constitution.* No. 26 of 1963.

Government of the Malayan Union   *Constitutional Proposals for Malaya—Report of the Consultative Committee.* Kuala Lumpur: Malayan Union Government Press, 1947.

—— *Malayan Union and Singapore—Summary of Proposed Constitutional Arrangements.* Kuala Lumpur: Malayan Union Government Press, 1946.

—— *Summary of Revised Constitutional Proposals Accepted by His Majesty's Government, 24th July, 1947.* Kuala Lumpur: Malayan Union Government Press, 1947.

Great Britain   *Statutory Rules and Orders,* 1946, Vol. 1 (London: H.M. Stationery Office, 1947), 543–571 (O. in C. No. 463), 1539–1557 (O. in C. No. 464). (Constitutions for Malayan Union and Singapore.)

Hickling, R. H.   *An Introduction to the Federal Constitution.* Kuala Lumpur: Federation of Malaya Information Services, 1960.

Singapore Legislative Assembly   *Memorandum Setting Out Heads of Agreement For a Merger Between the Federation of Malaya and Singapore.* Cmd. 33 of 1961.

PUBLIC PAPERS AND DOCUMENTARY SOURCES

Alliance National Council   *Constitution and Rules of the Alliance Party (As amended 20th May, 1958).* Kuala Lumpur: Printcraft Ltd., n.d.

—— *Menuju Kearah Kemerdekaan.* Kuala Lumpur: Alliance National Council, n.d. [1955].

—— *What the Alliance Offers You, 1959 Parliamentary Election Manifesto.* Kuala Lumpur: Alliance Headquarters, n.d.

AMCJA   "Constitutional and Political Developments from September 1945 to September 1947." AMCJA, 1947 (mimeographed).

BIBLIOGRAPHY

Benham, F. C.	*The National Income of Malaya, 1947–49.* Singapore: Government Printing Office, 1951.
Colony of North Borneo	*Annual Report, 1961.* Jesselton: Government Printing Department, 1962
——	*The Local Elections Ordinance, 1962.* No. 2 of 1962.
Colony of Singapore	*The Communist Threat in Singapore.* Legislative Assembly Paper No. 33 of 1957.
——	*Criminal Law (Temporary) Amendment Bill, 1958.*
——	*The Immigration Ordinance, 1952.* Singapore: Government Printer, 1952.
——	*Preservation of Public Security Ordinance, 1958.*
——	*Singapore Chinese Middle Schools Students' Union.* Legislative Assembly Paper No. 53 of 1956.
——	*Weekly Digest of the Non-English Press.* Singapore: Public Relations Office.
Federation of Malaya	*Action Taken by the Federation Government on the Report of the Rice Production Committee.* No. 30 of 1954.
——	*Annual Report on Education.* Vols. 1953–1955. Kuala Lumpur: Government Press.
——	*The 1957 Census—A Preliminary Report Based on "First Count Total" Returns.* Kuala Lumpur: Government Press, 1957.
——	*Central Advisory Committee on Education, First Report.* No. 29 of 1950.
——	*Citizenship Laws—A Short Guide.* Kuala Lumpur: 1954.
——	*The Communist Threat to the Federation of Malaya.* No. 23 of 1959.
——	*Courts of the Federation of Malaya.* No. 43 of 1948.
——	*Criminal Procedure Committee Report.* No. 59 of 1953.
——	*Daily Press Summary Vernacular Papers.* Kuala Lumpur: Department of Information.
——	*The Danger and Where It Lies.* Kuala Lumpur: Government Press, 1957.
——	*Detention and Deportation during the Emergency in the Federation of Malaya* No. 24 of 1953.
——	*The Education Ordinance, 1952.* No. 63 of 1952.
——	*Educational Policy.* No. 67 of 1954.
——	*Election Offences Law—A Short Guide.* Kuala Lumpur: 1954.
——	*Elections Ordinance, 1958.* No. 30 of 1959.
——	*Establishment, Organisation and Supervision of Local Authorities in Federation of Malaya.* No. 14 of 1953.
——	*Establishment of a Public Service Commission.* No. 9 of 1954.
——	*Evasion of Income Tax.* No. 64 of 1953.
——	*Internal Security Act, 1960.* No. 18 of 1960.
——	*The 1957 Population Census of the Federation of Malaya.* Report Nos. 1–18. Kuala Lumpur: Department of Statistics, 1960.
——	*The Progress of the Co-operative Consumers Movement, June 1952–September 1953.* No. 95 of 1953.
——	*Progress Report on the Development Plan of the Federation of Malaya, 1950–1952.* No. 86 of 1953.
——	*Registration of Schools Ordinance, 1950.* No. 16 of 1950.
——	*Report on the Barnes Report on Malay Education and the Fenn-Wu Report on Chinese Education.* (No number indicated), 1951.
——	*Report by the Chief Minister of the Federation of Malaya on the Baling Talks.* No. 25 of 1956.
——	*Report of a Commission to Enquire into Matters Affecting the Integrity of the Public Services, 1955.* Kuala Lumpur: Government Press, 1955.
——	*Report of the Committee Appointed to Examine the Question of Elections to the Federal Legislative Council.* No. 20 of 1954.
——	*Report of the Committee to Consider the Problem of Malay Education* (Barnes Report). No. 23 of 1951.

—— *Report of the Committee on the Malayanisation of the Government Service.* No. 59 of 1954.

—— *Report of the Committee on Malayanisation of the Public Service.* Kuala Lumpur: Government Press, 1956.

—— *Report on Community Development in the Federation of Malaya.* No. 39 of 1954.

—— *Report on the Conference on Community Development.* No. 87 of 1958.

—— *Report of the Constituency Delineation Commission.* No. 36 of 1954.

—— *Report on Economic Planning in the Federation of Malaya in 1956.* Kuala Lumpur: Government Press, 1957.

—— *Report of the Fenn Mission on Chinese Education.* No. 35 of 1951.

—— *Report of the Land Administration Commission.* Kuala Lumpur: Government Press, 1958.

—— *Report of the Mission of Enquiry into the Rubber Industry of Malaya.* Kuala Lumpur: Government Press, 1954.

—— *Report on the Parliamentary and State Elections, 1959.* Government Press, 1960.

—— *Report of the Registrar-General on Population, Births and Deaths for the year 1953.* No. 44 of 1954.

—— *Report of the Registrar-General on Population, Births, Deaths, Marriages and Adoptions, 1956.* Kuala Lumpur: Government Press, 1958.

—— *Federation of Malaya Annual Report.* Vols. 1952–1958. Kuala Lumpur: Government Press.

—— *Federation of Malaya Election Commission Report.* Kuala Lumpur: Election Commission, 1959.

—— *Federation of Malaya Official Year Book, 1962.* Kuala Lumpur: Government Press, 1962.

—— *First Annual Report of the Member for Education on the Education Ordinance, 1952.* No. 29 of 1954.

—— *Fortnightly Press Digests.* No. 1/55–No. 5/58. Kuala Lumpur: Department of Information.

—— *Future Development and Site of the University of Malaya.* No. 87 of 1953.

—— *Government Trading in Rice.* No. 27 of 1954.

—— *Grouping of Departments under Members Appointed from Unofficials.* No. 49 of 1950.

—— *Immigration Ordinance.* No. 68 of 1952.

—— *Internal Security Act, 1960.* No. 18 of 1960.

—— *Introduction of Elections to the Federal Legislative Council.* No. 21 of 1954.

—— *Local Authority Elections 1961, Results & Statistics of Voting.* Kuala Lumpur: Election Commission, 1961.

—— *Legislative Council Debates* (1954–1959). Kuala Lumpur: Government Press.

—— *Malay Participation in the Road Transport Industry.* No. 17 of 1954.

—— *Malayanisation of the Public Service—A Statement of Policy.* Kuala Lumpur: Government Press, 1956.

—— *Memorandum on the Introduction of Elections to the Federal Legislative Council.* Issued by command of His Excellency the High Commissioner, 26th May, 1954.

—— *National Service.* No. 39 of 1953.

—— *An Outline of the Principles for the Domestic Implementation of the International Tin Agreement.* No. 76 of 1954.

—— *Parliamentary Debates.* Vols. I–V (1957–1963).

—— *Report of the Education Committee, 1956* (Dato Abdul Razak, Chairman). No. 21 of 1956.

—— *Report of the Education Review Committee, 1960* (Enche' Talib, Chairman). Kuala Lumpur: Government Press, 1960.

BIBLIOGRAPHY

Federation of Malaya | *Report on the First Election of Members to the Legislative Council of the Federation of Malaya* (by T. E. Smith). Kuala Lumpur: Government Press, 1955.

—— *Report on the Parliamentary and State Elections, 1959.* Federation of Malaya: Government Press, 1960.

—— *Report on Registration and Licensing of Business Bill, 1953, with Bill.* No. 9 of 953.

—— *Report of the Rice Production Committee.* No. 52 of 1953.

—— *Report of the Select Committee on Policy to Provide for Election to Local Government Authorities.* No. 26 of 1950.

—— *Report of the Special Committee Appointed on the 20th Day of September, 1951, to Recommend Legislation to Cover All Aspects of Educational Policy for the Federation of Malaya.* No. 70 of 1952.

—— *Report by Mr. B. J. Surridge, C.M.G., O.B.E., Adviser on Co-operation for the Secretary of State for the Colonies, on Cooperation in the Federation of Malaya.* No. 41 of 1953.

—— *Report on the Village Council Bills, 1952, with Bill.* No.40 of 1952.

—— *Resettlement and the Development of New Villages in the Federation of Malaya, 1952.* No. 33 of 1952.

—— *Rules for the Conduct of Ministers.* No. 72 of 1954.

—— *Scheme for the Reorganization of the Rural Industrial Development Authority.* No. 10 of 1951.

—— *Second Five-Year Plan, 1961–1965.* Cmd. 3 of 1961.

—— *The Squatter Problem in the Federation of Malaya.* No. 14 of 1950.

—— *Taxation and Replanting in the Rubber Industry.* No. 36 of 1955.

—— *Trade Unions (Accounting Procedure) Regulations, 1958.* No. 17 of 1958.

Federation of Malaya, Attorney-General's Department | *General Index of Acts, Ordinances, Enactments, Proclamations, Etc.* Government Printer, 1962.

Federation of Malaya, Department of Information | *Malaysia.* No. 2 (April 1962).

—— *The Federation of Malaya Year Book, 1962.* Singapore: Straits Times Press, 1962.

Government of Malaysia | *Background to Indonesia's Policy Towards Malaysia.* Kuala Lumpur: Department of Information, 1963.

—— *Communism in the Nanyang University.* Kuala Lumpur: Government Press, 1964.

—— *Communist Threat to Sarawak.* Kuala Lumpur: Jabatan Chetak Kerajaan, 1966.

—— *Emergency (Federal Constitution and Constitution of Sarawak) Bill, 1966.*

—— *Indonesian Intentions Toward Malaysia.* Kuala Lumpur: Government Press, 1964.

—— *Malaysia/Indonesia Relations.* Kuala Lumpur: Government Printing Office, 1963.

—— *Malaysia's Case in the United Nations Security Council.* Kuala Lumpur: Ministry of External Affairs, 1964.

—— *The Militant Communist Threat to West Malaysia.* Kuala Lumpur: Jabatan Chetak Kerajaan, 1966.

—— *Parliamentary and State Elections, 1964.* Kuala Lumpur: Jabatan Penerangan Malaysia, 1964.

—— *Pilehan Raya Parlimen dan Negeri, 1964.* Kuala Lumpur: Jabatan Penerangan Malaysia, 1964.

—— *A Plot Exposed.* Cmd. 12 of 1965.

Government of
Sarawak

Report of the Land Committee, 1962. Kuching, Sarawak: Government Printer, 1963.

Great Britain

Parliamentary Debates—Commons (Fifth Series). Vols. 414–427 (1945–1946).

———

Statutory Rules and Orders—1946. Vol. I. London: H.M. Stationery Office, 1947.

Great Britain,
Colonial Office

British Dependencies in the Far East, 1945–1949. Cmd. London: H.M. Stationery Office, 1949.

———

The Colonial Empire (1939–1947). Cmd. 7167. London: H.M. Stationery Office, 1947.

———

Malayan Union and Singapore. Cmd. 6724. London: H.M. Stationery Office, 1946.

International Bank
for Reconstruction
and Development

Report on the Economic Aspects of Malaysia (Rueff Report). Singapore: Government Printing Office, 1963.

Labour Party of
Malaya

"Manifesto of the Labour Party of Malaya." (Mimeographed, n.d. [1955]).

Leach, Lionel
(Chairman)

Report of the Singapore Riots Inquiry Commission, 1951. Singapore: Government Printing Office, 1951.

Leigh, Michael B.

"The Chinese Community of Sarawak, A Study of Communal Relations." University of Melbourne, B.A. Thesis, 1963 (mimeographed).

MacGillivray, Sir
Donald

Installation Speech by His Excellency the High Commissioner. Kuala Lumpur: Government Press, 1954.

Malayan Chinese
Association

Malayan Chinese Association, Annual Report Seventh Annual General Committee Meeting (January 1955).

———

Malayan Chinese Association, Paper No. 1 of 1953.

McMichael, Sir
Harold

Report on a Mission to Malaya. Colonial No. 194. London: H.M. Stationery Office, 1946.

Moore, Daniel
Eldredge

"The United Malays National Organization and the 1959 Malayan Elections." University of California, unpublished Ph.D. dissertation, 1960.

Nyce, Ray

"The 'New Villages' of Malaya: A Community Study." Hartford, Conn.: unpublished Ph.D. dissertation, Hartford Seminary Foundation, 1962.

Pan-Malayan Labour
Party

Towards a New Malaya. Butterworth: Phoenix Press, 1952.

Parliament of the
Federation of
Malaya

Standing Orders of the Dewan Ra'ayat, 1959. Kuala Lumpur: Government Printer, 1960.

Perak Progressive
Party

Perak Progressive Party, Federal Elections 1955 Manifesto, Onward to Freedom. Ipoh: Mercantile Press, 1955.

Sarawak Government

Sarawak Annual Report, 1960. Kuching: Sarawak Government Printing Office, n.d.

Singapore Legislative
Assembly

Report of the Select Committee on the National Referendum Bill. No. 7 of 1962.

Smith, T. E.

Report on the First Election of Members to the Legislative Council of the Federation of Malaya. Kuala Lumpur: Government Press, 1955.

431

BIBLIOGRAPHY

State of Brunei   *State of Brunei, Annual Report, 1960.* Kuala Belait, Brunei: Brunei Press, 1962.

——   *Brunei Report on the Census of Population Taken on 10th August, 1960.* Kuching, Sarawak: Government Printing Office, 1961.

State of Trengganu   *Administration of Islamic Law Enactment, 1955.* No. 4 of 1955.

Tilman, Robert O.   "The Public Services of the Federation of Malaya." Durham, N.C.: unpublished Ph.D. dissertation, Duke University, 1961.

del Tufo, M. V.   *Malaya—A Report on the 1947 Census of Population.* Singapore: Government Printing Office, 1948.

United Malays National Organization   *Undang2 Tuboh Pertubohan Kebangsaan Melayu Bersatu.* Kuala Lumpur: Life Printers, 1960.

United Nations   *Introduction to the Annual Report of the Secretary-General on the Work of the Organization, 16 June 1963–15 June 1964.* General Assembly Official Records: Nineteenth Session, Supplement No. 1A (A/5801/Add.1), pp. 8–9.

PERIODICALS

Armstrong, Hamilton Fish   "The Troubled Birth of Malaysia", *Foreign Affairs*, XLI, no. 4 (July 1963), pp. 673–693.

Bradley, C. Paul   "Leftist Fissures in Singapore Politics", *Western Political Quarterly*, XVIII, no. 2, part 1 (June 1965), pp. 292–308.

Barnett, A. Doak   "A Chronology of Three Months of Unrest in Singapore", *American Universities Field Staff Reports*, III, no. 20, Singapore ADB-10-'55 (July 1955), pp. 1–11.

——   "Notes on Three Growing Forces Among Singapore Chinese: Political Parties, Students, and Workers", *American Universities Field Staff Reports*, III, no. 19, Singapore ADB-9-'55 (July 1955), pp. 1–18.

——   "Self-Rule and Unrest: Overseas Chinese in Singapore", *American Universities Field Staff Reports*, III, no. 18, Singapore ADB-8-'55 (July 1955), pp. 1–11.

Blythe, W. L.   "Historical Sketch of Chinese Labour in Malaya", *Journal of the Malayan Branch, Royal Asiatic Society*, XX, part 1 (June 1947), pp. 64–114.

——   "The Interplay of Chinese Secret and Political Societies in Malaya", *Eastern World*, IV, no. 3 (March 1950), pp. 14–15; IV, no. 4 (April 1950), pp. 10–13.

Brown, C. C.   "Sĕjarah Mĕlayu or 'Malay Annals' ", *Journal of the Malayan Branch Royal Asiatic Society*, XXV (parts 2 & 3, October 1952), pp. 1–173.

Carnell, Francis G.   "Communalism and Communism in Malaya", *Pacific Affairs*, XVI (June 1953), pp. 99–117.

——   "Political Ferment in Singapore", *Far Eastern Survey*, XXIV (1955), pp. 97–102.

——   "The Malayan Elections", *Pacific Affairs*, XXVIII (December 1955), pp. 315–330.

Dobby, E. H. G.   "Resettlement Transforms Malaya", *Economic Development and Cultural Change*, I (1952), pp. 163–189.

Enloe, Cynthia H.   "Issues and Integration in Malaysia", *Pacific Affairs*, XLI, no. 3 (Fall 1968), pp. 372–385.

Feith, Herbert, and Lev, Daniel S.	"The End of the Indonesian Rebellion", *Pacific Affairs*, XXXVI, no. 1 (Spring 1963), pp. 32–46.
Freedman, Maurice	"Colonial Law and Chinese Society", *Journal of the Royal Anthropological Institute*, LXXX, parts 1 and 2 (1950), pp. 97–126.
——	"The Growth of a Plural Society in Malaya", *Pacific Affairs*, XXXIII, no. 2 (June 1960), pp. 158–168.
Gamba, C.	"Rural Development in Malaya", *Eastern World*, VI (1952), pp. 20–21.
Gordon, Bernard K.	"Potential for Indonesian Expansionism", *Pacific Affairs*, XXXVI, no. 4 (Winter 1963–64), pp. 378–393.
Grossholtz, Jean	"An Exploration of Malaysian Meanings", *Asian Survey*, VI, no. 4 (April 1966), pp. 227–240.
Hanna, Willard A.	"The Malays' Singapore", *American Universities Field Staff Reports*, XIV, nos. 2–6, parts I–5 (1966).
Hawkins, Gerald	"First Steps in Malayan Local Government", *Pacific Affairs*, XXVI (June 1953), pp. 155–158.
——	"Reactions to the Malayan Union", *Pacific Affairs*, XIX (September 1946), pp. 279–285.
Heidhues, Mary F. Somers	"Peking and the Overseas Chinese: The Malaysian Dispute", *Asian Survey*, VI, no. 5 (May 1966), pp. 276–287.
Hindley, Donald	"Foreign Aid to Indonesia and Its Political Implications", *Pacific Affairs*, XXXVI, no. 2 (Summer 1963), pp. 107–119.
——	"Indonesia's Confrontation With Malaysia: A Search for Motives", *Asian Survey*, IV, no. 6 (June 1964), pp. 904–913.
——	"Political Power and the October 1965 Coup in Indonesia", *The Journal of Asian Studies*, XXVI, no. 2 (February 1967), pp. 237–249.
——	"President Sukarno and the Communists: The Politics of Domestication", *American Political Science Review*, LVI (December 1962), pp. 915–926.
Ishak bin Tadin	"Dato Onn and Malay Nationalism, 1946–1951", *Journal of Southeast Asian History*, I, no. 1 (March 1960), pp. 56–88.
Kahin, George McT.	"Malaysia and Indonesia", *Pacific Affairs*, XXXVII, no. 3 (Fall 1964), pp. 253–270.
van der Kroef, J. M.	"Communism in Sarawak Today", *Asian Survey*, VI, no. 10 (October 1966), pp. 568–579.
——	"Communism and Chinese Communalism in Sarawak", *China Quarterly*, XX (October–December 1964), pp. 38–66.
——	"The Dynamics of Communism in Malaysia", *Communist Affairs*, III, no. 3 (May–June 1965), pp. 4–10.
——	"Indonesian Communism and the Changing Balance of Power", *Pacific Affairs*, XXXVI, no. 4 (Winter 1964–65), pp. 357–383.
Lee Ting Hui	"Singapore Under the Japanese", *Journal of the South Seas Society*, XVI, part 1 (1961), pp. 31–69.
Leifer, Michael	"Communal Violence in Singapore", *Asian Survey*, IV, no. 10 (October 1964), pp. 115–121.
——	"Hopes and Tensions Follow a New Alignment", *The Times*, August 31, 1966, p. 20.
——	"Indonesia and Malaysia: The Diplomacy of Confrontation", *The World Today*, XXI, no. 6 (June 1965), pp. 250–260.

BIBLIOGRAPHY

Leifer, Michael

"Politics in Singapore", *Journal of Commonwealth Political Studies*, II, no. 2 (May 1964), pp. 102–119.
—— "Singapore in Malaysia: The Politics of Federation", *Journal of Southeast Asian History*, VI, no. 2 (September 1965), pp. 54–70.

Lev, Daniel S.

"The Political Role of the Army in Indonesia", *Pacific Affairs*, XXXVI, no. 4 (Winter 1963–64), pp. 349–364.

Lim, Beda

"Malaya, A Background Bibliography", *Journal of the Malayan Branch Royal Asiatic Society*, XXXV, parts 2 and 3 (1962).
—— "Manifesto of the Malayan National Liberation League", *Peking Review*, VIII, no. 27 (July 2, 1965), pp. 18–20.

McGee, T. E.

"The Malayan Elections of 1959, A Study in Electoral Geography", *The Journal of Tropical Geography*, XVI (October 1962), pp. 70–99.

Meadows, Martin

"The Philippine Claim to North Borneo", *Political Science Quarterly*, LXXVII, no. 3 (September 1962), pp. 321–335.

Means, Gordon P.

"The Internal Challenge to Malaysia", *Journal of the Minnesota Academy of Science*, XXXIII, no. 2 (1966), pp. 141–145.
—— "Malaysia—A New Federation in Southeast Asia", *Pacific Affairs*, XXXVI, no. 2 (Summer 1963), pp. 138–159.
—— "The Role of Islam in the Political Development of Malaysia", *Comparative Politics*, I, no. 2 (January 1969), pp. 264–284.

Milne, R. S.

"Malaysia: A New Federation in the Making", *Asian Survey*, III, no. 2 (February 1963), pp. 76–82.
—— "Singapore's Exit From Malaysia: The Consequences of Ambiguity", *Asian Survey*, VI, no. 3 (March 1966), pp. 175–184.

Ness, Gayl D.

"Modernization and Indigenous Control of the Bureaucracy in Malaysia", *Asian Survey*, V, no. 9 (September 1965), pp. 467–473.

Parmer, J. Norman

"Constitutional Change in Malaya's Plural Society", *Far Eastern Survey*, XXVI (October 1957), pp. 145–152.
—— "Malaysia 1965: Challenging the Terms of 1957", *Asian Survey*, VI, no. 2 (February 1966), pp. 111–118.
—— "Trade Unions and Politics in Malaya", *Far Eastern Survey*, XXIV (March 1955), pp. 33–39.

Png Poh Seng

"The Kuomintang in Malaya, 1912–1941", *Journal of Southeast Asian History*, II, no. 1 (March 1961), pp. 1–32.

Rahman, Tunku Abdul

"Malaysia: Key Area in Southeast Asia", *Foreign Affairs*, XLIII, no. 4 (July 1965), pp. 659–670.

Reid, Anthony

"Nineteenth Century Pan-Islam in Indonesia and Malaysia", *The Journal of Asian Studies*, XXVI, no. 2 (February 1967), pp. 267–283.

Sendut, Hamzah

"Contemporary Urbanization in Malaysia", *Asian Survey*, VI, no. 9 (September 1966), pp. 484–491.

Silcock, T. H.

"Policy for Malaya, 1952", *International Affairs*, XXVIII, no. 4 (October 1952), pp. 445–451.

Smith, T. E.

"The Malayan Elections of 1959", *Pacific Affairs*, XXXIII, no. 1 (March 1960), pp. 38–47.

Soenarno, Radin

"Malay Nationalism, 1900–1945", *Journal of Southeast Asian History*, I, no. 1 (March 1960), pp. 9–15.

Soh Eng Lim — "Tan Cheng Lock, His Leadership of the Malayan Chinese", *Journal of Southeast Asian History*, I, no. 1 (March 1960), pp. 29–55.

Spector, Stanley — "Students and Politics in Singapore", *Far Eastern Survey*, XXV, no. 4 (May 1956), pp. 65–73.

Starner, Frances L. — "Malaysia and the North Borneo Territories", *Asian Survey*, III, no. 11 (November 1963), pp. 519–534.

Thant, U — "Mission to Sarawak and Sabah, Secretary-General's Conclusions", *United Nations Review*, X, no. 9 (October 1963), pp. 14–15.

Tilman, Robert O. — "The Alliance Pattern in Malaysian Politics: Bornean Variations on a Theme", *The South Atlantic Quarterly*, LXIII, no. 1 (Winter 1964), pp. 60–74.

—— "Elections in Sarawak", *Asian Survey*, III, no. 10 (October 1963), pp. 507–518.

—— "Malaysia: The Problems of Federation", *Western Political Quarterly*, XVI, no. 4 (December 1963), pp. 897–911.

—— "The Non-lessons of the Malayan Emergency", *Asian Survey*, VI, no. 8 (August 1966), pp. 407–419.

—— "The Sarawak Political Scene", *Pacific Affairs*, XXXVII, no. 4 (Winter 1964–65), pp. 412–425.

Tinker, Irene — "Malayan Elections: Electoral Pattern for Plural Societies", *Western Political Quarterly*, IX (June 1956), pp. 258–282.

Turner, G. E. — "Indian Immigration", *The Malayan Historical Journal*, I (1954), pp. 80–84.

Tweedie, M. W. F. — "The Stone Age in Malaya", *Journal of the Malayan Branch of the Royal Asiatic Society*, XXVI, part 2 (October 1953), pp. 1–100.

Wang Gungwu — "Sun Yat-Sen and Singapore", *Journal of the South Seas Society*, XV, part 2 (December 1959), pp. 55–68.

Index

ABANG Haji Openg, Dato, 304, 384
abangan tradition, 369n
Abdul Aziz bin Ishak, 96n, 195, 218n, 247, 248, 249, 263n, 264n, 336, 338, 340, 341
Abdul Hamid, Mr. Justice, 173
Abdul Hamid bin Haji Ishak, Haji, 248
Abdul Mahmud, Inche, 386
Abdul Mohamed Abdul Karim Ghani, 119
Abdul Rahman, Tunku
    as Chief Minister, 167, 169n, 176, 266, 267, 268
    as Prime Minister, 211, 249, 251, 270, 278, 292, 293, 365, 413
    election to UMNO presidency, 126, 131n
    family background, 218n
    leadership of Alliance, 135, 173, 174, 199, 204, 205, 206, 208, 211, 215, 222n, 223n, 247, 251
    leadership of UMNO, 133, 141, 162, 174, 197, 198, 241, 249
    relations with Borneo states, 299, 358, 371, 377, 378, 379, 383, 384, 385, 386, 388n, 389n, 404, 405, 413
    relations with British, 66n, 148, 149, 152n, 161, 169n, 170, 171, 176, 295, 309n, 310n, 398
    relations with Indonesia, 315, 319, 320, 324, 362
    relations with Malayan parties, 133, 141, 159, 165, 233
    relations with Singapore, 292, 293, 297, 298, 337, 342, 343, 344, 345, 347, 351n, 353, 354, 355, 364, 404, 407, 408
    role of, 359
Abdul Rahman bin Haji Talib, 217
Abdul Rashid bin Mydin, 267
Abdul Razak, Dato, 148, 202, 211, 218n, 330n, 338, 346, 353, 358, 363, 365, 366, 380, 385
Abdul Samad, 122
Abdul Taib bin Mahmud, Inche, 384
Abdullah Abbas, Haji, 169n
Aborigines, 15, 57, 255n
Aborigines Department, 255n
Advisory Councils, 86, 99
Afro-Asian Conferences
    Algeria (1965), 341
    Bandung (1955), 154
    Tanganyika (1963) 314, 323
Ahmad Daud, 261n
Ahmad, Tuan Haji, 166, 260n
Aidit, D.N., 327, 360, 361
Al'Azhar University, 18, 230
Algeria, 323
Ali Haji Ahmad, 367n
All-Malaya Islamic Association, see: Pan-Malayan Islamic Party
Alliance Party (Malaya)
    appeals of, election campaigning, 137, 153, 170, 227, 400
    boycott, 149, 161, 169n, 397
    corruption charges, 367n
    election proposals, 62, 63, 67n, 142, 143, 144, 335
    election results, 166–167, 168n, 251, 252, 253, 263n, 399
    formation of, 133–134, 150n
    internal politics of, 193–218, 247, 268, 396, 410
        Action Committee, 368n
        Constitution, 210, 211
        Executive Council, 211, 197
        "July Crisis", 212–215
        National Council, 130n, 162, 163, 164, 193, 194, 210, 211, 212, 218n, 220n, 222n, 407
        problems of strengthening, 210, 211, 386
    manifesto, 164, 166, 223n
    policies of, 157, 164, 165, 175, 179, 187, 193, 203
    relations with colonial administration, 61, 66n, 148, 152n, 267, 397, 398

Alliance Party (Malaya)—*continued*
    relations with Malayan parties, 136, 140, 147, 151n, 156, 158, 159, 160, 222n, 225, 231, 233, 235, 236, 237, 241, 244, 246, 280, 282, 337, 342, 344, 345, 349n. 353, 354, 359, 365, 402, 412
    relations with Sabah, 309n, 383–387, 406
    relations with Singapore, 286, 334, 343, 347, 348, 349n, 356, 357, 407, 408
    relations with Rulers, 171, 190n
    supremacy in Malaysia, 366
Alliance Party (Malaysia), 384
Alliance Party (Sabah), 302–304, 374–376, 378–380, 406
    platform, 388n
Alliance Party (Sarawak), 303, 305, 359, 381, 382, 384, 387, 389n, 406
Alliance Party (Singapore), 334, 344
Allied Southeast Asia Command, 69
All Malay Round Table Conference, 142
All-Malaya Chinese Mining Association, 169n
All-Malaya Chinese Schools Management Association (AMCSMA), 203, 221n
All-Malaya Council of Joint Action (AMCJA), 55, 56, 75, 83–88, 90, 94n, 95n, 96n, 102, 105, 106, 107, 109, 113, 117, 120, 121, 129n, 138, 394
    policies of, 85
All-Malaya Malay League, 96n
All-Malaya Malay Youth Congress, 154, 155, 260n
All-Malaya Muslim Missionary Society, 39, 226
All-Malaya National Congress, 146–147, 154, 260n, 394
All-Malaya Nattukottai Chettiars Chamber of Commerce, 39
All-Malaya Peasants Organization, 156, 157
All-Malaya Youth Congress, 160
All-Malayan Islamic Association, 151n
    see also: Pan-Malayan Islamic Party
Al-Manar Circle, 25n
AMCJA, see: All-Malaya Council of Joint Action
AMCSMA, see: All-Malaya Chinese Schools Management Association
amendment process, 178
amnesty, 157, 165, 166, 265, 266, 268, 283, 287n
Ang Bin Hoey, 29, 34n
Angkatan Desa Bersatu, 307
Angkatan Pemuda Insaf (API), 91–93, 94n, 119, 128n, 156, 160, 239, 240, 260n
    declared illegal, 92
    manifesto, 96n
Angkatan Pemuda Revolusione Malaysia (APREMA), 339, 350n
Angkatan Ra'ayat Anak Sabah (ARAS), 307
Angkatan Revolusi Tentera Islam Singapore (ARTIS), 350
Anglo-Indians, 40
Anglo-Malayan Defense and Mutual Assistance Treaty (1957), 310n
Anglo-Siamese Treaty (1909), 42
Annamalai, K., 209, 236
Anti-British League, see: Singapore Peoples Anti-British League
anti-colonialism, 40, 71, 87, 90, 91, 113, 394, 396, 397
Anti-Malaysia United Front, 310n
API, see: Angkatan Pemuda Insaf
APREMA, see: Angkatan Pemuda Revolusione Malaysia
ARAS, see: Angkatan Ra'ayat Anak Sabah
ARTIS, see: Angkatan Revolusi Tentera Islam Singapure
ASA, see: Association of Southeast Asia
Asian Students Association, 76

Associated Chinese Chambers of Commerce, see: Chinese Chambers of Commerce
Association of Southeast Asia (ASA), 314
Attorney General, 58, 172, 174
Australia, 173, 183, 187, 233
Azad Hind Fauj, see: Indian National Army
Azahari, A. M., 305, 306, 307, 308, 310n, 311n, 312n, 314, 318, 329n, 363

BAJAUS, 300, 374
Baling Talks, 267–271, 272, 277, 282, 287n
Ball, Humphrey, 246
Bandung Declaration, 316
Bangkok Agreement, 362, 363
Bangkok Conference, 319–320
Bani, S. T., 335
banishment, 73, 118
banking, 31
Barisan Kebangsaan Melayu, see: Malay Nationalist Front
Barisan Pemuda, 306
Barisan Ra'ayat Jati Sarawak (BARJASA), 300, 311n, 381, 383, 384, 386, 389n
Barisan Sosialis (Singapore), 280, 296, 297, 298, 299, 307, 308, 333, 334, 335, 341, 348n, 349n, 352n
BARJASA, see Barisan Ra'ayat Jati Sarawak
"barter trade center", 357
Batu Arang coal mine, 72, 79n
Bella, Ben, 323
Bengal, 37
Berita Malai, 97n
Bin Seng Rubber Factory, 77
Blythe, W. L., 10
Bodhisattvas, 30
Boestamam, Ahmad, 44, 50, 91, 239, 240, 242, 245, 254n, 261n, 262n, 307, 309, 312n, 338, 340, 350
    arrest of, 92
Bong Kahar, 340
Borneo, 293, 294, 299–301, 309n
    regional issues and grievances, 371–373
    see also: Brunei; Sabah; Sarawak
"Borneo Federation", 310n
Borneo tribal people, 373, 381, 405, 419n
Borneo United Labour Front, 311n
Borneo Utara National Party, 300, 303, 311n, 374
Bose, Rash Behari, 47, 48
Bose, Subhas Chandra, 48, 50n, 108
"boundary-makers", 408
boycotts, 63, 84, 142, 149, 163, 169n, 196, 206, 240, 282, 317, 411
Braddell, Sir Roland, 65n, 130n
Brazier, John, 74
Bridge on the River Kwai, 48
British, see: United Kingdom; colonial government
British administration, see: colonial government; colonial policy
British Advisers, 172
British Government, see: United Kingdom
British colonial adminstration, see: colonial government
British East India Company, 189
British Labour Party, 156
British Military Administration, 49, 51, 53, 69, 73, 82, 103
British North Borneo Company, 314, 315
British policy, see: colonial policy
Brockway, Fenner, 129n
Brooke, James, Rajah, 306, 381
Brooke, Vyner, Rajah, 305
Brunei, 299
    revolt in (1962), 262n, 305–308, 309, 310n, 339
Brunei Shell Petroleum Company, 305
Bruneis, 374, 405
Buddhism, 30
"bumiputera unity", 380
Burhanuddin, Al-Helmy, Dr., 46, 50n, 89, 95n, 96n, 119, 154, 155, 156, 160, 220n, 226, 229, 230, 240, 254n, 255n, 338, 241, 349n, 350n
Burma, 45, 48, 76, 107, 108

CABINET, 59, 180, 218n, 407
Cairo Conference of Non-Aligned Nations, 340
Calcutta, 76
Calcutta Conference, 87
Canada, 173, 187
capitation grant, 192n
Catholics, 40
Celebes, 45
Central Indian Association of Malaya (CIAM), 39
Central Java, mass killings in, 361

Ceylon, 69, 176
    population, 110
    1958 race riots, 117n
Ceylon Federation of Malaya, 40, 110, 121, 129n, 130n, 151n
Ceylon Government, 117n
Ceylon Tamils, 38, 39, 40, 41n, 109
Ceylon Tamils Association, 94n
Ceylonese, 39, 40, 41n, 117n, 207, 222n, 235
Chamber of Mines, 112
Chambers of Commerce, 112
Chan Swee-hoh, 259n
Chapman, Spencer, 78n
Cheah Toon-lok, Dr., 214
Chen Ping, see: Chin Peng
Chen Tien, 267
Chettiars, 38, 41n
Chiang Kai-shek, 29, 68
Chief Minister (Federation of Malaya), 172, 178, 180, 181
    of states, 178, 180, 181
    see also: Mentri Besar
Chief Secretary, 58, 60, 66n, 172, 174
Chi Kung Society, 29
Chin Peng, 76, 266, 267, 268, 269, 270, 271, 283, 364
Chin See-yin, 248, 263n
China, 27, 33, 34n, 46, 71, 104, 176, 220n, 265, 269, 277, 284, 391
    Communist, see: Peoples Republic of China
    Nationalist, see: Nationalist Chinese Government
Chinese
    collaborators, 103
    culture, 30, 33, 104, 168n
    economic position, 30
    education, 138, 196, 203, 212, 223n, 246, 252, 273–277, 295, 299, 359
    festivals, 30
    immigration, 26, 27, 33, 259
    languages, 31, 35n, 174
    political rights, 106
    registration of for citizenship, 212
    religion, 30
    rural, 118, 120, 121
    social problems, 28, 29
    "squatters", 118
    see also: Chinese schools; elites; nationalism
Chinese Advisory Boards, 102
Chinese Chambers of Commerce, 75, 86, 103, 104–105, 106, 107, 116n, 120, 121, 169n, 201
Chinese Communist Government, see: Peoples Republic of China
Chinese Communist Party, 68, 71, 77, 269, 271, 281
Chinese Consulate, 103
Chinese Nationalist Government, see: Nationalist Chinese Government
Chinese guilds, 139, 163, 199, 200, 201, 204, 205, 206, 220n, 222n, 223n
Chinese leaders, see: elites
Chinese Protectorate, 28
"Chinese rights", 103
Chinese schools, 27, 70, 104, 202, 217, 224n, 288n
    Communist subversion of, 164, 273–277
    see also: Chinese, education
Chinese university, 139
Cho Yew-fai, 220n
Christian missionaries, 38, 372
Christians, 30, 40, 41n, 128n
CIAM, see: Central Indian Association of Malaya
citizenship, 21, 31, 33, 51, 52, 53, 54, 57, 65n, 66n, 83, 85, 89, 91, 96n. 98, 102, 106, 117n, 123, 124, 125, 133, 137, 139, 147, 155, 164, 174, 175, 177, 192n, 193, 198, 202, 206, 211, 228, 235, 236, 246, 254n, 297, 311n, 359
civil rights, 186, 188, 236, 290n, 412, 413
    see also: Emergency Regulations; Internal Security Act; Malay special rights
civil service, 20, 21, 25n, 37, 41n, 53, 56, 57, 62, 82, 112, 115n, 145, 158, 172, 198, 219n, 234
    Borneanization of, 372, 383, 384
    Malaysianization of, 371, 372, 377
Clandestine Communist Organization (CCO), (Sarawak), 310n, 381
Clarke, Sir Andrew, 34n
Clementi, Sir Cecil, 22, 34n
Clerical Union, 94n
Cobbold, Lord, 301
collaborators, 106, 108, 111
collective punishment, 118
Colombo Conference, 330n
colonial government and administration, 52–64, 83, 88, 105, 108, 112, 114, 129n, 391, 396, 397, 398
    see also: Colonial Office; colonial policy

Colonial Office (British), 51, 54, 55, 56, 65n, 74, 84, 90, 93, 99, 139, 170, 171, 175, 246, 309n, 310n
  see also: colonial government; Colonial Secretary
colonial policy, 21, 27, 32, 42, 43, 50n, 53
Colonial Secretary, 53, 55, 56, 59, 63, 65n, 115n, 148, 170, 171, 201
Cominform, 76, 80n, 271
Comintern, 71
  Far Eastern Bureau, 68
Committee on Elections (Hogan Committee), 145
Common Market, 344, 356, 357
Commonwealth, 127, 141, 172, 176, 357
Commonwealth Parliamentary Association, 300
Commonwealth Prime Ministers Conference, 353
communalism, 12, 31, 44, 54, 87, 104, 118–132, 134, 136, 158, 159, 166, 193–194, 208, 213, 342, 343, 346, 351n, 353, 399, 403, 410, 416, 418, 419n
  Chinese, 217, 258n, 280
  communal social structure, 414, 415, 418
  Indian, 208
  Malay, 127, 162, 168n, 212, 227, 347, 365
  see also: non-communalism; rioting
Communism
  in China, 107, 116n
  in Malaya, 23, 39, 46, 68, 239, 364
  see also: Chinese Communist Party; Clandestine Communist Organization; Cominform; Comintern; Indonesian Communist Party; Malayan Communist Party
Communist guerrillas, see: Malayan Communist Party
Communist Party. see Malayan Communist Party
Communist Party of the Soviet Union (CPSU), Twentieth Party Congress, 272
Communities Liaison Committee, 122–124, 125, 127, 130n, 150n, 395
Conference of the Youth and Students of Southeast Asia Fighting for Freedom and Independence, 80n
Confrontation, 318, 323–325, 326, 327, 331n, 336, 357, 362, 374, 378
  cease fire, 319, 323
Confucianism, 30
Congress Party of India, 50n, 108
Constituency Delineation Commission, 63
Constitutional Commission, see: Reid Commission
constitutionalism, 412, 416
Consultative Committee on the Constitutional Proposals, 56, 65n, 84, 91, 96n
cooperative movement, 249
Council of Joint Action, see: All-Malaya Council of Joint Action
Council of Rulers, see: Rulers, Conference of
counter-insurgency measures, 118, 127n
Courts, 186, 384, 385, 420n
  see also: judicial review
The Crown (British), 55, 57, 58, 59, 99, 175, 187, 189, 304, 381
"Crush Malaysia" campaign, 318, 320, 321, 362
  see also: Confrontation
curriculum, national, 202
Czechoslovakia, 322, 331n

Da Chung, 74
Dalam, Jusuf Muda, 360
Dalforce, 46, 78n
Darul Islam, 255n
Dass, K. R., 209
Daud bin Samad, Inche, 256n
David, V., 209, 262n, 278, 279, 338, 341
Dayaks, see: Ibans
D'Cruz, Leon, 246
"death railway", Bangkok to Rangoon, 48
Declaration of Human Rights, 246
delegation of powers, 183
democracy, 124, 415–417
Democratic Action Party (DAP), 359
Democratic Party (Sabah), 374
Department of Statistics, 222n
deportation, see: banishment
Deputy High Commissioner, 62, 124
Deputy Paramount Ruler, 180
Deputy Prime Minister, 211
Devaser, K. L., 150n, 153, 192n, 209, 222n
development projects, 377
  see also: rural development; economic development
Dewan Bahasa dan Pustaka, 352n
Dewan Negara, see: Senate
Dewan Ra'ayat, see: House of Representatives
Dhani, Omar, Air Vice Marshall, 360
district councils, 375

district offices, 100
"divide and rule", 113
Divisional Advisory Councils, 303
Djatikusumo, Brigadier General, 339, 340
Douglas-Home, Sir Alec, 345
dual nationality, 176
Ducroux, Joseph, 68
Duff Development Co. v. Government of Kelantan, 50n
Dusing, John, 377
Dusuns, see: Kadazans
Dutch, 111, 128n, 324, 325
Dutch East Indies, 44, 95n
Dutch New Guinea, 112
  see also: West Irian

EBER, John, 82, 83, 94n, 122, 129n, 279, 289n, exile, 95n
economic development, 232, 358, 366, 371, 373, 376, 383, 413
  see also: rural development
Education Ordinance, 135, 138, 139
educational grants-in-aid, 38, 203
educational policy, 82, 123, 183, 193, 198, 202–203, 212, 217, 218, 228, 244, 245, 247, 276
Egypt, 44
Election Commission, 152n, 180, 181, 191n, 222n, 264n
Election Committee, 147, 148
  report of, 62, 63
election days as holidays, 161
elections, federal
  1955, 153–167, 225
  1957, 246
  1959, 225, 250–253, 261n, 281, 285
  1964, 335
elections, introduction of, 29, 61–64, 123, 127, 137, 141, 142, 143, 144
  provisions for in Federation Agreement, 59
  federal election plans, 147–150
elections, local council and municipal
  1951, 132, 137
  1952, 132–134, 138, 143, 157
  1953, 143
  1954, 168n
  1955, 234
  1956, 251
  1957, 209, 243, 246, 251
  1958, 234, 251
  1961, 232, 251
  1963, 349n
elections, Sabah and Sarawak
  1963, 302, 303, 304, 376, 381
  1967, 378, 379, 386
elections, Singapore
  1948, 75
  1957, 285
  1963, 333
elections, state (Malaya)
  1954, 168n
  1955, 212, 234
  1958, 212
  1959, 231, 233, 234, 250–253, 258n, 261n
  1963, 250, 349
  1964, 335–341, 342
electoral colleges (three tiered system), 375, 419n
Electoral Commission, 223n
electorate, ethnic composition of, 158, 222n, 252
elites
  Chinese, 47, 104, 105, 106, 123
  English-educated, 37, 82–83, 280, 285, 391, 416–418
  Indian, 37, 107, 108
  Malay, 18, 53, 55, 88, 90, 98, 123, 194, 226, 229, 417
"The Emergency", 78, 87, 93, 107, 118, 119, 120, 121, 122, 127n, 165, 166, 197, 236, 239, 271, 277, 282, 385
  casualty figures, 290n
  costs, 287n
  Emergency powers, 188, 373
emergency detention, see: preventive detention
Emergency Regulations, 109, 119, 157, 158, 160, 165, 240, 262n, 265, 281, 283, 290n
  Emergency Regulations Ordinance, 78, 95n
Emigration Commissioner, 36
England, see: United Kingdom
English-educated, see: elites
English-media schools, 19, 38, 41n, 82, 105, 196, 202, 218
equality, 125, 187, 221n, 239, 246
  demands for, 74, 83, 133
  equal rights, 93, 105, 235, 237, 245, 254n
Eu Chooi-yip, 369n
Eurasian Association, 130n, 151n

Eurasians, 111, 168n, 207
  special rights for, 111
Eurasian Union, 111, 117n
Europeans, 127
  interests of, 112
  political activity, 112
Executive Council, Federal, 58
Executive Councils, State, 43, 120, 145, 172
export duty, 192n
External Affairs Service, 25n
Ex-Service Comrades Association, 70, 72, 78n, 80n, 94n
external affairs, control of, 172, 297

FABIAN socialists, 156, 238
federal grants to states, 184
Federal Land Development Authority (FLDA), 16, 216, 224n
federal powers, 57, 182–186, 373
federalism, 55, 57, 182–186, 342, 380, 381
Federated Malay States, 42, 51, 182, 192n
Federation Agreement, see: Federation of Malaya Agreement
Federation of Chinese Guilds and Associations, 192n, 201, 203, 236, 246
Federation of Chinese Teachers Associations, 236
Federation of Democratic Youth, 96n
Federation of Indian Organizations, 151n, 167n
Federation of Malay School Teachers Association (FMSTA), 196, 228
Federation of Malaya Agreement, 55–59, 74, 75, 83, 84, 86, 87, 91, 93, 100, 102, 105, 107, 108, 109, 112, 118, 122, 123, 127, 134, 138, 164, 170, 176, 177, 178, 182, 185, 187, 190n
  Executive Council, 58
  Legislative Council, 61–64, 120, 135, 142, 221n, 225, 251
Federation of Malaysia, 9, 129n, 188, 192n, 225, 230, 237, 247, 248, 253, 255n, 262n, 289n
  consequences of, 404–408
  democracy in, 411–413
  finances, 351n
  Parliamentary representation, 311n, 337
  peace settlement with Indonesia, 362
  proposal for, 292
  reasons for, 292
Federation of Selangor Chinese Guilds and Associations, 169n
federation proposals, 85, 87, 90, 101, 106, 110, 111, 114
Financial Secretary, 58, 172
First World War, 27
fitrah, 24n
FLDA, see: Federal Land Development Authority
FMSTA, see: Federation of Malay School Teachers Association
Fong Swee-suan, 280
Foong Seong, 257n
Force 136, 69
Ford Foundation, 9
franchise, 62, 83, 137, 145, 155
free trade policy, 105
freedom of the press, 413, 420n
freedom of speech, 187, 236
Front Nasional, 318, 326
fundamental rights, see: civil rights
Fujiwara, Major, 44, 47

GAMMONS, L. D., 54, 115n
Gandhi, Prime Minister Indira, 365
General Employees Union, 280
General Labour Union, 70, 72, 73, 74, 77, 79n
general strike, 72, 73
Geneva Conference (1954), 272
Gent, Sir Edward, 54, 55
Gerakan Angkatan Pemuda Melayu (GERAM), 92, 96n, 263n, 306n
Gerakan Permuda Islam Singapura, 370n
GERAM, see: Gerakan Angkatan Pemuda Melayu
German attack on Russia, 68
Gloucester, Duke of, 189
Goh Keng-swee, 351n, 368n
Goonting, J. S., 130n
gotong royong, (self-help), 250, 264n
"Government of Kalimantan Utara", 318
government service, see: civil service
Governors, 178, 180, 181
  see also: Yang di-Pertua Negara
Greater East Asia Co-Prosperity Sphere, 44, 45, 47
Greater Indonesia, see: Indonesia Raya
  see also: Melayu Raya

guerrillas
  in Brunei, 307, 308, 312n
  Communist, 29, 46, 47, 69, 70, 77, 78n, 80n, 88, 113, 118, 119, 120, 129n, 266, 267, 268, 269, 272, 277, 280, 284, 285, 290n, 293, 364
  demobilization of, 69, 70
  hiding arms, 78n
  Indonesian, 307, 317, 318, 319, 320, 322, 323, 338, 339, 340, 363, 368n
  landings in Johore, 321
  Kuomintang, 78n, 103
  warfare, tactics, 76, 270, 271, 272, 277, 280, 284, 323, 331n
Gurney, Sir Henry, 150n
Gurupatham, K., 209

hadith, 230, 256n
Hall, George, 98
Hang, Benjamin, 10
Hang Tuah, 350n
Hanif Shah bin Rajah Abdul Rahman, Rajah, 257n
Harbour Board (Singapore), 73
Harian Rakyat, 361
hartals, 32, 85, 86, 138, 139, 393
Harrisson, Tom, 312n
Hasan Manan, 50n
Hashim Ghani, Inche, 125, 146
Hasnul bin Abdul Hadi, 340, 341
Head of State, see: Paramount Ruler; Yang di-Pertua Negara
Heah Joo-seang, 105, 233, 262n
Hertog, Maria, 119, 125, 126, 128n
High Commissioner, 55, 57, 58, 59, 60, 61, 62, 63, 66n, 138, 145, 147, 148, 169n, 171, 172, 174
Hinduism, Hindus, 38, 41n
His Majesty, see: The Crown (British)
Hitler, Adolph, 48
Ho Chi-minh, 78n
Hoalim, Philip, 82
Holland, see: Dutch
Hor Lung, 290n
House of Commons (United Kingdom), 53, 61
House of Lords (United Kingdom), 53
House of Representatives (Dewan Ra'ayat), 181, 182, 252, 264n, 297, 301, 354
Hsueh Hsih, 274, 275
Hussain Yaacob, 350n
Hyderabad, 76

IBANS, 300, 381, 386
Ibrahim Fikri bin Mohammed, Inche, 256n
Ibrahim Mohamed, 369n
Ibrahim Yaacob, 23, 44, 45, 46, 97n, 190n, 340
Idris bin Hakim, Inche, 169n
IIL, see: Indian Independence League
Ikatan Pembela Tanah Ayer Malaya (PETA), 80n, 88, 89, 96n, 119
Illanuns, 374
immigrants, 26, 27, 33, 36, 37, 40n, 74, 88, 159
immigration, 26, 27, 33, 36, 37, 40n, 56, 57, 74, 88, 96n, 106, 135, 159, 165, 168n, 235, 301, 356
  restrictions, 159
  Sabah, Sarawak control over, 376, 388n
Immigration Control Bill, 135
IMP, see: Independence of Malaya Party
INA, see: Indian National Army
income taxation, 86, 87, 106
independence, 127, 133, 164, 394, 396
  see also: merdeka
Independence of Malaya Party (IMP), 126, 127, 131n, 132, 133, 134, 136, 137, 138, 141, 142, 143, 147, 150n, 151n, 157, 158, 219n, 261n, 396
independents, 214, 251
India, 36, 39, 40n, 48, 69, 108, 122, 173, 176, 183, 237, 391
Indian Association, 108, 121
Indian Chamber of Commerce, 39, 94n, 121
Indian Communist Party, 76
Indian Immigration Committee, 40n
Indian Immigration Fund, 40n
Indian Independence League (IIL), 39, 47, 48, 50n, 107, 108, 109
  trials, 107
Indian Merchants Association, 39
Indian National Army (INA), 47, 48, 107, 110
Indian National Army Defence Committee, 107, 108
Indians
  collaboration charges, 36, 168n
  economic activities, 37–38, 41n
  education, 37, 38, 41n, 143

Indians—*continued*
  immigration, 36, 37, 40n
  languages, 41n
  labor, 36, 37, 208
  nationalism, 39, 47
  religion, 38
  Sepoy troops, 36
  traders, 36, 37
  see also: elites
indirect rule, 28, 34n
Indo-China, 108
Indonesia, 305, 307, 309, 318, 324, 329n, 367n
  army, 325, 326, 327, 340, 360, 361
  example of, 89, 292, 255n
  exiles in, 119, 289n
  impact of Indonesian politics, 23, 195, 229, 231
  independence of, 45, 46
  internal politics and political movements, 68, 71,
    76, 88, 92, 117, 170, 360–362
  relations with Singapore, 357
  subversive activities in Malaysia, 262n, 313–314,
    319, 328n, 330n, 335, 338, 350n
  sympathy for, 108, 260n, 263n
  union with, see: *Indonesia Raya*
  and West Irian, 294
  withdrawal from United Nations, 322–323
Indonesia Raya, 45, 46, 89, 93, 96n, 155, 221n, 227,
    230, 241, 317, 327, 329n
  see also: *Melayu Raya*
Indonesia-Malaysia Treaty of Peace (1966), 363
Indonesia's Provisional People's Consultative Con-
    gress, 362
Indonesian Communist Party (Partai Komunis
    Indonesia, PKI), 68, 95n, 286, 307, 313, 325, 326,
    332n, 360, 361, 363, 368n, 369n
Indonesian Parliament, 314
insurrection, see: guerrillas; revolution
Inter-Governmental Committee (on Malaysia), 301
internal security, 267, 285, 297, 373
  Internal Security Act (1960), 236, 241, 245, 290n,
    341, 347
  Internal Security Council, 309, 348n
International Union of Students, 80n
international Communism, see: Cominform; Comin-
    tern
Ishak bin Haji Mohammad, Inche, 23, 44, 93, 97n,
    127n, 244, 262n, 338, 341, 350n
Islam
  Islamic schools, 226, 228
  legal status of, 34n, 45, 57, 85, 94n, 147, 179, 180,
    197, 198, 227, 228, 301, 371, 372, 376, 383, 413
  non-Malay Muslims, 30, 38
  as a political force, 119, 128n, 229, 255n, 336, 347
  reform movement and revivalism, 22, 119, 230, 231
  role of in Malay society, 17–18
Ismail, A. E. Mohamed, 209
Ismail bin Abdul Rahman, Dr., 66n, 161, 321, 338
Ismail, Tunku, 22
Israeli advisers, 364

Ja'afar Tan, 261n
Japan, 320
  defeat of, 48, 69
Japanese, 51, 69, 71, 72, 78n, 80n, 82, 91, 95n, 96n,
    114, 128n, 292, 305, 329n
  invasion, 23, 44, 46, 69, 111
  occupation, 32, 39, 44–51, 81, 88, 103, 104, 105, 106,
    189, 267, 299, 309n, 391
  prisoners, 96n
Japanese Emperor, 46
Japanese Military Administration, 44
Java, 45, 361
Jay, Douglas, 171
Jek Yeun-thong, 344
Jennings, Sir Ivor, 173
Joffe, Adolphe A., 68
Johore Rubber Workers Union, 369n
Judicial Committee of the Privy Council, 187
judicial review, 186–188, 189, 192n, 420n
judiciary, 416
  see also: courts
Jugah anak Barieng, Temenggong, 304, 305, 383, 386
Jumabhoy, R., 109
jus soli, 164, 175, 198, 209, 220n, 226, 239, 240

Kadazans, 300, 373
Kampo Radjo, Dato, 341
kampongs, 98
  headmen, see: *penghulus*
kangany system, 36, 37, 40n

"Kapitan China", 27, 28
kathis, 256n
Kaum Ibu, see: United Malays National Organization
Kaum Muda, 22
Kaum Tua, 22
Kedayans, 308, 312n, 374
Kehidupan Dunia Akhiral, 95n
Kekuatan Ra'ayat Istimewa (KRIS), 45, 46, 88, 89
Kennedy, Senator Robert, 319, 323
Kesatuan Melayu Merdeka (KMM), 340, 350n
Kesatuan Melayu Muda (KMM), 23, 44, 45, 88, 89,
    95n, 96n, 160, 262n
Kesatuan Melayu Singapura, 22
Kesatuan Ra'ayat Indonesia Semenanjong, 45, 46,
    50n, 115n
khalwat law, 230, 256n
Khir Johari, 344
Khoman, Thanat, 330n
Khong, Koh-yat, 259n
Khrushchev, Nikita, 272
King, see: Paramount Ruler
"the King's Chinese", 105
Kiram Corporation, 315
KMM, see: Kesatuan Melayu Merdeka; Kesatuan
    Melayu Muda
Konfrontasi, see: Confrontation
Konggres Melayu Sa-Tanah Melayu, 99
Koran, 230, 256n, 257n
Korean truce, 272
KRIS, see: Kekuatan Ra'ayat Istimewa
Krisher, Bernard, 364
Kuo Yu, 35n, 104, 202
Kuomintang (KMT), 34n, 46, 68, 71, 75, 103–104,
    116n, 139, 204, 221n
  banning of, 104
  guerrilla force, see: Malayan Overseas Chinese
    Self-Defence Army

Labor contractors, 73
"labor lines", 36
labor union laws, 79n
labor union movement, 70, 273
Labour Department, 74
Labour Front (Singapore), 276, 279, 285
Labour Government (United Kingdom), see: Labour
    Party (British)
Labour Party (British), 53, 83, 129n, 166
Labour Party of Malaya, 157, 158, 160, 168n, 238,
    242, 243, 244, 250, 260n, 261n, 282, 283, 336,
    340, 350n
  manifesto, 157, 259n
Laksamana, H., 311n
land administration and policy, 57, 185, 186, 190n,
    192n, 198, 224n, 376
Land Dayaks, 300, 381
language issue, 82, 85, 123, 159, 162, 175, 179, 202,
    228, 235, 372
  national language, 162, 164, 168n, 193, 198, 201,
    217, 221n, 301, 347, 359, 367, 371, 376, 383, 410,
    418
  see also: multilingualism
Larut Wars, 34n
Lau Pak-khuan, 200, 201, 220n, 223n
Lee, Hau-shik, Col., 66n, 107, 116n, 161, 199, 204,
    214, 220n, 223n
Lee Kuan-yew, Prime Minister, 284, 285, 295, 296,
    297, 298, 309n, 310n, 317, 333, 337, 343, 344, 345,
    346, 347, 348, 351n, 352n, 356, 357, 358, 362, 364,
    365, 367n, 368n
Legislative Council, Federal, 58, 59, 60–64, 66n, 110,
    120, 123, 135, 138, 140, 142, 145, 147, 149, 167,
    170, 172, 175, 188, 189, 190n, 203, 221n, 225,
    232, 251
Legislative Councils, State, 43
Lembaga Kesatuan Melayu, 94n
Lennox-Boyd, A., 170
Leong Chee-cheong, 169n, 220n
Leong Kee-nyean, 235
Leong Kew-yoh, 257n
Leong Mun-tong, 10
Leong Yew-koh, 120, 129n, 199, 235
Liberal Party, 387n
liberties, fundamental, see: civil rights
license tax, 138
Licensing and Registration of Business Ordinance,
    138
Lim Chin-joo, 290n
Lim Chin-siong, 280, 290n, 291n
Lim Chong-eu, Dr., 202, 204, 205, 206, 212, 213, 214,
    221n, 223n, 247, 248, 263n, 338, 350n
Lim Kean-siew, 261n, 262n, 338, 350n

Lim Oon-kiat, 275
Lim Yew-hock, Tun, 309n, 419n
local government, 185, 186
Loh, Peter, 388n
Loi Tak, 46, 71, 76, 80n
  Communist Party charges against, 80n
London Agreement (1963), 317
London Conference (1957), 178, 180, 186
London School of Economics, 312n
Lopez, Salvador, 330n
lotteries, 121, 129n, 135, 137–139, 161, 257n
  government operated, 372
Lyttelton, Oliver, 62, 148

MACAPAGAL, President Diosdado, 315, 318, 320
Macdonald, Malcolm, 55, 122, 130n
MacGillivray, Sir Donald, 67n, 142, 149, 152n
MACHINDA of Sarawak, 346, 352n, 381, 386
McKell, Sir William, 173
MacMichael, Sir Harold, 51, 52, 98
MacMichael mission, 99, 100
MacMichael Treaties, 51–53, 55, 56, 90, 93, 99, 115n
Macmillan, Prime Minister Harold, 310n
Madras, 36
Madrasah Aljunied, 95n
Mahmud bin Mat, Dato, 66n
Majlis, 130n
Majlis Amanah Ra'ayat (MARA), 16
Majlis Agama Tertinggi (Supreme Religious Council), 226
Malacca, status of, 175, 178, 190n
Malacca Chinese Chamber of Commerce, 104, 246
Malacca Chinese Union, 106
Malay Chambers of Commerce, 112
Malay-Chinese Goodwill Committee, 123
Malay College (Kuala Kangsar), 18
Malay Congress, 23, 233, 241–242, 254n
Malay Council of Action, 96n
Malay elites, see: elites
Malay-German Shipping Company, 350n
Malay League, 156, 160, 254n
Malay Mail, 151n
"Malay Malaysia", 344
Malay National Congress, 220n
Malay National Youth, 92
Malay nationalism, see: nationalism
Malay Nationalist Front (Barisan Kebangsaan Melayu), 155, 156, 160, 168n, 240, 254n, 260n, 394
Malay Nationalist Party, 46, 89–90, 91, 92, 93, 94n, 154, 155, 160, 227, 231, 240, 254n, 258n, 262n, 267
  policies of, 93, 96n
  outlawed, 119
Malay Otherwise-Trained Teachers Union, 219n
Malay Regiment, 96n
Malay Reservations, 57, 177, 178, 383
  see also: Malay special rights
Malay Rulers, 19, 20, 21, 23, 24n, 25n, 34n, 42, 43, 44, 45, 51, 52, 54, 55, 56, 57, 59, 61, 62, 63, 64n, 65n, 74, 83, 84, 85, 90, 92, 93, 94n, 95n, 98, 99, 100, 101, 102, 106, 111, 124, 127, 146, 148, 165, 168n, 170, 171, 172, 174, 175, 178, 228, 243, 257n, 260n, 391, 392
  position and powers, 179–181
Malay Sinhalese Association, 110
Malay special rights, 16, 22, 25n, 43, 54, 83, 90, 91, 93, 104, 125, 162, 172, 174, 177, 180, 187, 192n, 193, 198, 209, 219n, 220n, 221n, 228, 235, 239, 240, 243, 245, 260n, 298, 302, 336, 342, 343, 346, 371, 372, 388n, 399, 400, 410, 411
  see also: Malay Reservations
Malay States, 57, 105, 182, 185
Malay Union of Singapore, 125
Malay Youth Action League, 218n
Malaya and Singapore, union of, see: merger
"Malaya for the Malays", 124
Malaya-United Kingdom Defence Treaty, see: Treaty of Defence and Mutual Assistance (Malaya-United Kingdom)
Malayali, 37
Malayan Chinese Association (MCA)
  and Chinese education, 202–203, 359
    Central Education Committee, 203
  and Chinese guilds, 192n, 199–201, 220n, 222n, 246
  constitution of, 206, 207, 210
  formation of, 116n, 120–121, 150n
  internal politics of, 204–207
  "July Crisis", 212–215, 223n

Malayan Chinese Association (MCA)—*continued*
  lotteries, 121, 129n, 137–139
  MCA Youth, 368n
  relations with Alliance, 133–136, 141–146, 149–150, 162–166, 173, 174, 194, 199–203, 212–215, 223n, 334, 337, 396
    Malay Welfare Fund, 135, 151n
    Malay welfare projects, 138
  relations with other parties, 130n, 131n, 139–140, 151n, 155, 159, 246, 247, 263n, 342, 379, 408
  in Singapore, 356
Malayan Chinese League, 116n, 129n
Malayan Civil Service, see: civil service
Malayan Communist Party (MCP)
  during Japanese occupation, 46, 47, 49
  Examination Committee, 76
  formation of, 29, 68
  guerrillas, see: guerrillas, Communist
  insurrection, 78, 92, 103, 107, 111, 115, 118, 122, 157, 265, 394
  military defeat of, 283
  outlawed, 78, 80n
  peace talks, 267–271
  relations with colonial government, 35, 72–74
  relations with other parties, 87, 92, 93, 120, 128n, 236, 239, 240, 241, 245, 258n, 296, 297, 298, 309
  in Sarawak, see: Clandestine Communist Organization
  strategy and tactics, 34n, 71–77, 113, 129n, 258n, 271–286, 288n, 290n
    appeals of, 114, 119
    "Chinese line", 71, 77
    "Humiliation Day", 72
    and labor unions, 72–74, 86, 277–286
    liberated areas, 71
    manifesto, 70–71, 79n
    moderate policy, 76
    "open front", 280, 285, 291n
    and schools, 273–277, 335
    in Singapore, 284–286, 295–299
    Singapore Town Committee, 289, 368n
    united front tactics, 71, 72, 83, 87, 239, 240, 268, 279, 282, 283, 284, 285
  trial of Communists, 72
  see also: Ex-Service Comrades Association; Malayan National Liberation League; Malayan Peoples Anti-Japanese Army; Malayan Races Liberation Army; Malayan Races Liberation League; Singapore Peoples Anti-British League; Socialist Youth League; Workers Protection Corps
Malayan Constitution Bill, 54
Malayan Democratic Union, 82, 86, 87, 93, 94n, 95n, 106, 107, 111, 118, 122, 279, 369n
  manifesto of, 82
"Malayan Government in Exile", see: Nasional Republik Malaya
Malayan independence, see: *merdeka*
Malayan Indian Association (MIA), 39, 109, 143, 151n, 154, 167n
Malayan Indian Congress, 40, 94n, 108, 109, 110, 117, 121, 143, 150n, 151n, 153, 154, 161, 163, 164, 167n, 173, 194, 207–210, 222n, 236
  platform, 108
  MIC Youth, 209
Malayan Merdeka, 346
Malayan Monitor, 129n
Malayan Muslim College, 18, 226, 255n
Malayan Muslim Party, 168n, 226
Malayan National Liberation League (MNLL), 286, 363
Malayan National Progressive Party, 151n
Malayan nationalism, see: nationalism
Malayan Overseas Chinese Self-Defence Army, 78n, 103, 116n
Malayan Party, 220n, 245–247, 248, 250, 251, 262n
Malayan Peoples Anti-Japanese Army (MPAJA), 46, 69, 70, 72, 80n, 116n
  MPAJA Ex-Comrades Association, see: Ex-Service Comrades Association
Malayan Peoples United Front (PUTERA-AMCJA), 129n
Malayan Peoples United Labour Front, 157
Malayan Races Liberation Army, 166
  see also: guerrillas, Communist
Malayan Races Liberation League, 283
Malayan Railways, 40n, 48
Malayan Revolutionary Committee of the KMT, 68
Malayan Sinhalese Association, 40
Malayan Teachers Union, 122, 129n
Malayan Trade Union Congress, 127, 157, 262n, 278

Malayan Union, 51–57, 74, 75, 79n, 83, 84, 89, 90, 93, 96n, 98–103, 106, 109, 110, 113, 124, 134, 182, 194, 242, 391
Malay boycott of, 99
Malayan Union Advisory Council, 65n
"Malayanization", "Malaysianization", 164, 168n, 383, 390n
Malays
custom and culture, 57, 85, 88, 94n, 101
definition of, 13n
economic position of, 15–17, 98, 101, 255n, 400
education, 18–20, 25n, 196, 218, 228, 229, 233
migrations, 15
origin, 15, 23n
peasants, 16, 43, 45, 156, 195, 216, 227, 249, 250
raja class, 21, 98
see also: Malay Rulers
religion, see: Islam
rights and privileges, see: Malay special rights
role of women, 18, 24n, 25n
see also: elites; nationalism
Malaysia, see: Federation of Malaysia
Malaysia Agreement, 376
Malaysia-Indonesia Peace Pact (1966), 390n
Malaysia referendum, 298–299
Malaysia-Singapore-United Kingdom Defence Treaty (1965), 357
"Malaysian Malaysia", 347, 348, 354, 355, 372
Malaysian Solidarity Consultative Committee, 255n, 300, 301
Malaysian Solidarity Convention, 345–347, 348, 359, 406, 407
"Malaysianization", see: "Malayanization"
Malik, Adam, 363, 369n
Malik, B., 173
Malinau, 307
"Malindo", 410
Manchu dynasty, 34n
Maniam, A. K. S., 209
Manickasavasagam, V., 209
Manila Agreements (1963), 316–319, 362
Manila Conference (1963), 315–318, 331n
"Manipol", 326
Mao Tse-tung, 274, 284
Maphilindo, 316, 317, 318, 329n, 331n, 336, 354, 364, 410
MARA, see: Majlis Amanah Ra'ayat
Marshall, David, 267, 296, 298, 309n
Marshall Plan, 76
Martin, Dr. Charles E., 10
Marxism, 76, 81, 113, 122, 240, 274
masok Melayu, 17
MCA, see: Malayan Chinese Association
MCP, see: Malayan Communist Party
MDU, see: Malayan Democratic Union
Melanaus, 389n
Melayu Raya, 89, 229, 230, 241, 292, 408, 410
also see: Indonesia Raya
Member System, 59–61, 66n, 397
Mentri Besar, 115n, 124, 137, 141, 143, 146, 178, 180, 181
merdeka, 124, 141, 167, 170, 283
see also: independence
Merdeka Day, 189, 269
Merdeka Constitution, 170–189, 193, 225, 228, 240, 246, 398
ratification of, 188–189
Merdeka Mission, 171
merger (Singapore and Malaya), 164, 206, 221n, 230, 242, 281, 286, 293, 295, 296, 297, 298, 309n, 408
MIA, see: Malayan Indian Association
MIC, see: Malayan Indian Congress
military bases, 357, 364
military service, compulsory, 330n
Ming Shin Pao, 74
mining, 121
Ministry of Agriculture, 249
Ministry of External Affairs, 219n
Mitra, A. M., 94n
MNLL, see: Malayan National Liberation League
MNP, see: Malay Nationalist Party
Mobilization Committee, 69
MOCSDA, see: Malayan Overseas Chinese Self-Defence Army
modernization, 418
Mohamed Khir Johari, 419n
Mohamed Sopiee, Inche, 141, 149, 156, 157
Mohamed Tahar, 94n
Mohammad Eunos bin Abdullah, 22
Mohammed, The Prophet, 343
Mohammed Yamin, 324, 329n
Mojuntin, Peter, 378

Mokhtar U'd-din, 89, 95n
Mountbatten, Lord, 51
Movement for Colonial Freedom, 129n
Movement of Peninsular Malays (Pergerakan Melayu Semenanjong), 99
MPAJA, see: Malayan Peoples Anti-Japanese Army
multilingualism, 162, 163, 179, 236, 239, 245, 263n
multiple member constituencies, 62, 67n
Muruts, 301
Musa bin Ahmad, 269
Muslim courts, 17, 24n
Muslim Indians, 41n, 108
Muslim law, 24n, 128n, 255n
Muslim League (India), 108
Muslim League of Malaya, 39, 108, 137, 254n
Muslim Religious Councils, 24n, 256n
Muslim schools, 24n, 226, 228, 229
Muslim Youth Congress, 226
Mustapha bin Dato Harun, Tun Dato, 311n, 376, 377, 378, 379, 380
Mustaza, M., 92

"NADRA", see Hertog, Maria
Nair, C. Devan, 122, 280, 355, 356
Namazie, M. J., 108
Nanyang Communist Party, 68
Nanyang University, 275, 335, 351n
Dramatic Research Society, 275
History and Geography Society, 275
Political Science Society, 275
Social Science Research Society, 275
Nanyang University Guild of Graduates, 275
Nanyang University Students Union, 275
"Nasakom", 326
Nasional Republik Malaya, 340, 341, 412
Nasser, Gamal Abdul, 230
Nasution, General, 360, 361, 362
Natal, 108
nation-building, 331n, 387, 406, 407, 415
National Association of Perak (NAP), 160, 166, 220n, 226, 234–235, 253n, 257n, 260n, 395
National Conference, 141, 142, 143–144, 147, 151n, 394
National Convention, 142, 144–145, 147, 148, 149, 152n, 156, 226, 394
National Convention Party (NCP), 219n, 247, 248–250, 336, 340, 341, 411
National Finance Council, 184, 186
national income, 24n, 31
National Land Code, 185
National Land Council, 185, 186, 232
national language, see: language issue, national language
National Language Action Front, 368n
National Registration system, 276
National Service Act, 276
National Union of Factory and General Workers, 262n, 278
National Union of Teachers, 262n
"National Unity League", 107
Nationalist Chinese Government, 73, 103, 107
nationalism, 44, 49, 81, 104, 122, 126, 280, 281, 391, 396, 398
Chinese nationalism, 32, 33, 35n, 47, 104, 116n
Malay nationalism, 22, 23, 45, 46, 71, 81, 85, 87, 88, 89, 93, 95n, 98, 101, 106, 113, 114, 146, 154, 155, 160, 195, 229, 395
nationalists, 55, 81, 82, 110, 127, 394
nationality question, 165, 172, 201
"Native Alliance", 383
native land laws, 372
"Native Reservations", 383
native rights (Sabah and Sarawak), 302, 382
naturalization, 123
Nazar Nong, 261n
NCP, see: National Convention Party
"Nefos", 323
Negapatam, 36
negative response, 392–393
Nehru, Prime Minister Jawaharlal, 108, 154, 167n
neo-colonialism, 250, 324
Netherlands, see: Dutch
New Democracy, 74
New Democratic Youth League, 72, 76, 80n, 94n
newspapers, periodicals, see: Berita Malai; Da Chung; Harian Rakyat; Kehidupan Dunia Akhiral; Majlis; Malay Mail; Malayan Merdeka; Malayan Monitor; Ming Shin Pao; New Democracy; Petir; Shi Tai Jih Pao; Singapore Standard; Straits Times; Suara Ra'ayat; Taman Bahagia; Tamil Murasu; University Tribune; Utusan Melayu; Warta Melayu; Warta Negara

new villages, 118, 120, 128n, 138, 252, 275, 283
New Zealand, 187
Ng Thow-lin, 261n
Nik Ahmad Kamil, Dato, 233
Ningkan, Dato Stephen Kalong, 304, 381, 382, 383, 386, 389n, 420n
"no confidence" letter, 384
suit against Governor Openg, 384
"non-communalism", communal harmony, 82, 127, 159, 160
North Borneo, see: Sabah
North Borneo United Party, 263n
Norway, 322

OFFICIAL language, see: language issue, national language
Official Members, 59, 66n, 151n
Ogmore, Lord, 171
Old Comrades Association, see: Ex-Service Comrades Association
one-party dominance, 397, 411
Ong Eng-guan, 296
Ong Kee-hui, 310n
Ong Yoke-lin, 200, 204, 206, 221n
Onn bin Ja'afar, Dato, 50n, 99, 100, 101, 115n, 124, 125, 126, 127, 129n, 130n, 131n, 132, 133, 134, 136, 137, 140, 142, 146, 151n, 155, 158, 159, 160, 167, 168n, 219n, 220n, 232, 233, 252, 254n, 263n, 392, 395, 396
resignation from UMNO, 125
attempt to censure, 139–140
defeat of, 233
Ooi Thiam-siew, 262n
Osmena, Nicasio, 315, 329n
Osmena, Sergio, 315
Othman bin Wok, 342
Overseas Chinese Association, 129n

PAKISTAN, 37, 108, 122, 173, 176, 320
PANAS, see: Party Negara Sarawak
Pangkor Engagement, 34n, 50n
Panglima Bukit Gantang, Dato, 139, 140, 141, 156, 226, 234
Pan-Islamic nationalism, 155
see also: Islam; Pan-Malayan Islamic Party
Pan-Malay Congress, 22, 90, 96n, 99, 100
Pan-Malayan Chinese Chamber of Commerce, see: Chinese Chambers of Commerce
Pan-Malayan Council of Joint Action (PMCJA), see: All-Malaya Council of Joint Action (AMCJA)
Pan-Malayan Federation of Trade Unions, 74, 77, 79n, 94n, 95n, 277
Pan-Malayan Islamic Association, see: Pan-Malayan Islamic Party
Pan-Malayan Islamic Party
education memorandum, 254n
electoral support, 166, 251, 252, 264n
founding, 168n, 226
internal politics, 229–230
manifesto, 254n, 256n
policies, appeals of, 226–230, 250, 255n, 257n, 336, 354
relations with Indonesia, 340–341, 351n, 411
relations with other parties, 145, 155, 160, 197, 212, 224n, 226, 231–232, 237, 240, 241, 242, 244, 260n, 261n, 308, 347, 354, 403
Pan-Malayan Labour Party, 141, 145, 149, 151n, 156, 157
Pan-Malayan Rubber Workers Union, 278
Pan-Malayan Students Federation, 288n
PAP, see: Peoples Action Party
Paramount Ruler, 24n, 178–181, 187, 191n, 304, 348, 385
Parkinson, Professor C. Northcote, 10
Parliament, 112, 179, 181–182, 183, 186, 192n, 235, 264n, 283, 302, 335, 354, 375, 380, 385
Committee of the Whole, 412
role of, 407, 412
see also: House of Representatives; Senate
Parliamentary mission (1946), 54
parliamentary supremacy, 187
Partai Komunis Indonesia, see: Indonesian Communist Party (PKI)
Partai Nasionalis Indonesia (PARTINDO), 255n, 261n
PARTINDO, see: Partai Nasionalis Indonesia
Party Bumiputera, 386
Party Kebangsaan Melayu Sa-Malaya, 89
Party Negara (Malaya), 66n, 67n, 144, 147, 153, 154, 155, 157, 158–161, 164, 167, 226, 231, 232–234, 241, 242, 250, 251, 254n, 256n, 257n
manifesto, 186n

Party Negara Sarawak (PANAS), 300, 303, 304, 305, 311n, 352n, 381, 383, 384, 386, 389n
Party Pesaka Anak Sarawak (Pesaka), 300, 305, 311n, 381, 383, 386, 389n, 390n
Party Ra'ayat (Malaya), 239–241, 242, 244, 254n, 256n, 260n, 261n, 283, 307, 308, 309, 336, 339, 340, 341, 350n, 352n, 411
Party Ra'ayat (Singapore), 285, 339, 340
Party Rakyat (Brunei), 261n, 282, 300, 306, 307, 308, 309, 310n, 311n, 312n
Pasokan Gerak Chepat Bumiputra Singapura, 370n
patronage, 377
"peaceful co-existence", 272
Pembela Tanah Ayer (PETA), 44, 45
Pemuda Radikal Melayu, 92, 93
Pemuda Rakyat, 360, 361
Penang, status of, 175, 178, 190n
Penang Chinese Association, 116n
Penang Labour Party, 132, 137, 156
penghulus, 21, 100, 115n, 392
Peninsular Malays Union (PMU), 125, 142, 145, 146, 147, 150n, 151n, 154, 241, 254n, 339, 340, 350n, 351n
Peoples Action Party (PAP), 221n, 237, 279, 284, 285, 289n, 290n, 295, 298, 333, 334, 335, 336, 337, 342, 344, 345, 346, 347, 349n, 353, 354, 406, 408
censure motion against Alliance, 347–348, 352n
Communist infiltration of, 290n
"People's Constitutional Proposals", 85, 86, 91
Peoples Progressive Party (PPP), 209, 221n, 234, 235, 236, 242, 243, 247, 248, 250, 257n, 258n, 260n, 261n, 262n, 282, 336, 337, 346, 349n, 354, 395
manifesto, 258n
see also: Perak Progressive Party
Peoples Republic of China, 116n, 239, 243, 258n, 313, 318, 328n, 332n, 357
attack on India, 237
Overseas Chinese Affairs Commission, 116n
see also: Chinese Communist Party
People's Revolutionary Party of Singapore, 368n
People's Socialist Youth League, 282
Perak Labour Party, 156
Perak National Party, 140, 151n, 156
Perak Progressive Party, 151n, 156, 160, 235
see also: Peoples Progressive Party
PERAM, see: Pemuda Radikal Melayu
Pergerakan Melayu Semenanjong, 99
Perikatan Melayu Perak, 254n
Permentah Revolusione Republic Indonesia (PRRI), 324, 331n, 350n
Persatuan Aislam Sa-Melayu, see: Pan-Malayan Islamic Party
Persatuan Melayu Selangor, 22
Persatuan Melayu Semenanjong, see: Peninsular Malays Union
Persatuan Permuda Melayu, 119, 306
Persatuan Persetiaan Melayu Kelantan, 254n
Persatulak Sekarang, 97n
Pertubohan Bumi Putera, 304
Pertubohan Kebangsaan Melayu Bersatu, 115n
Pesaka, see: Party Pesaka Anak Sarawak
PETA, see: Ikatan Pembela Tanah Ayer
Petir, 290n
Philippine claim to Sabah, 314–316, 318, 320, 388n
The Philippines, 45, 76, 230, 241, 255n, 303, 307, 311n, 312n, 314–315, 318, 320, 329n
pirates, 311n
PKI, see: Indonesian Communist Party
plebiscite issue in Borneo, 323, 331n, 354, 380
PMCJA, see: All-Malaya Council of Joint Action
PMFTU, see: Pan-Malayan Federation of Trade Unions
PMIP, see: Pan-Malayan Islamic Party
PMU, see: Peninsular Malays Union
political mobilization, 21, 100, 391, 392, 393, 394
pondok schools, 226
Portugal, 26, 40, 111
PPP, see: Peoples Progressive Party; Perak Progressive Party
Preservation of Public Security Ordinance, 1958, 291n
preventive detention, 118, 122, 279, 290n, 291n
see also: Emergency Regulations
Prime Minister, 178, 180, 181, 211
see also: Abdul Rahman, Tunku
"prismatic society", 420n
Privy Council, 187, 190n
pro-Indonesian underground, 339
Provisional Indian Government, 48
PRRI, see: Permentah Revolusione Republic Indonesia
public servants, see: civil service
Public Services Commission, 180

Punjabis, 37
Purcell, Dr. Victor, 135
Pusat Tenaga Ra'ayat (PUTERA), 86, 90–91, 96n, 102, 129n, 394
   boycott, 91
PUTERA, see: Pusat Tenaga Ra'ayat

RA'AYAT, see: Malays, peasants
Ra'ayat School Teachers Association, 219n
radical nationalists, 81–97
Radical Party, 127, 132, 137, 168n
Radio Malaysia, 389n
Radio Moscow, 328n
Rahman, Tunku Abdul, see: Abdul Rahman, Tunku
railways, 36, 72
   see also: Malayan Railways
Raja Abu Hanifa, Dato, 341, 350n
Raja Uda bin Raja Muhammad, 22
Rajah, T. T., 284, 290n
Rajaratnam, S., 344, 347
Ramachandran, M. K., 39
Ramanatha, D. S., 238, 242, 244, 261n, 262n
Ramani, P., 154, 167n
"Razak Plan", 202, 203, 217, 236
Razak Report, 263n
Rees-Williams, D. R., 54, 115n
referendum on Malaysia (Singapore), 377
Registrar of Societies, 28, 168n, 206, 221n, 254n, 356
Registrar of Trade Unions, 73, 278
Registration and Licensing of Business Bill, 135
Reid Commission, 172, 173–175, 177, 179, 182, 184, 186, 187, 189, 190n, 193, 194, 198, 200, 228, 233, 240, 254n
Reid, Lord, 173
Reid Report, 174, 175, 178, 183, 185, 192n, 241, 246
religious freedom, 24n, 179, 187
Religious School Teachers Association, 219n
reserved powers of Governor and High Commissioner, 59, 60, 86, 170
reserved seats, 169n
resettlement program, see: new villages
Residential system, 42, 43
residual powers, 183
   see also: states rights
revenues, 183, 185
revolution, 71, 73, 75–78, 87, 88, 92, 109, 113, 114, 115, 119, 121, 122, 165, 195, 268, 278, 306, 307, 312n, 339, 394, 411
   see also: guerrillas
Riggs, Professor Fred, 420n
riots, 32, 403, 411, 416
   Communist, 72, 164, 276, 279, 288n
   in Indonesia, 361
   racial, 126, 342, 343, 350n, 351n, 365, 367n
   religious, 126, 128n
   student, 196, 276, 288n
road grant, 192n
roads, 36
Rome, 173
rubber, 26, 27, 31, 36, 37, 38, 48, 112, 118, 185, 216
Rubber Producers Council, 169n
Ruler of Negri Sembilan, 191n
Rulers, Conference of, 24, 55, 56, 63, 65n, 117n, 148, 149, 171, 174, 178, 179, 180, 181, 188, 190n, 191n, 228
Rural and Industrial Development Authority (RIDA), 16, 130n
rural development, 130n, 216, 217, 224n, 400
   see also: economic development
Rusk, Dean, 368n
Russia, see: Soviet Union

SABAH, 253, 300, 301, 302, 306, 311n, 359, 375
Sabah Alliance, see: Alliance Party (Sabah)
Sabah Chinese Association (SCA), 374, 379, 380
Sabah Indian Congress, 374
Sabah National Party (SANAP), 374
Sambanthan, V. T., 153, 208, 209, 222n
Samsuddin Nur bin Nurut, Sergeant-Major, 340
San Min Chu I Youth Corps, 103
sanctions against British goods, 344
Sandys, Duncan, 309n
santri tradition 369n
Sarawak, 253, 299, 300, 301, 302, 303, 306, 310n, 381–387
   indirect elections, 303
Sarawak Alliance, see: Alliance Party (Sarawak)
Sarawak Chinese Association (SCA), 300, 311n, 381, 386, 389n
Sarawak Communist Party, see: Clandestine Communist Organization

Sarawak Muslim Council, 304
Sarawak National Party (SNAP), 300, 304, 305, 311n, 380, 381, 383, 384, 385, 389n
   expelled from Sarawak Alliance, 384
Sarawak United Peoples Party (SUPP), 263n, 299, 300, 303, 304, 307, 308, 312n, 346, 354, 381
Sardon bin Haji Jubir, Dato, 196, 197, 249
Sarekat Islam, 18
Sarma, P. V., 122, 363
SATU, see: Singapore Association of Trade Unions
"Save Democracy Fund", 237
SCA, see: Sabah Chinese Association; Sarawak Chinese Association
Schattschneider, Dr. E. E., 11
schools, see: educational policy
SCMSSU, see: Singapore Chinese Middle School Students' Union
Second Five Year Plan, 217
Second World War, 11, 68, 129n
secret societies, 28, 29, 30, 34n, 46, 75, 102
   election activities, 29
Secretary for Chinese Affairs, 102
Secretary for Defence, 172
Secretary-General of the United Nations, see: Thant, U
Secretary of State for the Colonies, see: Colonial Secretary
Security Forces, 165, 266, 283, 289n, 290n
sedition trials, 74
See Toh-fatt, 261n
Seenivasagam, D. R., 234, 235, 236, 243, 247, 258n, 338
Seenivasagam, S. P., 338
Selangor Labour Party, 127, 133, 134, 136, 157
Selangor National Independence League, 283
Selangor Pakistan Association, 143
Selangor Peoples Anti-Japanese Union, 72
self-government
   demands for, 43, 49, 53, 61
   steps toward, 59, 102, 170, 391, 397
Selkirk, Lord, 308
Semangat Permuda Islam, 254n
Semangat Permuda Melayu, 254n
Senate, 181, 182, 252, 354
Senu bin Abdul Rahman, Inche, 344, 364
"September 30 Movement", 361
Sharkey, L. L., 76
Shi Tai Jih Pao, 74
SHLU, see: Singapore Harbour Labourers' Union
Siam, see: Thailand
Siamese, 42
Sikhs, 37
Silcock, Professor T. H., 31
Sim Siew-lin, 368n
Singapore
   expulsion from Malaysia, 355–358, 377, 388n, 420n
   fall of, 23, 47, 72
   independence of, 356
Singapore Government, 72, 73, 129n, 293
   Internal Security Council, 291n, 293
   Legislative Assembly, 86, 221n, 285, 295, 297
   Municipal Council, 221n
   treaty with Britain and Malaysia, 357
Singapore Alliance, see: Alliance Party (Singapore)
Singapore Association of Trade Unions (SATU), 280, 335, 349n
Singapore Chinese Chamber of Commerce, 116n
Singapore Chinese Middle School Students' Union (SCMSSU), 274, 275, 276
Singapore Co-operative Stores Society, 129n
Singapore Federation of Trade Unions, 77, 79n, 94n, 277
Singapore Harbour Board, 72, 77
Singapore Harbour Labourers' Union (SHLU), 73, 77
"no strike" truce, 77
Singapore Indian Association, 109
Singapore Islamic Revolutionary Armed Forces, see: Angkatan Revolusi Tentera Islam Singapure
Singapore Malay National Action Committee, 351n
Singapore Malayan Chinese Association, 206
Singapore Muslim League, 119
Singapore People's Alliance (SPA), 333, 334
Singapore Peoples Anti-British League, 95n, 122, 129n, 279, 289n
Singapore Progressive Party, 130n
Singapore Rubber Workers' Union, 77
Singapore Shop and Factory Workers Union, 280, 289n
Singapore Standard, 163
Singapore Teachers' Union, 82

Singapore Town Committee, see: Malayan Communist Party, Singapore Town Committee
Singapore Trade Union Congress, 279, 280, 289n, 296
Singapore Work Brigade, 343
Singh, Budh, 153
Singh, Karam, 261n, 262n
Sinhalese, 39
sin-kueh system, 27
SNAP, see: Sarawak National Party
Social Democratic Party, 387n
Socialist Front, 209, 242–245, 248, 250, 251, 262n, 279, 282, 308, 336, 337, 340, 341, 350n, 352n, 400
    manifesto, 261n
Socialist Party, 311n
Socialist Youth League, 239, 242, 261n, 283
Societies Ordinance (1889), 28, 29
Soenita, R. M., 350
Soong Kwong, 72
South Africa, 108
Southeast Asia Treaty Organization (SEATO), 229, 310n, 318, 328n
Southeast Asian Youth Conference, 76, 92
Soviet Union, 68, 71, 76, 313, 322, 328n, 357
Speaker, 61, 161
Special Constabulary Force, 118, 128n
special privileges, see: Malay special rights
Special Training School, 78n
State Executive Councils, 180, 197
"State of Kalimantan Utara", 307
State Legislative Councils and Assemblies, 59, 99, 179, 181
    Brunei, 307
    Johore, 190n
    Perak, 140, 248
    Sabah (North Borneo), 302, 375
    Sarawak, 303, 384
    Singapore, 295
    Straits Settlements, 22, 116n, 169n
    Trengganu, 231, 232
states rights and powers, 57, 182, 183, 372, 373, 376, 380, 381, 383, 387
Stephens, Dato Donald, 300, 311n, 373, 375, 376, 378, 380, 386
    request for direct elections, 388n
Stewart, Sir Duncan, 306
Straits Chinese British Association, 94n, 103, 105, 129n, 143, 151n, 262n
Straits Settlement Repeal Bill, 53
Straits Settlements, 22, 105, 116n, 246
Straits Times, 94n, 138
strikes, 73, 77, 79n
student enrolment statistics, 19
Suara Ra'ayat, 95n, 258n
Subandrio, Dr., 314, 328n, 329n, 330n, 331n, 357, 360
Sudjarwo, Dr., 321, 322
Suharto, General, 361, 364, 369n
Sukarno, President A., 46, 255n, 313, 314, 315, 317, 318, 320, 321, 322, 324, 325, 326, 327, 329n, 331n, 336, 360, 361, 362, 363, 369n
Sultan Idris Teachers Training College, 18
Sultan of Brunei, 306, 307, 308, 312n, 314
Sultan of Johore, 171, 190n, 191n
Sultan of Kedah, 189
Sultan of Pahang, 191n
Sultan of Perak, 54, 140, 234
Sultan of Selangor, 99
Sultan of Sulu, 314, 315
Sultan Saifuddin, see: Sultan of Brunei
Sulut, 300, 374
Sumatra, 45
Sun Yat-sen, 29, 68
Sundang, G. S., 388n
SUPP, see: Sarawak United Peoples Party
supremacy clause, 183
Supreme Court of Malaya, 187, 188
Supreme Court of Malaysia, 302
Surrender Campaign, 268–271, 283, 287n
Switzerland, 246
Syed Ja'afar Albar, 338, 342, 343, 344, 352n
Syed Nasir bin Ismail, 352n, 367n

TAHA Karim Ghani, 119
Taib Sabree, Inche, 156n
Tajuddin Kahar, 261n, 341
Talib Report, 217, 244
Taman Bahagia, 95n
Tamils, 36, 40
Tamil Murasu, 163

Tan, C. C., 130n
Tan Cheng-lock, 64n, 65n, 85, 94n, 104, 106, 107, 116n, 120, 130n, 131n, 134, 138, 139, 163, 199, 200, 204, 205, 213, 221n, 223n, 247, 266, 267
    assassination attempt, 121
    exile in Bangalore, 129n
Tan Chong-kin, 290n
Tan Kah-kee, 69, 107, 116n
Tan Kee-gak, 200, 220n, 246, 247
Tan Phock-kin, 261n
Tan Siew-sin, 140, 163, 164, 199, 206, 221n, 247, 263n, 338, 342, 345, 351n, 419n
Tan Tuan-boon, 238
Tan, T. H., 120, 148, 199
Taoism, 30
tariffs, 105, 356
Tawi Sli, Penghulu, 384, 386, 390n
taxes, 183, 184, 351n
    tax program, 345
    see also: income tax; Registration and Licensing of Businesses Bill
Telegu, 37
Temenggong Jugah, see: Jugah anak Barieng, Temenggong
Templer, Sir Gerald, 66n, 139, 140
Tentera Nasional Kalimantan Utara (Northern Borneo National Army), 307, 363
    see also: guerrillas, Indonesian
Tentera Republik Nasional Malaya, 340
terrorism, see: guerrillas
Thailand, 48, 229, 314, 319, 320, 330n, 364
Thant, U, 316, 317, 318, 319, 322, 323, 324, 330n
Tharmalingam, A., 209
Thaver, G. V., 39, 109, 167n
Thivy, J. A., 108, 153
Thuraisingham, E. E. C., 110, 129n, 130n, 143, 159, 160, 233
timber concessions (Sabah), 376, 377, 388n
tin, 26, 27, 31, 33n, 38, 192n
Toh Chin-chye, Dr., 284, 337, 344, 346, 355
Tokyo Conferences
    (1963), 315
    (1964), 320–321
Too Joon-hing, 247, 248, 263n
Trade Union Adviser, 74
trade unions, 73, 75, 77, 83, 199, 238, 279, 280, 295
Trade Unions Ordinance (1946), 77, 79n
Treaty of Defence and Mutual Assistance (Malaya-United Kingdom), 242–243, 280
Treaty of Friendship, 1959 (Malaya-Indonesia), 315
Treaty of Holland, 246
Trotsky, Leon, 94n
Truman Doctrine, 76
Tugau United Peoples Party (TUPP), 389n
T'ung Meng Hui, 29
TUPP, see: Tugau United Peoples Party
Turkey, 44
"20 points", 376, 378, 380, 383
    see also: states rights and powers
"two year political truce" (Alliance-PAP), 344

UCSTA, see: United Chinese School Teachers Associations
ulamas, 197, 230, 256n
UMNO, see: United Malays National Organization
UMNO Youth, see: United Malays National Organization
Unfederated Malay States, 42, 51, 192n
Union of Malay Teachers in Non-Malay Vernacular Schools, 219n
United Arab Republic, 230
United Chinese School Teachers Associations (UCSTA), 203, 217, 221n
United Democratic Party (UDP), 247–248, 250, 263n, 336, 337, 346, 350n, 354
united front, see: Malayan Communist Party
United Kingdom, 40, 47, 95n, 112, 127, 170, 173, 229, 233, 265, 287n, 295, 310n, 315, 357
    armed forces, 69, 330n, 365
    government of, 51, 52, 54, 55, 56, 62, 108, 174, 189
    relations with Malaya, 242–243, 280, 291n, 293, 295
    relations with Singapore, 291n, 293, 357
    quota on textiles, 344
    see also: colonial government
United Malays National Organization, 115n
    founding of, 99, 100, 395
    internal politics, 124–127, 131n, 194–199, 216, 220n, 248, 263n
    Kaum Ibu (women's section), 162, 197, 219n

United Malays National Organization—*continued*
  policies, 100, 101, 119, 174, 177, 197–199, 408
  relations with Alliance, 133–135, 141, 142, 144–149,
    150n, 161–166, 210, 211, 212, 213, 222n, 337,
    338, 396, 406
  relations with British, 55, 56, 65n, 99, 102, 113ʻ
    173, 174
  relations with other parties, 74, 84, 85, 90, 93, 95n,
    96n, 102, 106, 112, 114, 126–127, 130n, 132,
    136–149, 151n, 155, 159, 226, 227, 241, 248,
    254n, 305, 351n, 379
  relations with Singapore, 342–347, 349n, 408
  Ulama Section, 197
  UMNO Youth, 146, 195, 197, 219n, 249, 367n,
    368n
United Malays National Organization (Singapore),
  333, 334, 356
United National Kadazan Organization (UNKO),
  300, 303, 310n, 373
  see also: United Pasok-momogun Kadazan
    Organization (UPKO)
United National Pasok Momogun Organization, 300,
  303, 374
  see also: United Pasok-momogun Kadazan
    Organization (UPKO)
United Nations, 308, 323, 325, 380
  admission of Malaya, 281
  Commission, 316, 317
  investigating team, 317, 323
  Malaysia's case in, 321–322
  Security Council, 321, 322, 323, 330n, 331n
United Party (Sabah), 374
United Pasok-momogun Kadazan Organization
  (UPKO), 374, 377, 378, 379, 380
  decision to "dissolve", 380
  demand for new Malaysia negotiations, 377
  demand for referendum, 380
  policy statement, 388n
United Peoples Party (UPP), 296, 297, 298, 299, 333,
  334, 348n
United Planting Association of Malaya, 112
United Sabah National Organization (USNO), 300,
  303, 374, 376, 377, 378, 379
United States of America, 233, 265, 293, 318, 319,
  325
  CIA agents, 358, 368n
  US Information Service, 341
University of Malaya, 9, 20, 122, 139, 218
University Tribune, 288n
UNKO, see: United National Kadazan Organization
Unofficials, 59, 60, 172
urea fertilizer plant, 249
USNO, see: United Sabah National Organization
USSR, see: Soviet Union

Ustaz Ahmad Azam bin Napiah, 231, 256n
Utusan Melayu, 60, 98, 122, 219n, 220n, 256n, 263n,
  343, 346, 347, 350n, 352n

VEERASAMY, S. N., 39
Viet Nam, 71, 76, 284, 364
violence, see: guerrillas; revolution; riots

WAH Kei, 29, 34n
Wahhabi movement, 18, 25n
Wan Hussain Azmi bin Wad Kadir, Inche, 256n
Wang Gung-wu, Professor, 10
War Executive Committee, 165
wars of national liberation, 80n, 271, 330n
Warta Melayu, 115n
Warta Negara, 115n
West Irian, 117n, 294, 313, 324, 325
  volunteers for, 339
westernized left, 82–83
  see also: elites
Whitehall, see: Colonial Office
Wilson, Sir Samuel, 64
women's rights, 197
Wong Pow-nee, 199
Workers Party, 261n, 285, 296, 298
Workers' Protection Corps, 70, 73, 77
Working Committee (Federation of Malaya), 55, 56,
  65n, 84, 91, 96n, 100, 101, 110, 174, 179, 180,
  185, 186, 187
World Federation of Democratic Youth, 80n, 313
Wyatt, Woodrow, 171

YAHAYA bin Sheikh Ahmad, Tuan Haji
Yang di-Pertuan Agong, see: Paramount Ruler
Yang di-Pertuan Negara (Singapore), 263n, 372
Yang di-Pertua Negara, Sarawak (Governor), 304,
  372, 384, 385, 386
Yang di-Pertua Negara, Sabah (Head of State), 375,
  377, 379
Yap Mau-tatt, 220n
Yap Yin-fah, 257n
Yeong Kuo, 268, 287n
Yong Kong-yin, 261n
Yong Pung-how, 214
Yong, S. M., 192n
Yong, Stephen K. T., 312n, 420n
Young Men's Indian Association (YMIA), 39
Yusof bin Ishak, 263n

ZAHARIE M. Hassan, 258n
Zaini Haji Ahmad, 312n, 328n
zakat, 24n, 226, 254n
Zhdanov, A. A., 76
Zulkiflee bin Mohammad, 339